The Economic Value of Information

Springer
New York
Berlin
Heidelberg
Barcelona
Hong Kong
London
Milan
Paris
Singapore
Tokyo

David B. Lawrence

The Economic Value of Information

With 45 Figures

Springer

David B. Lawrence
College of Business and Public Administration
Drake University
Des Moines, IA 50311
USA

Library of Congress Cataloging-in-Publication Data
Lawrence, David B., 1929–
The economic value of information / David B. Lawrence.
p. cm.
Includes bibliographical references and index.
ISBN 0-387-98706-1 (alk. paper)
1. Business information services. 2. Information resources management—Economic aspects. I. Title.
HF54.5.L38 1999
658.4′038—dc21 98-51179

Printed on acid-free paper.

Production managed by Allan Abrams; manufacturing supervised by Jacqui Ashri.
Photocomposed copy prepared using the author's Microsoft Word files.
Printed and bound by Braun-Brumfield, Inc., Ann Arbor, MI.
Printed in the United States of America.

9 8 7 6 5 4 3 2 1

ISBN 0-387-98706-1 Springer-Verlag New York Berlin Heidelberg SPIN 10707206

To Gail, Sarah, and Dan

Preface

The Scope of This Book

Popular culture often refers to current times as the Information Age, classifying many of the technological, economic, and social changes of the past four decades under the rubric of the Information Revolution. But similar to the Iron Age before it, the description "Information Age" suggests the idea that information is a commodity in the marketplace, one that can be bought and sold as an item of value. When people seek to acquire information yet complain about information overload, and when organizations invest millions in information systems yet are unable to pinpoint the benefits, perhaps this reflects a difficulty with the assessment of the value of this commodity relative to its cost, an inability to discern the useless from the useful from the wasteful. The Information Age requires us to assess the value, cost, and gain from information, and to do it from several different viewpoints.

At the most elementary level is the individual who perceives a need for information—her current state of knowledge is insufficient and something needs to be understood, or clarified, or updated, or forecast. There is a universe of alternative information sources from which to choose, some more informative than others, some more costly than others. The individual's problem is to evaluate the alternatives and choose which sources to access.

An organization comprising many information-seeking employees and agents must take a somewhat broader viewpoint. The organization's problem is to design and manage a system for information that can meet the needs of diverse groups of individuals as those needs arise, while maximizing the organization's net gain from the services the system provides.

This is a book about the evaluation and choice of information sources by individuals and the design and management of information systems by organizations. These topics are unified by the thesis that both information sources and information systems are valuable to the extent they contribute to better decision making. Since the incorporation of information is costly in terms of money, time, and effort, optimal information use and system design involves classic economic tradeoffs between value and cost. This book studies the determinants of the value and cost of information, both to the individual and to the organization, provides techniques for the assessment of the value of information and the comparison of informativeness among alternative sources, and presents principles for the optimal design and management of information systems.

Decision theory is a ready-made methodology for assessing the economic value of information. Since many activities can be cast into a decision making framework, applications of decision theory are widespread, ranging from the notorious [the Ford Pinto gas tank decision, Gioia (1992)] to the nutritious [the foraging decisions of bumblebees, Real (1993)]. Applications of decision theory to the evaluation of information appear in such diverse scientific disciplines as accounting, economics, engineering, environmental science, geology, information science, management information systems, medical science, meteorology, operations research, psychology, and statistics. As Chapter 1 demonstrates, nowadays the applications are becoming more multidisciplinary in nature—decisions to study the banning of a potential carcinogen or the consequences of global warming necessarily require contributions from many fields.

Unfortunately, much of the existing literature tends to be highly specialized and technical, with little notational uniformity. Even basic words such as data, knowledge, information, and information system have different meanings in different contexts. An integrative understanding of the many aspects of information evaluation, choice, and system design requires consistency and precision in the definition of terms. One of the purposes of this book is to provide students and researchers with a unified and coherent notation and approach to this diverse multidisciplinary literature.

Research described in Chapter 9 indicates that as individuals and teams face more complex and multidisciplinary decision problems, the role of the information system becomes more critical. It is my belief that decision theory has not yet achieved its potential as a tool for corporations, governments, and other organizations to use when evaluating their information systems. One of the goals of this book is to improve the integration of the decision-theoretic approach to information value with the knowledge from information science on the design, management, and cost of cooperative information systems.

This book concentrates on a subset of a vast literature known collectively as the economics of information. The focus is on the evaluation and incorporation of information by a single decision maker, and on the cooperative facilitation of that task by an organization; with only a few exceptions, strategic and noncooperative uses of information, along with the market consequences of differential information, are excluded.

A Reader's Guide

The basic plot of this book is to move from the assessment of the economic value of a specific source, to the choice of source or sources, to the design of an organization's system for information. Although the mathematical prerequisite for the material is no more than undergraduate courses in calculus and probability theory, there may be different ways to read this book depending upon the reader's background and interest. A student who desires to learn decision theory and its application to the evaluation of information will find Chapters 1 through 4, Sections 5.1, 5.2, 5.4, 6.1, 6.2, 7.1, 7.3, and 8.1 to be most helpful. The reader interested primarily in information systems will find Chapters 1 and 9 most pertinent. Indeed, the book is written so that those interested primarily in information science can skip directly from Chapter 1 to Chapter 9 without loss, picking up the material in between as need be. Researchers who are already familiar with decision theory and who are interested in a particular application or in the more theoretical aspects of information value will find this in Chapters 5 through 8. The primarily technical and mathematical material of this book is constrained to these four chapters; there is a detailed symbol glossary beginning on page 365 to help with the notation. Subsections that are marked with an asterisk (*) contain either peripheral or highly technical material that can be bypassed without loss of continuity.

The ideas and techniques are illustrated throughout the book by means of examples which are set off from the text by black diamonds (♦). Since they may continue through several chapters, the examples are numbered according to the section in which they first appear: Example 4.2 first appears in Section 4.2. Each example hones in on the substance of the most recently introduced topic; the purpose is to fix ideas and not to provide immediate generality. The proximate text, however, presents citations for models and theories that offer more general, technical, complex, or realistic applications.

The book holds to a number of conventions throughout. The first definition of an important term is indicated by placing that term in italics. In equations, parentheses () always denote functional dependence, and brackets [] and braces {} always indicate separation for arithmetic operation. Finally, the protagonist in this book is the decision maker. The decision maker is considered to be a person and it is convenient to use a pronoun for reference; in many languages such pronouns are indicative of gender. We can use that to our advantage by adopting the following convention from the principal–agent literature: in this book the decision maker is the principal and so is always referred to as "she," and the information source, when human, is the agent and so is always "he."

Acknowledgments

In the several years it has taken to write this book, many individuals have provided me with valuable information, advice, and encouragement. I owe special gratitude to Stuart Klugman, along with Newton Bowers, John Rozycki, Rahul Parsa, C. Kenneth Meyer, Harry Wolk, Rick Trieff, and Brent Stuart. Numerous researchers have contributed to the pure theory of the economic value of information, but because of depth, rigor, and clarity, in my view the greatest contributor is Jacob Marschak (1974). "It's all in Marshall" students of microeconomic theory often say; students of the economics of information and organization can equally say, "It's all in Marschak!" I would also like to thank Karl A. Fox, who introduced me to the topic, Anne Mayère of ENSSIB, whose 1995 conference on the economics of information stimulated me in several directions, and Drake University, whose generous sabbatical policy gave me the time to do this work. Special appreciation and love go to Gail, Sarah, and Dan, who tolerated a lot and to whom this book is dedicated. Finally, there are the people who put me on the right track from the very beginning: Alpha, Louise, George, Jackie, George, Annette, and Doug. Thank you.

David B. Lawrence
Des Moines, Iowa
August, 1998

Contents

1
Introduction and Overview

This introductory chapter lays out a basic framework for the evaluation of information and information systems; subsequent chapters provide increasing generality and detail. The chapter presents the vocabulary of the book: the basic definitions, categorizations, and institutional descriptions upon which the sequel builds. It also previews the book's analytical approach and discusses some examples of real-world applicability. The introduction ends by applying the framework to a broader social science context, providing perspective for recent events in the information economy.

1.1 Information in Decision Making

1.1.1 The Basic Framework for Decision

Decision making is an almost continuous activity in the everyday business of living our lives. The vast majority of these decisions are trivial, decisions such as what to have for breakfast, when to read the newspaper, and which route to take to work. A few require some thought, and some may even seem difficult to make. A decision that necessitates a thoughtful solution is a *decision problem*; the decision problem, either actual or potential, is the fundamental unit of analysis in this book. The decision making unit or, more simply, the decision maker (DM), may be an individual or a team acting in concert. To say that a *decision* is to be made is to say that one from two or more alternative courses of action is to be chosen. Given that the DM has under control a set of available and feasible actions, termed the *action space* $\mathbf{a} = \{a\}$, a *pure decision* is a choice of the specific action $a_0 \in \mathbf{a}$ that is in some sense optimal.

Decision theory is the study of the solution to a decision problem, including the analysis of the option to seek the services of an information source. A framework and collection of techniques for making meaningful decisions, the normative purpose of decision theory is to impose logic and structure on the reasoning process that underlies the solution of the problem by the decision maker. At a minimum, the goal is to help the DM avoid illogical or inconsistent behavior. Although this approach is quite general, Section 2.2 points out that it may not be trivial to define and frame a model for the decision that captures the essence of the problem while retaining both tractability and intuition.

The identifying characteristic of decision making under uncertainty is that the DM does not know precisely the outcome of actions chosen because of the occurrence of events that are not under control, events that can only properly be viewed as a random variable X. Although the specific realization of the random variable is generally not known prior to the choice of action, in decision theory the DM identifies the possibilities and catalogues them into a nonempty set of mutually exclusive state descriptions, the *state space* $\mathbf{X} = \{x\}$, with the typical element $x \in \mathbf{X}$ being a specific state of nature that may occur. Examples of such variables include the realized future demand and price for a commodity, the political situation five years hence, the action chosen by an opponent, a scientific hypothesis, the precise distance in kilometers between your current location and the Eiffel Tower in Paris, and the values of a vector of unknown statistical parameters. As several of the examples illustrate, a state description can be multicategory.

Machlup (1962) defines knowledge as "anything that is known by somebody," and classifies it under these headings: 1) practical knowledge, 2) intellectual knowledge, 3) small-talk or pastime knowledge, 4) spiritual knowledge, and 5) unwanted knowledge. Since he defines practical knowledge as knowledge for the sake of action or control, decision making presents a need for practical or pragmatic knowledge. It is most convenient in the current context to define the DM's *knowledge* as her stock of beliefs about the state space $\mathbf{X}$, as assessed in $p(x)$, her current probability distribution over all possible states of nature.

In its simplest formulation, the outcome of the decision problem is a *payoff function* $\pi(x, a)$ that depends upon the combination of a, the action the DM chooses, and x, the ultimate realization of X. In a well-framed decision problem, the DM can either 1) immediately choose an optimal action a_0, or 2) exercise an option to change her knowledge about the random state variable by seeking information relevant to X.

1.1.2 Information and Information Sources

The concept of information plays an important role in a wide variety of scientific disciplines, and its precise meaning varies by subject and application; see Losee (1990). Dictionary definitions commonly contain phrases such as "knowledge communicated" or "knowledge acquired," implying the receipt of some kind of stimulus by an individual. For the purposes of this book on the economic value of information, *information* is defined as any stimulus that has changed the recipient's knowledge, that is, that has changed the recipient's probability distribution over a well-described set of states.

Boulding (1966) provides an analogy with the economic theory of capital that helps clarify the distinction between knowledge and information. Physical capital is a stock; at any point in time it is all produced means of further production. Knowledge can also be conceived of as a stock; at any point in time it is the stock of what is known and is embodied in the current probability distribution on the state space. Items known with certainty have a probability of one. In capital theory, investment is a flow; as it occurs it alters the stock of capital. Information is in a sense a flow—as it reveals itself it alters the stock of what is known by altering the probability of different states of the world. Finally, analogous to the depreciation of capital is the forgetting of knowledge.

Information may be an internally generated epiphany ("Eureka!") or, more likely, the result of the receipt and cognitive processing of a message from a data source. A *message* is the final form output of a data source, a specific package of data, accessible for processing into information. *Data* are symbols, images, sounds, and ideas that can be encoded, stored, and transmitted; a *data source* offers data with the intention or anticipation that they may be processed into information by some recipient at some time. The message remains as data until a recipient processes its semantic content and incorporates it into her knowledge of the world, at which time the message becomes information. The distinction between a data source and an information source is a fine one, based upon the intent of the user of the source: an *information source* is any data source from which a user seeks to obtain a message with the intention of processing it into information.

It is fundamental to maintain the distinction between an information source and a message that emanates from that source. The source the DM accesses is a matter of choice, but she cannot know beforehand the content of the resulting message; if the content were known, the message would already be incorporated into knowledge. To illustrate the distinction, consider the following examples of sources and their typical messages. Because they may have different implications for cost, it is useful in the sequel to group the sources themselves into four categories: interpersonal, data producing, broadcast, and archival.

1. *Interpersonal Sources.* These sources make direct human contact with the seeker of information and are typically able to get "close" to the perceived need. The messages are often original and verbal, hence not always documented.

- A doctor is a source; the diagnosis is a message.
- A friend or colleague is a source; advice is a message.
- A teacher is a source; an explanation is a message.
- A stockbroker is a source; stock recommendations are a message.
- A staff meeting is a source; a report from a subordinate is a message.

2. *Data Producing Sources.* These sources provide original data, often produced by individual creativity, by compiling from other sources, or by gathering and recording, for example, the responses to a survey, the documentation from a transaction, or the readings on a device in an experiment.

- An Internet search engine is a source; a listing of Websites is a message.
- A government agency is a source; last quarter's GDP growth rate is a message.
- A periodic sales report is a source; last week's sales are a message.
- A sphygmomanometer is a source; a blood pressure reading is a message.
- An author is a source; a manuscript is a message.
- An experiment to sample 43 bolts out of a production batch of 100 is a source; the observation that 6 bolts are defective is a message.

3. *Broadcast Sources.* These are instruments characterized by their active distribution of identical messages to a broad, but generally well-defined, audience. The potential user often needs to obtain some right or ability to receive the messages prior to dissemination, for example, by prepaying a subscription fee or belonging to the organization.

- A newspaper is a source; the news is a message.
- A browsing display is a source; a collection of recent issues is a message.
- A current awareness service is a source; a journal's contents page is a message.
- An investment advisory letter is a source; a list of stock recommendations is a message.
- A convention is a source; a seminar presentation is a message.

4. *Archival Sources.* These are sources from which stored data (from some other original source) may be retrieved as a message.

- The library catalogue is a source; the location of a book is a message.
- Personal files are a source; an extracted document is a message.
- The phone book is a source; a phone number is a message.
- A numerical database is a source; extracted historical data are a message.
- A competitor's new product is a source; the technology encoded within it is a message.
- A retailer's Internet home page is a source; the listed price on one of its products is a message.

The *common record*, a term used by Bush (1945), is the universe of publicly available data sources. To access a source from the common record and obtain its message, the individual must first find out that the source exists, then find out how and where it may be accessed. This access is always costly in terms of time and effort, and perhaps in other terms: the message may be for sale with payment in money and/or data about the individual; on the Internet, the individual may have to look at an advertisement before the message appears. In contrast to the common record are the *proprietary records* that are not intended to be available for common access.

1.1.3 Statistical and Pragmatic Information

In a decision problem under uncertainty, the prior distribution p(x) embodies all the DM's initial knowledge concerning the state realization. Suppose the DM identifies and chooses a specific information source, and subsequently obtains and cognitively processes a resulting message y. This message may lead the DM to eliminate the possibility of some states, decrease the probability of others, and increase the probability of still other states. With this new probability distribution of the state, called the *posterior distribution* and denoted $p(x \mid y)$, it may be that a new course of action appears to be best, one that may result in a different payoff. This is the fundamental way that information generates economic value—via its impact upon the solution to a decision problem.

The preceding paragraph in fact describes two distinct stages of information: statistical information and pragmatic information. *Statistical information* concerns only the properties of the probability distributions involved, for example, the cognitive transformation of knowledge from the prior to the posterior distribution. *Pragmatic information* involves the application of the statistical information; it concerns the potential impact of the statistical information on choice and payoff in a specific decision problem. This distinction [Cherry (1966), page 244] separates nouns commonly associated with the statistical attributes of information, such as coherence, format, and accuracy, from pragmatic attributes such as relevance, completeness, and timeliness. Statistical information affects what the individual knows; pragmatic information affects what the individual does.

Not all messages convey information. A necessary condition for a message to be statistical information is that it be news, that is, something not already known. When the content of the message is already known, the impact of the message is already incorporated into the initial probability assessment p(x) and the message is not statistical information. Another necessary condition for a message to be statistical information is that it be comprehensible. If a message is so garbled, or technical, or voluminous, or poorly expressed (e.g., bad teaching) that the recipient cannot assess the impact of the message upon the probability distribution of the states, the message cannot be statistical information.

A message can convey statistical information but not pragmatic information. A message stating your aunt's birthday is statistical information to me; it alters my probability assessment over that event. It is not pragmatic information to me and has no value to me because it is not relevant to the outcome of any of my actions. The same message may be pragmatic information to you, as your decision on sending a birthday gift may affect your payoffs via inheritance. Thus, the evaluation of pragmatic information requires reference to a specific decision problem and a specific decision maker.

One important alternative characterization of statistical information, associated with the pioneering work of Shannon (1948) in *information theory*, involves precise engineering measures of the quantity or amount of information—the amount of information in storage (measured, for example, in bytes), the amount of information transmitted over a period of time (for example, in bits per second), and the capacity or bandwidth of a communication channel that performs such transmission. It is preferable in the context of this book to think of information theory as studying the storage and transmission of data, rather than information. It turns out that these engineering measures relate directly to the costs of obtaining and incorporating information in decision making, but relate to the value of information only in very special cases (see Section 5.4).

1.1.4 Ex-Post Value and Gain

Let a_y denote the optimal response to the specific message y under the present knowledge $p(x \mid y)$. After the choice of action the state x occurs. An important quantity for information evaluation is the *ex-post value of the message* y:

$$\upsilon(x, y) = \pi(x, a_y) - \pi(x, a_0), \tag{1.1}$$

that is, the difference, in the realized state x, between the terminal payoff under action a_y and the terminal payoff that would have resulted under the prior action a_0. The ex-post value of a message can be positive, negative, or zero. The message could have resulted in an action more appropriate for the state that actually occurred; it could have steered the DM wrong and led to a less favorable outcome than would otherwise have been achieved; or it could have had no effect as, for example, when $a_y = a_0$. Dedicated and logical application of the ideas of decision theory does not guarantee that the DM always achieves a favorable outcome at the end of the day. Decision theory offers no defense against bad luck.

The ex-post value of the message y measures the gross impact of the message on the DM's payoff. To assess the net impact, there must be careful consideration of the costs of accessing, cognitively processing, and applying the message y. If $\mathcal{C}$ is the properly defined and measured cost, in the final accounting of the situation the *realized incremental gain* from incorporating information into the decision problem is

$$\mathcal{G} = \upsilon(x, y) - \mathcal{C} = \pi(x, a_y) - \pi(x, a_0) - \mathcal{C}. \tag{1.2}$$

The incorporation of information is an option for the DM, an option with the potential for generating value, but the certainty of generating cost. To build a framework for investigating the costs of information, let us presume that the DM is an agent or employee of a cooperative organization that is willing to facilitate the incorporation of information into her decision problem. This is not a constraining assumption, as the organization may well comprise a single individual, the DM herself. The next section considers such an organization's system for information.

1.2 Information in the Organization

1.2.1 Information Systems

Information produces value for the organization when it improves the solutions to decision problems whose outcomes are consequential to the organization. In its broadest definition, the organization's *information system* is the entire collection of data sources and related service capabilities, both internal and external to the organization, from which the users of the system may obtain messages. The fundamental presumption is that the system is user-centered: it serves the mission of the organization by serving the information needs of its users. The core function of the information system is to provide potential users with efficient accessibility to a cogent collection of sources and their concomitant messages.

For a single-person organization, the entire information system may simply be a personal collection of documents, the ability to access library facilities and the Internet, a set of friends and advisors, and any commercial vendors of data/information. For an organization comprising many information-seeking employees and agents, the information system can be quite complex.

It is natural for the organization to collect and link sources of all types into formal information subsystems intended to serve the needs of particular classifications of users, such as scientists, engineers, management executives, lawyers, and lobbyists. Common examples include:

- accounting and management information systems, set up to produce messages relevant to managerial control;
- special libraries, set up to assist in the solution of scientific/technical problems as they arise;
- market research departments, set up to produce studies of customers and products, along with finding and forecasting business opportunities;
- the legal department and law library, set up to address legal problems as they arise (litigation support subsystems);
- espionage subsystems, set up to obtain messages from proprietary records that other organizations do not want disseminated; and

- lobbying organizations, set up to monitor and influence government.

These formal subsystems are sometimes called *collective* or "*quasi-firm*" sources.

1.2.2 User Information Processing

User information processing is the procedure by which a user of the system seeks, identifies, chooses, obtains, understands, and applies information. It begins with a perceived need for information, which may arise from a specific and well-defined decision problem or merely reflect a desire to monitor or scan a particular environment in anticipation of potential future decision problems.

The purposes of *monitoring* are to obtain information for current awareness, professional development, education, and clearer general understanding of selected environments potentially relevant in future decision making situations. The incorporation of information via monitoring is similar in procedure to decision making, but since there is no active decision problem, there is no decision application of the message. Whereas successful decision making ends with pragmatic information, monitoring ends with statistical information. In Machlup's (1962) schema, the need that gives rise to monitoring is a need for intellectual knowledge. Monitoring initially engenders cost but not value; the benefit arises subsequently should the knowledge gained 1) reduce the cost of information processing in future decision making, or 2) lead to the identification of new opportunities (i.e., new decision problems with potentially favorable outcomes). In this sense, monitoring is an investment.

Facing the system with a well-framed need, the employee or agent of the organization views a multitude of alternative data sources; the problem is to process this universe of sources in the optimal way, appropriately defined. User information processing comprises three broad processes: user access, user cognition, and, when relevant, user application.

The first is *user access*, a problem involving the mechanics of how best to obtain an acceptable message for cognitive processing. The first activity of user access is the decision whether to seek information; when affirmative, the user enters the system as either a decision maker or a monitor. Access is successfully completed when the user has identified alternative data sources that could provide messages, chosen specific sources, obtained the message, and decided whether to accept the message for cognitive processing.

After user access comes *user cognition*, a complex intellectual process in which the user transforms the data into information and thereby views the environment with a new state of knowledge. Understanding the semantic content of the message can demand a time-consuming combination of cognitive activities such as reading, thinking, synthesizing, and interpreting, and sometimes requires sophisticated statistical data analysis.

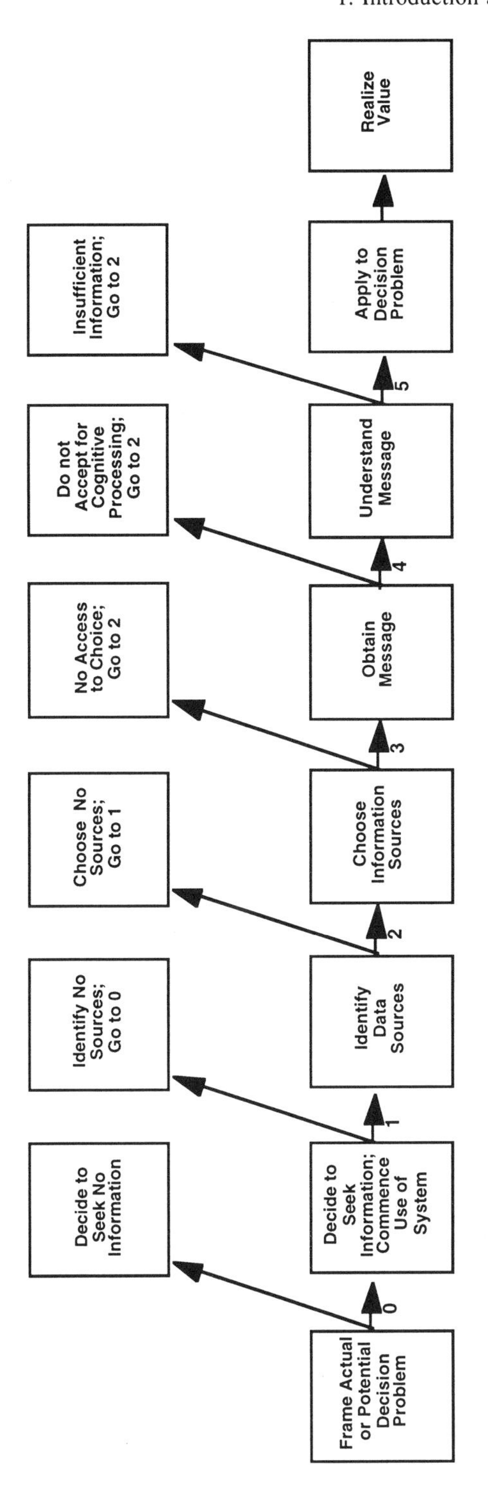

Figure 1.1. User information processing.

The assessment of statistical information is the end of the processing for the monitoring user. For the decision maker, the final process is *user application*, the determination of how best to respond to this new understanding within the context of the current decision problem, choosing the action now optimal in light of the message y.

Figure 1.1 presents the entire procedure for user information processing, detailing the various steps in what Kantor (1995) calls the *chain of value*: decision to seek, identification of alternative sources, choice of source, message access, cognition of the meaning and significance of the message, and application of the message to the decision problem at hand. Each step is costly to the DM and/or her organization, yet there is no guarantee at the time the costs are borne that the information will prove valuable.

Given an affirmative decision to seek information and enter the system, the flowchart illustrates that a complete terminal use of the system involves answers to the following questions, each of which has an associated cost. 1) Which potential information sources can I identify? 2) Which source do I choose? 3) Having chosen the source, how do I obtain the message? 4) Having accessed a specific message, what does this message mean in the context of my uncertain view of the environment? 5) For decision making uses, what action do I undertake in light of my new understanding of the environment? If this state of knowledge is deemed insufficient for meeting the original need, the user may choose to access another source. The user cognitively processes each source's message one by one until arriving at the decision to stop processing information and solve the decision problem by choosing the action a_y.

A false start occurs if, after having decided to seek information, 1) no potentially informative sources are identified, 2) none of the identified choices are judged worthy of being chosen, 3) a source is chosen but cannot be accessed, 4) a message is obtained but not processed because upon sight it is judged not to be valuable, or 5) the message is cognitively processed but contains no statistical information. A false start means there has been a waste of time and effort, and the more steps the user takes before either restarting or aborting the search, the more costs are borne for no gain. The cost of a terminal use of the information system is the sum of the cost of an efficient use plus the cost of false starts.

The user knows the procedure by which she identifies, chooses, obtains, understands, and applies information, but she cannot have full prior knowledge of the details. The initial decision to seek information, indicated by node 0) in the flowchart, is the overarching activity of user information processing because its proper execution requires ex-ante consideration of all subsequent activities and their prospective costs. It involves gathering information about the various potential information sources, making it essentially a problem of assessing *foreknowledge of information*, that is, of obtaining information about the alternative information sources. One motivation for monitoring is to obtain and update foreknowledge.

Unfortunately, the data and effort required for a formal decision-theoretic analysis of the choice from among multiple sources can be very demanding upon the DM. The completion of this task often requires simplified and heuristic decision making approaches, and is an activity to which the organization's information system can make key practical contributions.

Suppose the user enters the system with a more or less well-defined need. The organization facilitates the incorporation of information by designing and offering a system that allows the user to satisfy this perceived need efficiently. In perhaps the most simple modern use of the system, she types a keyword into a search engine (a data producing source)[1] and obtains a message, a list of titles and perhaps other descriptors. Each of these titles is now an archival data source, and the ones she chooses to access become information sources. Any document, once obtained, is a message to be cognitively processed.

1.2.3 Information System Accounting

The information system is costly to build and operate. Figure 1.2 depicts the framework for the accounting analysis of an information system from the organization's viewpoint. To the organization, it is system design that is overarching, as the optimal offer to the users requires proper consideration of all subsequent system and user activities and costs. Considering system design as itself a process, the top row of the flowchart indicates five system processes that contribute in their own way to the generation of information cost and value. The second row of Figure 1.2 identifies four classes of cost for a given information system. A cost may be fixed or variable, depending upon whether it increases directly with the number of terminal uses of the system. All costs are ultimately borne by the organization, but the incidence of a cost can be either on the system or on the user. Analysis in Chapter 9 indicates that the division between system-borne costs and user-borne costs is an important design characteristic because it affects user behavior within the system and ultimately the organization's information gain. As the final two rows of Figure 1.2 depict, subtracting the organization's total information cost from the total information value of all decision making uses yields the organization's information gain.

Note that in this framework, the only source of information value is user application in decision making. All other processes and activities contribute solely to the cost of information. Denoting each terminal use of the system with the subscript τ, the *organization's realized information gain* is

---

[1] Alternately, she could go first to an interpersonal source such as an information professional or to an archival source such as the card catalogue.

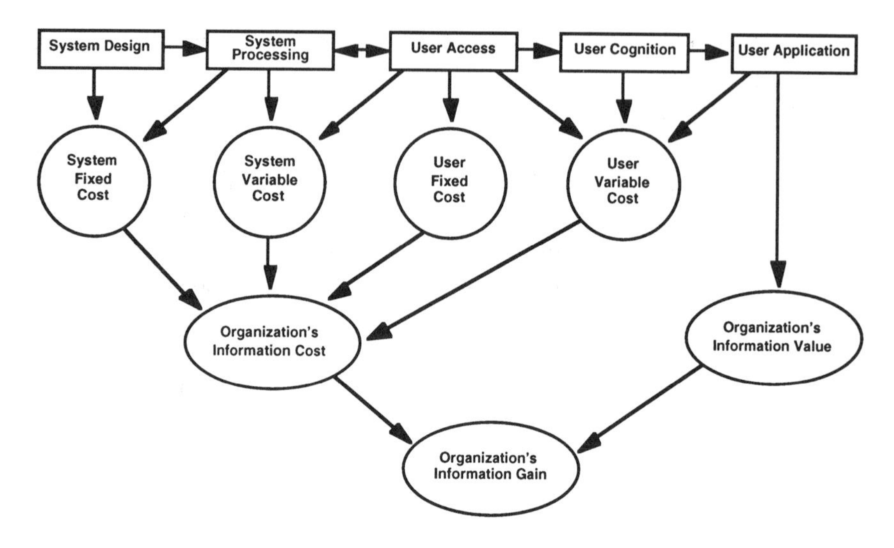

Figure 1.2. Information system accounting.

$$\mathcal{OG} = -\mathcal{FC} + \Sigma_\tau \mathcal{G}_\tau, \tag{1.3}$$

where $\mathcal{FC}$ is the total fixed cost of the system, $\mathcal{G}_\tau = \upsilon_\tau(x, y) - \mathcal{C}_\tau$ as in (1.2) for a decision making use, and $\mathcal{G}_\tau = -\mathcal{C}_\tau$ for a monitoring use of the information system. From the organization's viewpoint, there is no bottom-line difference between a \$1 increase in the value of information produced at the same cost and a \$1 decrease in the cost of information that provides the same value: both increase the organization's gain by \$1.[2]

1.3 Economics of the Incorporation of Information

1.3.1 The Criterion

Although accounting equations such as (1.2) and (1.3) are useful in the final analysis of the utilization of information sources and systems, they belie most of the economic complexities of optimal information provision, access, cognition, response, and consequence. The fundamental analytical difficulty in the study of information processing by the user and system design by the organization is the ex-ante nature of the decision making: actions must be chosen before states occur, sources must be evaluated, costed, and chosen before the receipt of

[2] See Figure 9.1 and the surrounding discussion for more specificity on the gain-producing activities within the information system.

any message, and the system must be designed before the specific information needs arise.

In the face of these uncertainties, users and system designers require a criterion upon which to evaluate and compare the available options. The *criterion* defines the characteristics of the best, or optimal, choice among alternatives. Perhaps the simplest and most popular is the criterion of expected value: evaluate and compare the expected value of the relevant objective function, using a specified probability distribution for the random variable generating the uncertainty.

The *expected value*, or *mathematical expectation*, of a function g(x) with respect to a random variable X having probability distribution p(x) is denoted as $E_x\, g(x)$. If the state space **X** is countable and p(x) discrete,

$$E_x\, g(x) \;=\; \Sigma_i\, g(x_i)\, p(x_i), \tag{1.4a}$$

and if **X** is uncountable and p(x) continuous,

$$E_x\, g(x) \;=\; \int_{\mathbf{X}} g(x)\, p(x)\, dx. \tag{1.4b}$$

In practice, it is always assumed that the sum or integral converges absolutely and hence that the expectation exists.

1.3.2 Ex-Ante Components of Decision Making

Choice of Action

Applying this criterion to the choice of action, the discussion in Section 1.1 describes the actions a_0 and a_y somewhat vaguely as the DM's optimal choice. The simplest, but certainly not the only, way to operationalize this is to use the DM's payoff in the decision problem as the relevant objective function. Given initial knowledge p(x), the optimal choice under the expected value criterion is identified by calculating the expectation of the payoff function $\pi(x, a)$ for every $a \in \mathbf{a}$ and choosing the action a_0 that maximizes it:

$$\max_a \int_{\mathbf{X}} \pi(x, a)\, p(x)\, dx \;=\; \max_a E_x\, \pi(x, a) \;=\; E_x\, \pi(x, a_0). \tag{1.5}$$

To avoid technical complications, it is assumed that such a maximum exists and can be achieved. The level of the maximum expected payoff in (1.5) is called the *value of the prior decision.*

Likewise, if the DM has processed the message into $p(x \mid y)$, the optimal action posterior to the receipt of the message y is defined by

$$\max_a \int_{\mathbf{X}} \pi(x, a)\, p(x \mid y)\, dx \;=\; \max_a E_{x|y}\, \pi(x, a) \;=\; E_{x|y}\, \pi(x, a_y), \tag{1.6}$$

where $E_{x|y}$ denotes expectation with respect to $p(x \mid y)$. The action a_y is a *conditional decision rule* that tells the DM what to do, conditional upon the cognitive processing of the received message y into the new state of knowledge embodied in $p(x|y)$.

Evaluation of a Source

Since the source must be chosen before any message is obtained, the relevant time period for assessing the pragmatic value of a particular information source is prior to the receipt of any message. For example, the source might be an economic forecasting firm, and the message a direct forecast of the future realization of the state. Before obtaining the forecast from the source, the DM must recognize that many different forecasts are possible, each of which might lead her to choose a different action in response, thereby altering her payoff.

The upcoming Section 1.4 discusses the evaluation and incorporation of one information source within the context of one decision problem. A review of several real-world case studies illustrates the applicability and versatility of the basic framework. At this stage the costs of information move into the background; the primary concern is the measurement of the gross or before-cost expected value of pragmatic information and the study of the determinants of that value. These topics comprise the bulk of this book, with Chapters 2 through 7 providing the details.

Choice of Sources

Section 1.5 and Chapter 8 concern the choice of which sources to access. It is at this point that tradeoffs between the value and cost of information play a major role. Choosing sources efficiently is important because many of the costs of information processing are borne prior to the completion of cognition and application to decision. In the preceding example, the forecaster is unlikely to provide any specific message until after the DM has agreed to pay for the service. Likewise, an archived document is merely a collection of data until a user accesses it, reads it, and processes its message into statistical and pragmatic information. The reader of this chapter has at this point already borne cost in terms of time spent, and may still be processing whether the data of these words amounts to a message containing any information.

Depending upon the specific decision problem, the DM may anticipate the selection of only one source (e.g., a doctor) or the selection of many sources (e.g., document titles) from among the universe of alternatives. In this auxiliary problem of optimal user access, an appropriate objective is to use (1.2) and evaluate the expected incremental gain from each combination of potential sources, choosing the one that maximizes this expectation. Section 1.5 ends by reviewing some case studies involving the tradeoffs between information cost and information value.

Design of the System

Finally, with regard to the ex-ante nature of system design, the organization has only general knowledge of the users' needs for information before they arise, and even less knowledge of which source or sources each user will ultimately choose. Despite the lack of knowledge about the specifics, the organization must design, fund, build, and manage the system in anticipation of future uses. An appropriate objective for design is to use (1.3) and maximize the organization's expected information gain. Section 1.6 and Chapter 9 investigate the design by the organization of an information system that intends to meet the myriad needs for information as those needs arise.

1.4 The Expected Value of an Information Source

1.4.1 Information Structure and Informativeness

Since the seeker of information cannot know the specific message before committing to the source and bearing some expense, it is proper to view the message to be received as itself a random variable. The *message space* $\mathbf{Y} = \{y\}$ formally enumerates all potentially receivable messages from the information source.

For example, suppose a military decision problem involves the deployment of tanks, and an officer is considering a reconnaissance mission to count the number of enemy tanks in a particular area. The officer cannot know, before the mission, the precise count that will result from this data producing source; the message is the set of integers from zero to some conceivable maximum. Likewise, in modern day weather forecasting of the dichotomous state space "rain" or "no rain," the messages are alternative probabilities of rain, stated in a range from zero to 100% in increments of 10%; there are eleven potential messages in this message space.

It is convenient when assessing statistical informativeness, the value of information, and the cost of user cognition to classify the message space $\mathbf{Y}$ by relevance and by type. The source's message space is *direct* if the messages concern the state variable in the decision problem at hand; the messages are *indirect* if the semantic content can be related to the matter at hand by means of inference, study, reflection, and related forms of cognitive processing. Roughly speaking, the interpersonal and data producing sources have greater capability to provide message spaces directly relevant to a specific decision problem, whereas the archival and broadcast sources tend to offer documents requiring semantic processing to establish relevance.

The messages can also be classified by type or form. An individual message is *probabilistic* if it expresses a probability distribution over some exhaustive collection of events ("The probability of rain tonight is 40%."). A *categorical* message simply makes a statement ("Long-term interest rates will be 4% in 2002." "An increase in demand will cause an increase in the price."), leaving to the user the determination of the appropriate posterior probability distribution over the payoff-relevant events. An *interval* message, most commonly occurring when the random variable is on the real line, identifies a range of values within which the realization lies and may or may not have a probability associated with it ("There is a good chance the stock's price will fall." "The high tomorrow will be between 70 and 75 degrees.").

Prior to the choice of source and receipt of message, both the state and the message are random variables, and presumably the two are interrelated; the joint probability distribution p(x, y), defined on $\mathbf{X} \times \mathbf{Y}$, expresses the probabilistic relationship between the states that might occur and the messages that might be obtained and processed. A source's *information structure* **I** comprises the message space and the joint measure on messages and states:

$$\mathbf{I} = \{\mathbf{Y}, p(x, y)\}. \tag{1.7}$$

The information structure, describing both the current and all potential states of knowledge about the unknown random variable X, is relevant in the analysis of both decision making and monitoring situations.

In the military example, because of enemy camouflage or certain inadequacies in the design of the reconnaissance mission, any resulting count of enemy tanks may not correspond exactly to the true state of the enemy's strength. The information structure quantifies the extent of the correspondence; in principle, it embodies the statistical informativeness the information source is capable of delivering. The *statistical informativeness* of an information structure is a latent measure of the structure's potential to provide pragmatic information value within the general context of any potential user interested in the state space **X**. Statistical informativeness can range from null (no) information to perfect information; anything in between is termed imperfect information. When appropriately defined, a parameter θ can serve as an index of the statistical informativeness of an information structure.

Depending upon the circumstances, the statistical informativeness of a structure may be exogenous or endogenous to the user. If informativeness is exogenous, the problem is to assess it. If it is endogenous, the problem is to control it.

1.4.2 The Measurement of Information Value: Chapters 2 and 3

The quantity $E_{x|y}\,\pi(x, a_y)$, defined in (1.6), gives the DM's expected payoff posterior to the optimal response to the message y, but prior to the realization of the state variable X. Assessing this quantity for every y that might be received, and weighing it by p(y), the marginal probability of ultimately receiving y, the DM's expected payoff prior to the receipt of any message is

$$E_y\, E_{x|y}\, \pi(x, a_y) \;=\; E_y\, \max_a E_{x|y}\, \pi(x, a). \tag{1.8}$$

If the DM expects the payoff $E_y\, E_{x|y}\, \pi(x, a_y)$ prior to choosing and using the source, and without the source can expect the payoff $E_x\, \pi(x, a_0)$ given by (1.5) anyway, then the simplest measure of the expected value of a source with information structure **I** is the incremental expected payoff attributable to the source:

$$V(\mathbf{I}) \;=\; E_y\, E_{x|y}\, \pi(x, a_y) - E_x\, \pi(x, a_0). \tag{1.9}$$

Under the criterion of maximizing the expected payoff in the decision problem, the quantity V(**I**) represents the maximum amount the DM could pay for a source with structure **I** and still expect to be better off from incorporating information into the problem solution. If the actual variable cost of incorporating **I** is known and fixed at $\mathcal{C}$, and $\mathcal{C} < V(\mathbf{I})$, then the expected gain from the structure **I** is $V(\mathbf{I}) - \mathcal{C}$. If $\mathcal{C} > V(\mathbf{I})$, then the DM expects to be worse off by incorporating information; the DM should not access this source.

This particular measure of the value of information can also be developed in another way: it is the ex-ante expectation of the ex-post value of the message y, defined by (1.1). That is,

$$\begin{aligned} E_y\, E_{x|y}\, \upsilon(x, y) \;&=\; E_y\, E_{x|y}\, [\pi(x, a_y) - \pi(x, a_0)], \\ &=\; E_y\, E_{x|y}\, \pi(x, a_y) - E_y\, E_{x|y}\, \pi(x, a_0) \\ &=\; E_y\, E_{x|y}\, \pi(x, a_y) - E_x\, \pi(x, a_0) \;=\; V(\mathbf{I}), \end{aligned} \tag{1.10}$$

where the third equality uses the law of iterated expectation presented in Section 2.3.

The measure V(**I**), ex-ante in nature because it is assessed prior to deciding whether to choose this source, exemplifies the basic idea of the expected value of information. There are, however, numerous generalizations, extensions, complications, and mitigating circumstances to this approach, especially involving the framing of the problem and the choices of objective and criterion. Chapter 2 presents the more general model for analyzing informed decision making; this chapter's introductory framework is a special case. Section 2.1 details the elements of decision making under uncertainty, and Section 2.2 discusses some of the practical difficulties involved in the framing of the decision problem for an information analysis.

Evaluating and applying information structures requires facility with multivariate probability distributions; Section 2.3 contains a brief review. From p(x, y) the DM can obtain the marginal distribution p(y) that describes the probability that she receives any specific message y, along with all potential posterior distributions of the state, p(x | y) for every $y \in \mathbf{Y}$ that may be received.

Section 2.4 generalizes the idea of (1.8), describing the determination of the *value of the informed decision*, the ex-ante gross expected benefit to the DM from incorporating information into the problem solution. Section 2.4 also considers the upper and lower bounds for the value of the informed decision.

By viewing the decision problem as a commodity that can be bought and sold, Chapter 3 studies various measures of the incremental or marginal value of decisions, messages, and information sources. The *buying price* of a decision is the maximum amount someone would be willing to pay in order to obtain the rights to receive the outcome of the problem. Similarly, the *reservation price* is the minimum amount the current owner of a decision would accept in a sale of the rights to another party. The comparison of the buying and selling prices of decisions with and without the use of information provides several alternative measures of the ex-ante value of incorporating a particular information source. The measure V(**I**) in (1.9) is an example of a buying price for an information structure.

The DM can assess these measures at any of four stages: 1) prior to any consideration of incorporating information; 2) *ex-post*, which is posterior to both the application of the message from a specific source and the realization of the state; 3) *conditional*, which is posterior to the processing and application of the message, but prior to the realization of the state; and 4) *preposterior*, which is prior to the processing of any of the source's potential messages. Chapter 3 shows that only in special cases do the various conceptualizations produce the same measure of value. The measure V(**I**) is a preposterior assessment.

1.4.3 The Assessment of Information Value: Chapters 4 and 5

Chapters 4 and 5 consider the practical problems of assessment. This covers two matters: assessment of the required probability distributions, and assessment of the problem-related factors necessary to determine the value of pragmatic information in a specific decision. These two chapters provide a compendium of tractable techniques for these assessments and calculations—methods for eliciting beliefs, problem framings with convenient functional forms and utility functions, and models for assessment with minimal initial foreknowledge of information.

Chapter 4 covers techniques for the assessment of foreknowledge of the information structure, a difficult task that requires the coherent assessment of probabilities and/or the estimation of statistical parameters. This activity may or may not be associated with a specific decision problem; the motivation may be to monitor in anticipation of future decisions. Monitoring can involve 1) reassessing one's prior knowledge (i.e., keeping p(x) current by obtaining information about the environment) and 2) obtaining foreknowledge about the informativeness of one or more alternative potential sources. In both cases, monitoring may reduce the cost of future decision making should the need arise.

The DM's most basic assessment is to figure out exactly what she already knows, that is, to express her prior knowledge of the state in the form of p(x). This task may be purely subjective and personal in nature, it may be based on auxiliary data such as historical relative frequencies of relevant events, or it may be based on some combination of the two. This assessment is fundamental to the solution of the problem, whether or not the DM decides to incorporate information. Determining exactly what she knows may require a significant amount of work, including sophisticated statistical analysis, and hence can be costly; it is a practical matter to determine when the assessment of foreknowledge ends and the incorporation of information begins.

The necessity for framing problems and assessing initial knowledge are costly activities that are independent of the decision to incorporate information, but the assessment of the prior distribution has an important side-benefit: p(x) is the only aspect of the information structure that the DM needs to calculate the *expected value of perfect information*, which answers the question, "If I were able to find out exactly which state will occur before I choose the optimal action, what do I expect that ability to be worth?" This quantity is an upper bound on information value that is independent of all the alternative sources.

The input for assessing a source's information structure, $\mathbf{I} = \{\mathbf{Y}, p(x, y)\}$ as in (1.7), may be the user's experience-based subjective beliefs about what a source might be able to do for her in a specific context, or it may be based upon historical relative frequencies such as a track record, or there may be a well-defined statistical model. The user may intend to extract the information herself, for example, by obtaining and reading documents or performing experiments. Alternately, she may elicit messages from vendors and other interpersonal sources, called *informants*. In any case, part of cognitive processing is to translate or calibrate whatever message is obtained into the user's own posterior beliefs.

Taking the foreknowledge as given, Chapter 5 presents a series of special case models with convenient assessment and interpretation that can help the DM clarify which probabilities, expectations, and economic parameters she needs to assess. For example, the problem structure may involve a number of economic parameters, but not all of them need to be assessed for the purpose of valuing a potential information source. Sections 5.1 through 5.6 investigate the determination and interpretation of the value of information in the context of several important types of economic problems, including production, pricing, sampling, inventory, investing, bidding, and control decisions. Section 5.7 presents some useful techniques for approximating information value in more complex decision situations.

1.4.4 Case Studies of Information Value

The techniques for assessing the economic value of an information source in the context of a specific decision problem are quite general, and despite their inherent complexity, find wide multidisciplinary application. The purpose of this subsection is to document this variety by reviewing several case studies that assess the value of various types of information. Several of the studies involve decision problems faced by business organizations, where the payoff is bottom-line profitability, whereas others involve public policy decisions in which the payoff is some measure of social welfare, such as public health.

Lave (1963) is an early case study, investigating the value of weather forecasts to a California raisin grower. The grower's action is to determine the best time in the fall to pick the grapes, and the unknown state variable is the timing of the first rainfall greater than a tenth of an inch. The grower's payoff (profit) is adversely affected by rain, but to different degrees depending upon whether the grapes are still on the vine or are being dried. Using a decision tree format (see Section 2.1) and taking the climatological probabilities as the prior distribution of the state, Lave finds the prior optimal decision is to wait a short while before harvesting, giving an expected profit of \$233.70/acre. Suppose now the grower has singular access to an information source that predicts perfectly when the first rain will occur, three weeks in advance of the event. The potential for changing the harvest time creates the economic value of this source. For example, if it should occur that the rain holds off until later in the fall, the grower can keep the grapes on the vine longer than she would otherwise dare, creating a larger crop. The value of the informed decision is \$314.65/acre, making the expected value of perfect information \$90.95/acre.

Baquet, Halter, and Conklin (1976) estimate the value of nightly forecasts of frost to eight specific pear orchardists in Jackson County, Oregon. The state space is 16 possible nightly low temperatures, and the orchardist's action is to light heaters which raise the orchard's temperature by an amount that depends on how many are lit. The decision rule stating how many heaters to light depends upon a nightly message from the National Weather Service, a broadcast source that offers a direct and categorical forecast of the low. Hence the information structure is the finite one discussed in Section 2.3.2, and the statistical informativeness is assessed using historical data of past forecasts and past realizations. The prior distribution of the state is climatologically based. The payoff is each orchardist's profit measured from a base, a daily table that varies according to the development of the pears over the two-month at-risk season. The value of the informed decision varies for each orchardist, illustrating the problem-specific and person-specific nature of the value of information. The government forecasts have an average value for all profit-maximizing orchardists of $4.73 per day per acre.

Davis and Dvoranchik (1971) investigate an engineering problem regarding the design of a bridge over Rillito Creek in Arizona. The decision is the depth of the bridge's piles; the deeper the piles the stronger the bridge. The state variabl is the maximum annual streamflow under the bridge. The payoff involves th cost of sinking deeper piles versus the cost of repairing the bridge should th streamflow be too great and the bridge be damaged. The message space is t possible flows that could be observed in additional years. Davis and Dvoranc concentrate on obtaining better estimates for the parameters of the probabi distribution of the maximum flow. Given 40 years of historical data, the pected value of knowing the "true" parameters of the distribution is $331.

Swinton and King (1994) provide an example of the trend toward integ multidisciplinary approaches to the valuation of information. This study ass the value of weed-scouting information in the context of a complete manag model for a 480-acre cash grain farm in southwestern Minnesota. The state population of weeds on the farm; the actions are various techniques for c ling the weeds. The model is multiperiod (see Section 5.6.1), as decisi weed control in one year affect the weed seed bank the next. The payoff fı is the discounted profits of the farm enterprise. A bioeconomic model a the effect of weed population on yield, and then determines the decision rule for optimal weed control, given perfect information at some point about the weed count. If initial knowledge is that the weed count is relatively low, Swinton and King estimate a perfect count of emerged seedlings is expected to increase annual farm income by $3,957, or $8.24 per acre, over the prior decision. As does Baquet et al. (1976), the paper also assesses the information value if the DM is not neutral towards risk (see Section 2.1.1), in this case for DMs exhibiting the exponential utility function discussed in Sections 5.3 and 7.1.3.

Adams et al. (1995) assess the aggregate economic value of improved forecasts of the El Niño weather phenomenon to the southeastern United States. The state space is finite with three possibilities: an El Niño pattern, a La Niña (or El Viejo) pattern, and neither pattern. The message space is a direct categorical forecast of one of the states, hence the information structure is the straightforward finite model of Section 2.3.2. The assessment of the expected payoff under alternative information structures is quite sophisticated, drawing upon meteorological, agronomic, and economic effects. The model estimates the temperature and precipitation conditions under the three states in 13 geographic locations, estimates the consequences of these changes on various crops using an agronomic model, determines how this affects the cropping, irrigation, and livestock decisions of farmers in the region, and finally assesses the aggregate economic effects on society's payoff, as measured by total producer and consumer surplus.[3] The value of perfect information is assessed at $144.5 million, and the value of a specified improvement in informativeness over current forecasts is assessed at $96 million, assuming no federal farm programs.

Dakins et al. (1996) apply the decision theory framework to the cleanup of PCB contamination in New Bedford Harbor, Massachusetts. The action is the volume of the harbor's sediment to be cleaned up in order to make the biota fit for human consumption. The state variable is the correct amount to be cleaned up. The payoff is asymmetric: if too little is cleaned up the harbor must be closed longer, with great economic loss; if too much is cleaned up, cost has been borne unnecessarily. The formal structure of the problem is similar to the inventory problem covered in Section 5.2.4. The information source is a data producing experiment to observe the body burden of PCB in the flounder of the harbor. This is an example of a message space offering indirect probabilistic messages. Given a sample of fish and a frequency distribution of PCB body burden, complex biological and engineering analysis is necessary to relate the message to the posterior probability distribution for the state. The expected value of perfect information about the PCB body burden is given as $15.6 million; the authors give several reasons why this estimate seems high and should be viewed as an upper bound.

Decision theory finds considerable application in medicine; see Weinstein (1996) for a recent review. Decisions on a patient's health are perhaps the clearest example of the individual-specific nature of the value of information. In order to decide whether to incorporate an information source such as a biopsy on a person suspected of having herpes encephalitis [Barza and Pauker (1980)] or an amniocentesis to detect Down's syndrome [Pauker and Pauker (1987)], the payoff function is typically assessed by the patient in consultation with the physician; payoff is rarely measured in the monetary unit.

On the public health front, information evaluation techniques offer a methodology for allocating limited funds among alternative research projects (i.e., information sources). Weinstein (1983) studies research funding for cancer prevention. Here, the actions are alternative policies to alter the public's exposure to specific chemicals, and a natural unit for payoff is the aggregate number of premature deaths prevented or the years of life saved, per dollar expended on the project. Weinstein estimates that a rodent bioassay to study the carcinogenic potency of the chemical p-Dichlorobenzene is expected to cost $11,000 per year of life saved, whereas a study of the health benefits of the dietary supplement β-

---

[3] See Section 8.1.2 for discussion and references about market feedback effects from broadcast-source information provided to individual DMs.

carotene would cost $91 per year of life saved. Hence, studying β-carotene is more cost-effective.

Hammitt and Cave (1991) go one step further by recognizing that policies to alter the exposure to one chemical can cause behavioral responses by consumers and businesses that may alter exposure to other chemicals. They consider the unknown loss of life attributable to the consumption of coffee that has been decaffeinated using the solvent Dichloromethane (DCM). If DCM were banned, businesses would use other processes for decaffeination, but these alternatives themselves may have an unknown impact upon human health. Furthermore, in a more detailed analysis for any one chemical, the loss of life can be factored into several components, each of which can itself be viewed as a random variable: the carcinogenic potency or toxicity, the exposure or dose per person, and the number of people exposed. Joint consideration of all possibilities sets up a multi-categorical state space; information analysis can then investigate the value of complete information about all of the categories taken together, or the value of *incomplete information* about one random variable only, accomplished by assuming only prior knowledge about all others. This is straightforward if all the variables are statistically independent—if not, information about one category can provide information about the others. Section 5.5 covers these issues.

In the preceding example, if the prior decision were to permit the use of DCM, Hammitt and Cave estimate that perfect information about both health impacts is expected to save 510 life-years, perfect information about the DCM category alone would save 501, and perfect information about the substitutes would save 469. Note that the value of incomplete information taken one at a time does not add up to the value of complete information. This is typically the case, even when the random variables involved are statistically independent. The recommendation of this type of analysis is that resources be targeted to the individual categories about which the value of incomplete information is the highest; in the preceding example, it would be better to study the health impacts of DCM than the alternatives, if the cost of each research program were the same and funds were limited.

If one is willing to put a monetary value on a human life saved or lost, then it becomes straightforward to compare alternative actions that differ both in their cost of implementation and in their effectiveness for reducing loss of life. In an often-applied approach [Finkel and Evans (1987)], the state variable is the number of deaths per year from exposure to a specific substance in the absence of any controls. This sets up a model in which the payoff is linear in the state variable for each of several alternative actions intended to affect exposure. Information takes the form of making better assessments of the state variable; in its simplest version, this is the model of Section 5.2.1. Evans, Hawkins, and Graham (1988) use this approach to calculate the expected value of radon testing for various types of families and different prior knowledge about previous test results from other locations. Using techniques described in Section 4.1.3, the authors elicit probability judgments from experts on radon exposure and potency. One of their assessments is that the expected value of a radon test to a young childless couple in an untested region in the northern United States is $333. Incidentally, the test costs about $50.

The recent decline in the cost of computation is facilitating more frequent application of highly complex models with multicategorical state spaces. These approaches typically require probabilistic and economic assessments that draw from many disciplines and can only be analyzed by means of simulation and/or sampling techniques. A good example is Thompson and Evans (1997), who study the value of information about the potency of and exposure to Perchloroethylene (Perc), a compound used in dry cleaning. Carcinogenic potency is one random variable, and current exposures are also unknown, differing for dry cleaners, customers, and the general public, and varying by the type of equipment the facility currently employs. This sets up a model with well over a dozen random state variables. The various actions differ by their cost of implementation and their effectiveness in reducing exposure; furthermore, the action spaces differ by the type of equipment in use. Generally, Thompson and Evans find that perfect incomplete information about potency is more valuable than that about exposure. Perfect complete information for one particular facility is $370/year when life is valued at $3 million each. Finding out about potency alone is worth $340/year to this facility. Nationally, the value of perfect complete information is $7.6 million, if regulatory standards are set by facility.

Better understanding of global warming is an important current issue that requires complex modeling and multidisciplinary knowledge. Global warming is the possibility that the emission of carbon dioxide and other greenhouse gases (GHG) will change the Earth's climate, and that any climate change could have profound effects upon the future history of the planet. Decisions taken today to reduce GHG emissions seem very expensive, but the payoff from actions today are long-term, and the random variables are manifold: among others, the effects GHG have on climate, the damage that would occur if the climate changes, the costs of reducing emissions today or in the future, the ability of the environment to cleanse itself, and the technological progress that will occur in the future. The number of possible states of the world are almost unimaginable. Two integrated models of world economic development and climate change, Peck and Teisberg's (1996) CETA-R model and Nordhaus and Popp's (1997) PRICE model, are being applied to assess the value of complete and incomplete information about the random variables of importance.

The most interesting informational issue is the assessment of the value of learning about the realization of one or more of the random variables today as opposed to many years into the future. The sooner we know one way or the other, the sooner we can make the appropriate investments and enforce the appropriate controls. The expected impact of this on the discounted present value of worldwide income is the value of more timely information.[4]

The Peck and Teisberg analysis is the simpler of the two. They look at three random variables: the effect of GHG on climate, the economic effect of global climate change, and the discount rate. If each variable can take on one of two values, there is a grand total of only $2^3 = 8$ states. Nordhaus and Popp consider eight variables, each of which can take on five values, giving $5^8 = 390{,}625$ states. This is unmanageable and requires sampling techniques to assess information value. The technique of Latin hypercube sampling is popular in these cases; see Section 5.7 for further discussion of both the Nordhaus–Popp approach and information evaluation in large complex models more generally.

On the basis of a sample of 200 model runs, compared to finding out in 50 years, Nordhaus and Popp assess the value of perfect complete information today at $85.8 billion. The Peck and Teisberg estimates are higher, but it is interesting to note that both studies rank the value of incomplete information similarly: both assess the value of answering the question of the damages from global warming to be about four times the value of learning about the impact of GHG on global temperature.[5]

1.4.5 The Theory of Information Value: Chapters 6 and 7

Many applied studies use sensitivity analysis to quantify the effects on the value of information from changes in the level of certain critical parameters; the assumed value of a life and the appropriate rate of time preference are just two important examples. These are, generally speaking, problem-specific results with effects on information value that are not monotonic. The trend away from simple models with closed form solutions to highly complex models that can only be analyzed by means of simulation makes it harder to isolate the determinants of the value of information. The value of information depends upon many factors, not only upon the specific pragmatic uses to which the source is to be put, but also upon the preferences and initial knowledge of the DM and the general statistical properties of the information structure. Chapters 6 and 7 are primarily theo-

---

[4] Two technical issues are interesting here: Section 5.6.1 discusses the role of the discount rate, and Section 4.2.3 considers the reconciliation of divergent expert opinion about the prior probability distribution of the economic effects of global climate change.

[5] Compare Table 5 of Nordhaus and Popp (1997) with Table 6 of Peck and Teisberg (1996).

retical chapters whose motivation is to investigate more closely the determinants of the economic value of information.

As an illustration of the practical importance of this, Hammitt and Cave (1991) present an alternative approach to the allocation of a research budget, based upon an assessment of the various characteristics of a project that are believed to be the determinants of the value of the project's information, factors such as the prior uncertainty, the statistical informativeness, the potential for the resulting message to affect action, and the consequential impact upon payoff. The factors are then combined and the scores compared by project using methods developed by Keeney and Raiffa (1976). The application of this kind of holistic approach requires a thorough understanding about the determinants of information value.

Most people have an intuitive feel for how various attributes of a decision problem ought to affect the value of information. Some assertions are empty, true by definition: "Better information is more valuable." "More timely information is more valuable." "More relevant information is more valuable." Other statements are meaningful, in the sense that their validity can be investigated: "The greater the stakes of the problem, the more valuable is information." "The more risky the situation, the more valuable is information." "More accurate information is more valuable." "Less delayed information is more valuable." "When the DM has more options from which to choose, the information is less valuable." "Information value increases with the amount of information transmitted." "The more you dislike risk, the more you value information." "Wealthier individuals are willing to pay more for information." "The more informative the information structure, in the sense of Blackwell, the more valuable the structure."

Certainly the validity and generality of these statements depend upon precise definitions and measurements of concepts such as informativeness, risk, and stochastic preference. Chapters 6 and 7 show that, under reasonable definitions, none of the preceding statements is universally true.[6] Many are valid under some conditions, forcing the analyst to specify "more valuable to whom?" and "more valuable under what circumstances?" The goal is to describe the widest class of decision problems within which a certain property or relationship holds, but with a few notable exceptions, the success at identifying general results is not

[6] The text identifies nine meaningful statements. Counterexamples or counterarguments can be found in Arrow (1972, page 134) for stakes; Gould (1974, page 77) for environmental uncertainty; Demski (1972, page 122) for accuracy; Marschak (1974, page 294) for delay; Hirshleifer and Riley (1992, page 207) for range of options; Marschak (1974, page 324) for information transmitted; Lawrence (1992, page 207) for attitude towards risk; LaValle (1967, page 275) for initial wealth; Hilton (1990) for Blackwell-informativeness.

very great. Most changes in the parameters of the decision problem affect both the value of the informed decision and the value of the prior decision, making it difficult to sort out the net impact on the value of information. Nevertheless, understanding why there are so few general statements about the determinants of information value is itself a useful exercise.

To help understand both the importance of precise definitions and the lack of general results, consider the concept of riskiness. When a DM talks of risk, does she mean the riskiness of the underlying state variable X, or the riskiness of the outcomes she faces? At least three different sources of risk can be identified: the prior riskiness of the underlying state variable p(x), by construction completely exogenous to the DM; the riskiness of the information structure p(x, y), that is, the specific message to be received and the riskiness of the resulting posterior distribution of the state (this risk is under some control via the DM's choice of source); and the riskiness of the outcomes she faces, which are induced by the actions she chooses and hence also under some control. The risks cannot be viewed in isolation; changes in the riskiness of the state, combined with the DM's attitude toward that risk, influence the risk characteristics of the decision the DM chooses, both with and without information. Hence we are interested in two distinct sets of probability distributions: not only the distributions of the random state variable X, but also the distributions of the DM's terminal wealth that she chooses to accept when she makes a specific decision. These latter distributions are called the DM's *prospects*.

For example, suppose there is a wagering game in which you double your bet with probability 51%, and lose your bet with probability 49%. If you elect not to play, you have chosen to take no risk. If now the rules of the game change so that the prior probability of winning is 80%, this is a less risky environment in some intuitive sense, but if you change your mind and decide to play, you are choosing to bear more risk than if you sit out. Suppose instead the rules stay the same, but there is an informant who will tell you how to win with an 80% chance. If your prior decision is not to play, but now you choose to gamble, then the use of information has led you to a more risky prospect. Alternately, if your prior decision under the original odds is to play, then the use of the information is affording you a less risky prospect. How this nets out to information value depends upon a precise definition of risk, and a precise definition of the DM's attitude toward bearing that risk.

Chapter 6 concentrates on the statistical characteristics of information structures as determinants of information value. Section 6.1 presents an approach developed in statistics that goes as far as possible in analyzing the decision before invoking the prior knowledge p(x). This provides a focus for investigating the influence of p(x) on the value of information. More importantly, it allows for a precise definition of statistical informativeness and a criterion, due to

Blackwell (1951; 1953), for the formal comparison of information structures by their informativeness. In any standard decision problem with the state space **X**, greater statistical informativeness in the sense of Blackwell is sufficient to ensure greater (more correctly, not less) pragmatic information value. Section 6.2 covers these issues and presents a simple model for statistical informativeness that is subsequently useful. Section 6.3 defines Rothschild–Stiglitz variability, the notion of riskiness that is appropriate for the comparison of probability distributions, and applies it to investigate the role of uncertainty about the underlying state variable as a determinant of information value.

To the extent that the state realization is uncertain at the time the action is taken, the outcome of the decision is also unknown and hence also a random variable. In the analysis of the determinants of the expected value of information, it is often convenient to suppress the state space **X** and work directly with the DM's prospects, the probability distributions of the DM's terminal wealth as a consequence of alternative solutions to the decision problem. In Chapter 7, the comparison of the optimal prospects with and without the incorporation of information allows for the study of the role of the DM's preferences as a determinant of information value.

Section 7.1 presents the analysis of decisions in terms of their prospects. Two aspects of preference are particularly important to the individual DM's valuation of information: Section 7.2 investigates the role of the DM's attitude toward risk, and Section 7.3 concerns the possible assessment of negative information value when the DM does not insist her choices conform with the standard expected utility criterion.

1.5 Information Value, Cost, and Procurement

1.5.1 The Optimal Information Structure

Every accessible source from the universe of sources, common and proprietary, can provide the DM with a certain degree of informativeness, if it were chosen and processed. As Section 1.4.5 mentions, greater informativeness in the sense of Blackwell is usually sufficient to ensure greater information value in any decision problem with state space **X**, but most information structures are not comparable in Blackwell's sense. In the context of a specific decision problem, information sources can still be compared and ranked by their *pragmatic informativeness*: their potential to provide pragmatic information value within the context of a specific need by a specific DM. The parameter θ can serve as an index of the pragmatic value of an information structure; the index may also index the Blackwell-informativeness of the alternative information structures under consideration. The notation $\mathbf{I}(\theta)$ denotes that the structure **I** has informativeness θ.

In Chapters 2 through 7 the informativeness is considered exogenous, the problem being to assess it for a given source. More generally, the informativeness of a specific source may be endogenous or exogenous, but the informativeness applied in the decision problem is ultimately determined by the DM and hence endogenous. Informativeness becomes endogenous to the DM when she chooses specific sources from among the alternatives, or offers incentives to an informant to achieve a specific level of informativeness. Chapter 8 takes up these issues.

Choosing which information sources to access is a problem that in principle requires the DM to assess a measure of the expected net gain from every possible (composite) information structure that could be procured. Antecedent to this activity, of course, is the decision to seek information and the identification of alternative sources. Since the costs of access and cognition must be borne before the decision application of the message, optimal access requires up-front consideration of the costs of achieving any given level of informativeness.

For a number of reasons, the cost of incorporating information varies among the alternative structures. The postulate is that it is more costly for a DM to incorporate a more informative information structure into her decision problem. A "quick and dirty" study is less expensive than a careful considered analysis, but it is also likely to be less informative. Adding and processing more sources (e.g., accessing and reading additional documents on a specific topic) are likely to increase the informativeness of such a composite information structure, but they also increase costs.

The cost of an information structure may be random, ex-ante. For a structure with informativeness θ, let $\mathbf{C}(\theta)$ be the sum of the expected variable costs of identification, choice, access, and cognition, properly allocated to this problem. Under the optimal management of the DM-user, the cost function $\mathbf{C}(\theta)$ describes the minimum expected variable cost to the organization of achieving the informativeness θ. The ultimate realization of $\mathbf{C}(\theta)$ will be the accounting observation $\mathcal{C}$. The expected gain from information $\mathbf{G}(\theta)$ is the expectation of (1.2) using the information structure $\mathbf{I}(\theta)$:

$$\mathbf{G}(\theta) = E_y E_{x|y} \mathcal{G} = E_y E_{x|y} [\upsilon(x, y) - \mathcal{C}] = V(\theta) - \mathbf{C}(\theta), \qquad (1.11)$$

where the final equality uses (1.10) and $V(\theta)$ is shorthand for $V(\mathbf{I}(\theta))$.

As is typical in economic matters, the problem of finding the best information structure is a problem of comparing benefits and costs, and it requires an economic, not a technical solution. The technical, or ideal, solution is to use the information system to find and incorporate the sources that "maximize the informativeness and minimize the cost," a solution unlikely to be operational. For example, the most informative source might be the world-renowned expert on the particular subject, available only at prohibitive expense. A more economic (i.e., cost effective) solution might be to access a book written by that expert, perhaps a slightly less informative source, but much less costly.

Since both expected value and expected cost increase with θ, there is a classic economic tradeoff between benefit and cost. There is an optimum effort to undertake and informativeness to incorporate into the decision problem, the informativeness θ* that maximizes the expected gain to the organization. The optimal informativeness solves

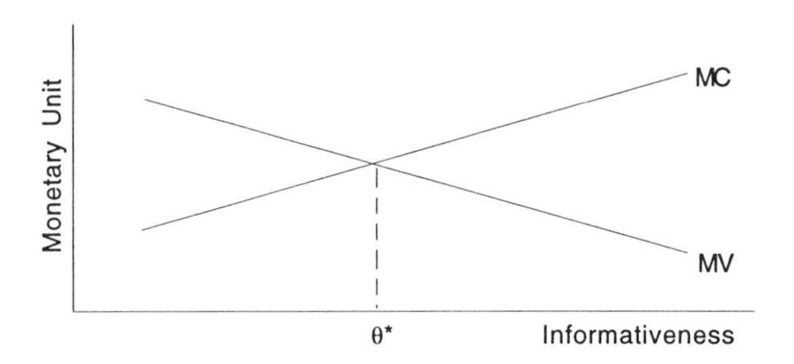

Figure 1.3(a). Optimal informativeness with an interior solution.

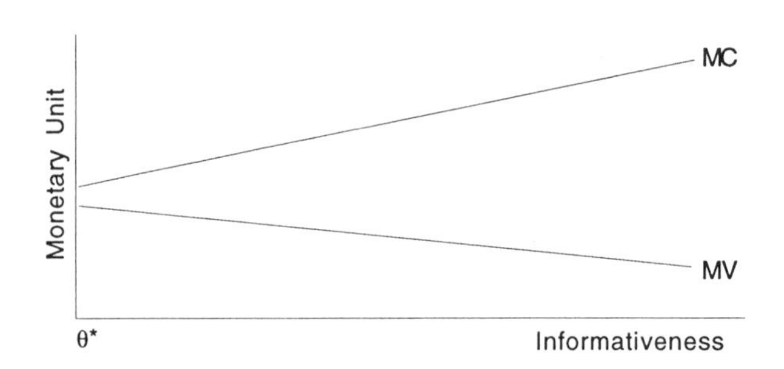

Figure 1.3(b). This situation leads to a decision not to seek information.

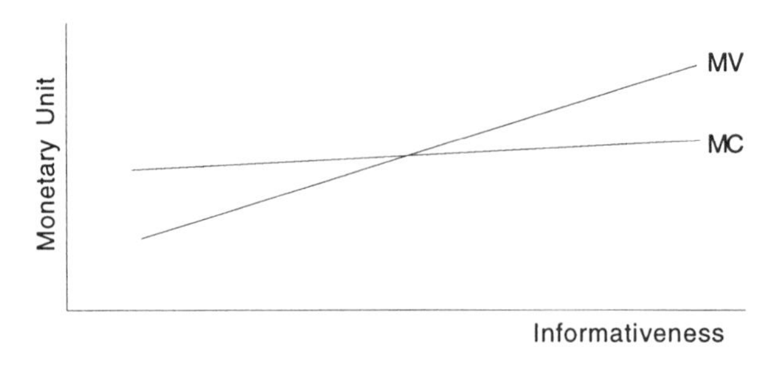

Figure 1.3(c). Here, maximum informativeness is economically feasible.

$$\max_{\theta} \mathbf{G}(\theta) = \mathrm{V}(\theta) - \mathbf{C}(\theta), \tag{1.12}$$

yielding the optimal choice θ^*. Should $\theta^* = 0$, the optimal decision is not to seek information.

If $\mathrm{V}(\theta)$ and $\mathbf{C}(\theta)$ are continuous and differentiable in θ, and the second-order conditions are met, the (interior) solution to (1.12) advises the DM to choose the level of informativeness at that point where the marginal value (MV) of the last scintilla of informativeness is equal to the marginal cost (MC) of that scintilla:

$$\mathrm{MV}(\theta) = \frac{d\,\mathrm{V}(\theta)}{d\theta} = \frac{d\,\mathbf{C}(\theta)}{d\theta} = \mathrm{MC}(\theta). \tag{1.13}$$

Figure 1.3(a) shows an interior solution, and Figure 1.3(b) depicts a situation in which it is advisable not to incorporate information. The second-order condition is important in this model because, over at least some of its range, $\mathrm{V}(\theta)$ may be convex in θ, making $\mathrm{MV}(\theta)$ increasing in θ. Figure 1.3(c) illustrates a possible consequence of this: there are increasing returns to informativeness and it is optimal to choose the most informative source available. The crossing point represents a minimum rather than a maximum information gain.

For the situation in Figure 1.3(a), Figure 1.4 shows an idealization of the relationship between the informativeness incorporated and the organization's information gain. The organization can expect to lose money from the purchase of information when it buys a structure that has little capacity to affect decisions and hence has low value, or when the structure is highly informative, but costs more than it is worth. In characterizing the optimal and suboptimal possession of information, the more general approach in Section 8.1 is able to identify null, useless, uneconomic, economic, and wasteful levels of information ownership.

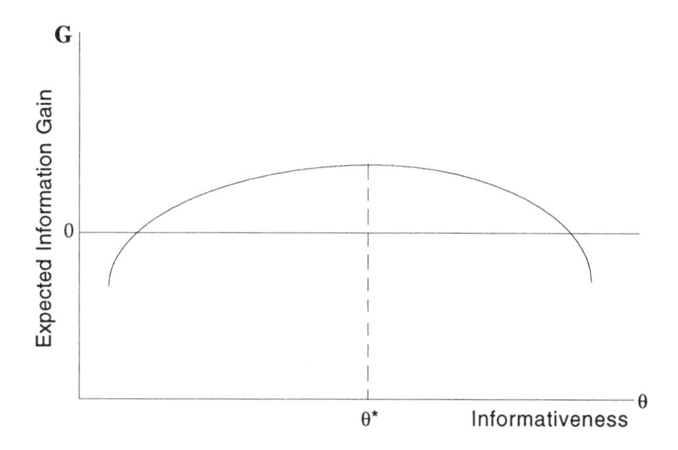

Figure 1.4. An idealization of the expected gain from information as it depends on the informativeness incorporated. See also Figure 8.3.

Varying the cost of informativeness in a systematic way generates the demand curve for informativeness. As examples in Section 8.1 show, the demand curve for θ-information may have a discontinuity but is otherwise well behaved.

1.5.2 Procuring Direct Information

Most of this book describes cooperative relationships for incorporating information—the user and the organization work together as a team to achieve the common goal. Sections 8.2 and 8.3 consider the problem of hiring a single source, an informant from outside the organization. When the DM and the informant do not share the same goal, there is the potential for an adversarial relationship. Mischief can arise when a procurement contract is poorly designed.

In contracting for and ultimately using the services of an informant, the DM faces multiple uncertainties due to lack of knowledge. Anyone can make forecasts or give advice, and a DM taking action based upon the messages she receives can not observe the informant's effort, the cost efficiency of effort, nor whether the informant is transmitting the messages he truly believes as a result of his inquiry. As Osband (1989) stresses, these characteristics are not immutable and can be influenced by the contract's incentives. A consultant, for example, may have an incentive to overstate his costs and efforts, while not revealing what he really knows or believes.

The consequences can be significant should there be a discrepancy between the information structure the informant produces and the one the DM uses to determine her choice of action. If the assessed information structure differs from the true one, the DM can be led to actions that differ from optimal, resulting in either real or opportunity losses. If the stockbroker is always wrong, the optimal decision rule is to sell when the recommendation is to buy. The problem is that if the DM does not know this statistical characteristic beforehand, she will lose some money before learning the optimal response to that message. This lack of foreknowledge about the statistical properties of the information structure puts quite a burden on the DM, especially if the source is only to be accessed once or a very small number of times and there is insufficient opportunity for significant learning.

Section 8.2 offers a solution to this problem using a modification of the kind of contingency contract an individual might have with a lawyer. Consider a contractual agreement between the DM and the source specifying that 1) the source will produce an information structure $\mathbf{I}$, transmitting messages $y \in \mathbf{Y}$ asserted to come from the joint distribution $p(x, y)$, 2) the DM will take any received forecast y at face value and choose the action a_y that is optimal under $p(x \mid y)$, and 3) the DM and the informant agree to the payment of a fixed amount s plus a fraction α of the ex-post value of the message defined in (1.1). The cost equation for the information is

$$\mathcal{C} = s + \alpha\upsilon(x, y) = s + \alpha[\pi(x, a_y) - \pi(x, a_0)]. \tag{1.14}$$

Since (1.14) can be negative, the realized information cost of any specific message can very well be negative, meaning the informant must pay the DM. However, if the informant produces and delivers messages according to the agreed upon structure, (1.10) shows the expected cost function of the complete information source is

$$\mathbf{C}(\mathbf{I}) = E_y E_{x|y} \mathcal{C} = s + \alpha[V(\mathbf{I})], \tag{1.15}$$

and, combining this with (1.11), the DM's expected gain is

$$\mathbf{G}(\mathbf{I}) = [1 - \alpha][V(\mathbf{I})] - s. \tag{1.16}$$

Section 8.3 solves the technical problem of determining the two compensation parameters s and α. Not surprisingly, a contractual scheme in which the two parties share the value-in-use of the information the DM receives and acts upon is quite helpful in ensuring the information source's honesty and effort.

1.5.3 Case Studies of Information Cost, Value, and Choice

This subsection reviews some representative case studies and practical applications that highlight the cost of information and the choice of information source. The examples illustrate the variety of informativeness measures that have been applied in specific circumstances.

Lave and Omenn (1986; 1988) fit a cost curve for the informativeness of various investigations about the carcinogenicity of untested chemicals. The animal bioassay is a common data producing information source for determining carcinogenic potency. A thorough study on one substance using rodents can take several years and cost millions of dollars; even at that such studies cannot offer perfect information about potency. Meanwhile, there are tens of thousands of untested chemicals, with new ones being introduced every year. There are, however, a number of short-duration, less expensive in vitro and in vivo tests that are also available, having varying ability to classify a chemical as carcinogenic or not. Lave and Omenn use a data set containing the results of a large number of different short-term tests done on up to 38 chemicals whose carcinogenic classification has already been established. Measuring informativeness by the probability that a chemical is correctly classified as either a true positive or a true negative carcinogen, Lave and Omenn show how to use a logistic regression technique to determine the battery of these tests that can achieve various levels of informativeness at the minimum cost. The "shape" of this empirical cost function is quite similar to the illustrative cost function used in Sections 8.3.4 and 9.4.2.

The most well-known and well-developed application of optimal information choice is to problems of experimental design in statistics. Typically, the index of informativeness is the sample size, the cost function increases linearly in this index, and within the context of the specified statistical decision problem (as in Section 5.2.2), the choice of the optimal information source amounts to the determination of the sample size that maximizes the expected information gain. Chapters 14 through 16 of Pratt, Raiffa, and Schlaifer (1995) provide several examples.

Reichard and Evans (1989) assess the value of testing the drinking water from private wells near the Whitehouse Waste Oil Pits in Florida. The nearby homeowners' possible actions are to do nothing or treat the water individually at home. The model is basically the Finkel and Evans (1987) approach, with the state variable being the incremental deaths per year if no action were taken. There are about 60 people who may be exposed to arsenic contamination, and the value of perfect information to the neighborhood is \$10,600 when life is valued at \$1 million each. Several data producing information sources, involving different numbers of wells checking for contaminants over different time periods, are compared by a problem-specific informativeness index which the authors call an index of monitoring efficiency. In the language of Section 8.1, the most informative source considered provides wasteful information (cost > value). Another is inefficient, as it offers both lower informativeness and greater cost than the optimal source, which is to sink one well, 60 meters from the source of the contamination, and draw a message from it every other year for the next seven. Here, $V(\theta^*) = \$8{,}300$ and $\mathbf{C}(\theta^*) = \$2{,}800$, making $\mathbf{G}(\theta^*) = \$5{,}500$.

James and Freeze (1993) study the containment of contaminants at the Savannah River, South Carolina radioactive site. The state variable involves whether a specific geologic formation, an aquitard, is continuously strong enough to protect deep aquifers from toxic contaminants closer to the surface. The DM's action is whether to contain the contamination by other means. If contained, at an up-front cost, it is not relevant to payoff whether the aquitard is continuously strong enough. If the decision is not to contain and the aquitard has "windows" through which contaminants may seep, the costs are very high. A cored borehole can determine the situation at one location in the region, providing a message space with two messages: at this location there is an aquitard or there is a window. One experiment (information source) is to drill a specified number of boreholes at specified distances from one another. For various sample outcomes (messages), a geological model calculates the expected payoff from each action. James and Freeze estimate the value of perfect information about the key aquitard to be \$780,000, given prior knowledge from the results of previous boreholes and other, less informative, sources. They are able to determine the most cost-effective location for one additional borehole; this source has an expected value of $65,000 and, with a cost of $20,000 per borehole, the expected information gain is $45,000. The authors then estimate the information gain from various experiments of adding more boreholes at various spacings, providing a diagram akin to Figure 1.4. A larger sample size is of course more informative, but if the holes are too close together the messages are redundant and gain decreases; if they are too far apart the value also doesn't increase fast enough to compensate for the drilling costs, as the chance increases that a window is being missed. The optimal information source among those reported is to bore five holes with 261-meter spacing. This offers an information gain of about $110,000.

Bernknopf et al. (1997) study the value of replacing the existing geologic map of Loudoun County, Virginia with a new and more detailed one. In a regulatory decision concerning the siting of a waste disposal facility, a key state variable is the permeability of the subsurface rocks, and the payoff involves the effects on property values should contamination occur. Bernknopf et al. assess the value of this improved map for this decision at $1.5 million. It cost the United States Geological Survey about $1.16 million to produce the map.

This is not, however, a full measure of the value and gain from this specific map. Once this package of data has been produced, it may be used again and again for unknown future purposes—perhaps by a DM needing to site an airport or to mine for aggregate, or perhaps by a teacher explaining some principle of geology or geography. The potential for reusability at low marginal cost gives public good characteristics to many kinds of data. Presumably, various organizations will choose to archive this map and index its existence in their information systems, in anticipation that someone will identify and access it at some future time. The questions of whether and in what form an organization should archive the map, how it should be indexed and identified, and where it may be accessed, are just some of the matters that are important in the broad problem of information system design and management.

1.6 System Design for Information Gain

1.6.1 Decision Theory, Information Science, and System Design

Having completed the study of the value and demand for information in a single decision problem, Chapter 9 considers the role of a sponsoring organization that designs, finances, builds, and manages a system to facilitate the processing of information by the users it desires to serve, the information-seeking employees and agents of the organization. As decision problems arise, the information system must have the capability to produce net gain, and the optimal system maximizes the organization's expected information gain: the excess of total expected information value over total expected information cost (see Figure 1.2). To address issues of system design, it is necessary to aggregate from informativeness and information gain at the level of the single decision problem to a broader, organization-wide viewpoint.

Whereas decision theory concentrates on the incorporation of information in the context of a single problem, information science is concerned with the design and management of a system intended to serve a population of users facing myriad information needs. Information science takes a holistic approach to system design [Cronin and Davenport (1991); Best (1996); Wilson (1997)], including recognition that the organization's information system is more than a library that stores documents, more than a mechanism for generating reports about the organization's transactions, and more than investments in computers, telecommunications, and other modern information technology. A common thread that runs through both decision theory and information science is that the primary orientation is on the user of the information, rather than on the technological instruments that assist the user's information processing. In decision theory, the user is the DM; in information science the user is the patron, either as a DM or as a monitor.

Information science has its roots in library science and, as a discipline, it is part operations research and part social science. The work in operations research [Kantor (1979); Kraft and Boyce (1991)] concerns quantitative problems of managing libraries and other information-providing entities. Much of this research is directly relevant to the cost side of the organization's information gain. For example, Getz (1988) studies the economics of the decision to automate cataloguing; Kingma (1996) studies the currently relevant decision whether to subscribe to journals or merely arrange the ability to access journal articles. In both cases, costs include not only monetary expenditures, but also the opportunity cost of patron time. Snyder and Davenport (1997) present some simple costing analyses for libraries.

For the purposes of this book, user orientation is the preferred philosophy for system design, as it puts the focus on the efficient provision of pragmatic information. The technological orientation, disparagingly called "technocratic utopianism" by Davenport, Eccles, and Prusak (1992), tends to focus more on the efficient provision of statistical information. Powell (1992) identifies 17 approaches to the evaluation of the technological components of an information system; surprisingly few of them are financial in nature and amenable to ex-ante analysis. Indeed, some seem more oriented toward the ex-post justification of technological investments than the ex-ante evaluation of information systems. Even generally accepted ex-ante techniques, such as cost/benefit analysis, concentrate in application on the cost-saving benefits of system design, offering little more than lip service and platitudes about the value side. This neglect is understandable, as cost savings are without question easier to identify and assess, but disregarding value is not necessary and certainly not optimal.

Chapter 9 investigates whether the decision-theoretic approach to information value can be integrated with information science's understanding of information cost to provide a sound user-oriented framework for the empirical evaluation and design of information systems. The assimilation of the decision theory paradigm into general information management requires consideration of several broad matters: 1) the economic analysis of the processes and activities the information system can undertake in order to increase information value and/or decrease cost in any given situation, thereby producing information gain for the organization; 2) a resolution of the empirical questions revolving around the consistency of observed individual behavior with the theory of information evaluation and choice; and 3) a model to explain how the organization's expected information gain is determined by the interaction of the nature of the decision problems the users face, the behavior of the users, the incentives the design of the system gives to those users, and the investments the organization makes.

1.6.2 Information Use Environments

Pointing out the ex-ante nature of the design process, Taylor (1986, pages 4–5) states:

> A message has potential for value. And therein, of course, lies the trouble. We cannot determine a priori the value of an individual message. We must work at the system level, not at the level of the individual message. What we can do . . . is to analyze the population who will be users . . . . In this way we can make estimates as to the probable utility of certain kinds of information, the preferred modes of access, and the kinds of enhancements or signals the system can provide so that use can be facilitated in that particular context.

Taylor is describing the basic framework for modeling information needs within the organization, the *information use environment.* The information use environment goes beyond simply identifying the subject matter of the problems the users face. Taylor (1991) suggests that potential users can be grouped by professional and/or social characteristics, with each group being characterized by the class of decision problems it faces, the work and social settings in which the group finds itself,[7] and the group's perceptions of what constitutes the resolution of a problem.

Section 9.1 reviews empirical studies of the information use environments for two groups within a business organization: managers and scientific/technical personnel. An interesting common theme is the users' observed preference for

[7] Davenport, Eccles, and Prusak (1992) add the political setting to this mix.

interpersonal information sources (e.g., meetings) over data producing and archival ones. This preference is another justification for recommending a holistic user-centered approach to system design over the narrower information technology orientation that concentrates more on document provision and data mining.

Activity logs, survey instruments, and direct interviews are the common techniques for studying information use environments and the information processing behavior of users. Perhaps the most enlightening empirical work investigates the environment and behavior of scientists and engineers, along with the subsystems that serve their needs. To the extent that scientific and technical personnel face decision problems that are well-defined, self-contained, and have outcomes that are consequential to the organization's profitability, they offer a relatively uncluttered environment for the application of decision theory. Two large long-term studies are particularly relevant: Allen's (1977) comparative study of information use and performance by matched teams of engineers, and the King Research Inc. [Griffiths and King (1993)] surveys of special library patrons who are asked to report the value and cost of the information obtained from their most recent use of the subsystem.

The information use environment provides important clues about optimal information system design. The design of the system determines the organization's "offer" to the users, the cost allocations in Figure 1.2, and ultimately the efficiency of the users' movement through the information processing steps that Figure 1.1 depicts. Section 9.2 catalogues and analyzes the kinds of enhancements the system can provide: the value-adding and cost-reducing processes and activities that facilitate the provision and use of information in decision making and monitoring contexts.

Decision theory offers normative techniques for the assessment of information value and the choice of sources to access, but it is a different matter to ask if users are actually observed to behave in ways consistent with the basic theory. If users are unable to assess information value and cost, or do not alter their behavior in response to incentives that affect value and cost, then a decision-theoretic approach to system design is unlikely to be insightful or successful. Section 9.3 takes up these issues. Fortunately, the empirical evidence indicates that individuals value and choose their information sources, at least qualitatively, in ways consistent with the theory of Chapters 6, 7, and 8.

1.6.3 A Model of System Design and User Behavior

The final section of Chapter 9 sketches a model that allows system design to influence user behavior and ultimately the organization's information gain. Section 9.4 begins with an economic model for the production of informativeness inside the organization. A fundamental assumption is that it takes effort to generate informativeness, effort undertaken by some combination of the individual, the internal resources of the organization, and external resources under contract, such as consulting firms. This is the DM/user's control over the cost of information: altering the effort she and the organization undertake in performing the processing, thereby affecting the informativeness she extracts from the system.

Since design takes place before any use of the system, the goal of system design is to configure the sources and services in the way that maximizes the expectation of the organization's information gain. In the approach of Section 9.4, a set of canonical decision problems models the revenue side of the gain. A canonical problem is a very simple 2-act, 2-state problem with one additional component: the magnitude of the payoff, the stakes of the problem, is a random variable from the organization's viewpoint. In addition to studying the optimal incorporation of information into the canonical sequence of problems, Section 9.4.4 investigates what a user survey of such a hypothetical organization would observe. Whenever users estimate the value of information, it is important to identify precisely the concept they are reporting; it could be an ex-post, conditional, or preposterior value, depending upon the timing of the survey relative to the completion of the decision problem.

The informativeness of a given application is a function of both the user's effort and the contribution of the organization; the latter is summarized in the model as the system's effectiveness. System *effectiveness* is a design characteristic that directly affects the productivity of the user, involving such factors as the physical proximity of sources, the accessibility of messages from each source, laborsaving computer hardware and software, the knowledge and training of information professionals and other interpersonal sources, and the flexibility, security, and simplicity of use. Greater system effectiveness, by lowering the variable cost of incorporating information, is likely to increase the informativeness the users incorporate, but require greater fixed investment and costs. Since both user costs and system costs are ultimately borne by the organization, the optimal system design involves trading off the four classes of cost in Figure 1.2 against one other and against the value the informativeness is expected to produce. Section 9.4.5 characterizes the optimal information system in these terms.

1.7 Information Social Science

1.7.1 The Information Society

One phenomenon of the 1990s, reported in the popular press [*Economist* (1996)], is a significant decline in the costs of information. The impacts of this decline are profound, important not only to system designers, but also to society as a whole. This warrants a brief excursion into the social science of information.

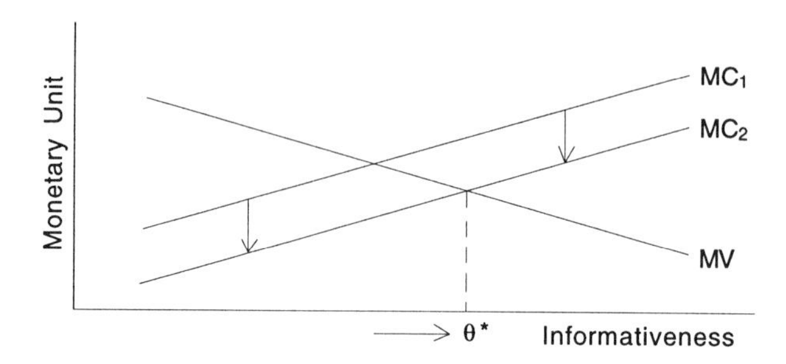

Figure 1.5(a). Lower cost of information increases optimal informativeness.

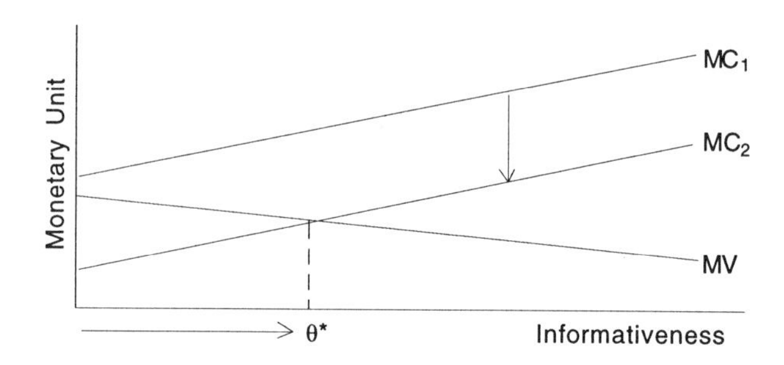

Figure 1.5(b). Lower cost of information can change the decision to seek.

Information social science studies the relationships between human beings and the rapidly changing environment of information products, markets, and industries. Many view these changes as leading to what they call the *information society*, a society in which data availability, access, and application, more so than the physical production of goods, are key driving forces for economic and social change. The information society puts the focus on informed management.

Many years ago, Porat (1977) provided an empirical basis for this belief. In an accounting analysis of the United States economy, Porat identified four sectors—agriculture, industry, services, and information—and using a rather broad definition, found that about half the work force is employed in the information sector. However broadly one wishes to define the information sector, there is little question that its share of total GDP continues to increase. The Porat analysis is also applicable to the study of local and regional economic development; see Hayes (1995) and Ellger (1991).

Today we see a dramatic decrease in the costs of communicating and computing, and a concomitant increase in the supply of data. Among the causes are 1) technological advances in the storage and transmission of data, 2) the ability to apply greater computing power to that data, 3) software that gives individuals with little technical training the ability to both access and supply these data, allowing virtually anybody to contribute to the common record, 4) deregulation of the telecommunications industry, and 5) increased willingness of government to disseminate and exchange technical data, perhaps brought about by the end of the cold war.

These events have led to a decline in the cost of incorporating information into decision. Not all the components of information cost have declined; the costs of choosing sources goes up to the extent DMs must filter through more alternatives. Nevertheless, it is reasonable to assert that whatever the cost of achieving a given level of informativeness used to be, that cost is now lower.

Declining cost of information is nothing new; the computer as a communication device is just the latest in a long series of innovations. The invention of writing removed communication from the shackles of being face-to-face and synchronous in time; it became possible for Moses and Homer to communicate with us over a span of thousands of years. The telegraph for the first time allowed for the movement of data at a speed faster than either a human or a carrier pigeon. The first transatlantic cable was laid in 1858. Casson (1997) investigates some of the economic consequences of this long-term decline in information costs.

1.7.2 How Monumental Are Recent Events?

Mokyr (1997), an economic historian, asks if we are today in the middle of a new industrial revolution, with technological progress bursting forth in a multitude of areas, not just in what gets lumped together under the word "computers." We live in fascinating times, but it is interesting to wonder if, 50 years from now, historians will view the changes of the 1990s, especially the rise of the Internet, as truly monumental.

Visualizing the future is a risky business. Incorrect insights become famous ("There is no business application for the telephone."), but the current information environment was foreseen: Bush (1945) conceived a machine, the memex, that finds and applies information from the common record in the same way we use the Web today.[8] Bawden (1997) writes of the prescience of Arthur C. Clarke, author of *2001, A Space Odyssey* and creator of HAL, the thinking computer. The pitfalls notwithstanding, designers of today's information systems must operate with some vision of the information future, if for no other reason than to try to avoid costly reworking of the system too soon after implementation.

The social consequence of the current events should be, at least in theory, a more informed society. Data that were available before are still available, but at lower cost. An investor can obtain financial data on corporations instantly, and

---

[8] It was all to be available in a personal microfilm collection!

without monetary cost, via the Internet and the Securities and Exchange Commission. A doctor can discover if there is a tumor via imaging rather than surgery. Figure 1.5(a) illustrates how the lower MC leads to a more informed optimal decision. Furthermore, the lower costs lead at the margin to more affirmative decisions to seek information, as opposed to accepting the prior decision: in other words, a greater desire to incorporate information. Figure 1.5(b) shows how lower costs can change the decision to seek, making it now economically feasible to incorporate information. For example, there may be an increased belief by individuals that there must be something out there on the Internet that can help them solve this or that problem, leading them to search for it. As another example, the lower costs can make health providers willing to fund more screenings to find tumors before they become unmanageable. In these ways, lower marginal cost for informativeness makes for the possibility of a more informed society.

In an introductory economics course, students learn that for a product to be produced in the market it must be technically possible, and it should be economically feasible and socially permissible. Technical possibility is the only really binding constraint; goods that are not economically feasible can still be produced if there is sufficient subsidy from somewhere, and socially impermissible goods are still produced outside the law. Suppose, in the not too distant future, it becomes technically possible for all data in existence to be digitized and accessible simply, instantaneously, and locally. To believe this requires a certain confidence that there will be solutions to current practical problems of computing, storing, and transmitting data, along with resolution of legal problems involving ownership and copyright. Even so, the specific information products that would be available in such an environment depend upon economic feasibility, upon the value of the data as information relative to the properly allocated cost.

To be sure, some of what passes for information today has value only as entertainment. This has proven value in the marketplace [see Hayes (1997)], and Hollywood is currently a major developer of new technologies. But for today's events to be judged as truly monumental, there has to be more than just the ability to access movies, games, celebrity gossip, and books on demand in the home. We must understand better the marginal product of information as it relates to the allocation of society's scarce resources. This is the social importance of the subject matter of this book. The topics here should be of interest not only to decision makers and organizations, but also to policy makers concerned with the technological, economic, and social challenges the Information Age brings into the twenty-first century; see Braunstein (1982).

There are certainly many examples of the allocational gain from greater application of information. Just-in-time inventory management reduces the need for working capital. Lower communication cost increases the span of what one individual can manage or supervise, and with fewer supervisors needed, the bureaucratic hierarchy flattens. Factories can be far-flung, located more efficiently. To the extent that symbols move rather than people, transportation costs and related negative externalities (e.g., congestion and pollution) are reduced. Indeed, the Internet itself provides an alternative forum for retail transactions. We have already seen how lower computation costs are allowing meaningful value of information analyses of highly complex problems, potentially allowing for more efficient allocations of research budgets.

Although the volume of data is increasing and the cost of transmitting it declining, the real constraint lies in the ability of human beings to cognitively process the data into information. Bush (1945) bemoaned "information overload" at a time of much lower data supply; Radner (1993) sees the modern problem as reflective of the relative cheapness of communication compared to the cost of cognition. How fast people cognitively process data depends upon the data and the context. Consider the symbol $\overline{W}_{I\uparrow}^{A_1}(V_{I\uparrow}^{A_1})$. It will take the diligent reader longer to figure out the meaning of this symbol when it appears in Section 7.2.2 than it took to process that same symbol just now—and the ability to speed read will not help!

Along with an increased supply of data comes an increased supply of uninformative and useless information. This makes efficient filtering critical; somehow the wheat must be separated from the chaff. Education on how to perform searches in this environment will become more important; if seekers know what to ask and how to ask a filter such as a search engine, they can save time and money. Although there is much talk about the decline in the need for traditional intermediaries such as travel agents and retailers [Gates (1995)], there may be an increased demand for knowledgeable information intermediaries who can perform a filtering function.

A contract akin to the one discussed in Section 1.5.2 could provide incentives for data producers to self-identify their informativeness by forcing them to invest in themselves. Consider an arrangement with three parties: the producer of the data (e.g., the author of a journal article), a firm that offers an information product which collects many different data sources into one database (e.g., a publishing house or a document delivery service), and a user who is willing to pay a fee to be able to access any source the firm indexes, if she so desires. Suppose to get his data indexed in the database so they can be identifiable and accessible, the producer must pay a fixed fee to the firm, and then receives a payment every time the data are accessed. If the firm offers the data producer an appropriately designed menu of contracts with different combinations of fixed fee and per-access revenue, the data producer can then be induced to reveal his true informativeness by the specific compensation scheme he chooses. The user observes the access fee, and maybe a good executive summary and other metadata, and makes her judgment to access accordingly.

Finally, the effect of a new information economy on the worldwide distribution of income and wealth is a matter of great concern and debate; see Menou (1993). Section 8.1 analyzes a very simple model that illustrates a reason for concern. To the extent that wealthier individuals can afford more informative information structures, they can make better decisions and obtain better outcomes on average than poorer individuals who can afford only less informative options. On the other hand, the globalization of business, facilitated by declining information costs, is bringing more promising employment prospects to emerging nations worldwide. The lower cost segments of the world's common record are now available in places they were never available before, making data available to anyone who can get on the Web and read the language in which it was written. One thing never changes: education is one of the most important information products. With minimal communication costs and fair access worldwide to the common record, if the citizens of a nation are education-rich, there is no reason why they cannot be information-rich.

2
The Value of the Informed Decision

This chapter presents the general model for decision making under uncertainty with the option to incorporate information. The chapter introduces several of the analytical tools that are useful in the sequel, and shows that the incorporation of information cannot make the expected-utility-maximizing decision maker worse off.

2.1 Elements of a Decision Problem Under Uncertainty

2.1.1 Utility of Outcome

For decision problems in which the outcome is quantifiable and measurable in the monetary unit, the terminal level of the DM's total wealth is often a more proper objective than the simple payoff function $\pi(x, a)$. In this class of problem framings, the outcome is that the DM's fixed and known initial wealth w changes to the random terminal wealth W. Let $\mathbf{W}$ represent the set of potential terminal wealths of the DM, so that $W \in \mathbf{W}$. In its most general form, the *outcome function* ω, a real-valued function defined on $\mathbf{W} \times \mathbf{X} \times \mathbf{a}$, assesses the terminal wealth when the DM with initial wealth w chooses the action $a \in \mathbf{a}$ and the state $x \in \mathbf{X}$ occurs:

$$W = \omega(w, x, a). \tag{2.1}$$

In an important and commonly occurring special case, the initial wealth enters into the problem only as a base level from which wealth is changed. When the payoff from the decision problem is explicitly assumed to be additively separable from the initial wealth, the terminal wealth outcome is

$$W = w + \pi(x, a). \tag{2.2}$$

The DM's utility of the outcome is a more general objective function than either terminal wealth or payoff. A Von Neumann–Morgenstern *utility function* u, defined on $\mathbf{W}$, indicates the DM's preferences toward alternative sums of money. It is assumed the utility function u(W) is strictly increasing and continuous in W; the former assumption asserts that more money is always preferred to less, the latter is simply a technical convenience. In general, the utility of terminal wealth, measured in utiles, is

$$u(W) = u(\omega(w, x, a)). \tag{2.3}$$

For the special case in which there is a finite set of K actions, $\mathbf{a}^K = \{a_1, \cdots, a_k, \cdots, a_K\}$, and a countable finite set of m states, $\mathbf{X}^m = \{x_1, \cdots, x_i, \cdots, x_m\}$, the utility of the outcome can be expressed conveniently as the $K \times m$ matrix $\mathbf{u}$ stating the utility of wealth from each action a_k and each state x_i:

$$\mathbf{u} = \begin{bmatrix} u(\omega(w, x_1, a_1)) & \cdots & u(\omega(w, x_m, a_1)) \\ \vdots & u(\omega(w, x_i, a_k)) & \vdots \\ u(\omega(w, x_1, a_K)) & \cdots & u(\omega(w, x_m, a_K)) \end{bmatrix}. \tag{2.4}$$

The DM's attitude towards bearing risk is a characteristic of preference embedded in the utility function, and is indicated by the shape of the utility function as it varies with wealth. Section 7.1 presents the justification for the following terminology, due to Friedman and Savage (1948): if u(W) is concave[1] in W, the DM is said to be *risk averse*, if u(W) is convex in W, the DM is a *risk lover*. In the important intermediate case when the utility function is linear in wealth, utility can be taken as the outcome function itself,

$$u(\omega(w, x, a)) = \omega(w, x, a); \tag{2.5}$$

here the DM is *neutral towards risk* and the unit of measurement can be the monetary unit. Figure 2.1 depicts the three characteristic shapes for the utility function on wealth.

2.1.2 Decision Problems

The information structure available to the DM,

$$\mathbf{I} = \{\mathbf{Y}, p(x, y)\}, \tag{2.6}$$

---

[1] A real-valued function f defined on an interval (C, D) of the real line is *concave* on (C, D) if, for any two points c and d in the interval and any number $0 < \alpha < 1$,

$$\alpha f(c) + [1-\alpha]f(d) \leq f(\alpha c + [1-\alpha]d).$$

In geometric terms, the function is concave if the line segment joining any two points in the interval does not lie above the curve. The function is strictly concave over the interval if strict equality holds above. The negative of a concave function is *convex*. A function linear over the entire range is both concave and convex. These notions generalize to higher dimensions.

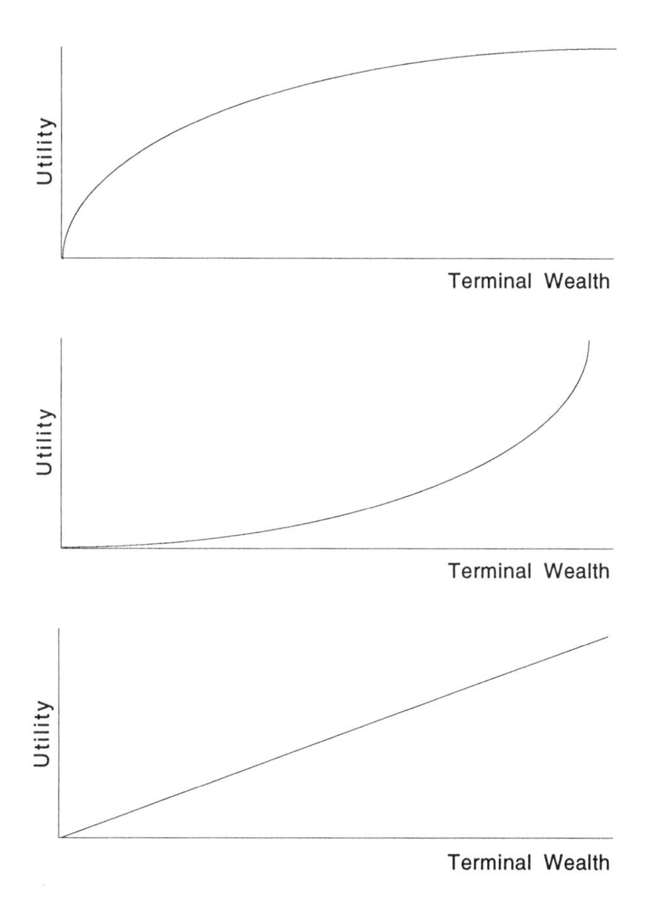

Figure 2.1. Alternative attitudes towards bearing risk. The concave utility function in the top graph illustrates a risk averse DM, the convex function in the middle is that of a risk lover, and the linear function at the bottom indicates neutrality towards risk.

as in (1.7), has an associated cost function $\mathbf{C(I)}$ for information processing. In total, a *decision problem* $\mathbf{D}$,

$$\mathbf{D} = < \mathbf{a}, \mathrm{X}, \omega, \mathrm{u}, \mathrm{w}, \mathbf{I}, \mathbf{C(I)} >, \tag{2.7}$$

comprises the following elements: a space of actions, a space of possible states of nature, an outcome function defined on $\mathbf{W} \times \mathbf{X} \times \mathbf{a}$, the DM's utility function for terminal wealth, the initial wealth, the available information about the random variables, and an information cost function.

In decision problems not involving the incorporation of information, the class of *decision problems under uncertainty*, the only available knowledge is a proper prior probability measure p(x) defined on **X**. This situation of minimal initial information is denoted **I**↓ and is defined by the set

$$\mathbf{I}{\downarrow} = \{p(x)\}. \tag{2.8}$$

It is assumed this initial information is available at no cost. A decision problem under uncertainty is therefore a special case of (2.7) in which $\mathbf{I} = \mathbf{I}{\downarrow} = \{p(x)\}$ and $\mathbf{C}(\mathbf{I}{\downarrow}) = 0$.

It is often convenient to summarize a decision problem by its *decision tree*, a pictorial device that allows the DM to keep track of the timing of the possible choices, the potential state realizations, and the resulting outcomes. Each of the DM's choices at a given point in the problem emanates from a *choice node*, symbolized with a square. Each of nature's potential realizations emanates from a *chance node*, symbolized with a circle. Figure 2.2 illustrates a typical choice node and chance node. Concatenating the choice nodes and the chance nodes in a way that describes the specific decision problem produces the decision tree. Following through on a particular branch from a choice node and then a chance node leads to a particular outcome according to the function ω, and a particular utility according to u. Figure 2.3 presents the decision tree for the simplest type of problem.

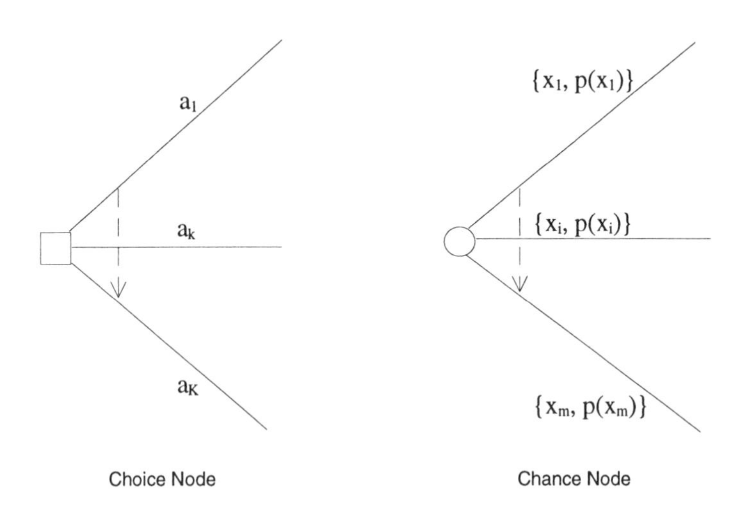

Figure 2.2. The basic elements for a decision tree. The arrows signify unwritten actions or states.

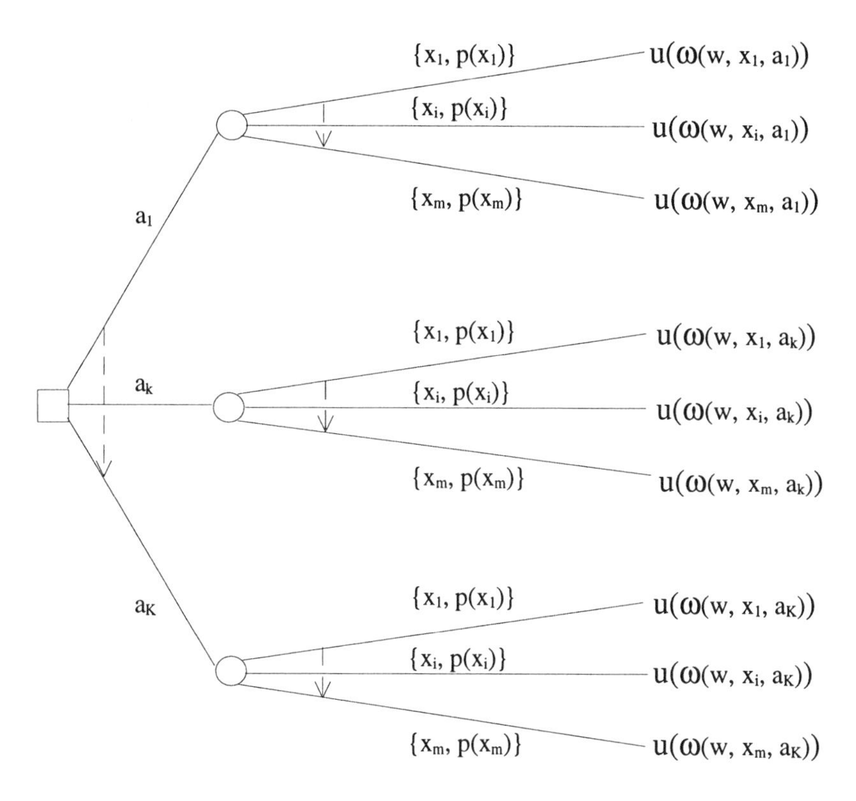

Figure 2.3. A decision tree for a simple problem.

2.1.3 Decision Making

The DM can immediately eliminate some actions from consideration. Given two alternative actions a_j and a_k, a_k *dominates* a_j when

$$\omega(w, x, a_k) \geq \omega(w, x, a_j) \text{ for every } x \in \mathbf{X}, \text{ and}$$

$$\omega(w, x, a_k) > \omega(w, x, a_j) \text{ for at least one } x \in \mathbf{X}. \qquad (2.9)$$

Regardless of which state occurs, the dominated action a_j cannot compete with a_k as the choice of any DM with a utility function not decreasing in wealth. Hence the DM can immediately drop dominated actions from further consideration.[2]

[2] There are two other bases upon which a DM may be able to drop specific actions from consideration: admissibility and stochastic dominance, which are taken up in Chapters 6 and 7.

To solve the decision problem, the expected utility criterion proposes that the DM choose the nonrandomized or pure action that maximizes the mathematical expectation of utility. The expected utility of a decision **D**, conditional on the initial information structure **I**↓ and an action $a \in \mathbf{a}$, is written $\mathbf{U}(\mathbf{D} \mid \mathbf{I}\downarrow, a)$:[3]

$$\mathbf{U}(\mathbf{D} \mid \mathbf{I}\downarrow, a) = E_x\, u(\omega(w, x, a)). \tag{2.10}$$

The *optimal prior decision* is the choice of action a_0 that maximizes (2.10):

$$\begin{aligned} \mathbf{U}(\mathbf{D}^* \mid \mathbf{I}\downarrow) &= \max_a \mathbf{U}(\mathbf{D} \mid \mathbf{I}\downarrow, a) \\ &= \max_a E_x\, u(\omega(w, x, a)) \\ &= E_x\, u(\omega(w, x, a_0^u)). \end{aligned} \tag{2.11}$$

The quantity $\mathbf{U}(\mathbf{D}^* \mid \mathbf{I}\downarrow)$ is called the *value of the prior decision.*

The notation in (2.11) includes the superscript u in the optimal action a_0^u to stress the dependence of the choice upon the specific utility function. Whenever it is useful or necessary to distinguish, the notation replaces the superscript u with A to identify a risk averse DM, L to identify a risk lover, and N to identify a risk neutral DM. For example, when the DM is neutral towards risk and the utility function is the outcome function itself, a_0^N signifies the optimal prior decision of the risk neutral DM.

♦*Example 2.1 A Farmer's Planting Decision*

This example illustrates the calculation of the value of the prior decision and shows that both the choice of optimal action and the value of the decision depend upon an intertwining of the problem structure, the utility function, the initial wealth, and the initial knowledge.

A farmer, with initial wealth w = \$100 thousand dollars, must decide which crop to plant. There are three choices, a_1: plant corn, which flourishes when the weather is wet, but does poorly when the weather is dry, a_2: plant sorghum, which is less profitable than corn in a wet year but more profitable in a dry year, or a_3: plant oats, which does equally well in either type of weather. Denote x_1: the weather turns out dry, and x_2: the weather turns out wet. In this problem the terminal wealth outcome is separable between initial wealth and payoff, as in (2.2). In thousands of dollars, the following matrix **u** shows the farmer's assessment of the utility of terminal wealth from each state-action pair,

$$\mathbf{u} = \begin{bmatrix} u(\omega(w, x_1, a_1)) & u(\omega(w, x_2, a_1)) \\ u(\omega(w, x_1, a_2)) & u(\omega(w, x_2, a_2)) \\ u(\omega(w, x_1, a_3)) & u(\omega(w, x_2, a_3)) \end{bmatrix}$$

[3] This notation suppresses the other components of **D** that are not of current interest.

$$= \begin{bmatrix} u(100+\pi(x_1,a_1)) & u(100+\pi(x_2,a_1)) \\ u(100+\pi(x_1,a_2)) & u(100+\pi(x_2,a_2)) \\ u(100+\pi(x_1,a_3)) & u(100+\pi(x_2,a_3)) \end{bmatrix} = \begin{bmatrix} u(110) & u(150) \\ u(125) & u(115) \\ u(105) & u(105) \end{bmatrix}. \quad (2.12)$$

It is apparent that, regardless of the state of the weather, the terminal wealth from the action a_3 is less than the terminal wealth from both a_1 and a_2. The action a_3: plant oats is dominated both by a_1 and by a_2 and can be dropped from further consideration.

The choice now boils down to a_1 or a_2. A natural way of thinking is to consider the relative chances of each type of weather. The farmer thinks, "This is a wet climate most of the time, but droughts do occur. In fact, these things tend to run in cycles, with dry years often following dry years. Last year was dry. Hence, in my experience, I think there is a 60 percent chance that it will be dry, and a 40 percent chance of a wet year." This assessment is the DM's initial knowledge and serves as the prior probability distribution: $p(x_1) = .60$ and $p(x_2) = .40$.

Figure 2.4 presents the decision tree for Example 2.1. The action that is dominated is included, but marked by a //, indicating that this portion of the tree can be "pruned."

Suppose the farmer is risk neutral and has the simple linear utility function $u(W) = W$. Given the prior distribution $p(x_1) = .6$ and $p(x_2) = .4$, initial wealth w = 100, and the profits implied by (2.12), the expected outcomes from the two undominated actions are

$$\mathbf{U}(\mathbf{D} \mid \mathbf{I}\!\downarrow, a_1) = E_x\, \omega(w, x, a_1)$$

$$= E_x\,\{100 + \pi(x, a_1)\} = [.6][110] + [.4][150] = 126,$$

$$\mathbf{U}(\mathbf{D} \mid \mathbf{I}\!\downarrow, a_2) = E_x\, \omega(w, x, a_2)$$

$$= E_x\,\{100 + \pi(x, a_2)\} = [.6][125] + [.4][115] = 121.$$

Hence the expected wealth maximizing action is $a_0^N = a_1$, and the value of the prior decision is $\mathbf{U}(\mathbf{D}^* \mid \mathbf{I}\!\downarrow) = \$126$ thousand dollars.

Under this objective function, changing the initial wealth by any amount does not change the relative desirability of the two actions. However, note that if the DM had the alternative initial knowledge that $p(x_1) = .95$ and $p(x_2) = .05$, then the optimal prior decision is $a_0^N = a_2$, and $\mathbf{U}(\mathbf{D}^* \mid \mathbf{I}\!\downarrow) = [.95][125] + [.05][115] = \$124.5$ thousand dollars.

Suppose instead the DM is risk averse and has the logarithmic utility function $u(W) = \log[W - 90]$, defined only for $W > 90$. Returning to the original initial knowledge and with all other elements in the problem the same, the calculation of the expected utility from each action:

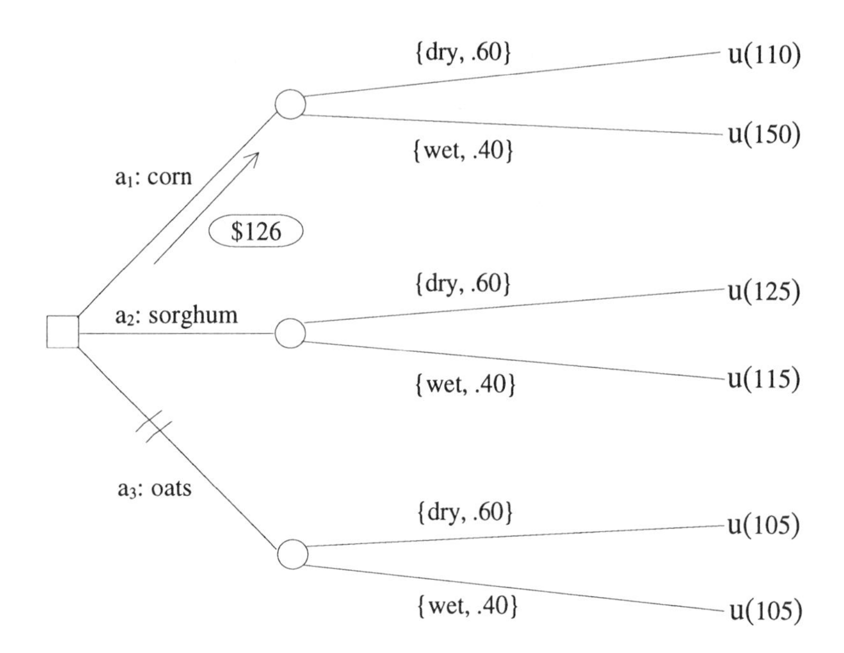

Figure 2.4. The decision tree for Example 2.1. The arrow indicates the optimal decision for a risk neutral DM, and the circled amount is the expected wealth from that choice. A DM with a different utility function might choose a different action.

$$E_x\, u(\omega(100, x, a_1)) = E_x \log[\omega(100, x, a_1) - 90]$$

$$= E_x \log[10 + \pi(x, a_1)] = [.6] \log[20] + [.4] \log[60] = 3.43518,$$ [4]

and

$$E_x\, u(\omega(100, x, a_2)) = E_x \log[\omega(100, x, a_2) - 90]$$

$$= E_x \log[10 + \pi(x, a_2)] = [.6] \log[35] + [.4] \log[25] = 3.42076,$$

shows the optimal action is $a_0^A = a_1$, with $\mathbf{U(D^* | I\downarrow)} = 3.43518$ utiles.

Under this objective function, the initial wealth w plays an important role in the solution to the problem. Suppose initial wealth is lowered to w = 95. This leads to the following calculations,

$$\mathbf{U(D | I\downarrow}, a_1) = E_x \log[\omega(95, x, a_1) - 90]$$

---

[4] Throughout this book, log[z] denotes the natural logarithm of z, that is, the logarithm to the base e.

$$= E_x \log[5 + \pi(x, a_1)] = [.6] \log[15] + [.4] \log[55] = 3.22776,$$

and

$$\mathbf{U(D \mid I\downarrow}, a_2) = E_x \log[\omega(95, x, a_2) - 90]$$

$$= E_x \log[5 + \pi(x, a_2)] = [.6] \log[30] + [.4] \log[20] = 3.23901,$$

which shows the optimal action is now $a_0^A = a_2$. The change in initial wealth has altered the relative desirability of the available actions.

It is interesting to compare the previous decisions with an alternative solution using the *maximin criterion*, which in its purest form advises the DM to choose the action, or probabilistic mixture of actions, that maximizes the minimum possible wealth. The maximin criterion does not make use of the initial knowledge, and is most useful when nature is an opponent and is actively choosing the state for her own benefit. It is thus quite useful in game theory. On the other hand, when nature is dispassionate and uncaring, use of this criterion can lead to overly pessimistic decisions. Adjustments can be made to mitigate this problem somewhat, but maximin-type criteria are seldom considered in this book. Borch (1968, Chapter 7) discusses in this context several maximin-type alternatives, and Szaniawski (1967) considers the information evaluation problem under this class of criteria.

In Example 2.1, a maximin DM might reason as follows. "There's a black cloud always hanging over me, and it's not necessarily a rain cloud. If I choose a_1: plant corn, it's sure to be dry and I'm worth \$110. If I choose a_2: plant sorghum, it's sure to be wet, and I'm worth \$115. My best decision is a_2." This line of reasoning, that nature's choice of weather depends upon this farmer's decisions, does not seem advisable. Example 2.1 continues in Section 2.4.1.♦

2.2 The Framing of the Decision Problem

2.2.1 Practical Issues in Framing

The DM frames the problem by identifying the alternative actions $\mathbf{a}$, enumerating the possible states $\mathbf{X}$, and determining the stakes involved by assessing the terminal wealth outcome of each initial wealth-state-action triplet, $\omega(w, x, a)$. Included in this assessment is the cost associated with framing the problem, a cost that must be borne regardless of whether the DM chooses to incorporate information into the solution. The DM also assesses her utility function and knows or chooses the information structure and its associated cost.

This brief presentation of the elements of decision making under uncertainty belies the practical difficulties of actually formulating, assessing, calculating, and analyzing the solution to a particular decision problem under uncertainty.

One such difficulty involves problems with significant nonmonetary aspects such as ethical dilemmas. It is not easy, for example, to formulate decision models for doctors involved in questions of life and death. In a sense, the assessments of problem structure, utility functions, and probability distributions are themselves decision problems. The situation in Example 2.1 can quite easily be made more complex, by adding the many details that would make it more realistic. The "art" of applied quantitative decision theory is to obtain tractability without sacrificing the essential characteristics of the problem. In general, the amount of thought, effort, and detail that a problem warrants increases in proportion to the magnitude of the problem's consequences; but see Horowitz and Thompson (1995).

One of the best studies of these practical matters is Schlaifer (1969); also quite useful are Lindley (1985) and Smith (1988). For business decision problems, Newman (1971) presents several case studies from marketing that illustrate many of the complexities that arise when solving practical problems. Brown, Kahr, and Peterson (1974) and Clemen (1991) are nice intermediate-level texts. Willemain (1995) presents an interesting empirical study of how experts go about framing a decision model.

Keeney (1992) approaches the framing of a decision by beginning with the delineation of the fundamental objectives, followed by the identification of alternative actions to achieve those objectives.[5] Keeney argues that this sequencing is useful not only in problem solving, but also in identifying opportunities.

LaValle (1978) and Schlaifer (1969) present some of the techniques for translating the DM's often vague preferences into a specific functional form for her utility function. Certainly the risk neutral case is the most simple, since no utility function need be assessed. If the DM must exhibit risk aversion, the concave-exponential function has certain practical conveniences; see the upcoming Example 2.2 along with Sections 5.3 and 7.1.3. The decision problem associated with the assessment of the DM's utility function is beyond the scope here, but one recurring theme in Chapter 7 is the study of conditions and relationships that are valid for any, say, risk averse DM, the purpose being to avoid the need for assessing a specific utility function.

Sometimes it is easier to frame the problem in terms of minimizing the DM's opportunity loss rather than maximizing her payoff. This is especially common in certain decision problems that arise in statistics; see Raiffa and Schlaifer (1961, Section 4.4) and the upcoming Section 5.2.4.

In the types of decision problems facing a single-person organization such as an individual investor or single proprietorship, it is often necessary to frame the

---

[5] Or, first figure out what you want, then figure out how to get it [Keeney (1992), page 4].

problem such that both risk aversion and the level of initial wealth play an important role. At the other extreme, in the setting of a large organization it is likely that any particular decision is merely one of many, a small contributor to overall corporate net worth. In this circumstance it is reasonable to frame all decision makers as being risk neutral, and to consider only the contribution each decision makes to organizational profits.[6] For this reason the Chapter 9 analysis of information within organizations generally frames the criterion as the maximization of the organization's expected profit.

2.2.2 *Framing the State Space and Initial Knowledge*

The initial structure **I**↓ must reflect the DM's best assessment of her beliefs about the probabilities of the possibilities in the state space **X**. Free from both wishful thinking and paranoia, this probability assessment embodies the DM's prior knowledge concerning the state, and may well be the output from a previous analysis. The viewpoint in this book is that this is a subjective, or personal probability measure, subjective in the sense that two reasonable DMs could very well disagree on its "correctness." Adopting such a view does not preclude the use of relative frequency data as a tool of assessment; see Chapter 4.

The state space **X** may be countable or uncountable. When **X** is countable, the probability measure p(x) is a discrete mass function and it is meaningful to talk about $p(x_i)$ as the probability of state x_i. When **X** is uncountable, the measure p(x) is a density function and not directly a probability; however, the quantity p(x)dx is the probability element near state x. In either case p(x) is often somewhat loosely called a probability distribution.

Whether the DM's beliefs about **X**, especially subjective beliefs, should be admitted into the problem is not without controversy. Indeed, for decision problems in statistics in which the state variable is a statistical parameter, the acceptance of this probability measure is a prime identifying characteristic of a Bayesian statistician. In the business-type decision problems considered in this book the prior measure is often an important component of the knowledge the DM brings to the problem, and its acceptance is less controversial. The approach here is Bayesian primarily in the sense that it makes extensive use of Bayes' Theorem, equation (2.17). Nonetheless, the purpose of several sections in Chapter 6 is to seek results that are not dependent upon the assessment of any specific prior.

Apparently, the formulation and construction of the decision problem, in other words, the preparation of the problem for analysis, is itself a decision problem. The expected utility criterion requires that the formulated problem exhibit several characteristics. First, probability assessments must be *coherent*, that is,

---

[6] Arrow and Lind (1970) argue why public policy should also exhibit risk neutrality.

obey all the mathematical laws of probability. Second, tastes and beliefs must be independent; that is, the preferences for outcomes embodied in u(W) must be independent of both the means of realizing them and the probability of realizing them. Third, for state-space analysis both the probability measure p(x) on the state and the utility function u(W) must not depend on the DM's choice of a particular action a. See LaValle (1980) for further discussion.

♦ *Example 2.2 Style vs. Substance?*

As the owner of a small advertising agency, you must make a presentation to win a contract from a potential client, and need to decide whether to hire the services of a graphic design specialist for $1,000. If the client accepts your campaign proposal, you can add $20,000 to your initial wealth of $2,000; if the proposal is rejected you add nothing to your wealth. The graphic designer promises slick multicolored charts, graphs, and overheads for you to use in a multimedia presentation, but the expense for these services must be paid out of initial wealth.

A natural attempt to formulate this decision problem is to define the state as whether or not the proposal is accepted, giving the outcomes shown in Table 2.1. In this framing, not buying the graphics is a dominating action and must be chosen. But this formulation misses the essence of the situation and cannot be the best way to look at the problem.

Table 2.1. A Poor Framing for Example 2.2

	x_1 = proposal accepted	x_2 = proposal rejected
a_1 = buy graphics	$21	$1
a_2 = don't buy graphics	$22	$2

The error in the preceding approach is that it violates one of the previous construction principles for applying the expected utility criterion. Specifically, the probability of the state is clearly influenced by the choice of action, in the same way that, say, the action of seeding clouds affects the chances of rain. The state space **X** needs to be defined so that p(x) does not depend upon any $a \in \mathbf{a}$.

A correct formulation defines the state space $\mathbf{X}^4 = \{x_1, x_2, x_3, x_4\}$, with

x_1 = the proposal is accepted on its merits no matter what we do,
x_2 = the proposal is rejected on its merits no matter what we do,
x_3 = the proposal is accepted if and only if it is graphically slick,
x_4 = the proposal is rejected if and only if it is graphically slick.

The assessed probabilities of each of the possibilities no longer depends upon the choice of action. The idea is to make the state variable the mindset of the client, allowing for the possibility that the graphical presentation affects the way the client makes the decision. Naturally, the graphic designer would like to convince us that state x_3 is quite likely. The rationale for the state x_4 is that a slick presentation might lead the client to decide our services are all style and no substance.

This framing leads to the following table of monetary outcomes.

Table 2.2. Proper Framing for Example 2.2

	x_1	x_2	x_3	x_4
a_1 = buy graphics	\$21	\$1	\$21	\$ 1
a_2 = don't buy graphics	\$22	\$2	\$ 2	\$22

Suppose the DM assesses the following prior probabilities for the four states: $p(x_1) = .50$, $p(x_2) = .25$, $p(x_3) = .20$, and $p(x_4) = .05$. If the DM's utility function is $u(W) = W$, it is straightforward to calculate the expected utility of each alternative as $\mathbf{U(D\,|\,I\!\downarrow}, a_1) = \$15$ and $\mathbf{U(D\,|\,I\!\downarrow}, a_2) = \$13$. Hence the optimal action is $a_0^N = a_1$, and $\mathbf{U(D^*\,|\,I\!\downarrow)} = \$15$.

Suppose instead the DM has the interesting and important concave-exponential utility function $u(W) = -\exp[-bW]$, with $b = .8$. Calculating $\mathbf{U(D\,|\,I\!\downarrow}, a_k)$ as in (2.10),

$$\mathbf{U(D\,|\,I\!\downarrow}, a_1) = .50\{-\exp[-[.8][21]]\} + .25\{-\exp[-[.8][1]]\} + .20\{-\exp[-[.8][21]]\} + .05\{-\exp[-[.8][1]]\} = -.1348,$$

$$\mathbf{U(D\,|\,I\!\downarrow}, a_2) = .50\{-\exp[-[.8][22]]\} + .25\{-\exp[-[.8][2]]\} + .20\{-\exp[-[.8][2]]\} + .05\{-\exp[-[.8][22]]\} = -.0909,$$

so this DM chooses an action different from the risk neutral counterpart: here, $a_0^A = a_2$ with $\mathbf{U(D^*\,|\,I\!\downarrow)} = -.0909$ utiles. Example 2.2 continues in Section 7.1.2. ♦

2.2.3 The Incorporation of Information

As a final component in the framing of the problem, the DM can consider the potential benefits of incorporating information into the solution. The DM can control the action, can assess the outcome of each action in each state, knows the utility of alternative sums of money, but cannot control the realization of the state. The DM may, however, be able to affect beliefs about the probability measure on the state through the utilization of an information source. The possible augmentation of the problem via the use of information creates a new decision situation that may very well be preferable to the DM.

As Hirshleifer (1973) points out, the incorporation of information is an active approach to decision making, whereas decision making under uncertainty is a passive approach. In fact, decision making under uncertainty is a special case, one in which the information source provides only one message: "no further information."

2.3 Useful Facts About Statistical Information

2.3.1 *Statistical Properties of the Information Structure*

Since the relevant time period for deciding whether to incorporate information is prior to the accessing of any message, and the DM cannot know beforehand with certainty what the specific message y will be, the DM assesses an information structure $\mathbf{I} = \{\mathbf{Y}, p(x, y)\}$ to embody the statistical aspects of the information source; this assessment is a key subject matter of this book. Before considering the incorporation of information into the problem, this section collects some definitions and results from probability theory that are useful in the sequel.

The assessment and application of statistical informativeness is often facilitated by utilizing the marginal and conditional components of the joint measure, as developed coherently with the laws of probability. The joint measure p(x, y) induces the *marginal probability measure on the message space* $\mathbf{Y}$, denoted p(y). This is

$$p(y_j) = \Sigma_i\, p(x_i, y_j) \tag{2.13a}$$

or

$$p(y) = \int_{\mathbf{X}} p(x, y)\, dx, \tag{2.13b}$$

in the discrete and continuous cases, respectively. This measure gives the unconditional probability that the information source produces any potential message in the message space. Likewise, the marginal probability measure on the state space (the prior measure) is obtained analogously as

$$p(x_i) = \Sigma_j\, p(x_i, y_j) \tag{2.14a}$$

or

$$p(x) = \int_{\mathbf{Y}} p(x, y)\, dy. \tag{2.14b}$$

Two important conditional distributions also derive from p(x, y). The probability measure of the messages, conditional on each state, is called the *likelihood of the message space* and is denoted $p(y \mid x)$. By the definition of conditional probability, with $p(x) > 0$, the likelihood is

$$p(y \mid x) = p(x, y)/p(x). \tag{2.15}$$

For a fixed x, $p(y \mid x)$ is a proper probability distribution on $\mathbf{Y}$. Fixing y and viewing $p(y \mid x)$ as a function of x defines the *likelihood function*, which is not a proper probability distribution. Analogously, when $p(y) > 0$ the posterior of the state, conditional on the message, is

$$p(x \mid y) = p(x, y)/p(y). \tag{2.16}$$

Rearranging (2.15) and combining it with (2.16) yields

$$p(x \mid y) = p(y \mid x)\, p(x)/p(y). \tag{2.17}$$

The formula (2.17) shows the relationship between all the induced distributions and is known as *Bayes' Theorem.*

For many purposes the statistical evaluation of the information structure involves the assessment and interpretation of the relationship between the prior distribution and the set of posterior distributions, one for each $y \in \mathbf{Y}$. In a rearrangement of (2.17),

$$p(x \mid y) = [p(y \mid x)/p(y)]\, p(x). \tag{2.18}$$

The quantity in brackets, the ratio of the conditional distribution $p(y \mid x)$ to the marginal distribution $p(y)$, can be thought of as a function of each y that transforms, or processes, the prior distribution $p(x)$ into the posterior distribution $p(x \mid y)$.

When the prior marginal measure $p(x)$ has already been assessed in the prior decision, combining the likelihood with the prior is a common, although certainly not the only, method for assessing $p(x, y)$. Raiffa and Schlaifer (1961) catalogue a number of pairings of priors and likelihoods that combine with convenience and mathematical tractability; these *natural conjugates* are especially useful in statistical decision problems such as the upcoming Example 5.2.

2.3.2 The Finite Model

An important special case, especially for illustrative purposes, is the situation in which both the state space and the information structure are finite. When the state space is finite and contains m elements, $\mathbf{X}^m = \{x_1, \cdots, x_i, \cdots, x_m\}$, the prior probability distribution of the state variable is discrete and can conveniently be written as the $1 \times m$ vector $\mathbf{r}$:

$$\mathbf{r} = [p(x_1), \cdots, p(x_i), \cdots, p(x_m)]. \tag{2.19}$$

Adopting the convention that any impossible state is purged from the description $\mathbf{X}^m$ ensures that $p(x_i) > 0$, and coherence requires $\Sigma_i\, p(x_i) = 1$.

When the information structure is finite, $\mathbf{I} = \{\mathbf{Y}^n, p(x_i, y_j)\}$, the information source provides one from a finite space $\mathbf{Y}^n$ of potential messages, $\mathbf{Y}^n = \{y_1, \cdots, y_j, \cdots, y_n\}$. The marginal probability measure on the messages is the $1 \times n$ vector

$$\mathbf{q} = [p(y_1), \cdots, p(y_j), \cdots, p(y_n)], \tag{2.20}$$

having typical element $p(y_j) \geq 0$ with $\Sigma_j\, p(y_j) = 1$. The message y_j is *receivable* if $p(y_j) > 0$.

The joint measure, a discrete distribution on $\mathbf{X}^m \times \mathbf{Y}^n$, is expressed as the m $\times$ n matrix ρ:

$$\rho = \begin{bmatrix} p(x_1, y_1) & \cdots & p(x_1, y_n) \\ \vdots & p(x_i, y_j) & \vdots \\ p(x_m, y_1) & \cdots & p(x_m, y_n) \end{bmatrix}. \tag{2.21}$$

A relabeling of messages amounts to a permutation of the columns of ρ.

The probability of message y_j conditional on state x_i is

$$p(y_j | x_i) = p(x_i, y_j)/p(x_i) \geq 0, \tag{2.22}$$

and the likelihood is the m $\times$ n matrix λ,

$$\lambda = \begin{bmatrix} p(y_1|x_1) & \cdots & p(y_n|x_1) \\ \vdots & p(y_j|x_i) & \vdots \\ p(y_1|x_m) & \cdots & p(y_n|x_m) \end{bmatrix}. \tag{2.23}$$

The rows of λ sum to one: $\Sigma_j\ p(y_j | x_i) = 1$; such a matrix is called a *row-stochastic Markov matrix*. The information structure is *noiseless* if each row of λ contains exactly one "1"—conditional on the occurrence of state x_i, only one message can be received. Note also that for the fixed message y_j, reading down the column gives the likelihood function; the columns do not in general sum to one.

Finally, the posterior distribution of the state given each receivable message

$$p(x_i | y_j) = p(x_i, y_j)/p(y_j) \geq 0, \tag{2.24}$$

is shown as the m $\times$ n matrix Π:

$$\Pi = \begin{bmatrix} p(x_1| y_1) & \cdots & p(x_1| y_n) \\ \vdots & p(x_i| y_j) & \vdots \\ p(x_m| y_1) & \cdots & p(x_m| y_n) \end{bmatrix}. \tag{2.25}$$

The matrix Π is *column-stochastic*, since $\Sigma_i\ p(x_i | y_j) = 1$.

2.3.3 *Some Specific Expectations*

This subsection catalogues for future application the mathematical expectation of a number of specific functions. The mean and the variance of a random variable are two well-known examples; the additional concepts of partial expectation and entropy are also useful in the sequel. Jensen's inequality is the basis for several subsequent results of both theoretical and practical importance. Finally, the order in which the analyst performs joint expectations is a matter of choice that leads to alternative approaches to the incorporation of information.

Unconditional and Conditional Means

The unconditional mean of the random variable X, $\overline{x}$, is defined in the discrete and continuous cases, respectively, as

$$\overline{x} \equiv E_x\, x = \Sigma_i\, x_i\, p(x_i), \tag{2.26a}$$

and

$$\overline{x} \equiv E_x\, x = \int_{\mathbf{X}} x\, p(x)\, dx.^{7} \tag{2.26b}$$

The mean of X, conditional on the processing of the message y, $\overline{x}_y$, is the analogous concept using the posterior distribution $p(x \mid y)$:

$$\overline{x}_y \equiv E_{x\mid y}\, x. \tag{2.27}$$

Partial Expectations

When assessing the pragmatic value of information, certain outcome functions give rise to the need for calculating the partial expectation of a random variable, the expectation when the random variable is constrained to some subset of its normal range. When the state space **X** is continuous on the real line, the left-hand unconditional and conditional partial expectations up to t are defined as

$$\overline{x}^{(\ell)}(t) = \int_{-\infty}^{t} x\, p(x)\, dx \tag{2.28a}$$

and

$$\overline{x}_y^{(\ell)}(t) = \int_{-\infty}^{t} x\, p(x \mid y)\, dx, \tag{2.28b}$$

respectively. Likewise, the right-hand unconditional and conditional partial expectations from t are

$$\overline{x}^{(r)}(t) = \int_{t}^{\infty} x\, p(x)\, dx \tag{2.29a}$$

and

$$\overline{x}_y^{(r)}(t) = \int_{t}^{\infty} x\, p(x \mid y)\, dx. \tag{2.29b}$$

[7] The symbol "≡" indicates a new notation for a previously defined concept or quantity; it links two symbols that are simply different notations for precisely the same thing.

Measures of Uncertainty

If the probability distribution of the state (prior or posterior) describes the DM's current knowledge, it is natural to seek measures of the DM's uncertainty about what she knows. The unconditional variance of the random variable X, σ_x^2, is defined as the expectation of the function

$$\sigma_x^2 = E_x[x - \bar{x}]^2 = E_x[x^2] - \bar{x}^2; \tag{2.30}$$

this can be calculated as

$$\sigma_x^2 = \Sigma_i [x_i - \bar{x}]^2 p(x_i) \tag{2.31a}$$

or

$$\sigma_x^2 = \int_{\mathbf{X}} [x - \bar{x}]^2 p(x)\, dx, \tag{2.31b}$$

depending upon the nature of **X**. Likewise, the conditional variance posterior to y is

$$\sigma_{x|y}^2 = E_{x|y}[x - \bar{x}_y]^2 = E_{x|y}[x^2] - \bar{x}_y^2. \tag{2.32}$$

In the definitions (2.30) and (2.32), the final equality is an algebraic manipulation that is often convenient.

Entropy is another useful quantification of the amount of uncertainty in a probability distribution. For a univariate distribution such as the prior p(x), *entropy* is defined as

$$H(\mathbf{I}\downarrow) = -\Sigma_i\, p(x_i) \log[p(x_i)] \tag{2.33a}$$

or

$$H(\mathbf{I}\downarrow) = -\int_{\mathbf{X}} p(x) \log[p(x)]\, dx, \tag{2.33b}$$

as the case may be. It can be shown [Theil (1967)] that the entropy of a statistical distribution is maximized by the uniform distribution and is zero when there is no uncertainty about the realization of the random variable, since log[1] = 0.

Given the entropy of each conditional distribution p(x | y), the *expected entropy* of an information structure, also called the *equivocation* of **I**, is

$$H(\mathbf{I}) = -\int_{\mathbf{Y}} p(y) \int_{\mathbf{X}} p(x\,|\,y) \log[p(x\,|\,y)]\, dx\, dy, \tag{2.34}$$

and the difference

$$J(\mathbf{I}) = H(\mathbf{I}\downarrow) - H(\mathbf{I}) \tag{2.35}$$

ranges from 0 when $\mathbf{I} = \mathbf{I}\downarrow$ to $H(\mathbf{I}\downarrow)$ when the structure always precisely identifies the state. The quantity J(**I**) is called the *information transmitted*, or the *uncertainty removed.* However, as Sections 5.4 and 6.2.2 show, only in certain special cases does J(**I**) relate directly to the pragmatic valuation of the information structure. It may, however, relate to the cost of information transmission [Marschak (1971)] and storage [Bookstein and Klein (1990)].

Jensen's Inequality

Many of the functions that arise in the analysis of information are known to be either concave or convex over their entire range. If f(x) is a function defined on the interval (C, D), and the random variable X is such that its entire support of probability is also within that range, taking on at least two values with nonzero probability, then assuming that $\overline{x} \equiv E_x\, x$ and $E_x\, f(x)$ exist, Jensen's inequality ensures that

$$E_x\, f(x) \geq f(\overline{x}) \tag{2.36a}$$

if f(x) is convex, and

$$E_x\, f(x) \leq f(\overline{x}) \tag{2.36b}$$

if f(x) is concave. A proof can be found in DeGroot (1970, Section 7.6).

Extensive and Normal Form Analysis

To begin to tie statistical information in with its pragmatic uses, there are several useful facts involving the expectations of functions of the random variables. When a function, $g(x, y, \bullet)$ (where the "$\bullet$" indicates any other item not a function of x or y) is bounded the analyst can perform the double expectation $E_{x,y}$ $g(x, y, \bullet)$ in the more convenient order; in particular,

$$\begin{aligned} E_{x,y}\, g(x, y, \bullet) &= \Sigma_i\, \Sigma_j\, g(x_i, y_j, \bullet)\, p(x_i, y_j) \\ &= \Sigma_j\, \Sigma_i\, g(x_i, y_j, \bullet)\, p(x_i, y_j) \end{aligned} \tag{2.37a}$$

in the discrete case, and

$$\begin{aligned} E_{x,y}\, g(x, y, \bullet) &= \int_X \int_Y g(x, y, \bullet)\, p(x, y)\, dx\, dy \\ &= \int_Y \int_X g(x, y, \bullet)\, p(x, y)\, dy\, dx \end{aligned} \tag{2.37b}$$

in the continuous case. This maneuver is called a *change in the order of summation/integration.*

The relationships between the joint, conditional, and marginal distributions imply that

$$E_{x,y}\, g(x, y, \bullet) = E_x\, E_{y|x}\, g(x, y, \bullet) = E_y\, E_{x|y}\, g(x, y, \bullet). \tag{2.38}$$

For example, in the continuous case,

$$E_{x,y}\, g(x, y, \bullet) = \int_Y \int_X g(x, y, \bullet)\, p(x, y)\, dy\, dx$$

$$= \int_Y p(y) \left\{ \int_X g(x, y, \bullet)\, p(x \mid y)\, dx \right\} dy$$

$$= E_y E_{x \mid y}\, g(x, y, \bullet). \tag{2.39}$$

As an application of (2.38), Raiffa and Schlaifer (1961) identify two methods for finding the solution to the decision problem with information: the extensive form and the normal form. The *extensive form* of analysis conditions first on the message, as in (2.39); the *normal form* conditions first on the state. Both methods ultimately result in the same answer under the expected utility criterion. The extensive form is the more useful in practice and is presented in the next section, but it has come under criticism [Machina (1989)] as inappropriate for decision makers with certain types of preferences; see Section 7.3. The normal form is the more useful for statistical study, and is presented in Chapter 6.

Law of Iterated Expectation

A final useful fact is the *law of iterated expectation*: for any integrable function $g(x, \bullet)$, not depending upon y,

$$E_y E_{x \mid y}\, g(x, \bullet) = E_x\, g(x, \bullet). \tag{2.40}$$

To prove this in the discrete case, by definition,

$$E_{x \mid y}\, g(x, \bullet) = \Sigma_i\, g(x_i, \bullet)\, p(x_i \mid y_j)$$

and

$$E_y E_{x \mid y}\, g(x, \bullet) = \Sigma_j \Sigma_i\, g(x_i, \bullet)\, p(x_i \mid y_j)\, p(y_j).$$

Interchanging the order of summation and combining the posterior and marginal yields

$$E_y E_{x \mid y}\, g(x, \bullet) = \Sigma_i \Sigma_j\, g(x_i, \bullet)\, p(x_i, y_j).$$

Since the function $g(x_i, \bullet)$ is constant when summing with respect to y, the preceding becomes, using (2.14a),

$$E_y E_{x \mid y}\, g(x, \bullet) = \Sigma_i\, g(x_i, \bullet)\, \Sigma_j\, p(x_i, y_j)$$

$$= \Sigma_i\, g(x_i, \bullet)\, p(x_i) = E_x\, g(x_i, \bullet).$$

As an application of this, consider the expectation of the conditional mean $\bar{x}_y$ with respect to the marginal density p(y): $E_y\, \bar{x}_y = E_y E_{x \mid y}\, x$. Here, $g(x_i, \bullet) =$ x, so by a direct application of (2.40),

$$E_y\, \bar{x}_y = E_y E_{x \mid y}\, x = E_x\, x = \bar{x}; \tag{2.41}$$

although $\bar{x}_y$ is a function of y via the posterior distribution p(x | y), the mean of the conditional posterior measures is always the unconditional mean of X.

2.4 Value of the Informed Decision

2.4.1 Extensive Form Analysis

Suppose the information structure **I** were available cost-free. Having processed the specific message y and now believing the relevant probability distribution of the state to be p(x | y), the DM with utility function u takes the optimal action a_y^u defined by

$$\mathbf{U(D^* \mid I}, y) = \max_a E_{x|y}\, u(\omega(w, x, a)) = E_{x|y}\, u(\omega(w, x, a_y^u)), \quad (2.42)$$

where in the discrete case,

$$E_{x|y_j}\, u(\omega(w, x_i, a_{y_j}^u)) = \Sigma_i\, u(\omega(w, x_i, a_{y_j}^u))\, p(x_i \mid y_j), \quad (2.43a)$$

and in the continuous case

$$E_{x|y}\, u(\omega(w, x, a_y^u)) = \int_{\mathbf{X}} u(\omega(w, x, a_y^u))\, p(x \mid y)\, dx. \quad (2.43b)$$

The quantity $\mathbf{U(D^* \mid I}, y)$ measures the before-cost utility the DM expects to achieve prior to the realization of the state but posterior to the cognitive processing of the message y.

The optimal choice a_y^u is a conditional decision rule that tells the decision maker how to respond, conditional on the message y. The extensive form of analysis finds this action for each message that might be received and processed, thereby building up the optimal decision rule as the collection of optimal conditional decision rules:

$$a_{\mathbf{I}}^u = \{\, a_y^u \text{ for all } y \in \mathbf{Y} \}. \quad (2.44)$$

Raiffa and Schlaifer (1961) call this first stage *terminal analysis.*

The second stage is *preposterior analysis,* in which these maximum conditional expected utilities are averaged over all potential messages to obtain the *value of the informed decision,* $\mathbf{U(D^* \mid I)}$. Using (2.42),

$$\mathbf{U(D^* \mid I)} = E_y\, \mathbf{U(D^* \mid I}, y) = E_y \max_a E_{x|y}\, u(\omega(w, x, a))$$

$$= E_y\, E_{x|y}\, u(\omega(w, x, a_y^u)). \quad (2.45)$$

Writing (2.45) out in full,

$$\mathbf{U(D^* \mid I)} = \int_{\mathbf{Y}} \int_{\mathbf{X}} u(\omega(w, x, a_y^u))\, p(x \mid y)\, p(y)\, dx\, dy$$

$$= \int_{\mathbf{Y}} p(y) \int_{\mathbf{X}} u(\omega(w, x, a_y^u))\, p(x \mid y)\, dx\, dy. \quad (2.46)$$

Extensive form analysis provides a straightforward way of showing that, for an expected-utility-maximizing DM, the value of the informed decision is not less than the value of the prior decision. To show $\mathbf{U(D^* \mid I)} \geq \mathbf{U(D^* \mid I\downarrow)}$, the definition of the conditional decision rule says

$$\max_a E_{x \mid y}\, u(\omega(w, x, a)) \geq E_{x \mid y}\, u(\omega(w, x, a))$$

for any action other than a_y^u, including the action a_0^u that is optimal under the prior distribution:

$$\max_a E_{x \mid y}\, u(\omega(w, x, a)) \geq E_{x \mid y}\, u(\omega(w, x, a_0^u)).$$

The utility function on the right-hand side of the inequality no longer depends in any way on the variable y; multiplying both sides by p(y) (all nonnegative, so the direction of the inequality cannot change) and summing or integrating to obtain the expectation with respect to p(y) yields

$$\mathbf{U(D^* \mid I)} = E_y \max_a E_{x \mid y}\, u(\omega(w, x, a)) \geq E_y E_{x \mid y}\, u(\omega(w, x, a_0^u)). \quad (2.47)$$

Since the function on the right-hand side of (2.47) does not depend upon the specific y, the law of iterated expectation (2.40) ensures

$$E_y E_{x \mid y}\, u(\omega(w, x, a_0^u)) = E_x\, u(\omega(w, x, a_0^u)) = \mathbf{U(D^* \mid I\downarrow)}. \quad (2.48)$$

Combining (2.47) with (2.48) shows that

$$\mathbf{U(D^* \mid I)} = E_y \max_a E_{x \mid y}\, u(\omega(w, x, a))$$

$$\geq E_x\, u(\omega(w, x, a_0^u)) = \mathbf{U(D^* \mid I\downarrow)}. \quad (2.49)$$

The economic interpretation (2.49) is important: under these conditions, the expected-utility-maximizing DM cannot be made worse off by a cost-free movement from the prior uninformed decision to a decision situation that makes use of an information structure **I**.

♦ *Example 2.1 A Farmer's Planting Decision (Continued)*
To illustrate the incorporation of information, suppose the farmer decides to utilize the services of a local firm that offers to provide a categorical forecast of the weather situation, an information structure with the message space

$$\mathbf{Y} = \{y_1, y_2\} = \{\text{the weather will be dry, the weather will be wet}\}.$$

The analysis requires knowledge of the joint probability p(x, y). The actual assessment of this distribution is a critical problem in the evaluation of information; Chapter 4 takes up the practical issues. For now assume the DM already knows that the joint distribution of states and messages in terms of the matrix ρ defined in (2.21) is

$$\rho = \begin{bmatrix} p(x_1, y_1) & p(x_1, y_2) \\ p(x_2, y_1) & p(x_2, y_2) \end{bmatrix} = \begin{bmatrix} .48 & .12 \\ .16 & .24 \end{bmatrix}. \tag{2.50}$$

The analysis of the informed decision via the extensive form requires use of the marginal distribution p(y) and the posterior distribution p(x | y). The marginal distribution of the messages is derived by adding up each column of ρ to form the vector **q**:

$$\mathbf{q} = [p(y_1), p(y_2)] = [.64, .36]. \tag{2.51}$$

Using (2.24) the posterior distribution in matrix form is

$$\Pi = \begin{bmatrix} p(x_1|y_1) & p(x_1|y_2) \\ p(x_2|y_1) & p(x_2|y_2) \end{bmatrix} = \begin{bmatrix} .75 & .33\bar{3} \\ .25 & .66\bar{6} \end{bmatrix}. \tag{2.52}$$

Recall that the DM has also assessed the prior distribution of the states as the vector

$$\mathbf{r} = [p(x_1), p(x_2)] = [.60, .40]. \tag{2.53}$$

Although the extensive form analysis does not make use of this prior, note that the entire package of probability assessments obeys the laws of probability and hence is coherent in the sense of Section 2.3. However, the assessment is biased, or uncalibrated. For example, the probability of state x_1 is .60, but the probability that the structure produces a message predicting state x_1 is .64.

Figure 2.5 presents the decision tree for Example 2.1 when the problem includes the option to incorporate information. The approach of extensive form analysis is to "fold back" the decision tree, beginning with the rightmost choice nodes and working backwards to the beginning. The DM's reasoning process involves planning decisions along the lines of, "If I should find myself in the precise circumstances this choice node represents, what decision would I make?" Whether the DM ever reaches any given choice node depends upon nature's choice at previous chance nodes.

Given message y_1, the expected utility from taking action a_1 is $[.75]u(110) + [.25]u(150)$, and the expected utility of taking a_2 is $[.75]u(125) + [.25]u(115)$. Under risk neutrality $a^N_{y_1} = a_2$, with $E_{x|y_1} u(\omega(w, x_i, a^N_{y_1})) = \$122.50$. Likewise, given message y_2, the expected utility of a_1 is $[.333]u(110) + [.667]u(150)$ and of a_2 is $[.333]u(125) + [.667]u(115)$. Under risk neutrality $a^N_{y_2} = a_1$ and $E_{x|y_2} u(\omega(w, x_i, a^N_{y_2})) = \$136.667$. Thus the optimal decision rule is

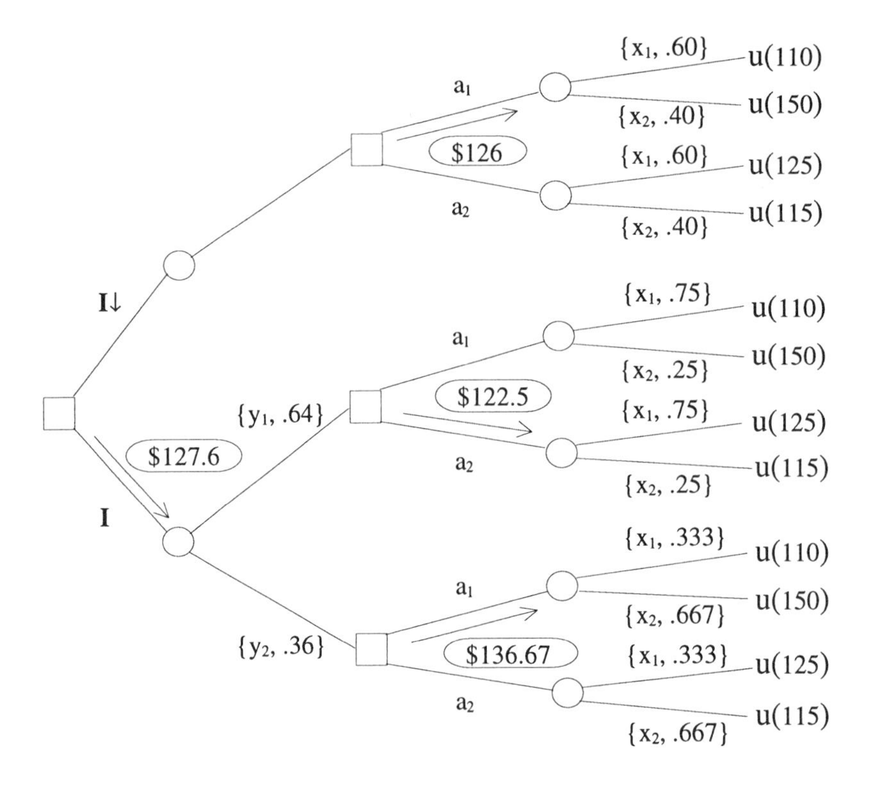

Figure 2.5. This decision tree for Example 2.1 indicates the optimal choices for the risk neutral DM with arrows, and circles the expected terminal wealth from each choice.

$$a_{\mathbf{I}}^{N} = \{ a_{y_1}^{N},\ a_{y_2}^{N} \} = \{a_2,\ a_1\}. \tag{2.54}$$

Assessing now (2.45) using (2.54), the value of the informed decision under risk neutrality is

$$\begin{aligned} \mathbf{U(D^* \,|\, I)} &= E_y\, E_{x\,|\,y}\, u(\omega(w,\ x,\ a_y^N)) \\ &= [.64][122.50] + [.36][136.667] = \$127.60. \end{aligned}$$

In words, the preceding calculation says: taking the optimal response to whatever message is received, the DM has a 64% chance of being worth \$122.50 and a 36% chance of being worth \$136.667; before the receipt of any message this expected wealth is \$127.60. Comparing this with the value of the prior decision, **U(D* | I↓)** = 126, the DM expects to be better off through the cost-free incorporation of **I**.

It is straightforward to show that the risk averter with utility function $u(W) = \log[W - 90]$ chooses the decision rule a_I^A identical to (2.54), that $E_{x|y_1} u(\omega(100, x_i, a_2)) = 3.47123$ utiles, and that $E_{x|y_2} u(\omega(100, x_i, a_1)) = 3.72814$ utiles. Hence, the value of the informed decision for this DM is, in utiles,

$$\mathbf{U(D^* | I)} = [.64][3.47123] + [.36][3.72814] = 3.56372,$$

an improvement from the previously calculated $\mathbf{U(D^* | I\downarrow)} = 3.43518$ utiles. ♦

2.4.2 *Perfect Information*

The maximum potential value of information, and incidentally the easiest for the DM to assess, is perfect information. *Perfect information* occurs when the information structure provides categorical direct messages that identify precisely and unequivocally the state that occurs. Under perfect information the message space is identical to the state space, $\mathbf{Y} = \mathbf{X}$, the DM receives the categorical message "state x occurs," and the posterior distribution is such that the probability of this event is one. Knowing this with certainty, the optimal choice is action a_x defined by

$$\max_a u(\omega(w, x, a)) = u(\omega(w, x, a_x)). \tag{2.55}$$

Under perfect information the messages exhibit *categorical calibration* with the state variable: the prior chance of state x occurring, p(x), is identical to the probability that the perfect information structure produces a message identifying the state x. That is, there is a lack of bias in message provision; the marginal probability distribution of the messages is the same as the prior probability distribution of the state: p(y) = p(x).

In summary, the perfect information structure is characterized by

$$\mathbf{I}\uparrow = \{\mathbf{Y} = \mathbf{X}, x, p(y) = p(x)\}. \tag{2.56}$$

Replacing p(y) with p(x) in (2.45) and taking advantage of the posterior certainty, the gross expected utility of the decision using the perfect information structure $\mathbf{I}\uparrow$ is

$$\mathbf{U(D^* | I\uparrow)} = E_x \max_a u(\omega(w, x, a)) = E_x u(\omega(w, x, a_x)). \tag{2.57}$$

Thus, a great practical advantage of perfect information is that assessment requires only the unconditional probability distribution p(x), that is, the initial information $\mathbf{I}\downarrow$ given in (2.8).

There is no structure more valuable than perfect information. This statement can be justified by showing that the value of the informed decision is greater under the perfect information structure $\mathbf{I}\uparrow$ than any other structure $\mathbf{I}$:

$$\mathbf{U}(\mathbf{D}^* \mid \mathbf{I}\uparrow) = \mathrm{E_x} \max_a u(\omega(w, x, a))$$

$$\geq \mathrm{E_y} \max_a \mathrm{E_{x|y}}\, u(\omega(w, x, a)) = \mathbf{U}(\mathbf{D}^* \mid \mathbf{I}). \qquad (2.58)$$

To show (2.58), for a given x the optimal action a_x satisfies

$$\max_a u(\omega(w, x, a)) \geq u(\omega(w, x, a)) \text{ for any } a \neq a_x.$$

Taking the expectation of the preceding inequality with respect to the (nonnegative) conditional measure p(x | y) gives

$$\mathrm{E_{x|y}} \max_a u(\omega(w, x, a)) \geq \mathrm{E_{x|y}}\, u(\omega(w, x, a)).$$

Since this is true for any a on the right-hand side of the inequality, it is true for the a that maximizes the right-hand side:

$$\mathrm{E_{x|y}} \max_a u(\omega(w, x, a)) \geq \max_a \mathrm{E_{x|y}}\, u(\omega(w, x, a)).$$

The expectation of this inequality with respect to the (nonnegative) marginal measure p(y) yields

$$\mathrm{E_y}\, \mathrm{E_{x|y}} \max_a u(\omega(w, x, a)) \geq \mathrm{E_y} \max_a \mathrm{E_{x|y}}\, u(\omega(w, x, a)).$$

The right-hand side of the preceding inequality is $\mathbf{U}(\mathbf{D}^* \mid \mathbf{I})$, as in (2.45); applying the law of iterated expectation to the left-hand side yields $\mathbf{U}(\mathbf{D}^* \mid \mathbf{I}\uparrow)$, as in (2.57). Hence, $\mathbf{U}(\mathbf{D}^* \mid \mathbf{I}\uparrow) \geq \mathbf{U}(\mathbf{D}^* \mid \mathbf{I})$.

2.4.3 Worthless Information

At the opposite end of the informativeness spectrum is statistically null information. An information structure **I** provides *null information* if the posterior probability function resulting from every receivable message is identical to the prior measure:

$$p(x \mid y) = p(x) \text{ for all } y \in \mathbf{Y}. \qquad (2.59)$$

This is the least useful information structure because such an information source is doing nothing statistically and not surprisingly has no pragmatic value.

The information structure $\mathbf{I} = \{\mathbf{Y}, p(x, y)\} = \{\mathbf{Y}, p(y), p(x \mid y)\}$ becomes, by invoking the null information criterion (2.59), $\{\mathbf{Y}, p(y), p(x)\}$. This structure is equivalent to $\mathbf{I}\downarrow$ because the message space **Y** and the marginal measure p(y) are arbitrary and extraneous under null information. Because the two are equivalent in all essential ways, denote the null information structure $\mathbf{I}\downarrow$, the same symbol as the initial information defined in equation (2.8):

$$\mathbf{I}\downarrow = \{\mathbf{Y}, p(y), p(x)\}. \qquad (2.60)$$

To prove this assertion, note first that the semantic meaning of **Y** is irrelevant, since no matter what message y is received, the probability measure on **X** does not change. Starting in extensive form, the value of the informed decision

$$\mathbf{U(D^* \mid I)} = E_y \max_a E_{x \mid y} u(\omega(w, x, a)),$$

becomes under (2.59)

$$\mathbf{U(D^* \mid I)} = E_y \max_a E_x u(\omega(w, x, a)).$$

For any $y \in \mathbf{Y}$, the optimal action under this "posterior" distribution is a_0^u, the optimal action in the uninformed decision:

$$\max_a E_x u(\omega(w, x, a)) = E_x u(\omega(w, x, a_0^u)).$$

Since a_0^u is optimal for each $y \in \mathbf{Y}$, the right-hand side is constant for every y; using (2.11)

$$E_y E_x u(\omega(w, x, a_0^u)) = E_x u(\omega(w, x, a_0^u)) = \mathbf{U(D^* \mid I\downarrow)}.$$

In other words, the precise distribution p(y) does not matter because the expectation of a constant is a constant.

Nonnull statistical information is a necessary but not sufficient condition for pragmatic information value. That is, decision problems can be constructed in which there is statistical information, $\mathbf{I} \neq \mathbf{I\downarrow}$, but the informativeness is not great enough for $\mathbf{U(D^* \mid I)} > \mathbf{U(D^* \mid I\downarrow)}$. Marschak (1971) uses the term *useless information* to describe a structure that offers statistical information but not pragmatic information. The following continuation of Example 2.1 presents a simple illustration; Radner and Stiglitz (1984) and Section 6.3.3 consider this phenomenon in more general circumstances.

♦ *Example 2.1 (Continued)*
Suppose the farmer's information source precisely identifies the state. The matrices (2.61) provide the joint and posterior distributions for this source:

$$\rho = \begin{bmatrix} 1 & 0 \\ 0 & 1 \end{bmatrix}; \quad \Pi = \begin{bmatrix} p(x_1 \mid y_1) & p(x_1 \mid y_2) \\ p(x_2 \mid y_1) & p(x_2 \mid y_2) \end{bmatrix} = \begin{bmatrix} 1 & 0 \\ 0 & 1 \end{bmatrix}. \tag{2.61}$$

Given the message y_1 that state x_1 is a certainty, the optimal action is $a_{x_1}^u = a_2$ with utility u(125). Given y_2, $a_{x_2}^u = a_1$ and utility is certain to be u(150). Under perfect information the chance of receiving y_j is identical to the chance of state x_j occurring, so with $p(y_1) = p(x_1) = .60$ and $p(y_2) = p(x_2) = .40$, the value of the perfectly informed decision is $\mathbf{U(D^* \mid I\uparrow)} = [.60]u(125) + [.40]u(150)$. For the risk neutral DM, $\mathbf{U(D^* \mid I\uparrow)} = \$135$. For the risk averse DM with $u(W) = \log[W - 90]$, the value of the perfectly informed decision is $\mathbf{U(D^* \mid I\uparrow)} = 3.77095$ utiles.

Returning to the situation of imperfect information, let the assessments of **q** and **r** remain as in (2.51) and (2.53), respectively. Consider the following two joint distributions of messages and states, A and B, along with their associated posteriors.

$$\rho_A = \begin{bmatrix} .384 & .216 \\ .256 & .144 \end{bmatrix}; \quad \Pi_A = \begin{bmatrix} p(x_1|y_1) & p(x_1|y_2) \\ p(x_2|y_1) & p(x_2|y_2) \end{bmatrix} = \begin{bmatrix} .60 & .60 \\ .40 & .40 \end{bmatrix}; \quad (2.62)$$

$$\rho_B = \begin{bmatrix} .40 & .20 \\ .24 & .16 \end{bmatrix}; \quad \Pi_B = \begin{bmatrix} p(x_1|y_1) & p(x_1|y_2) \\ p(x_2|y_1) & p(x_2|y_2) \end{bmatrix} = \begin{bmatrix} .625 & .55\bar{5} \\ .375 & .44\bar{4} \end{bmatrix}. \quad (2.63)$$

Comparing, in order, the posterior distributions (2.62), (2.63), (2.52), and (2.61), casual observation indicates this is a ranking of the four information structures by increasing "informativeness." The source A offers null information; no matter what the message is, $p(x_i|y_j) = p(x_i)$, $a^u_{y_1} = a^u_{y_2} = a^u_0$, and this source can never generate any value for any DM.

The source B seems to be more informative, giving higher probabilities to "correct" identifications of the state [cf. $p(x_1, y_1) = .40$ in ρ_B with $p(x_1, y_1) = .384$ in ρ_A], but it offers useless information in this problem if the DM is risk neutral. To show this, recall that $a^N_0 = a_1$ and $\mathbf{U(D^*|I\downarrow)} = 126$. Upon hearing y_1, calculation shows $a^N_{y_1} = a_1$, with $E_{x|y_1} u(\omega(w, x_i, a^N_{y_1})) = [.625]u(110) + [.375]u(150) = \$125.00$. Likewise, given message y_2, $a^N_{y_2} = a_1$, with $E_{x|y_2} u(\omega(w, x_i, a^N_{y_2})) = [.55\bar{5}]u(110) + [.44\bar{4}]u(150) = \$127.78$. This gives the value of the informed decision as $\mathbf{U(D^*|I)} = [.64][125] + [.36][127.78] = \$126 = \mathbf{U(D^*|I\downarrow)}$. Although this source may be useless to this decision maker in this problem, other situations can be constructed where this source does provide value; uselessness is a problem-specific characteristic. Example 2.1 continues in Section 3.1.1. ♦

Having shown that an expected utility maximizer assesses $\mathbf{U(D^*|I)} \geq \mathbf{U(D^*|I\downarrow)}$, the natural next step is to quantify the incremental value to the DM from using the information structure **I**. This is the subject of the next chapter.

3 Measures of the Value of Information

This chapter investigates the measurement of the changes in the DM's well-being that result from making a prior decision, processing a message, or incorporating an information source. To do this it is convenient to view a decision as a commodity, making it meaningful to consider the buying and selling prices for decisions with and without the incorporation of information.

3.1 Measures of the Value of a Message

3.1.1 Cash-Equivalent Values of a Decision

This subsection addresses some modeling issues and introduces several alternative measures of the incremental value of a decision to an expected utility maximizing DM. Some of the subsequent definitions intend to measure how much better (or worse) off the DM is as a consequence of the decision. Others intend to measure the demand price, that is, the maximum amount the DM should pay for the rights to the outcome of the decision.

Suppose the DM owns, or is committed to, a specific decision problem. The *reservation price of the prior decision* is the deterministic terminal wealth that makes the DM indifferent between the optimal solution with expected utility $\mathbf{U(D^* \mid I\downarrow)}$ and the sale of the entire situation for a cash-equivalent payment of a certain amount. Dependent upon the DM's specific utility function, the reservation price, also called the *certainty equivalent*, is written R_0^u and defined implicitly as the solution to

$$u(R_0^u) = \mathbf{U(D^* \mid I\downarrow)} = E_x\, u(\omega(w, x, a_0^u)). \tag{3.1}$$

A related idea is the *prior incremental gain in the reservation price*, which is defined as the difference

$$G_0^u = R_0^u - w. \tag{3.2}$$

This quantity can be positive or negative and measures the change in the DM's sell-out price attributable to this specific decision. Another important cash summarization is the DM's *prior expected terminal wealth* $\overline{W}_0^u$, which is

$$\overline{W}_0^u = E_x\{\omega(w, x, a_0^u)\}. \tag{3.3}$$

The reservation price and the expected wealth are generally not identical; the difference between the two is called the *risk* or *insurance premium*:

$$\iota = \overline{W}_0^u - R_0^u. \tag{3.4}$$

There are important definitive relationships between the reservation price and the expected terminal wealth that depend upon the DM's attitude towards risk; these are taken up in Chapter 7.

Before turning to demand price measures, it is necessary to clarify the functional treatment of the DM's terminal wealth after provision for any expense of a decision and/or information source. Let ψ denote a fixed nonstochastic cost, perhaps the bill or invoice for the information source (e.g., the cost $\mathcal{C}$), or perhaps simply a hypothetical quantity. The sequel uses three distinct formulations for modeling the terminal wealth from decisions with expense. Most commonly, cost is viewed as an up-front reduction in initial wealth, payable before undertaking any action, and hence making the DM's de facto initial wealth $w - \psi$. In this case terminal wealth is

$$W = \omega(w - \psi, x, a). \tag{3.5}$$

Less commonly, it may be convenient to model the cost as being paid after the fact, with posterior rather than prior dollars. In this case

$$W = \omega^{\#}(w, x, a, \psi) = \omega(w, x, a) - f(\psi). \tag{3.6}$$

One circumstance where this can arise is if the seller provides credit, payable at the end of the problem. Example 5.4a provides an illustration. Finally, when the outcome function is separable as in (2.2), initial wealth enters additively and terminal wealth is simply

$$W = w - \psi + \pi(x, a). \tag{3.7}$$

This latter modeling situation is often the most tractable and generally applied, but blind application of it can lead to mistakes in certain investing and betting problems such as the upcoming Example 3.1b.

The fundamental difficulty is that any change in initial wealth changes the expected utility of alternative actions in a way that may affect their ordering. This phenomenon comes into play and must be dealt with in the evaluation of information because the cost of purchasing a decision and/or information source is generally assumed to be paid out of initial wealth.

Suppose the DM with initial wealth w does not yet own the prior decision but is merely eyeing the opportunity. The *prior buying price* of the decision is the up-front change in initial wealth that makes the DM indifferent between owning the prior decision and standing pat with nonstochastic initial wealth w. The prior buying price B_0^u solves the equation

$$u(w) = \max_a E_x u(\omega(w - B_0^u, x, a)). \tag{3.8}$$

This quantity can be positive or negative. As Example 2.1 illustrates in Section 2.1, a reduction of initial wealth may change the relative desirability of alternative actions, so the maximizing action used to define B_0^u in (3.8) is not necessarily the same action as a_0^u in (2.11). In fact, iterative search methods may be necessary to find the buying price; the subsequent Example 3.1a illustrates a situation in which it is difficult to write down analytically the solution to (3.8). This type of computational difficulty is a recurring problem in the assessment of the value of information.

To treat this matter formally, consider the prior expected utility of an arbitrary action a_k, viewed as a function of a nonstochastic reduction in initial wealth of ψ:

$$\mathbf{U}(\mathbf{D} \mid \mathbf{I}\downarrow, \psi, a_k) = E_x u(\omega(w - \psi, x, a_k)). \tag{3.9}$$

For the values of ψ under which the utility function is defined and the expectation exists, the function $\mathbf{U}(\mathbf{D} \mid \mathbf{I}\downarrow, \psi, a_k)$ is continuous and strictly decreasing as ψ traverses the real line. For proof of this type of result, see LaValle (1978, Section 8.2). Define analogously $R_k^u(\psi)$, the prior reservation price of action a_k as a function of ψ, as the implicit solution to

$$u(R_k^u(\psi)) = \mathbf{U}(\mathbf{D} \mid \mathbf{I}\downarrow, \psi, a_k) = E_x u(\omega(w - \psi, x, a_k)). \tag{3.10}$$

The expected terminal wealth is

$$\overline{W}_k(\psi) = E_x \omega(w - \psi, x, a_k). \tag{3.11}$$

Both $R_k^u(\psi)$ and $\overline{W}_k(\psi)$ are continuous and strictly decreasing in ψ.

Furthermore, the functions

$$\mathbf{U}(\mathbf{D}^* \mid \mathbf{I}\downarrow, \psi) = \max_a E_x u(\omega(w - \psi, x, a)), \tag{3.12}$$

and

$$u(R_0^u(\psi)) = \mathbf{U}(\mathbf{D}^* \mid \mathbf{I}\downarrow, \psi) = \max_a E_x u(\omega(w - \psi, x, a)), \tag{3.13}$$

are the upper envelopes of (3.9) and the implicit solution to (3.10), respectively, and are also continuous and strictly decreasing in ψ. However, as the next continuation of Example 2.1 shows, the mean of the optimal prior wealth $\overline{W}_0^u(\psi)$ is not necessarily continuous in ψ, nor therefore is the risk premium $\iota(\psi)$ defined in (3.4).

♦ *Example 2.1 (Continued)*

If the farmer has initial wealth w = 100 and the logarithmic utility function $u(W) = \log[W - 90]$, the optimal prior decision is $a_0^A = a_1$, and the value of the prior decision is $\mathbf{U}(\mathbf{D}^* \mid \mathbf{I}\downarrow) = 3.43518$. Using the definition (3.1), the reservation price of this optimal decision is the solution to the equation

$$\log[R_0^A - 90] = 3.43518;$$

$$R_0^A - 90 = \exp[3.43518],$$

which is $R_0^A = \$121.04$. The prior incremental gain is \$21.04, and the DM's expected wealth from the decision is $\overline{W}_0^A = \$126$, giving an expected increase in wealth from the decision of \$26. The risk premium is $\iota = \overline{W}_0^A - R_0^A = \$4.96$.

If $\psi = 1$ so $w - \psi = 99$, the optimal action remains a_1, $\overline{W}_0^A = \$125$, $R_0^A = \$119.89$, and the risk premium rises to \$5.11. The more interesting circumstance arises when $\psi = 5$, making $w - \psi = 95$. The calculation in Section 2.1.3 shows the optimal action is now $a_0^A = a_2$, meaning the change in wealth has altered the relative desirability of the available actions. With $\mathbf{U}(\mathbf{D}^* \mid \mathbf{I}\downarrow) = 3.23901$, $R_0^A = \$115.51$ and $\overline{W}_0^A = \$116$; the risk premium is only \$0.49. The change in de facto initial wealth can affect choice because it changes the DM's degree of risk aversion.[1]

The upper graph in Figure 3.1 shows the two functions

$$\mathbf{U}(\mathbf{D} \mid \mathbf{I}\downarrow, \psi, a_1) = E_x \log[\omega(100 - \psi, x, a_1) - 90]$$

$$= [.6]\log[20 - \psi] + [.4]\log[60 - \psi]$$

and

$$\mathbf{U}(\mathbf{D} \mid \mathbf{I}\downarrow, \psi, a_2) = E_x \log[\omega(100 - \psi, x, a_2) - 90]$$

$$= [.6]\log[35 - \psi] + [.4]\log[25 - \psi].$$

The solid line, the upper envelope, is the graph of (3.12). The breakeven value of ψ at which the optimal action changes is $\psi = 3.235$. The lower graph in Figure 3.1 shows $R_k^A(\psi)$, with the upper envelope being $R_0^A(\psi)$. Figure 3.2 shows

[1] In the language of Section 7.1.3, this utility function exhibits the characteristic of decreasing absolute risk aversion.

that $\overline{W}_0^A(\psi)$ is strictly decreasing but not continuous and that the risk premium under the optimal decision, $\iota(\psi)$, is neither strictly decreasing nor continuous.

The buying price solves

$$\log[100 - 90] = \max_a E_x \log[100 - B_0^A + \pi(x, a) - 90].$$

The solution, found using a spreadsheet program, is $B_0^A = \$19.71$. That is, if the DM pays \$19.71 out of her initial wealth w = 100, it is now optimal for her to choose action $a_0^A = a_2$, giving her expected utility of [.60]log[125 – 19.71 – 90] + [.40]log[115 – 19.71 – 90] = 2.3026. This is equal to her original utility with certainty of log[10]. Example 2.1 continues in Section 3.2.2 ♦

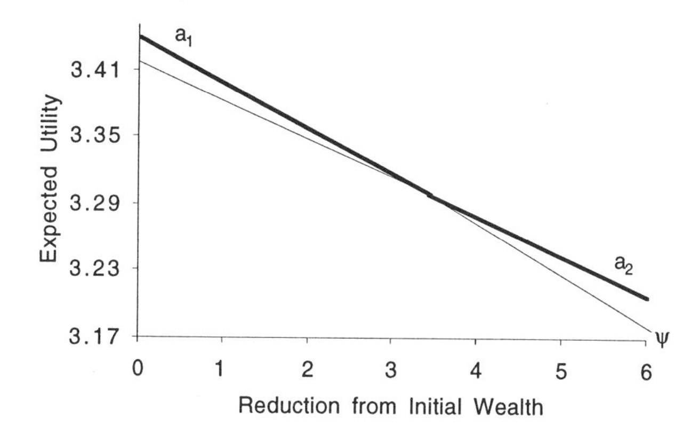

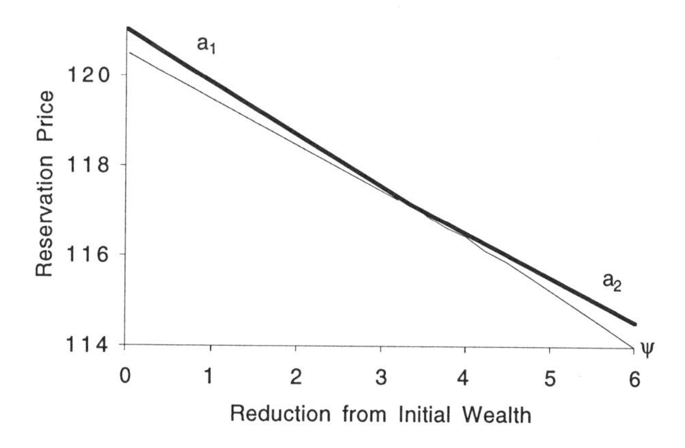

Figure 3.1. The optimal action in Example 2.1 is indicated by the darkened line, and changes at $\psi = \$3.235$. The maximum expected utility and the optimal reservation price are continuous in ψ.

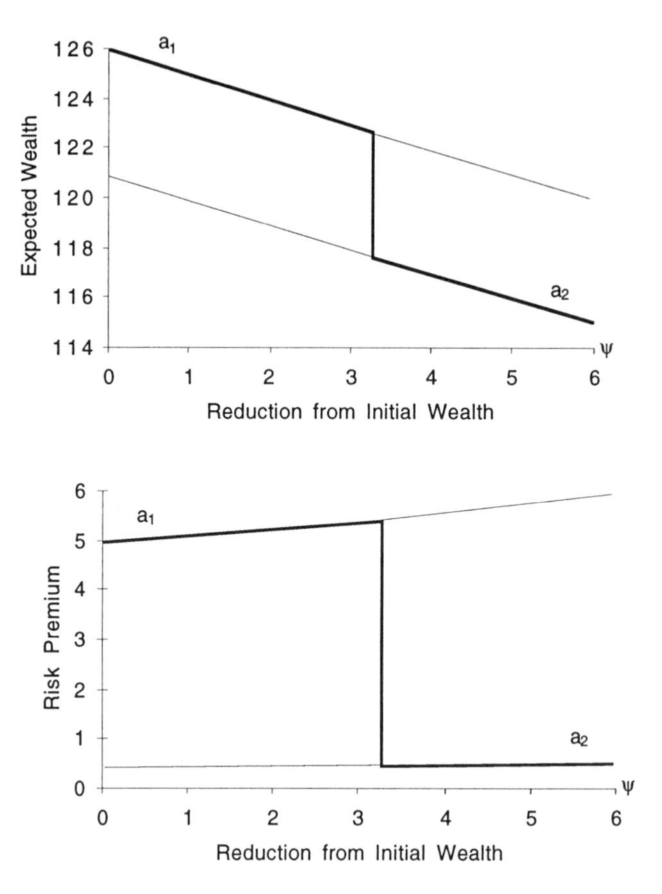

Figure 3.2. When initial wealth in Example 2.1 is reduced by more than $\psi = \$3.235$, the optimal action has lower expected wealth and a lower risk premium. With this utility function, the DM chooses to take less risk.

3.1.2 Value of Decisions Posterior to the Message

Turning to the analysis of the informed decision, suppose the DM accesses an information source, processes the message y, and applies it to the decision problem. After making the choice a_y^u, the state x_i occurs. Posterior to the message and the state, the DM's terminal wealth is $\omega(w, x_i, a_y^u)$, and without using the message it would have been $\omega(w, x_i, a_0^u)$. Generalizing (1.1), the change in the terminal wealth is the ex-post value of the message y, denoted $\hat{\upsilon}^u(x_i, y)$:

$$\hat{\upsilon}^u(x_i, y) = \omega(w, x_i, a_y^u) - \omega(w, x_i, a_0^u). \tag{3.14}$$

The ex-post value of the message y may be positive or negative. This characterization is of interest in an ex-post accounting of the situation, and is helpful in Chapter 8 for designing incentive contracts to procure information, but is of little use in assessing the value of the message y prior to the realization of the state.

Before the realization of the state the DM can calculate the various summary measures and compare them with the analogous quantities in the prior decision. When the DM takes the optimal response to the message, the *conditional reservation price* of the message y is the solution for R_y^u in the equation

$$u(R_y^u) = \mathbf{U}(\mathbf{D}^* \mid \mathbf{I}, y) = E_{x|y}\, u(\omega(w, x, a_y^u)). \tag{3.15}$$

The *conditional incremental gain* from the message y is

$$G_y^u = R_y^u - R_0^u. \tag{3.16}$$

The *conditional expected wealth* of the message y is

$$\overline{W}_y^u = E_{x|y}\, \{\omega(w, x, a_y^u)\}. \tag{3.17}$$

The difference between $\overline{W}_y^u$ and $\overline{W}_0^u$, the expected wealth under the prior decision, measures the *conditional incremental expected wealth* of the message y,

$$g_y^u = \overline{W}_y^u - \overline{W}_0^u. \tag{3.18}$$

Compared to ownership of the prior decision, the quantities g_y^u and G_y^u attempt to measure how much better off the DM is under knowledge of y. Both quantities can be positive or negative. There is no guarantee the DM expects to be "happier" after hearing the message; even by taking the optimal action in response to the message, the message may be "bad news."

The *conditional buying price* for the message y, B_y^u, is directly analogous to the prior buying price in equation (3.8). Compared to the pre-message situation, the conditional buying price is the solution for B_y^u in the equation

$$E_x\, u(\omega(w, x, a_0^u)) = \max_a E_{x|y}\, u(\omega(w - B_y^u, x, a)). \tag{3.19}$$

Again, this measure may be positive or negative.

An alternative and ultimately more useful approach to valuing the message starts with the optimal action a_y^u defined as

$$E_{x|y}\, u(\omega(w, x, a_y^u)) \geq E_{x|y}\, u(\omega(w, x, a)) \text{ for all } a \neq a_y^u.$$

Since this is true for all actions other than a_y^u, it is true for the action a_0^u that is optimal under the prior distribution:

$$E_{x|y}\, u(\omega(w, x, a_y^u)) \geq E_{x|y}\, u(\omega(w, x, a_0^u)). \tag{3.20}$$

The idea of (3.20) is to compare the expected utility of the new and the prior actions in light of current beliefs about the state variable.

This approach leads to an unambiguously nonnegative value of the message that can be interpreted as a demand price. With ψ denoting a nonstochastic subtraction from initial wealth, define the conditional value of the decision given ψ and y as the function

$$\begin{aligned} \mathbf{U}(\mathbf{D}^* \mid \mathbf{I}, \psi, y) &= \max_a E_{x|y}\, u(\omega(w - \psi, x, a)) \\ &= E_{x|y}\, u(\omega(w - \psi, x, a_y^u(\psi))). \qquad (3.21) \end{aligned}$$

In (3.21), the optimal action given y when initial wealth is reduced by $\$\psi$ is denoted

$$a_y^u(\psi) \in \mathbf{a}. \qquad (3.22)$$

As a matter of notation, if the information source were free the functional dependence on ψ in statements like (3.22) is omitted. Except in special cases,

$$a_y^u(\psi) \neq a_y^u.$$

In general, as the information bill ψ differs, so does $w - \psi$, which in turn may change the relative desirability of the alternative actions available for choice. Thus, the payment of $\$\psi$ has both an indirect and a direct impact upon the DM's well-being: indirectly by affecting the optimal action chosen, and directly by reducing all potential terminal wealths by the amount of the bill.

It can be shown [e.g., LaValle (1978, Section 8.2)] that $\mathbf{U}(\mathbf{D}^* \mid \mathbf{I}, \psi, y)$ is strictly decreasing and continuous as ψ traverses the real line, and that for any finite quantity $\mathfrak{I}$ in which

$$\max_a E_{x|y}\, u(\omega(w, x, a)) \geq \mathfrak{I},$$

there exists a number $\psi^* \geq 0$ such that

$$\max_a E_{x|y}\, u(\omega(w - \psi^*, x, a)) = \mathfrak{I}.$$

These facts allow for the definition of the *conditional value of the message* y, V_y^u. This quantity is a type of buying price, the nonnegative subtraction from initial wealth that produces equality in (3.20):

$$\max_a E_{x|y}\, u(\omega(w - V_y^u, x, a)) = E_{x|y}\, u(\omega(w, x, a_0^u)). \qquad (3.23)$$

The action that optimizes the left-hand side of (3.23) can be denoted $a_y^u(V_y^u)$.

3.1.3 The Simplest Special Case

The literature on the value of information commonly highlights decision problems in which the outcome function is separable between wealth and profit, that is, decision problems having terminal wealth given by equation (2.2) and its costly analogue (3.7). In this special case the preceding measures of the value of the message y simplify when the DM's preferences exhibit neutrality towards risk because $a_y^N(\psi) = a_y^N$.[2]

For example, under risk neutrality and nonstochastic initial wealth, the conditional reservation price is

$$R_y^N = \max_a E_{x|y}\{w + \pi(x, a)\} = w + \max_a E_{x|y}\pi(x, a)$$

$$= w + E_{x|y}\pi(x, a_y^N), \tag{3.24}$$

where the second equality follows from the linearity of the function and the fact that the expectation of a constant is a constant. With initial wealth also "factoring out" in the prior reservation price,

$$R_0^N = E_x\{w + \pi(x, a_0^N)\} = w + E_x\pi(x, a_0^N), \tag{3.25}$$

the conditional incremental gain is simply the difference in expected profit before and after the message:

$$G_y^N = E_{x|y}\pi(x, a_y^N) - E_x\pi(x, a_0^N). \tag{3.26}$$

Likewise, the buying price is the solution for B_y^N in the risk neutral, separable version of (3.19):

$$E_x\{w + \pi(x, a_0^N)\} = \max_a E_{x|y}\{w - B_y^N + \pi(x, a)\}. \tag{3.27}$$

Again, under risk neutrality and separability both w and B_y^N factor out; the optimal action is not affected by any subtraction from initial wealth, so the best action remains a_y^N, as in (3.24). Solving (3.27) for the buying price and comparing it with (3.26) shows that the buying price is identical to the conditional gain:

$$B_y^N = E_{x|y}\pi(x, a_y^N) - E_x\pi(x, a_0^N) = G_y^N. \tag{3.28}$$

Finally, in the risk neutral, separable version of (3.23), the conditional value of the message solves

---

[2] An analysis in Section 5.3 shows that this simplification generalizes to the class of preferences that exhibit constant absolute risk aversion, of which neutrality towards risk is a special case.

$$\max_a E_{x|y} \{w - V_y^N + \pi(x, a)\} = E_{x|y} \{w + \pi(x, a_0^N)\},$$

which is the nonnegative quantity

$$V_y^N = E_{x|y} \{\pi(x, a_y^N) - \pi(x, a_0^N)\}. \tag{3.29}$$

In other words, the conditional value of y is the increase in expected payoff (and, for that matter, expected wealth), evaluated under current probabilistic beliefs, that results when the DM learns at no cost the message y and alters the prior choice of action.

The quantity defined in (3.29) is well-known in the literature; Raiffa and Schlaifer (1961) call it the *conditional value of information.* Antonovitz and Roe (1986) work directly with this measure.

3.1.4 Two Examples

This subsection presents two examples that illustrate the evaluation of a message. The first is a traditional economic model, and the second demonstrates the difficulties that arise when the outcome function (2.1) is not separable as in (2.2).

♦ *Example 3.1a The Quadratic Perfect Competitor*

This example differs from the previous examples because it contains an infinite action space. This type of framing is advantageous to the extent that the powers of the calculus can be brought to bear in the analysis of the optimization aspects of the problem. This particular example, which is a special case of the useful model in Section 5.1, intends to illustrate 1) some of the computational problems that can arise with certain nonlinear utility functions, and 2) that, as ex-ante indicators of the value of information, the preceding conditional posterior measures are inadequate.

A perfectly competitive firm must choose a nonnegative production quantity $a \in \mathbf{a}$ prior to the realization of the random price $x \in \mathbf{X}$. Total revenue is xa, and suppose total cost is given by FC + $.5a^2$, where FC is the fixed cost. Hence, the payoff is the profit function $\pi(x, a) = xa - FC - .5a^2$. Given that initial wealth w is separable from the profit function, terminal wealth is

$$W = w + \pi(x, a) = w - FC + xa - .5a^2. \tag{3.30}$$

Assume there are two possible prices, so $\mathbf{X} = \{4, 8\}$ and that the initial knowledge is that $p(x_1) = .75$ and $p(x_2) = .25$. Finally, let w = \$9 and FC = \$3.

If the DM is risk neutral, desiring to choose the course of action that maximizes expected profit and hence expected terminal wealth, then the optimal production level a_0^N is the solution to

$$\max_a \mathbf{U}(\mathbf{D} \mid \mathbf{I}\downarrow, a) = .75[6 + 4a - .5a^2] + .25[6 + 8a - .5a^2]. \quad (3.31)$$

Using the calculus, the optimum solves

$$\frac{d\mathbf{U}(\mathbf{D} \mid \mathbf{I}\downarrow, a)}{da} = 6 + 5a - .5a^2 = 0,$$

which is $a_0^N = 5$. Plugging this solution into (3.31) yields the expected terminal wealth $\mathbf{U}(\mathbf{D}^* \mid \mathbf{I}\downarrow) = \overline{W}_0^N = \$18.50$. The reservation price or certainty equivalent is $R_0^N = \$18.50$. The prior incremental gain in the reservation price, the increase in the DM's certainty equivalent due to ownership of the decision, is $G_0^N = R_0^N - w = \$9.50$. The prior buying price (3.8) is the solution to the equation

$$w = \max_a E_x \{w - B_0^N - FC + xa - .5a^2\}.$$

Substituting the specific values, the prior buying price solves

$$9 = \max_a \{.75[6 - B_0^N + 4a - .5a^2] + .25[6 - B_0^N + 8a - .5a^2]\}.$$

Despite the subtraction of B_0^N from initial wealth, the optimal prior action remains $a_0^N = 5$, so $B_0^N = \$9.50$. Note that in this special case, risk neutrality combined with an outcome function separable as in (3.7), $\overline{W}_0^N = R_0^N$ and $G_0^N = B_0^N$.

Consider instead a risk averter with the concave utility function $u(W) = [W]^{\frac{1}{2}}$. Now the optimal prior course of action a_0^A is the solution to

$$\max_a E_x u(6 + xa - .5a^2) = \max_a \{.75[6 + 4a - .5a^2]^{\frac{1}{2}} + .25[6 + 8a - .5a^2]^{\frac{1}{2}}\}.$$

This is difficult to solve analytically, but a computer search using a spreadsheet program finds $a_0^A = 4.7118$. This choice gives the DM expected wealth

$$\overline{W}_0^A = E_x \{6 + x a_0^A - .5[a_0^A]^2\} = \$18.458,$$

and expected utility

$$\mathbf{U}(\mathbf{D}^* \mid \mathbf{I}\downarrow) = E_x u(6 + x a_0^A - .5[a_0^A]^2) = 4.2080.$$

The reservation price is $R_0^A = \$17.707$, the solution to $[R_0^A]^{\frac{1}{2}} = 4.2080$, and the prior incremental gain is $G_0^A = \$17.707 - \$9 = \$8.707$.

This DM's risk aversion makes the calculation of the prior buying price somewhat difficult. Starting with w, the up-front expenditure to purchase the decision problem makes this DM more risk averse, which in turn feeds back upon the choice of course of action.[3]

A first estimate for B_0^A is the quantity $B_\bullet^A$, the solution to

---

[3] This utility function also exhibits the characteristic of decreasing absolute risk aversion.

$$u(w) = E_x u(6 - B_{\bullet}^A + x a_0^A - .5[a_0^A]^2),$$

or

$$3 = .75[6 - B_{\bullet}^A + 4a_0^A - .5[a_0^A]^2]^{\frac{1}{2}} + .25[6 - B_{\bullet}^A + 8a_0^A - .5[a_0^A]^2]^{\frac{1}{2}}, \quad (3.32)$$

which is $B_{\bullet}^A = \$8.206$. This quantity cannot be the buying price because if $B_{\bullet}^A$ were paid, the DM could obtain expected utility greater than 3 utiles by altering the production level to the action a that maximizes

$$.75[6 - 8.206 + 4a - .5a^2]^{\frac{1}{2}} + .25[6 - 8.206 + 8a - .5a^2]^{\frac{1}{2}}, \quad (3.33)$$

which is $a_{\bullet}^A = 4.558$. This buying price and action gives the DM an expected utility of 3.0023172 utiles. Now finding the buying price to solve (3.32), with $a_{\bullet}^A$ replacing a_0^A, yields a new buying price estimate $B_{\bullet}^A = \$8.219$. At this point the iteration between (3.32) and (3.33) can be over because the action that maximizes

$$.75[6 - 8.219 + 4a - .5a^2]^{\frac{1}{2}} + .25[6 - 8.219 + 8a - .5a^2]^{\frac{1}{2}}$$

is essentially a = 4.558 and its expected utility is essentially 3. Thus, if the DM pays $B_0^A = \$8.219$ and chooses production level a = 4.558, the DM receives the same expected utility as the utility of simply standing pat with initial wealth w = \$9.

Suppose next that the DM receives the message y = "it is an absolute certainty that the price will be \$4." Assuming this message is "correct," the posterior distribution is degenerate with $p(x_1 | y) = 1$. Since there is no risk posterior to the receipt of this message, the DM's utility function and attitude towards risk are no longer relevant for choosing a_y^u; the action that maximizes (3.30) when x = 4 also maximizes any strictly increasing function of (3.30). Using the calculus, the optimal production decision is $a_y^u = 4$ for any utility function. Any DM has terminal wealth W = \$14.

Under the prior belief that $p(x_1) = .75$ and $p(x_2) = .25$, the optimal production decision for the risk neutral DM is $a_0^N = 5$. Knowing now that x_1 occurs, the ex-post value of this message, (3.14), is

$$\hat{\upsilon}^N(x_1, y) = \{6 + [4][4] - .5[4]^2\} - \{6 + [4][5] - .5[5]^2\} = + \$0.50.$$

Since the price turns out low, the message is valuable because it saves the firm from overproducing.

The ex-post value of the message to the DM with utility function $u(W) = [W]^{\frac{1}{2}}$ is lower than $\hat{\upsilon}^N(x_1, y)$. This risk averter initially chooses the more conservative production plan $a_0^A = 4.7118$, and since this is closer to the posterior optimum, it turns out $\hat{\upsilon}^A(x_1, y) = + \$0.2533$.

In this problem the quantities g_y^u, G_y^u, and B_y^u are nonpositive because the message informs the DM that the economic situation is unfavorable and profits are not going to be as high as previously expected. For example, the risk neutral DM now knows $\overline{W}_y^N$ = \$14, as compared with the prior expectation $\overline{W}_0^N$ = \$18.50. Calculating (3.18) and (3.28) shows $G_y^N = B_y^N = g_y^N = -$ \$4.50. This negative value certainly does not mean the DM should ignore the message and continue with the old production plan. To do so would lead to overproduction. It does mean that g_y^u, G_y^u, and B_y^u are not particularly good measures of the message's economic value.

Finally, as it must be by definition, the conditional value of the message y, V_y^N as in (3.29), is nonnegative for any DM. Under risk neutrality and the posterior knowledge that price is certain to be \$4, the new production plan gives posterior expected wealth \$14, and the old production plan gives posterior expected wealth \$13.50, so V_y^N = \$0.50. This seems to be a reasonable measure of how much better off the DM is as a result of the message. That $V_y^N = \hat{\upsilon}^N(x_1, y)$ in this case is coincidental, a consequence of the assumption that the message gives perfect knowledge of the state. If there is any uncertainty posterior to the receipt of the message y (the usual case), then assessment of $\hat{\upsilon}^N(x, y)$ must await the final realization of x. Example 3.1a continues in Section 7.2.2. ♦

♦ *Example 3.1b The Celebrity Informant*

This example illustrates the additional complications that arise when the outcome function is not separable as in (2.2). There is a new TV show in which two contestants predict whether the next ball drawn randomly from an urn will come up red or green. Everyone knows that 60% of the balls are red, 40% green. Each contestant starts with a grubstake of a fresh w each play, and can wager up to available wealth each time. If the prediction is correct, the contestant receives double the bet; if incorrect, the wager is lost. In addition, each player has the option of buying the services of a humorous celebrity informant who can identify one of the two balls before the contestant makes the bet and actually sees the final realization. Sandwiched between the celebrity clowning around, the audience clapping, and the advertising time-outs, each contestant gets to make four choices per half-hour show. The producers see great humor potential in having the celebrity lie about the ball's color in one of each contestant's four plays. The producers also see great economic drama in allowing the contestants to make side payments of cash to each other and swap decisions at any point in the game. The players can keep coming back to the show as long as they want until the show is canceled, which is not likely to be long.

In this decision problem the state space is

$$\mathbf{X} = \{x_1, x_2\} = \{\text{ball is red, ball is green}\},$$

with the prior probability on the state being $p(x_1) = .60$ and $p(x_2) = .40$. The action a is the fraction of wealth bet. Model the action space as $\mathbf{a} = \{-1 \leq a \leq +1\}$, adopting the convention that $a > 0$ is a bet on x_1 and $a < 0$ is a bet on x_2. The outcome function

$$\omega(w, x_1, a) = w + aw = w[1 + a];$$

$$\omega(w, x_2, a) = w - aw = w[1 - a], \tag{3.34}$$

cannot be written in the separable form (2.2).

Assume that both contestants are risk neutral. The expected utility from the action a is

$$E_x \{\omega(w, x, a)\} = [.60]w[1 + a] + [.40]w[1 - a] = w[1 + .20a],$$

and hence the optimal prior action is to bet everything on red: $a_0^N = +1$. The value of the prior decision and the prior reservation price are identical in this risk neutral case:

$$\mathbf{U(D^* \mid I\downarrow)} = E_x \{\omega(w, x, a_0^N)\} = 1.2w = R_0^N. \tag{3.35}$$

If there were no option to use the informant, the contestant would accept no less than $G_0^N = R_0^N - w = .2w$ in cash to walk away from the play.

Contestant 1 gets the first play of the game, with contestant 2 observing, and let 1 elect to utilize the informant. The drawing takes place, and suppose the celebrity tells the contestants the message y = "the ball will be green." Each contestant knows that one time in four this is a lie, so current beliefs about the color of the ball are $p(x_1 \mid y) = .25$ and $p(x_2 \mid y) = .75$. Now,

$$E_{x \mid y} \{\omega(w, x, a)\} = [.25]w[1 + a] + [.75]w[1 - a] = w[1 - .5a],$$

so the optimal action changes to $a_y^N = -1$; bet it all on green. If this message is free, the contestant's expected utility, expected wealth, and reservation price are

$$\mathbf{U(D^* \mid I}, y) = E_{x \mid y} \{\omega(w, x, a_y^N)\} = 1.5w = R_y^N. \tag{3.36}$$

This message is statistical information that has definite pragmatic value. Statistically, the message has altered the DM's beliefs about the state. Pragmatically, the message has allowed the DM to make a different bet, one more appropriate (in a statistical sense) to the state that will occur. Contestant 1 expects higher wealth and utility; she would accept no less than $R_y^N - w = .5w$ to walk away from the play.

Suppose, however, that her only option at this point is to return to the prior decision. Having heard this message, how much better off is contestant 1? The conditional incremental gain from the message,

$$G_y^N = R_y^N - R_0^N = .30w,$$

is not the minimum selling price to accept the results of a new drawing without the informant; betting 1.3w on the prior decision with the factor 1.2 yields expected wealth of 1.56w. The minimum selling price is .25w, since [1.25w][1.2] = 1.5w, the current expectation.

To find the buying price for moving from the prior decision to this position, the expected utility and wealth given ψ is

$$\begin{aligned} \mathbf{U}(\mathbf{D}^* \mid \mathbf{I}, \psi, y) &= \max_a E_{x|y} \{\omega(w - \psi, x, a)\} \\ &= \max_a \{[.25][w - \psi][1 + a] + [.75][w - \psi][1 - a]\} \\ &= \max_a \{[w - \psi][1 - .5a]\} \\ &= 1.5[w - \psi], \end{aligned} \tag{3.37}$$

since $a_y^N(\psi) = -1$ for any $\psi \geq 0$. Applying (3.35) and (3.37) to (3.19), the buying price is the solution to

$$1.2w = 1.5[w - B_y^N],$$

which is $B_y^N = .2w$.

Because of nonseparability, the buying price, the minimum selling price, and the conditional incremental gain are not identical. One interpretation of this buying price is that it is the maximum amount contestant 2 would pay contestant 1 to take 1's current opportunity and return 1 to the uninformed prior decision. If contestant 2 pays .2w, the bet .8w gives contestant 2 expected wealth [.8w][1.5] = 1.2w, the same situation that 2 currently has. Since 2's buying price is less than 1's selling price, the swap is not going to take place. If the producers of this show expect any side payments, they are not going to get it at this stage of the game if they recruit risk neutral, expected-utility-maximizing contestants.

The ex-post value of the message turns on whether the celebrity informant is lying. Hearing the message and betting green, if the ball is red, the "incorrect" information turns the contestant from a winner to a loser and costs $\hat{\upsilon}^N(x_1, y) = \omega(w, x_1, a_y^N) - \omega(w, x_1, a_0^N) = 0 - 2w = -2w$. Likewise, if the ball turns out green the message saves the contestant $\hat{\upsilon}^N(x_2, y) = \omega(w, x_2, a_y^N) - \omega(w, x_2, a_0^N) = +2w$.

Finally, to determine V_y^N, the conditional value of the celebrity's message under the prior decision $a_0^N = +1$ and the new posterior distribution, the contestant's expected wealth is now

$$E_{x|y} \{\omega(w, x, a_0^N)\} = .50w. \tag{3.38}$$

Setting up the solution to (3.23) by combining (3.37) with (3.38),

$$1.5[w - V_y^N] = .50w,$$

and solving gives $V_y^N = 2w/3$. If the contestant pays this amount to receive this message, then betting w/3 on $a_y^N = -1$ yields expected wealth .50w, the same amount she now expects from betting w on the prior decision. ♦

Example 3.1b illustrates clearly the differences between measures of the financial improvement as a consequence of the message and the DM's demand price for the message. It is incorrect to argue that under the new knowledge and the prior action the contestant expects .50w, and under the new knowledge and the new action the contestant expects 1.5w − .50w = w dollars more, so therefore w is the demand price. This definition of the value of the message y,

$$E_{x|y}\{\omega(w, x, a_y^N) - \omega(w, x, a_0^N)\}, \tag{3.39}$$

amounts to a hybrid between the general definition (3.23) and the risk neutral, separable special case (3.29). Perhaps this quantity is a good measure of how much better off the contestant is courtesy of the message, but if w were paid, the contestant would have nothing left to bet! Equation (3.39) does not measure the demand price for the message when the outcome function is nonseparable.

3.1.5 The Need for Preposterior Evaluation

To consider more thoroughly the idea of the demand price for a message, suppose an informant comes to the DM and says, "How much would you pay me if I told you y?" The DM should think, "If I hear the message y and it makes me believe that $p(x|y)$ is the proper way for me to view the probability distribution on the state, then this message is saving me from taking the action a_0^u, an action I now see as suboptimal. If I pay \$$\psi$ for this message, and ψ is less than some maximum, then I can find another action, defined by (3.21), that is better suited to my current beliefs. The maximum amount I can pay is V_y^u. If the message costs more, I might as well pay nothing and keep the prior decision." At this point the DM should ask the informant, "Are you actually telling me y?" If the informant answers in the affirmative, then the DM has just received free information and should make a choice accordingly. The informant is more likely to respond, "Maybe, but maybe my message is y', or maybe y''. Pay me first." Apparently V_y^u, being a function of y, is still not what the DM should actually pay the informant.

None of the preceding conditional approaches provides an adequate measure of the demand price for the information, in the sense of the maximum amount the DM should pay the information source. It is likely the message must be paid for out of initial wealth, but not knowing beforehand the specific message, it is advisable for the DM to consider the preposterior comparison of the value of the informed decision, $\mathbf{U}(\mathbf{D}^*|\mathbf{I})$, with the value of the prior decision, $\mathbf{U}(\mathbf{D}^*|\mathbf{I}\downarrow)$.

3.2 Measures of the Value of a Source

3.2.1 Incremental Value from Incorporating Information

The first such measure is the *utility increment*, the increase in the DM's expected utility due to the informational augmentation of the decision. This quantity,

$$\hat{V}_I^u = \mathbf{U}(\mathbf{D}^* \mid \mathbf{I}) - \mathbf{U}(\mathbf{D}^* \mid \mathbf{I}\downarrow), \tag{3.40}$$

plays a major role in the theoretical analysis in Chapter 6, but has several practical deficiencies. An obvious problem is that, unless the DM is risk neutral, $\hat{V}_I^u$ is measured in utiles rather than dollars.

One way around the units problem is to translate the expected utilities into reservation prices and measure the increment in reservation price from using the information. The *reservation price of the informed decision* is the solution to

$$u(R_I^u) = \mathbf{U}(\mathbf{D}^* \mid \mathbf{I}) = E_y E_{x\mid y} u(\omega(w, x, a_y^u)). \tag{3.41}$$

The *cash-equivalent gain* from the cost-free use of the information structure **I** is defined as

$$G_I^u = R_I^u - R_0^u. \tag{3.42}$$

This measure is directly analogous to (3.16) but is nonnegative; from the definitions of the reservation prices given by (3.41) and (3.1), and the result (2.49),

$$u(R_I^u) = \mathbf{U}(\mathbf{D}^* \mid \mathbf{I}) \geq \mathbf{U}(\mathbf{D}^* \mid \mathbf{I}\downarrow) = u(R_0^u). \tag{3.43}$$

Hence, $R_I^u \geq R_0^u$ by the nondecreasingness of the utility function.

The *preposterior expected wealth* of **I** is

$$\overline{W}_I^u = E_y E_{x\mid y} \{\omega(w, x, a_y^u)\}. \tag{3.44}$$

Subtracting $\overline{W}_0^u$, the expected wealth under the prior decision, from $\overline{W}_I^u$ measures the *preposterior incremental expected wealth* of **I**:

$$g_I^u = \overline{W}_I^u - \overline{W}_0^u. \tag{3.45}$$

A more commonly used methodology for evaluating the pragmatic benefits from the information structure **I** is to assess the demand price. The demand price for information is the maximum nonstochastic cost that the DM is willing to pay in order to move from the uninformed decision to the informed one. As such it is a buying price, defined in the informed decision problem **D**.

For each $y \in \mathbf{Y}$ and any up-front cost $\psi \geq 0$, the DM determines the optimal response $a_y^u(\psi)$. The optimal decision rule is

$$a_I^u(\psi) = \{ a_y^u(\psi) \text{ for all } y \in \mathbf{Y} \}. \tag{3.46}$$

Define

$$\mathbf{U(D^* \mid I, \psi)} = E_y \max_a E_{x\mid y} u(\omega(w - \psi, x, a))$$

$$= E_y E_{x\mid y} u(\omega(w - \psi, x, a_y^u(\psi))). \tag{3.47}$$

Analogous to the definition (3.8) of the buying price of the prior decision, the buying price of moving from the prior decision to the cost-free informed decision is the *expected value of information*, defined as the solution $\psi = V_I^u$ in the extensive form equation[4]

$$E_y \max_a E_{x\mid y} u(\omega(w - V_I^u, x, a)) = \max_a E_x u(\omega(w, x, a)). \tag{3.48}$$

Equivalently, in terms of (3.47) and (2.11), the value of information is the V_I^u that equates

$$\mathbf{U(D^* \mid I, V_I^u)} = \mathbf{U(D^* \mid I\downarrow)}. \tag{3.49}$$

Alternative names for the quantity V_I^u include the *demand price*, the *demand value*, the *Willing-to-Pay (WTP) value*, and the *compensating variation*.

To prove in general that $V_I^u \geq 0$, it is sufficient to prove that

$$E_y \max_a E_{x\mid y} u(\omega(w - V_I^u, x, a)) \leq E_y \max_a E_{x\mid y} u(\omega(w, x, a)), \tag{3.50}$$

because the left-hand side is strictly decreasing in $\psi = V_I^u$, so the inequality can hold only if $V_I^u \geq 0$. The proof of (3.50) uses the definition of V_I^u and the result (2.49):

$$E_y \max_a E_{x\mid y} u(\omega(w - V_I^u, x, a)) = \max_a E_x u(\omega(w, x, a))$$

$$\leq E_y \max_a E_{x\mid y} u(\omega(w, x, a)).$$

In the simplest case, when the DM is risk neutral and the outcome function is separable in wealth and profit, the value of information solves

$$E_y \max_a E_{x\mid y} \{w - V_I^N + \pi(x, a)\} = \max_a E_x \{w + \pi(x, a)\}.$$

Indeed, in this situation the initial wealth w is not relevant and can be canceled out of the preceding equation, yielding

$$V_I^N = E_y \max_a E_{x\mid y} \pi(x, a) - \max_a E_x \pi(x, a). \tag{3.51}$$

---

[4] This is a notation change from Chapter 1: $V_I \equiv V(\mathbf{I})$. The original notation returns in Chapter 8, when it again becomes necessary to consider choice from among a sequence of ordered and costly information structures.

This is precisely the value of information defined in equation (1.9), Section 1.4. In addition, substituting the risk neutral, separable special cases of the reservation prices defined in (3.41) and (3.1), the value of information is equal to the cash-equivalent gain defined in (3.42):

$$V_I^N = R_I^N - R_0^N = G_I^N. \tag{3.52}$$

This characterization is important because, as shown in Section 5.3.1, it also holds under constant absolute risk aversion when the outcome function is separable.

A final measure of information value goes under the alternative names of the *supply value*, the *supply price*, the *Willing-to-Accept (WTA) value*, and the *equivalent variation*. It is the solution for $\tilde{V}_I^u$ in the equation

$$E_y \max_a E_{x|y} u(\omega(w, x, a)) = \max_a E_x u(\omega(w + \tilde{V}_I^u, x, a)). \tag{3.53}$$

If the DM owns the information structure, the supply value is the minimum amount she would be willing to accept to forgo its use. If she does not have access to the structure, the supply value is the minimum side payment or bribe necessary to keep her uninformed; this has application in game theory. The supply value is not in general equal to the demand value V_I^u, but it may be easier to solve for in specific problems. LaValle (1967) compares $\tilde{V}_I^u$ and V_I^u; the two are identical under constant absolute risk aversion with separable outcome function. In a continuation of Example 2.1 in Section 6.1.2, Figure 6.1 depicts the relationship among $\tilde{V}_I^A$, V_I^A, and G_I^A as they vary with the initial probability assessment p(x).

3.2.2 *The Range of the Expected Value of Information*

The utility increment from perfect information is

$$\hat{V}_{I\uparrow}^u = \mathbf{U(D^* \mid I\uparrow) - U(D^* \mid I\downarrow)}, \tag{3.54}$$

Defining a costly version of (2.57), the value of perfect information is the solution to

$$E_x u(\omega(w - V_{I\uparrow}^u, x, a_x)) = E_x u(\omega(w, x, a_0^u)). \tag{3.55}$$

Under risk neutrality this is, in general,

$$E_x \omega(w - V_{I\uparrow}^N, x, a_x) = E_x \omega(w, x, a_0^N). \tag{3.56}$$

When the outcome function is separable into initial wealth and profit

$$V_{I\uparrow}^N = E_x \pi(x, a_x) - E_x \pi(x, a_0^N). \tag{3.57}$$

To prove $V^u_{I\uparrow} \geq V^u_I$, it is sufficient to prove

$$E_x \max_a u(\omega(w - V^u_{I\uparrow}, x, a)) \leq E_x \max_a u(\omega(w - V^u_I, x, a)). \quad (3.58)$$

By the definition of $V^u_{I\uparrow}$,

$$\begin{aligned} E_x \max_a u(\omega(w - V^u_{I\uparrow}, x, a)) &= \max_a E_x u(\omega(w, x, a)) \\ &= E_y \max_a E_{x|y} u(\omega(w - V^u_I, x, a)) \\ &\leq E_x \max_a u(\omega(w - V^u_I, x, a)), \end{aligned}$$

where the second equality is the definition of V^u_I, for an arbitrary **I**, and the inequality is a direct application of the costly analogue to the result (2.58), evaluated at $\psi = V^u_I$.

The value of null information, the solution for $V^u_{I\downarrow}$ in the equation

$$E_x u(\omega(w - V^u_{I\downarrow}, x, a^u_0)) = E_x u(\omega(w, x, a^u_0)), \quad (3.59)$$

is obviously $V^u_{I\downarrow} = 0$.

The following summarization justifies the statement that perfect information provides the highest information value and null information the lowest.

$$V^u_{I\uparrow} \geq V^u_I \geq V^u_{I\downarrow} = 0. \quad (3.60)$$

Combining the meaning of (3.58) with (3.50) and (3.59) yields (3.60).

♦ *Example 2.1 A Farmer's Planting Decision (Continued from Section 3.1.1)* For the risk neutral farmer using the joint density function given by (2.50) and the optimal decision rule (2.54), the determination that **U(D* | I)** = \$127.60 establishes that $\overline{W}^N_I = R^N_I = \$127.60$, and since $R^N_0 = \$126$, the cash-equivalent gain and value of information are, in light of (3.52), $V^N_I = G^N_I = R^N_I - R^N_0 = \$1.60$. With the value of the perfectly informed decision given in Section 2.4 as **U(D* | I↑)** = \$135, the value of perfect information is $V^N_{I\uparrow} = \$135 - \$126 = \$9$.

The calculations are a bit more complicated for the DM with utility function $u(W) = \log[W - 90]$. The decision rule is the same as (2.54), so $\overline{W}^A_I = \$127.60$. Given **U(D* | I)** = 3.5637 utiles, the reservation price of the informed decision solves $\log[R^A_I - 90] = 3.5637$, which is $R^A_I = \$125.29$. The cash-equivalent gain is $G^A_I = \$125.29 - 121.04 = \$4.25$. With **U(D* | I↓)** given in Section 2.1.3 as 3.4352 utiles, the value of information solves (3.48) for V^u_I; this is the solution to

$$E_y \max_a E_{x|y} \log[10 - V^A_I + \pi(x, a)] = \mathbf{U(D^* | I\downarrow)};$$

$$\begin{aligned} &[.64]\{ \max_a E_{x|y_1} \log[10 - V^A_I + \pi(x, a)]\} \\ &\qquad + [.36]\{ \max_a E_{x|y_2} \log[10 - V^A_I + \pi(x, a)]\} = 3.4352. \end{aligned}$$

The solution, found by spreadsheet calculation, is $V_I^A = \$3.97$. If the DM pays \$3.97 for the right to use this information source, leaving her with wealth of \$100.00 – \$3.97 = \$96.03, she will take a_2 if she receives y_1 [i.e., $a_y^A(3.97) = a_2$, yielding expected utility 3.3377 utiles], action a_1 if y_2 (yielding expected utility 3.6087 utiles), and prior to any message her expected utility is [.64][3.3377] + [.36][3.6087] = 3.4353, essentially the same as $\mathbf{U(D^* \mid I\downarrow)}$.

Finally, the expected value of perfect information solves $[.60]\log[35 - V_{I\uparrow}^A] + [.40]\log[60 - V_{I\uparrow}^A] = \mathbf{U(D^* \mid I\downarrow)}$. The solution is $V_{I\uparrow}^A = \$11.84$.

Table 3.1 summarizes the decisions and value measurements for Example 2.1 when the information structure is given by (2.50). Example 2.1 continues in Section 4.1.1. ♦

It is interesting to observe that the risk averse DM values the same information in the same problem by more than the risk neutral counterpart. Intuition might suggest this should generally be the case, but it is not. Chapter 7 considers in detail the role of the DM's attitude towards risk as a determinant of information value.

Table 3.1. Summary of Results for Two Utility Functions in Example 2.1

	$u(W) = W$	$u(W) = \log[W-90]$
Prior Decision	$a_0^N = a_1$	$a_0^A = a_1$
Value of Prior Decision	$\mathbf{U(D^* \mid I\downarrow)} = \$126$	$\mathbf{U(D^* \mid I\downarrow)} = 3.4352$
Prior Mean Wealth	$\overline{W}_0^N = \$126$	$\overline{W}_0^A = \$126$
Prior Reservation Price	$R_0^N = \$126$	$R_0^A = \$121.04$
Prior Buying Price	$B_0^N = \$26$	$B_0^A = \$19.71$
Decision Rule a_I^u	$\{a_{y_1}^N, a_{y_2}^N\} = \{a_2, a_1\}$	$\{a_{y_1}^A, a_{y_2}^A\} = \{a_2, a_1\}$
Value of Informed Decision	$\mathbf{U(D^* \mid I)} = \$127.60$	$\mathbf{U(D^* \mid I)} = 3.5637$
Expected Terminal Wealth	$\overline{W}_I^N = \$127.60$	$\overline{W}_I^A = \$127.60$
Reservation Price of **I**	$R_I^N = \$127.60$	$R_I^A = \$125.29$
Cash-Equivalent Gain	$G_I^N = \$1.60$	$G_I^A = \$4.25$
Value of Information	$V_I^N = \$1.60$	$V_I^A = \$3.97$
Supply Value	$\tilde{V}_I^N = \$1.60$	$\tilde{V}_I^A = \$3.79$
Value of Perfect Information	$V_{I\uparrow}^N = \$9.00$	$V_{I\uparrow}^A = \$11.84$

With these issues of definition, modeling, calculation, and measurement out of the way, the next two chapters turn to the problem of assessment. Chapter 4 considers the assessment of a necessary ingredient for measuring information value—the probability distributions that comprise the information structure.

4 The Assessment of Statistical Information

The formal analysis of the option to incorporate a given information source into a decision problem requires the DM to enumerate the potential messages, ascertain the statistical relationship between each potential message and each possible state of nature, decide upon the optimal decision rule conditional on each message, and recognize that information processing has costs that may depend upon any and all of these activities. Optimal incorporation requires considerable specificity in the framing of the problem; one of the key ingredients is the specification of the statistical characteristics of the random variables. Under the prerequisite that the resulting assessments are coherent with the laws of probability, this chapter offers an overview of techniques for eliciting prior knowledge and for developing foreknowledge of the information structure.

4.1 Coherent Assessment of Probability Distributions

4.1.1 Coherence and Consistency

The practical problem of adequately assessing or eliciting even a univariate probability distribution such as p(x) is generally no trivial endeavor. One pitfall that arises, especially with novice assessors of probabilities, is *incoherence* of the assessment, that is, an incompatibility with the laws of probability. Since $\mathbf{X}$ is an exhaustive listing of the possibilities, one $x \in \mathbf{X}$ must ultimately occur; coherence requires that the assessed distribution p(x) either sums or integrates to one; in the discrete case the assessment of the probability of every possibility must be such that $\Sigma_i p(x_i) = 1$. There is considerable empirical evidence [Staël von Holstein (1970); Hogarth (1975); Slovic, Fischhoff, and Lichtenstein (1977); Wallsten and Budescu (1983)] that people in general are not very good at this, often making incoherent assessments that do not add up to one. Fortunately, there is also evidence [Winkler (1967); Staël von Holstein (1970)] that people can learn how to better assess probabilities, not only via experience but also via instruction. Lindley, Tversky, and Brown (1979) present techniques for reconciling incoherent assessments.

When the state space **X** and the message space **Y** are countable and the number of alternatives is not too large, direct assessment of each $p(x_i)$, $p(y_j)$, and $p(x_i, y_j)$ is often a straightforward tack to take. The joint distribution $p(x, y)$ can also be assessed indirectly in terms of its constituent conditional and marginal distributions. Since $p(x)$ is likely to be assessed anyway, a convenient technique is to assess the conditional distribution $p(y|x)$ and combine the two using the laws of probability (see Section 2.3). This technique is very useful in statistical decision problems such as the upcoming Example 5.2, but in general it is not very natural to think in terms of the chances of receiving each possible message given a specific state. It seems more natural to think first in terms of what each message would mean as far as the state distribution is concerned, followed by an assessment of the chances of receiving each message. This technique, assessing $p(x|y)$ and $p(y)$ directly, requires care because, even though coherent, it can lead to an inconsistent package of probability assessments. The following continuation of Example 2.1 illustrates.

♦ *Example 2.1 A Farmer's Planting Decision (Continued from Section 3.2.2)* The DM facing this binary decision problem with two states, two acts, and two messages has assessed the prior distribution as $\mathbf{r} = [p(x_1), p(x_2)] = [.60, .40]$. Consider the following assessment of the posterior distribution.

$$\Pi = \begin{bmatrix} p(x_1|y_1) & p(x_1|y_2) \\ p(x_2|y_1) & p(x_2|y_2) \end{bmatrix} = \begin{bmatrix} .90 & .40 \\ .10 & .60 \end{bmatrix}.$$

In this assessment, if message y_1 is received, the forecast of dry weather has a 90% chance of being correct, and the forecast of wet weather in message y_2 has only a 60% chance of coming to pass. If the assessor then reasons that the chance each message is received should equal the corresponding chance of the state it forecasts, the assessment of the marginal distribution of the messages is $\mathbf{q} = [p(y_1), p(y_2)] = [.60, .40]$. At this point there is trouble because the resulting joint distribution

$$\rho = \begin{bmatrix} p(x_1, y_1) & p(x_1, y_2) \\ p(x_2, y_1) & p(x_2, y_2) \end{bmatrix} = \begin{bmatrix} .54 & .16 \\ .06 & .24 \end{bmatrix}$$

implies prior probabilities such as $p(x_1) = p(x_1, y_1) + p(x_1, y_2) = .70$, an assessment that is inconsistent with the original statement of prior beliefs. Example 2.1 continues in Section 6.1.2 ♦

Assessing $p(y|x)$ to go along with $p(x)$ is one way to avoid this inconsistency, but then the assessor must accept the implied marginal distribution $p(y)$. The source of the difficulty is that coherence requires the prior distribution and the set of posterior distributions to be tied together in an important way: the expectation of the posterior probability of each state x, expected over all receivable messages, must equal the prior probability of the state x. In the expectation notation,

$$E_y\, p(x\,|\,y) \;=\; p(x). \tag{4.1}$$

To show this in the discrete case using (2.14a), $\Sigma_j\, p(x_i|y_j)\, p(y_j) = \Sigma_j\, p(x_i, y_j) = p(x_i)$. Similarly, coherence also requires

$$E_x\, p(y\,|\,x) \;=\; p(y), \tag{4.2}$$

since $\Sigma_i\, p(y_j|x_i)\, p(x_i) = p(y_j)$. Coherence does not insist that $p(x) = p(y)$, even when $\mathbf{X} = \mathbf{Y}$.

4.1.2 Families of Probability Densities

A naturally coherent technique is to pick a family of probability distributions and assess the parameters using whatever foreknowledge is at hand. In an important class of decision problems, the state space **X** is a subset of the real line; the random variable is a set of possible numerical values (e.g., a price, a temperature, a proportion), perhaps within a specified range. A convenient method for such cases is to assume that p(x) or p(x, y) belongs to some parameterized family of probability functions; assessment becomes the task of specifying the distribution by choosing the parameters. There are a large number of such parameterized functions from which to choose; the multivolume work of Johnson and Kotz (1970) is a excellent compendium of alternatives. Functions with considerable flexibility, mathematical tractability, and an economy of parameters are particularly desirable; the normal and the beta distributions are often good practical choices, along with certain other functions that arise naturally via some observable process, such as the binomial and the Poisson distributions. This subsection presents some facts that prove useful in the sequel about the beta and normal families.

When working with parameterized families of densities, write $p(x) = f_*(x\,|\,\bullet)$, with the "*" holding a place for any identifying attributes and the "•" holding a place for the required parameters. In many applications the need for the cumulative distribution function (cdf) arises. Define

$$F_*(x\,|\,\bullet) \;=\; \int_{-\infty}^{x} f_*(s\,|\,\bullet)\, ds \tag{4.3}$$

as the left-tail, and

$$\Gamma_*(x\,|\,\bullet) \;=\; \int_{x}^{\infty} f_*(s\,|\,\bullet)\, ds \tag{4.4}$$

as the right-tail cumulative distribution function.

The Beta Distribution

The general beta distribution, also called the Pearson Type I distribution, is a four-parameter family with a finite range from B to C. The density function is

$$p(x) = f_{\beta*}(x \mid r', n', B, C) = \frac{1}{\beta(r', n' - r')} \frac{[x - B]^{r'-1}[C - x]^{n'-r'-1}}{[C - B]^{n'-1}},$$

$$\text{with } n' > r' > 0 \text{ and } B \leq x \leq C. \tag{4.5}$$

An important special case is B = 0 and C = 1, yielding the standard beta distribution

$$p(x) = f_{\beta}(x \mid r', n') = \frac{1}{\beta(r', n' - r')} x^{r'-1}\left[1 - x\right]^{n'-r'-1},$$

$$\text{with } n' > r' > 0 \text{ and } 0 \leq x \leq 1. \tag{4.6}$$

The standard beta distribution is especially useful when the random variable of interest is a proportion or a probability. Raiffa and Schlaifer (1961, Section 7.3.2) show that the expected value of a variable with density (4.6) is $\overline{x} = r'/n'$.

In both (4.5) and (4.6), the term $\beta(r', n' - r')$ is the complete beta function discussed in books on calculus. The primes on the parameters are at this point unnecessary, but prove to be convenient in applications such as Example 5.2.

The cumulative distribution function is not analytically tractable except in special cases,[1] but is extensively tabled by Pearson (1968). Pearson tables the left-tail cumulative function as the quantity $I_x(r', n' - r')$ defined by

$$F_{\beta}(x \mid r', n') = \int_0^x f_{\beta}(s \mid r', n')\, ds = I_x(r', n' - r'), \tag{4.7}$$

for $r' \geq n' - r'$ and $0 \leq x \leq 1$. In a specific application, the practical difficulty is to determine the relevant entry from the tables. The upcoming Example 5.2 illustrates. Approximations due to Peizer and Pratt (1968) are also useful in practice.

The Normal Distribution

A second useful class is the normal distribution, a two-parameter family with density function

$$p(x) = f_N(x \mid \overline{x}, \sigma_x^2) = \frac{1}{\sigma_x\sqrt{2\pi}} \exp\left\{-\frac{1}{2\sigma_x^2}\left[x - \overline{x}\right]^2\right\}. \tag{4.8}$$

---

[1] Two convenient yet somewhat flexible situations are when $n' - r' = 1$ and $n' - r' = 2$.

Here, the first parameter $\overline{x}$ is the mean of the random variable, and the second parameter σ_x^2 is the variance. To indicate that a random variable X is normally distributed with a specified mean and variance, write

$$p(x) \sim \mathbf{N}(\text{mean of X, variance of X}).$$

Random variables obeying this distribution arise naturally in many varied circumstances.

An important special case is the random variable Z defined by the transformation $z = [x - \overline{x}]/\sigma_x$, which has mean $\overline{z} = 0$ and variance $\sigma_z^2 = 1$. These specific parameters define the standard normal distribution, written $p(z) \sim \mathbf{N}^*(0, 1)$. Virtually every textbook in statistics provides a table of the cumulative distribution function for the standard normal; from this the cumulative function of any normal variate can be obtained.

The Bivariate Normal Distribution

The assessment of statistical information is particularly straightforward when the message space **Y** is categorical and direct and the joint distribution p(x, y) obeys the bivariate normal distribution,

$$p(x, y) \sim \mathbf{BN}(\overline{x}, \sigma_x^2;\ \overline{y},\ \sigma_y^2;\ \rho), \tag{4.9}$$

a five-parameter family comprising the two unconditional means, the two unconditional variances, and the correlation coefficient ρ that ties them together. The great practical advantage is that all necessary marginal and conditional distributions are also normally distributed [e.g., Hogg and Craig (1978), Chapter 3].

Specifically, the marginal distributions are

$$p(x) \sim \mathbf{N}(\overline{x},\ \sigma_x^2); \tag{4.10}$$

$$p(y) \sim \mathbf{N}(\overline{y},\ \sigma_y^2), \tag{4.11}$$

and the conditional distributions are

$$p(y\,|\,x) \sim \mathbf{N}(\overline{y}_x, \sigma_{y|x}^2) \sim \mathbf{N}(\overline{y} + \rho\,\sigma_y[x - \overline{x}]/\sigma_x,\ \sigma_y^2[1 - \rho^2]); \tag{4.12}$$

$$p(x\,|\,y) \sim \mathbf{N}(\overline{x}_y, \sigma_{x|y}^2) \sim \mathbf{N}(\overline{x} + \rho\,\sigma_x[y - \overline{y}]/\sigma_y,\ \sigma_x^2[1 - \rho^2]). \tag{4.13}$$

In subsequent applications the most convenient properties of the conditional posterior distribution derive from the facts that the conditional posterior mean,

$$\overline{x}_y = \overline{x} + \rho\,\sigma_x[y - \overline{y}]/\sigma_y, \tag{4.14}$$

is a linear function of the particular y that is received, and the conditional posterior variance

$$\sigma_{x|y}^2 = \sigma_x^2[1 - \rho^2] \tag{4.15}$$

does not depend upon y. Hence,

$$E_y \sigma^2_{x|y} = \sigma^2_x[1 - \rho^2]. \tag{4.16}$$

Bivariate Copulas

For situations in which the normal densities are clearly not appropriate, copula models offer a flexible variety of families. The idea is that the bivariate joint cumulative distribution of the random variables X and Y, denoted $F_{X,Y}(x, y)$, can be expressed in terms of the marginal cdfs $F_X(x)$ and $F_Y(y)$ and an associated dependence function, the copula function $C(\bullet)$ defined by

$$F_{X,Y}(x, y) = C(F_X(x), F_Y(y)). \tag{4.17}$$

The copula can be estimated and studied separately from the marginals, which is useful in the current context because the marginal distribution p(x) is the same for all potential information structures. Important families of copulas, many of which can be characterized by one parameter, have been introduced by Gumbel (1960), Plackett (1965), Clayton (1978), Cook and Johnson (1981), and Frank (1979). Although generally not as analytically tractable as the normal model, copulas are becoming more popular and applicable as inexpensive computing power becomes more readily available.

4.2 Assessment of Beliefs and Foreknowledge

The property of coherence is not sufficient for a good probability assessment; the goal is to incorporate whatever experience and evidence the DM has from the real world into a coherent assessment that best expresses her true beliefs and foreknowledge. This section reviews a number of techniques and considerations for achieving this goal; see also Huber (1974) and Spetzler and Staël von Holstein (1975).

4.2.1 Assessing a Univariate Distribution

When X is a continuous variable on the real line, one naturally coherent method is to directly assess the cumulative distribution function of X, prior or posterior as the case may be, from which the density function is then obtained. In the method of equally likely subintervals [Pratt, Raiffa, and Schlaifer (1995, Chapter 7)], the beliefs are extracted by looking at the entire range of X and first determining the value x* at which the assessor believes the realization is equally as likely to be below x* as above x*. This creates two subintervals, and for each subinterval the assessor again determines the value of x for which she believes it equally likely the realization will be above or below. Repeating this procedure as often as necessary, the end result is a partitioning of the range of X into n subintervals, each being equally likely. By plotting the points the assessor can fair or smooth a curve that amounts to the cumulative distribution function. This curve can then serve as the basis for choosing from among a parameterized family as discussed previously. Alternately, the entire analysis can serve as the basis for chopping up or "discretizing" the random variable and perhaps even the entire decision problem; this type of approximation [see Schlaifer (1969, Sections 7.4 and 9.4)] trades off accuracy for convenience.

If there are no auxiliary data to aid the assessment, another technique is to apply a computer program that pictures the members of a family of probability densities as a function of the distribution parameters. The assessor chooses a specific density by viewing the screen and altering the parameters until she observes the shape that best fits her foreknowledge and beliefs.

Probability assessment includes, whenever possible, the use of empirical evidence; special techniques can apply when auxiliary data such as historical relative frequencies of indistinguishable trials are available. *Indistinguishable* means that, in the assessor's opinion, there is no prior reason for believing that the probability law explaining any trial differs among trials.

In a sense, the unconditional distribution p(x) reflects the broad spectrum of potential forces that operate to determine the realization of X. For example, in some problems of meteorological forecasting, long-term historical frequencies of realizations provide base-rate frequencies that serve as reasonable "objective" proxies for the prior distribution of the state [e.g., Katz, Brown, and Murphy (1987)]. Care must be taken; the probability distribution of the daily high temperature in July is likely to be distinguishable from the same concept in January.

Successive observations on certain economic time series are likely to be distinguishable because of autocorrelation: the probability of the next observation may depend upon past observations. If, for example, the daily closing price of a share of stock has ranged over the past two years between $50 and $100 and the most recent close is $95, then it is reasonable to assess the probability distribution of tomorrow's close with considerable probability volume around $95. The identical distribution would seem less reasonable if the most recent close were $55. An oftentimes fruitful solution to this problem is to redefine the state space as the change, or first difference, of the time series between two observation points. The assessor may feel more confident that the probability distribution of the change in share price does not depend upon the current level of the share price. Indeed, the assessor can test, using standard statistical techniques [Fuller (1996)], whether there is historical evidence of autocorrelation in the price changes. In the upcoming Example 4.2, the assessor appeals to the economic theory of efficient markets to justify the belief that observations on the change in a price represent realizations of indistinguishable trials.

Pearson's System

Let the random variable X be suitably defined or transformed so that any observed realization $\tilde{x}_h$ is an independent drawing from an unconditional probability distribution p(x). If the number of trials is relatively small, there may be "gaps" in the data where no realization has been observed despite the belief that such an event could very well happen. This calls for techniques to smooth out such irregularities; Pearson's system is a time-honored method for achieving this. For a modern presentation, see Johnson, Kotz, and Balakrishnan (1994).

To apply Pearson's system to a snapshot set of state realizations $\{\tilde{x}_1, \cdots, \tilde{x}_h, \cdots, \tilde{x}_N\}$, the assessor calculates the empirical mean $\mu_1 = [1/N] \Sigma_h \tilde{x}_h$ and three empirical moments about the mean, $\mu_k = [1/N] \Sigma_h [\tilde{x}_h - \mu_1]^k$ for k = 2, 3, and 4. Then, based upon the resulting values of a skewness measure $\beta_1 = \mu_3^2 / \mu_2^3$ and a kurtosis measure $\beta_2 = \mu_4 / \mu_2^2$, the assessor can determine which density function from among a large and flexible set of alternatives bests fits the observed frequency data. Elderton and Johnson (1969) identify 12 families, including the beta, normal, and exponential densities. Once a particular family is chosen, the requisite parameters can then be estimated using any of several standard statistical techniques. Maximum likelihood estimation and the method of moments are two well-known classical techniques; Bayesian techniques ask the assessor for another input, a prior distribution for the parameters.

♦ *Example 4.2 Random Market Price*

As an example of the assessment of a prior distribution using historical data, Lawrence (1991a) assesses a prior distribution for the year-to-year change in the price of hogs in Iowa. This is a partitioning of a more general random variable, a time series of the price at every point in time. One can imagine a class of decision problems for which this state variable is relevant to payoff. The change in price could be relevant to a farmer concerned about output prices, a packer concerned about input prices, a speculator concerned about a market position, and a policy maker concerned about income tax receipts from farm income.

The basic data are 179 observations of the 12-month difference in the price of hogs in Iowa between 1968 and 1986 [United States Department of Agriculture (1968–1987)], excluding 1973 to 1974. All data are adjusted for the changing price level by inflating them to 1988 prices using the Producer Price Index. Lawrence (1991a) provides a histogram of the real price change. The distribution is unimodal but negatively skewed. The data indicate a surprising number of large declines in the real price of hogs in Iowa over this period.

The first four moments of the historical data are μ_1 = \$ −.382, μ_2 = 243.73, μ_3 = −1000.48, and μ_4 = 170,878. The mean change in price, a decline of only 38 cents per hundredweight, is reasonably consistent with the efficient markets hypothesis, although the serial correlation coefficient of −0.19 with a t-value of −2.48 is a bit larger than ideal. Assuming the marginal distribution fits within Pearson's system, the skewness and kurtosis measures $\beta_1 = .069$ and $\beta_2 = 2.877$ for the data indicate a platykurtic Type I distribution. The Pearson Type I is the beta distribution $f_{\beta*}(x \mid r', n', B, C)$ given by (4.5). Using the formulae given by Elderton and Johnson [1969, Chapter 5], estimation of the four parameters r′, n′, B, and C by the method of moments yields r′ = 15.7932, n′ = 23.8785, B = −109.21, and C = +55.33.

The preceding calculations provide an assessment for the prior distribution. In this case, it represents the base-rate frequencies of changes in the real price of hogs, reflecting the potential economic forces that could be at work for any single realization. As often occurs in this type of analysis, this assessment gives a positive probability to the impossible event that the price falls below zero. Since even when the price is in the low end of its range (the \$30s) this chance is 1 in 333, this problem is of little practical importance. Example 4.2 continues in Section 4.2.4 ♦

Markowitz and Usmen (1996) apply a Bayesian approach to the assessment of the probability distribution of the logarithm of the change in the closing value of a stock market index. Using data from 1962 to 1983, their evidence points toward the Pearson Type IV distribution and away from the more commonly assumed normal one.

4.2.2 Obtaining Qualitative Foreknowledge of Information

Turning now to consideration of the joint distribution p(x, y), the matter-of-fact discussion in Section 4.1.1 makes the task of assessing the information structure appear deceivingly simple—just assess two distributions, a conditional and a marginal, and combine them using the laws of probability. In fact, unless there is a well-defined and generally agreed upon likelihood function, as in certain problems of statistical sampling, the assessment task is, simply put, not simple. This subsection discusses some of the factors relevant for qualitative judgment about source informativeness.

In the end, there is no escape from assessing and synthesizing the various determinants of an information source's informativeness, such as credibility, skill, accuracy, validity, presentation, relevance, timeliness, and so on. A common way of obtaining foreknowledge of informativeness is through a track record of past performance. After years of experience with my doctor, I can judge him as an information structure, and feel confident when assessing the posterior distribution of my health, given his diagnosis. Without a direct performance record, *vouching* is another technique for obtaining foreknowledge. For a personal advisor, finding out about the individual's reputation, educational credentials, and the like, can help assess abilities. In the case of a document, the reputation of the author, the journal, and the publisher, along with other descriptors attached to the document such as an abstract or executive summary, can help assess validity and relevance at minimal cost. The credibility of a source is always an important dimension of informativeness. Special skepticism is often warranted about statistics thrown out in political debate; the credibility of messages is reduced when the source has a political agenda.

It is useful to delineate the type of message space the source provides. A message can be direct and categorical, direct and probabilistic, indirect and categorical, or indirect and probabilistic. Consider a decision problem in which the state variable is the demand next year for a specific product. A forecast that demand will be 1,200 units next year is a direct and categorical message. If the message is that demand will be normally distributed with mean 1,900 and standard deviation 200, then it is direct and probabilistic. A document containing a textbook analysis of the general economic determinants of the demand for a commodity is an indirect categorical message with informativeness that depends upon the prior knowledge of the DM. The DM must process such a message further in order to make it relevant to the demand for this specific product. Another indirect categorical message is a forecast that the nation's Gross Domestic Product (GDP) will rise by 3% next year. Here, one possible processing mechanism would be a regression model with product demand expressed as a function of GDP. Finally, if the forecast takes the form of a probability distribution of GDP, the message is indirect and probabilistic.

Categorical message spaces are more common than probabilistic ones, despite the fact that in the informant's own mind the outcome may be probabilistic. Categorical statements can lead to economy in presentation; probability messages have more detail to transmit and hence are likely to be more expensive in terms of time and money. In addition, we know from the literature of behavioral decision theory [e.g., Slovic, Fischhoff, and Lichtenstein (1977)] that many individuals have a rather shaky ability to use the ideas of probability, and hence probability statements may be more difficult to process into the decision rule. In forecasting practice, probability statements are most common in the dichotomous state situation (rain/no rain), but forecasts of today's high temperature and of many economic variables (especially when disseminated in published form) are often expressed in categorical terms. For example, when Whiteman (1996) forecasts state tax revenues in Iowa, he produces a posterior distribution, but state policy makers have little interest in it. State law requires a point estimate, a number that binds the spending decisions of the legislature.

Hildreth (1963) discusses many of the possible types of message space a source might provide, from raw data itself to direct recommendations of action ("sell all stocks," "stop smoking"). Marschak (1971, Section 4.4) states that in the ideal, the source should provide the complete likelihood function, letting the DM combine it with her own prior and apply it to assess her own posterior distribution. Assuming the informant knows the likelihood function and is willing to reveal it, this might work for a sophisticated DM, but some users will become uninterested in the face of technical computation and analysis. If instead each message takes the form of a posterior distribution, the DM must still process it into her own beliefs, and needs to be concerned with how the source generated the message and whether the informant is expressing his true beliefs (see Section 8.2). If the message is categorical, knowledge of the criterion the informant uses to generate the particular statement is germane to the assessment of informativeness.

In choosing to summarize the posterior distribution into a categorical or interval statement, the informant faces a decision problem in which the action space $\mathbf{a}$ relates to the state space $\mathbf{X}$, and the question is the informant's choice of criterion in naming a specific value, or range of values. Marschak (1963) points out that it is not in general optimal to reduce a posterior distribution to a small set of parameters, chosen on the basis of some auxiliary criterion such as maximum likelihood, minimum sum of squared error, unbiasedness, and the like, unless those estimates happen to be the ones called for under the objective function of the decision problem at hand. Whiteman (1996) uses an asymmetric loss function from the forecast error as his criterion; since state government believes the loss from overforecasting tax revenue is greater than from underforecasting it, Whiteman does not name the mean of his posterior; he names a particular fractile of the cumulative distribution function. The same type of result arises in the inventory problem in Section 5.2.4.

It is also helpful to consider how the informant sees his task; are the messages meant to be general purpose, or for monitoring, or are they customized to a particular decision? Some of the standard applications of statistical inference are not tailored to specific decision problems. Indeed, both Schlaifer (1969, page 442) and Lindley (1972) view statistical inference in a monitoring context, arguing that most samples are taken to provide "background information" for informal thinking and data for prospective application. Lindley (1972, page 9) writes

> My view is that the purpose of an inference is to enable decision problems to be solved using the data upon which the inference is based, though at the time at which the inference is based no decisions may be envisioned.

For a given posterior distribution in the mind of the informant, customizing the message space for the user can improve informativeness by offering *decision relevance*. A speculator is more interested in whether the price will rise or fall by more than the transaction cost than whether the price will merely rise or fall [Marschak, (1959)]. In the case of a government meteorological forecast, the same forecasts will be disseminated to a multitude of different users, each with a different decision problem. Because it offers the potential to improve decisions and provide pragmatic value, a DM may be quite willing to buy a tailored weather forecast from a private vendor. As an example, the general-purpose forecast lacks relevance in a decision to incorporate a herbicide when the farmer is more interested in whether it will rain by more than a certain amount, rather than whether it will rain at all. The marketplace offers such customized information structures.

4.2.3 Expert Resolution

Consider the situation in which the information structure is a composite of separate sources of messages about the same state space: a group of "expert" informants or a collection of alternative documents. For example, needing to assess a prior distribution for the economic consequences of global warming, Nordhaus (1994b) surveys 19 experts, both economists and scientists. Among other questions, Nordhaus asks the experts to assess the probability of a 25% reduction in global output, as a function of various scenarios about the magnitude of the warming. Because of skewness, the means of the assessments are considerably higher than the medians, and remarkably, the assessments of the natural scientists are 20 to 30 times higher than the economists'. The question is how best to resolve such informed yet divergent messages. A similar circumstance arises when a DM wants to combine her intuition and beliefs with the output of a system-supplied Decision Support System (DSS). Studying some forecasting situations, Blattberg and Hoch (1990) make a case for combining the two sources with equal weighting, but there are other alternatives.

There is a large literature [e.g., Genest and Zidek (1986); Clemen, Murphy, and Winkler (1995)] on how to combine probability forecasts from multiple sources into a single "consensus" posterior distribution for the (usually dichotomous) state. P. A. Morris (1983) attempts to deal with this problem without assessing the rather complicated likelihood function. Without the likelihood as an anchor, there is a lot of freedom in doing this resolution: in the probability calculus, probabilities can combine both by addition and by multiplication. Winkler (1986) brings together several comments on Morris' approach. Jouini and Clemen (1996) show that copula models generate a flexible class of distributions that may be helpful when the normal distribution is clearly not appropriate.

The statements of the separate providers may not be independent of one another; the questions are how the assessor should form a consensus and how any multiple dependency affects the value of information. Using a multivariate normal distribution for states and categorical messages, Clemen and Winkler (1985) investigate both these issues. P. A. Morris (1974) presents the general theory of how to assess an information structure that is a composite of sources.

4.2.4 *Analysis of a Track Record*

This subsection concentrates on information structures that offer direct messages about the state space, either categorical statements such as, "state x_h will occur," in which case $\mathbf{Y} = \mathbf{X}$, or probability messages asserting a distribution over $\mathbf{X}$. Perhaps the most straightforward assessment occurs when there is an available track record that can be compared with corresponding realizations of the state. Let $\tilde{x}_h$ denote a specific realization of a random state variable of interest, and $\tilde{y}_h$ the corresponding statement by the informant. If there are N such occurrences, the assessor has available for evaluation the data set

$$\{(\tilde{x}_1, \tilde{y}_1), \cdots, (\tilde{x}_h, \tilde{y}_h), \cdots, (\tilde{x}_N, \tilde{y}_N)\}.$$

This special case often arises in forecasting problems, and techniques for analysis are well developed.

Consider first the case in which each message is a categorical statement of the state realization. As far as the assessment of the joint distribution p(x, y) is concerned, simple tabular enumeration of the data is useful when there is extensive experience on the joint relative frequencies and the relevant range of the state variable is relatively short. This is the method used by Baquet, Halter, and Conklin (1976) in assessing some temperature forecasts around 0°C, the temperature that is decision relevant to orchardists. For a wide-ranging state variable, many conveniences arise when it is appropriate to assume the joint distribution is bivariate normal. Krzysztofowicz (1992) presents some assessment and evaluation techniques for the bivariate normal case, and applies them to categorical forecasts of snowmelt runoff. Gnanadesikan (1996) provides several methods for testing if empirical data are distributed bivariate normal; even when data cannot be transformed to pass a formal test, the computational and conceptual advantages can often make it reasonable to so assume.

For a bivariate track record that is clearly not normal, Genest and Rivest (1993) offer a technique for selecting which family of copulas best fits an available sample from an unknown bivariate population. Although they are not illustrations of information structure assessment, Frees and Valdez (1997) and Klugman and Parsa (1999) show how to fit a copula to bivariate insurance data.

The prototype examples of message spaces that transmit probability statements occur in meteorological forecasting, where there is no shortage of forecasters and forecasts to study, and since the state realizations are generally measured promptly and accurately, there is no shortage of track records. Murphy and Winkler (1992) assess several joint distributions by tabular enumeration, and analyze various aspects of statistical informativeness by factoring each empirical joint density p(x, y) into its conditional and marginal components.

Rather than assess p(x, y) in its entirety, several techniques aspire to assess characteristics of $p(x \mid y)$ for any y that might be received. Schlaifer [(1969), Sections 8.3 and 9.7] suggests the direct assessment of the probability distribution of the forecast error as measured by the ratio of the state realization to the forecast. The idea is to assess p(x/y). The forecaster is unbiased if the mean of p(x/y) is 1; if the forecaster offers perfect information, $\text{Prob}[[x/y] = 1] = 1$. Given the assessment of p(x/y), the posterior distribution can be immediately processed for any subsequent forecast $y = y^*$. For example, the posterior probability $\text{Prob}[x \leq b \mid y = y^*] = \text{Prob}[[x/y^*] \leq [b/y^*]]$.

Lawrence (1991a) presents a technique that uses Cox's (1958; 1970) logistic regression model to assess the source's ability to transform prior probabilities into posterior ones. Given the prior density p(x), consider a single point forecast $\tilde{y}_h$ from the track record. Defining a tolerance range b units either side of $\tilde{y}_h$, the prior probability that the realization falls within the tolerance range is

$$\Re_h = \int_{\tilde{y}_h - b}^{\tilde{y}_h + b} p(x)\, dx, \tag{4.18}$$

and the odds of this occurring are $\Re_h/1 - \Re_h$. Under the unknown posterior density $p(x \mid \tilde{y}_h)$, the posterior probability that the realization falls within the tolerance range is

$$\Pi_h = \int_{\tilde{y}_h - b}^{\tilde{y}_h + b} p(x \mid \tilde{y}_h)\, dx, \tag{4.19}$$

with odds $\Pi_h/1 - \Pi_h$. The idea is to estimate these posterior odds by running a logistic regression of the form

$$\log[\Pi_h/1 - \Pi_h] = \alpha + \beta \log[\Re_h/1 - \Re_h]. \tag{4.20}$$

In (4.20), the dependent variable is an indicator z_h from the track record, where $z_h = 1$ if the realization falls within the tolerance range, and $z_h = 0$ if it does not. If $\alpha = 0$ and $\beta = 1$, then the track record is consistent with a source that offers null information. Cox (1958) provides the appropriate test statistic.

From a track record the assessor can calculate (and compare with competitor sources and against benchmarks) several interesting summary statistics that intend to measure the "quality" of the track record. For categorical messages, measures such as the mean forecast error $\Sigma_h [\tilde{y}_h - \tilde{x}_h]/N$, the mean square error, and Theil's U-statistic are well known [see Theil (1965, especially Chapter 2)].

For probability statements, there are a number of *scoring rules* and related criteria [Pearl (1978); Murphy and Daan (1985)] that compare the messages with the state realizations. Scoring rules are of interest not only as performance measures, but also as feedback mechanisms when training probability assessors, and as incentive mechanisms to induce the informant to reveal his true beliefs [Hendrickson and Buehler (1971)]. Section 8.2 takes up this latter issue when considering incentive contracts to hire a source. In a slightly different vein, Lawrence and Watkins (1986) forecast the probability of entry into certain banking markets using logistic regression, and use a χ^2 test to assess the validity of the model in light of subsequently observed market entry.

However, it is important to point out that these are auxiliary criteria; what matters to the DM is the expected value that the information structure can produce. Leitch and Tanner (1991) compare the profitability of some interest rate forecasts with several summary measures of quality, and conclude that the profitability bears little relationship to the conventional size-of-error criteria. Murphy and Thompson (1977) illustrate the same thing for probability statements. The following continuation of the empirical Example 4.2 helps explain why.

♦ *Example 4.2 (Continued)*

This example continues with an analysis of the track record of long-range hog price forecasts by Dr. Gene Futrell, a veteran analyst of the Iowa hog market. These forecasts, published in the *Iowa Outlook Letter* [Futrell (1968–1986)], were never generated solely from an econometric model; they were judgmental and based mostly upon the analyst's view of the specific market forces expected to be in operation on the forecast dates. Construction of the data set was complicated by the fact that the forecaster did not have these purposes in mind when making the forecasts. The long-range forecasts were made irregularly, seldom available precisely one year in advance, sometimes categorical point forecasts and sometimes interval statements, and oftentimes not for one specific month but for two or three. The author tried as dispassionately as possible to translate the published statements into a set of categorical 12-month-ahead forecasts, ultimately finding 46 acceptable messages. Thus, from a population of 179 realizations, we have a track record of 46 combinations of forecast and state. Table 4.1 presents the raw data. With a mean forecast of a price decline of \$5.06, this forecaster was somewhat bearish. The sample mean change in the state is a price decline of 83 cents, not far from the "population" mean of down 38 cents. The standard deviation of the price changes in the sample is \$17.54, \$1.93 greater than for the 179 realizations. Figure 4.1 shows a scatter diagram of each forecast and the corresponding realization; if the forecasts were always perfect, all observations would lie on the diagonal line. The sample correlation coefficient between the state and forecast is $\rho = .4749$. The mean forecast error is –\$4.23 with a standard deviation of \$15.86.

Table 4.1. Forecast and State Realization Data for Example 4.2

Date of Realization	Forecast	Realization	Forecast Error
5-69	$ -0.29	$ 10.49	$ -10.78
11-69	-7.04	19.75	-26.79
10-70	-17.63	-22.94	5.31
2-71	-27.13	-24.11	-3.02
6-71	-4.12	-16.57	12.45
7-71	-8.41	-14.89	6.48
11-71	5.40	8.64	-3.24
2-72	-1.01	15.10	-16.11
6-72	8.94	18.85	-9.91
8-72	10.92	23.83	-12.91
11-72	5.91	18.23	-12.32
2-73	-7.90	17.00	-24.90
5-73	-10.60	14.98	-25.58
8-73	-16.95	50.18	-67.13
11-73	-17.59	20.68	-38.27
4-76	12.31	10.77	1.54
8-76	-29.47	-27.77	-1.70
11-76	-13.13	-33.40	20.27
2-77	-21.33	-18.56	-2.77
4-77	-25.52	-23.29	-2.23
6-77	-27.78	-16.47	-11.31
8-77	-16.08	-3.83	-12.25
11-77	-0.61	8.35	-8.96
8-78	-18.69	1.75	-20.44
11-78	-14.01	9.39	-23.40
5-79	-12.14	-14.94	2.80
8-79	-7.32	-22.79	15.47
11-79	-16.01	-26.41	10.40
5-80	-16.24	-24.21	7.97
8-80	-3.37	4.89	-8.26
11-80	-1.16	8.72	-9.88
2-81	1.43	0.57	0.86
5-81	14.33	9.59	4.74
8-81	3.57	-0.40	3.97
11-81	4.61	-7.97	12.58
5-82	11.28	15.74	-4.46
11-82	6.02	10.87	-4.85
5-83	1.18	-11.45	12.63
8-83	-6.41	-14.95	8.54
11-83	-6.19	-16.02	9.83
5-84	2.41	0.08	2.33
8-84	4.47	2.78	1.69
11-84	12.09	9.10	2.99
2-85	10.19	3.38	6.81
8-85	5.29	-6.90	12.19
11-85	1.09	-3.91	5.00
Mean	$ - 5.06	$ - 0.83	$ - 4.23
Standard Deviation	$ 11.96	$ 17.54	$ 15.86

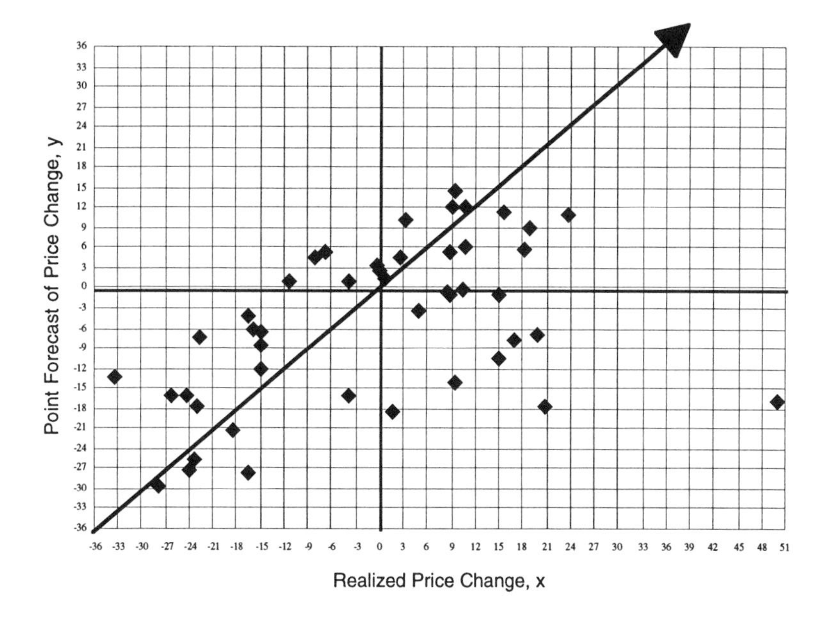

Figure 4.1. Frequency distribution of states and forecasts in Example 4.2.

In and of itself, forecast accuracy is not the same thing as statistical informativeness. Any forecast source can randomly supply forecasts yet still know nothing more than the prior distribution. For example, a simple benchmark forecaster who every time forecasts the mean change in the price from the underlying prior, $\mu_1 = -\$0.38$, knows nothing but for 179 forecasts would have a mean error of zero with a standard deviation of \$15.61. If Professor Futrell would have forecast a 38-cent decline for each of these 46 occasions, his mean forecast error would have been + 45 cents.

The real question is not the measured accuracy, but whether the source offers statistical information. Lawrence (1991a) applies the logistic regression model (4.20) to these data, and reports results that are not consistent with the null hypothesis that Professor Futrell's forecasts contain null information.

Professor Futrell was tailoring his forecasts, and this policy cost him in terms of accuracy measure. An analysis [Lawrence (1991b)] shows that this forecaster called for large price drops and moderate price changes about as often as those events occurred, but never forecast large price increases. Not only did this forecaster have a slight bearish bias, but in the language of Kahneman and Tversky (1979b), the judgmental predictions exhibited a kind of asymmetric predictive regression to the prior mean: when the forecaster was highly bearish he said so,[2] when he was bullish he tempered his enthusiasm and predicted a smaller price increase. In an interview with the author, Professor Futrell said he thought it was better for the farmers. He said that if he is bullish and wrong, farmers will have over-expanded their production and will lose real dollars; if he is bearish and wrong, farmers will not have expanded and their loss will be in the form of opportunity cost. In his forecasts, the informant was not expressing his true beliefs; instead he was making a judgment on how hypothetical dollars lost should be valued relative to real dollars lost.

The consequence of this bias is that the case for bivariate normality of the information structure is not strong. Research currently underway using Genest and Rivest's (1993) procedure suggests that Clayton's copula model best fits these data. Example 4.2 continues in Section 5.1.2. ♦

Users of these forecasts other than local hog farmers are unlikely to appreciate this bias and are interested in what the forecaster really believes. Knowing the bias, they can calibrate or tune the forecasts they receive to serve as the basis for their decision making. A source that is generally wrong can still be informative, but the assessor must process the message with this in mind. As an example, inaccurate opinion is the idea behind contrarian indicators of the stock market.

Calibration

Regarding this issue of bias, as the old saying goes, the assessor must "consider the source" when contemplating the meaning of the messages received. *Calibration*, or lack of bias, is a well-defined systematic relationship between messages and state realizations. It is a property of statistical information that is independent of the decision problem; whether a source is calibrated is neither necessary nor sufficient to ensure informativeness and information value. It is a property, however, that can be beneficial to the extent it reduces the cost of cognitive processing. Two types of calibration are of interest, corresponding to the two types of message space: categorical calibration and probabilistic calibration.

Categorical calibration is a relationship between the distribution of the categorical forecasts and the distribution of the realizations. A reasonable attribute for an information source to exhibit is a lack of bias in forecast provision: rare events should be forecast rarely, common events should be forecast often. A forecaster that successfully forecasts a rare event (e.g., the stock market crash of October 1987) becomes a guru, one that consistently forecasts rare events (The

---

[2] The forecaster was not afraid to go out on a limb, in several cases with remarkable results. Two forecasts jump out: both the forecast for the realization in August 1976 (published in August 1975), and the forecast for April 1977 (published in July 1976), were for huge price declines—events with very low prior probability that came to pass.

world will end tomorrow!) is a crackpot. In fact, such a property is a necessary condition for the achievement of perfect information. Since the distribution of the realizations is embodied in the prior measure p(x), the information structure exhibits *categorical predictive calibration* when $\mathbf{X} = \mathbf{Y}$ and the chance of receiving a forecast of a particular state is equal to the prior chance of that state occurring: $p(y) = p(x)$. There are a number of statistical tests for the equality of two distributions based upon sample data; see D'Agostino and Stephens (1986).

Categorical predictive calibration does not imply statistical informativeness, as an informant can offer calibrated null information simply by randomly choosing forecasts from the underlying distribution p(x). Also, a source need not exhibit this type of calibration to generate value; the information structure (2.50) in Example 2.1 is not calibrated, yet valuable. For finite information structures, Section 6.2.4 presents a formal model for statistical informativeness that ensures categorical calibration.

Turning to probabilistic message spaces, if the message y_j is a statement that the probability of state x_i is $y_j(x_i)$, one version of *probabilistic calibration* is the condition that, from the DM's viewpoint,

$$p(x_i | y_j) = y_j(x_i). \tag{4.21}$$

In other words, for all receivable messages, after the DM's processing, the conditional posterior probability of each state is as expressed by the message. If a weather forecaster states the probability of rain is 20%, then if the DM believes the probability is 20%, the source is calibrated. Otherwise it must be tuned. This property saves costs of cognitive processing, if the DM believes it holds. See Dawid (1982) for further discussion from a Bayesian point of view.

In the preceding example, a forecaster of rain can exhibit probabilistic calibration yet offer null information, simply by always stating the climatological probability of rain. Nevertheless, calibration has a useful role to play in the practical problem of assessing the relative quality of probability forecasts [Murphy (1973)]. It is also important in the formal comparison of statistical informativeness [DeGroot and Fienberg (1982; 1986); Vardeman and Meeden (1983)], a subject matter that Section 6.2 takes up.

4.3 Simplifying the Assessment

Perhaps the best practical advice for a DM desiring to assess the value of information is to start first with the decision problem at hand and work backwards to the statistical assessment, because the structure of the decision problem helps determine the probability assessments the DM needs. As the upcoming Chapter 5 documents, there may be characteristics of the problem structure that, on a case-by-case basis, can be exploited to improve tractability in the assessment of the value of information. The DM can then assess as little about the statistical aspects of the information structure as necessary in order to assess the value of information with the precision that the circumstances warrant. This section considers some different types of simplifications that may be useful. The first is a single random variable that arises naturally in several problem framings; the DM may choose to assess this particular distribution directly. The second is a simple approach for modeling imperfect information using only the prior knowledge p(x).

4.3.1 The Preposterior Mean

Several of the subsequent examples in this book demonstrate the considerable simplifications that arise in framings in which the conditional posterior mean of the random variable X plays a major role. Defining, as in (2.27), $E_{x|y}\, x \equiv \bar{x}_y$, and viewing this quantity as a random variable, a function of the as yet unknown message y, the distribution $p(\bar{x}_y)$ is called the *prior distribution of the posterior mean*, or the *preposterior mean*. The behavior of this distribution, as a function of the informativeness of the information structure, is curious. If the structure offers null information, then $\bar{x}_y$ is the same for all y and $p(\bar{x}_y)$ is a degenerate distribution with all its mass at that value (which is simply the unconditional mean $\bar{x}$). If the source offers perfect information, then $\bar{x}_y$ is simply x itself and has prior probability p(x). The increase in informativeness has caused the distribution $p(\bar{x}_y)$ to "spread out" from degeneracy to p(x); this behavior is somewhat opposite from what the notion "being more informed" connotes. The general theory of such distributions appears in Raiffa and Schlaifer (1961, Chapter 5). As Section 5.2.1 discusses, these ideas are useful in statistical decision problems where being more informed is associated with taking a larger sample.

This approach is most tractable when the joint density p(x, y) is bivariate normal. In this case, in light of (2.41), $p(\bar{x}_y)$ is normally distributed with mean

$$E_y\, \bar{x}_y = \bar{x}. \tag{4.22}$$

The variance of $p(\bar{x}_y)$ can be found by applying the general equation 5-28 of Raiffa and Schlaifer (1961) to the normal distribution:

$$\sigma^2_{\bar{x}_y} = \sigma^2_x - E_y\, \sigma^2_{x|y} = \sigma^2_x - \sigma^2_x[1-\rho^2] = \sigma^2_x\rho^2. \tag{4.23}$$

In summary, the preposterior mean

$$p(\bar{x}_y) \sim N(\bar{x},\, \sigma^2_x\rho^2); \tag{4.24}$$

that is,

$$p(\bar{x}_y) = \frac{1}{\sigma_x \rho \sqrt{2\pi}} \exp\left\{-\frac{1}{2\sigma_x^2 \rho^2}\left[\bar{x}_y - \bar{x}\right]^2\right\}. \tag{4.25}$$

4.3.2 *The Calibrated Noiseless Model*

Finally, the decision maker may be in an early stage of information assessment, not considering a specific source but desiring instead simply to obtain a rough estimate of what imperfect information would be worth in a particular situation. Alternately, the track record on the performance of a specific information source may be insufficient for adequate assessment of the joint distribution p(x, y). This motivates consideration of the assessment of an imperfect information structure using nothing more than the prior unconditional distribution p(x). Progress in this case can be facilitated by adopting a modeling technique intended not to mimic or describe any real or achievable information structure, but rather designed as a decision heuristic which, as Tversky and Kahneman (1974, page 1124) explain, intends to reduce the complex tasks of assessment to simpler judgmental operations.

One such methodology derives from generalizing an approach first presented in simple form by Marschak (1954, Section 5). Given a state space **X** on the real line, assume that the message space,

$$\mathbf{Y}^n = \{y_1, \cdots, y_j, \cdots, y_n\},$$

is a partitioning of **X** into n mutually exclusive and exhaustive intervals within which the realization of the state is forecast to lie. The typical forecast y_j is a statement of the form $b_j \leq x \leq c_j$, where b_j and c_j are the endpoints of the stated interval. The information structure $\mathbf{I}^n$ combines the message space $\mathbf{Y}^n$ with the probabilistic assumptions that the forecast intervals are calibrated and noiseless. The structure is noiseless if, for every $y_j \in \mathbf{Y}^n$, it is a certainty that the realization will fall within the stated interval:

$$\int_{b_j}^{c_j} p(x \mid y_j)\, dx = 1. \tag{4.26}$$

The structure is calibrated if the chance of naming the interval is equal to the prior probability of a realization within the stated interval:

$$p(y_j) = \int_{b_j}^{c_j} p(x)\, dx. \tag{4.27}$$

By altering n, the number of intervals, in a systematic way, the assessor alters the precision of the information structure.

Lawrence (1991b) shows this approach is tractable for a variety of prior probability distributions and payoff functions. Depending upon the structure of the outcome function and the construction of the intervals, the value of information does not necessarily increase with the precision measure n. Hausch and Ziemba (1983) use a similar technique to build bounds on information value in complex stochastic programming problems. Wilson (1975) uses this model to study returns to scale from information acquisition.

The notion of linking the statistical assessments to the decision problem at hand serves as a prelude for the next chapter. Under the assumption that the required probability distributions either are or can be available, Chapter 5 takes up the calculation of information value in a number of specific problem framings.

5 Models with Convenient Assessment and Interpretation

Both the economic structure of the outcome and the DM's personal preferences are factors that affect the tractability of assessing and interpreting the value of information. This chapter covers practical or prescriptive techniques for quantitatively assessing the value of an information structure in the context of a number of convenient problem framings. Such models are also useful in the early stages of user information processing, when the DM has no specific source in mind but is merely interested in what information would be worth, if it had given properties.

The results in several of the subsections of this chapter are well known in the literature, but complete derivations can be difficult to find. This technical chapter offers the benefit of filling in and explaining some of the steps that journal articles often skip; the downside for some readers is an increase in the cost of cognitive processing in the form of greater diligence, patience, and cross-referencing than has been required before. Specifically, the presentation relies heavily on statistical facts developed in Sections 2.3, 4.1.2, and 4.3.1.

5.1 Models with Payoff Quadratic in the Action

A tractable, flexible, and economically interesting payoff function is quadratic and concave in the action a:

$$w + \pi(x, a) = w + \omega_1 + \omega_2 x + \omega_3 a + \omega_4 xa + \omega_5 x^2 - \omega_6 a^2, \qquad (5.1)$$

with $\omega_6 > 0$. A standard application of this class of model is to the monopolistic or perfectly competitive firm whose stochastic profit is quadratic in the production decision. Nelson (1961) and Marschak (1954) study information value in this model when price is the random variable; Hilton (1979) provides a thorough analysis, including allowance for capacity constraints and shutdown, when the uncertainty arises in cost rather than price. Using a cost function quadratic in production, Ijiri and Itami (1973) study the tradeoffs between promptness and accuracy of reports about demand, the information value arising from the ability to stabilize production rates and save on costs. The upcoming Section 5.6 also consider promptness and accuracy in a stochastic control model in which the payoff is quadratic and the state variable moves over time according to a well-defined stochastic process.

5.1.1 The General Case

The first step in the valuation of information in the quadratic model is the determination of the decision rules. By differentiation of the relevant expectation of (5.1), the optimal prior choice for the risk neutral DM is

$$a_0^N = [\omega_3 + \omega_4 \bar{x}]/2\omega_6, \tag{5.2}$$

and the optimal conditional decision rule is

$$a_y^N = [\omega_3 + \omega_4 \bar{x}_y]/2\omega_6. \tag{5.3}$$

Hence, the advantage of (5.1) is that the optimal decision rule is linear in the expectation of X. Substituting (5.2) into (5.1) shows that the value of the prior decision is

$$\mathbf{U(D^* \mid I\downarrow)} = \max_a E_x \pi(x, a) = \kappa_1 \bar{x}^2 + \kappa_2 E_x[x^2] + \kappa_3 \bar{x} + \kappa_4, \tag{5.4}$$

and putting (5.3) into (5.1) gives the conditional value of the decision, given the message y, as

$$\mathbf{U(D^* \mid I}, y) = \max_a E_{x|y} \pi(x, a) = \kappa_1 \bar{x}_y^2 + \kappa_2 E_{x|y}[x^2] + \kappa_3 \bar{x}_y + \kappa_4. \tag{5.5}$$

In (5.4) and (5.5), the κ_h are constants; $\kappa_1 = \omega_4^2/4\omega_6$.

The assessment of V_I^N requires the expectation of (5.5) with respect to the marginal distribution p(y). Using the law of iterated expectation, equation (2.40), the substitution of (5.4) and the expectation of (5.5) into the value definition (3.51) yields

$$V_I^N = \kappa_1\{E_y \bar{x}_y^2 - \bar{x}^2\}. \tag{5.6}$$

Thus, when the problem can be framed in this manner, the decision maker needs to assess only the joint distribution p(x, y) and the two economic parameters that comprise κ_1: ω_4 and ω_6.

Economic insights into the value of information problem for the quadratic payoff function can be obtained from further manipulation of (5.6). Replacing $\bar{x}^2$ and $\bar{x}_y^2$ with their equivalents by rearranging the definitions of the unconditional and conditional variances given in (2.30) and (2.32), respectively, and then applying the law of iterated expectation (2.40), the value of information is

$$V_I^N = \kappa_1\{E_y[E_{x|y}[x^2] - \sigma^2_{x|y}] + \sigma^2_x - E_x[x^2]\}.$$

$$= \kappa_1\{\sigma^2_x - E_y \sigma^2_{x|y}\}. \tag{5.7}$$

From (5.7), if the information is perfect (i.e., the source reveals precisely which x will occur), then the posterior variance of X is zero and the value of information is proportional to the variance of X itself. The information value is diminished if the information is imperfect and variance in X remains for some message y.

5.1.2 The Bivariate Normal Case

When p(x, y) is bivariate normal, (4.16) shows that $E_y \sigma^2_{x|y} = \sigma^2_x[1 - \rho^2]$, so

$$V_I^N = \kappa_1\{\rho^2 \sigma^2_x\}. \tag{5.8}$$

The value of information is proportional to the variance of the state variable and the square of the correlation coefficient. Information value increases with ρ^2; this parameter indexes the statistical informativeness of the information structure.

A transformation of the variables X and Y to standard normal amounts to a choice of origins such that $\bar{x} = \bar{y} = 0$ and a choice of units such that $\sigma^2_x = \sigma^2_y = 1$; this calibrates to p(x) = p(y) has no effect upon ρ. In the bivariate standard normal case,

$$V_I^N = \kappa_1 \rho^2. \tag{5.9}$$

With a reinterpretation of the semantic meaning of the potential messages, this bivariate normal model also applies in the evaluation of probabilistic interval forecasts. Interpret each categorical message y as a statement of the mean of the forecaster's posterior probability distribution on the state. This posterior distribution is well defined; in the bivariate standard normal case it is normal with mean y and variance $1 - \rho^2$. Under this distribution it is straightforward to calculate the probability that the realization falls within any arbitrary interval of length L; intervals symmetric in length about the stated mean y are a natural choice. Winkler (1972) provides conditions under which interval estimates symmetric about the mean in both length and probability are appropriate. If the contained probability is to be 95%, the length of such an interval is given by $L = 2[1.96][1 - \rho^2]^{\frac{1}{2}}$. Solving for ρ^2 to obtain (5.9), the value of the information structure **I** as a function of the length of the forecast interval L is:

$$V^N_{I(95)} = \kappa_1 \rho^2 = \kappa_1\{1 - [L^2/15.3664]\}, \tag{5.10}$$

recognizing that the length cannot be so long as to imply information value less than zero. Similarly, the value of the structure if it offers 99% posterior probability of forecast coverage, $V^N_{I(99)}$, is given by

$$V^N_{I(99)} = \kappa_1\rho^2 = \kappa_1\{1 - [L^2/26.543]\}. \tag{5.11}$$

The value of information indicated in (5.10) or (5.11) has two economic uses. Equation (5.10) measures the value of information in a structure offering forecast intervals of length L that have 95% probability of forecast coverage, or it indicates the ρ^2 necessary between X and Y in order to achieve forecast intervals of length L with 95% probability of coverage.

♦ *Example 4.2 Random Market Price (Continued from Section 4.2.4)*
This example concludes with a pragmatic application of Professor Futrell's forecasts, an analysis of the value of these forecasts to a specific farrow-to-finish hog enterprise in Iowa. In the perfectly competitive business of producing hogs farrow-to-finish, biological factors lead to production decisions being made well in advance of knowledge of sales price. Giving time for decisions on sow herd size, breeding, gestation, and feeding to market weight, there is about a 12-month production lag. The price of hogs in 12 months is the decision-relevant random variable today.

The perfectly competitive firm with a quadratic cost function has an outcome function described by (5.1). Monthly profits are

$$\pi(x, a) = [\tilde{x} + x]a - \omega_1 - \omega_3 a - \omega_6 a^2, \tag{5.12}$$

where $\tilde{x}$ is the observable price today, x is the random 12-month change in that price, and a is the quantity of production, assumed to be determinable with certainty today. The parameter ω_6 is the slope of the average variable cost curve and also is one-half the slope of the marginal cost curve. Unfortunately, strict use of the calculus fails here to produce the optimal decision rule: if price falls below average variable cost, then the optimal production decision is to shut down. This discontinuity results in a loss of tractability that we wish to avoid; one simple way of dealing with the problem is to assume $\omega_3 = 0$, in which case there is no shutdown as long as the price is positive.

The value of an information structure **I** is

$$V^N_I = \tfrac{1}{4}\omega_6\{E_y\bar{x}^2_y - \bar{x}^2\}.$$

Since the economics of the problem make $\omega_4 = 1$, the parameter ω_6 is the only one needed to set the scale for the value of information.

The estimate of ω_6 is from the linear programming study by Hanrahan (1972) on a farrow-to-finish operation, the Brenton Hog Farm in Dallas County, Iowa. This facility has 11 pens in the breeding and gestating building, 40 farrowing stalls and 32 pens in the farrow barn and nursery, and 72 pens in the grower and finisher building. Hanrahan's model allows a breeding, feeding, and marketing decision to be made every two weeks throughout the year. Conveniently for our purposes, his production solutions assume perfect information concerning future price. Comparison of his optimal production solutions with the realized prices yields, after differencing, the optimal linear decision rule, per hundredweight per month, $\Delta a_x = x/2\omega_6 = 2.685x$. This implies $\omega_6 = .1862$. At the mean production level of 588.3 cwt/month and inflation-adjusted mean price of \$60.55/cwt, the elasticity of the enterprise's supply is [2.685][60.55]/588.3 = +.276. This inelastic response is consistent with most estimates of the short-run price elasticity of hog supply, as catalogued in Hayenga et al. (1985).

The value of perfect information to this enterprise is $V_{I\Gamma}^N = \sigma_x^2/4\omega_6 = 243.73/4[.1862]$ = \$327.24/month. When valued per hundredweight at the mean enterprise production level of 588.3 cwt/month, the value of perfect information is \$0.556/cwt.

The sample correlation coefficient for the data is $\rho = .4749$. Gnanadesikan (1996) provides several methods for assessing if the data are distributed bivariate normal; without further transformation of these data, the case is not very strong. Nevertheless, assuming for tractability that the joint distribution is bivariate normal, then the value of information to this enterprise is given by, utilizing (5.8), $V_I^N = \rho^2\sigma_x^2/4\omega_6$ = \$73.80/month or \$0.125/cwt at mean production, a little over two bits per pig. This implies the 95% forecast intervals have length L = \$53.86. ♦

*5.1.3 The Quadratic Team

A *team* is a collection of decision makers working to achieve a common objective and sharing information in a coordinated manner. An organizational form first described by Marschak (1954), Radner (1962) and Marschak and Radner (1972) analyze in detail the team with a payoff function that is quadratic in the team's action variables. Ohlson (1975; 1979) applies this model to an investing problem; see Section 5.7.1.

The team has H individual actions to choose; suppose each teammate h chooses one optimal action, based upon the message she receives. A team action is a vector describing the choice of each teammate:

$$a = [a_1, \cdots, a_h, \cdots, a_s, \cdots, a_H]. \tag{5.13}$$

The team's quadratic payoff function is

$$\pi(x, a) = g(x) + 2\Sigma_h x a_h - \Sigma_h \Sigma_s v_{hs} a_h a_s$$

$$= g(x) + 2xa_h - v_{hh} a_h^2 + 2\Sigma_{s\neq h} x a_s - 2\Sigma_{s\neq h} v_{hs} a_h a_s - \Sigma_{s\neq h} \Sigma_{\ell\neq h} v_{s\ell} a_s a_\ell, \tag{5.14}$$

where, to ensure a maximum the coefficient matrix $[v_{hs}]$ is symmetric and positive definite.

The message space for the hth DM,

$$\mathbf{Y}_h = \{y_{h1}, \cdots, y_{hj}, \cdots, y_{hn^h}\}, \tag{5.15}$$

contains n^h potential messages; if h receives the message y_{hj}, the optimal action conditional on that message is written $a_{hy_{hj}}$. From the organizational design of the information system, the DM also knows that when she receives y_{hj}, the chance that teammate s receives message $y_{sJ} \in \mathbf{Y}_s$ is $p(y_{sJ} | y_{hj})$, for $J = 1, \cdots, n^s$. Each teammate chooses the optimal action $a_{hy_{hj}}$ by maximizing the expected payoff of the team, conditional on the message y_{hj}. The expected payoff to the team depends upon h's choice of action, the conditional distribution of X, given y_{hj}, and the optimal actions chosen by the teammates, based upon their messages. Teammate h doesn't know a_s, but knows that teammate s will make the right decision given the message y_{sj}; as far as h is concerned,

$$E_{a_s | y_{hj}} a_s = \Sigma_J\, a_{sy_{sJ}}\, p(y_{sJ} | y_{hj}), \tag{5.16}$$

where $a_{sy_{sJ}}$ is the optimal response of teammate s to message y_{sJ}.

Evaluating the derivative of the expectation of (5.14) conditional on y_{hj},

$$\frac{\partial \bullet}{\partial a_h} = 2E_{x | y_{hj}} x - 2v_{hh}a_h - 2\Sigma_{s \neq h} v_{hs}\, \Sigma_J\, a_{sy_{sJ}}\, p(y_{sJ} | y_{hj}) = 0;$$

the optimal actions are characterized by the conditions

$$a_{hy_{hj}} v_{hh} + \Sigma_{s \neq h} v_{hs}\, \Sigma_J\, a_{sy_{sJ}}\, p(y_{sJ} | y_{hj}) = E_{x | y_{hj}} x, \tag{5.17}$$

for each $y_{hj} \in \mathbf{Y}_h$, and for every teammate $h = 1, \cdots, H$. If the state is countable and finite, then Radner (1962) and Marschak and Radner (1972) show that the preceding conditions amount to $n^1 + n^2 + \cdots + n^H$ linear equations whose solution is optimal for the team and, for each individual separately, *person-by-person satisfactory*.

The evaluation of information becomes tractable for the quadratic team when the joint distribution of states and messages is multivariate normal, with known correlation between each message and the state, and known correlation between the messages the various teammates receive. In this case, the optimal decision rules are linear in the received message, with coefficients determinable from a system of linear equations. The value of the informed decision and value of information can then be calculated using the results in Section 6.3 of Marschak and Radner (1972).

5.2 Models with Payoff Linear in the State

There are a number of popular decision models that can be framed with the payoff function linear in a continuous state variable. In addition to the standard statistical decision and inventory problems that this section discusses, several of the case studies in Sections 1.4.4 and 1.5.3 apply this framework to environmental cleanup and the evaluation of information about toxic chemical potency and exposure. For example, Taylor, Evans, and McKone (1993) use this linear model to investigate the value of various animal testing procedures as information sources about the carcinogenic potential of untested chemical compounds.

5.2.1 Raiffa and Schlaifer's Approach

Raiffa and Schlaifer (1961) study in detail the class of decision problems in which the action space is finite, $\mathbf{a}^K = \{a_1, \cdots, a_k, \cdots, a_K\}$, the state space is on the real line and can be unbounded, $\mathbf{X} = \{-\infty < x < \infty\}$, the DM is risk neutral, and the payoff from each action $a_k \in \mathbf{a}$ is linear in the state realization x with the form

$$\pi(x, a_k) = \omega_{1k} + \omega_{2k}x \quad \text{for all } a_k \in \mathbf{a}. \tag{5.18}$$

The advantage of this functional form is that only the mean of the random variable is relevant for choice among the available actions. Specifically, the expected payoff from action a_k under the prior decision is

$$E_x\, \pi(x, a_k) = \omega_{1k} + \omega_{2k}\,\bar{x}, \tag{5.19}$$

and conditional on the message y,

$$E_{x|y}\, \pi(x, a_k) = \omega_{1k} + \omega_{2k}\,\bar{x}_y. \tag{5.20}$$

The analysis for the case of two actions $\mathbf{a} = \{a_1, a_2\}$ is instructive and generalizes in a straightforward manner. Adopting the labeling convention that $\omega_{21} < \omega_{22}$, the strict inequality ensures that each action is optimal for some value in $\mathbf{X}$. There is a breakeven level where the optimal action changes from a_1 to a_2; this breakeven value is denoted x_b and defined by $\pi(x_b, a_1) = \pi(x_b, a_2)$. Hence,

$$\omega_{11} + \omega_{21}x_b = \omega_{12} + \omega_{22}x_b, \tag{5.21a}$$

or

$$x_b = [\omega_{11} - \omega_{12}]/[\omega_{22} - \omega_{21}]. \tag{5.21b}$$

In this model it is simplest to evaluate the expected value of information as the ex-ante expectation of the ex-post value, as in (1.10). To evaluate first the value of perfect information, note that the optimal action given x is

$$a_x = \begin{cases} a_1 & \text{if } x \le x_b \\ a_2 & \text{if } x \ge x_b, \end{cases} \tag{5.22}$$

and that the optimal prior decision, taking advantage of (5.19),

$$a_0^N = \begin{cases} a_1 & \text{if } \overline{x} \leq x_b \\ a_2 & \text{if } \overline{x} \geq x_b, \end{cases} \tag{5.23}$$

turns only upon the prior mean. There are therefore these cases to distinguish: (1) $\overline{x} \leq x_b$ and (2) $\overline{x} \geq x_b$. In Case (1) the ex-post value of the perfect information x (i.e., the increment in payoff) is, following (1.1) when y = x,

$$\upsilon^N(x, x) = \begin{cases} \pi(x, a_1) - \pi(x, a_1) = 0 & \text{if } x \leq x_b \\ \pi(x, a_2) - \pi(x, a_1) & \text{if } x \geq x_b. \end{cases} \tag{5.24}$$

This statement can be simplified using the definition of x_b given by (5.21b):

$$\begin{aligned} \pi(x, a_2) - \pi(x, a_1) &= [\omega_{12} - \omega_{11}] + [\omega_{22} - \omega_{21}]x \\ &= -\, x_b[\omega_{22} - \omega_{21}] + [\omega_{22} - \omega_{21}]x \\ &= [\omega_{22} - \omega_{21}]\,[x - x_b]. \end{aligned} \tag{5.25}$$

Thus, the statement (5.24) can be written most succinctly in Case (1) as

$$\upsilon^N(x, x) = [\omega_{22} - \omega_{21}] \max(x - x_b, 0) \quad \text{if } \overline{x} \leq x_b. \tag{5.26}$$

By similar reasoning, the ex-post value of the message x under Case (2) is

$$\upsilon^N(x, x) = [\omega_{22} - \omega_{21}] \max(x_b - x, 0) \quad \text{if } \overline{x} \geq x_b. \tag{5.27}$$

The economic meaning here is that if the prior optimal action is a_0^N, then any identification of x that results in a_0^N remaining optimal offers no gain to the DM over and above what would have been earned anyway; all such messages are useless. Those identifications that lead the DM to change away from a_0^N do have incremental value, and this value increases with x. Figure 5.1 depicts this for Case (1).

Weighing $\upsilon^N(x, x)$ by p(x), the prior chance that realization x comes to pass, and summing them up gives the expected value of these incremental gains, $V_{I\uparrow}^N$:

$$V_{I\uparrow}^N = \begin{cases} [\omega_{22} - \omega_{21}] \displaystyle\int_{x_b}^{\infty} [x - x_b]\, p(x)\, dx & \text{if } \overline{x} \leq x_b \\ [\omega_{22} - \omega_{21}] \displaystyle\int_{-\infty}^{x_b} [x_b - x]\, p(x)\, dx & \text{if } \overline{x} \geq x_b. \end{cases} \tag{5.28}$$

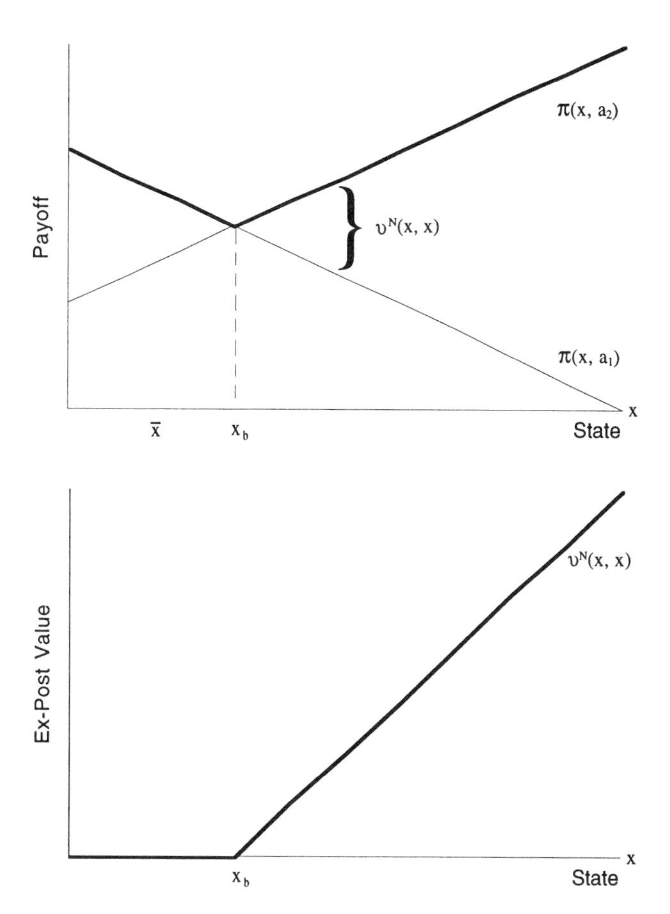

Figure 5.1. The ex-post value of perfect information in Case (1). The optimal prior action is a_1 when $\overline{x} \leq x_b$. For realizations of X less than x_b, the prior optimal action remains unchanged. Any realizations of X greater than x_b give the DM a higher ex-post payoff than she would have received without the information.

Raiffa and Schlaifer (1961, Section 5.2) call the integrals in (5.28) *linear-loss integrals*, show how to evaluate them for commonly occurring functional forms for p(x), and table the function for the case in which p(x) is standard normal.

Evaluating next the value of imperfect information under this linear payoff function, note first that the breakeven value x_b and the prior optimal action a_0^N do not change. Using (5.20), the optimal choice given y turns only on the posterior mean $\overline{x}_y$, so

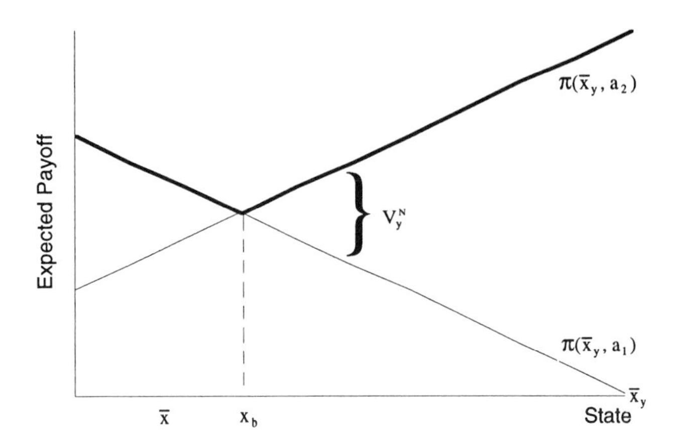

Figure 5.2. The conditional value of the message y in Case (1). The message informs the DM that the mean of X is $\bar{x}_y$; all messages that $\bar{x}_y \leq x_b$ are useless.

$$a_y^N = \begin{cases} a_1 & \text{if } \bar{x}_y \leq x_b \\ a_2 & \text{if } \bar{x}_y \geq x_b. \end{cases} \tag{5.29}$$

Thus, in Case (1) (when $\bar{x} \leq x_b$ and $a_0^N = a_1$), the conditional value of the message y is, using (3.29),

$$V_y^N = \begin{cases} E_{x|y}\,\pi(x, a_1) - E_{x|y}\,\pi(x, a_1) = 0 & \text{if } \bar{x}_y \leq x_b \\ E_{x|y}\,\pi(x, a_2) - E_{x|y}\,\pi(x, a_1) & \text{if } \bar{x}_y \geq x_b. \end{cases} \tag{5.30}$$

This statement is written more succinctly by using the definition of x_b and replacing x with $\bar{x}_y$ in an equation analogous to (5.26):

$$V_y^N = [\omega_{22} - \omega_{21}]\max(\bar{x}_y - x_b, 0) \quad \text{if } \bar{x} \leq x_b. \tag{5.31}$$

See Figure 5.2. Similarly, the conditional value of the message y under Case (2) is

$$V_y^N = [\omega_{22} - \omega_{21}]\max(x_b - \bar{x}_y, 0) \quad \text{if } \bar{x} \geq x_b. \tag{5.32}$$

In this model with a risk neutral DM and a separable outcome function, the value of imperfect information is the expectation of (5.31) and (5.32) with respect to the marginal distribution p(y). It is at this stage that Raiffa and Schlaifer (1961, Section 5.3.1) present the following simplifying insight that offers computational advantages in several types of application: the function V_y^N depends upon y only via the conditional mean $\bar{x}_y$ associated with y. Prior to the receipt of y, $\overline{x}_y$ is itself a random variable with its own probability distribution $p(\overline{x}_y)$, the preposterior mean described in Section 4.3.1. Using $\overline{x}_y$ as the random variable, the value of imperfect information is, when $p(\overline{x}_y)$ is a continuous density,

$$V_I^N = E_{\overline{x}_y} V_y^N = \begin{cases} [\omega_{22} - \omega_{21}] \int_{x_b}^{\infty} [\overline{x}_y - x_b]\, p(\overline{x}_y)\, d\overline{x}_y & \text{if } \overline{x} \le x_b \\ [\omega_{22} - \omega_{21}] \int_{-\infty}^{x_b} [x_b - \overline{x}_y]\, p(\overline{x}_y)\, d\overline{x}_y & \text{if } \overline{x} \ge x_b. \end{cases} \tag{5.33}$$

Raiffa and Schlaifer (1961, Table 5.2) work out the preposterior mean and its approximations for several combinations of $p(y\,|\,x)$ and $p(x)$ that are natural conjugate pairs.

5.2.2 Application to Statistical Decision Problems

Raiffa and Schlaifer's approach has proven particularly useful in the solution to statistical decision problems. A statistical decision problem is one in which prior probabilities are processed into posterior probabilities by means of gathering or observing sample data that are known to obey a specific conditional distribution $p(y\,|\,x)$. Example 5.2 illustrates.

♦ *Example 5.2 A Statistical Sampling Problem*
An intricate component is produced in lots of size N, and any one of a large number of potential causes could make any one individual defective. Let x be the fraction defective in the batch; this fraction varies by batch and is hence a random variable. Management, the DM, can choose between two actions, either a_1: ship the entire lot to the customer, with a money-back guarantee for each defective piece, or a_2: closely inspect each component, determine the cause of the problem for each defective piece, repair it, and ship a defect-free batch. The DM also has the option to take a sample from the lot and make it available to an independent testing house. The test can determine exactly how many defectives are in the sample, but it is not an inspection and tells nothing about the cause of any defect. Via the sampling, the DM can estimate the fraction defective in the entire batch. Remarkably, the sampling does not tag the specific components in the sample that are defective, so after having received the report that "y pieces are defective out of n," the DM is back to the original choice of either shipping the entire batch or inspecting and repairing them one at a time.

The profit from each action is

$$\pi^{\#}(x, a_1) = N\alpha[1 - x] - \beta N x = N\alpha - [N\alpha + N\beta]x;$$

$$\pi^{\#}(x, a_2) = N\alpha - IC - \gamma N x,$$

where x is the proportion defective, $0 \le x \le 1$, α is the profit per good piece, β is the money-back guarantee per defective piece shipped and returned, γ is the cost of repairing an inspected defective, and IC is the fixed cost of inspecting the entire batch. Taking advantage of the assumption of neutrality towards risk, payoff can be measured as the deviation from $N\alpha$, the exogenous profit from shipping a defect-free lot. The payoff function is

$$\pi(x, a_1) = -[N\alpha + N\beta]x = \omega_{21}x;$$

$$\pi(x, a_2) = -IC - \gamma Nx = \omega_{12} + \omega_{22}x.$$

The breakeven value, using (5.21b), is

$$x_b = IC/[N\alpha + N\beta - \gamma N].$$

For specificity, let $N = 100$, $\alpha = \$1$, $\beta = \$2$, $\gamma = \$0.50$, and $IC = \$15$. Then $x_b = .06$ and the optimal prior decision is to ship if $x \le .06$, and inspect and repair if $x \ge .06$. The payoff from each action as a function of x is $\pi(x, a_1) = -300x$ and $\pi(x, a_2) = -15 - 50x$.

Let $\bar{x} = .05 < x_b$, so Case 1 holds. Given perfect information that x is the actual proportion defective, the ex-post value of this message is

$$\upsilon^N(x, x) = \begin{cases} \pi(x, a_1) - \pi(x, a_1) = 0 & \text{if } x \le x_b \\ \pi(x, a_2) - \pi(x, a_1) = -15 + 250x & \text{if } x \ge x_b. \end{cases}$$

The ex-post value is an increasing function of x: the more defectives there are, the more it pays to avoid the expensive money-back guarantee.

Rewriting in terms of x_b using the idea of (5.25),

$$\upsilon^N(x, x) = [250] \max(x - .06, 0) \quad \text{if } \bar{x} \le .06.$$

The expected value of perfect information is the expectation of $\upsilon^N(x, x)$ with respect to p(x); this is

$$V_{I\uparrow}^N = [250] \int_{.06}^{1} [x - .06]\, p(x)\, dx. \tag{5.34}$$

Since the prior optimal action has been to ship without inspection, there is considerable historical data on the proportion returned by batch, which serves as the basis for assessing p(x). The standard beta distribution (4.6), $p(x) = f_\beta(x|r', n')$, has mean $\bar{x} = r'/n'$, so the choice of prior can be limited to those beta distributions with $r'/n' = .05$. As an indicator of the flexibility of this family of distributions, Raiffa and Schlaifer (1961, pages 218–219) picture a large number of potential candidates with mean $\bar{x} = .05$. Suppose $r' = 2$ and $n' = 40$ best fit the historical data.

To evaluate the integral in (5.34), Raiffa and Schlaifer (1961, Section 9.1.3) show that for any beta prior,

$$\int_{x_b}^{1} [x - x_b]\, p(x)\, dx \;=\; \bar{x}[\Gamma_\beta(x_b \mid r' + 1, n' + 1)] - x_b[\Gamma_\beta(x_b \mid r', n')], \quad (5.35)$$

where $\Gamma_\beta(x \mid r', n')$ is the right-tail cumulative density function of the beta distribution. To assess $V_{I\Gamma}^{N}$ using Pearson's tables, Raiffa and Schlaifer (1961, Section 7.3.2) show that the correct tabulated value in this case is $\Gamma_\beta(x_b \mid r', n') = I_{1-x_b}(n' - r', r')$, so,

$$\begin{aligned} V_{I\Gamma}^{N} &= [250]\{.05\,[I_{.94}(38,3)] - .06[I_{.94}(38,2)]\} \\ &= [250]\{.05[.5665] - .06[.3124]\} \;=\; \$2.395/\text{batch}. \end{aligned}$$

Let the message y_j state the number of defective components in the sample. In a sample of size n, the message space contains n + 1 messages,

$$\mathbf{Y}^{n+1} = \{y_0, y_1, \cdots, y_j, \cdots, y_n\},$$

where the semantic meaning of message y_j is "j defects observed." This message space is categorical, but not direct—the statement is about the sample, not the state space.

Under these circumstances, with the sample size predetermined and the number of defectives left to chance, virtually everyone would agree that the conditional distribution $p(y \mid x)$ is binomial with parameters x and n:

$$p(y_j \mid x) \;=\; f_{bi}(y_j \mid x, n) \;=\; \frac{n!}{y_j!\,[n - y_j]!}\, x^{y_j}\, [1 - x]^{n - y_j}. \quad (5.36)$$

This conditional distribution is a natural conjugate to the beta prior, and Raiffa and Schlaifer (1961, Section 9.1.3) show the posterior distribution is beta

$$p(x \mid y_j) \;=\; f_\beta(x \mid r' + y_j, n' + n),$$

yielding the posterior mean, conditional on the message y_j, as simply

$$\bar{x}_{y_j} \;=\; [r' + y_j]/[n' + n].$$

In general, with this information structure the conditional value of the message y_j becomes, using (5.31) and the preceding conditional mean,

$$V_{y_j}^{N} \;=\; [\omega_{22} - \omega_{21}]\, \max([r' + y_j]/[n' + n] - x_b, 0). \quad (5.37)$$

From (5.37) the DM can determine the sample sizes that would result in useless information, the situation in which no potential message could have any value. The information structure would be useless if $[r' + y_j]/[n' + n] \leq x_b$ for all $y_j \leq n$. For this to hold it must hold for $y_j = n$. In other words, if in a sample of size n all observations are a success, yet $\bar{x}_y < x_b$, then no message can change the prior optimal action and the source (experiment) is useless. If $[r' + y_j]/[n' + n] \leq x_b$, then all sample sizes $n \leq [x_b n' - r']/[1 - x_b]$ are useless. In this example the condition calculates to $n \leq .426$, so even $n = 1$ could have value, due to the low prior probability of success and the low breakeven value.

The message space $\mathbf{Y}^{n+1}$ is countable and the marginal distribution of the messages is discrete. Pratt, Raiffa, and Schlaifer (1995, Section 14.4.2) show p(y) has the hyperbinomial distribution

$$p(y_j) = f_{hb}(y_j \mid r', n', n) = \frac{[y_j + r' - 1]!\,[n + n' - y_j - r' - 1]!\, n!\,[n' - 1]!}{y_j!\,[n - y_j]!\,[r' - 1]!\,[n' - r' - 1]!\,[n + n' - 1]!},$$

$$\text{for } n \geq y_j;\ n' > r' > 0;\ y_j = 0, 1, \cdots;\ \text{and } n = 1, 2, \cdots. \quad (5.38)$$

This distribution, also called the beta-binomial by Raiffa and Schlaifer (1961, Section 7.11), is not very convenient and is best handled on a computer spreadsheet. Because $p(y_j)$ is a discrete distribution and $\bar{x}_{y_j}$ is linear in y_j, it is simplest to evaluate V_I^N by directly taking the expectation of $V_{y_j}^N$ with respect to $p(y_j)$, rather than transforming to $p(\bar{x}_y)$.

Given a sample of size n, partition the message space $\mathbf{Y}^{n+1}$ by identifying the message y* such that if $y_j < y^*$, $V_{y_j}^N = 0$, and if $y_j > y^*$, $V_{y_j}^N > 0$. This is defined by the condition $[r' + y^*]/[n' + n] \geq x_b$, or $y^* \geq x_b[n' + n] - r'$.

Using the marginal $p(y_j)$, the expected value of information is

$$V_{I(n)}^N = [\omega_{22} - \omega_{21}]\ \Sigma_{y_j > y^*} \{[r' + y_j]/[n' + n] - x_b\}\ p(y_j).$$

In the example, with $p(y_j) = f_{hb}(y_j \mid r', n', n) = f_{hb}(y_j \mid 2, 40, n)$, $y^* = .06[40 + n] - 2 = .40 + .06n$. The value of information, as a function of n, is

$$V_{I(n)}^N = [250]\ \Sigma_{y_j > y^*} \{[2 + y_j]/[40 + n] - .06\}\ f_{hb}(y_j \mid 2, 40, n).$$

Information value is nondecreasing in n; the sample size summarizes the informativeness of the information structure. For n = 10, y* = 1, so assessment using the marginal distribution $f_{hb}(y_j \mid 2, 40, 10)$ yields

$$V_{I(10)}^N = [250]\ \Sigma_{y_j > 1}\ [.02y_j - .02]\ f_{hb}(y_j \mid 2, 40, 10) = \$0.65. \ \blacklozenge$$

In a problem similar to Example 5.2, Gaba and Winkler (1995) study the impact on the value of sampling information when the inspection procedure might misclassify any component as good or defective. The error probabilities may themselves have to be viewed as random variables and, not surprisingly, this garbling of the messages lowers $V_{I(n)}^N$.

5.2.3 Application in a Dichotomy

For decision problems with dichotomous state space, $\mathbf{X} = \{x_1, x_2\}$, the techniques of Section 5.2.1 apply if there is a suitable redefinition of the state variable. To illustrate the idea with a minimum of notational burden, consider a two-action, two-state problem with the following payoff matrix.

$$\begin{bmatrix} \pi(x_1,a_1) & \pi(x_2,a_1) \\ \pi(x_1,a_2) & \pi(x_2,a_2) \end{bmatrix} = \begin{bmatrix} 1 & 0 \\ 0 & \gamma \end{bmatrix}.$$

Under the prior beliefs about X, suppose the prior optimal action is a_2, implying that $[1]p(x_1) \leq [\gamma]p(x_2)$ or $[1 + \gamma]^{-1} \leq p(x_2)$, since $p(x_1) = 1 - p(x_2)$. The analogous case, with $[1 + \gamma]^{-1} \geq p(x_2)$ so that $a_0^N = a_1$, is symmetric with the following analysis.

Consider now a source with an arbitrary and unspecified information structure. Upon the processing of the message y, the expected payoff from each action, $E_{x|y}\, \pi(x, a_1) = 1 - p(x_2|y)$ and $E_{x|y}\, \pi(x, a_2) = \gamma p(x_2|y)$, are both linear in the conditional probability $p(x_2|y)$. Without specification of the information structure, this is a random variable ex-ante, because the DM does not know which y will be received and what its statistical information would be. The approach is to reframe the problem with a new state variable $z = p(x_2|y)$, a random variable ranging from 0 to 1, stating the posterior probability of x_2 that will result at the end of the day from incorporating this source into the original problem. The payoff function in this recast problem,

$$\pi^{\#}(z, a_1) = \omega_{11} + \omega_{21}z;$$

$$\pi^{\#}(z, a_2) = \omega_{12} + \omega_{22}z,$$

with $\omega_{11} = 1$, $\omega_{21} = -1$, $\omega_{12} = 0$, and $\omega_{22} = \gamma$, is of the form studied by Raiffa and Schlaifer. There is a breakeven probability z_b defined by $\pi^{\#}(z_b, a_1) = \pi^{\#}(z_b, a_2)$, such that if the ultimate $p(x_2|y) \leq z_b$, the optimal action changes to $a_y^N = a_1$; otherwise it remains at the prior optimal choice a_2. Here, $z_b = [1 + \gamma]^{-1}$, and the conditional value of the "message" z is, analogous to Case 2, equation (5.32) under the assumption $p(x_2) \geq [1 + \gamma]^{-1} = z_b$,

$$V_z^N = [\omega_{22} - \omega_{21}] \max(z_b - z, 0) = [1 + \gamma] \max(z_b - z, 0).$$

The idea is for the DM to provide as foreknowledge a probability distribution for Z, p(z), a prior distribution for the posterior probability of x_2. Given this input, the expected value of the information source is

$$V_I^N = [\omega_{22} - \omega_{21}] \int_0^{z_b} [\, z_b - z]\, p(z)\, dz$$

$$= [1 + \gamma] \int_0^{z_b} \{[1 + \gamma]^{-1} - z\} \, p(z) \, dz. \qquad (5.39)$$

The distribution p(z) is the only input asked of the DM; there is no other assessment of the information structure $\mathbf{I} = \{\mathbf{Y}, p(x, y)\}$.

As usual, the DM can always assess the value of perfect information using only the prior p(x). In terms of the variable Z, perfect information is the knowledge that either $z = 1$ or $z = 0$. Prior to the incorporation of information, $\text{Prob}[z = 1] = p(x_2)$ and $\text{Prob}[z = 0] = 1 - p(x_2)$. The expected value of the perfect source, using the discrete version of (5.28), is

$$V_{I\uparrow}^{N} = [1 + \gamma]\{[1 + \gamma]^{-1} - 0\}[1 - p(x_2)] = 1 - p(x_2),$$

the same value that standard techniques assess.

More generally, the DM's task is to express her beliefs about p(z) when the posterior probability could be between zero and one, that is, to assess the extent to which the distribution p(z) "falls away" from its extreme values. As a random variable ranging from zero to one, inclusive, the standard beta distribution (4.6) is a tractable and flexible model for p(z). The choice of specific p(z) requires a holistic approach, but there are heuristics the DM can apply to assist in the assessment.

First, from (2.14b), the mean of the assessed p(z) must be

$$\bar{z} = \int_Y p(x_2 | y) \, p(y) \, dy = \int_Y p(x_2, y) \, dy = p(x_2),$$

so the DM can limit consideration to those p(z) for which $\bar{z} = p(x_2)$. For the standard beta distribution, this constrains the choice of parameters along the line $r'/n' = p(x_2)$.

Next, given the prior optimal action, it is apparent from (5.39) that the only portion of p(z) that is relevant to the value of information is the segment of the domain of p(z) associated with the choice of a different action. That is, the entire distribution of p(z) is not required, only the portion associated with posterior probabilities that would lead to a change from the prior decision. Given the assumption that $p(x_2) = \bar{z} \geq z_b = [1 + \gamma]^{-1}$, the expected value of information depends only on the payoff function and the distribution of p(z) between 0 and z_b. This suggests the following heuristic for the DM to use in assessing p(z): the probability she will change her mind as a result of incorporating the information. The proposed heuristic is to fix the quantity

$$\mathfrak{Z} = \int_0^{z_b} p(z) \, dz.$$

The heuristic in and of itself is not sufficient to determine information value; it merely puts further constraints on the choice of parameters r′ and n′. The value depends on how the cumulative probability $\mathfrak{Z}$ is distributed within the range 0 to

z_b. This in turn depends upon the DM's assessment of the perceived accuracy of the source: the more definitive the message the greater the chance Z will be near zero and the greater the expected value of information. This is the stage at which the DM assesses the informativeness of the source.

Once r′ and n′ are chosen, the integral (5.39) can be calculated using Pearson's (1968) tables. Raiffa and Schlaifer (1961, Section 9.1.3) show that

$$\int_0^{z_b} [z_b - z]\, f_\beta(z \mid r', n')\, dz \;=\; z_b[F_\beta(z_b \mid r', n')] - \;\bar{z}\,[F_\beta(z_b \mid r' + 1, n' + 1)], \quad (5.40)$$

where $F_\beta(z_b \mid r', n') = \mathfrak{I}$ is the left-tail cumulative distribution function for $p(z) = f_\beta(z \mid r', n')$.

Lawrence (1987) presents a numerical example and compares this technique with the standard approach. The primary practical problem is that it does not generalize well beyond the dichotomy.

5.2.4 The Inventory Problem

In a typical inventory problem, the DM must determine the quantity of a commodity to stock in the face of a random demand for the product. Here the state space and the action space measure the same nonnegative quantity; the state x is the amount of the product sold, and the action a is the amount stocked. The problem in all its generality can be complex, but in its simplest form it can be framed as a problem with an outcome function linear in both the state and the action variables. The following illustration, involving the stocking of a perishable commodity, is sometimes called the *newsboy problem.*

T-shirts commemorating a big athletic victory cost β to make and sell for γ each. The fans being fickle, the commodity is in demand for a short period only; a random total of $x \geq 0$ will be sold quickly, and none thereafter. The decision variable a is the number of shirts to print up. The profit function is $\pi(x, a) = \gamma x - \beta a$, but in this situation it is easier to frame the problem in terms of the loss function. If $x < a$, $a - x$ shirts are unsold and destroyed; the DM has lost $\beta[a - x]$. If $x > a$, the DM has an opportunity loss, having foregone profit of $[\gamma - \beta][x - a]$. The loss function is piecewise linear in x:

$$\mathbf{L}(x, a) = [\gamma - \beta][x - a] \qquad \text{if } x > a;$$

$$\mathbf{L}(x, a) = \beta[a - x] \qquad \text{if } x < a.$$

Under the prior density function p(x), the expected loss from a is

$$E_x\,\mathbf{L}(x, a) = \int_{-\infty}^{a} \beta[a - x]\,p(x)\,dx + \int_{a}^{\infty} [\gamma - \beta][x - a]\,p(x)\,dx$$

$$= \gamma \int_{a}^{\infty} [x - a]\,p(x)\,dx - \beta[\bar{x} - a]. \quad (5.41)$$

Differentiating with respect to a characterizes the optimal prior action as the solution to

$$\int_{a_0^N}^{\infty} p(x)\,dx = 1 - F_*(a_0^N \mid \bullet) = \beta/\gamma,$$

that is, stock to a fractile of the cumulative distribution function that depends upon the cost and price per unit. Figure 5.3 depicts this situation. Substituting this solution into (5.41) gives the expected loss of the prior decision as

$$E_x\, \mathbf{L}(x, a_0^N) = \gamma \int_{a_0^N}^{\infty} [x - a_0^N]\, p(x)\, dx - \beta[\bar{x} - a_0^N] = \gamma \bar{x}^{(r)}(a_0^N) - \beta \bar{x}, \quad (5.42)$$

where $\bar{x}^{(r)}(a_0^N)$ is the partial expectation of X evaluated at a_0^N, as defined in (2.29a).

Likewise, having observed the signal y, a point forecast of the realization of X, the DM stocks the a_y^N that solves

$$\int_{a_y^N}^{\infty} p(x \mid y)\, dx = 1 - F_*(a_y^N \mid \bullet) = \beta/\gamma,$$

which yields the expected loss

$$E_{x\mid y}\, \mathbf{L}(x, a_y^N) = \gamma \bar{x}_y^{(r)}(a_y^N) - \beta \bar{x}_y. \quad (5.43)$$

The preposterior expected loss is the expectation of (5.43) with respect to the marginal p(y):

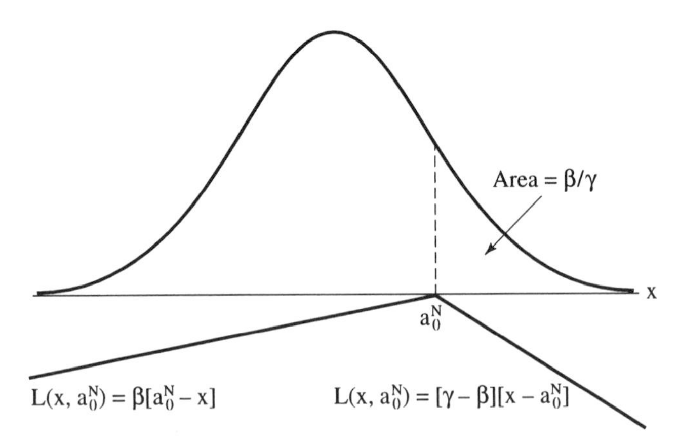

Figure 5.3. Above the horizontal axis is the probability density for X; below the axis is the DM's realized loss from the decision a_0^N, should the state x occur. Whatever the DM's current knowledge of X, she chooses the optimal action such that the probability of a greater value is β/γ.

$$E_y\, E_{x\,|\,y}\, \mathbf{L}(x,\ a_y^N) = \int_{-\infty}^{\infty} [\gamma\, \overline{x}_y^{(r)}(a_y^N) - \beta\, \overline{x}_y]\, p(y)\, dy$$

$$= \int_{-\infty}^{\infty} [\gamma\, \overline{x}_y^{(r)}(a_y^N)]\, p(y)\, dy - \beta\, \overline{x}, \qquad (5.44)$$

using the law of iterated expectation. Since the incorporation of information reduces losses, the expected value of information is the difference between (5.42) and (5.44):

$$V_I^N = E_x\, \mathbf{L}(x,\ a_0^N) - E_y\, E_{x\,|\,y}\, \mathbf{L}(x,\ a_y^N). \qquad (5.45)$$

When X is normally distributed, these calculations are tractable. When X is standard normal, $p(x) \sim \mathbf{N}^*(0, 1)$, so that

$$p(x) = f_{N^*}(x\,|\,0, 1) = \frac{1}{\sqrt{2\pi}} \exp\{-\tfrac{1}{2}x^2\};$$

the optimal action a_0^N is characterized by

$$1 - F_{N^*}(a_0^N\,|\,0, 1) = \beta/\gamma. \qquad (5.46)$$

The partial expectation $\overline{x}^{(r)}(a_0^N)$, required in (5.42), evaluates to [see Raiffa and Schlaifer (1961), Section 7.8.1]

$$\overline{x}^{(r)}(a_0^N) = f_{N^*}(a_0^N\,|\,0, 1),$$

and with $\overline{x} = 0$, the prior expected loss is

$$E_x\, \mathbf{L}(x,\ a_0^N) = \gamma\, f_{N^*}(a_0^N\,|\,0, 1). \qquad (5.47)$$

For example, when $\beta = \$0.33$ and $\gamma = \$1.00$, a table of the cumulative distribution function of the standard normal shows $a_0^N = .44$; the ordinate of the density function at a_0^N gives $E_x\, \mathbf{L}(x,\ a_0^N) = .3621$.

Turning now to the information analysis, suppose the joint density p(x, y) is bivariate normal with correlation parameter ρ. The conditional density $p(x\,|\,y) \sim \mathbf{N}(\overline{x}_y, \sigma_{x|y}^2) \sim \mathbf{N}(\rho y, 1 - \rho^2)$. The optimal decision rule a_y^N is characterized by

$$\int_{a_y^N}^{\infty} p(x\,|\,y)\, dx = 1 - F_N(a_y^N) = \beta/\gamma.$$

Transforming X evaluated at a_y^N to the standard normal variate $z = [a_y^N - \rho y]/\sigma_{x|y}$, the characterization becomes

$$1 - F_{N^*}(z\,|\,0, 1) = \beta/\gamma;$$

this is identical to (5.46) with $z = a_0^N$. Hence, $a_0^N = [a_y^N - \rho y]/\sigma_{x|y}$, meaning $a_y^N = a_0^N\, \sigma_{x|y} + \rho y$.

The partial expectation required in (5.44) is, from Section 7.8.2 of Raiffa and Schlaifer (1961),

$$\bar{x}_y^{(r)}(a_y^N) = \rho y[1 - F_{N*}(u)] + \sigma_{x|y} f_{N*}(u|0, 1),$$

where $u = [a_y^N - \rho y]/\sigma_{x|y}$. But since $u = a_0^N$ by the previous argument,

$$\bar{x}_y^{(r)}(a_y^N) = \rho y[1 - F_{N*}(a_0^N)] + \sigma_{x|y} f_{N*}(a_0^N|0, 1).$$

By the first-order condition (5.46), $1 - F_{N*}(a_0^N) = \beta/\gamma$, yielding

$$\bar{x}_y^{(r)}(a_y^N) = \rho y\beta/\gamma + \sigma_{x|y} f_{N*}(a_0^N|0, 1).$$

Finally, the conditional expected loss (5.43) becomes

$$E_{x|y}\,\mathbf{L}(x, a_y^N) = \gamma\{\rho y\beta/\gamma + \sigma_{x|y} f_{N*}(a_0^N|0, 1)\} - \beta\rho y$$

$$= \sigma_{x|y}\gamma f_{N*}(a_0^N|0, 1) = \sigma_{x|y} E_x\,\mathbf{L}(x, a_0^N),$$

using (5.47). This quantity does not depend upon the specific y, so the preposterior expectation is

$$E_y\,E_{x|y}\,\mathbf{L}(x, a_y^N) = \sigma_{x|y} E_x\,\mathbf{L}(x, a_0^N),$$

and the expected value of information as in (5.45) is

$$V_I^N = E_x\,\mathbf{L}(x, a_0^N) - \sigma_{x|y} E_x\,\mathbf{L}(x, a_0^N)$$

$$= [1 - \sigma_{x|y}]\,E_x\,\mathbf{L}(x, a_0^N),$$

where $\sigma_{x|y} = \sqrt{1 - \rho^2}$.

Similar to the analysis in Section 5.1.2, ρ indexes the value of information in this bivariate normal model. The prior expected loss, $E_x\,\mathbf{L}(x, a_0^N)$, is the value of perfect information, occurring when $\rho = 1$. Null information, $\rho = 0$, has no value, and there is no range of useless information in this problem.

5.3 Models with Concave-Exponential Utility

The previous two sections analyze information valuation in risk neutral situations. If aversion towards risk is a major consideration in the framing of the problem, the analytics generally become more difficult. There are, however, a few important special cases under which tractability can be retained. This section considers the most convenient risk averse functional form, the concave-exponential utility function.

5.3.1 Information Value with Separable Outcome

Consider a DM with the risk averse concave-exponential utility function

$$u(W) = -\exp[-bW]. \tag{5.48}$$

As Section 7.1.3 shows, the parameter $b > 0$ is an index of the DM's risk aversion—the larger is b, the more averse towards risk is the DM. In a decision problem with additively separable outcome as in (2.2), the value of the prior decision is

$$\begin{aligned} \mathbf{U}(\mathbf{D}^* \mid \mathbf{I}\!\downarrow) &= \max_a E_x\, u(w + \pi(x, a)) \\ &= \max_a E_x \{-\exp[-b[w + \pi(x, a)]]\} \\ &= \{\exp[-bw]\}\{\max_a E_x\{-\exp[-b\pi(x, a)]\}\}. \end{aligned} \tag{5.49}$$

Note that the prior optimal choice of action is independent of initial wealth. The reservation price of the prior decision, defined in equation (3.1) as the solution to

$$u(R_0^A) = \mathbf{U}(\mathbf{D}^* \mid \mathbf{I}\!\downarrow),$$

is explicitly in this case, by combining (5.48) with (5.49) and taking logarithms,

$$-\exp[-b\, R_0^A] = \{\exp[-bw]\}\{\max_a E_x\{-\exp[-b\pi(x, a)]\}\};$$

$$R_0^A = w - b^{-1}\log[-\max_a E_x\{-\exp[-b\pi(x, a)]\}]. \tag{5.50}$$

Given now an information structure **I**, conditional on each message,

$$\begin{aligned} \mathbf{U}(\mathbf{D}^* \mid \mathbf{I}, y) &= \max_a E_{x\mid y}\, u(w + \pi(x, a)) \\ &= \{\exp[-bw]\}\{\max_a E_{x\mid y}\{-\exp[-b\pi(x, a)]\}\}, \end{aligned}$$

and the value of the informed decision is

$$\begin{aligned} \mathbf{U}(\mathbf{D}^* \mid \mathbf{I}) &= E_y \max_a E_{x\mid y}\, u(w + \pi(x, a)) \\ &= \{\exp[-bw]\}\{E_y \max_a E_{x\mid y}\{-\exp[-b\pi(x, a)]\}\}. \end{aligned} \tag{5.51}$$

The reservation price R_I^A, defined in (3.41), solves

$$-\exp[-b\, R_I^A] = \{\exp[-bw]\}\{E_y \max_a E_{x\mid y}\{-\exp[-b\pi(x, a)]\}\},$$

which is

$$R_I^A = w - b^{-1}\log[-E_y \max_a E_{x\mid y}\{-\exp[-b\pi(x, a)]\}]. \tag{5.52}$$

The calculation of the value of information uses the characterization given by (3.49); setting $\mathbf{U}(\mathbf{D}^* \mid \mathbf{I},\ V_I^A) = \mathbf{U}(\mathbf{D}^* \mid \mathbf{I}\!\downarrow)$ gives, using (5.49) and the costly version of (5.51),

$$\{\exp[-b[w - V_I^A]]\}\{E_y \max_a E_{x\mid y}\{-\exp[-b\pi(x, a)]\}\}$$

$$= \{\exp[-bw]\}\{\max_a E_x\{-\exp[-b\pi(x, a)]\}\}.$$

Multiplying both sides by −1, this solves to

$$V_I^A = -b^{-1}\log[-E_y \max_a E_{x|y}\{-\exp[-b\pi(x, a)]\}]$$

$$+ b^{-1}\log[-\max_a E_x\{-\exp[-b\pi(x, a)]\}]. \quad (5.53)$$

Hence, comparing (5.53) with (5.52) and (5.50),

$$V_I^A = R_I^A - R_0^A. \quad (5.54)$$

Just as in the risk neutral case described by equation (3.52), under the concave-exponential utility function with separable outcome, the value of information is simply the difference between the reservation price using the informed decision and the reservation price of the prior decision.

5.3.2 Applications with the Bivariate Normal Information Structure

When X is normally distributed, the following fact is useful for evaluating the expected utility of the risk averse DM having the concave-exponential utility function. When $p(x) \sim \mathbf{N}(\bar{x}, \sigma_x^2)$,

$$E_x \exp\{\kappa + cx + ex^2\}$$

$$= [1 - 2e\sigma_x^2]^{-\frac{1}{2}} \exp\{[1 - 2e\sigma_x^2]^{-1}[\kappa + c\bar{x} + \tfrac{1}{2}c^2\sigma_x^2 + e\bar{x}^2 - 2\kappa e\sigma_x^2]\}. \quad (5.55)$$

This follows after rearrangement, completion of the square, and straightforward but tedious algebraic evaluation of the integral

$$\int_{-\infty}^{\infty} \frac{1}{\sigma_x\sqrt{2\pi}} \exp\{\kappa + cx + ex^2\}\exp\left\{-\frac{1}{2\sigma_x^2}[x - \bar{x}]^2\right\}dx.$$

This fact, although stated previously for the prior distribution p(x), is general and also holds for the normally distributed posterior density $p(x\,|\,y)$, and the normally distributed preposterior mean $p(\bar{x}_y)$ as in (4.25).

Consider a decision problem with an outcome function having one of the following forms, linear in the state variable x.

$$W = w + \pi(x, a_k) = w + \omega_{1k} + \omega_{2k}x \text{ for all } a_k \in \mathbf{a}^K;$$

$$W = w + \pi(x, a) = w + \omega_1 + \omega_2 x + \omega_3 a + \omega_4 xa \text{ for } a \in \mathbf{R}. \quad (5.56)$$

Working with the second specification, note that the outcome function is certainly unbounded and the optimal action under risk neutrality is either plus or minus infinity. It is convenient, and there is no loss of generality, to choose the monetary unit so that $w_4 = 1$.

Substituting the outcome function (5.56) into the utility function (5.48) and rearranging to put it in the form (5.55) gives

$$u(W) = -\exp\{-bw - b\omega_1 - b\omega_3 a + [-b\omega_2 - ba]x\} = -\exp\{\kappa + cx\}.$$

Using (5.55) the expected utility with respect to the normally distributed random variable X is

$$\mathbf{U}(\mathbf{D} \mid \mathbf{I}\downarrow, a)$$
$$= -\exp\{-bw - b\omega_1 - b\omega_3 a - b\omega_2 \overline{x} - ba\overline{x} + [b^2 \sigma_x^2 [\omega_2 + a]^2/2]\}. \quad (5.57)$$

The optimal action is characterized by

$$\frac{d\mathbf{U}(\mathbf{D} \mid \mathbf{I}\downarrow, a)}{da} = \mathbf{U}(\mathbf{D} \mid \mathbf{I}\downarrow, a)\,[-b\omega_3 - b\overline{x} + b^2\sigma_x^2[\omega_2 + a]] = 0,$$

which solves to

$$a_0^A = [\omega_3 + \overline{x} - b\omega_2\sigma_x^2]/b\sigma_x^2.$$

Substituting the optimal action into (5.57) and solving gives the value of the prior decision as

$$\mathbf{U}(\mathbf{D}^* \mid \mathbf{I}\downarrow) = -\exp\{-bw - b\omega_1 + b\omega_3\omega_2 - [[\omega_3 + \overline{x}]^2/2\sigma_x^2]\}. \quad (5.58)$$

Turning now to the informed decision, suppose the DM has received the message y. The posterior distribution is normally distributed with mean $\overline{x}_y$ and variance $\sigma_{x|y}^2 = \sigma_x^2[1 - \rho^2]$; analogous to (5.57), the conditional expected utility

$$\mathbf{U}(\mathbf{D} \mid \mathbf{I}, y, a) = -\exp\{-bw - b\omega_1 - b\omega_3 a - b\omega_2 \overline{x}_y - ba\overline{x}_y$$
$$+ [b^2\sigma_x^2[1 - \rho^2][\omega_2 + a]^2/2]\}, \quad (5.59)$$

is maximized at

$$a_y^A = [\omega_3 + \overline{x}_y - b\omega_2\sigma_x^2[1 - \rho^2]]/b\sigma_x^2[1 - \rho^2].$$

Substituting this into (5.59) and rearranging to put the equation in the same form as (5.55) results in

$$\mathbf{U}(\mathbf{D}^* \mid \mathbf{I}, y) = -\exp\{-bw - b\omega_1 + b\omega_3\omega_2 - \omega_3^2[2\sigma_x^2[1 - \rho^2]]^{-1}$$
$$- \omega_3[\sigma_x^2[1 - \rho^2]]^{-1}\,\overline{x}_y - [2\sigma_x^2[1 - \rho^2]]^{-1}\,\overline{x}_y^2\}$$
$$= -\exp\{\kappa + c\overline{x}_y + e\overline{x}_y^2\}. \quad (5.60)$$

The value of the informed decision is the expectation of (5.60) with respect to the marginal p(y). Here, just as in Section 5.2.1, the message y enters only via the posterior mean $\bar{x}_y$. Hence, the value of the informed decision is most conveniently calculated by taking the expectation of (5.60) with respect to $p(\bar{x}_y)$, a normally distributed variable given by (4.25), with mean $\bar{x}$ and variance $\sigma^2_{\bar{x}_y} = \sigma^2_x \rho^2$:

$$\mathbf{U(D^*\,|\,I)} = E_{\bar{x}_y} \mathbf{U(D^*\,|\,I}, y) = E_{\bar{x}_y} -\exp\{\kappa + c\bar{x}_y + e\bar{x}_y^2\}$$

$$= \left[1 - 2e\sigma^2_{\bar{x}_y}\right]^{-\frac{1}{2}} \left\{-\exp\left\{\left[1 - 2e\sigma^2_{\bar{x}_y}\right]^{-1}\left[\kappa + c\bar{x} + \tfrac{1}{2}c^2\sigma^2_{\bar{x}_y} + e\bar{x}^2 - 2\kappa e\sigma^2_{\bar{x}_y}\right]\right\}\right\}$$

$$= \left[1 - \rho^2\right]^{-\frac{1}{2}} \left\{-\exp\{-bw - b\omega_1 + b\omega_3\omega_2 - [[\omega_3 + \bar{x}]^2/2\sigma^2_x]\}\right\}. \tag{5.61}$$

The third equality in (5.61) comes from the expectation of (5.60) using the result (5.55); the fourth equality derives algebraically from replacing the quantities κ, c, and e with their counterparts in terms of the original parameters.

Translating (5.58) and (5.61) to their respective reservation prices and then applying (5.54), the value of information in this risk averse case is

$$V_I^A = -[2b]^{-1} \log[1 - \rho^2]. \tag{5.62}$$

This quite simple result states that the value of information depends only upon the statistical informativeness of the information structure (as measured by ρ) and the DM's risk aversion parameter b; information value does not depend in any way on the parameters of the outcome function. Perfect information is infinitely valuable!

These conclusions are primarily a consequence of the unboundedness of the outcome function. If information were perfect, the DM would always "totally plunge," setting a equal to either plus or minus infinity [depending on the signs of the parameters in (5.56)]. Conservatism, in the sense of the choice of an action that is finite, results because of the risk aversion and, in the informed decision, because of imperfection in the information structure. From the decision rules a_0^A and a_y^A, the more risk averse the DM (i.e., the greater is b), and the more imperfect the information, the closer the optimal decision is to zero. The other determinants of the terminal wealth cancel out in the equation (5.62) defining the value of information.

Ho and Michaely (1988) analyze a financial problem with the outcome function given by (5.56). In this model an investor can hold cash with zero return or invest in a common stock with current price per share s; the future unknown share price is x and the action a is the number of shares bought (a > 0) or sold (a < 0) at the current price. Stochastic terminal wealth is

$$W = w - as + ax.$$

This is a special case of (5.56), with $\omega_1 = \omega_2 = 0$, $\omega_3 = -s$, and $\omega_4 = 1$. The value of information about the share price is given by (5.62).

There are several practical constraints that limit the applicability of this model. Since the total number of outstanding shares must be finite, perfect information cannot be allowed to occur because then the DM would want to borrow an infinite amount of money or an infinite number of shares (at no cost!) to take an infinite long or short position in the stock. Ho and Michaely deal with this by assuming perfect information is infinitely costly. Furthermore, the actual number of shares the investor could buy or short without affecting the market price is likely to be considerably less than the number of outstanding shares. Such constraints considerably complicate the information analysis of the investor's problem.

5.4 Models with Nonseparable Outcome; Betting and Investing Models

This section studies the value of information in financial-type problems involving the direct application of initial wealth, a framing that generally makes the outcome function nonseparable between wealth and payoff. It turns out that the logarithmic utility function provides the most tractable mechanism for incorporating risk aversion into the information valuation of investors and gamblers.

5.4.1 Nonseparability and Information Value: Two Examples

As Example 3.1b in Section 3.1.4 indicates, care must be taken in problem framings having an outcome function that is not separable, even when the DM is risk neutral. This subsection presents two illustrative examples. Both continue in Chapter 8 when they are applied to the problem of choosing the optimal information structure.

♦ *Example 5.4a Fed Watching and Investing*

The profitability of traders in the financial markets is affected by movements in interest rates, which in turn are highly dependent on policy changes by the Federal Reserve. The importance of foreknowledge about monetary policy has led to the establishment of literally scores of information sources, each engaging in "Fed watching," that is, the technique of studying in detail each reported statistic and utterance by a Board member, with the intention of gleaning signals about future policy intentions. The recent change in Fed procedures to announce policy decisions publicly does little to solve the basic problem: predicting what the Fed will do before they do it. This section models the factors affecting the choice of a Fed watching service in the context of a decision problem faced often by traders. Trading profits are certainly not the only source of value from the Fed revealing its intentions; see Friedman (1979).

An investor with a one-period planning horizon is deciding between purchasing a Treasury Bill that matures at the end of the horizon and a longer term Treasury Bond that would have to be sold at the end of the horizon at an unknown future price. If k is the risk-free interest rate, [1+k] is the risk-free terminal wealth per dollar invested in the bill. The terminal wealth per dollar invested in the bond is a random variable, a function of any Federal Reserve policy changes between now and the end of the holding period. Let the states be x_1: Fed tightens monetary policy, and x_2: Fed loosens monetary policy. If the Fed tightens, the return per dollar invested in the bond is $z_1[1+k]$; if the Fed loosens it is $z_2[1+k]$, where z_1 and z_2 are parameters such that $z_1 \leq 1 \leq z_2$. Given the prior probabilities $p(x_1)$ and $p(x_2)$, assume the equilibrium situation that the risky asset has higher prior expected payoff per dollar of invested wealth:

$$\bar{z}[1+k] = p(x_1)z_1[1+k] + p(x_2)z_2[1+k] > [1+k]. \tag{5.63}$$

The economics of (5.63) makes the quantity $\bar{z} = p(x_1)z_1 + p(x_2)z_2 > 1$.

The action is a, the fraction of wealth placed in the bill (asset 1). Given initial wealth w, the outcome function is

$$\omega(w, x_1, a) = aw[1+k] + [1-a]wz_1[1+k] = w[1+k][a + [1-a]z_1];$$

$$\omega(w, x_2, a) = aw[1+k] + [1-a]wz_2[1+k] = w[1+k][a + [1-a]z_2],$$

where $\mathbf{a} = \{a: 0 \leq a \leq 1\}$. Under risk neutrality, the expected utility of a prior decision a is, using the summarizing quantity $\bar{z}$,

$$E_x\, \omega(w, x, a) = w[1+k][a + [1-a]\bar{z}].$$

Under risk neutrality the optimal action is a corner solution; since $\bar{z} > 1$, the optimal prior action is to put all initial wealth in the risky asset. Hence, $a_0^N = 0$ and

$$\mathbf{U}(\mathbf{D}^* \,|\, \mathbf{I}\downarrow) = \max_a E_x\, \omega(w, x, a) = w[1+k]\bar{z}. \tag{5.64}$$

To illustrate a specific situation, suppose $p(x_1) = .25$, $p(x_2) = .75$, $z_1 = .8$, $z_2 = 1.2$, $w = \$100$, and $k = .08$. Then $\bar{z} = 1.10$ and $\mathbf{U}(\mathbf{D}^* \,|\, \mathbf{I}\downarrow) = \$118.80$.

The value of information is the cost ψ that equates the expected utility with and without the use of the information structure. Let ψ be the cost of information, subtracted from initial wealth prior to the receipt of any message. Under risk neutrality, the expected terminal wealth from taking action a is

$$\omega(w-\psi, x_1, a) = [w-\psi][1+k][a + [1-a]z_1];$$

$$\omega(w-\psi, x_2, a) = [w-\psi][1+k][a + [1-a]z_2].$$

Under the perfect information structure $I\uparrow$, there are two messages, both undoubtedly correct: y_1: "the Fed will tighten," and y_2: "the Fed will loosen." Hearing message y_1 and knowing x_1 will occur, the optimal action is to put everything left into the bill: $a^N_{y_1} = a^N_{x_1} = 1$, and

$$\omega(w - \psi, x_1, a^N_{x_1}) = [w - \psi][1 + k].$$

Likewise, $a^N_{y_2} = a^N_{x_2} = 0$ and

$$\omega(w - \psi, x_2, a^N_{x_2}) = [w - \psi][1 + k]z_2.$$

The expected utility from paying ψ and using the perfect information structure is

$$U(D^* \mid I\uparrow, \psi) = E_x\, \omega(w, x, a_x) = [w - \psi][1 + k][p(x_1) + p(x_2)z_2]. \quad (5.65)$$

Using (3.49), the value of perfect information is the solution for $\psi = V^N_{I\uparrow}$ in the equation

$$[w - V^N_{I\uparrow}][1 + k][p(x_1) + p(x_2)z_2] = w[1 + k]\,\bar{z}.$$

This solves to

$$V^N_{I\uparrow} = wp(x_1)[1 - z_1][p(x_1) + p(x_2)z_2]^{-1}.$$

Notice that this is an increasing function of the DM's initial wealth; the wealthier the investor, the more valuable the perfect information structure.

A slightly different information value obtains if the model is changed so that the information cost can be paid out of posterior dollars. Suppose the information source provides credit: the informant lends the cost ψ to the DM at the risk-free rate k. That is, the full amount w can be invested and the DM pays $\psi[1+k]$ at the end of the period. Here we can write

$$\omega^{\#}(w, x_1, a^N_{x_1}, \psi) = [w - \psi][1 + k];$$

$$\omega^{\#}(w, x_2, a^N_{x_2}, \psi) = [wz_2 - \psi][1 + k].$$

The value of the perfectly informed decision is

$$E_x\, \omega^{\#}(w, x, a_x, \psi) = w[1 + k][p(x_1) + p(x_2)z_2] - \psi[1 + k],$$

and the value of perfect information is the solution $\psi = \mathcal{V}^N_{I\uparrow}$ to the equation

$$w[1 + k][p(x_1) + p(x_2)z_2] - \mathcal{V}^N_{I\uparrow}[1 + k] = w[1 + k]\,\bar{z},$$

which is simply

$$\mathcal{V}^N_{I\uparrow} = wp(x_1)[1 - z_1].$$

Clearly $\mathcal{V}_{I\uparrow}^{N} \geq V_{I\uparrow}^{N}$ by an amount depending upon the parameter z_2. This granting of credit allows the DM to invest the full amount of wealth and some of that incremental wealth invested can earn a return greater than the rate k. Example 5.4a continues in Section 8.1.3. ♦

♦ *Example 5.4b A Betting Model*

The following betting model is similar in structure to Example 3.1b, the Celebrity Informant, and to the more serious model developed by Kelly (1956) and studied by J. R. Morris (1974). Given initial wealth w, a gambler can bet a proportion of her wealth on the occurrence of either state x_1 or state x_2. For example, x_1 might be the event "team 1 beats the point spread," and event x_2 "team 2 beats the point spread." Model the space of actions as $\mathbf{a} = \{a: -1 \leq a \leq 1\}$, adopting the convention that $a > 0$ is a bet on x_1, and $a < 0$ is a bet on x_2. A correct bet returns twice the amount bet; an incorrect bet returns nothing. The terminal wealth from action a in state x_i is

$$\omega(w, x_1, a) = w + aw = w[1 + a];$$

$$\omega(w, x_2, a) = w - aw = w[1 - a].$$

Suppose the gambler has the risk averse logarithmic utility function

$$u(\omega(w, x_1, a)) = \log[w[1 + a]];$$

$$u(\omega(w, x_2, a)) = \log[w[1 - a]].$$

This betting model with logarithmic utility illustrates a situation in which the value of information is directly related to J(**I**), the information transmitted or uncertainty removed defined by (2.35).

The expected utility of the prior decision

$$\mathbf{U}(\mathbf{D} \,|\, \mathbf{I}\!\downarrow, a) = p(x_1) \log\big[w[1 + a]\big] + p(x_2) \log\big[w[1 - a]\big], \qquad (5.66)$$

is maximized where

$$\frac{d\mathbf{U}(\mathbf{D} \,|\, \mathbf{I}\!\downarrow, a)}{da} = p(x_1)[1 + a]^{-1} - p(x_2)[1 - a]^{-1} = 0.$$

Solving,

$$a_0^A = 2p(x_1) - 1.$$

The optimal prior decision depends only upon the state probability. Substituting this decision into (5.66) yields the value of the prior decision as, using (2.33a),

$$\mathbf{U}(\mathbf{D}^* \,|\, \mathbf{I}\!\downarrow) = p(x_1) \log[2wp(x_1)] + p(x_2) \log[2wp(x_2)]$$

$$= \log[2w] + \Sigma_i\, p(x_i) \log[p(x_i)] \;=\; \log[2w] - H(\mathbf{I}{\downarrow}). \qquad (5.67)$$

After paying ψ for the information structure **I** and receiving the message y_j,

$$\begin{aligned} &E_{x\,|\,y_j}\, u(\omega(w - \psi, x, a)) \\ &\quad= p(x_1\,|\,y_j)\log[[w - \psi][1 + a]] + p(x_2\,|\,y_j)\log[[w - \psi][1 - a]] \\ &\quad= \log[w - \psi] + p(x_1\,|\,y_j)\log[1 + a] + p(x_2\,|\,y_j)\log[1 - a]. \end{aligned}$$

The optimal decision rule is

$$a^{A}_{y_j} \;=\; 2p(x_1\,|\,y_j) - 1;$$

note that it does not depend upon ψ. Hence,

$$\max_a E_{x\,|\,y_j}\, u(\omega(w - \psi, x, a)) \;=\; \log[2[w - \psi]] + \Sigma_i\, p(x_i\,|\,y_j) \log[p(x_i\,|\,y_j)].$$

The value of the informed decision is

$$\begin{aligned} U(\mathbf{D}^* \mid \mathbf{I}, \psi) &= \Sigma_j\, p(y_j)\{\log[2[w - \psi]] + \Sigma_i\, p(x_i\,|\,y_j) \log[p(x_i\,|\,y_j)]\} \\ &= \log[2[w - \psi]] + \Sigma_j\, p(y_j)\, \Sigma_i\, p(x_i\,|\,y_j) \log[p(x_i\,|\,y_j)] \\ &= \log[2[w - \psi]] - H(\mathbf{I}), \qquad (5.68) \end{aligned}$$

where the final equality uses the definition of equivocation in (2.34). The value of information is the solution for $\psi = V^{A}_{\mathbf{I}}$ in the equation

$$\log[2[w - V^{A}_{\mathbf{I}}]] - H(\mathbf{I}) \;=\; \log[2w] - H(\mathbf{I}{\downarrow}).$$

This solves to, using the definition (2.35),

$$V^{A}_{\mathbf{I}} \;=\; w[1 - \exp[-J(\mathbf{I})]]. \qquad (5.69)$$

Thus, the value of information in this risk-averse case depends only upon the initial wealth and the statistical information transmitted. The quantity $J(\mathbf{I})$ can serve as an index of informativeness in this problem. Information value ranges from 0 at null information when $J(\mathbf{I}) = 0$ to perfect information

$$V^{A}_{\mathbf{I}\uparrow} \;=\; w[1 - \exp[-H(\mathbf{I}{\downarrow})]].$$

Note that the wealthier the individual, the larger the bet each time, and the more valuable is the information structure. Example 5.4b continues in Section 8.1.1.♦

5.4.2 *Arrow's Contingent Securities Model*

As a generalization of the preceding model, suppose an investor has available m securities, each priced at \$1, and there are m states, $\mathbf{X}^m = \{x_1, \cdots, x_i, \cdots, x_m\}$. The payoff from security i is x_i if state i occurs, zero if it does not. The investor has w initial dollars, out of which she has the option of paying ψ for an information structure **I**. The action variable is to choose a portfolio of securities out of remaining wealth. Let a_i be the proportion of remaining wealth placed in security i. A portfolio a is

$$a = [a_1, \cdots, a_i, \cdots, a_m],$$

and the space of actions is the simplex,

$$\mathbf{a} = \{a: \Sigma_i a_i = 1\}. \tag{5.70}$$

If state i occurs, the terminal wealth of the investor will be

$$W = \omega(w - \psi, x_i, a) = a_i x_i[w - \psi].$$

If the DM has the logarithmic utility function $u(W) = \log[W]$, the expected utility from portfolio a after receiving message y_j is

$$\mathbf{U(D \mid I}, \psi, y_j, a) = \Sigma_i p(x_i \mid y_j) \log[a_i x_i[w - \psi]]. \tag{5.71}$$

The optimal portfolio maximizes (5.71) with respect to the a_i, subject to the constraint (5.70). The Lagrangian function $\mathcal{L}$ is

$$\mathcal{L} = \Sigma_i p(x_i \mid y_j) \log[a_i x_i[w - \psi]] - \lambda[\Sigma_i a_i - 1],$$

so the first-order conditions are

$$\frac{\partial \mathcal{L}}{\partial a_i} = [p(x_i \mid y_j)/ a_i] - \lambda = 0, \quad i = 1, \cdots, m;$$

$$\frac{\partial \mathcal{L}}{\partial \lambda} = \Sigma_i a_i - 1 = 0.$$

To solve, start with $p(x_i \mid y_j) = a_i \lambda$, and sum over i to obtain

$$\Sigma_i p(x_i \mid y_j) = \lambda \Sigma_i a_i,$$

meaning $\lambda = 1$. Hence, the optimal proportion is $a_i^{\wedge} = p(x_i \mid y_j)$, and the best portfolio is to hold the securities in proportions equal to their posterior probabilities:

$$a_{y_j}^{\wedge} = [p(x_1 \mid y_j), \cdots, p(x_i \mid y_j), \cdots, p(x_m \mid y_j)],$$

The expected utility of the conditional optimal decision is

$$\begin{aligned}\mathbf{U(D^* \mid I}, \psi, y_j) &= \Sigma_i p(x_i \mid y_j) \log[p(x_i \mid y_j)x_i[w - \psi]] \\ &= \log[w - \psi] + \Sigma_i p(x_i \mid y_j) \log[p(x_i \mid y_j)] + \Sigma_i p(x_i \mid y_j) \log[x_i].\end{aligned}$$

Taking the expectation with respect to p(y) and using the law of iterated expectation gives

$$\mathbf{U(D^* | I, \psi)} = \log[w - \psi] + \{\Sigma_j \, p(y_j) \, \Sigma_i \, p(x_i | y_j)\log[p(x_i | y_j)]\} + \{\Sigma_i \, p(x_i)\log[x_i]\}$$
$$= \log[w - \psi] + J(\mathbf{I}) - H(\mathbf{I}\downarrow) + \{\Sigma_i \, p(x_i)\log[x_i]\}, \quad (5.72)$$

using the definition of $J(\mathbf{I})$.

In the uninformed decision it is easy to show that

$$a_0^A = [p(x_1), \cdots, p(x_i), \cdots, p(x_m)],$$

and

$$\mathbf{U(D^* | I\downarrow)} = \log[w] - H(\mathbf{I}\downarrow) + \{\Sigma_i \, p(x_i)\log[x_i]\}. \quad (5.73)$$

Comparing (5.72) and (5.73), the value of information is again

$$V_\mathbf{I}^A = w[1 - \exp[-J(\mathbf{I})]].$$

The value increases with the DM's wealth and the information transmitted, but is independent of the x_i, the payoffs or stakes of the problem.

Applying the definition (3.53), it is easy to show that the supply value of the information is $\tilde{V}_\mathbf{I}^A = w[\exp[J(\mathbf{I})] - 1]$. Murota (1988) also considers the information value in this model when the cost is paid from posterior wealth, as in the outcome function (3.6). Nadiminti, Mukhopadhyay, and Kriebel (1996) study conditional economic value in this contingent decision model when the utility function is concave-exponential, investigating the effect that the risk aversion parameter b has on the value of information.

5.5 Models with Multicategorical State Description

This section and the next consider the value of information in model framings having multidimensional state descriptions: in this section, problems with a state description having more than one distinct category; in the next, dynamic problems in which the dimension of time enters into the state description. Recalling the discussion in Section 1.4.4, the availability of inexpensive computing power is making information value analysis in complex multidimensional problems more common. An excellent example is global warming, a decision problem involving many separate categories of random state variables evolving with consequences that stretch over the course of centuries. As Nordhaus (1994b, page 45) puts it, the extent of alternative state realizations overwhelms even the most fertile imagination. Such models can rapidly become intractable in the sense that an analytical solution describing the precise value of information in the model cannot be written down. Section 5.7 takes up the problem of approximating information value for highly complex situations; the current interest is to apply tractable models to investigate more precisely how and why these complicating factors affect the value of information.

5.5.1 *Multicategorical Information Structures*

In the simplest decision problem for which the state variable has more than one distinct category, the state space **X** is a vector containing a two-dimensional description, with each $x \in \mathbf{X}$ being an ordered pair $[\times, z]$. In general, the two categories are not statistically independent; denote the prior measure on the state as $p(\times, z)$. Should the two categories be independent, then $p(\times, z) = p(\times)p(z)$. Even with independence the DM's analysis of the option to incorporate information into the solution is complex, as the available information structures can be quite detailed and difficult to assess. The value of the informed decision is maximized by perfect information about all categories. Under *incomplete information*, the information source is capable of providing messages about only a subset of the categories. Most likely, the available sources can offer only imperfect incomplete information.

Marschak (1954), in one of the earliest studies on the economics of information value, points up the role of statistical dependence between the categories as a determinant of the comparative values of alternative information structures. He conjectures that the greater the statistical dependence between the state descriptions, as assessed in the multivariate prior on the state, the smaller the gain from learning about all categories over learning about a subset of them. For example, if my payoffs depend upon economic conditions in Paris, Lyon, and Beijing, and I can process the data from only two of the three local business newspapers, economic conditions in Paris are likely to be more highly correlated with conditions in Lyon than in Beijing. Subscribing to the papers in Paris and Beijing (and indirectly finding out about Lyon) may lead to better decisions than subscribing to Paris and Lyon, using these sources to obtain information about Beijing. Marschak and Radner (1972) build upon this conjecture.

5.5.2 *Bidding Models*

Problems involving the submission of sealed bids provide a most interesting application of a two-category state space. There are two similar types of bidding problem: (a) bidding to obtain an item of uncertain value, such as a radio frequency or oil drilling rights, and (b) bidding to obtain a contract to perform a well-defined task at uncertain cost. In both cases, the second random variable is the unknown high [Case (a)] or low [Case (b)] bid of the other participants.

The economics of this problem is quite different from the previous models, for now the realization of the random variable depends upon the deliberate decisions of an opponent, not the benign revelations of nature. When the various protagonists possess different knowledge, new decision strategies arise concerning the gathering of information and the dissemination of the resulting message. Indeed, as Akerlof (1970) shows, in such environments the possession of superior knowledge, appropriately defined, can have negative value to the DM.

Game theory is the appropriate paradigm to address such issues; see, for example, Part II of Hirshleifer and Riley (1992). Milgrom and Weber (1982) provide a straightforward analysis of information value in a game-theoretic approach to sealed-bid auctions. However, such an investigation would take us too far afield from the primarily normative motivation of quantitatively assessing the value of information to an individual DM. LaValle (1967) makes the case for applying the techniques of decision theory for prescriptive purposes in sealed-bid English auctions. Ward and Chapman (1988) consider practical issues involving the application of information in bid preparation.

Example 5.5 generalizes Howard's (1966) information analysis of a contract-bidding problem. The example illustrates the workings of the nonadditivity of pragmatic information value, a phenomenon that many case studies (see Section 1.4.4) with multiple categories exhibit: the sum of the values of perfect but incomplete information about each component may be different from the value of perfect complete information about all components.

♦ *Example 5.5 Bidding with Incomplete Information*
Consider a competitive bidding problem in which the action variable a is the DM's bid on a contract and the two unknowns are the opportunity costs of performing on the contract $\times$, and the unknown lowest bid of all competitors z. Assuming our DM wins the contract in the event of a tie for the lowest bid, the profit function is

$$\pi(\times, z, a) = \begin{cases} a - \times & \text{if } a \leq z \\ 0 & \text{if } a > z. \end{cases} \tag{5.74}$$

There are two types of circumstances that can have a negative impact upon profits: the DM wins with the lowest bid but realized costs turn out so high that the DM is worse off than if she had not won the bid, and the DM bids lower than necessary to win, thereby leaving money on the table. If the DM can obtain perfect information about costs, she can ensure no money-losing bids, but may still underbid. If she can obtain perfect information about the competitors' low bid, then she can win the contract with that identical bid, but still may lose money if costs overrun. Only with complete perfect information on both X and Z can the DM guarantee that she wins the bid only when she desires, and when she wins, she never underbids.

The initial information structure for the prior decision is the joint distribution of $\times$ and z:

$$\mathbf{I}\downarrow = \{p(\mathsf{x}, z)\}.$$

Since the contract is won only for those realizations of Z that are greater than or equal to the bid, the expected payoff from bidding a is

$$\mathbf{U}(\mathbf{D} \mid \mathbf{I}\downarrow, a) = E_{\mathsf{x},z}\, \pi(\mathsf{x}, z, a) = \int_0^\infty \int_a^\infty [a - \mathsf{x}]\, p(\mathsf{x}, z)\, dz\, d\mathsf{x}.$$

Factoring the joint distribution,

$$\begin{aligned} \mathbf{U}(\mathbf{D} \mid \mathbf{I}\downarrow, a) &= E_{\mathsf{x}}\, E_{z|\mathsf{x}}\, \pi(\mathsf{x}, z, a) \\ &= E_{\mathsf{x}} \left\{ [a - \mathsf{x}] \int_a^\infty p(z|\mathsf{x})\, dz \right\} \\ &= \int_0^\infty [a - \mathsf{x}]\, \Gamma_{z|\mathsf{x}}(a)\, p(\mathsf{x})\, d\mathsf{x}, \end{aligned} \tag{5.75}$$

where $\Gamma_{z|\mathsf{x}}(a)$ is the right-tail cumulative distribution function of the conditional density $p(z|\mathsf{x})$, evaluated at a.

Should X and Z be stochastically independent, so that $p(\mathsf{x}, z) = p(\mathsf{x})\, p(z)$ and $\Gamma_{z|\mathsf{x}}(a) = \Gamma_z(a)$, the optimal prior bid,

$$\max_a \mathbf{U}(\mathbf{D} \mid \mathbf{I}\downarrow, a) = \max_a E_{\mathsf{x}} \{[a - \mathsf{x}]\, \Gamma_z(a)\} = \max_a [a - \bar{\mathsf{x}}]\, \Gamma_z(a),$$

maximizes the difference between the DM's bid and expected cost, weighted by the probability of winning the bid. Differentiating with respect to a characterizes the optimal bid a_0^N as the solution to

$$a_0^N - \bar{\mathsf{x}} = \Gamma_z(a_0^N)/f_z(a_0^N), \tag{5.76}$$

writing $f_z(a_0^N)$ for the density function p(z) evaluated at a_0^N. When p(z) is normally distributed, the solution can be found using tables of Mills' Ratio [Mills (1926)], the quantity on the right-hand side of (5.76).

The assumption of stochastic independence between the competitors' bids and the DM's costs may not be warranted. The competitors' bids depend upon their cost assessments, required profit margins, and general aggressiveness toward getting the job. All parties are bidding to perform the same task; presumably the costs of the various bidders are positively correlated with one another. If our DM's costs are higher, so may be the competitors' costs, which in turn may lead to higher bids by those competitors.

A bivariate uniform distribution for $p(\mathsf{x}, z)$ provides a tractable way to investigate the role of this dependence on the value of incomplete and complete perfect information. Suppose the DM's costs are uniformly distributed between A and B. Choosing the origin for the analysis at A = 0 and defining the monetary unit so that B = 1, the marginal density on the costs is simply $p(\mathsf{x}) = 1$. If the DM's realized costs are x, let the competitors' minimum bid be distributed uniformly between γx and $D + \gamma x$, where $D > 1$, and $0 \le \gamma \le 1$ models the dependence between the DM's costs and the competitors' bids. The conditional distribution $p(z|x) = D^{-1}$, since the length of Z does not depend upon x. The joint distribution $p(x, z) = p(z|x)p(x) = D^{-1}$.

The assessment of the densities $p(x|z)$ and $p(z)$ is more involved. If knowledge of x provides information about Z, then knowledge of z should provide information about X. For example, if word comes out that the minimum bid is close to 0, this indicates to the DM that her costs are low; in fact, certain high costs would no longer even be possible in this model framing.

Figure 5.4 depicts the support of (X, Z); the support of Z ranges from 0 (when $x = 0$) to $D + \gamma$ (when $x = 1$). Assuming $\gamma > 0$, the range of X depends upon which of three regions the specific realization of Z falls. Reading horizontally for a given z, when z is low, $0 < z \le \gamma$, the range of X is constrained to between 0 and z/γ. Under the uniform distribution, this makes $p(x|z) = \gamma/z$. The marginal probability of any z within this first region can be found by integrating x out of the joint distribution $p(x, z)$:

$$p(z) = \int_0^{z/\gamma} p(x, z)\, dx = z/\gamma D. \tag{5.77}$$

In the second region, when z falls between the dotted lines in Figure 5.4, there is no constraint on the range of X other than it be between 0 and 1. Hence, $p(x|z) = 1$ and $p(z) = D^{-1}$. In the third region, when $D \le z \le D + \gamma$, only high realizations of X are possible: X ranges from $[z - D]/\gamma$ to 1, making $p(x|z) = \gamma/[D + \gamma - z]$. Proceeding as in (5.77), the marginal on Z is $p(z) = [D + \gamma - z]/\gamma D$. Note that, in total, the marginal distribution $p(z)$ is not uniform.

The application of (5.75) to determine the value of the prior decision requires $\Gamma_{z|x}(a)$; here

$$\Gamma_{z|x}(a) = \int_a^{D+\gamma x} p(z|x)\, dz = D^{-1}\int_a^{D+\gamma x} dz = D^{-1}\left[D + \gamma x - a\right].$$

Hence,

$$\begin{aligned} \mathbf{U(D\,|\,I}\!\downarrow\!, \gamma, a) &= \int_0^1 \left[a - x\right]\left[D^{-1}\right]\left[D + \gamma x - a\right] dx \\ &= D^{-1}\left\{-a^2 + \left[D + \tfrac{1}{2}\gamma + \tfrac{1}{2}\right]a - \left[\tfrac{1}{2}D + \tfrac{1}{3}\gamma\right]\right\}. \end{aligned}$$

Differentiation shows

$$a_0^N = \tfrac{1}{2}\left[D + \tfrac{1}{2}\gamma + \tfrac{1}{2}\right],$$

yielding the value of the prior decision as

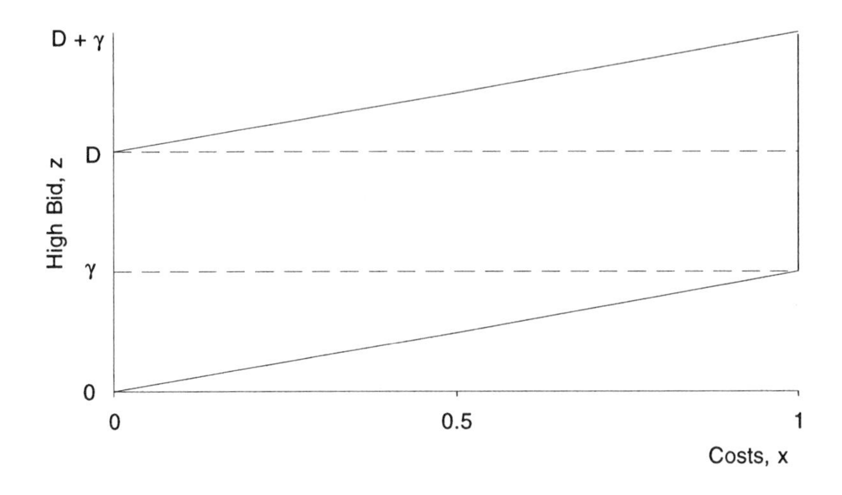

Figure 5.4. The support of (X, Z).

$$\mathbf{U(D^* \,|\, I\!\downarrow,\, \gamma)} \;=\; D^{-1}\left\{\tfrac{1}{4}\left[D + \tfrac{1}{2}\gamma + \tfrac{1}{2}\right]^2 - \left[\tfrac{1}{2}D + \tfrac{1}{3}\gamma\right]\right\}. \tag{5.78}$$

Next, suppose the DM can obtain complete and perfect information, knowing both the cost x and the competitors' lowest bid z. The optimal decision rule is to bid z if $x < z$, and decline to participate if it is not:

$$\max_a \pi(x, z, a) = \begin{cases} z - x & \text{if } x < z \\ 0 & \text{if } x \geq z. \end{cases} \tag{5.79}$$

The value of the perfectly informed decision is

$$\begin{aligned} \mathbf{U(D^* \,|\, I\!\uparrow,\, \gamma)} &= E_{x,z} \max_a \pi(x, z, a) \\ &= \int_0^1 \int_x^{D+\gamma x} [z - x]\, p(x, z)\, dz\, dx \\ &= D^{-1}\left\{\tfrac{1}{2}D\left[D + \gamma - 1\right] + \tfrac{1}{6}\left[\gamma - 1\right]^2\right\}. \end{aligned} \tag{5.80}$$

The value of complete perfect information, given the framing parameter γ, $V^N_{I\uparrow}(\gamma)$, is the utility increment, the difference between (5.80) and (5.78):

$$V^N_{I\uparrow}(\gamma) \;=\; \mathbf{U(D^* \,|\, I\!\uparrow,\, \gamma)} - \mathbf{U(D^* \,|\, I\!\downarrow,\, \gamma)}.$$

Suppose next that the DM can determine by inquiry her own costs x with certainty, but not the lowest competitor bid. Write this incomplete information structure as $\mathbf{I}^{(x)}$. To calculate the value of this incompletely informed decision, the outcome function continues to be given by (5.74) and the expected profit given $\times$ and a is

$$\max_a E_{z|\times} \pi(\times, z, a) = \max_a \int_a^{D+\gamma\times} [a - \times]\, p(z|\times)\, dz$$

$$= \max_a D^{-1}\{-a^2 + [D + \gamma\times + \times]a - [D + \gamma\times]\times\}. \quad (5.81)$$

The optimal decision rule given $\times$ is

$$a_\times^N = \tfrac{1}{2}[D + \gamma\times + \times].$$

With $\times$ still a random variable prior to the inquiry, substituting this rule into (5.81) and taking the expectation with respect to the marginal $p(\times)$, the value of the decision using the incomplete structure $\mathbf{I}^{(\times)}$ is

$$\mathbf{U}(\mathbf{D}^* | \mathbf{I}^{(\times)}, \gamma) = D^{-1}\int_0^1 \left\{\tfrac{1}{4}[D + \gamma\times + \times]^2 - [D + \gamma\times]\times\right\} d\times$$

$$= D^{-1}\left\{\tfrac{1}{4}D[D + \gamma - 1] + \tfrac{1}{12}[\gamma - 1]^2\right\}. \quad (5.82)$$

Comparing (5.82) with (5.80), it is interesting to note that $\mathbf{U}(\mathbf{D}^* | \mathbf{I}^{(\times)})$ is precisely one half of $\mathbf{U}(\mathbf{D}^* | \mathbf{I}\uparrow)$. Hence,

$$V_{\mathbf{I}^{(\times)}}^N(\gamma) = \tfrac{1}{2}V_{\mathbf{I}\uparrow}^N(\gamma) - \tfrac{1}{2}\mathbf{U}(\mathbf{D}^* | \mathbf{I}\downarrow, \gamma);$$

the value of perfect but incomplete information about costs is less than half the value of complete perfect information.

Suppose finally that the DM cannot obtain information on the costs, but can hire a mole who will provide the lowest competitor bid. Denote this incomplete information structure $\mathbf{I}^{(z)}$. Defining $\overline{\times}_z \equiv E_{\times|z}\times$ as the conditional mean given z, the optimal decision rule is to bid z if $\overline{\times}_z < z$; otherwise do not bid. Expected profit conditional on z is

$$\max_a E_{\times|z} \pi(\times, z, a) = \begin{cases} z - \overline{\times}_z & \text{if } \overline{\times}_z < z \\ 0 & \text{if } \overline{\times}_z \geq z. \end{cases} \quad (5.83)$$

To calculate $\mathbf{U}(\mathbf{D}^* | \mathbf{I}^{(z)}, \gamma)$, the expectation of (5.83) with respect to p(z) requires the evaluation of $\overline{\times}_z$ and p(z) in each of the three regions in the range of Z. This evaluation depends, in turn, on the value of the parameter γ.

Consider first the case of stochastic independence, $\gamma = 0$. Here, $\overline{\times}_z = 1/2$, and with $p(z) = D^{-1}$, the value of the decision is

$$\mathbf{U}(\mathbf{D}^* | \mathbf{I}^{(z)}, \gamma = 0) = \int_{\frac{1}{2}}^{D} \left[z - \tfrac{1}{2}\right]\left[D^{-1}\right] dz = D^{-1}\left[\tfrac{1}{2}D^2 - \tfrac{1}{2}D + \tfrac{1}{8}\right].$$

Let D = 2. Evaluating the information values $V^N_{I\uparrow}(0)$, $V^N_{I^{(\times)}}(0)$, and $V^N_{I^{(z)}}(0)$ shows that the value of the two incomplete information structures taken separately is different from the value of the complete structure: $V^N_{I\uparrow}(0) = 7/12 - 9/32 = 29/96$, $V^N_{I^{(\times)}}(0) = 29/192 - 9/64 = 1/96$, and $V^N_{I^{(z)}}(0) = 9/16 - 9/32 = 27/96$. The pragmatic information value is not additive: knowing × prevents the DM from losing money, knowing z prevents her from underbidding, but not knowing both simultaneously causes the DM to decline to participate in situations in which a profit could have been made by bidding.

In this framing, an increase in the parameter γ means that knowledge of z provides information about X, narrowing down the range of potential costs and improving the decision to participate. In fact, when $\gamma = 1$, the DM can never err and the value of the structure $\mathbf{I}^{(z)}$ is as valuable as $\mathbf{I}\uparrow$; there is no need to spend resources evaluating costs.

For $0 < \gamma \leq 1$, in region 1 of the support of Z, $z \in (0, \gamma]$, the conditional is $p(\times|z) = \gamma/z$ for $0 \leq x \leq z/\gamma$, and $p(z) = z/D\gamma$. The mean $\bar{\times}_z$ being $z/2\gamma$, the participation criterion $z - \bar{\times}_z > 0$ for all $\gamma > 1/2$. Hence, for values of z within this range, the DM always bids for $\gamma > 1/2$, and never bids for $\gamma \leq 1/2$. This results in a loss from complete perfect information for all γ except $\gamma = 1$, when the DM cannot lose money because the range of X is constrained to be less than or equal to z. Evaluating the expectation of (5.83) with respect to p(z) for this range, the contribution to $\mathbf{U}(\mathbf{D}^* | \mathbf{I}^{(z)}, \gamma)$ is

$$\int_0^{\gamma} [\max_a E_{\times|z}\, \pi(\times, z, a)]\, p(z)\, dz = \begin{cases} 0 & \text{for } \gamma \leq 1/2 \\ [6D]^{-1}\left[2\gamma^2 - \gamma\right] & \text{for } \gamma > 1/2. \end{cases} \tag{5.84}$$

In the second region, when $z \in [\gamma, D]$, $p(\times|z) = 1$ for $0 \leq x \leq 1$, and $p(z) = D^{-1}$. Here, $\bar{\times}_z = 1/2$, so $z - \bar{\times}_z > 0$ for all $z > 1/2$. Hence the DM bids whenever $z > 1/2$; for $\gamma > 1/2$ this is all z in the range; for $\gamma \leq 1/2$, she does not bid for small values of z. The contribution to $\mathbf{U}(\mathbf{D}^* | \mathbf{I}^{(z)}, \gamma)$ in this range of Z is

$$\int_{\frac{1}{2}}^{D}\left[z - \tfrac{1}{2}\right]\left[D^{-1}\right]dz = D^{-1}\left[\tfrac{1}{2}D^2 - \tfrac{1}{2}D + \tfrac{1}{8}\right] \quad \text{for } \gamma \leq 1/2,$$

$$\int_{\gamma}^{D}\left[z - \tfrac{1}{2}\right]\left[D^{-1}\right]dz = D^{-1}\left[\tfrac{1}{2}D^2 - \tfrac{1}{2}D - \tfrac{1}{2}\gamma[\gamma - 1]\right] \quad \text{for } \gamma > 1/2. \tag{5.85}$$

Finally, in the third region with $z \in [D, D + \gamma)$, $p(\times|z) = \gamma/[D + \gamma - z]$ for $[z - D]/\gamma \leq x \leq 1$, and $p(z) = [D + \gamma - z]/\gamma D$. Since maximum possible costs are 1 unit and $D > 1$ by the model specification, the DM always bids and cannot lose money when the competitors' bids are on the high end. Here, $\bar{\times}_z = [\gamma + z - D]/2\gamma$, so the contribution is

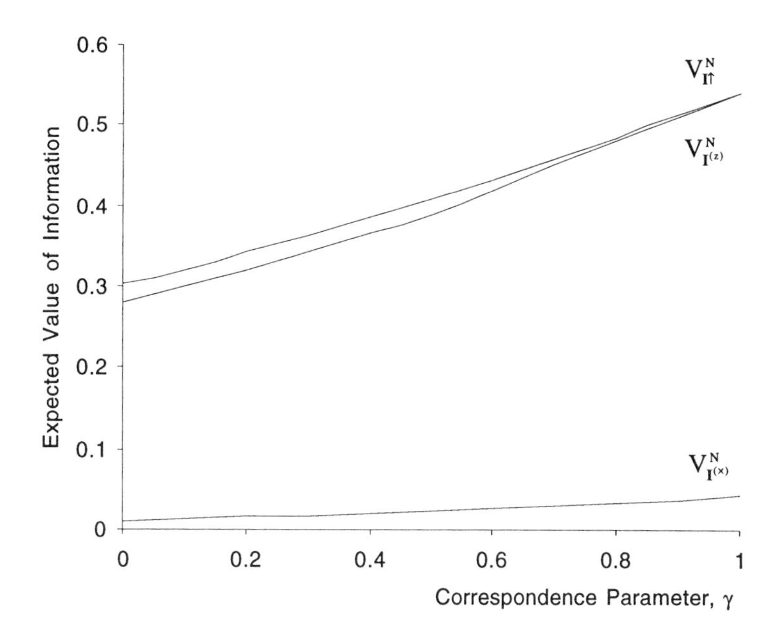

Figure 5.5. The value of complete and incomplete perfect information.

$$\int_{D}^{D+\gamma}\left[z-\frac{\gamma+[z-D]}{2\gamma}\right]\left[\frac{\gamma-[z-D]}{\gamma D}\right]dz\,. \tag{5.86}$$

For $0<\gamma\leq 1$, $\mathbf{U}(\mathbf{D}^*\,|\,\mathbf{I}^{(z)},\gamma)$ is the sum of (5.84), (5.85), and the evaluation of (5.86). The value of the incomplete information structure $\mathbf{I}^{(z)}$ is

$$V^N_{\mathbf{I}^{(z)}}(\gamma)\;=\;\mathbf{U}(\mathbf{D}^*\,|\,\mathbf{I}^{(z)},\gamma)-\mathbf{U}(\mathbf{D}^*\,|\,\mathbf{I}\!\downarrow,\gamma).$$

Figure 5.5 graphs $V^N_{\mathbf{I}\uparrow}(\gamma)$, $V^N_{\mathbf{I}^{(z)}}(\gamma)$, and $V^N_{\mathbf{I}^{(\times)}}(\gamma)$ as a function of γ. In all cases, $\mathbf{I}^{(z)}$ is considerably more valuable than $\mathbf{I}^{(\times)}$, and nearly as valuable as $\mathbf{I}\!\uparrow$. Via its ability to mitigate underbidding decisions, in this model intelligence about competitors' actions is a very valuable commodity. ♦

5.6 Dynamic Models and the Role of Timeliness

In many important decision problems, the outcomes evolve in stages that involve the passage of time. This section examines some of the special features that influence the value of information in dynamic decision problems where time enters in a meaningful way; of particular interest is the role of promptness (or its negative, delay) in the receipt of direct messages about the current state.

5.6.1 Dynamic Decision Problems

Dynamic decision models generally require multidimensional state and act descriptions. If x(s) denotes the realization of the state at time stage s, s = 0, 1, ⋯, t, ⋯, T, then the complete state description x is the vector

$$x = [x(0), x(1), \cdots, x(t), \cdots, x(T)], \tag{5.87}$$

where T denotes the end of the planning horizon. Letting stage t represent the current situation, each $x \in \mathbf{X}$ describes a past history ($s < t$) and a future history ($s > t$), a complete unfolding of the state realization over time. Likewise, let a(s) denote the action chosen by the DM at time s. Each $a \in \mathbf{a}$ describes the sequence of actions the decision maker takes over the horizon T:

$$a = [a(0), a(1), \cdots, a(t), \cdots, a(T)]. \tag{5.88}$$

Each time stage need not have the same chronological length, but inherent in the everyday concept of time is the successive nature of the realizations and choices. Each x(s) is called a *successive state*, and each a(s) a *successive action.*

One interesting economic issue that arises in dynamic models concerns the impact on choice from the possible temporal resolution of uncertainty prior to the end of the planning horizon. Actions chosen in one period may constrain the set of feasible actions in subsequent periods: some choices may involve commitments that in the extreme are irreversible; others may retain flexibility. Suppose, for example, in a two-stage model it is not feasible to obtain any information about the random variables in period 1, when a(1) must be chosen, but after this choice, the uncertainty is completely resolved and the DM chooses a(2) under perfect information. How much recourse the DM has to affect the outcome in period 2 may depend upon the flexibility she left herself after the period 1 choice.

Drèze and Modigliani (1972), Henry (1974), Epstein (1980), Jones and Ostroy (1984), and Freixas and Laffont (1984) investigate the role of the value of subsequent information on earlier period decisions. The hypothesis is that the greater the subsequent value of information, the more desirable is a flexible initial decision, as it makes it easier to exploit the information not yet received. In an empirical study of a realistic dynamic version of the farmer's planting decision (Example 2.1), Chavas, Kristjanson, and Matlon (1991) conclude that the phenomenon of early planting of short-cycle sorghum varieties by farmers in the Sahel can be explained as a choice that permits flexible responses to subsequent rainfall realizations. Kelly (1991) uses the continuous version of the Kalman filter (see Section 5.6.4) to assess the value of information about the present value of an irreversible investment. Pethig (1994) studies the value of future information revelation in an optimal control model for damaging pollution emissions when the consequences of the damage are not known today.

This section studies a simpler situation in which there is no interaction between actions at different times, no constraints linking them, and an outcome function $\omega(w, x, a)$ that is separable between wealth and payoffs. In this framing, the payoff function is additive,

$$\pi(x, a) = \sum_{s=t}^{T} \mathcal{D}^{s-t} \pi(x(s), a(s)), \tag{5.89}$$

and the sequential decision problem can be dealt with as a succession of one-period problems. The discount, or "impatience" coefficient $\mathcal{D}$ generally reflects the time value of money. With the exception of perfect information, the DM makes the choice a(s) prior to knowledge of the realization x(s). The multivariate nature of the probability distributions on **X** is managed by modeling the movement of each successive event x(s) as a stochastic process, calculating the probability distribution of any future history as a function of all remembered past history.

The DM takes the first successive action a(t) using the optimal decision rule $a_{y_t}(t)$ based upon y_t, the message available at time t. The message y_t includes a new component and all past remembered messages, potentially revised in period t:

$$y_t = [y(t; t), y(t-1; t), \cdots, y(t-M_t; t)], \tag{5.90}$$

where y(t; t) is the new component available in period t, y(t − 1; t) is the component received last period, but potentially revised this period, and M_t is the length of the memory at time t. If the information structure does not discard messages, the dimension of y_t increases with t.

In general, the problem of this section is to choose the future sequence of optimal successive actions $a_{y_s}(s)$, s = t, t + 1, ··· T, and to determine the value of information as it depends upon characteristics of the information structure such as delay, memory, and the accuracy of the messages. This, in turn, depends upon the model and the specification of the stochastic process defining the relationship over time between the successive states. See Miyasawa (1968) and Marschak and Radner (1972, Chapter 7).

Dynamic stochastic programming [Bellman (1961)] is a time-honored procedure for solving this type of problem. The procedure is recursive, beginning with the optimal solution in the terminal period T and proceeding backwards to the current period t. The resulting functional equation characterizes the grand solution.

Dynamic stochastic decision models have proven quite successful in applied economics, operations research, and engineering. Indeed, most of the models in this chapter have more sophisticated dynamic versions. The multiperiod model with quadratic payoff is particularly successful, in part because of the Simon–Theil theorem [Simon (1956); Theil (1957)] that allows the simple determination of the first-period action a(t) by merely replacing the random variable with its current mean. Statistical problems such as in Section 5.2 have well-developed sequential sampling analogues [DeGroot (1970); Berger (1985)].[1] The dynamic inventory problem, with a storable commodity, has a long history going back at least to Arrow, Harris, and Marschak (1951). Karlin (1960) is pertinent here; Song and Zipkin (1996) is a recent contribution that considers the value of information about stochastic order leadtimes. Important techniques of time-series forecasting use the available message y_t to forecast future values of X; the problem of subsequent data revision is particularly vexing [Whiteman (1996)]. Bellman and Kalaba (1957) present a dynamic programming formulation of Kelly's (1956) wagering problem in which the criterion is to maximize the expected value of the utility of terminal wealth. Samuelson (1969) discusses this and also presents a model for multiperiod consumption-investment decisions. McCall (1965) applies dynamic programming to incorporate the expected value of information into the choice from among investment opportunities that appear over time.

Although the functional equation of dynamic programming characterizes the optimal solution to the problem, it does not always lead to a simple identification of that solution. In such cases simulation analysis can provide assessments of the value of information, as long as it is economical to solve the model with sufficient repetitions. Swinton and King (1994) simulate optimal weed management by risk averse farmers over a six-year horizon under alternative weed-count information structures. In a discretized framing, Zacharias, Huh, and Brandon (1990) investigate the value of sampling the plant tissues of the rice crop when deciding on the timing and level of fertilizer application over the course of the growing season. Kiefer (1989) studies the monopolist with quadratic payoffs and random demand coefficients in a dynamic context.

Kiefer's simulations illustrate the influence of the discount rate on the value of the informed decision. In multiperiod dynamic models, the discount rate changes the relative importance of present outcomes versus future outcomes; this can have significant influence upon decisions and expected outcomes in both the prior and the informed situations. In problems such as global warming with very long time horizons, the discount rate is critically important for determining the proper actions and research programs today [see Nordhaus (1994a), Peck and Teisberg (1996), and Nordhaus and Popp (1997)]. In light of the profound inter-

---

[1] Wald (1947, page 3) states that the earliest version of sequential sampling was seen as so valuable, as a technique, that it was classified information during World War II!

generational transfer of well-being that some researchers see as a potential consequence of current and postponed decisions, Schelling (1996) discusses the proper philosophy for discounting costs and benefits in this type of circumstance.

5.6.2 Delay

In dynamic formulations, there are two types of delay that can influence the economic value of information: implementation delay and observation delay. If an information source or system is expected to be valuable, but its incorporation into decision problems cannot begin until a period of time passes, the DM is forced to continue with the prior decision. The loss over time that comes from not being able to make informed decisions is the cost of *implementation delay.* In Example 4.2, the expected value of the forecast source is $73.80/month. Discounting this expected value as an annuity over the time horizon gives the expected present value of this source; if for some reason the DM must wait a period of time before being able to incorporate the forecasts into managerial decisions, additional expected profits are foregone and the discounted expected present value of the source is lower.

An abundance of decision problems have relatively short time horizons, and the more commonly studied information issues revolve around the losses from delaying the receipt of messages in a changing environment—*observation delay.* Observation delay is caused by the time it takes to perform the various activities of information processing by the system and the individual; see the subsequent Figure 9.1. When the state changes over time, delay can produce losses for the DM to the extent it causes the DM to continue an action that is suboptimal under the current state, if it were known.

Observation delay can often be reduced, but typically by either incurring higher costs or sacrificing accuracy in the observation. Clearly there are tradeoffs between the two; see Chapter 7 of Marschak and Radner (1972) and Hilton (1979). To investigate this with a minimum of complication, the next subsection considers a one-period decision problem at time stage t, with the quadratic payoff function of Section 5.1. It turns out that the value of information partitions into two terms, one depending only on the observation delay, and the other reflecting the additional loss due to observation inaccuracy.

Here, a critical aspect of the framing of a dynamic model is the specification of how the state moves through time. Two of the simplest specifications are the autoregressive process

$$x(s) = \phi x(s-1) + \varepsilon(s), \tag{5.91}$$

and the first-order moving average process

$$x(s) = \varepsilon(s) + \phi\varepsilon(s-1), \tag{5.92}$$

where $\varepsilon(s)$ is a sequence of independently and identically distributed random variables with mean $\bar{\varepsilon} = 0$ and variance σ_ε^2. It is assumed that $0 \le \phi \le 1$.

Concentrating on direct messages about the state, let $\mathbf{Y}_t$ be the set of currently available potential messages on the past state history. If each realization $y_t \in \mathbf{Y}_t$ is such that each component of y_t,

$$y(s; t) = x(s - \Delta),$$

is a perfect measurement of the successive event $x(\bullet)$, Δ periods ago, then the information structure offers *perfect information with delay* Δ. The special case $\Delta = 0$ is *prompt perfect information.* If each component $y_t \in \mathbf{Y}_t$ is an inaccurate observation of $x(\bullet)$, Δ periods ago, such that

$$y(s; t) = f(x(s - \Delta); t),$$

then the information structure offers *delayed imperfect information.* When $\Delta = 0$, it is *prompt imperfect information.*

5.6.3 The Value of Timeliness and Accuracy

For the quadratic payoff function (5.1), but now with time scripts, equation (5.7) shows that the value of information at time period or stage t is

$$V_{\mathrm{I}}^{\mathrm{N}}(t) = \kappa_1\{\sigma_{x(t)}^2 - E_{y_t}\sigma_{x(t)|y_t}^2\}. \tag{5.93}$$

Let the environment be generated according to (5.91); then by successive substitution back in time,

$$x(t) = \phi^t x(0) + \sum_{m=0}^{t-1} \phi^m \varepsilon(t - m). \tag{5.94}$$

Assuming that x(0) is known, and choosing units so that x(0) = 0, the unconditional mean is $\bar{x}(t) = 0$ and the unconditional variance $\sigma_{x(t)}^2$ is

$$\sigma_{x(t)}^2 = \sigma_\varepsilon^2 \sum_{m=0}^{t-1} \phi^{2m}. \tag{5.95}$$

The value of perfect information is then

$$V_{\mathrm{I\dagger}}^{\mathrm{N}}(t) = \kappa_1\{\sigma_{x(t)}^2\} = \kappa_1 \sigma_\varepsilon^2 \sum_{m=0}^{t-1} \phi^{2m}.$$

Suppose the message available at time t is $x(t - \Delta)$, an exact measurement of the state, but delayed Δ periods. By successive substitution on (5.91), x(t) relates to $x(t - \Delta)$ according to

$$x(t) = \phi^\Delta x(t - \Delta) + \sum_{m=0}^{\Delta-1} \phi^m \varepsilon(t - m). \tag{5.96}$$

In this way the observation $x(t-\Delta)$ serves as a benchmark for the current location of $x(t)$. The mean conditional on the delayed observation is

$$E_{x(t)\,|\,x(t-\Delta)}\, x(t) \;=\; \phi^{\Delta} x(t-\Delta),$$

and the conditional variance is

$$\sigma^2_{x(t)|x(t-\Delta)} \;=\; \sigma^2_{\varepsilon} \sum_{m=0}^{\Delta-1} \phi^{2m}\,. \tag{5.97}$$

Since this does not depend upon the specific $x(t-\Delta)$ observed, the value of the information structure with delay Δ is, subtracting (5.97) from (5.95) in (5.93),

$$V^{N}_{I(\Delta)}(t) = \kappa_1\{\, \sigma^2_{\varepsilon} \sum_{m=\Delta}^{t-1} \phi^{2m} \,\} \;=\; \kappa_1\{\, \sigma^2_{\varepsilon}\phi^{2\Delta} \sum_{m=0}^{t-\Delta-1} \phi^{2m} \,\}. \tag{5.98}$$

The value of perfect but delayed information is an increasing function of σ^2_{ε} and ϕ, and a decreasing function of Δ. Note that the loss attributable to the delay, $\kappa_1 \sigma^2_{x(t)|x(t-\Delta)}$, is a function of the model parameters and the delay, but not the specific time period t. The dependence on the variance σ^2_{ε} is a typical result for the quadratic payoff function. The role of ϕ deserves further comment.

Given a certain delay, the larger ϕ is, the more valuable the information. Roughly speaking, ϕ measures the amount of information about the current environment that can be gleaned from past observations. A more precise measure of how the current state depends upon past values of the state is the autocorrelation function of the stochastic process [see Part 3 of Pindyck and Rubinfeld (1991)],

$$\rho_{\Delta} = \mathrm{Cov}(x(t),\, x(t-\Delta))/\,\sigma_{x(t)}\,\sigma_{x(t-\Delta)},$$

which for the stochastic process (5.91) is ϕ^{Δ}. The larger ϕ is, the more the autocorrelation function stays "up," and the more valuable is information with delay Δ.

The effect of delay is very much a function of the underlying movement of the x-process. If the state moves according to the process (5.92), it can be shown that the perfect measurement has no value to the DM if $\Delta \geq 2$; the autocorrelation function reaches zero at that time and the delayed message is worthless. If the underlying environment is periodic, more delay may be more valuable; if, in July, the DM seeks to forecast the demand for heating oil next January in North America, the observation of last January's demand ($\Delta = 6$ months) is probably more valuable than the observation of last June's ($\Delta = 1$ month). In a slightly different vein, the state itself might be unchanging, but suppose the information structure is exogenous and capable of providing complete information only periodically. A past component of y_t may be more valuable than a nearby one; if the DM is searching for an apartment on Wednesday, in many cities she is likely to find more valuable information in last Sunday's newspaper than in today's or yesterday's. Finding and buying this dated message may be costly; we see here an example of the kinds of net information value (i.e., economic efficiency) that continuously available, updated, and complete messages on the Internet can generate.

Now suppose the message y(t), received at time t, is an inaccurate observation of the state Δ periods ago:

$$y(t) = \gamma x(t - \Delta) + \eta(t), \tag{5.99}$$

where $\eta(t)$ is a sequence of independently and identically distributed random variables with mean $\bar{\eta} = 0$ and variance σ_η^2. Identify the informativeness characteristics of **I** as **I**(Δ, η'), where $\eta' \equiv \sigma_\eta^2$.[2] This information structure does not allow for data revisions, hence y(t; t) in (5.90) is simplified to y(t). There are certain special cases of interest:

1) $\Delta = 0,\ \sigma_\eta^2 = 0$ prompt perfect information;
2) $\Delta = 0,\ \sigma_\eta^2 > 0$ prompt imperfect information;
3) $\Delta > 0,\ \sigma_\eta^2 = 0$ delayed perfect information;
4) $\Delta > 0,\ \sigma_\eta^2 > 0$ delayed imperfect information.

To simplify the presentation, write $\bar{x}_t(s) \equiv E_{x(s)|y_t} x(s)$, and $\sigma_{s|t}^2 \equiv \sigma_{x(s)|y_t}^2$. Then the conditional mean and variance for (5.96) are

$$\bar{x}_t(t) = \phi^\Delta \bar{x}_t(t - \Delta),$$

and

$$\sigma_{t|t}^2 = \phi^{2\Delta} \sigma_{t-\Delta|t}^2 + \sigma_\varepsilon^2 \sum_{m=0}^{\Delta-1} \phi^{2m}, \tag{5.100}$$

since the state variation subsequent to $t - \Delta$ is independent of events at $t - \Delta$. The quantity $\sigma_{t-\Delta|t}^2$ is the currently held estimate of the variance of where the state was Δ periods ago.

Substituting (5.100) into (5.93), rearranging, and using (5.95), the value of potentially delayed and inaccurate information partitions into two parts: the value of delayed perfect information given by (5.98), and a reduction attributable to the inaccuracy:

$$\begin{aligned} V_{\mathbf{I}(\Delta,\eta')}^N(t) &= \kappa_1 \{ \sigma_t^2 - E_{y_t} \phi^{2\Delta} \sigma_{t-\Delta|t}^2 - E_{y_t} \sigma_\varepsilon^2 \sum_{m=0}^{\Delta-1} \phi^{2m} \}. \\ &= \kappa_1 \{ \sigma_\varepsilon^2 \sum_{m=0}^{t-1} \phi^{2m} - \sigma_\varepsilon^2 \sum_{m=0}^{\Delta-1} \phi^{2m} \} - \kappa_1 \{ \phi^{2\Delta} E_{y_t} \sigma_{t-\Delta|t}^2 \} \end{aligned}$$

---

[2] Alternately, to remain consistent with the convention of ordering the informativeness of the information structure as a nondecreasing function of an index θ, write **I**(θ_1, θ_2), where $\theta_1 = t - \Delta$ measures the promptness, and $\theta_2 = 1/\eta'$ is the precision of the observations.

$$= V^N_{I(\Delta,0)}(t) - \kappa_1\phi^{2\Delta}\{E_{y_t}\sigma^2_{t-\Delta|t}\}. \qquad (5.101)$$

The remaining task is to calculate the quantity in brackets, the current expectation of the variance of where the state was Δ periods ago. It is at this point convenient to specify that the random variables $\varepsilon(t)$ and $\eta(t)$ are normally distributed, in addition to being independent both mutually and over time; we have several times seen the advantages of the fact that, under normality, the conditional variances do not depend upon the specific message.

*5.6.4 *Assessing the Joint Distribution of Messages and States Via the Kalman Filter*

This subsection concerns the probability assessments necessary to calculate equation (5.101); as such, it might properly be considered an appendage to Chapter 4. The problem of interest here concerns inferences about a state variable moving through time according to (5.91) with the message available at time t being as in (5.90), but ignoring revisions:

$$y_t = [y(t), y(t-1), \cdots, y(t-M_t)].$$

The new component of the message this period is an observation on the x-process delayed Δ periods and generated according to (5.99). In (5.91) and (5.99), the variables $\varepsilon(\bullet)$ and $\eta(\bullet)$ are a sequence of independent, identically distributed, and now assumed to be normal random variables with $p(\varepsilon(\bullet)) \sim \mathbf{N}(0, \sigma^2_\varepsilon)$, $p(\eta(\bullet)) \sim \mathbf{N}(0, \sigma^2_\eta)$, $\text{cov}(\varepsilon(s), \eta(s)) = 0$, and both $\text{cov}(\varepsilon(t), \varepsilon(s))$ and $\text{cov}(\eta(t), \eta(s)) = 0$ for all $s \neq t$.

The Kalman filter [Kalman (1960); Kalman and Bucy (1961)] is a popular iterative technique for determining the posterior probability distribution of the location of the state variable, given inaccurate measurements of that location. There are several ways to develop the Kalman Filter, but the following approach, due to Meinhold and Singpurwalla (1983), makes direct use of the properties of the normal distribution presented in Section 4.1.2.

The expression (5.94) shows that the state at any time is the sum of a sequence of normal random variables and is therefore also normally distributed. The same statement holds for the messages, via a similar successive substitution into (5.99). The goal is to obtain the normal density $p(x(t-\Delta)\,|\,y_t)$, which is completely described by its mean and variance:

$$p(x(t-\Delta)\,|\,y_t) = p(x(t-\Delta)\,|\,y(t), y_{t-1}) \sim \mathbf{N}(\bar{x}_t(t-\Delta), \sigma^2_{t-\Delta|t}). \quad (5.102)$$

The equality in (5.102) is suggestive of the iterative procedure: beginning with the known previous period's density,

$$p(x(t-\Delta-1)\,|\,y_{t-1}) \sim \mathbf{N}(\bar{x}_{t-1}(t-\Delta-1), \sigma^2_{t-\Delta-1|t-1}), \qquad (5.103)$$

the idea is to update the distribution using the statistical information contained in the new component y(t). At t – 1, prior to the receipt of y(t), the DM makes two forecasts: a probability distribution for x(t – Δ), and a point forecast of the expected message, $\bar{y}_{t-1}(t)$. First,

$$p(x(t-\Delta)\,|\,y_{t-1}) \sim \mathbf{N}(\bar{x}_{t-1}(t-\Delta),\ \sigma^2_{t-\Delta|t-1})$$

$$\sim \mathbf{N}(\phi\,\bar{x}_{t-1}(t-\Delta-1),\ \phi^2\sigma^2_{t-\Delta-1|t-1} + \sigma^2_{\varepsilon}), \quad (5.104)$$

using (5.91) with s = t – Δ. The forecast of the expected message is, taking the conditional expectation of (5.99) and substituting from (5.104),

$$\bar{y}_{t-1}(t) = \gamma\bar{x}_{t-1}(t-\Delta) = \gamma\phi\,\bar{x}_{t-1}(t-\Delta-1). \quad (5.105)$$

At time period t, rather than using the message y(t) directly, the procedure makes use of the *innovation* $\tilde{y}(t)$, defined as the difference between the ultimately observed y(t) and its previous-period expectation, $\bar{y}_{t-1}(t)$. The innovation captures the statistical information contained in the observation y(t). Indeed, since from (5.105),

$$\tilde{y}(t) = y(t) - \bar{y}_{t-1}(t) = y(t) - \gamma\phi\,\bar{x}_{t-1}(t-\Delta-1). \quad (5.106)$$

Since γ, φ, and $\bar{x}_{t-1}(t-\Delta-1)$ are all known, observing $\tilde{y}(t)$ is equivalent to observing y(t). This justifies rewriting (5.102) as

$$p(x(t-\Delta)\,|\,y(t), y_{t-1}) = p(x(t-\Delta)\,|\,\tilde{y}(t), y_{t-1}).$$

Furthermore, $\tilde{y}(t)$ and y_{t-1} are independent.

As far as the probability distribution for $\tilde{y}(t)$ is concerned, it is the sum of normals and so is itself normal; substituting (5.99) into (5.106) and rearranging shows

$$\tilde{y}(t) = \gamma[x(t-\Delta) - \phi\,\bar{x}_{t-1}(t-\Delta-1)] + \eta(t), \quad (5.107)$$

yielding the conditional density

$$p(\tilde{y}(t)\,|\,x(t-\Delta), y_{t-1}) \sim \mathbf{N}(\gamma[x(t-\Delta) - \phi\,\bar{x}_{t-1}(t-\Delta-1)],\ \sigma^2_{\eta}).$$

Now, since $p(x(t-\Delta)\,|\,y_{t-1})$ in (5.104) and $p(\tilde{y}(t)\,|\,x(t-\Delta), y_{t-1})$ in the preceding are both normally distributed, so is the joint distribution of states and messages, conditional on y_{t-1}:

$$p(x(t-\Delta),\ \tilde{y}(t)\,|\,y_{t-1})$$

$$\sim \mathbf{BN}(\bar{x}_{t-1}(t-\Delta),\ \sigma^2_{t-\Delta|t-1};\ \bar{y}_{t-1}(t),\ \sigma^2_{\tilde{y}(t)|t-1};\ \rho). \quad (5.108)$$

Each parameter in (5.108) can be "built up" from the initial forecast (5.104) and (5.107):

$$\overline{x}_{t-1}(t-\Delta) = \phi\,\overline{x}_{t-1}(t-\Delta-1);$$
$$\sigma^2_{t-\Delta|t-1} = \phi^2\sigma^2_{t-\Delta-1|t-1} + \sigma^2_\varepsilon;$$
$$\overline{\tilde{y}}_{t-1}(t) = 0;$$
$$\sigma^2_{\tilde{y}(t)|t-1} = \gamma^2\sigma^2_{t-\Delta|t-1} + \sigma^2_\eta;$$
$$\mathrm{cov}(x(t-\Delta), \tilde{y}(t)\,|\,y_{t-1}) = \gamma\sigma^2_{t-\Delta|t-1};$$
$$\rho = \mathrm{cov}(x(t-\Delta), \tilde{y}(t)\,|\,y_{t-1})/\sigma_{t-\Delta|t-1}\,\sigma_{\tilde{y}(t)|t-1} = \gamma\sigma_{t-\Delta|t-1}/\sigma_{\tilde{y}(t)|t-1}. \quad (5.109)$$

Using (4.13), the posterior distribution the DM needs is

$$p(x(t-\Delta)\,|\,\tilde{y}(t), y_{t-1}) = p(x(t-\Delta)\,|\,y_t) \sim N(\overline{x}_t(t-\Delta), \sigma^2_{t-\Delta|t})$$
$$\sim N(\overline{x}_{t-1}(t-\Delta) + \rho\,\sigma_{t-\Delta|t-1}[\sigma_{\tilde{y}(t)|t-1}]^{-1}\tilde{y}(t), \sigma^2_{t-\Delta|t-1}[1-\rho^2]). \quad (5.110)$$

Substituting ρ and $\sigma^2_{\tilde{y}(t)|t-1}$ from the collection (5.109) gives the state estimation under the Kalman filter:

$$\overline{x}_t(t-\Delta) = \overline{x}_{t-1}(t-\Delta) + \gamma\sigma^2_{t-\Delta|t-1}[\gamma^2\sigma^2_{t-\Delta|t-1} + \sigma^2_\eta]^{-1}\tilde{y}(t). \quad (5.111)$$

This period's forecast of the state is last period's forecast plus an adjustment reflecting the observation obtained this period. The adjustment factor on the innovation is called the Kalman gain; note that it does not depend upon the observation itself and can be assessed beforehand. This period's variance of the state is

$$\sigma^2_{t-\Delta|t} = \sigma^2_{t-\Delta|t-1}\,\sigma^2_\eta\,[\gamma^2\sigma^2_{t-\Delta|t-1} + \sigma^2_\eta]^{-1}. \quad (5.112)$$

Again, this key determinant of the value of information does not depend upon the specific message and can be calculated beforehand. When applying (5.112) into the assessment of the value of information in (5.101), the expectation over the message space is unnecessary. The posterior distribution characterized by (5.110) now takes over for (5.103) as the initial knowledge for next period's iteration.

To begin the iterations, the procedure requires appropriate startup values, allowing for the delay. As a simple example of the recursive calculations, suppose $\Delta = 0$ and the state at period 0 is known, making $\overline{x}_0(0) = 0$ and $\sigma^2_{0|0} = 0$. Then $\sigma^2_{1|0} = \sigma^2_\varepsilon$, $\overline{x}_0(1) = 0$, and $\overline{y}_0(1) = 0$. Now observing $\tilde{y}(1) = y(1) - \overline{y}_0(1) = y(1)$, the density (5.110) has a mean which is a fraction of the observation,

$$\overline{x}_1(1) = 0 + \gamma\sigma^2_\varepsilon[\gamma^2\sigma^2_\varepsilon + \sigma^2_\eta]^{-1}y(1),$$

and the variance is

$$\sigma^2_{1|1} = \sigma^2_\varepsilon\,\sigma^2_\eta[\gamma^2\sigma^2_\varepsilon + \sigma^2_\eta]^{-1}.$$

5.6.5 *Stochastic Control Theory*

The results of the previous section generalize in several ways. The Linear-Quadratic-Gaussian (LQG) stochastic control model is an approach with significant applicability, offering tractable, albeit complex, solutions and interpretations in a wide class of dynamic decision problems. The approach is somewhat different from the standard decision model in that the state variable is not completely exogenous; instead, it is at least partially under the influence of the DM via the choice of control variable a(s). A typical specification has a linear stochastic state model,

$$x(t) = \phi x(t-1) + \zeta a(t) + \varepsilon(t),$$

an objective function that is quadratic in x(t) and a(t), an observation equation such as (5.99), and errors $\varepsilon(t)$ and $\eta(t)$ that are independent and obey the normal (Gaussian) distribution. The state may be multicategory, as in Section 5.5, there may be multiple actions to choose each time period, and the parameters may be time varying. Such generalizations are easily handled by shifting to the techniques of matrix algebra. The Simon–Theil theorem allows for the separation of the optimal control problem from the problem of state estimation using the Kalman filter.

Chow (1975) is a classic text in this area. The theory of quantitative economic policy [Fox, Sengupta, and Thorbecke (1973)] offers a straightforward application of control theory to economics. Here, the state is various components of the condition of the economy [GDP(t), unemployment(t), inflation(t), etc.], possibly observed with delayed and noisy statistics. The actions are various policy tools such as tax rates and interest rates that presumably influence the movement of the state. The objective function includes two types of cost, the costs of deviating from desired state targets and the costs (political and otherwise) of changing the actions.

Engineering applications are very well developed. Åström (1970) is an excellent text with accessible notation that directly considers the value of alternative information structures.

5.7 Approximations and Bounds for the Value of Information

In many situations the structure of the decision problem is much more complex than in the tractable models just considered, making it difficult analytically to determine decision rules, the values of the informed and uninformed decisions, and the value of information. A problem may contain scores of actions and random variables, operating together in complex ways that the DM may not even fully understand. This section considers three approaches for assessing the value of information in complex decision problems: approximations based upon a Taylor series expansion of the outcome function, bounds based upon Jensen's inequality, and estimates inferred from statistical samples.

*5.7.1 *Use of the Taylor Series Expansion*

Consider a DM with a risk averse, thrice continuously differentiable utility function $u(W)$, with $u'(W) > 0$ and $u''(W) < 0$. Let the utility of the outcome function be given by $u(\omega(w, x, a) - \psi)$, where, as in (3.6), the outcome is not necessarily separable between wealth and payoff, but any costs are paid from posterior dollars. The Taylor series expansion of u about initial wealth w is

$$u(\omega(w, x, a) - \psi) = u(w) + u'(w)[\omega(w, x, a) - w - \psi] + .5u''(w)[\omega(w, x, a) - w - \psi]^2 + R_2, \quad (5.113)$$

where R_2 is the error term reflecting the error in the two-term approximation. If conditions are sufficient to ensure that $R_2 = 0$, the expansion (5.113), combined with the proper decision rules $a_y^u(\psi)$, can serve as a basis for assessing information value. As an example, Ohlson (1975; 1979) studies a more general and realistic (= complex) version of the investment problems considered in Sections 5.3 and 5.4.

Suppose the investor faces H assets, one of which is risk free. Let x_h be the total return per dollar invested in asset h; a state realization is an H-tuple $x = [x_1, \cdots, x_h, \cdots, x_H]$, and a typical realization of x_h is denoted x_{hb}. The investor divides up initial wealth by investing $a_h w$ into asset h. A portfolio is a division of wealth amongst alternatives, an action $a = [a_1, \cdots, a_h, \cdots, a_H]$ with $\Sigma_h a_h = 1$. Denote a typical portion of wealth placed in asset h as a_{hk}; the prior optimal action is a_{h0}^u, and the optimal choice conditional on message y is a_{hy}^u. Assume that the message space $\mathbf{Y}$ is finite and countable.

The outcome function is $\omega(w, x, a) = w\Sigma_h a_h x_h$, and $\omega(w, x, a) - w = w\Sigma_h a_h[x_h - 1]$, since $\Sigma_h a_h = 1$. The quantity $[x_h - 1]$ is the rate of return on asset h. Substituting this outcome function into the Taylor series (5.113), and scaling the utility function so that $u(w) = 0$,

$$u(\omega(w, x, a) - \psi) = u'(w)[w\Sigma_h a_h[x_h - 1] - \psi] + .5u''(w)[w\Sigma_h a_h[x_h - 1] - \psi]^2 + R_2. \quad (5.114)$$

The simplifications arise by assuming that the multivariate distribution of returns belongs to a family of what Samuelson (1970) calls "small-risk" or "compact" distributions, defined so that

$$\lim_{t \to 0} \frac{1}{t} E_{x|y;t} [x_h - 1] = \bar{x}_{hy};$$

$$\lim_{t \to 0} \frac{1}{t} E_{x|y;t} [x_h - 1][x_s - 1] = \sigma_{hs};$$

and all higher-order moments are zero. Here t can be interpreted as the trading interval: $t \to 0$ allows for virtually immediate portfolio revision. The quantity $\bar{x}_{hy}$ is the instantaneous expected rate of return on h, conditional on y, and σ_{hs} is the instantaneous variance-covariance among the returns. The σ_{hs} do not depend upon the specific message y.

Ohlson (1975) then shows that, under small risk,

$$\mathbf{U}(\mathbf{D} | \mathbf{I}, \psi, y, a) = \lim_{t \to 0} \frac{1}{t} E_{x|y;t} u(\omega(w, x, a) - \psi)$$

$$= u'(w)[w\Sigma_h a_h \bar{x}_{hy} - \psi] + .5u''(w)[w^2 \Sigma_h \Sigma_s a_h a_s \sigma_{hs}]$$

$$= -\psi u'(w) + u'(w)[\Sigma_h a_h \bar{x}_{hy}]w + .5u''(w)[\Sigma_h \Sigma_s a_h a_s \sigma_{hs}]w^2.$$

That is, both the remainder and the ψ in the quadratic term of (5.114) disappear under small risk, leaving a decision problem that can be handled within the framework of the standard quadratic team, as in Section 5.1.3. Given now the optimal conditional decision rules a^u_{hy}, the value of the informed decision is

$$\mathbf{U}(\mathbf{D}^* | \mathbf{I}, \psi) = E_y \mathbf{U}(\mathbf{D}^* | \mathbf{I}, \psi, y)$$

$$= E_y\{-\psi u'(w) + u'(w)[\Sigma_h a^u_{hy} \bar{x}_{hy}]w + .5u''(w)[\Sigma_h \Sigma_s a^u_{hy} a^u_{sy} \sigma_{hs}]w^2\}. \quad (5.115)$$

The analogous value of the prior decision is

$$\mathbf{U}(\mathbf{D}^* | \mathbf{I}\downarrow) = u'(w)[\Sigma_h a^u_{h0} \bar{x}_h]w + .5u''(w)[\Sigma_h \Sigma_s a^u_{h0} a^u_{s0} \sigma_{hs}]w^2. \quad (5.116)$$

The value of information is the ψ that equates (5.115) and (5.116):

$$V^u_{\mathbf{I}} = E_y\{ [\Sigma_h a^u_{hy} \bar{x}_{hy} - \Sigma_h a^u_{h0} \bar{x}_h]w$$

$$+ .5 \frac{u''(w)}{u'(w)} [\Sigma_h \Sigma_s a^u_{hy} a^u_{sy} \sigma_{hs} - \Sigma_h \Sigma_s a^u_{h0} a^u_{s0} \sigma_{hs}]w^2\}. \quad (5.117)$$

The first term in (5.117) is simply the change in the expected terminal wealth from using the information source. The second term adjusts for additional impacts from risk and risk aversion; as Section 7.1.3 covers, the quantity $u''(w)/u'(w) < 0$ measures the DM's degree of risk aversion.

The full power of the theory of the quadratic team becomes available if all distributions are multivariate normal. In this case, all optimal decision rules become linear in the message, and the value of information can be calculated using formulas given on page 513 of Ohlson (1979).

Working with Taylor series expansion of the outcome function about the mean, Howard (1971) provides another approach for approximating the value of information in complex problems that do not admit a tractable solution. He illustrates his approach in a pricing problem with risk aversion and stochastic demand and cost. Iman and Helton (1988) compare the combination of Taylor series expansion and Monte Carlo simulation with other techniques for sensitivity analysis in three large computer models; they state a preference for Latin hypercube sampling (see Section 5.7.3) over such differential analysis.

5.7.2 Bounds for Stochastic Programming Problems

Some large-scale decision problems can be framed and solved using the techniques of *mathematical programming*. In this general framework, the DM desires to maximize a potentially nonlinear objective function subject to a number of potentially nonlinear constraints on the actions. This becomes a *stochastic program* when some of the coefficients and limitations are random variables. Kall and Wallace (1994) and Birge and Louveaux (1997) present several methods for solving such problems; a popular formulation is to set it up as a stochastic program with recourse.

In a *recourse problem*, the action variables are chosen, the state realized, and then there is recourse—the opportunity to take additional actions that try to make the best of the situation. For example, in the inventory problem, the action is to stock a certain amount, the random demand is then realized, and the recourse is either an emergency purchase if there is a shortage or storage/disposal if there is a surplus. Baron (1971) presents a Bayesian analysis of the value of information in a simple recourse problem. Wagner, Shamir, and Nemati (1992) assess information value in a stochastic programming with recourse model for containing groundwater contamination in the face of unknown conductivity in the aquifer; see also the discussion in Section 1.5.3.

Although computation is certainly much cheaper than it used to be, the calculations necessary to assess the value of information can still be formidable, requiring multiple solutions to the stochastic program and numerical integrations. To illustrate how quickly the situation can get out of hand, suppose that in the finite state description $\mathbf{X}^m = \{x_1, \cdots, x_i, \cdots, x_m\}$, each state x_i is a vector of realizations from each of H categories in each of T time periods:

$$x_i = [\chi_1(1), \cdots, \chi_H(1), \cdots, \chi_h(t), \cdots, \chi_1(T), \cdots, \chi_H(T)]. \tag{5.118}$$

If any category h in time t can have one of B(h, t) possible values, that is,

$$\chi_h(t) \in \{\chi_{h1}(t), \cdots, \chi_{hb}(t), \cdots, \chi_{hB(h,t)}(t)\},$$

then the dimension of $\mathbf{X}^m$ can quickly exhibit what is sometimes called the *curse of dimensionality*: if B(h, t) = B for all categories and times, then $m = [B^H]^T$. The computational burden arises even in the relatively simple case of risk neutrality and motivates Madansky (1960), Avriel and Williams (1970), Ziemba and Butterworth (1975), and Hausch and Ziemba (1983) to seek more readily computable bounds on the value of information in stochastic programming.

The computation of the risk neutral value of the prior decision with separable outcome,

$$\mathbf{U}(\mathbf{D}^* \mid \mathbf{I}\downarrow) = \max_a E_x \{w + \pi(x, a)\},$$

requires the stochastic program be solved for the optimal prior decision, followed by an integration to determine the expected value of the objective function at the optimum. One simplification is to replace all random variables with their means, a technique that is commonly criticized [see Birge (1995)] as leading to a solution that lacks proper diversification in light of the true uncertainty.

The perfectly informed decision, sometimes called the wait-and-see problem, with value

$$\mathbf{U}(\mathbf{D}^* \mid \mathbf{I}\uparrow) = E_x \max_a \{w + \pi(x, a)\},$$

requires the solution of a *distribution problem.* This is burdensome because the optimal action a_x must be determined for every x, and then the expectation assessed [see Bereanu (1966) for discussion and techniques].

Bounds for the Risk Neutral Case

A bound on the value of complete perfect information,

$$V^N_{I\uparrow} = \mathbf{U}(\mathbf{D}^* \mid \mathbf{I}\uparrow) - \mathbf{U}(\mathbf{D}^* \mid \mathbf{I}\downarrow),$$

arises by exploiting an assumption that the payoff function $\pi(x, a)$ is concave in both x and a on the convex set $\mathbf{X} \times \mathbf{a}$. If this is true, then Jensen's inequality (2.36b) comes into play, guaranteeing that

$$E_x \{w + \pi(x, a)\} \leq w + \pi(\bar{x}, a).$$

Also, the function $\max_a \{w + \pi(x, a)\}$ is concave, so

$$E_x \max_a \{w + \pi(x, a)\} \leq \max_a \{w + \pi(\bar{x}, a)\}. \tag{5.119}$$

Writing $a_{\bar{x}}$ as the solution to the deterministic problem

$$\max_a \{w + \pi(\bar{x}, a)\} = w + \pi(\bar{x}, a_{\bar{x}}), \tag{5.120}$$

the risk neutral value of perfect information can be bounded by

$$V_{IT}^{N} = E_x \max_a \{w + \pi(x, a)\} - \max_a E_x \{w + \pi(x, a)\}$$

$$\leq \pi(\bar{x}, a_{\bar{x}}) - \max_a E_x \pi(x, a), \quad (5.121)$$

after canceling out w and applying (5.119). Finally, since $a_{\bar{x}}$ is suboptimal for the uninformed decision,

$$E_x \pi(x, a_{\bar{x}}) \leq \max_a E_x \pi(x, a),$$

(5.121) becomes

$$V_{IT}^{N} \leq \pi(\bar{x}, a_{\bar{x}}) - E_x \pi(x, a_{\bar{x}}). \quad (5.122)$$

This computation requires the determination of only the optimal action when the random variable X is replaced by its expected value, and the evaluation of one expectation. Even the evaluation of this one expectation may be difficult; researchers continue to devote effort toward finding bounds on the expectation of complex functions; see, for example, Madansky (1959), Dulá (1992), and Edirisinghe and Ziemba (1994).

Wagner and Berman (1995) assess the preceding quantities in the context of alternative stochastic programming models to plan for the expansion of a chain of convenience stores in the face of uncertain demand. One of their illustrative problems has five time periods and three possible demand scenarios each period, for a total of $3^5 = 243$ distinct demand scenarios. Even with this moderate size, the dynamic stochastic programming version of their model becomes too large to solve.

Bounds for the Risk Averse Case

There are analogous bounds on the value of perfect information when the decision maker's utility function is risk averse. If both the payoff function $\pi(x, a)$ and the utility function $u(\bullet)$ are concave, then the function $\max_a u(w - \psi + \pi(x, a))$ is a composition of concave functions and is concave in x, a, and ψ [see Lemma 2 of Ziemba and Butterworth (1975)]. Hence, by Jensen's inequality,

$$E_x \max_a u(w - \psi + \pi(x, a)) \leq \max_a u(w - \psi + \pi(\bar{x}, a)). \quad (5.123)$$

Since the choice of action that maximizes the right-hand side of (5.123) is obtainable by solving a nonstochastic problem in which the random variable X is replaced by its expectation $\bar{x}$, the optimal choice $a_{\bar{x}}$ defined by

$$\max_a u(w - \psi + \pi(\bar{x}, a)) = u(w - \psi + \pi(\bar{x}, a_{\bar{x}})), \quad (5.124)$$

is identical to the $a_{\bar{x}}$ defined in the risk neutral case (5.120) because of the continuity and strict increasingness of the utility function.

The value of perfect information is the solution for $\psi = V_{I\uparrow}^{A}$ in the equation

$$E_x \max_a u(w - V_{I\uparrow}^{A} + \pi(x, a)) = \max_a E_x u(w + \pi(x, a)). \qquad (5.125)$$

To obtain the bound, apply (5.123) evaluated at $\psi = V_{I\uparrow}^{A}$ to the definition (5.125),

$$\max_a u(w - V_{I\uparrow}^{A} + \pi(\bar{x}, a)) \geq \max_a E_x u(w + \pi(x, a)),$$

and then invoke (5.124) to yield

$$u(w - V_{I\uparrow}^{A} + \pi(\bar{x}, a_{\bar{x}})) \geq \max_a E_x u(w + \pi(x, a)). \qquad (5.126)$$

Substituting the definition of the prior reservation price,

$$u(R_0^A) = \max_a E_x u(w + \pi(x, a)),$$

into the right-hand side of (5.126) gives

$$u(w - V_{I\uparrow}^{A} + \pi(\bar{x}, a_{\bar{x}})) \geq u(R_0^A),$$

and this implies by the continuity and strict increasingness of the utility function that

$$V_{I\uparrow}^{A} \leq w + \pi(\bar{x}, a_{\bar{x}}) - R_0^A.$$

Finally, since $a_{\bar{x}}$ is suboptimal for the prior decision, define the suboptimal prior reservation price $\tilde{R}_0^A$ as

$$u(\tilde{R}_0^A) = E_x u(w + \pi(x, a_{\bar{x}})) \leq u(R_0^A),$$

so

$$V_{I\uparrow}^{A} \leq w + \pi(\bar{x}, a_{\bar{x}}) - \tilde{R}_0^A. \qquad (5.127)$$

This computation requires finding $a_{\bar{x}}$, evaluating one expectation, and inverting the utility function to obtain the suboptimal reservation price.

As Section 3.1.2 covers, one of the computational difficulties in assessing V_I^A is that the optimal conditional decision rule $a_y^A(\psi)$ generally varies with any change in initial wealth brought about by an expenditure on information. As in (3.48), the demand value for imperfect information is the V_I^A that solves

$$E_y E_{x|y} u(w - V_I^A + \pi(x, a_y^A(V_I^A))) = E_x u(w + \pi(x, a_0^A)),$$

and it generally requires an iterative recalculation of the optimal decision rules for each ψ until the solution V_I^A is found. LaValle (1978) provides an algorithm for this iterative search.

A bound for V_I^A is derived by forcing the DM to use the decision rule a_y^A despite having to pay ψ for the information source. Define the hypothetical demand value $\breve{V}_I^A$ as the solution to

$$E_y E_{x|y} u(w - \breve{V}_I^A + \pi(x, a_y^A)) = E_x u(w + \pi(x, a_0^A)). \quad (5.128)$$

This measure is a lower bound for V_I^A. The suboptimality of a_y^A is to the detriment of the value of the informed decision for any $\psi > 0$:

$$E_y E_{x|y} u(w - \psi + \pi(x, a_y^A)) \leq E_y E_{x|y} u(w - \psi + \pi(x, a_y^A(\psi))).$$

Specifically, evaluated at $\psi = V_I^A$,

$$E_y E_{x|y} u(w - V_I^A + \pi(x, a_y^A)) \leq E_y E_{x|y} u(w - V_I^A + \pi(x, a_y^A(V_I^A)))$$

$$= E_x u(w + \pi(x, a_0^A)). \quad (5.129)$$

Now since $\breve{V}_I^A$ is also defined in terms of the value of the prior decision, combining (5.129) and (5.128) yields

$$E_y E_{x|y} u(w - V_I^A + \pi(x, a_y^A)) \leq E_y E_{x|y} u(w - \breve{V}_I^A + \pi(x, a_y^A)).$$

With the strictly increasing utility function, this inequality can only hold true if $\breve{V}_I^A \leq V_I^A$.

5.7.3 Approximating Information Value by Sampling

In complex multidimensional models, sampling techniques offer a feasible way to estimate the expected value of complete and incomplete perfect information. Knowing the prior optimal action a_0^N, recall from the special case of (1.10) that the value of perfect complete information is the expectation of $\upsilon^N(x, x) = \pi(x, a_x) - \pi(x, a_0^N)$ with respect to the marginal distribution p(x). When the number of states is extremely large and it becomes impractical to find a_0^N in the decision problem without information, and/or to determine a_x for every $x \in \mathbf{X}^m$, then techniques that sample from among the states can estimate the mean of $\upsilon^N(x, x)$ using fewer model runs.

The validity of the frequency distribution of the output depends upon the extent to which the sampled joint distribution of the states agrees with the prior p(x). McKay, Conover, and Beckman (1979) discuss and compare three sampling techniques: traditional random sampling from p(x); stratified sampling in which the sample space is partitioned and a sample is taken from each stratum in the partition; and the technique that has become quite popular for these purposes, *Latin hypercube sampling*, or LHS. The idea of LHS is to ensure that every portion of the range of each category random variable X_h is represented in the sample.

Suppose the large model can handle no more than $m' < m$ discrete possible state descriptions, where a given state description is a vector of one realization from each of H categories:

$$x_i = [x_1, x_2, \cdots, x_h, \cdots, x_H], \quad i = 1, 2, \cdots, m'.$$

Latin hypercube sampling [see Iman and Conover (1980)] divides the range of each X_h into m' strata of equal marginal probability $1/m'$.[3] Then choose one value from each stratum. Doing this for all H of the X_h, a stratum value from X_1 is matched with a stratum value from X_2 and so on through X_H; this creates the multicategory state realization x_1. Then one of the remaining values from each X_h are matched, creating state realization x_2. This continues until m' state realizations have been created.

For example, suppose the model can handle $m' = 5$ states, and each state describes $H = 3$ categories of random variable. Partitioning the range of each X_h into equiprobable quintiles and obtaining a representative value from each quintile/stratum, represent the five possible realizations as

$$x_h \in \{x_{h1}, x_{h2}, x_{h3}, x_{h4}, x_{h5}\} = \{1, 2, 3, 4, 5\}.$$

One possible sampled state space might be

	X_1	X_2	X_3
x_1	1	2	5
x_2	3	5	1
x_3	2	3	4
x_4	5	1	3
x_5	4	4	2

Reading down a column, note that each category realization appears once and only once. Using these data to calculate a_0^N and a_{x_i}, the expected value of perfect information can be estimated for this state space. The model can be rerun as often as desired by sampling additional state spaces.

If there are H categories each taking on m' values, the grand state space has $m = [m']^H$ possible state realizations; $m = 125$ in the preceding illustration. Iman and Helton (1988, page 73) count $[m'!]^{H-1}$ distinct state spaces for a Latin hypercube sample of size m'; in the illustration this is $[5!]^2 = 14{,}400$ different potential state spaces for a given run.

As Section 5.4 details, the various categories may or may not be statistically dependent. Iman and Conover (1982) show how to induce desired rank correla-

---

[3] Recall the method of equally likely subintervals in Section 4.2.1 as a way to assess the marginal distribution $p(X_h)$.

tion among the categories in the context of LHS by restricting the possible state spaces. This is accomplished by rearranging the values of the variables in each of the preceding columns, that is, by adjusting the matching that creates each state description. Although the adjustment is not exact and may produce bias, it can both allow for dependence and eliminate any undesired pairwise correlation that might sneak in.

In their study of the value of research on the issue of global warming, Nordhaus and Popp (1997) illustrate several applications of LHS to the assessment of the value of information. The authors perform a number of experiments on a stochastic extension of a deterministic growth model that allows for five states of the world, each representing a different realization with up to eight categories.

Recall from the review in Section 1.4.4 that the primary focus of the Nordhaus and Popp study is the value of earlier information (or the related idea, the cost of implementation delay). For the time horizon T, suppose society takes the prior action a_0^N for the first t' years, then finds out that state x_i is the truth and chooses state a_{x_i} for the remaining $T - t'$ years. The case $t' = T$ is the uninformed decision; the case $t' = 0$ is perfect immediate information; the difference in the expected value of the objective function between a model run with $t' < T$ and the base-case run with $t' = T$ is the expected value of earlier resolution of the uncertainty.

Dividing each of the eight random variables into equiprobable quintiles creates $5^8 = 390{,}625$ possible states; the authors sample 625 of them using LHS and solve the deterministic problem to obtain a frequency distribution for a_{x_i} and $\pi(x, a_{x_i})$. The mean of this distribution is an estimate of the value of the perfectly informed decision. If the model cannot calculate a_0^N for as many as 625 states, the assessment of the value of information can proceed with smaller samples developed by LHS.

The Nordhaus–Popp model can handle five states, so the authors sample from the grand state space five at a time. Running the model for each of 200 sampled state spaces gives a sample of 200 estimates of the value of earlier information. Interestingly, the distribution of values is highly skewed, with the mean considerably larger than the median. The authors also utilize an alternative methodology in which they create one representative state space using the larger sample, based upon an auxiliary criterion.

Nordhaus and Popp offer two approaches for estimating the value of earlier resolution of incomplete information (i. e., finding out at time t' about only one of the categories of random variables). One approach is simply to set the realizations of all categories other than the targeted category equal to their respective median levels while varying the target over its five possibilities. The other approach samples 100 draws of combinations of nontargeted categories. This again creates a frequency distribution for the value of incomplete perfect information, done for various implementation delay.

Nordhaus and Popp also run some sensitivity analyses of the effects of changes in the mean or the standard deviation of the targeted variables on the value of incomplete information. This brings up a more general question about the factors that determine information value. Returning to tractable models with analytical solutions, the next two chapters concentrate on the statistical characteristics and personal preferences as determinants of the economic value of information.

6 Statistical Determinants of Information Value

The special models in Chapter 5 define problems with particular outcome and/or utility functions, assessing and explaining the value of information for all decision problems within that class. Chapters 6 and 7 study the determinants of the value of information in a broader sense than in Chapter 5 by identifying various classes Ω of decision problems $\mathbf{D}$, such that for all $\mathbf{D} \in \Omega$ it can be assured that information value increases or decreases with particular characteristics of $\mathbf{D}$ such as environmental riskiness, statistical informativeness, stochastic preference, and initial wealth. Some results hold for very broad classes of decision problems, others hold only for subclasses of DMs such as risk averters, or subclasses of problem structure such as those with utility of outcome functions that are increasing and/or convex in particular variables. This chapter focuses on the information structure and the exogenous environment as determinants of information value; Chapter 7 covers the role of the decision maker's preferences.

Studying the decision theory of the value of information is more than simply an intellectual exercise; the methodologies themselves find wide application outside decision and information per se. Understanding the determinants of information value, and the extent of their generality, is applicable in approaches that indirectly assess the value of sources and systems; see King and Epstein (1983) and Hammitt and Cave (1991). As Chapter 9 demonstrates, the theory of informativeness provides several insights for information system design, and in empirical analyses of information use and valuation, the theory can guide the experimental design and assist in the interpretation of the results.

6.1 The Normal Form of Decision Analysis

Chapter 6 begins with the alternative approach to the analysis of decision making under uncertainty, the normal form introduced in Section 2.3.3. The normal form is the original framework for the development of decision theory; the material in this section is standard fare for a course in statistical decision theory, such as in Berger (1985) or Ferguson (1967). In the normal form of analysis, the decision maker first considers all potential decision rules or strategies and evaluates each one conditional on the state x, performing the evaluation for every possible $x \in \mathbf{X}$. This allows the DM to go as far as possible without the need to invoke a specific prior. At the final stage of the analysis, the DM applies the prior probability distribution of X and selects the optimal strategy. The normal form allows for a more detailed examination of the roles the prior and posterior state distributions play in the DM's choice of action and her ultimate well-being. As a by-product, it provides an additional principle the expected-utility maximizer can use to eliminate certain actions from further consideration—the notion of admissibility.

6.1.1 *Randomized Courses of Action*

In a decision problem under uncertainty, the DM ultimately chooses one action a from among the space of mutually exclusive actions $\mathbf{a}$. For theoretical reasons it is convenient to frame the situation more generally and define the phrase *choice of a course of action* to mean, "choice of a probability measure p(a), defined on $\mathbf{a}$, that expresses the probability the DM undertakes each action $a \in \mathbf{a}$." It is possible to think of a DM who has chosen the course of action p(a) as having decided to utilize a random device (e.g., a random number generator) that chooses to undertake the action a according to p(a).

The set of possible courses of action is the set δ of possible proper probability measures defined on $\mathbf{a}$. That is, δ defines the simplex on the action space $\mathbf{a}$: if the action space is countable and finite with K members, the simplex on $\mathbf{a}^K$ is the set

$$\delta = \{p(a_k): p(a_k) \geq 0, \Sigma_k \, p(a_k) = 1\}; \tag{6.1a}$$

in the continuous case it is

$$\delta = \{p(a): p(a) \geq 0, \int_{\mathbf{a}} p(a) = 1\}. \tag{6.1b}$$

An important special case is the *pure or deterministic course of action* in which p(a) is degenerate with all its probability confined to the specific action a = a′. In other words, the course of action is deterministic if

$$p(a) = \begin{cases} 1 & \text{if } a = a' \\ 0 & \text{if } a \neq a'. \end{cases}$$

Otherwise, the DM is said to adopt a *mixed or randomized course of action.*

Many people find the idea of a randomized course of action to be somewhat unappealing, questioning whether any truly important decision problem should be solved with the aid of a randomizing device. Perhaps it makes sense when the unknown state of nature is the action of an intelligent opponent and the DM wants to keep the opponent guessing, but if nature is dispassionate the randomization seems superfluous. Dvoretzky, Wald, and Wolfowitz (1951) show that this intuition is good: in virtually all single-person decision problems under the expected utility hypothesis, only pure or deterministic courses of action need to be considered. [There are a few anomalous cases; see Ferguson (1967, page 142)]. As long as decision making is cost-free, this simplifies the DM's task because without randomization the optimal choice from among the set of courses of action amounts to the choice of one a from $\mathbf{a}$. Nevertheless, at times there are both theoretical and practical reasons for viewing the problem more generally by allowing for randomized courses of action and considering the choice problem as the choice of $p(a) \in \delta$.

For now the outcome function ω is not of current interest, so it is convenient to subsume it into the utility function. Write the *utility of outcome function* as

$$u(w, x, a) \equiv u(\omega(w, x, a)). \tag{6.2}$$

Suppose the DM can choose from among any course of action $p(a) \in \delta$, pure or randomized. Conditional on the occurrence of the specific state x_i, the expected utility of the course of action $p(a)$ is $E_a\, u(w, x_i, a)$, and the unconditional expected utility of $p(a)$ is

$$\mathbf{U}(\mathbf{D} \mid \mathbf{I}\downarrow, p(a)) = E_x\, E_a\, u(w, x, a). \tag{6.3}$$

The optimal course of action and the resulting value of the prior decision are then given by

$$\mathbf{U}(\mathbf{D}^* \mid \mathbf{I}\downarrow) = \max_{p(a) \in \delta} \mathbf{U}(\mathbf{D} \mid \mathbf{I}\downarrow, p(a)), \tag{6.4}$$

but, as has been asserted, there will not be any gain from using a randomized course of action, so

$$\mathbf{U}(\mathbf{D}^* \mid \mathbf{I}\downarrow) = \max_a \mathbf{U}(\mathbf{D} \mid \mathbf{I}\downarrow, a),$$

as in (2.11).

6.1.2 Decision Rules

The DM puts the information structure to use by means of a decision rule that gives a response in terms of action to every $y \in \mathbf{Y}$ that may be received. The generalization of the definition of a course of action, a *conditional decision rule* is a function $\mathbf{d}(y)$ that gives for each $y \in \mathbf{Y}$ a conditional probability measure over the action space $\mathbf{a}$:

$$\mathbf{d}(y) = p(a \mid y) \in \delta. \tag{6.5}$$

A conditional decision rule is deterministic if it ascribes with probability one a specific action a′ in response to the message y. That is,

$$p(a \mid y) = \begin{cases} 1 & \text{if } a = a' \\ 0 & \text{if } a \neq a'. \end{cases}$$

The *decision rule* **d** is a listing of conditional decision rules for each message:

$$\mathbf{d} = \{\mathbf{d}(y) \text{ for all } y \in \mathbf{Y}\}. \tag{6.6}$$

Any decision rule **d** is a member of the set $\delta_{\mathbf{I}}$ of feasible decision rules available to the DM using information structure **I**.

Conditional on the occurrence of a specific state x_i and message y_j, the expected utility of adopting the conditional decision rule $\mathbf{d}(y_j)$ in response to y_j is $E_{a \mid y_j}\, u(w, x_i, a)$, and the expected utility of an informed decision given the information structure **I** and a decision rule **d** is

$$\mathbf{U}(\mathbf{D} \mid \mathbf{I}, \mathbf{d}) = E_{x,y}\, E_{a \mid y}\, u(w, x, a). \tag{6.7}$$

The maximum expected net utility occurs when the DM employs the optimal decision rule given **I**:

$$\mathbf{d}^{u}_{\mathbf{I}} = \{\mathbf{d}^{u}_{\mathbf{I}}(y) \text{ for all } y \in \mathbf{Y}\}, \tag{6.8}$$

yielding the value of the informed decision:

$$\mathbf{U}(\mathbf{D}^* \mid \mathbf{I}) = \max_{\mathbf{d} \in \delta} \mathbf{U}(\mathbf{D} \mid \mathbf{I}, \mathbf{d}) = \max_{\mathbf{d} \in \delta} E_{x,y}\, E_{a \mid y}\, u(w, x, a). \tag{6.9}$$

The Dvoretzky, Wald, and Wolfowitz (1951) result is that when certain technical conditions on the problem structure hold true, as they do in all the decision problems considered in this book, the search for the optimal decision rule can be limited to the class of deterministic rules. Let $\mathbf{d}_\kappa$ denote the κth deterministic decision rule, with $\mathbf{d}_\kappa(y)$ identifying the specific action taken in response to y under $\mathbf{d}_\kappa$. Then in (6.7) the expectation with respect to the conditional distribution $p(a \mid y)$ drops out and it is appropriate to write

$$\mathbf{U}(\mathbf{D} \mid \mathbf{I}, \mathbf{d}_\kappa) = E_{x,y}\, u(w, x, \mathbf{d}_\kappa(y)). \tag{6.10}$$

Under the optimal deterministic decision rule $\mathbf{d}^{u}_{\mathbf{I}}$ and utility function u, the optimal action to choose in response to the message y is $\mathbf{d}^{u}_{\mathbf{I}}(y) = a^{u}_{y}$. Hence, the value of the informed decision is

$$\mathbf{U}(\mathbf{D}^* \mid \mathbf{I}) = \max_{\mathbf{d} \in \delta} \mathbf{U}(\mathbf{D} \mid \mathbf{I}, \mathbf{d}) = E_{x,y}\, u(w, x, a^{u}_{y}),$$

just as in the extensive form approach given by (2.45).

♦ *Example 2.1 A Farmer's Planting Decision (Continued from Section 4.1.1)* This continuation of Example 2.1 solves the farmer's decision problem using the normal form of analysis. With the utility of outcome given by (2.12), and the message space binary,

$$\mathbf{Y} = \{y_1, y_2\} = \{\text{the weather will be dry, the weather will be wet}\},$$

consider the normal form analysis of the information structure with joint distribution given by (2.50), repeated here for convenience:

$$\rho = \begin{bmatrix} p(x_1,y_1) & p(x_1,y_2) \\ p(x_2,y_1) & p(x_2,y_2) \end{bmatrix} = \begin{bmatrix} .48 & .12 \\ .16 & .24 \end{bmatrix}.$$

Table 6.1 presents the four possible pure decision rules that result from the two states and two messages.

Table 6.1. Decision Rules in Example 2.1

Rule	Response to y_1	Response to y_2
$\mathbf{d}_1$:	$\mathbf{d}_1(y_1) = a_1$	$\mathbf{d}_1(y_2) = a_1$
$\mathbf{d}_2$:	$\mathbf{d}_2(y_1) = a_1$	$\mathbf{d}_2(y_2) = a_2$
$\mathbf{d}_3$:	$\mathbf{d}_3(y_1) = a_2$	$\mathbf{d}_3(y_2) = a_1$
$\mathbf{d}_4$:	$\mathbf{d}_4(y_1) = a_2$	$\mathbf{d}_4(y_2) = a_2$

Discovering the optimal decision rule requires the assessment of (6.10) for each d_κ; writing this out in full,

$$\begin{aligned} U(\mathbf{D} \mid \mathbf{I}, \mathbf{d}_\kappa) &= u(w, x_1, \mathbf{d}_\kappa(y_1))\, p(x_1, y_1) + u(w, x_1, \mathbf{d}_\kappa(y_2))\, p(x_1, y_2) \\ &\quad + u(w, x_2, \mathbf{d}_\kappa(y_1))\, p(x_2, y_1) + u(w, x_2, \mathbf{d}_\kappa(y_2))\, p(x_2, y_2), \end{aligned}$$

for $\kappa = 1, 2, 3$, and 4. Calculation using the data in (2.12) and (2.50) gives the following expected utility and expected wealth for each decision rule:

$$U(\mathbf{D} \mid \mathbf{I}, \mathbf{d}_1) = u(110)[.48] + u(110)[.12] + u(150)[.16] + u(150)[.24],$$

a decision with expected wealth $\overline{W}_\mathbf{I} = \$126$;

$$U(\mathbf{D} \mid \mathbf{I}, \mathbf{d}_2) = u(110)[.48] + u(125)[.12] + u(150)[.16] + u(115)[.24],$$

a decision with expected wealth $\overline{W}_\mathbf{I} = \$119.40$;

$$U(\mathbf{D} \mid \mathbf{I}, \mathbf{d}_3) = u(125)[.48] + u(110)[.12] + u(115)[.16] + u(150)[.24],$$

a decision with expected wealth $\overline{W}_\mathbf{I} = \$127.60$;

$$U(\mathbf{D} \mid \mathbf{I}, \mathbf{d}_4) = u(125)[.48] + u(125)[.12] + u(115)[.16] + u(115)[.24],$$

a decision with expected wealth $\overline{W}_\mathbf{I} = \$121$.

If the DM is risk neutral, the optimal decision maximizes expected wealth, so $\mathbf{d}_\mathbf{I}^N = \mathbf{d}_3$ and $\mathbf{U(D^* \mid I)}$ = \$127.60 = $\overline{W}_I^N$. Under the risk averse utility function $u(W) = \log[W - 90]$, the calculation shows $\mathbf{d}_\mathbf{I}^A = \mathbf{d}_3$, $\mathbf{U(D^* \mid I)} = 3.5637$ utiles, and expected wealth $\overline{W}_I^A$ = \$127.60. In both cases, the optimal decision rule $\mathbf{d}_3$ is identical to the decision rule (2.54) found by the extensive form of analysis. ♦

Comparing this solution with the extensive form analysis in Section 2.4, the normal form is not particularly intuitive or enlightening, nor is it very efficient for actually finding the optimal decision rule and assessing the value of the informed decision. Much of the work in statistical decision theory is carried out in normal form; for information evaluation in business-type decision problems, the extensive form analysis is more commonly applied.

The normal form comes into its own by allowing for randomized decisions and performing the double expectation in (6.9) by first conditioning on the state:

$$\mathbf{U(D^* \mid I)} = \max_{\mathbf{d} \in \delta} \mathbf{U(D \mid I, d)} = \max_{\mathbf{d} \in \delta} E_x E_{y \mid x} E_{a \mid y} u(w, x, a). \quad (6.11)$$

This method, by invoking p(x) last, is useful for analyzing the characteristics of alternative decision rules conditional on each state and before averaging the conditional expected utilities with a specific prior. The normal form is handy when the DM wishes to restrict consideration of decision rules to some feasible subset of δ_I, such as the class of linear decision rules, and also is appropriate when, for philosophical or other reasons, the DM is unwilling to provide a prior.

In addition, normal form analysis is useful for investigating the sensitivity, or robustness, of the optimal choice and the value of information to the assessment of a specific prior. Especially in relatively simple decision problems, such an analysis can influence the precision with which the DM needs to assess the initial knowledge. As the following continuation of Example 2.1 shows, initial beliefs can have a significant effect on the expected value of information; for another illustration, see Finkel and Evans (1987, especially page 1168).

♦ *Example 2.1 (Continued)*

With the state space $\mathbf{X} = \{x_1, x_2\}$ a dichotomy, the prior distribution of X is fully characterized by the probability $p(x_1)$. For the logarithmic utility function $u(W) = \log[W - 90]$ and the fixed likelihood matrix

$$\lambda = \begin{bmatrix} p(y_1 \mid x_1) & p(y_2 \mid x_1) \\ p(y_1 \mid x_2) & p(y_2 \mid x_2) \end{bmatrix} = \begin{bmatrix} .80 & .20 \\ .40 & .60 \end{bmatrix},$$

Figure 6.1 shows the three information value measures G_I^A, V_I^A, and $\tilde{V}_I^A$ as a function of the prior probability $p(x_1)$. When $p(x_1) = .6$, the preceding likelihood combines with the prior to produce the joint distribution ρ in (2.50).

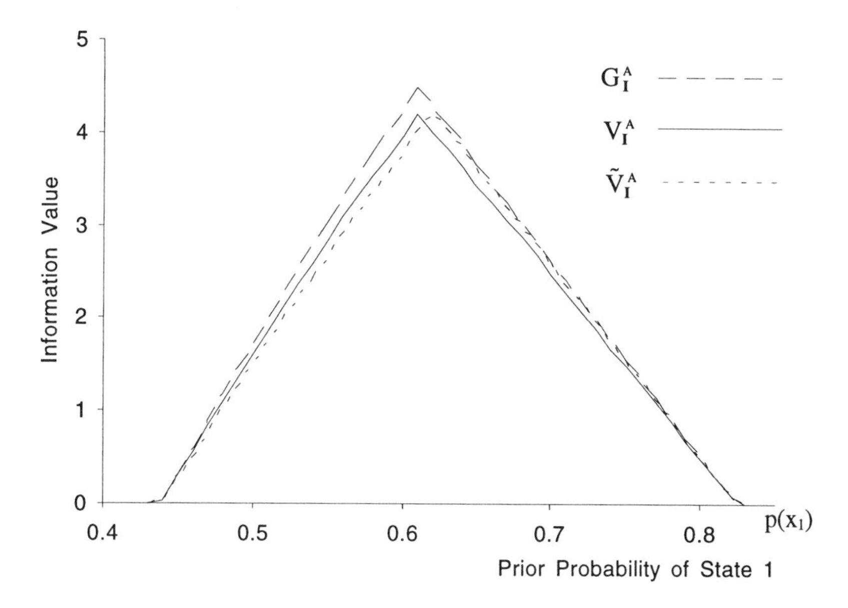

Figure 6.1. Three alternative measures of the value of information in Example 2.1, as a function of the decision maker's initial knowledge.

The three measures of value, the cash-equivalent gain $G_I^A = R_I^A - R_0^A$ given by (3.42), the demand value V_I^A, and the supply value $\tilde{V}_I^A$ as in (3.53), all track together closely. The gain is the easiest to calculate, and always measures the highest value in this problem. The demand value is not less than the supply value for $p(x_1) < .615$, but $\tilde{V}_I^A \geq V_I^A$ for all $p(x_1) \geq .615$. The difference between the two measures has to do with wealth effects and the risk attitude specific to the utility function. Note that the variation in value among the three measures is small relative to the variation in value as $p(x_1)$ changes.

For prior beliefs that indicate both low and high probability of the state, this information source has no value; it is useless in the sense of Section 2.4.3. Here the DM is so confident about the state that no message from this source can change her prior decision. However, the important matter here is not her confidence in the state, it is her confidence in the appropriateness of her prior decision, given this information structure. For intermediate assessments of the prior probability, the value of information rapidly rises and falls. The demand value is \$1.61 at $p(x_1) = .5$, the prior distribution with the highest "uncertainty" as measured by the entropy, but demand value is at its maximum of \$4.19 when $p(x_1) = .61$. The prior probability $p(x_1) = .61$ is the breakeven prior, where the prior optimal action changes from a_1 to a_2. In this example, the value of information is maximized when prior beliefs make the prior decision a close call for the DM. ♦

6.1.3 Utility Possibilities and Admissibility

Consider the special case in which there is a finite set of K actions, $\mathbf{a}^K = \{a_1, \cdots, a_k, \cdots, a_K\}$, and a countable finite set of m states, $\mathbf{X}^m = \{x_1, \cdots, x_i, \cdots, x_m\}$. For any specified action a_k, define the *utility consequence* of a_k, denoted $\breve{\mathbf{u}}(a_k)$, as the set:

$$\breve{\mathbf{u}}(a_k) = \{u(w, x_i, a_k) \text{ for every } x_i \in \mathbf{X}\}$$

$$= [u(w, x_1, a_k), \cdots, u(w, x_i, a_k), \cdots, u(w, x_m, a_k)]. \quad (6.12)$$

For any given action a_k, viewed as function of the state x_i the utility consequence defines a point in an m-dimensional Euclidean space $\mathbf{R}^m$; it is nothing more than the kth row of the $K \times m$ utility matrix $\mathbf{u}$ in (2.4).

Define the set τ comprising the vectors $\breve{\mathbf{u}}(a_k)$ for each $a_k \in \mathbf{a}^K$:

$$\tau = \{\breve{\mathbf{u}}(a_1), \cdots, \breve{\mathbf{u}}(a_k), \cdots, \breve{\mathbf{u}}(a_K)\}. \quad (6.13)$$

In words, τ is the set of *available utility consequences.*

The *convex hull* of τ is the set of all points that are convex combinations of the points in τ. The convex hull, denoted CVXH(τ), is defined as the set of all vectors of the form

$$\Sigma_k\ \breve{\mathbf{u}}(a_k)\ \alpha_k, \quad (6.14)$$

where each $\breve{\mathbf{u}}(a_k) \in \tau$ is a point in $\mathbf{R}^m$, and the α_k are a set of numbers such that $0 \le \alpha_k \le 1$ and $\Sigma_k\ \alpha_k = 1$. It can be shown that the convex hull of a set is the smallest convex set containing all of the points in τ. The importance of this definition becomes apparent when the set of numbers α is interpreted as a course of action p(a).

♦ *Example 6.1 The Land Speculator*

A land speculator/developer must choose to purchase one from five alternative tracts of land. The utility of the outcomes depends upon which of two routes is chosen for a new freeway bypass. The government agency deciding on the route is impeccably honest and concerned only with the general public welfare; therefore, as far as the speculator is concerned, the route of the highway is an uncontrollable random variable. The DM faces a problem with two states: x_1 = route one and x_2 = route two, and five actions corresponding to the choice of one of the five tracts of land. The DM assesses the following utilities of outcome for each action-state pair.

Table 6.2. Utility of Outcome for Example 6.2

	x_1	x_2
a_1	10	1
a_2	6	6
a_3	3	7
a_4	4	2
a_5	1	10

Comparing the utility consequences of the five actions, the purchase of the tract of land identified with a_2 is a risk-free action—the location of the highway does not affect the utility of outcome. The action a_4 is dominated in the sense of (2.9) by a_2. The most interesting action is the purchase of the tract identified with a_3. In the event of route two, a_3 offers the second highest utility. Under route one, a_3 does not offer the lowest utility. Is a_3 an alternative worthy of further consideration?

The set τ of available utility consequences is

$$\tau = \{[10,1], [6,6], [3,7], [4,2], [1,10]\}.$$

Figure 6.2 pictures this set in $\mathbf{R}^2$, and also shows its convex hull. Intuitively, the convex hull is formed by connecting each point in the set by straight lines; in this problem CVXH(τ) is the boundary of the quadrilateral and all points inside. ♦

Conditional on x_i, the expected utility of p(a) is

$$\mu_{x_i}(p(a)) = E_a\, u(w, x_i, a) = \Sigma_k\, u(w, x_i, a_k)\, p(a_k). \qquad (6.15)$$

Collecting the $\mu_{x_i}(p(a))$ for every $x_i \in \mathbf{X}^m$, define the *expected utility characteristic* of the course of action p(a) as the vector

$$\mu(p(a)) = [\mu_{x_1}(p(a)), \cdots, \mu_{x_i}(p(a)), \cdots, \mu_{x_m}(p(a))], \qquad (6.16)$$

a point in $\mathbf{R}^m$. Note that when the course of action is deterministic, the expected utility characteristic is simply the utility consequence $\breve{\mathbf{u}}(a_k)$ of the pure action a_k.

In principle the DM can choose to own the expected utility characteristic associated with any $p(a) \in \delta$. Define the *utility possibility set* $\aleph$ to be the set of all potential expected utility characteristics:

$$\aleph = \{\mu(p(a)) \text{ for every } p(a) \in \delta\}. \qquad (6.17)$$

In this finite case, it can be shown that the set $\aleph$ is a closed, bounded, and convex subset of the m-dimensional Euclidean space $\mathbf{R}^m$. The key fact here is that $\aleph$

is nothing more than the convex hull of the set τ of available utility consequences defined by equation (6.13):

$$\aleph = \text{CVXH}(\tau) = \text{CVXH}(\{ \breve{\mathbf{u}}(a_k) \text{ for all } a_k \in \mathbf{a}^K\}). \qquad (6.18)$$

Reference to Figure 6.2 assists in the economic interpretation of the set $\aleph$. For any point $\mu(p(a)) \in \aleph$, any other point in $\aleph$ that is north and/or east of $\mu(p(a))$ represents a utility possibility with greater expected utility in one state without a corresponding decrease in the expected utility conditional on any other state. Hence north and east is the direction of preference for any expected utility maximizer, and the optimal course of action must be associated with a point on the northeast boundary of the set $\aleph$.

The type of dominance described in the previous paragraph is called *admissibility*. The course of action $p^{\#}(a)$ is inadmissible if there is another course of action p(a) such that

$$\mu_{x_i}(p(a)) \geq \mu_{x_i}(p^{\#}(a)) \text{ for every } x_i \in \mathbf{X}^m, \qquad (6.19)$$

with strict inequality holding at least once. An equivalent statement in terms of vectors is $\mu(p(a)) \geq \mu(p^{\#}(a))$ but $\mu(p(a)) \neq \mu(p^{\#}(a))$.

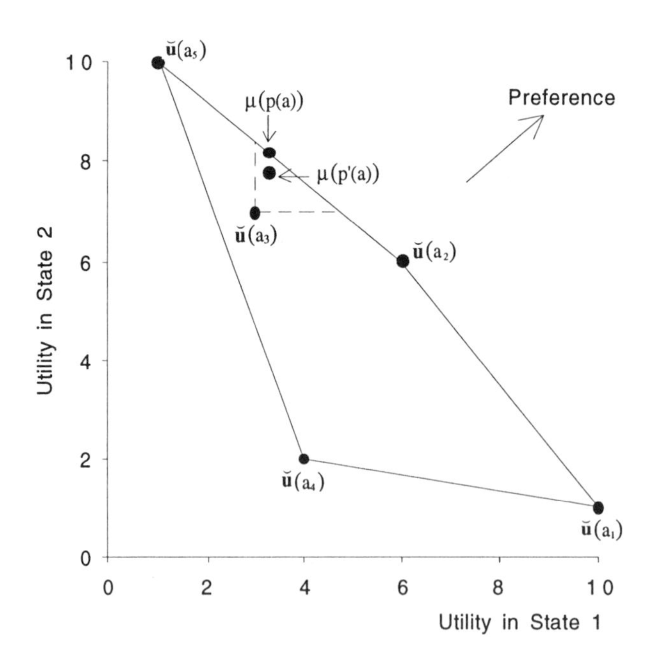

Figure 6.2. The set τ and its convex hull $\aleph$.

♦ *Example 6.1 (Continued)*

Figure 6.2 shows that the otherwise reasonable appearing action a_3 is inadmissible. Any course of action that leads to a utility possibility inside the dashed triangle in Figure 6.2 is preferred to a_3 by any expected utility maximizer. That is, the deterministic course of action described by the vector $p^{\#}(a) = [p(a_1), p(a_2), p(a_3), p(a_4), p(a_5)] = [0,0,1,0,0]$, with $\mu(p^{\#}(a)) = [3, 7]$, is inferior to a mixture of a_1 and a_5 such as $p'(a) = [.25, 0, 0, 0, .75]$ because $\mu(p'(a)) = [3.25, 7.75]$. Furthermore, $p'(a)$ is itself inadmissible, because the randomized course of action $p(a) = [0, .45, 0, 0, .55]$ offers $\mu(p(a)) = [3.25, 8.20]$, which is even better. The course of action $p(a)$ is on the boundary of $\aleph$ and is admissible. ♦

Admissibility of a course of action generalizes to the notion of admissibility for a decision rule. The quantity

$$\mu_{x_i}(\mathbf{d}, \mathbf{I}) = E_{y|x_i}\, \mu_{x_i}(\mathbf{d}(y)), \tag{6.20}$$

is a scalar, a function of x and the likelihood $p(y\,|\,x_i)$ of **I**. Define the *conditional expected utility characteristic* of the decision rule **d** under information structure **I** as the set

$$\mu(\mathbf{d}, \mathbf{I}) = \{E_{y|x_i}\, \mu_{x_i}(\mathbf{d}(y)) \text{ for every } x_i \in \mathbf{X}^m\}. \tag{6.21}$$

A decision rule $\mathbf{d}_{\#}$ is inadmissible if there is another decision rule **d**, feasible for **I**, such that

$$E_{y|x_i}\, \mu_{x_i}(\mathbf{d}(y)) \geq E_{y|x_i}\, \mu_{x_i}(\mathbf{d}_{\#}(y)) \tag{6.22}$$

for every $x_i \in \mathbf{X}^m$, with strict inequality holding for some $x_i \in \mathbf{X}^m$.

♦ *Example 6.1 (Continued)*

In the problem of the speculator choosing among five tracts of land with the utility of outcome as in Table 6.2, suppose there is an information source **I** that offers a categorical prediction of which route the government will choose. Perhaps the source is a consultant's study to determine which route is in the greater public interest. The possible final conclusions create the message space $\mathbf{Y} = \{y_1, y_2\}$ = {route one is better, route two is better}. The DM assesses the likelihood $p(y_j\,|\,x_i)$ as

$$\lambda = \begin{bmatrix} p(y_1|x_1) & p(y_2|x_1) \\ p(y_1|x_2) & p(y_2|x_2) \end{bmatrix} = \begin{bmatrix} .80 & .20 \\ .30 & .70 \end{bmatrix}. \tag{6.23}$$

The prior distribution on the state is as yet unspecified.

The normal form analysis requires the assessment of the conditional expected utility characteristic $\mu(\mathbf{d}, \mathbf{I})$ for every decision rule $\mathbf{d} \in \delta_{\mathbf{I}}$. The first step is to identify all possible pure or deterministic decision rules. Since the action a_4 is dominated in the sense of (2.9), there are four undominated actions. Combined with two messages, there are 16 pure decision rules.

For each pure decision rule $\mathbf{d}_\kappa$, the next step is to calculate the scalar quantity (6.20):

$$\mu_{x_i}(\mathbf{d}_\kappa, \mathbf{I}) = u(w, x_i, \mathbf{d}_\kappa(y_1))\, p(y_1 \mid x_i) + u(w, x_i, \mathbf{d}_\kappa(y_2))\, p(y_2 \mid x_i) \quad (6.24)$$

for i = 1, 2. For each pure decision rule, the expected utility characteristic of **I** is the vector

$$\mu(\mathbf{d}_\kappa, \mathbf{I}) = [\mu_{x_1}(\mathbf{d}_\kappa, \mathbf{I}), \mu_{x_2}(\mathbf{d}_\kappa, \mathbf{I})]. \quad (6.25)$$

Table 6.3 gives the results of the calculations specified by (6.24).

Table 6.3. The Conditional Expected Utility Characteristics in Example 6.1

κ	$\mathbf{d}_\kappa(y_1)$	$\mathbf{d}_\kappa(y_2)$	$\mu_{x_1}(\mathbf{d}_\kappa, \mathbf{I})$	$\mu_{x_2}(\mathbf{d}_\kappa, \mathbf{I})$	Inadmissible by
1	a_1	a_1	10.0	1.0	--
2	a_1	a_2	9.2	4.5	--
3	a_1	a_3	8.6	5.2	mixture of $\mathbf{d}_2$ and $\mathbf{d}_4$
4	a_1	a_5	8.2	7.3	--
5	a_2	a_1	6.8	2.5	$\mathbf{d}_2$
6	a_2	a_2	6.0	6.0	$\mathbf{d}_4$
7	a_2	a_3	5.4	6.7	$\mathbf{d}_4$
8	a_2	a_5	5.0	8.8	--
9	a_3	a_1	4.4	2.8	$\mathbf{d}_2$
10	a_3	a_2	3.6	6.3	$\mathbf{d}_4$
11	a_3	a_3	3.0	7.0	$\mathbf{d}_4$
12	a_3	a_5	2.6	9.1	mixture of $\mathbf{d}_8$ and $\mathbf{d}_{16}$
13	a_5	a_1	2.8	3.7	$\mathbf{d}_2$
14	a_5	a_2	2.0	7.2	$\mathbf{d}_4$
15	a_5	a_3	1.4	7.9	$\mathbf{d}_8$
16	a_5	a_5	1.0	10.0	--

The decision rules $\mathbf{d}_3$ and $\mathbf{d}_{12}$ are inadmissible because there are randomizations of other pure decision rules that have better conditional expected utility characteristics. Consider, for example, the decision rule $\mathbf{d}_\bullet$ described in matrix format:

$$\mathbf{d}_\bullet = \begin{bmatrix} p(a_1 \mid y_1) & p(a_2 \mid y_1) & p(a_3 \mid y_1) & p(a_5 \mid y_1) \\ p(a_1 \mid y_2) & p(a_2 \mid y_2) & p(a_3 \mid y_2) & p(a_5 \mid y_2) \end{bmatrix} = \begin{bmatrix} 1.0 & 0 & 0 & 0 \\ 0 & .60 & 0 & .40 \end{bmatrix}.$$

In words, $\mathbf{d}_\bullet$ says: take a_1 if y_1, and if y_2, take a_2 with probability .60 and a_5 with probability .40. Calculating first (6.15),

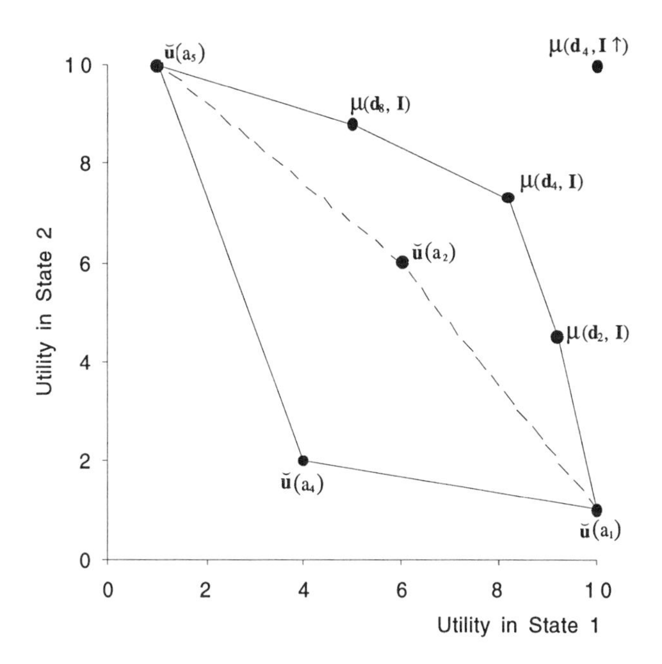

Figure 6.3. As a consequence of the incorporation of information, the utility possibilities set expands in the preferred direction. Perfect information, the most informative structure, would expand the convex hull out to the upper right-hand corner.

$$\mu_{x_1}(\mathbf{d}_\bullet(y_1)) = 10.0 \qquad \mu_{x_1}(\mathbf{d}_\bullet(y_2)) = 4.0$$

$$\mu_{x_2}(\mathbf{d}_\bullet(y_1)) = 1.0 \qquad \mu_{x_2}(\mathbf{d}_\bullet(y_2)) = 7.6.$$

Using λ in (6.23) to calculate (6.20) yields

$$\mu(\mathbf{d}_\bullet, \mathbf{I}) = [\mu_{x_1}(\mathbf{d}_\bullet, \mathbf{I}), \mu_{x_2}(\mathbf{d}_\bullet, \mathbf{I})] = [8.80, 5.62],$$

which dominates $\mu(\mathbf{d}_3, \mathbf{I})$.

Describing the utility possibility set is about as far as the DM can go before finally choosing the optimal point in $\aleph$ by utilizing the probability distribution on the state. Figure 6.3 superimposes the set of undominated conditional expected utility characteristics under **I** upon Figure 6.2, the set of expected utility characteristics in the uninformed decision. Comparing the convex hulls of the two sets shows the expansion of the utility possibilities in the preferred direction as a result of using the information structure **I**. In fact, Section 6.2.2 shows how the characteristics of this expansion can be used to measure and compare the informativeness of alternative information structures. In the limiting case of perfect information, the convex hull expands to include the point $\mu(\mathbf{d}_4, \mathbf{I}\uparrow) = [10,$

10]; with this structure it is a sure deal that the DM receives utility of outcome = 10. ♦

6.1.4 The Finite Model in Normal Form

When the action, state, and message spaces are all finite, the value of the informed decision can be expressed in matrix form. This is particularly convenient for computer modeling.

In light of (6.2), the utility of the outcome is the K × m matrix **u** stating the utility of outcome from each action a_k and each state x_i:

$$\mathbf{u} = \begin{bmatrix} u(w, x_1, a_1) & \cdots & u(w, x_m, a_1) \\ \vdots & u(w, x_i, a_k) & \vdots \\ u(w, x_1, a_K) & \cdots & u(w, x_m, a_K) \end{bmatrix}. \tag{6.26}$$

The decision rule is most simply characterized in the finite model as an n × K Markov matrix that lists the responses the DM takes posterior to each message:

$$\mathbf{d} = \begin{bmatrix} p(a_1|y_1) & \cdots & p(a_K|y_1) \\ \vdots & p(a_k|y_j) & \vdots \\ p(a_1|y_n) & \cdots & p(a_K|y_n) \end{bmatrix}. \tag{6.27}$$

Each row of **d** is a conditional decision rule $\mathbf{d}(y_j)$ expressing the action strategy in response to message y_j. In this finite model the broadest set of potential decision rules available for choice is the set of all n × K Markov matrices. In the case of deterministic decision rules, each row of the matrix **d** contains one 1 and [K – 1] zeros. The matrix product **du** is an n × m matrix in which the typical element is the expected utility of a decision rule $\mathbf{d}(y_j)$:

$$\Sigma_k\, u(w, x_i, a_k)\, p(a_k | y_j) = \mu_{x_i}(\mathbf{d}(y_j)).$$

Next, premultiplying **du** by the m × n likelihood matrix (2.23) gives the m × m matrix $\lambda\mathbf{du}$. Only the main diagonal of the square matrix $\lambda\mathbf{du}$ has economic meaning; the typical component on the diagonal is $\mu_{x_i}(\mathbf{d}, \mathbf{I})$ as in (6.20), the expected utility of **d** under **I**, conditional on x_i:

$$\Sigma_j\, \Sigma_k\, u(w, x_i, a_k)\, p(a_k | y_j)\, p(y_j | x_i) = \mu_{x_i}(\mathbf{d}, \mathbf{I}).$$

The diagonalization of $\lambda\mathbf{du}$ is the 1 × m vector $\mu(\mathbf{d}, \mathbf{I})$, the conditional expected utility characteristic of **d** under **I**:

$$\text{diag}(\lambda\mathbf{du}) = [\mu_{x_1}(\mathbf{d}, \mathbf{I}), \cdots, \mu_{x_i}(\mathbf{d}, \mathbf{I}), \cdots, \mu_{x_m}(\mathbf{d}, \mathbf{I})] = \mu(\mathbf{d}, \mathbf{I}),$$

using (6.21).

The unconditional expected utility of the decision, given **d** and **I**, is the weighted average of each $\mu_{x_i}(\mathbf{d}, \mathbf{I})$, the weight being the prior distribution $p(x_i)$:

$$\mathbf{U(D \mid I, d)} = \Sigma_i \Sigma_j \Sigma_k u(w, x_i, a_k) p(a_k \mid y_j) p(y_j \mid x_i) p(x_i)$$

$$= \Sigma_i \mu_{x_i}(\mathbf{d}, \mathbf{I}) p(x_i).$$

This writes most conveniently in matrix form by defining the diagonalized prior **R** as the m × m matrix

$$\mathbf{R} = \begin{bmatrix} p(x_1) & \cdots & 0 \\ \vdots & p(x_i) & \vdots \\ 0 & \cdots & p(x_m) \end{bmatrix}. \tag{6.28}$$

In the matrix expression $\lambda\mathbf{duR}$, only the diagonal components come into play; $\lambda\mathbf{duR}$ is an m × m matrix whose trace (the sum of the diagonal terms) is

$$\mathbf{U(D \mid I, d)} = \text{tr}\, \lambda\mathbf{duR}. \tag{6.29}$$

The value of the informed decision is the choice of decision rule (matrix) **d** that maximizes (6.29):

$$\mathbf{U(D^* \mid I)} = \max_{\mathbf{d} \in \delta} \text{tr}\, \lambda\mathbf{duR}. \tag{6.30}$$

Ahituv and Wand (1984) conceive of this choice as the solution to a linear programming problem. With $a^u_{y_j}$ as the optimal deterministic response to y_j, (6.30) is equivalent to

$$\mathbf{U(D^* \mid I)} = \Sigma_i p(x_i) \Sigma_j u(w, x_i, a^u_{y_j}) p(y_j \mid x_i). \tag{6.31}$$

It is left as an exercise to show the equivalent matrix expression for extensive form analysis is $\mathbf{U(D^* \mid I)} = \max_{\mathbf{d} \in \delta} \text{tr}\, \mathbf{du\Pi Q}$, where **Q** diagonalizes **q**, the marginal on the message space.

♦ *Example 6.1 (Continued)*

The optimal decision rule depends upon the expectation of (6.25) with respect to the prior distribution p(x). If, for example, $p(x_1) = .35$ and $p(x_2) = .65$, then using the data in (6.23) for the likelihood, in Table 6.2 for (6.26), and the preceding prior, assessing (6.29) for every decision rule shows $\mathbf{d}^u_{\mathbf{I}} = \mathbf{d}_4$. The value of the informed decision is

$$\mathbf{U(D^* \mid I)} = \text{tr} \begin{bmatrix} .80 & .20 \\ .30 & .70 \end{bmatrix} \begin{bmatrix} 1 & 0 & 0 & 0 \\ 0 & 0 & 0 & 1 \end{bmatrix} \begin{bmatrix} 10 & 1 \\ 6 & 6 \\ 3 & 7 \\ 1 & 10 \end{bmatrix} \begin{bmatrix} .35 & 0 \\ 0 & .65 \end{bmatrix}.$$

Calculating from left to right, the final step leads to $\mathbf{U}(\mathbf{D}^* \mid \mathbf{I}) = [8.2][.35] + [7.3][.65] = 7.615$. Different priors, of course, lead to different optimal decision rules. ♦

6.1.5 Convexity in the Probabilities

The notation can be embellished further in order to concentrate on an information structure's abilities to transform, or process, prior probabilities into posterior probabilities. Let $\xi = \{\xi_1, \cdots, \xi_i, \cdots, \xi_m\}$ be any probability distribution (prior or posterior) defined on the finite set $\mathbf{X}^m = \{x_1, \cdots, x_i, \cdots, x_m\}$. Let Ξ be the set of all such probability distributions over $\mathbf{X}^m$, that is, the m − 1 dimensional simplex

$$\Xi = \{\xi: \xi_i \geq 0, \Sigma_i \xi_i = 1\}. \tag{6.32}$$

Again using the utility consequence from taking action a_k, the $1 \times m$ vector

$$\breve{\mathbf{u}}(a_k) = [u(w, x_1, a_k), \cdots, u(w, x_i, a_k), \cdots, u(w, x_m, a_k)],$$

write the expected terminal utility of outcome from a_k under the distribution ξ on $\mathbf{X}$ as

$$\breve{\mu}(a_k(\xi)) = \Sigma_i u(w, x_i, a_k) \xi_i. \tag{6.33}$$

Taking the optimum action under ξ, denoted $a_*(\xi)$, yields

$$\breve{\mu}(a_*(\xi)) = \max_a \Sigma_i u(w, x_i, a_k) \xi_i = t(\xi). \tag{6.34}$$

The notation $t(\xi)$ means to stress the dependency on the distribution ξ.

When ξ is the prior distribution over the state, ξ is the $1 \times m$ vector $\mathbf{r}$ given by (2.19). Since $\mathbf{r} \in \Xi$, $t(\mathbf{r})$ is

$$t(\mathbf{r}) = \breve{\mu}(a_0(\mathbf{r})) = \max_a \Sigma_i u(w, x_i, a_k) p(x_i) = \mathbf{U}(\mathbf{D}^* \mid \mathbf{I}\downarrow). \tag{6.35}$$

When ξ is the posterior distribution of the state, resulting from the receipt of message y_j, then ξ is the jth column of the matrix Π in (2.25); this is the $m \times 1$ column vector $[p(x_1 \mid y_j), \cdots, p(x_i \mid y_j), \cdots, p(x_m \mid y_j)]^T = \Pi_j$. With $\Pi_j \in \Xi$, and writing

$$a_j \equiv a_{y_j}$$

for the action optimal posterior to the receipt of message y_j, $t(\Pi_j)$ is

$$t(\Pi_j) = \breve{\mu}(a_j(\Pi_j)) = \max_a \Sigma_i u(w, x_i, a_k) p(x_i \mid y_j) = \mathbf{U}(\mathbf{D}^* \mid \mathbf{I}, y_j). \tag{6.36}$$

The expectation of the function $t(\Pi_j)$ with respect to the marginal on $\mathbf{Y}$ is of course $\mathbf{U}(\mathbf{D}^* \mid \mathbf{I})$:

$$E_y\, t(\Pi_j) = E_y\, \breve{\mu}(a_j(\Pi_j))$$

$$= \Sigma_j \max_a \Sigma_i u(w, x_i, a_k)\, p(x_i | y_j)\, p(y_j) = \mathbf{U}(\mathbf{D}^* | \mathbf{I}). \quad (6.37)$$

Several important results in the sequel follow from the fact that $t(\xi)$, defined on the convex set Ξ, is convex in ξ. For any two distributions ξ' and $\xi'' \in \Xi$, any number α such that $0 \le \alpha \le 1$, and a third distribution $\xi''' = \alpha\xi' + [1 - \alpha]\xi''$, it suffices to show that

$$t(\xi''') \le \alpha t(\xi') + [1 - \alpha]\xi''.$$

For any action a_k, from the definition (6.33),

$$\breve{\mu}(a_k(\xi''')) = \Sigma_i u(w, x_i, a_k)\, [\alpha\xi' + [1 - \alpha]\xi'']$$

$$= \Sigma_i u(w, x_i, a_k)\, \alpha\xi' + \Sigma_i u(w, x_i, a_k)\, [1 - \alpha]\xi''$$

$$= \alpha\, \Sigma_i u(w, x_i, a_k)\, \xi' + [1 - \alpha]\, \Sigma_i u(w, x_i, a_k)\, \xi''. \quad (6.38)$$

Now, using (6.34),

$$t(\xi''') = \max_a \Sigma_i u(w, x_i, a_k)\, [\alpha\xi' + [1 - \alpha]\xi''],$$

and substituting (6.38) yields

$$t(\xi''') = \max_a \{\alpha\, \Sigma_i u(w, x_i, a_k)\, \xi' + [1 - \alpha]\, \Sigma_i u(w, x_i, a_k)\, \xi''\}.$$

Since the maximum of the sum of two functions can never be greater than the sum of their individual maxima,

$$t(\xi''') \le \max_a \{\alpha\, \Sigma_i u(w, x_i, a_k)\, \xi'\} + \max_a \{[1 - \alpha]\, \Sigma_i u(w, x_i, a_k)\, \xi''\},$$

it follows that

$$t(\xi''') \le \alpha \max_a \Sigma_i u(w, x_i, a_k)\, \xi' + [1 - \alpha] \max_a \Sigma_i u(w, x_i, a_k)\, \xi'',$$

or, finally

$$t(\xi''') \le \alpha t(\xi') + [1 - \alpha]\xi''.$$

Since $t(\xi)$ is convex, we know from Jensen's inequality (2.36a) that

$$E_\xi\, t(\xi) \ge t(E_\xi\, \xi).$$

Jensen's inequality applied to $\mathbf{U}(\mathbf{D}^* | \mathbf{I})$ states

$$\mathbf{U}(\mathbf{D}^* | \mathbf{I}) = E_y\, \breve{\mu}(a_j(\Pi_j)) \ge \breve{\mu}(a_*(E_y\, \Pi_j))$$

or, in the notation as in (6.37),

$$\mathbf{U(D^* \mid I)} = \Sigma_j \Sigma_i u(w, x_i, a_j)\, p(x_i \mid y_j)\, p(y_j)$$

$$\geq \max_a \Sigma_i u(w, x_i, a)\, \Sigma_j p(x_i \mid y_j)\, p(y_j).$$

Since, as in (4.1), $\Sigma_j p(x_i \mid y_j)\, p(y_j) = p(x_i)$, the right-hand side of this inequality is

$$\max_a \Sigma_i u(w, x_i, a)\, p(x_i) = \mathbf{U(D^* \mid I\downarrow)}.$$

Thus, Jensen's inequality provides an alternative demonstration that $\mathbf{U(D^* \mid I)} \geq \mathbf{U(D^* \mid I\downarrow)}$.

The upcoming continuation of Example 6.1 illustrates the convexity of the function $t(\xi)$ for a dichotomy with a finite set of actions. If the action space $\mathbf{a}$ is infinite and no action is optimal for two distinct values of ξ, then the envelope function $t(\xi)$ becomes strictly convex.

♦ *Example 6.1 (Continued)*

When the state space is a simple dichotomy ($m = 2$) as in this example, the simplex Ξ is a straight line from zero to one and the distribution is fully characterized by the probability of one of the states, say x_1. Writing $r_1 \equiv p(x_1)$, the expected utility of any action a_k is, in general,

$$\mathbf{U(D \mid I\downarrow}, a_k) = u(w, x_1, a_k)\, r_1 + u(w, x_2, a_k)[1 - r_1]$$

$$= u(w, x_2, a_k) + [u(w, x_1, a_k) - u(w, x_2, a_k)]r_1.$$

Plugging in the specific utility numbers from Table 6.2 yields

$$\mathbf{U(D \mid I\downarrow}, a_1) = 1 + 9r_1,$$

$$\mathbf{U(D \mid I\downarrow}, a_2) = 6,$$

$$\mathbf{U(D \mid I\downarrow}, a_3) = 7 - 4r_1,$$

$$\mathbf{U(D \mid I\downarrow}, a_4) = 2 + 2r_1,$$

$$\mathbf{U(D \mid I\downarrow}, a_5) = 10 - 9r_1.$$

Figure 6.4 graphs these functions. The upper envelope of these straight lines identifies the optimal action and the maximum expected utility as a function of r_1. The inadmissible action a_3 and the dominated action a_4 are never optimal. The envelope function is $t(\mathbf{r})$ as in (6.35), and is convex in r_1. The optimal course of action is to choose

$$\begin{array}{ll} a_1 & \text{if } 5/9 \leq r_1 \leq 1, \\ a_2 & \text{if } 4/9 \leq r_1 \leq 5/9, \\ a_5 & \text{if } 0 \leq r_1 \leq 4/9. \end{array}$$

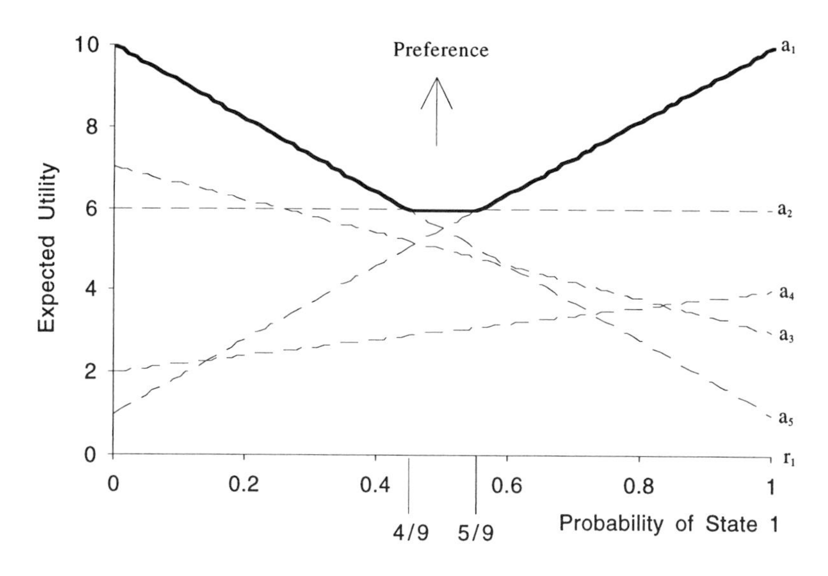

Figure 6.4. This graph shows the expected utility of each of the five actions in Example 6.1, as a function of the DM's initial probability assessment $p(x_1) \equiv r_1$. The darkened line is the convex function $t(\mathbf{r})$, which gives $\mathbf{U(D^* \,|\, I\downarrow)}$ for every prior probability r_1.

Note that the three possible optimal choices correspond to the actions associated with the three extreme points on the northeastern boundary of the set $\aleph$ in Figure 6.2. For the two breakeven prior distributions (i.e., r_1 = 4/9 and 5/9) in which the DM is indifferent between two actions, any randomized course of action mixing the two provides the same expected utility. The randomization does not help the DM's expected utility, but in this case it does not hurt it any either. In Figure 6.2, any such randomized course of action corresponds to a point on the line segment connecting the utility consequences of the two pure decisions. For example, when r_1 = 4/9, consider the course of action p(a) = [0, .45, 0, 0, .55], with $\mu(p(a))$ = [3.25, 8.20] as identified in Figure 6.2. This randomized choice has expected utility [3.25][4/9] + [8.20][5/9] = 6, the same as the expected utility of the pure decisions a_2 and a_5 that comprise it.

Equation (3.54) defines the utility increment from perfect information as the difference $\mathbf{U(D^* \,|\, I\uparrow)} - \mathbf{U(D^* \,|\, I\downarrow)}$. Figure 6.5 shows how this measure of information value depends upon the prior distribution. Regardless of the prior, the value of the perfectly informed decision is $\mathbf{U(D^* \,|\, I\uparrow)} = 10$; this value is shown by the dotted line in the figure. The vertical distance between the dotted line and the upper envelope is the utility increment from perfect information.

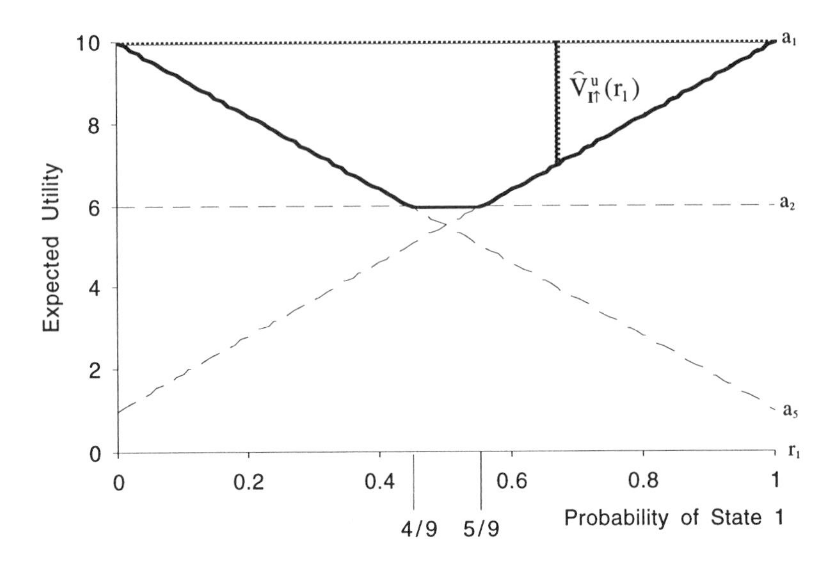

Figure 6.5. If the DM possesses the perfect information structure, she is assured of receiving utility of 10, regardless of her prior. The value of perfect information, as measured by the utility increment, is the indicated distance for any assessment of r_1.

The maximum utility increment of 4 occurs for priors with r_1 between 4/9 and 5/9; the increment declines with the DM's prior certainty about the state, reaching zero at $r_1 = 0$ and $r_1 = 1$. The value-maximizing prior distributions are distinguished by the breakeven values where the optimal prior action changes, and not by the entropy-maximizing prior of $r_1 = .5$. The upcoming continuation of Example 6.1 in Section 6.3.1 generalizes this analysis to consider less than perfect informativeness. ♦

Figure 6.5 is helpful for pointing up the sensitivity of information value to several types of changes in the situation. Note that if a very small amount were added to the payoff of a_1 in state x_1, there would be a unique prior that maximizes the utility increment, a belief very close to 5/9, and the increment would be larger. This illustrates that information value is sensitive to the parameters of the outcome function. Also, an alteration in the DM's technology—an expansion, deletion, or adjustment in the action space **a**—does not have an unambiguous effect on information value. Such changes can have an impact on the value of both the informed and the uninformed decisions in ways that are problem-specific and decision maker specific. In Figure 6.5, if there were a new and dominating action a_6 that offered utility of 20 in both states, the utility increment would be zero for any prior. Note also that this is a different phenomenon from the value of flexibility in dynamic decision models; see the preceding Section 5.6.1 and also Section 5.2.5 of Hirshleifer and Riley (1992).

Case studies commonly investigate the magnitude of the sensitivities by means of simulation analysis. As an example, perhaps the most morally difficult parameter is the assumed value of a human life in decision problems involving life and death. In Reichard and Evans' (1989) analysis of the value of information to a neighborhood facing potential contamination of its drinking water, information value first rises and then falls as the assumed value of a life increases; Finkel and Evans (1987) obtain a similar result. This is a problem-specific result, but the explanation is clear. When life is cheap, expensive actions to remediate are rejected regardless of most messages; when life is extremely dear, the action offering the most personal safety is chosen in the prior decision, and this decision is difficult for any information to change. For values of a life in which the decision to pay for remediation is a close call and messages can have a pragmatic impact on action, the value of information is greater.

6.2 Comparative Informativeness

The normal form of analysis lays the groundwork for investigating the role of the information structure **I** as a determinant of the value of information. Unlike the previous alterations of the outcome function or the action space, alterations in the information structure can affect only the informed decision. This allows for the identification of one of the most general determinants of information value, the statistical informativeness of the structure **I**. The concept of informativness, however, must be precisely defined. It is certainly not the same thing as accuracy; Section 4.2 describes several examples in which greater "accuracy," by one measure or another, is associated with less valuable information. This section presents the general results that are available under the precise definition of informativeness due to Blackwell (1953).

6.2.1 The Relation "More Informative Than"

Section 2.1.2 formulates a decision problem as comprising a space of actions, a space of possible states of nature, an outcome function, the DM's utility function for terminal wealth, the initial wealth, the available information structure $\mathbf{I} = \{\mathbf{Y}, p(x, y)\}$, and an information cost function:

$$\mathbf{D} = < \mathbf{a}, \mathbf{X}, \omega, u, w, \mathbf{I}, \mathbf{C}(\mathbf{I}) >.$$

The components u and w are specific to the decision maker. Consider a class of decision problems with a fixed state space $\mathbf{X}$, and a set of potential information structures Θ such that for each $\mathbf{I} \in \Theta$, $\mathbf{C}(\mathbf{I}) = 0$. Let $u^{\#}$ represent the class of all

DMs who use the expected utility criterion and have utility strictly increasing in wealth. With all other components of $\mathbf{D}$ arbitrary, define the class of decision situations Ω as

$$\Omega = \{\mathbf{D}: \mathbf{D} = < \bullet, \mathbf{X}, \bullet, u^{\#}, \bullet, \mathbf{I}, 0 >\}. \tag{6.39}$$

The *theory of comparative informativeness*, also called the *comparison of experiments* [Torgersen (1991)], seeks to analyze the conditions under which, before consideration of costs, one information structure is preferred to another by every potential user with a decision situation in Ω. This section studies the gross comparability of alternative information structures for all expected-utility decision makers facing decision problems using the state space $\mathbf{X}$ as a payoff-adequate description of the uncertain state of nature. See Marschak and Radner (1972) for a discussion of the concept of payoff-adequacy.

Identifying alternative information structures in Θ by the parameter θ, two structures

$$\mathbf{I}(\theta) = \{\mathbf{Y}(\theta), p(x, y; \theta)\},$$

and

$$\mathbf{I}(\theta') = \{\mathbf{Y}(\theta'), p(x, y'; \theta')\},$$

can differ from one another in the following ways.

1) $\mathbf{Y}(\theta) = \mathbf{Y}(\theta')$ but $p(x, y; \theta) \neq p(x, y'; \theta')$. Here the message spaces are identical but the joint distributions different. An important application of this case is to the comparison of alternative categorical and direct forecasts of a common state variable that is payoff-relevant in many different decision problems, such as the prime interest rate or tomorrow's temperature; see Section 6.2.4.

2) Both $\mathbf{Y}(\theta) \neq \mathbf{Y}(\theta')$ and $p(x, y; \theta) \neq p(x, y'; \theta')$. This situation can arise when comparing two sources with alternative indirect message spaces, such as two monographs by different authors. It also occurs when $\mathbf{Y}(\theta')$ is constructed from $\mathbf{Y}(\theta)$ by, for example, combining or suppressing some of the messages; see Section 6.2.3.

The theory of comparative informativeness studies the characteristics of $\mathbf{I}(\theta)$ and $\mathbf{I}(\theta')$ under which the value of any informed decision in Ω is greater using $\mathbf{I}(\theta)$ than from using $\mathbf{I}(\theta')$. The formal definition is:

Statistical Informativeness: $\mathbf{I}(\theta)$ is more statistically informative than $\mathbf{I}(\theta')$ if and only if $\mathbf{U}(\mathbf{D}^* \mid \mathbf{I}(\theta)) \geq \mathbf{U}(\mathbf{D}^* \mid \mathbf{I}(\theta'))$ for all $\mathbf{D} \in \Omega$.

Section 6.2.2 identifies a set of conditions fully equivalent to greater informativeness. Section 6.2.3 presents several special cases.

In comparing informativeness it is convenient to define the dual information structure combining both $\mathbf{I}(\theta)$ and $\mathbf{I}(\theta')$. The dual structure is written

$$\vartheta(\theta, \theta') = \{\mathbf{Y}(\theta) \times \mathbf{Y}(\theta'), p(x, y, y'; \theta, \theta')\}; \tag{6.40}$$

the interest lies especially in the properties of the trivariate distribution of the state and the alternative messages. For example, Ahituv and Ronen (1988) work with this trivariate distribution in order to investigate the value of a second opinion y', having already obtained y.

6.2.2 *Blackwell's Theorem*

To avoid technical distractions, assume that the state space and the two information structures are finite. At this stage there is no need for the notation to carry along the identifying parameters θ and θ'; write $\mathbf{I} \equiv \mathbf{I}(\theta)$ and $\mathbf{I}' \equiv \mathbf{I}(\theta')$. With the state space given by $\mathbf{X}^m = \{x_1, \cdots, x_i, \cdots, x_m\}$, write

$$\mathbf{I} = \{\mathbf{Y}^n, p(x_i, y_j)\} = \{\mathbf{Y}^n, p(y_j | x_i), p(x_i)\} = \{\mathbf{Y}^n, p(x_i | y_j), p(y_j)\}, \tag{6.41}$$

with

$$\mathbf{Y}^n = \{y_1, \cdots, y_j, \cdots, y_n\},$$

and

$$\mathbf{I}' = \{\mathbf{Y}'^{n'}, p(x_i, y'_J)\} = \{\mathbf{Y}'^{n'}, p(y'_J | x_i), p(x_i)\} = \{\mathbf{Y}'^{n'}, p(x_i | y'_J), p(y'_J)\}, \tag{6.42}$$

with

$$\mathbf{Y}'^{n'} = \{y'_1, \cdots, y'_J, \cdots, y'_{n'}\}.$$

In (6.42), the subscript J identifies the typical message among the n' members of $\mathbf{Y}'^{n'}$. The corresponding likelihood and posterior matrices are denoted λ' and Π', respectively. The trivariate density in (6.40) is written $p(x_i, y_j, y'_J)$.

This subsection presents a set of four conditions equivalent to greater informativeness; proofs and discussions can be found in Bohnenblust, Shapley, and Sherman (1949), Blackwell and Girshick (1954), Grettenberg (1964), Marschak and Miyasawa (1968), and McGuire (1972). The most important result, developed in work culminating with Blackwell (1951; 1953), is a condition relating the likelihoods $p(y_j | x_i)$ and $p(y'_J | x_i)$ that is valid for arbitrary $p(x_i)$, without the need to specify the exact trivariate distribution tying the two structures together.

Comparison via Likelihoods

To motivate the development of Blackwell's main theorem, Marschak and Radner (1972) suppose the existence of a random device. When the information source $\mathbf{I}$ produces message y_j the DM does not receive it; instead, the device transforms y_j into an alternative signal y'_J with probability b_{jJ}, $J = 1, \cdots, n'$. The stochastic transformation of y_j into y'_J characterized by this device can in the finite case be represented by the $n \times n'$ matrix

$$B = \begin{bmatrix} b_{11} & \cdots & b_{1n'} \\ \vdots & b_{jJ} & \vdots \\ b_{n1} & \cdots & b_{nn'} \end{bmatrix}. \tag{6.43}$$

Blackwell's Theorem: the satisfaction of the following two conditions, B_1 and B_2, is necessary and sufficient to ensure that **I** is more informative than **I′**.

$$B_1: b_{jJ} \geq 0, \text{ with } \Sigma_J\, b_{jJ} = 1;$$

$$B_2: p(y'_J \mid x_i) = \Sigma_j\, p(y_j \mid x_i)\, b_{jJ}, \text{ or } \lambda' = \lambda B.$$

The matrix B is said to *quasi-garble* λ into λ'. Condition B_1 says the matrix B must be Markov, that is, have rows summing to one. Economically, this means the device must not malfunction, in the sense that one of the messages in $\mathbf{Y}'^{n'}$ must be produced each time. Condition B_2 describes the likelihood of the generation of the message y'_J for each state via the likelihood of the structure **I** and the operation of the device. The sufficiency part of the theorem is pretty easy to understand; any DM would seem better off by directly receiving y_j and taking action on that basis than having the message y_j quasi-garbled into y'_J. The necessity part is a remarkable result. In words, it states that if **I** is to be more valuable than **I′**, then there must exist a stochastic transformation with matrix B such that the preceding conditions hold. The text shows only the sufficiency part; for proofs of necessity using game-theoretic methods see Blackwell (1953, Theorem 6), Blackwell and Girshick (1954, Theorem 12.2.2), Marschak and Miyasawa (1968, Theorem 8.1), and Crémer (1982).

The value of the informed decision using **I′** is

$$\mathbf{U}(\mathbf{D}^* \mid \mathbf{I}') = \Sigma_J\, \Sigma_i\, u(w, x_i, a_J)\, p(x_i, y'_J), \tag{6.44}$$

writing, as in Section 6.1.5, a_J as the optimal action given message y'_J. The joint distribution becomes, by invoking the hypothesis B_2 and reconditioning,

$$\begin{aligned} p(x_i, y'_J) &= p(y'_J \mid x_i)\, p(x_i) \\ &= \Sigma_j\, p(y_j \mid x_i)\, p(x_i)\, b_{jJ} \\ &= \Sigma_j\, p(x_i \mid y_j)\, p(y_j)\, b_{jJ}. \end{aligned} \tag{6.45}$$

Hence, substituting (6.45) into (6.44), changing the order of summation, and rearranging,

$$\mathbf{U}(\mathbf{D}^* \mid \mathbf{I}') = \Sigma_j\, p(y_j)\, \Sigma_J\, b_{jJ}\, \Sigma_i\, u(w, x_i, a_J)\, p(x_i \mid y_j).$$

Now, by the definition of a_j, the optimal action under y_j,

$$\Sigma_i u(w, x_i, a_J) p(x_i | y_j) \leq \Sigma_i u(w, x_i, a_j) p(x_i | y_j).$$

Using B_1,

$$\mathbf{U(D^* | I')} = \Sigma_j p(y_j) \Sigma_J b_{jJ} \Sigma_i u(w, x_i, a_J) p(x_i | y_j),$$

$$\leq \Sigma_j p(y_j) \Sigma_J b_{jJ} \Sigma_i u(w, x_i, a_j) p(x_i | y_j)$$

$$= \Sigma_j p(y_j) \Sigma_i u(w, x_i, a_j) p(x_i | y_j) = \mathbf{U(D^* | I)},$$

since the sense of the inequality does not change and $\Sigma_J b_{jJ} = 1$.

Note finally that B_2 also implies a specific relationship between the two marginal distributions on the message spaces. Summing (6.45) over the x_i shows

$$p(y'_J) = \Sigma_i p(x_i, y'_J) = \Sigma_i \Sigma_j p(x_i, y_j) b_{jJ} = \Sigma_j p(y_j) b_{jJ}. \qquad (6.46a)$$

In matrix notation,

$$\mathbf{q}' = \mathbf{q}B; \qquad (6.46b)$$

that is, the matrix B quasi-garbles the marginal on the messages.

Comparison via Posterior Probabilities

Blackwell's Theorem is a condition based upon the likelihoods λ and λ'; an equivalent condition compares the posterior distributions and marginal distributions of the messages. In the finite case define a matrix of conditional probabilities s_{jJ}

$$\mathbf{S} = \begin{bmatrix} s_{11} & \cdots & s_{1n'} \\ \vdots & s_{jJ} & \vdots \\ s_{n1} & \cdots & s_{nn'} \end{bmatrix},$$

such that

S_1: $s_{jJ} \geq 0$, with $\Sigma_j s_{jJ} = 1$;

S_2: $p(x_i | y'_J) = \Sigma_j p(x_i | y_j) s_{jJ}$, or $\Pi' = \Pi\mathbf{S}$;

S_3: $p(y_j) = \Sigma_J s_{jJ} p(y'_J)$, or $\mathbf{q}^T = \mathbf{S}[\mathbf{q}']^T$

The first condition requires that the Markov matrix be column-stochastic, so that the s_{jJ} can be interpreted as probabilities. The second condition describes the generation of the less informative posterior distributions as a scrambling of Π via the matrix $\mathbf{S}$. Unlike Blackwell's Theorem, this scrambling is not sufficient to ensure the comparative informativeness; the marginal distributions of the messages must relate to one another according to S_3. Marschak and Miyasawa (1968, Section 9) prove that when the columns of Π are linearly independent (i.e., when Π has rank = n), then S_3 is automatically satisfied and the comparative informativeness is revealed by the posterior probabilities only.

Having more messages than states is sufficient to open the door to *posterior-preserving* comparisons of information structures [Singh (1991)]. This approach compares two structures that generate identical posterior distributions for each message, but have different marginal distributions for those messages. The advantage is that conditional decision rules remain unchanged. Singh applies this approach to a principal-agent problem.

Comparison via Utility Possibilities

An equivalent condition with more direct economic motivation is due to Bohnenblust, Shapley, and Sherman (1949). This approach is based upon the conditional expected utility characteristic of each decision rule **d** defined by (6.21); under the use of λ this is a point in m-space

$$\mu(\mathbf{d}, \mathbf{I}) = [\mu_{x_1}(\mathbf{d}, \mathbf{I}), \cdots, \mu_{x_i}(\mathbf{d}, \mathbf{I}), \cdots, \mu_{x_m}(\mathbf{d}, \mathbf{I})],$$

with typical member as in (6.20):

$$\mu_{x_i}(\mathbf{d}, \mathbf{I}) = E_{y|x_i}\, \mu_{x_i}(\mathbf{d}(y)) = \Sigma_j \Sigma_k\, u(w, x_i, a_k)\, p(a_k | y_j)\, p(y_j | x_i).$$

Consider the utility possibility set $\aleph$ created by varying **d** over all possible decision rules [Markov matrices as in (6.27)]

$$\aleph = \{\mu(\mathbf{d}, \mathbf{I}) \text{ for every } \mathbf{d} \in \delta\}.$$

Under standard assumptions and allowing for randomized decision rules, the set $\aleph$ is a compact and convex subset of m-space [see Blackwell (1951; 1953)]. This set does not depend upon the prior distribution $p(x_i)$; the decision problem can be thought of as choosing a point $\mu(\mathbf{d}, \mathbf{I})$ from $\aleph$; that is, given any prior distribution on the m-dimensional simplex,

$$\mathbf{U}(\mathbf{D}^* | \mathbf{I}) = \max_{\mathbf{d} \in \delta} \Sigma_i\, \mu_{x_i}(\mathbf{d}, \mathbf{I})\, p(x_i) = \max_{\mu(\mathbf{d}, \mathbf{I}) \in \aleph} \Sigma_i\, \mu_{x_i}(\mathbf{d}, \mathbf{I})\, p(x_i).$$

Analogously, the information structure $\mathbf{I}'$ offers its own utility possibility set $\aleph'$ from which to choose the optimal expected utility characteristic $\mu(\mathbf{d}^u_{\mathbf{I}'}, \mathbf{I}')$ yielding $\mathbf{U}(\mathbf{D}^* | \mathbf{I}')$.

It is straightforward to show [e.g., Marschak and Miyasawa (1968), Section 13] that if $\aleph'$ is contained in the convex hull of $\aleph$, then **I** is more informative than $\mathbf{I}'$. Any conditional expected utility characteristic available from $\mathbf{I}'$ is also obtainable by using **I**, and even better is possible. In terms of Figure 6.3, a more informative information structure further pushes the boundary north and/or east. Writing

$$\mathbf{U}(\mathbf{D}^* \mid \mathbf{I}) = \Sigma_i \, \mu_{x_i}(\mathbf{d}_{\mathbf{I}}^u, \mathbf{I}) \, p(x_i) \geq \Sigma_i \, \mu_{x_i}(\mathbf{d}_{\mathbf{I}'}^u, \mathbf{I}') \, p(x_i) = \mathbf{U}(\mathbf{D}^* \mid \mathbf{I}')$$

indicates perhaps most clearly the irrelevance of the prior distribution to the question of comparative informativeness: whatever prior distribution p(x) the DM assesses, she cannot be worse off by moving from **I′** to **I**.

Comparison via Uncertainty Functions

In Section 6.1.5 the jth column of the matrix Π was written as the $m \times 1$ vector

$$\Pi_j = [p(x_1 \mid y_j), \cdots, p(x_i \mid y_j), \cdots, p(x_m \mid y_j)]^T;$$

this is the posterior distribution of the state given the message y_j, $\Pi_j \in \Xi$. The fourth equivalent condition is that if, for any convex function φ defined on Ξ,

$$\Sigma_j \, p(y_j) \, \varphi(\Pi_j) > \Sigma_J \, p(y_J') \, \varphi(\Pi_J'), \tag{6.47}$$

then **I** is more informative than **I′**. If this condition holds for every convex function on Ξ, it holds for the specific convex function $t(\Pi_j)$ defined by (6.36):

$$t(\Pi_j) = \max_a \Sigma_i \, u(w, x_i, a_k) \, p(x_i \mid y_j) = \mathbf{U}(\mathbf{D}^* \mid \mathbf{I}, y_j).$$

The condition then states that

$$\mathbf{U}(\mathbf{D}^* \mid \mathbf{I}) = E_y \, t(\Pi_j) \geq E_{y'} \, t(\Pi_J') = \mathbf{U}(\mathbf{D}^* \mid \mathbf{I}'), \tag{6.48}$$

so it is sufficient for greater informativeness. This condition, like the others, is also necessary: if one information source is to be more informative than another, then (6.47) must hold for all convex functions.

Note that if φ is any convex function, then $-\varphi$ is concave. When comparing concave functions, which DeGroot (1962) calls *uncertainty functions*, the preceding result holds but with the direction of the inequality reversed. The interpretation now is that information structure **I** is more informative if and only if it reduces expected uncertainty more than structure **I′**.

In particular, the entropy function defined in (2.33) is concave in any distribution ξ on the state space, making it eligible as an uncertainty function. If **I** is more informative than **I′**, then the expected entropy or equivocation of **I**, as in (2.34), must be lower than the expected entropy of **I′**. The converse does not follow; lower expected entropy does not imply higher informativeness. Unless the relationship holds for all concave functions, a decision problem can be constructed that combines lower expected entropy with lower information value. Lower equivocation, H(**I**) < H(**I′**), is necessary but not sufficient for greater informativeness.

When information structures are Blackwell-comparable, every decision maker facing a $\mathbf{D} \in \Omega$ given by (6.39) will order them in an identical way. This result is not universal, but it holds in the standard problem framing for the (large?) class of decision makers who obey the expected utility hypothesis. The result may also not be robust to problem framings that diverge from standard; Sulganik and Zilcha (1997) show that Blackwell's theorem does not necessarily hold if the action space varies with the message; that is, one information structure may be more Blackwell-informative than another, yet strictly not preferred.

6.2.3 Special Cases

Blackwell's Theorem describes the necessary and sufficient conditions for greater informativeness in terms of a stochastic transformation between the likelihoods $p(y'_J \mid x_i)$ and $p(y_j \mid x_i)$, captured by the matrix B. This subsection presents several special cases, including sufficient methods for constructing transformations that describe the randomized production of $\mathbf{I}'$ from $\mathbf{I}$ according to a specified probability distribution $p(y'_J \mid y_j)$ that is independent of the state. These special cases are particularly useful in practice, as they identify commonly occurring situations in which alternative information structures are Blackwell-comparable.

Garbling

Following Marschak and Miyasawa (1968), $\mathbf{I}$ is said to be *garbled* into $\mathbf{I}'$ if any of the following three equivalent conditions hold,

$$G_1\colon p(y'_J \mid y_j, x_i) = p(y'_J \mid y_j);$$

$$G_2\colon p(y_j, y'_J \mid x_i) = p(y_j \mid x_i)\, p(y'_J \mid y_j);$$

$$G_3\colon p(x_i \mid y_j, y'_J) = p(x_i \mid y_j).$$

Condition G_1 describes the formation of a message y'_J as being independent of the state, as if it were formed randomly from message y_j using an outside device. Condition G_2 describes the joint conditional distribution of the messages; the general identity is $p(y_j, y'_J \mid x_i) = p(y_j \mid x_i)\, p(y'_J \mid y_j, x_i)$, but the generation of y'_J becomes independent of the state due to G_1. Summing G_2 over j yields

$$\Sigma_j\, p(y_j, y'_J \mid x_i) = p(y'_J \mid x_i) = \Sigma_j\, p(y_j \mid x_i)\, p(y'_J \mid y_j), \text{ or } \lambda' = \lambda\Gamma, \quad (6.49)$$

where Γ is an $n \times n'$ row-stochastic Markov matrix with typical element $p(y'_J \mid y_j)$. Putting $b_{jJ} = p(y'_J \mid y_j)$ yields condition B_2, showing that garbling is sufficient for greater informativeness. Garbling is not a necessary condition, as the quasi-garbling matrix B in (6.43) is consistent with numerous trivariate distributions, including, for example, transformations that do depend upon the state [see Marschak and Radner (1972), pages 66–67].

Condition G_3 has a slightly different semantic interpretation, asserting that the augmentation of an already received signal y_j by any other message from the source $\mathbf{I}'$ has no effect upon the posterior probability of the state (There's nothing you can tell me!). To prove that G_3 is equivalent to G_1, multiply both sides of G_1 by $p(x_i, y_j) = p(x_i | y_j)\, p(y_j)$ to obtain $p(y_j, y'_J, x_i) = p(y'_J | y_j)\, p(y_j)\, p(x_i | y_j)$, and recondition to $p(x_i | y_j, y'_J)\, p(y_j, y'_J) = p(y_j, y'_J)\, p(x_i | y_j)$, implying G_3.

Multiplying both sides of G_3 by $p(y_j | y'_J)$, reconditioning, and summing over j to remove the message y_j shows

$$\Sigma_j\, p(x_i, y_j, | y'_J) = p(x_i | y'_J) = \Sigma_j\, p(x_i | y_j)\, p(y_j | y'_J), \text{ or } \Pi' = \Pi\Gamma^{\#},$$

where $\Gamma^{\#}$ is an $n \times n'$ column-stochastic Markov matrix with typical element $p(y_j | y'_J)$. Since replacing $\mathbf{S}$ with $\Gamma^{\#}$ satisfies the conditions S_1, S_2, and S_3 of the previous section, garbling as in G_3 is sufficient for comparison via posterior probabilities. The economic meaning is that if the augmentation of message y_j by y'_J has no effect on the posterior probability of the state, for any y_j and y'_J, then the replacement of y_j with y'_J results in less informativeness. Section 8.3.1 applies this interpretation.

Message Consolidation

Of particular special interest is the situation in which the message space,

$$\mathbf{Y}'^{n'} = \{ y'_1, \cdots, y'_J, \cdots, y'_{n'} \}$$

is consolidated from the message space $\mathbf{Y}^n$, independent of the state. This is constructed by a partitioning of $\mathbf{Y}^n$ in which several messages y_j are combined into one message y'_J.

Technically, a finite *partition* of an arbitrary set $\Phi = \{\phi\}$ is a division of Φ into nonnull, mutually exclusive sets whose union is Φ. A finite partition Φ' of Φ is a collection of subsets

$$\Phi' = \{ \phi'_1, \cdots, \phi'_h, \cdots, \phi'_H \},$$

such that

a) $\phi'_h \neq \varnothing$,
b) $\phi'_h \in \Phi'$,
c) $\phi'_h \cap \phi'_g = \varnothing$ for all $g \neq h$, and
d) $\cup_h\, \phi'_h = \Phi$.

A partition $\mathbf{Y}'^{n'}$ is *coarser* than $\mathbf{Y}^n$, or $\mathbf{Y}^n$ is *finer* than $\mathbf{Y}'^{n'}$, if each y_j in $\mathbf{Y}^n$ is contained in one y'_J from $\mathbf{Y}'^{n'}$. In the finite case, this is equivalent to

$$p(y'_J \mid y_j) = \begin{cases} 1 & \text{if } y_j \in y'_J \\ 0 & \text{if } y_j \notin y'_J. \end{cases}$$

To illustrate, let $\mathbf{Y}^4 = \{y_1, y_2, y_3, y_4\}$, and consider the message space $\mathbf{Y}'^2 = \{y'_1, y'_2\} = \{y_1 \cup y_4, y_2 \cup y_3\}$. In receiving a message from $\mathbf{Y}'^2$, whatever details that distinguish y_1 from y_4 and y_2 from y_3 are now suppressed. Under the assumption that information and decision are cost-free, intuition suggests that $\mathbf{I}'$ cannot be more informative than $\mathbf{I}$.

This intuition is correct because message consolidation is sufficient (but not necessary) for the garbling condition G_1. Specifically, the consolidation of the message space implies, via (6.49), $\lambda' = \lambda\Gamma$, where Γ is an $n \times n'$ "collection" matrix containing one 1 in each of its n rows, leading to

$$p(y'_J \mid x_i) = \Sigma_{y_j \in y'_J}\ p(y_j \mid x_i) \tag{6.50}$$

for every $y'_J \in \mathbf{Y}'^{n'}$. In the preceding illustration,

$$\Gamma = \begin{bmatrix} p(y'_1 \mid y_1) & p(y'_2 \mid y_1) \\ p(y'_1 \mid y_2) & p(y'_2 \mid y_2) \\ p(y'_1 \mid y_3) & p(y'_2 \mid y_3) \\ p(y'_1 \mid y_4) & p(y'_2 \mid y_4) \end{bmatrix} = \begin{bmatrix} 1 & 0 \\ 0 & 1 \\ 0 & 1 \\ 1 & 0 \end{bmatrix}.$$

Marschak (1971, Section 6.2) uses these results to prove that longer memory [M_t in (5.90)] in a dynamic model is more informative. For additional work on partitions and information value, see Gilboa and Lehrer (1991).

Sufficient Partitions

The number of potential messages in the message space n can become very large. For example, if each message y_j is a vector describing the results of a sample of size N, and each individual observation can take on H different values, then $n = H^N$; even if $H = 2$ as in binomial sampling, n can become quite cumbersome. Another example arises in economic theory, where the size of the message space, the number of messages necessary to ensure an efficient allocation of resources, plays a role in the comparison of economic systems [Hurwicz (1960; 1972); Mount and Reiter (1974)]. It is therefore of interest to investigate the conditions under which a message space can be consolidated without the loss of information value. A message space constructed to ensure that when $\mathbf{I}'$ is coarser than $\mathbf{I}$, $\mathbf{U}(\mathbf{D}^* \mid \mathbf{I}) = \mathbf{U}(\mathbf{D}^* \mid \mathbf{I}')$ for all $\mathbf{D} \in \Omega$, is called a *sufficient partition.*

Let $\mathbf{Y}^n$ be consolidated (garbled) into $\mathbf{Y}'^{n'}$ in a way such that each consolidated message y'_J is merely an abridged version of the original: shorter but retaining the essential content. The garbling condition G_3, $p(x_i \mid y_j,\ y'_J) = p(x_i \mid y_j)$, tells us that removing y'_J has no effect on the posterior knowledge of X, but suppose the same thing can be said about y_j: $p(x_i | y_j, y'_J) = p(x_i | y'_J)$; that is, removal of the unabridged message y_j has no effect on posterior knowledge of X. The definition of *statistical sufficiency* is

$$p(x_i | y'_J) = p(x_i | y_j), \text{ for every } y_j \in y'_J, \text{ and each } y'_J \in \mathbf{Y}'^{n'}. \tag{6.51}$$

The identical posterior distribution for all $y_j \in y'_J$ ensures that

$$a^u_{y_j} = a^u_{y'_J}, \text{ for every } y_j \in y'_J. \tag{6.52}$$

To show there is no loss in value from this sufficient consolidation, begin with the value of $\mathbf{I}'$ written in normal form as in (6.31), use the garbling relationship (6.50), and substitute the sufficiency conclusion (6.52):

$$\begin{aligned} \mathbf{U(D^* | I')} &= \Sigma_i\, p(x_i)\, \Sigma_J\, u(w, x_i, a^u_{y'_J})\, p(y'_J | x_i) \\ &= \Sigma_i\, p(x_i)\, \Sigma_J\, \Sigma_{y_j \in y'_J}\, u(w, x_i, a^u_{y'_J})\, p(y_j | x_i) \\ &= \Sigma_i\, p(x_i)\, \Sigma_j\, u(w, x_i, a^u_{y_j})\, p(y_j | x_i) = \mathbf{U(D^* | I)}. \end{aligned}$$

These ideas find great use in statistical sampling, where the identification and application of sufficient statistics offers considerable simplification. Sufficient statistics are identified through the famous factorization criterion on the likelihood; see Blackwell and Girshick (1954, Chapter 8) and Raiffa and Schlaifer (1961, Chapter 2). The framing in the sampling problem of Example 5.2 sets up the message space as a sufficient description of the experimental outcomes, in this case the number of defects observed, rather than the more complete listing stating whether each observation in the sample is defective. This consolidation costs nothing in terms of value, as long as we have total confidence that the sampling model is the correct one. However, Pratt, Raiffa, and Schlaifer (1995, page 455) caution that application of sufficient statistics when not appropriate results in loss of value.

On a problem-specific basis, there may be consolidations of a larger message space that do not satisfy (6.51), but still do not result in a loss. Consider the following simple example, based upon Marschak (1959).

♦ *Example 6.2 The Day-Trader*

A risk-neutral day trader can purchase one futures contract at the open of trading, and liquidate it at the end of the day. Let X be the daily price change; since there are daily limits on the change, $X = \{-\gamma \le x \le \gamma\}$. Suppose the random variable is uniformly distributed between these points, making $p(x) = 1/2\gamma$. If there are no transaction costs, $\pi(x, a) = ax$, where $a = +1$ means "long one contract," $a = -1$ means "short one contract," and $a = 0$ means "stand aside today."

The speculator will make her daily decision based upon a message provided by her broker. The broker can forecast price change perfectly; hence $a_x = +1$ for $x > 0$ and $a_x = -1$ for $x < 0$. The value of the perfectly informed decision is

$$\mathbf{U(D^* \mid I\uparrow)} = \frac{1}{2\gamma}\left[\int_{-\gamma}^{0} -x\,dx + \int_{0}^{\gamma} x\,dx\right] = \tfrac{1}{2}\gamma.$$

Now suppose the broker consolidates the message space into $y_1' = \{x: x \le 0\}$ and $y_2' = \{x: x \ge 0\}$. Here, $p(y_J' \mid x) = 1$ if $x \in y_J'$, and zero otherwise, $p(y_J') = .5$, and $p(x \mid y_J') = 1/\gamma$ for $J = 1, 2$. The optimal conditional decision rule is $a^N_{y_1'} = -1$ and $a^N_{y_2'} = +1$, making the value of the informed decision

$$\tfrac{1}{2}\left[\int_{-\gamma}^{0} -x\left[\tfrac{1}{\gamma}\right]dx\right] + \tfrac{1}{2}\left[\int_{0}^{\gamma} x\left[\tfrac{1}{\gamma}\right]dx\right] = \tfrac{1}{2}\gamma = \mathbf{U(D^* \mid I\uparrow)}.$$

This customization of the message space has the same value as $\mathbf{I\uparrow}$.

This lack of loss in value is problem-specific; note that (6.51) does not hold. It is easy to construct another decision problem in which this consolidation is detrimental: suppose there is a transaction cost of ψ for a round trip in the contract. Now the preceding message space, although noiseless, has the DM taking positions on occasions when she cannot cover transaction costs. With perfect information, she can simply stand aside when $|x| < \psi$, choosing $a = 0$. ♦

Useless Information

A final special case has $\mathbf{I}$ more informative than $\mathbf{I'}$, but $\mathbf{U(D^* \mid I) = U(D^* \mid I')}$. When $\mathbf{I' = I\downarrow}$, Section 2.4.3 refers to this as useless information; this is a problem-specific characteristic that may or may not arise.

The basic relationship comparing the value of the informed and uninformed decisions is, in extensive form,

$$\Sigma_j \Sigma_i\, u(w, x_i, a^u_{y_j})\, p(x_i \mid y_j)\, p(y_j) \ge \Sigma_j \Sigma_i\, u(w, x_i, a^u_0)\, p(x_i \mid y_j)\, p(y_j). \quad (6.53)$$

When equality holds in (6.53), $\mathbf{I}$ has the same gross value as $\mathbf{I\downarrow}$, and the information structure $\mathbf{I}$ is useless. The structure is useless if it is not informative enough to induce any change in action by the DM; this happens if and only if the posterior distribution from every message in $\mathbf{Y}^n$ leads the DM to continue choosing the prior optimal action: $a^u_{y_j} = a^u_0$ for all $y_j \in \mathbf{Y}^n$. Sufficiency is obvious; simply substitute a^u_0 for $a^u_{y_j}$ in the left-hand side of (6.53). Necessity can be proved by contradiction: if equality holds in (6.53), there cannot be a message y_h that is receivable $[p(y_h) > 0]$ such that $\Sigma_i\, u(w, x_i, a^u_{y_h})\, p(x_i \mid y_h) > \Sigma_i\, u(w, x_i, a^u_0)\, p(x_i \mid y_h)$ without contradicting the premise.

6.2.4 *Constructing a Sequence of Structures Ranked by Informativeness*

To investigate the role of statistical informativeness as a determinant of the value of information, and to be able to disentangle its effects from the other determinants, it is desirable to index a sequence of information structures, ordered by Blackwell-informativeness, that runs the gamut from null information to perfect information. For theoretical applications such as in the upcoming Section 6.3.2, we can simply posit such an index; the statistical informativeness of each structure in the sequence depends upon an index θ embodied in the joint probability measure $p(x, y; \theta)$ on $\mathbf{X} \times \mathbf{Y}(\theta)$. Typically θ has a finite range and $p(x, y; \theta)$ is assumed to be continuous and differentiable in θ, with $\theta > \theta'$ implying $\mathbf{I}(\theta)$ is more Blackwell-informative than $\mathbf{I}(\theta')$. Derived from this joint measure are the likelihood of receiving message y given state x, $p(y \mid x; \theta)$; the posterior probability of state x given message y, $p(x \mid y; \theta)$; and the unconditional distribution of the messages, $p(y; \theta)$. The prior distribution $p(x)$ does not vary with θ, but does influence $p(x \mid y; \theta)$ and $p(y; \theta)$ via Bayes' Theorem (2.17). As the likelihood $p(y \mid x; \theta)$ does not have to depend in any way on the prior, it is the fundamental repository of informativeness.

For applications and illustrations, there are several ways to construct an indexing model. An important special case is when the sets $\mathbf{Y}(\theta)$ and $\mathbf{X}$ stand in one-to-one correspondence to one another, with each message being a direct and categorical forecast of its respective state. When $p(x, y)$ is bivariate normal, a Blackwell-indexing is $\theta = \rho^2$: informativeness increases with the squared correlation coefficient between the message and state. This can be proven using the continuous version of Blackwell's Theorem, but DeGroot (1970, pages 438–439) provides a convincing demonstration. This should not be surprising, given that ρ^2 always plays a prominent role as a determinant of information value in the Chapter 5 models that use the bivariate normal structure.

Another important indexing arises in many sampling problems, where the sample size n indexes statistical informativeness. In a statistical decision problem such as Example 5.2, information value increases with n and the optimal choice of information structure is the determination of the optimal sample size.

In the finite case with m states and m messages, the likelihood of message y_j given state x_i is expressed as the $m \times m$ row-stochastic (Markov) matrix $\lambda(\theta) = [p(y_j \mid x_i; \theta)]$, the posterior distribution is expressed as the $m \times m$ column-stochastic matrix $\Pi(\theta) = [p(x_i \mid y_j; \theta)]$, and the unconditional distribution of the messages is shown as the $1 \times m$ vector $\mathbf{q}(\theta) = [p(y_j; \theta)]$. A convenient and flexible indexing model makes $\Pi(\theta)$ the following linear combination of the perfect information matrix $\Pi\uparrow$ and a compatible null information matrix $\Pi\downarrow$ that is based upon the prior distribution,

$$\Pi(\theta) = \theta\Pi\uparrow + [1-\theta]\Pi\downarrow. \tag{6.54}$$

Here, $0 \le \theta \le 1$, with $\theta = 0$ and $\theta = 1$ corresponding to null and perfect information, respectively.

With the interpretation that each message is direct, categorical, and precisely identifies a state, each column of $\Pi\uparrow$ contains one 1 and zeros elsewhere. By proper naming of variables, $\Pi\uparrow$ can be taken as the $m \times m$ identity matrix:

$$\Pi\uparrow = \begin{bmatrix} 1 & \cdots & 0 \\ \vdots & 1 & \vdots \\ 0 & \cdots & 1 \end{bmatrix}.$$

In this case the likelihood is noiseless and $\Pi\uparrow = \lambda\uparrow$. At the other end of the informativeness spectrum is null information, defined by (2.59). In the finite model when $p(x_i | y_j) = p(x_i)$ for every $y_j \in \mathbf{Y}^m$, each column Π_j of Π simply repeats the prior distribution $\mathbf{r}^T$, as in (2.19). The null matrix $\Pi\downarrow$ is then

$$\Pi\downarrow = \begin{bmatrix} p(x_1) & \cdots & p(x_1) \\ \vdots & p(x_i) & \vdots \\ p(x_m) & \cdots & p(x_m) \end{bmatrix}.$$

If $p(x_i | y_j) = p(x_i)$, then $p(x_i, y_j) = p(x_i)\, p(y_j)$, and $p(y_j | x_i) = p(y_j)$, so the likelihood matrix under null information is the $m \times m$ matrix $\lambda\downarrow$ with identical rows:

$$\lambda\downarrow = \begin{bmatrix} p(y_1) & \cdots & p(y_m) \\ \vdots & p(y_{j=i}) & \vdots \\ p(y_1) & \cdots & p(y_m) \end{bmatrix};$$

there is the same chance of receiving message y_j, regardless of which state occurs.

Writing out the matrix for the model (6.54),

$$\Pi(\theta) = \theta\begin{bmatrix} 1 & \cdots & 0 \\ \vdots & 1 & \vdots \\ 0 & \cdots & 1 \end{bmatrix} + [1-\theta]\begin{bmatrix} p(x_1) & \cdots & p(x_1) \\ \vdots & p(x_i) & \vdots \\ p(x_m) & \cdots & p(x_m) \end{bmatrix}$$

$$= \begin{bmatrix} \theta + [1-\theta]p(x_1) & [1-\theta]p(x_1) & \cdots & [1-\theta]p(x_1) \\ [1-\theta]p(x_2) & \theta + [1-\theta]p(x_2) & \cdots & [1-\theta]p(x_2) \\ \vdots & \vdots & \vdots & \vdots \\ [1-\theta]p(x_m) & [1-\theta]p(x_m) & \cdots & \theta + [1-\theta]p(x_m) \end{bmatrix}. \tag{6.55}$$

To find the vector $\mathbf{q}(\theta)$ describing the marginal distribution of the messages, use the coherence relationship (4.1), which is written in matrix form as $\Pi(\theta)[\mathbf{q}(\theta)]^T = \mathbf{r}^T$. The sth row of this equation is

$$[\theta + [1-\theta]p(x_s)]\, p(y_s;\theta) + [1-\theta]p(x_s)\, \Sigma_{j\neq s}\, p(y_j;\theta) = p(x_s).$$

Rearranging and using the fact that $\Sigma_j\, p(y_j;\theta) = 1$ shows that $p(y_s;\theta) = p(x_s)$ for each $s = 1, \cdots, m$, or $\mathbf{q}(\theta) = \mathbf{r}$. The chance of receiving a forecast of a particular state is equal to the prior chance of that state occurring; in the language of Section 4.2.2, the sequence of information structures exhibits categorical predictive calibration.

*Properties and Generalizations of the Model

A convenient computational property of the modeling system (6.54) is that, for a fixed $\mathbf{r}$, $\lambda(\theta)$ and $\Pi(\theta)$ are transposes of one another: $\lambda(\theta) = [\Pi(\theta)]^T$. The coherence requirement (4.2), $\Sigma_i\, p(y_j|x_i;\theta)\, p(x_i) = p(y_j;\theta)$, is written in matrix terms $\mathbf{r}\lambda(\theta) = \mathbf{q}(\theta) = \mathbf{r}$, where the final equality invokes the calibration characteristic. Thus, $\lambda(\theta)$ maps $\mathbf{r}$ back into itself. In the transpose of the matrix version of (4.1), $\mathbf{q}(\theta)[\Pi(\theta)]^T = \mathbf{r}$, substituting $\mathbf{q}(\theta) = \mathbf{r}$ gives $\mathbf{r}[\Pi(\theta)]^T = \mathbf{r}$. Hence, $\mathbf{r}\lambda(\theta) = \mathbf{r}[\Pi(\theta)]^T$, implying $\lambda(\theta) = [\Pi(\theta)]^T$.

The sequence of information structures has the following likelihood.

$$\lambda(\theta) = \begin{bmatrix} \theta+[1-\theta]p(x_1) & [1-\theta]p(x_2) & \cdots & [1-\theta]p(x_m) \\ [1-\theta]p(x_1) & \theta+[1-\theta]p(x_2) & \cdots & [1-\theta]p(x_m) \\ \vdots & \vdots & \vdots & \vdots \\ [1-\theta]p(x_1) & [1-\theta]p(x_2) & \cdots & \theta+[1-\theta]p(x_m) \end{bmatrix}. \quad (6.56)$$

That θ is a proper index of informativeness is guaranteed by Blackwell's Theorem if for any two members of the family $\lambda(\theta)$ and $\lambda(\theta')$, with $0 \le \theta' < \theta \le 1$, there is a nonnegative Markov matrix B such that $\lambda(\theta') = \lambda(\theta)B$. The matrix B that satisfies this criterion is

$$B = \frac{1}{\theta}\begin{bmatrix} \theta\, p(x_1)+\theta'[1-p(x_1)] & [\theta-\theta']p(x_2) & \cdots & [\theta-\theta']p(x_m) \\ [\theta-\theta']p(x_1) & \theta\, p(x_2)+\theta'[1-p(x_2)] & \cdots & [\theta-\theta']p(x_m) \\ \vdots & \vdots & \vdots & \vdots \\ [\theta-\theta']p(x_1) & [\theta-\theta']p(x_2) & \cdots & \theta\, p(x_m)+\theta'[1-p(x_m)] \end{bmatrix}.$$

This square $m \times m$ matrix is Markov because each element is nonnegative and the sum of the ith row is one:

$$1/\theta\, \{\theta\, p(x_i) + \theta'[1-p(x_i)] + [\Sigma_{s\neq i}\, p(x_s)\, [\theta-\theta']]\} = \theta/\theta = 1.$$

To show $\lambda(\theta') = \lambda(\theta)B$, multiply the ith row of $\lambda(\theta)$ by the ith column of B to obtain the diagonal term of $\lambda(\theta')$:

$$1/\theta\{[\theta + [1-\theta]p(x_i)]\ [\theta p(x_i) + \theta'[1-p(x_i)]]$$

$$+ [[\theta - \theta']\ [1-\theta]p(x_i)]\ [\Sigma_{s\neq i}\ p(x_s)]\} \ = \ \theta' + [1-\theta']\ p(x_i).$$

Next multiply the ith row by the jth column of B to yield the off-diagonal term of $\lambda(\theta')$:

$$1/\theta\{[\theta + [1-\theta]p(x_i)]\ [[\theta - \theta']p(x_j)] + [[1-\theta]p(x_j)]\ [\theta\ p(x_j) + \theta'[1-\ p(x_j)]]$$

$$+ [[\theta - \theta'][1-\theta]\ p(x_j)]\ [\Sigma_{s\neq i\neq j}\ p(x_s)]\} \ = \ [1-\theta']\ p(x_j).$$

The literature contains a number and variety of applications of this model; see Kwon, Fellingham, and Newman (1979), Bradford and Kelejian (1981), Jones and Ostroy (1984), and Lawrence (1992). Jones and Ostroy (1984) generalize the model to $m \neq n$, but care must be taken. When $n > m$, more messages than states, consider the following model with $m = 2$ and $n = 3$,

$$\Pi(\theta) \ = \theta\begin{bmatrix}1 & 0 & 1\\ 0 & 1 & 0\end{bmatrix} + [1-\theta]\begin{bmatrix}p(x_1) & p(x_1) & p(x_1)\\ p(x_2) & p(x_2) & p(x_2)\end{bmatrix}$$

$$= \begin{bmatrix}\theta+[1-\theta]p(x_1) & [1-\theta]p(x_1) & \theta+[1-\theta]p(x_1)\\ [1-\theta]p(x_2) & [1-\theta]p(x_2) & [1-\theta]p(x_2)\end{bmatrix}.$$

Columns 1 and 3 are identical. When framing the decision problem, all messages that offer exactly the same posterior distribution of the state might as well be consolidated into one, ultimately making $m = n$; this is the rationale for representing perfect information by the square identity matrix.

To model imperfect information when $n > m$, start with a Π from an information structure **I** that is less Blackwell-informative than **I**↑, and model $\Pi(\theta) = \theta\Pi + [1-\theta]\Pi\downarrow$. For example,

$$\Pi(\theta) \ = \theta\begin{bmatrix}1 & \gamma & 0\\ 0 & 1-\gamma & 1\end{bmatrix} + [1-\theta]\begin{bmatrix}p(x_1) & p(x_1) & p(x_1)\\ p(x_2) & p(x_2) & p(x_2)\end{bmatrix}$$

$$= \begin{bmatrix}\theta+[1-\theta]p(x_1) & \gamma\theta+[1-\theta]p(x_1) & [1-\theta]p(x_1)\\ [1-\theta]p(x_2) & [1-\gamma]\theta+[1-\theta]p(x_2) & \theta+[1-\theta]p(x_2)\end{bmatrix}. \tag{6.57}$$

Here, each message is distinct, but the maximum informativeness is Π, when $\theta = 1$. Jones and Ostroy (1984) make the model more flexible by allowing θ to depend upon y, but this creates multiple informativeness parameters.

Given an $m \times m$ matrix λ from a less than perfect information structure **I**, another method for generating a sequence of less informative matrices is to use λ

itself as the matrix B in Blackwell's Theorem. The information structure essentially characterized by the likelihood matrix λ' defined by

$$\lambda' = \lambda \lambda = \lambda^2 \tag{6.58}$$

is less informative than λ. This process can be applied as often as desired; ultimately the sequence converges to null information. The inverse of the number of multiplications can serve as the index θ. Hilton (1980) illustrates the use of this technique; note that it does not work when the first matrix is the identity matrix of perfect information.

6.3 Informativeness, Prior Knowledge, and Value

Suppose there is some factor β that varies in a systematic way and influences the value of a decision. The problem is to investigate how a change in β affects the utility increment

$$\hat{V}_I^u(\beta) = \mathbf{U}(\mathbf{D}^* \,|\, \mathbf{I}, \beta) - \mathbf{U}(\mathbf{D}^* \,|\, \mathbf{I}\!\downarrow, \beta), \tag{6.59}$$

or one of the other related measures of information value.[1] When a modeled change in the problem **D** affects both the value of the informed decision and the value of the prior decision, the effect on information value depends upon the difference between the two. Even if both $\mathbf{U}(\mathbf{D}^* \,|\, \mathbf{I}, \beta)$ and $\mathbf{U}(\mathbf{D}^* \,|\, \mathbf{I}\!\downarrow, \beta)$ are monotonically changing in β, the utility increment changes according to the relative slope of the two changing components. This is a basic reason why general results about the determinants of the value of information are rather scarce.

This section investigates the roles of statistical informativeness and prior knowledge of the state as determinants of the value of information. The first part of this section identifies β with the statistical informativeness index θ. Here the prior decision does not depend upon the parameter, facilitating the strong results of Blackwell's Theorem. The second part investigates the impact on information value of environmental uncertainty: the underlying riskiness of the prior distribution, appropriately defined. This affects both terms in (6.59), and the results are less general.

Changes in the informativeness of an information structure and in the underlying riskiness of the environment can be thought of as factors that redistribute the probabilities within the probability distributions the DM faces. Subsection

---

[1] Most theoretical analyses in the literature work with the utility increment; an exception is Chan (1981), who generalizes some results to the demand price measure V_I^u. Recall that the utility increment is the risk neutral demand value of information when the outcome function is separable.

6.3.2 covers various types of stochastic dominance, an important topic in general economic, statistical, and financial theory. *Stochastic dominance* sets forth conditions under which a redistribution of probabilities is certain to have either a beneficial or a detrimental effect upon the DM's expected utility. A special type of stochastic dominance, Rothschild–Stiglitz variability, provides the basic definition of riskiness that is relevant to the evaluation of information. The analysis in this section makes greater use of the calculus than has previously been the case, requiring additional technical assumptions such as continuity and differentiability, along with some new notation.

6.3.1 The Value of Statistical Informativeness: The Binary Case

This subsection uses the model (6.55) to investigate how the prior distribution and the statistical informativeness interact to determine the utility increment. A two-state, two-message binary decision model, such as Example 6.1, is the simplest nontrivial way to do this.

The informativeness index θ orders information value for an arbitrary, but fixed, prior distribution. In practice, this presents no problem because the prior knowledge is an elementary ingredient the DM provides. For the theoretical purpose of investigating how information value varies with the prior, the impact of the prior on the posterior distributions, via Bayes' Theorem, must explicitly be recognized. This is already implicit in the model (6.55), where the null matrix repeats the prior.

Equation (6.34) defines the function

$$t(\xi) = \max_a \Sigma_i u(w, x_i, a_k) \xi_i$$

as the maximized expected utility from using a probability distribution ξ defined on the state space $\mathbf{X}$. Whether the distribution ξ is prior or posterior, the function $t(\xi)$ is convex. In a dichotomy such as Example 6.1, the distribution of the state is fully characterized by the probability of state 1. Let ξ_1 denote any assignment of probability to state 1, and specifically let $r_1 \equiv p(x_1)$ be the prior probability. To allow for joint variation in both θ and r_1, let $\Pi_{ij}(\theta, r_1) \equiv p(x_i|y_j; \theta, r_1)$ denote the conditional probabilities of state i given message y_j, as a function of θ and r_1.

With this notation in hand, the model (6.55) for the posterior distributions becomes

$$\Pi(\theta, r_1) = \begin{bmatrix} p(x_1|y_1;\theta,r_1) & p(x_1|y_2;\theta,r_1) \\ p(x_2|y_1;\theta,r_1) & p(x_2|y_2;\theta,r_1) \end{bmatrix} = \begin{bmatrix} \Pi_{11}(\theta,r_1) & \Pi_{12}(\theta,r_1) \\ \Pi_{21}(\theta,r_1) & \Pi_{22}(\theta,r_1) \end{bmatrix}$$

$$= \begin{bmatrix} \theta+[1-\theta]r_1 & [1-\theta]r_1 \\ [1-\theta][1-r_1] & \theta+[1-\theta][1-r_1] \end{bmatrix}. \quad (6.60)$$

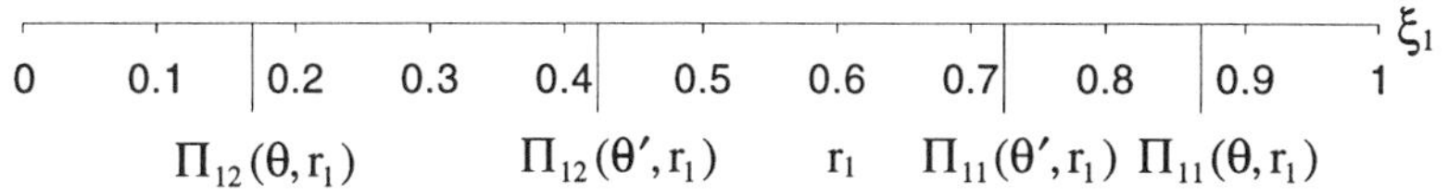

Figure 6.6. On the one-dimensional simplex, the posterior probabilities of more informative structures bracket the posterior probabilities of less informative ones. The specific numbers come from (6.60), with $r_1 = .6$, $\theta' = .3$, and $\theta = .7$.

The set of posterior distributions are completely characterized by the distributions of x_1 in the first row of $\Pi(\theta, r_1)$. Since the calibration property $p(y; \theta) = p(x)$ holds for all θ in this model, θ and r_1 completely determine the information structure.

The parameter θ orders all information structures in the class of decision situations defined by Ω in (6.39). If $\theta > \theta'$, the greater informativeness shows up on the one-dimensional simplex as in Figure 6.6. Starting with an arbitrary prior distribution r_1, the posterior probabilities associated with larger θ bracket the posterior probabilities associated with smaller θ. The length of a bracket is $\Pi_{11}(\theta, r_1) - \Pi_{12}(\theta, r_1) = \theta$; the brackets are symmetric around r_1 only in special cases.

The function $t(\bullet)$ measures the value of a decision; in particular $t(r_1) = \mathbf{U}(\mathbf{D}^* \,|\, \mathbf{I}\downarrow)$, $t(\Pi_{11}(\theta, r_1)) = \mathbf{U}(\mathbf{D}^* \,|\, \mathbf{I}(\theta, r_1), y_1)$, and $t(\Pi_{12}(\theta, r_1)) = \mathbf{U}(\mathbf{D}^* \,|\, \mathbf{I}(\theta, r_1), y_2)$. The value of the informed decision is

$$\begin{aligned} \mathbf{U}(\mathbf{D}^* \,|\, \mathbf{I}(\theta, r_1)) &= t(\Pi_{11}(\theta, r_1))[r_1] + t(\Pi_{12}(\theta, r_1))[1 - r_1] \\ &= t(\Pi_{12}(\theta, r_1)) + [t(\Pi_{11}(\theta, r_1)) - t(\Pi_{12}(\theta, r_1))]r_1. \qquad (6.61) \end{aligned}$$

The following continuation of Example 6.1 provides some specific numbers.

♦ *Example 6.1 (Continued)*

For this dichotomy, Figure 6.7 shows the maximized expected utility as a function of ξ_1 for the three admissible actions. Suppose initial beliefs are $r_1 = .7$. Reading from the figure, the optimal prior action is a_1, and the value of the prior decision is $t(.7) = 10[.7] + 1[.3] = 7.30$. Suppose an information structure with $\theta = .5$ is available. According to (6.60), this situation offers posterior probabilities $\Pi_{11}(.5, .7) = .85$ with expected payoff $t(\Pi_{11}(.5, .7)) = 10[.85] + 1[.15] = 8.65$, and $\Pi_{12}(.5, .7) = .35$ with $t(\Pi_{12}(.5, .7)) = 1[.35] + 10[.65] = 6.85$. Using (6.61), the value of the informed decision is $\mathbf{U}(\mathbf{D}^* \,|\, \mathbf{I}(.5, .7)) = 6.85 + [8.65 - 6.85][.7] = 8.11$, and the utility increment is $\hat{V}_I^u(.5, .7) = 8.11 - 7.30 = 0.81$.

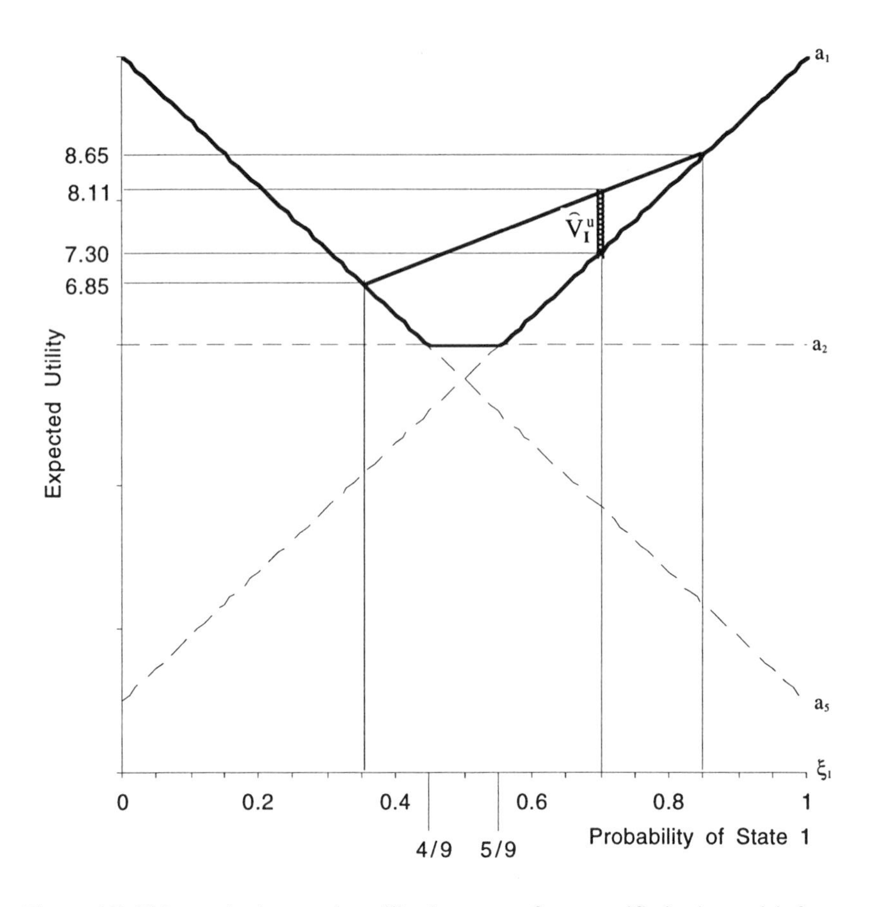

Figure 6.7. This graph pictures the utility increment for a specified prior and information structure. As the information structure becomes more informative, the posterior probabilities spread out from the prior, and the utility increment cannot decrease.

The value of the informed decision and the utility increment can be read directly from Figure 6.7 by using the following construction. Draw a chord connecting $t(\Pi_{12}(.5, .7)) = 6.85$ with $t(\Pi_{11}(.5, .7)) = 8.65$. The value of the informed decision is the height of this chord evaluated at r_1, so the utility increment is represented by the length of the thick vertical line segment in Figure 6.7.

To show this is generally true, observe that the slope of the chord is $[t(\Pi_{11}(\theta, r_1)) - t(\Pi_{12}(\theta, r_1))]/\theta$, so the equation of the line between these two points is

$$t(\Pi_{12}(\theta, r_1)) + \frac{t(\Pi_{11}(\theta, r_1)) - t(\Pi_{12}(\theta, r_1))}{\theta}[\xi_1 - \Pi_{12}(\theta, r_1)].$$

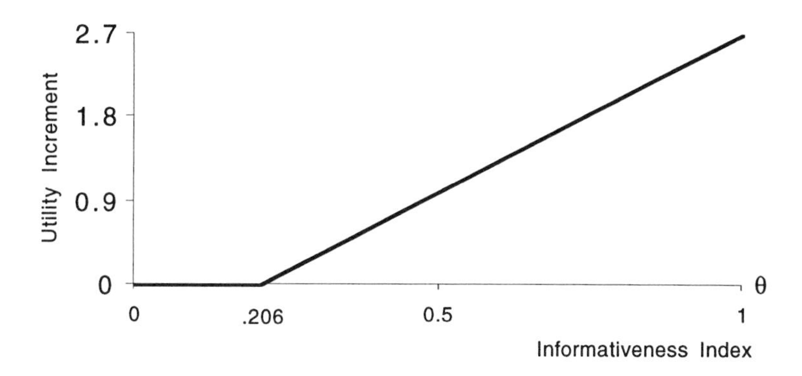

Figure 6.8. For the specified prior $r_1 = .7$, the value of information, as measured by the utility increment, increases with θ once the information structure achieves sufficient informativeness to affect actions.

Evaluated at $\xi_1 = r_1$, and observing that $r_1 - \Pi_{12}(\theta, r_1) = r_1\theta$, the value of the function is

$$t(\Pi_{12}(\theta, r_1)) + [t(\Pi_{11}(\theta, r_1)) - t(\Pi_{12}(\theta, r_1))]r_1 = \mathbf{U}(\mathbf{D}^* \,|\, \mathbf{I}(\theta, r_1)).$$

As θ increases in Figure 6.7, the posterior probabilities each move closer to the extreme values of ξ_1, as in Figure 6.6. Clearly, the utility increment increases. As θ falls from .5, the utility increment declines, and ultimately there comes a point when the optimal action remains a_1 regardless of the message. The information structure becomes useless when $\Pi_{12}(\theta, .7) = 5/9$, which is $\theta = .206$. Figure 6.8 shows the utility increment as a function of θ for $r_1 = .7$. All $\theta \leq .206$ are useless. The information value then steadily increases with θ, reaching its peak of $10 - 7.3 = 2.7$ utiles when $\theta = 1$.

Figure 6.9 shows the utility increment $\hat{V}_I^u(\theta, r_1)$ for every possible assessment of initial knowledge, $r_1 \in \Xi$, and all levels of the informativeness index θ between 0 and .50. It does not form a convex set. The ridges occur at $r_1 = 4/9$ and $r_1 = 5/9$, the breakeven priors. From Figure 6.7, it is apparent there is no region of useless information for the two breakeven priors; any $\theta > 0$ brackets two different actions and hence has value. The low point of the rising canyon is at the entropy-maximizing prior of $r_1 = .5$; for this initial knowledge the information is useless until $\theta = 1/9$, when it becomes informative enough to induce an action different from a_2. The darker lines in Figure 6.9 show the utility increment for θ fixed at .10, .20, .30, .40, and .50. For example, this information structure is useless for a wide range of priors when $\theta = .10$; the twin peaks of value are at $r_1 = 4/9$ and 5/9.

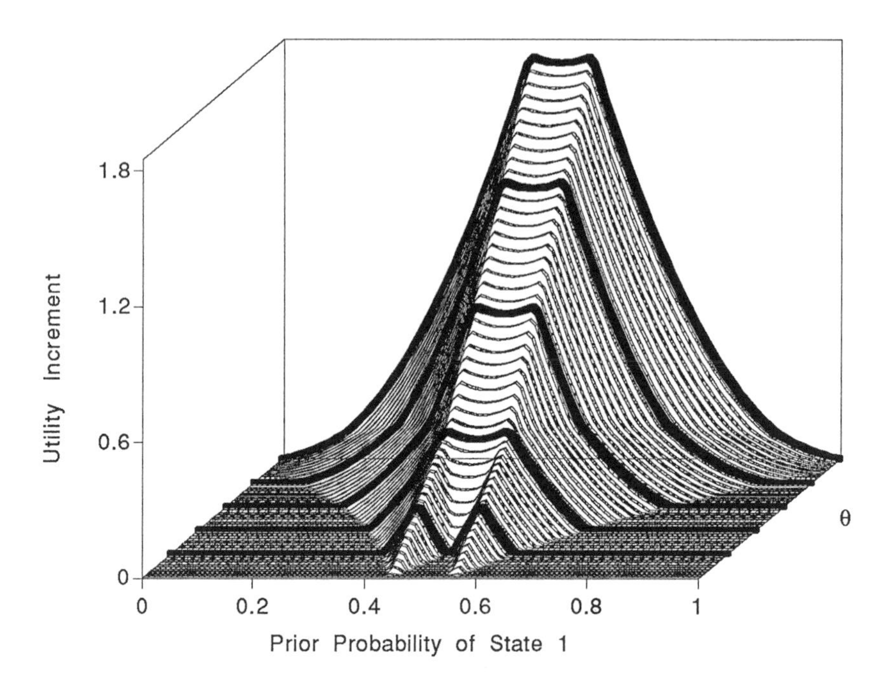

Figure 6.9. The value of information, as measured by the utility increment, depends upon both the DM's initial knowledge, as assessed by $r_1 \equiv p(x_1)$, and the informativeness θ of the information structure. The darker bands show the impact of r_1 on value for a given θ; Figure 6.8 shows the impact of θ for a given r_1.

The flat plain in Figure 6.9 is the region of useless information. As the DM becomes more certain of her initial beliefs (by assessing a prior closer to the extremes of ξ_1), notice that it takes larger and larger values of θ to provide valuable information. In a situation like this, with a small number of alternative actions, individuals with high prior confidence in what they know and what they should do are potential demanders of only highly informative information sources. ♦

6.3.2 The Value of Systematic Redistribution of the Probability: Stochastic Dominance

This subsection presents a technique for modeling systematic redistributions of probability and assessing the impact of such redistributions on expected utility.

Consider a random variable Z and an associated family of probability density functions $p(z; \beta)$ indexed by the parameter β. Typically, Z will either be the state variable, the likelihood of a message, or the terminal wealth of the DM; depending upon the application, this density may be marginal, conditional, or preposterior. For any integrable, monotonically increasing,[2] and otherwise well-behaved function $g(z)$ defined on **Z**, this subsection collects some results concerning the difference in the mathematical expectation of $g(z)$ as the probability distribution of Z changes in a systematic way. This analysis lays the groundwork for investigating several important factors that determine information value, with the interpretation being that as a factor changes, its consequence is to redistribute the probability. This redistribution can cause the DM to choose different optimal actions that may lead to outcomes with different expected utility.

Before proceeding, let us clarify some notation. First, throughout this book, a prime (′) appended to a variable or a parameter denotes the assignment of an alternative value to that item. However, when primes are appended to a function, it indicates the total derivative of that function. For a function $g(z)$, $g'(z) \equiv dg(z)/dz$ is the first total derivative, $g''(z)$ is the second, and so on. To avoid confusion, this section uses $\beta^{\#}$ to denote an alternative value of β. Second, for a function such as $p(z; \beta)$, let $p_\beta(z^*; \beta^*)$ denote the partial derivative of the function with respect to β, evaluated at $z = z^*$ and $\beta = \beta^*$; $p_{\beta\beta}$ is the second partial, $p_{\beta z}$ the cross-partial derivative, and so on, always evaluated at the specific values given by the arguments of the function.

The fundamental theorem of calculus says

$$g(z)\, dz = d \int_{-\infty}^{z} g(s)\, ds. \tag{6.62}$$

Applying this to the indexed probability density function for the random variable Z,

$$p(z; \beta)\, dz = d \int_{-\infty}^{z} p(s; \beta)\, ds = dF(z; \beta), \tag{6.63}$$

where $F(z; \beta)$ is the cumulative distribution function of Z, evaluated at z. For a continuous random variable, the symbols $p(z; \beta)\, dz$ and $dF(z; \beta)$ represent precisely the same thing: the probability of a small region near the point z.

For two members of the family β and $\beta^{\#}$, the difference in the probability that $p(z; \beta^{\#})$ and $p(z; \beta)$ assign to the neighborhood around z is

$$[p(z; \beta^{\#}) - p(z; \beta)]\, dz = [dF(z; \beta^{\#}) - dF(z; \beta)].$$

---

[2] This means $dg(z)/dz > 0$ for all $z \in \mathbf{Z}$. Results similar to the following hold when the function is monotonically decreasing in z; the key assumption is that the function be monotonic. Fortunately, this arises naturally in most applications.

Since each individual density must integrate to one, the accumulation of all the changes from the redistribution must be zero:

$$\int_Z [p(z;\beta^\#) - p(z;\beta)]\,dz = \int_Z [dF(z;\beta^\#) - dF(z;\beta)] = 0. \quad (6.64)$$

Now let the difference between $\beta^\#$ and β become very small. The impact of an infinitesimal change in the factor β on $p(z;\beta)$ is revealed by the partial derivative $p_\beta(z;\beta)$. The derivative tells us what the small changes depend upon, and it is of interest to study the conditions under which it can be signed, or shown to be unambiguously positive, negative, or zero. The (first) partial derivatives are formally defined as

$$p_\beta(z;\beta) = \lim_{\beta^\# \to \beta} \frac{p(z;\beta^\#) - p(z;\beta)}{\beta^\# - \beta}, \quad (6.65)$$

and

$$dF_\beta(z;\beta) = \lim_{\beta^\# \to \beta} \frac{dF(z;\beta^\#) - dF(z;\beta)}{\beta^\# - \beta}, \quad (6.66)$$

with

$$\int_Z p_\beta(z;\beta)\,dz = \int_Z dF_\beta(z;\beta) = 0. \quad (6.67)$$

A convenient assumption is that the support of the random variable Z is bounded from 0 to 1; this can be achieved by scaling the units appropriately and in fact loses little generality. The expected value of g(z), as a function of β, is written as

$$G(\beta) = E_{z;\beta}\, g(z) = \int_0^1 g(z)\,p(z;\beta)\,dz = \int_0^1 g(z)\,dF(z;\beta). \quad (6.68)$$

Integrating the final expression in (6.68) by parts,[3] the expectation evaluates to

$$E_{z;\beta}\, g(z) = g(z)\,F(z;\beta)\big|_0^1 - \int_0^1 F(z;\beta)\,g'(z)\,dz$$

$$= g(1) - \int_0^1 g'(z)\,F(z;\beta)\,dz, \quad (6.69)$$

since $F(1) = 1$ and $F(0) = 0$. Substituting $z = g(z)$ in (6.69) gives the mean of the random variable as

$$E_{z;\beta}\, z = 1 - \int_0^1 F(z;\beta)\,dz. \quad (6.70)$$

On the unit square, Figure 6.10 pictures the random variable Z and the cumulative distribution functions for two distributions $F(z;\beta)$ and $F(z;\beta^\#)$. Subtract-

[3] Let $u = g(z)$ and $v = F(z;\beta)$.

ing the area under the curve for each distribution from 1 gives each mean; for $F(z; \beta^{\#})$ the mean is the shaded area. Clearly $F(z; \beta)$ has a higher mean than $F(z; \beta^{\#})$, since $F(z; \beta)$ gives more probability weight to larger values of z. In fact, here $F(z; \beta)$ is the uniform distribution; its mean is .5, half the area of the unit square.

First-Degree Stochastic Dominance

For any two cumulative distribution functions in the family, $F(z; \beta)$ and $F(z; \beta^{\#})$, a change from β to $\beta^{\#}$ causes the expectation of g(z) to change by, applying (6.69),

$$\begin{aligned} \Delta E_z\, g(z) &= \int_0^1 g(z)\, dF(z; \beta^{\#}) - \int_0^1 g(z)\, dF(z; \beta) \\ &= -\int_0^1 g'(z)\, F(z; \beta^{\#})\, dz + \int_0^1 g'(z)\, F(z; \beta)\, dz. \\ &= -\int_0^1 g'(z)[F(z; \beta^{\#}) - F(z; \beta)]\, dz. \end{aligned} \tag{6.71}$$

As long as the function g(z) increases monotonically in z, the necessary and sufficient condition for the change to be detrimental, $\Delta E_z\, g(z) \leq 0$ is that

$$F(z; \beta) \leq F(z; \beta^{\#}) \text{ for all } z \in [0, 1]; \tag{6.72}$$

that is, the cumulative distribution function of $F(z; \beta)$ is never higher than $F(z; \beta^{\#})$, meaning $F(z; \beta)$ assigns more probability to larger values of g(z). When this is true, as in Figure 6.10, $F(z; \beta)$ has *first-degree stochastic dominance* over $F(z; \beta^{\#})$. An example is Blackwell's theorem, which asserts the first-degree stochastic dominance of a more informative information structure. Milgrom (1981) applies first-degree stochastic dominance to several interesting problems in information economics.

Second-Degree Stochastic Dominance

First-degree stochastic dominance implies that the accumulated area under $F(z; \beta^{\#})$ cannot be less than the accumulated area under $F(z; \beta)$, for every z:

$$T(z, \beta^{\#}, \beta) = \int_0^z [F(s; \beta^{\#}) - F(s; \beta)]\, ds \geq 0 \text{ for all } z \in [0, 1]. \tag{6.73}$$

This condition is not sufficient to ensure first-degree dominance, but a further development of (6.69) shows that the quantity $T(z, \beta^{\#}, \beta)$ has its own role to play.

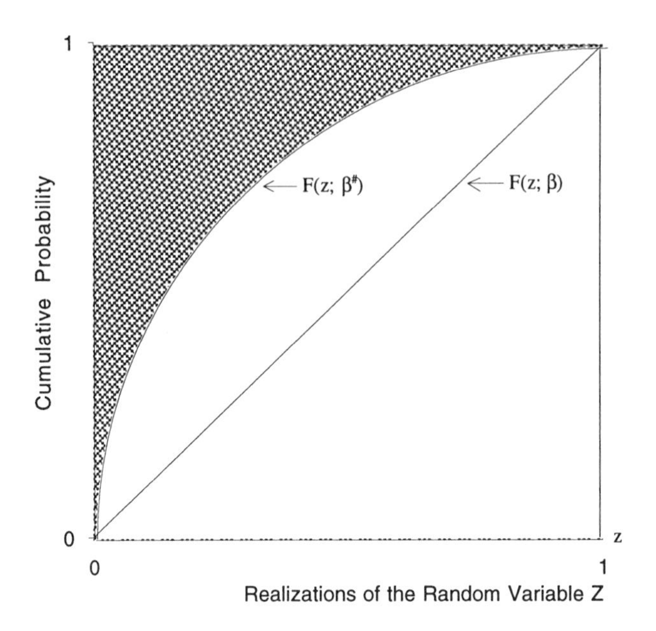

Figure 6.10. Comparing two alternative probability distributions for the random variable Z, the distribution $p(z;\beta)$ has first-degree stochastic dominance over $p(z;\beta^{\#})$, since its cumulative distribution function is everywhere lower. The mean of the uniformly distributed $p(z;\beta)$ is .5; the mean of $p(z;\beta^{\#})$ is given by the area of the shaded region.

Applying the fundamental theorem of calculus again, (6.69) can be rewritten as

$$E_{z;\beta}\, g(z) = g(1) - \int_0^1 g'(z) \left[d \int_0^z F(s;\beta)\, ds\right].$$

Integrating by parts again,

$$E_{z;\beta}\, g(z) = g(1) - g'(z) \int_0^z F(s;\beta)\, ds \,\Big|_0^1 + \int_0^1 g''(z) \left[\int_0^z F(s;\beta)\, ds\right] dz,$$

$$= g(1) - g'(1) \int_0^1 F(z;\beta)\, dz + \int_0^1 g''(z) \left[\int_0^z F(s;\beta)\, ds\right] dz. \qquad (6.74)$$

The difference in the expectation between $F(z;\beta^{\#})$ and $F(z;\beta)$ is then

$$\Delta E_z\, g(z) = -g'(1) \int_0^1 \left[F(z;\beta^{\#}) - F(z;\beta)\right] dz$$

$$+ \int_0^1 g''(z) \left[\int_0^z \left[F(s;\beta^{\#}) - F(s;\beta)\right] ds\right] dz. \qquad (6.75)$$

When (6.73) holds (including the special case when $z = 1$, which makes the first term in (6.75) nonpositive), $\Delta E_z\, g(z) \le 0$ for any increasing strictly concave function with $g'(z) > 0$ and $g''(z) < 0$. The integral condition (6.73) can hold without first-degree stochastic dominance; the two distributions can cross several times and yet $T(z, \beta^{\#}, \beta) \ge 0$. Should (6.73) but not (6.72) hold, and $g''(z) < 0$, then $F(z; \beta)$ gives the concave function greater expected value and exhibits *second-degree stochastic dominance* over $F(z; \beta^{\#})$.

Note that the first term in (6.75) is proportional to the difference in the means of the random variables. Using (6.70)

$$\Delta E_z\, g(z) = g'(1)[E_{z;\beta^{\#}}\, z - E_{z;\beta}\, z] + \int_0^1 g''(z) \left[\int_0^z [F(s; \beta^{\#}) - F(s; \beta)]\, ds\right] dz. \qquad (6.76)$$

Hence the change in the expected value of the function is a constant times the change in the mean, plus an adjustment factor that depends upon the curvature of the function and the effects of the redistribution of the probability.

Rothschild–Stiglitz Variability

Rothschild and Stiglitz (1970) use a special case of second-degree stochastic dominance to define a very important concept of riskiness. Suppose that when $z = 1$ in (6.73),

$$T(1, \beta^{\#}, \beta) = \int_0^1 [F(z; \beta^{\#}) - F(z; \beta)]\, dz = 0, \qquad (6.77)$$

stipulating that the two distributions $F(z; \beta^{\#})$ and $F(z; \beta)$ have identical means. In this case the first term of (6.75) drops out, leaving only the term involving $g''(z)$. The two integral conditions, $T(z, \beta^{\#}, \beta) \ge 0$ and $T(1, \beta^{\#}, \beta) = 0$, define a partial ordering between the two random variables that provides a natural way to compare riskiness. Rothschild and Stiglitz call satisfaction of the two integral conditions a *mean preserving spread* (an *MPS*) of the random variable Z, and give both a statistical and an economic interpretation. Statistically, an MPS redistributes the probability density of Z toward the tails, in such a way that the mean stays constant.

The economic interpretation provides the fundamental definition of the concept of comparative riskiness. When $g(z)$ can be interpreted as the utility of terminal wealth for a DM, $g''(z) < 0$ identifies that DM as a risk averter. With the means identical and $T(z, \beta^{\#}, \beta) \ge 0$, the MPS reduces the utility of outcome for every risk averter:

$$\Delta E_z\, g(z) = \int_0^1 g''(z)\, T(z, \beta^{\#}, \beta)\, dz \le 0. \qquad (6.78)$$

This is a natural method by which to compare riskiness: a situation is more risky if and only if all risk averters dislike it. If $p(z; \beta^{\#})$ is formed by an MPS of $p(z; \beta)$, then $p(z; \beta^{\#})$ has greater *Rothschild–Stiglitz* or *R–S variability*.

As is Blackwell-comparability, Rothschild–Stiglitz variability is a partial ordering. Two arbitrary probability distributions may not be comparable in this way, even when they have the same mean. The test is whether the integral condition $T(z, \beta^{\#}, \beta) \geq 0$ is satisfied. When it does not hold, the two distributions are not R–S comparable, and the sign of $\Delta E_z\, g(z)$ becomes problem-specific. See Figure 7.2 for an illustration of this test.

More generally from (6.78), an MPS of $p(z; \beta)$ causes the expected value of all concave functions of the random variable to decline, and the expected value of all convex functions to increase. The variance of the random variable is a convex function; an MPS causes the variance to increase. The converse is not true, an increase in the variance does not need to be associated with an MPS. Hence variance is not the best measure of risk; examples are easy to find in which the variance of a random variable rises, but some risk averters prefer it. A simple way to demonstrate this is to construct an example with a highly asymmetric probability distribution for Z; see Hanoch and Levy (1969, page 342).

We are interested in very small changes in β, especially those situations in which it is economically reasonable to assume a monotonic impact of changes in β on the cumulative distribution function. This suggests a differential format. Define the derivative

$$F_\beta(z; \beta) = \lim_{\beta^{\#} \to \beta} \frac{F(z;\beta^{\#}) - F(z;\beta)}{\beta^{\#} - \beta}. \tag{6.79}$$

Given a function $G(\beta)$ defined by an expectation of the form (6.68), the analogue of (6.75) is the derivative of $G(\beta)$ with respect to β:

$$\begin{aligned} G'(\beta) &= \frac{d\,E_{z;\beta}\, g(z)}{d\beta} \\ &= -g'(1) \int_0^1 [F_\beta(z; \beta)]\, dz + \int_0^1 g''(z) \left[\int_0^z F_\beta(s; \beta)\, ds \right] dz. \end{aligned} \tag{6.80}$$

When expressions involving $F_\beta(z; \beta)$ can be signed, the direction of the impact will depend upon the sign of $g''(z)$.

*6.3.3 *The Differential Approach to the Value of Statistical Informativeness*

The gain from incorporating information into a decision problem is a consequence of redistributing the probability of the alternative states, causing the DM to choose different optimal actions and decision rules that can lead to outcomes with higher expected utility. Let $p(x, y; \theta)$ denote a family of information structures ordered by their Blackwell-informativeness θ. Assume that the joint distribution, the likelihood $p(y \mid x; \theta)$, and the posterior $p(x \mid y; \theta)$ are continuous and differentiable in θ. Furthermore, let the utility of outcome $u(w, x, a)$ be a continuous, differentiable, and strictly concave function of a, meaning that $u_{aa}(w, x, a) < 0$. This subsection investigates the value of a scintilla of informativeness, the value of a differential change $d\theta$.

Under the information structure $\mathbf{I}(\theta)$, the value of the informed decision is

$$\mathbf{U}(\mathbf{D}^* \mid \mathbf{I}(\theta)) = \int_X \int_Y u(w, x, a_y^u(\theta))\, p(x, y; \theta)\, dy\, dx. \qquad (6.81)$$

Given y, the optimal conditional decision rule is found by taking the derivative of

$$\mathbf{U}(\mathbf{D} \mid \mathbf{I}(\theta), y, a) = \int_X u(w, x, a)\, p(x \mid y; \theta)\, dx$$

with respect to a. This first-order condition characterizes $a_y^u(\theta)$ as the unique solution to

$$\int_X u_a(w, x, a_y^u(\theta))\, p(x \mid y; \theta)\, dx = 0, \qquad (6.82)$$

assuming verification of the second-order condition $u_{aa}(w, x, a_y^u(\theta)) < 0$.

Consider now the effect of a differential change in θ on the value of the informed decision. Rewriting (6.81) in the following way segments the components of the problem that depend upon θ,

$$\mathbf{U}(\mathbf{D}^* \mid \mathbf{I}(\theta)) = \int_X \left\{ \int_Y u(w, x, a_y^u(\theta))\, p(y \mid x; \theta)\, dy \right\} p(x)\, dx. \qquad (6.83)$$

Using the product rule, the derivative of (6.83) with respect to θ is

$$\mathbf{U}'(\mathbf{D}^* \mid \mathbf{I}(\theta)) = \int_X \left\{ \int_Y \left[u(w, x, a_y^u(\theta))\, p_\theta(y \mid x; \theta) \right.\right.$$

$$\left.\left. + \, u_a(w, x, a_y^u(\theta)) \frac{d a_y^u(\theta)}{d\theta}\, p(y \mid x; \theta) \right] dy \right\} p(x)\, dx. \qquad (6.84)$$

For the original optimal decision rule given θ, the first term in (6.84) measures the accounting effect upon value due to the redistribution of the probabilities that comes from altering the informativeness. The second term measures the economic effect from changing informativeness: for the original probabilities, the change in θ causes a change in the optimal action, which in turn feeds back upon value via the impact of changed action on the utility of outcome. Although for discrete changes in informativeness the economic effect is likely to be significant, for this differential change its impact washes out to zero, leaving only the accounting effect. To see this rearrange (6.84) in the following way,

$$\mathbf{U}'(\mathbf{D}^* \mid \mathbf{I}(\theta)) = \int_X \int_Y \left[u(w, x, a_y^u(\theta))\, p_\theta(y \mid x; \theta)\, dy \right] p(x)\, dx$$

$$+\int_Y \frac{d a_y^u(\theta)}{d\theta}\left\{\int_X [u_a(w, x, a_y^u(\theta))\, p(x \mid y; \theta)]\, dx\right\} p(y; \theta)\, dy.$$

The foregoing second term is zero; it is the first-order condition (6.82) that characterizes the optimal decision rule $a_y^u(\theta)$. Thus the immediate impact of a differential change in θ is only the accounting effect

$$\mathbf{U'(D^* \mid I(\theta))} = \int_X \int_Y [u(w, x, a_y^u(\theta))\, p_\theta(y \mid x; \theta)\, dy]\; p(x)\; dx. \quad (6.85)$$

If the information structure is useless at θ, meaning $a_y^u(\theta) = a_0^u$ for every y, then the redistribution of probabilities has no effect on utility and, in light of (6.67),

$$\mathbf{U'(D^* \mid I(\theta))} = \int_X u(w, x, a_0^u)\, p(x)\; dx\; [\int_Y p_\theta(y \mid x; \theta)\, dy] = 0.$$

The continuation of Example 6.1 in Section 6.3.1 shows that there may be a range of low values of θ within which all structures are useless, and this range depends upon the prior distribution p(x).

A more fundamental result is due to Radner and Stiglitz (1984). If the utility of outcome $u(w, x, a_y^u(\theta))$ is continuous in a and θ, if the conditional distribution $p(y \mid x; \theta)$ is differentiable at $\theta = 0$, and if the change in θ has no effect upon the set of feasible actions, then evaluated at $\theta = 0$ where $a_y^u(0) = a_0^u$,

$$\mathbf{U'(D^* \mid I(0))} = \int_X u(w, x, a_0^u)\, p(x)\; dx\; [\int_Y p_\theta(y \mid x; 0)\, dy] = 0. \quad (6.86)$$

In the neighborhood of no information, the gross utility increment is zero to the first order. This result has nothing to do with whether there is a range of useless information; starting at null information, the marginal value of the first scintilla of information is zero. If that scintilla has positive marginal cost, then the net gain from information starts out negative. The implications of this are important in Chapter 8 for understanding the demand for informativeness and the choice of the optimal source. For now, we can simply conclude that the beneficial economic effects of greater informativeness start out slowly.

*6.3.4 *Environmental Uncertainty*

This subsection follows Gould (1974), Laffont (1976), and Hess (1982) to study the role of environmental uncertainty, that is, the comparative R–S variability of the prior distribution p(x), as a determinant of the value of information. As Chapter 9 details, the effects of the DM's environment on information search and choice are a major topic of research on the information use environment and information system design in organizations. Intuition suggests that greater environmental uncertainty should make a risk-averse DM worse off. Even if that were always so, the impact on information value and search would be unclear because the increased uncertainty affects the values of both the prior and the informed decisions. Chapter 5 presents several models in which the value of information increases directly with standard measures of risk such as the variance or the entropy of the state variable X, but it is easy to construct examples in which greater variance in the state leads to lower information value, even for risk neutral DMs. Furthermore, Gould (1974) presents an example in which the state distribution becomes more risky via an MPS, yet the value of perfect information declines.

To investigate this formally, let an increase in the index ζ indicate an increase in the Rothschild–Stiglitz variability of the state. If $p(x; \zeta)$ is a family of probability density functions with the range of X in the closed interval [0, 1], the cumulative distribution function for X is

$$F(x; \zeta) = \int_0^x p(s; \zeta)\, ds. \tag{6.87}$$

If $F(\bullet,\bullet)$ is twice differentiable, the condition for a mean preserving spread in a differential format is

$$T(x; \zeta) = \int_0^x F_\zeta(s; \zeta)\, ds \geq 0 \text{ for all } x \in [0, 1], \tag{6.88}$$

$$T(1; \zeta) = \int_0^1 F_\zeta(x; \zeta)\, dx = 0. \tag{6.89}$$

In general, redistribution of the probabilities associated with the prior distribution of X changes both $\mathbf{U(D^* \mid I}, \zeta)$ and $\mathbf{U(D^* \mid I{\downarrow}}, \zeta)$ in distinct ways: 1) there is an accounting impact; redistributing the probabilities changes the weights applied when assessing the expected utility of the various states, and 2) there is an economic impact, because changing the riskiness of the distribution, even with the mean unchanged, affects the optimal decisions chosen by the DM: the decisions $a_y^u(\zeta)$ and $a_0^u(\zeta)$ may depend upon ζ.

The prior expected utility of action a,

$$\mathbf{U(D \mid I{\downarrow}}, \zeta, a) = \int_0^1 u(w, x, a)\, dF(x; \zeta),$$

is maximized by the action $a_0^u(\zeta)$ characterized by the first-order condition

$$\int_0^1 u_a(w, x, a_0^u(\zeta))\, dF(x; \zeta) = 0,$$

with $u_{aa}(w, x, a_0^u(\zeta)) < 0$. Optimal prior expected utility is written as

$$\mathbf{U(D^* \mid I{\downarrow}}, \zeta) = \int_0^1 u(w, x, a_0^u(\zeta))\, dF(x; \zeta). \tag{6.90}$$

The question is how optimal expected utility changes with ζ. The derivative of (6.90) with respect to ζ is

$$\frac{d}{d\zeta}\mathbf{U}(\mathbf{D}^*\,|\,\mathbf{I}\!\downarrow,\zeta) = \int_0^1 u(w, x, a_0^u(\zeta))\, dF_\zeta(x;\zeta)$$

$$+ \int_0^1 u_a(w, x, a_0^u(\zeta))\, \frac{d a_0^u(\zeta)}{d\zeta}\, dF(x;\zeta)$$

$$= \int_0^1 u(w, x, a_0^u(\zeta))\, dF_\zeta(x;\zeta), \tag{6.91}$$

since the second term is again zero by the first-order condition. Thus, although there is a feedback from changed risk upon optimal action,[4] the effect on optimal expected utility is inconsequential, in the limit. The only impact is the accounting impact of the change in the distribution of X on expected utility. Laffont (1976) shows the remaining term in (6.91) can be signed; integrating by parts twice yields a result analogous to (6.80) with u replacing g. As long as the utility of outcome increases with x and is strictly concave, $u' > 0$ and $u'' < 0$, the term is negative. The increased uncertainty about the state of nature makes the expected utility of the prior decision lower for every risk averter, an intuitively reasonable result.

When $\mathbf{U}(\mathbf{D}^*\,|\,\mathbf{I}\!\downarrow,\zeta)$ decreases with ζ, the utility increment as in (6.59) is certain to increase with ζ if the value of the informed decision $\mathbf{U}(\mathbf{D}^*\,|\,\mathbf{I},\zeta)$ does not decrease with ζ. Perfect information is convenient for investigating this, as the optimal decision rules a_x are chosen under certainty and are identical for all DMs.

The notion that in the limit the slope of $\mathbf{U}(\mathbf{D}^*\,|\,\mathbf{I}\!\downarrow,\zeta)$ does not depend on the impact of ζ on a_0^u justifies studying the behavior of the ex-post utility increment from perfect information

$$\hat{\upsilon}(x, x) = u(w, x, a_x) - u(w, x, a_0^u) \geq 0. \tag{6.92}$$

The expectation of $\hat{\upsilon}(x, x)$ with respect to the prior distribution of X gives the utility increment from perfect information as it varies with ζ:

$$\hat{V}_{I\uparrow}^u(\zeta) = \mathbf{U}(\mathbf{D}^*\,|\,\mathbf{I}\!\uparrow,\zeta) - \mathbf{U}(\mathbf{D}^*\,|\,\mathbf{I}\!\downarrow,\zeta),$$

$$= E_{x;\zeta}\, u(w, x, a_x) - E_{x;\zeta}\, u(w, x, a_0^u)$$

$$= E_{x;\zeta}\, \hat{\upsilon}(x, x)$$

$$= \int_0^1 \hat{\upsilon}(x, x)\, dF(x;\zeta). \tag{6.93}$$

---

[4] The direction of this change can be signed as a function of the third derivative of u; see Diamond and Stiglitz (1974, Theorem 1).

Since this is in the same form as (6.68), with $\hat{\upsilon}(x, x)$ serving as the function g, definitive results turn on the ability to sign $\hat{\upsilon}''(x, x)$ over its entire range.

The first derivative with respect to x is

$$\hat{\upsilon}'(x, x) = u_x(w, x, a_x) + u_a(w, x, a_x)\frac{\partial a_x}{\partial x} - u_x(w, x, a_0^u) - u_a(w, x, a_0^u)\frac{\partial a_0^u}{\partial x}.$$

Differentiating again,

$$\hat{\upsilon}''(x, x) = u_{xx}(w, x, a_x) + u_{xa}(w, x, a_x)\frac{\partial a_x}{\partial x} + u_a(w, x, a_x)\frac{\partial^2 a_x}{\partial x^2}$$

$$+ \frac{\partial a_x}{\partial x}[u_{xa}(w, x, a_x) + u_{aa}(w, x, a_x)\frac{\partial a_x}{\partial x}] - u_{xx}(w, x, a_0^u).$$

The first-order condition that guarantees a_x is the optimal decision is $u_a(w, x, a_x) = 0$; taking the total differential tells us that $u_{aa}(w, x, a_x)\, da_x + u_{xa}(w, x, a_x)\, dx = 0$, giving the total derivative as

$$\frac{da_x}{dx} = -\frac{u_{ax}(w, x, a_x)}{u_{aa}(w, x, a_x)}.$$

Thus the second derivative is

$$\hat{\upsilon}''(x, x) = \frac{u_{aa}(w, x, a_x)u_{xx}(w, x, a_x) - [u_{xa}(w, x, a_x)]^2}{u_{aa}(w, x, a_x)} - u_{xx}(w, x, a_0^u). \quad (6.94)$$

Gould (1974) assumes that utility is linear in the state, meaning that altered riskiness does not matter and **U(D* | I↓,** ζ**)** is constant in ζ. Then $\hat{\upsilon}''(x, x) \geq 0$ since $u_{aa} < 0$. When $\hat{\upsilon}''(x, x)$ is strictly convex, **U(D* | I↑,** ζ**)** is increasing with ζ, and the value of information increases with R–S variability. Hess' (1982) result is that if $u_{aa}\, u_{xx} \leq u_{xa}^2$, and $u_{xx} < 0$, then $\hat{\upsilon}''(x, x) \geq 0$, and value increases with ζ. Sufficient for this conclusion are technical conditions on the utility of outcome function that $u(w, x, a_x)$ be strictly concave in x and a, but not concave in both (x, a). Greater environmental uncertainty is sure to increase information value only within the subset of Ω defined by the preceding requirements.

Hess (1982) also presents an example that illustrates the practical benefits of this type of theoretical analysis. Suppose a firm has K machines that break down randomly, with only xK available at any time. The firm combines the available machines with a quantity of labor a to produce goods according to a Cobb–Douglas production function $Q = [xK]^\alpha a^\gamma$. If the output price is 1, profits are $\pi(x, a) = [xK]^\alpha a^\gamma - rK - wa$, where r is the rental rate and w the wage rate. Here it is difficult to calculate the value of information about machine availability, but if there are increasing returns to scale, $\alpha + \gamma > 1$, it can be verified that information value increases as the R–S variability of equipment breakdown increases.

As a final word on this topic before turning explicitly to the role of the DM's preferences, there are no empirical data on the extent to which real-world decision problems do or do not meet any of the preceding sufficiency conditions. Hence, when some of the empirical studies in Section 9.1 assume that increased uncertainty leads to increased information value and search, the assumption may or may not be warranted. In experimental design, the theory cautions that when offering decision problems to subjects and observing their behavior, the framing of the problems should not be ignored.

7
Stochastic Preference and Information Value

As we have seen time and again, the economic value of information depends not only on the decision problem and the statistical characteristics of prior knowledge and informativeness; it also depends on the decision maker's preferences—preferences on the willingness to bear risk, and preferences on the choice of decision criterion. Chapter 7 brings these preferences to the forefront. The chapter begins by recasting the approach of Chapters 2 and 3 into an alternate, equivalent, and oftentimes enlightening viewpoint for formulating and analyzing decision problems under uncertainty. In this alternative formulation, the DM does not choose from among alternative actions, but rather from among the alternative probability distributions on wealth that are induced by the choice of a specific action or decision rule. Dealing directly with choice from among univariate probability measures over cash amounts puts the focus on the DM's attitude towards risk as a determinant of information value. The chapter concludes with the topic of aversion to information, which can arise when a DM does not obey the standard linear expected utility criterion.

7.1 Prospects and Attitude Towards Risk

Suppose you own a lottery ticket to the next drawing of a lotto game. What you really own is a prospect: a given chance you will lose and your wealth be the same as it is today, a given chance you will match all the balls and increase your wealth by the (present value of the) amount of the jackpot, and given chances you will win one of several sub-prizes. Your action to give up some current wealth and purchase this lotto ticket is equivalent to a choice of ownership of a specific *prospect*, a particular probability distribution over a set of potential terminal wealths. This section concentrates on the characteristics of the prospects the DM chooses to accept, a subject that intertwines the DM's attitude towards risk and initial wealth with the characteristics of the decision problem and the information source.

7.1.1 *Prospects Induced by Actions*

The reformulation of a decision problem into choice among prospects is accomplished by means of a change of variables in the problem, moving from probability measures defined on the state space **X** to measures defined on the wealth space **W**. For each $a_k \in \mathbf{a}$, the outcome function $\omega(w, x, a_k)$ defines a function from **X** to **W** that serves as the basis for the change in variables. Savage (1954) terms this function an *act*. When the DM chooses the action $a_k \in \mathbf{a}$, this induces ownership of a prospect denoted $\tilde{W}_k$. In this notation, the tilde indicates that the prospect is a random variable, and the subscript identifies the action that is inducing this random variable. Let the probability measure on **W** associated with $\tilde{W}_k$ be denoted $p(W | a_k)$. That is, $\mathbf{W} = \{W\}$ and $p(W | a_k)$ is the probability of obtaining terminal wealth W having chosen $a_k \in \mathbf{a}$.

The change of variables to prospects requires a partitioning of the state space **X** for each action $a_k \in \mathbf{a}$. The prospect from action a_k is determined from the outcome function and the (currently) relevant probability measure on **X** by partitioning **X** into subsets of the form

$$\mathbf{X} = \mathbf{X}'(a_k) = \{\{x'_w(a_k)\} \text{ for each } W \in \mathbf{W}\}, \tag{7.1}$$

within which the terminal wealth from action a_k is constant; that is,

$$x'_w(a_k) = \{x \colon \omega(w, x, a_k) = W\}. \tag{7.2}$$

With the terminal wealth from each $x \in x'_w(a_k)$ constant,

$$W = \omega(w, x'_w(a_k), a_k). \tag{7.3}$$

The probability distribution over $\mathbf{X}'(a_k)$ is the same as that of the prospect $\tilde{W}_k$:

$$p(W | a_k) = \text{Prob}(x \colon \omega(w, x, a_k) = W) = \text{Prob}(x'_w(a_k)). \tag{7.4}$$

Since by construction the elements of **X** are mutually exclusive, the probability of the union of elements described by (7.4) is simply the sum of the probability of each element:

$$\text{Prob}(x'_w(a_k)) = \sum_{x_i \in x'_w(a_k)} p(x_i). \tag{7.5}$$

In summary, the prospect associated with a_k is

$$\tilde{W}_k = \{W, p(W | a_k); \text{ for each } W \in \mathbf{W}\}. \tag{7.6}$$

The expected utility of $\tilde{W}_k$ can be written as

$$E_{W|a_k} u(W) = \Sigma_w u(W)\, p(W | a_k), \tag{7.7a}$$

or

$$E_{W\,|\,a_k}\, u(W) \;=\; \int_{\mathbf{W}} u(W)\; p(W\,|\,a_k)\; dW, \tag{7.7b}$$

depending upon whether **W** is countable. In fact, the new notation of Section 6.3.2 allows us to combine the two cases into

$$E_{W\,|\,a_k}\, u(W) \;=\; \int_{\mathbf{W}} u(W)\; dF(W\,|\,a_k), \tag{7.7c}$$

where $F(W\,|\,a_k)$ is the cumulative distribution function of $p(W\,|\,a_k)$, and the integral is properly interpreted in the Stieltjes sense.

Suppose the DM owns the prospect $\tilde{W}_k$. The exchange values that arise by characterizing decisions as commodities also apply directly to prospects. The *reservation price of the prospect*, also called the *certainty equivalent*, is the deterministic terminal wealth that makes the DM indifferent between the prospect $\tilde{W}_k$ and the sale of $\tilde{W}_k$ for a cash-equivalent payment with certainty of R_k^u. This selling price is defined implicitly in terms of the prospect as the solution to

$$u(R_k^u) \;=\; E_{W\,|\,a_k}\, u(W). \tag{7.8}$$

Another important cash summarization of $\tilde{W}_k$ is its mean $\overline{W}_k$, the expected terminal wealth of the prospect defined by

$$\overline{W}_k \;=\; E_{W\,|\,a_k}[W] \;=\; \int_{\mathbf{W}} [W]\; dF(W\,|\,a_k). \tag{7.9}$$

The definition of Rothschild–Stiglitz variability provides the natural method for investigating whether one prospect is more risky than another; replace $g(z)$ with $u(W)$ and $dF(z;\,\beta)$ with $dF(W\,|\,a_k)$ in the analysis of Section 6.3.2. To make the Rothschild–Stiglitz variability comparison, the prospects must be adjusted to the same mean; in general, the location of a prospect can be changed by subtracting a constant amount ψ from every terminal wealth. This adjusted prospect is denoted $\tilde{W}_k(\psi)$ and defined by

$$\tilde{W}_k(\psi) \;=\; \{W - \psi,\; p(W\,|\,a_k);\; \text{for each } W \in \mathbf{W}\}. \tag{7.10}$$

The expected utility of $\tilde{W}_k(\psi)$ is

$$E_{W\,|\,a_k}\, u(W-\psi) \;=\; \int_{\mathbf{W}} u(W-\psi)\; dF(W\,|\,a_k), \tag{7.11}$$

the reservation price is written $R_k^u(\psi)$, and the mean evaluates to

$$\overline{W}_k(\psi) \;=\; \int_{\mathbf{W}} [W-\psi]\; dF(W\,|\,a_k) \;=\; \overline{W}_k - \psi. \tag{7.12}$$

By appropriate choice of ψ, the mean of $\tilde{W}_k$ can be adjusted to an arbitrary value.

Given two prospects with the same mean, prospect $\tilde{W}_k$ is Rothschild–Stiglitz more variable (or more risky) than prospect $\tilde{W}_\ell$ if and only if the expected utility from prospect $\tilde{W}_\ell$ is at least as great as from prospect $\tilde{W}_k$ for any strictly concave utility function defined on **W**. Rothschild and Stiglitz (1970) show that this partial ordering is equivalent to forming prospect $\tilde{W}_k$ via a mean-preserving spread of prospect $\tilde{W}_\ell$. Not all prospects are comparable in this sense, but when it holds, every risk averse DM prefers $\tilde{W}_\ell$ to $\tilde{W}_k$. Recall that higher variance or entropy is necessary but not sufficient for this characteristic.

7.1.2 Cash Summarizations for Optimal Prospects

The optimal prior decision maximizes (7.7) with respect to a; the optimal prior action a_0^u leads to the optimal prior prospect $\tilde{W}_0^u$, a prospect with probability distribution $p(W \mid a_0^u)$ induced by a_0^u via a partitioning $\mathbf{X}'(a_0^u)$ defined by (7.1) and (7.2). The value of the prior decision is the same in terms of prospects as in the state space approach since, using (2.11), (7.2), (7.5), (7.4), and (7.7a),

$$\begin{aligned}
\mathbf{U}(\mathbf{D}^* \mid \mathbf{I}\downarrow) &= E_x\, u(\omega(w, x, a_0^u)) \\
&= \Sigma_i\, u(\omega(w, x_i, a_0^u))\, p(x_i) \\
&= \Sigma_w\, u(\omega(w, x'_w(a_0^u), a_0^u))\, \Sigma_{x_i \in x'_w(a_0^u)}\, p(x_i) \\
&= \Sigma_w\, u(\omega(w, x'_w(a_0^u), a_0^u))\, \mathrm{Prob}(x'_w(a_0^u)) \\
&= \Sigma_w\, u(W)\, p(W \mid a_0^u) \\
&= E_{w|a_0^u}\, u(W). \qquad (7.13)
\end{aligned}$$

The reservation price of the prior decision solves $u(R_0^u) = \mathbf{U}(\mathbf{D}^* \mid \mathbf{I}\downarrow)$ and, in light of (7.13) can be defined in either prospect space or state space as the solution to

$$\begin{aligned}
u(R_0^u) &= E_{w|a_0^u}\, u(W) \\
&= E_x\, u(\omega(w, x, a_0^u)). \qquad (7.14)
\end{aligned}$$

Likewise, the mean of the optimal prior prospect $\overline{W}_0^u$ is, in prospect space and state space, respectively,

$$\begin{aligned}
\overline{W}_0^u &= E_{w|a_0^u}[W] \\
&= E_x\, \{\omega(w, x, a_0^u)\}. \qquad (7.15)
\end{aligned}$$

Suppose now the DM receives a message y that changes beliefs about the state from p(x) to the posterior measure $p(x \mid y)$. If the message causes the DM to change the choice from a_0^u to a new optimal action a_y^u, then posterior to this message but prior to the state realization the DM now owns the conditional optimal prospect $\tilde{W}_y^u$, a prospect with probability distribution $p(W \mid a_y^u)$. In this notation the subscript y does double duty, indicating that the prospect is induced both by the choice of action a_y^u and by the conditional measure $p(x|y)$ on the state space. The expected utility of the conditional optimal prospect is

$$\mathbf{U(D^* | I}, y) = E_{W|a_y^u} u(W) = \int_{\mathbf{W}} u(W)\, p(W | a_y^u)\, dW. \qquad (7.16)$$

The prospect $\tilde{W}_y^u$ has reservation price R_y^u and mean $\overline{W}_y^u$.

Before the receipt of any message, the ability to make use of the information source provides the DM with an optimal informed prospect with properties that arise naturally. Since in extensive form each conditional optimal prospect $\tilde{W}_y^u$ has probability $p(y)$ of applying, the preposterior optimal informed prospect from the structure **I**, $\tilde{W}_{\mathbf{I}}^u$, is a mixture distribution

$$p(W | a_{\mathbf{I}}^u) = \int_{\mathbf{Y}} p(W | a_y^u)\, p(y)\, dy, \qquad (7.17)$$

where the optimal decision rule $a_{\mathbf{I}}^u = \{ a_y^u \text{ for all } y \in \mathbf{Y}\}$. For example, when **Y** is finite and there are n distributions $p(W | a_{y_j}^u)$ and another distribution $p(y_j)$, then $p(W | a_{\mathbf{I}}^u)$ is a distribution over **W** that assigns probability

$$\Sigma_j\, p(W | a_{y_j}^u)\, p(y_j)$$

to terminal wealth $W \in \mathbf{W}$.

The expected utility of the optimal informed prospect is derived by taking the expectation of (7.16) with respect to p(y) and using (7.17):

$$\begin{aligned} E_y\, E_{W|a_y^u} u(W) &= \int_{\mathbf{Y}} \left\{ \int_{\mathbf{W}} u(W)\, p(W | a_y^u)\, dW \right\} p(y)\, dy \\ &= \int_{\mathbf{W}} u(W) \left\{ \int_{\mathbf{Y}} p(W | a_y^u)\, p(y)\, dy \right\} dW \\ &= \int_{\mathbf{W}} u(W)\, p(W | a_{\mathbf{I}}^u)\, dW \\ &= E_{W|a_{\mathbf{I}}^u} u(W). \end{aligned} \qquad (7.18)$$

In terms of the optimal informed prospect, the reservation price of the informed decision, $R_{\mathbf{I}}^u$, is defined from (7.8) as

$$u(R_{\mathbf{I}}^u) = \mathbf{U(D^* | I)} = E_{W|a_{\mathbf{I}}^u} u(W). \qquad (7.19)$$

The overall preposterior mean [defined in state space by (3.44)],

$$\overline{W}_{\mathbf{I}}^u = E_{W|a_{\mathbf{I}}^u} [W] = E_y\, E_{W|a_y^u} [W] = E_y\, \overline{W}_y^u, \qquad (7.20)$$

is simply the mean of the conditional means.

These results hold up for costly optimal prospects. When assessing the demand value of information in terms of prospects, it is important to recall from Section 3.1.2 that the payment of ψ has a double impact: it reduces all terminal wealths by ψ, and it also changes the optimal conditional decision rule to $a_y^u(\psi)$ for every y. Thus the costly conditional prospect is

$$\tilde{W}_y^u(\psi) = \{W - \psi, p(W \mid a_y^u(\psi))\}, \tag{7.21}$$

and the costly informed prospect is written as

$$\tilde{W}_I^u(\psi) = \{W - \psi, p(W \mid a_I^u(\psi))\}. \tag{7.22}$$

Recall that the demand value in state space with separable payoff is the $\psi = V_I^u$ that solves

$$E_y E_{x|y} u(w - V_I^u + \pi(x, a_y^u(V_I^u))) = E_x u(w + \pi(x, a_0^u)). \tag{7.23}$$

In terms of prospects this is

$$E_{w|a_I^u(V_I^u)} u(W - V_I^u) = E_{w|a_0^u} u(W), \tag{7.24}$$

or

$$\int_W u(W - V_I^u) dF(W \mid a_I^u(V_I^u)) = \int_W u(W) dF(W \mid a_0^u). \tag{7.25}$$

Under risk neutrality, $a_I^N(\psi) = a_I^N$, so (7.25) solves to the familiar

$$V_I^N = \overline{W}_I^N - \overline{W}_0^N. \tag{7.26}$$

Finally, in terms of reservation prices, the demand value of information is defined by

$$u(R_I^u(V_I^u)) = u(R_0^u), \tag{7.27}$$

which implies

$$R_I^u(V_I^u) = R_0^u, \tag{7.28}$$

because of the assumed continuity and strict increasingness of the utility function.

♦ *Example 2.2 Style vs. Substance? (Continued from Section 2.2)*
This continuation reformulates Example 2.2 into a problem of valuing and choosing from among alternative informed and prior prospects. The example concludes with an illustration of the tests for first-degree stochastic dominance and Rothschild–Stiglitz variability.

In the decision problem whether the advertising agency should invest in slick graphics to improve a presentation to a potential client, recall the four states as

x_1 = the proposal is accepted on its merits no matter what we do,
x_2 = the proposal is rejected on its merits no matter what we do,
x_3 = the proposal is accepted if and only if it is graphically slick,
x_4 = the proposal is rejected if and only if it is graphically slick,

and the monetary outcomes as in the following repeat of Table 2.2.

Table 7.1. Framing for Example 2.2

	x_1	x_2	x_3	x_4
a_1 = buy graphics	\$21	\$1	\$21	\$ 1
a_2 = don't buy graphics	\$22	\$2	\$ 2	\$22

The partitions of $\mathbf{X}^4$ for the change of variables to prospects are

$$\mathbf{X}'(a_1) = \{\, x_1'(a_1) = \{x_2, x_4\};\ x_{21}'(a_1) = \{x_1, x_3\}\};$$

$$\mathbf{X}'(a_2) = \{\, x_2'(a_2) = \{x_2, x_3\};\ x_{22}'(a_2) = \{x_1, x_4\}\}. \tag{7.29}$$

Suppose the DM assesses the following prior probabilities for the four states: $p(x_1) = .50$, $p(x_2) = .25$, $p(x_3) = .20$, and $p(x_4) = .05$. Using (7.5), the probability of each constant-wealth union of states is

$$\text{Prob}(\, x_1'(a_1)) = p(x_2) + p(x_4) = .30;$$

$$\text{Prob}(\, x_{21}'(a_1)) = p(x_1) + p(x_3) = .70;$$

$$\text{Prob}(\, x_2'(a_2)) = p(x_2) + p(x_3) = .45;$$

$$\text{Prob}(\, x_{22}'(a_2)) = p(x_1) + p(x_4) = .55.$$

Hence, the prospects from the two actions are

$$\tilde{W}_1 = \{\$1, .30; \$21, .70\};$$

$$\tilde{W}_2 = \{\$2, .45; \$22, .55\}.$$

If the DM's utility function is $u(W) = W$, it is simple to calculate the expected utility of each prospect as $E_{w|a_1}u(W) = \$15$ and $E_{w|a_2}u(W) = \$13$. Hence the optimal prospect is $\tilde{W}_0^N = \tilde{W}_1$, and $\overline{W}_0^N = \mathbf{U}(\mathbf{D}^* \,|\, \mathbf{I}\downarrow) = \$15$. The optimal prior decision is to buy the graphics and accept a prospect giving a 70% chance of the client accepting the proposal.

Suppose instead the DM assesses a slightly different prior distribution $p^\#(x)$: $p^\#(x_1) = .50$, $p^\#(x_2) = .30$, $p^\#(x_3) = .10$, and $p^\#(x_4) = .10$. This prior assesses a slightly lower chance for the capricious behavior described in states x_3 and x_4. Now the two prospects are

$$\tilde{W}_1^\# = \{\$1, .40; \$21, .60\};$$

$$\tilde{W}_2^\# = \{\$2, .40; \$22, .60\}.$$

Many DMs would choose $\tilde{W}_2^\#$ over $\tilde{W}_1^\#$ without a lot of thought, because $\tilde{W}_2^\#$ clearly exhibits first-degree stochastic dominance over $\tilde{W}_1^\#$; the basic idea is that a stochastically dominating prospect unambiguously gives the DM a better chance of receiving a higher level of wealth.

The advertising agency now has the opportunity to obtain the following information: the graphical characteristics and final resolution of the most recent decision by the client on an unrelated advertising campaign. The space **Y** contains the following messages.

y_1 = the previous proposal was slick and rejected,
y_2 = the previous proposal was not slick and rejected,
y_3 = the previous proposal was not slick and accepted,
y_4 = the previous proposal was slick and accepted.

This information source provides indirect information, not purporting to reveal directly which of the four states occurs this time. Such information has the potential to be valuable because learning message y_3 means that state x_3 is no longer possible (the client is not rejecting nonslick presentations out of hand), and learning y_4 means x_4 is not possible.

The DM assesses the likelihood of each message conditional on the state as

$$\lambda = \begin{bmatrix} p(y_1|x_1) & p(y_2|x_1) & p(y_3|x_1) & p(y_4|x_1) \\ p(y_1|x_2) & p(y_2|x_2) & p(y_3|x_2) & p(y_4|x_2) \\ p(y_1|x_3) & p(y_2|x_3) & p(y_3|x_3) & p(y_4|x_3) \\ p(y_1|x_4) & p(y_2|x_4) & p(y_3|x_4) & p(y_4|x_4) \end{bmatrix} = \begin{bmatrix} \frac{1}{4} & \frac{1}{4} & \frac{1}{4} & \frac{1}{4} \\ \frac{1}{4} & \frac{1}{4} & \frac{1}{4} & \frac{1}{4} \\ 0 & \frac{1}{2} & 0 & \frac{1}{2} \\ \frac{1}{2} & 0 & \frac{1}{2} & 0 \end{bmatrix}.$$

The rationale for this assessment of likelihood is as follows. The semantic meaning of conditioning on x_1 or x_2 is the hypothesis that the client judges proposals solely on merit. If this is true then in the previous client decision any combination of graphical characteristics and final resolution—any of the four messages—could be observed. Without any additional knowledge, it is reasonable to assess each of the four possibilities as equally likely. In contrast, conditioning on x_3 means that the client only goes for style and does not care about substance, hence y_1 and y_3 cannot be observed. Likewise, conditional on x_4, messages y_2 and y_4 are not possible. In each case the DM decides to assess the probability evenly between the two remaining messages.

Combining the likelihood with the prior distribution on the state gives the matrix ρ, the joint distribution of messages and states:

$$\rho = \begin{bmatrix} p(x_1, y_1) & p(x_1, y_2) & p(x_1, y_3) & p(x_1, y_4) \\ p(x_2, y_1) & p(x_2, y_2) & p(x_2, y_3) & p(x_2, y_4) \\ p(x_3, y_1) & p(x_3, y_2) & p(x_3, y_3) & p(x_3, y_4) \\ p(x_4, y_1) & p(x_4, y_2) & p(x_4, y_3) & p(x_4, y_4) \end{bmatrix} = \begin{bmatrix} \frac{10}{80} & \frac{10}{80} & \frac{10}{80} & \frac{10}{80} \\ \frac{5}{80} & \frac{5}{80} & \frac{5}{80} & \frac{5}{80} \\ 0 & \frac{8}{80} & 0 & \frac{8}{80} \\ \frac{2}{80} & 0 & \frac{2}{80} & 0 \end{bmatrix}.$$

Adding up the probability in each column of ρ yields the marginal distribution of the messages, the vector **q**:

$$\mathbf{q} = [p(y_1), p(y_2), p(y_3), p(y_4)] = \left[\tfrac{17}{80} \;\; \tfrac{23}{80} \;\; \tfrac{17}{80} \;\; \tfrac{23}{80}\right]. \tag{7.30}$$

Finally, dividing the joint distribution by the marginal gives the matrix Π, the posterior distribution of the state, conditional on each message:

$$\Pi = \begin{bmatrix} p(x_1|y_1) & p(x_1|y_2) & p(x_1|y_3) & p(x_1|y_4) \\ p(x_2|y_1) & p(x_2|y_2) & p(x_2|y_3) & p(x_2|y_4) \\ p(x_3|y_1) & p(x_3|y_2) & p(x_3|y_3) & p(x_3|y_4) \\ p(x_4|y_1) & p(x_4|y_2) & p(x_4|y_3) & p(x_4|y_4) \end{bmatrix} = \begin{bmatrix} \tfrac{10}{17} & \tfrac{10}{23} & \tfrac{10}{17} & \tfrac{10}{23} \\ \tfrac{5}{17} & \tfrac{5}{23} & \tfrac{5}{17} & \tfrac{5}{23} \\ 0 & \tfrac{8}{23} & 0 & \tfrac{8}{23} \\ \tfrac{2}{17} & 0 & \tfrac{2}{17} & 0 \end{bmatrix}. \tag{7.31}$$

Table 7.2 presents the conditional optimal prospects and corresponding means for the risk neutral DM. As an example of the typical calculation leading to Table 7.2, consider the possible responses to message y_1. Given the outcomes in Table 7.1, the partitioning given in (7.29), and the posterior distribution (7.31), the probability of each constant-wealth union of states is

$$\text{Prob}(x_1'(a_1)) = p(x_2|y_1) + p(x_4|y_1) = \tfrac{7}{17};$$

$$\text{Prob}(x_{21}'(a_1)) = p(x_1|y_1) + p(x_3|y_1) = \tfrac{10}{17};$$

$$\text{Prob}(x_2'(a_2)) = p(x_2|y_1) + p(x_3|y_1) = \tfrac{5}{17};$$

$$\text{Prob}(x_{22}'(a_2)) = p(x_1|y_1) + p(x_4|y_1) = \tfrac{12}{17}.$$

Hence, the two prospects, conditional on y_1 are,

$$\text{if } a_1\text{: } \tilde{W}_1 = \{\$1, \tfrac{7}{17}; \$21, \tfrac{10}{17}\} \text{ with } \overline{W}_1 = \$12.7647,$$

$$\text{if } a_2\text{: } \tilde{W}_2 = \{\$2, \tfrac{5}{17}; \$22, \tfrac{12}{17}\} \text{ with } \overline{W}_2 = \$16.1176;$$

under risk neutrality the optimal conditional decision rule must be $a_{y_1}^N = a_2$, so the optimal conditional prospect is $\tilde{W}_2$.

Table 7.2. Conditional Optimal Prospects in Example 2.2

Message	Optimal Prospect	Mean Wealth
y_1	$\tilde{W}_{y_1}^N = \{\$2, \tfrac{5}{17}; \$22, \tfrac{12}{17}\}$	$\overline{W}_{y_1}^N = \$16.1176$
y_2	$\tilde{W}_{y_2}^N = \{\$1, \tfrac{5}{23}; \$21, \tfrac{18}{23}\}$	$\overline{W}_{y_2}^N = \$16.6522$
y_3	$\tilde{W}_{y_3}^N = \{\$2, \tfrac{5}{17}; \$22, \tfrac{12}{17}\}$	$\overline{W}_{y_3}^N = \$16.1176$
y_4	$\tilde{W}_{y_4}^N = \{\$1, \tfrac{5}{23}; \$21, \tfrac{18}{23}\}$	$\overline{W}_{y_4}^N = \$16.6522$

The optimal decision rule is

$$a_I^N = \{a_{y_1}^N, a_{y_2}^N, a_{y_3}^N, a_{y_4}^N\} = \{a_2, a_1, a_2, a_1\}.$$

Obtaining the preposterior optimal informed prospect under risk neutrality requires determination of (7.17) for each $W \in \mathbf{W}$. Using the results in Table 7.2 and the marginal distribution of the messages, (7.30),

$$\text{Prob}(W = 1 \mid a_I^N) = [0][\tfrac{17}{80}] + [\tfrac{5}{23}][\tfrac{23}{80}] + [0][\tfrac{17}{80}] + [\tfrac{5}{23}][\tfrac{23}{80}] = \tfrac{10}{80} = .125;$$

$$\text{Prob}(W = 2 \mid a_I^N) = [\tfrac{5}{17}][\tfrac{17}{80}] + [0][\tfrac{23}{80}] + [\tfrac{5}{17}][\tfrac{17}{80}] + [0][\tfrac{23}{80}] = \tfrac{10}{80} = .125;$$

$$\text{Prob}(W = 21 \mid a_I^N) = [0][\tfrac{17}{80}] + [\tfrac{18}{23}][\tfrac{23}{80}] + [0][\tfrac{17}{80}] + [\tfrac{18}{23}][\tfrac{23}{80}] = \tfrac{36}{80} = .45;$$

$$\text{Prob}(W = 22 \mid a_I^N) = [\tfrac{12}{17}][\tfrac{17}{80}] + [0][\tfrac{23}{80}] + [\tfrac{12}{17}][\tfrac{17}{80}] + [0][\tfrac{23}{80}] = \tfrac{24}{80} = .30.$$

Hence the optimal preposterior prospect is

$$\tilde{W}_I^N = \{\$1, .125; \$2, .125; \$21, .45; \$22, .30\},$$

a prospect with mean $\overline{W}_I^N = \$16.425$. This expected wealth can also be calculated directly from Table 7.2 using (7.20):

$$\overline{W}_I^N = [16.1176][\tfrac{17}{80}] + [16.6522][\tfrac{23}{80}]$$
$$+ [16.1176][\tfrac{17}{80}] + [16.6522][\tfrac{23}{80}] = \$16.425.$$

The value of the information structure is $V_I^N = \overline{W}_I^N - \overline{W}_0^N = \$1.425$.

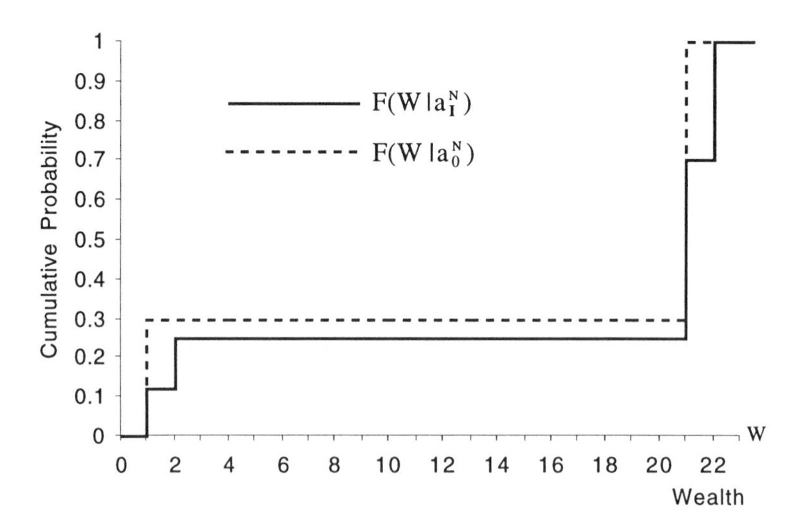

Figure 7.1. The cumulative distribution functions of the optimal prior and informed prospects show first-degree stochastic dominance for the decision with information.

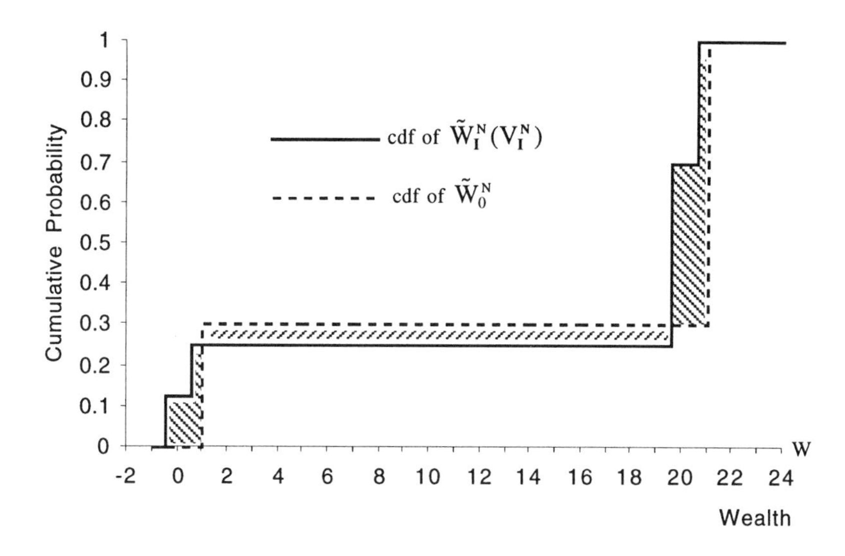

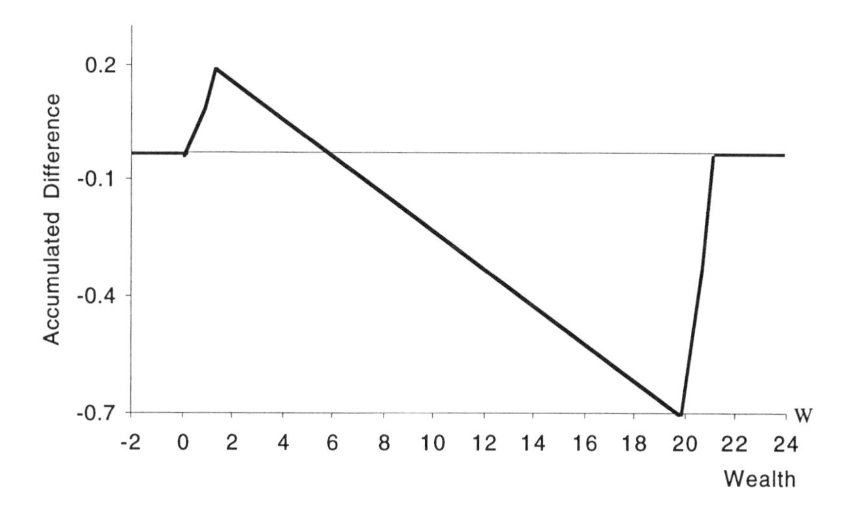

Figure 7.2. Rothschild–Stiglitz comparability between two prospects with the same mean requires satisfaction of the integral condition (6.73). The upper graph shows multiple crossings of the two cdfs, and the lower graph assesses the accumulated difference in the two areas. The integral condition is not met and the two prospects are not comparable.

Figure 7.1 graphs the cumulative distribution functions $F(W \mid a_I^N)$ and $F(W \mid a_0^N)$; $\tilde{W}_I^N$ is clearly first-degree dominant: the cdf of $\tilde{W}_I^N$ is never above, and sometimes below, the cdf of $\tilde{W}_0^N$. To perform an R–S variability comparison between $\tilde{W}_I^N$ and $\tilde{W}_0^N$, the two prospects must be adjusted to have the same mean. Here, if $\psi = V_I^N = \$1.425$, the resulting prospect

$$\tilde{W}_I^N(V_I^N) = \{-\$0.425, .125; \$0.575, .125; \$19.575, .45; \$20.575, .30\}$$

has the mean $\overline{W}_I^N(V_I^N) = \$15 = \overline{W}_0^N$. Figure 7.2 shows the two cumulative distribution functions and the accumulated value of the integral T(W, $a_I^N(V_I^N)$, a_0^N). For second-degree stochastic dominance, the integral must be positive for all values of W; it is not, so the two prospects are not comparable. Of course, the risk neutral DM is indifferent between the two prospects because she doesn't care about the riskiness. But if these prospects were offered as is to risk averse DMs, the lack of comparability means no conclusions can be drawn about which prospect is preferred. ♦

An alternative way of approaching a situation like Example 2.2 is to formulate and assess the problem directly in prospect space. This is the tack that Howard, Matheson, and North (1972) take when they assess the probabilities of alternative monetary losses due to hurricane damage, conditional upon whether the hurricane is seeded. The application of their model provides an interesting illustration of first-degree stochastic dominance between two resulting prospects.

7.1.3 *Attitude Towards Risk*

There are definite relationships between the reservation price and the mean of an arbitrary prospect that depend upon the DM's attitude towards bearing risk, a characteristic of preference that is indicated by the shape of the utility function as it varies with wealth. Figure 7.3 presents three basic shapes for the utility of wealth function u(W): concave and risk averse in the top graph, convex and risk loving in the middle, and linear and risk neutral at the bottom.

An application of Jensen's inequality provides the rationale for these designations. Jensen's inequality states that if u(W) is a concave function defined on the interval [C, D], and if $\tilde{W}_k$ is any arbitrary prospect having all its probability contained in that interval, and assuming as usual that all expectations exist, then the utility of the expectation is greater than the expectation of utility. In symbols,

$$u(E_{W|a_k}[W]) \geq E_{W|a_k} u(W). \tag{7.32}$$

Substituting the definitions (7.9) and (7.8), with A replacing u to signify risk aversion, shows

$$u(\overline{W}_k) \geq u(R_k^A),$$

and hence by the strict increasingness of the utility function

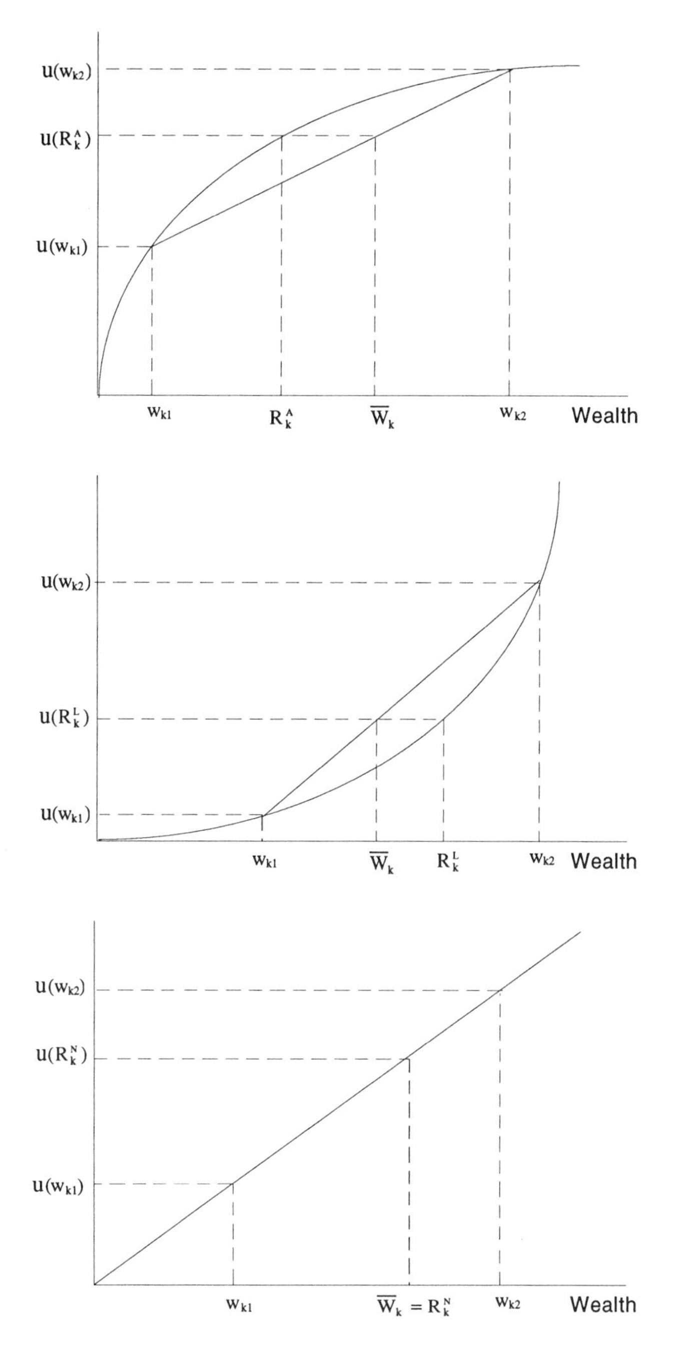

Figure 7.3. There are three pure shapes for the utility function on wealth: concave and risk averse in the top graph, convex and risk loving in the middle, and linear and risk neutral at the bottom.

$$\overline{W}_k \geq R_k^A. \tag{7.33}$$

This is the sense in which such a DM is averse towards risk: this DM is willing to accept less than the expected value of the prospect in order to avoid the risk inherent in that prospect. Put a different way, the DM is willing to pay a *risk* or *insurance premium* of

$$\iota = \overline{W}_k - R_k^A \tag{7.34}$$

to be protected from the prospect's risk.

If the utility function is linear over the interval, Jensen's inequality ensures

$$u(E_{w\,|\,a_k}[W]) = E_{w\,|\,a_k}\,u(W).$$

The risk neutral DM with the linear utility function for wealth cares only about the expected wealth generated by a prospect; the riskiness of the prospect is immaterial. Hence, applying (7.9) and (7.8) to the risk neutral case,

$$\overline{W}_k = R_k^N. \tag{7.35}$$

and the risk premium is zero.

Finally, if the utility function is convex in W,

$$u(E_{w\,|\,a_k}[W]) \leq E_{w\,|\,a_k}\,u(W),$$

and

$$\overline{W}_k \leq R_k^L. \tag{7.36}$$

With the risk premium negative, this DM would pay extra for the privilege of taking the risk. The risk loving case is seldom analyzed; it is presumed that most DMs are either risk averse or risk neutral.

Figure 7.3 gives the geometric interpretation when the DM owns a two-valued prospect $\tilde{W}_k = \{w_{k1}, p_{k1}; w_{k2}, p_{k2}\}$. For the risk averter in the top graph, the horizontal axis identifies the two wealth levels offered by $\tilde{W}_k$, and the vertical distances register their corresponding utility. The mean of the prospect

$$p_{k1}w_{k1} + [1 - p_{k1}]w_{k2} = \overline{W}_k$$

is a specific point on the horizontal axis, the point that divides the segment $[w_{k1}, w_{k2}]$ in the ratio $[1 - p_{k1}]/\,p_{k1}$. The graph also shows the line segment connecting the utilities of the two wealth levels, an equation of the form

$$\alpha\, u(w_{k1}) + [1 - \alpha]\, u(w_{k2}),$$

for $0 \leq \alpha \leq 1$. Replacing α with the probability p_{k1} shows that the expected utility of the prospect is a point on that line, a point that divides the line segment in the same ratio $[1 - p_{k1}]/p_{k1}$ as the preceding. On the graph the expected utility is the vertical distance from the point $\overline{W}_k$ to the line segment. The prospect's reservation price R_k^A is the fixed wealth level that provides the same utility as the expected utility. With $\overline{W}_k > R_k^A$, the difference $\overline{W}_k - R_k^A$ is the risk premium.

Similarly, for the risk lover pictured in the middle graph, $\overline{W}_k < R_k^L$, as the risk lover is willing to pay a premium for the right to take the risk. Finally, for the risk neutral DM, $\overline{W}_k = R_k^N$.

Concentrating on strictly concave utility functions, Pratt (1964) and Arrow (1965) investigate the relationship between the degree of concavity of the utility function, as measured by the risk aversion index

$$b(W) = -u''(W)/u'(W), \tag{7.37}$$

and the insurance or risk premium $\iota = \overline{W}_k - R_k^A$. Under certain circumstances, when the absolute risk aversion index tends towards infinity, the expected utility criterion converges to the maximin criterion. See, for example, Laffont (1989) for a demonstration.

Pratt (1964) considers a DM with initial wealth w facing a "small" risk in which her initial wealth has a 50–50 chance of increasing or decreasing by a minimal amount ε. Her prospect is

$$\tilde{W} = \{w - \varepsilon, \tfrac{1}{2}; w + \varepsilon, \tfrac{1}{2}\}, \tag{7.38}$$

where $\overline{W} = w$ and the variance is $Var(\tilde{W}) = \varepsilon^2$. The reservation price, defined by $u(R^A) = E_w u(W)$, is the minimum amount the DM would take to trade her entire position, small risk and all, for a risk-free position. The risk premium is $\iota = w - R^A$; rearranging so $R^A = w - \iota$ and substituting into the definition of R^A gives

$$u(w - \iota) = \tfrac{1}{2}u(w - \varepsilon) + \tfrac{1}{2}u(w + \varepsilon). \tag{7.39}$$

Pratt solves for the risk premium ι by expanding both sides of (7.39) in a Taylor series about initial wealth w. Cutting off the expansion after two terms for the left-hand side and three terms on the right-hand side, the approximation yields

$$u(w) + u'(w)[-\iota] = u(w) + \tfrac{1}{2}u''(w)[\varepsilon^2],$$

which solves to

$$\iota = -\tfrac{1}{2}\frac{u''(w)}{u'(w)}[\varepsilon^2] = \tfrac{1}{2}b(w)\,Var(\tilde{W}). \tag{7.40}$$

Rearranging (7.40) to isolate b(w), the coefficient of (absolute) risk aversion for the small risk is twice the risk premium per unit of variance.

Consider two risk averse DMs, 1 and 2, with utility functions $u_1(W)$ and $u_2(W)$, respectively. DM 1 is more risk averse than DM 2 in the Arrow–Pratt sense if $[u_1''(W)/u_1'(W)] \geq [u_2''(W)/u_2'(W)]$ for all W. Integrating this twice yields the direct expression that $u_1(W) = f(u_2(W))$, where f is a monotone increasing concave function. Thus a more risk averse utility function is a "concavification" of a less risk averse one. Pratt also proves that $\iota_1 \geq \iota_2$; the more risk averse DM will pay a higher premium to avoid the risk.

In Example 2.1, an R–S comparison of the prior prospects associated with the two actions, $\tilde{W}_1 = \{\$110, .60; \$150, .40\}$ for a_1 and $\tilde{W}_2 = \{\$125, .60; \$115, .40\}$ for a_2 shows that, after adjusting them to have equal means, the integral condition (6.73) is satisfied and $\tilde{W}_1$ is more risky than $\tilde{W}_2$. The actual choice, however, is between the unadjusted prospects, and the choice often boils down to one between a higher risk prospect with a higher mean, and a lower risk prospect with a lower mean. As the discussion in Section 2.1.3 shows, risk averters in different circumstances choose one or the other. The next section makes comparisons between the behavior of different individuals facing the same risky choices, and we need a measure of comparative aversion toward risk. Such a measure should have the following property. If one DM chooses, for example, the less risky prospect with a lower mean, then any more risk averse DM should make the same choice.

The Arrow–Pratt approach is based upon the choice between a risky prospect and one that is risk free. Ross (1981) points out that the Arrow–Pratt results may not hold up when comparing two DMs choosing between two risky prospects such as the informed and uninformed decisions. Ross presents the following definition. DM 1 is more risk averse than DM 2 if there is a positive number Λ such that for any two wealth levels W_1 and W_2, $[u_1''(W_1)/u_2''(W_1)] \geq \Lambda \geq [u_1'(W_2)/u_2'(W_2)]$. When DM 1 is more risk averse than DM 2 in Ross' sense, then if DM 2 chooses a lower risk prospect with lower mean, DM 1 makes the same choice. The Ross measure of risk aversion is the more appropriate for our purposes.

Another matter of importance is the extent to which the absolute level of wealth itself affects the DM's attitude towards risk. Suppose the absolute level of the terminal wealths is the only characteristic of the prospect to vary. This can occur, for example, by varying only the initial wealth of the DM and keeping the action constant. When the risk or insurance premium $\overline{W}_k - R_k^A$ decreases as wealth increases, the DM's preferences are said to exhibit decreasing absolute risk aversion, or DARA. The more wealthy is such an individual, the lower is the maximum insurance premium the DM would willingly pay to avoid the prospect's risk. Likewise, if $\overline{W}_k - R_k^A$ increases with W, the DM's preferences exhibit increasing absolute risk aversion. When the curvature index or the insurance premium does not depend upon the absolute level of wealth, the DM exhibits constant absolute risk aversion, or CARA. Pratt (1964) proves that the utility function exhibits decreasing, constant, or increasing absolute risk aversion if and only if the risk aversion index b(W) is, respectively, decreasing, constant, or increasing in W. LaValle (1968) shows by example that, regardless of this characteristic, the absolute level of the DM's initial wealth has no unambiguous impact on information value.

Pfanzagl (1959) and Pratt (1964) demonstrate that the DM exhibits constant absolute risk aversion if and only if the utility of terminal wealth function is linear (in which case the second derivative is always zero) or of the concave-exponential form in (5.48), $u(W) = -\exp[-bW]$. The coefficient of risk aversion in the latter case is $b(W) = -u''(W)/u'(W) = b$; hence, increases in b reflect increases in aversion towards risk in the Arrow–Pratt sense. Section 5.3.2 gives a problem using this utility function in which the value of information is a direct function of b: the greater the DM's coefficient of risk aversion, the lower her expected value of information.

The purpose of the Chapter 3 discussions surrounding Figures 3.1 and 3.2 was to show that reductions in initial wealth, from, for example, expenditure on information, affect the DM's decisions and decision rules. A calculation of the risk aversion index b(W) shows that the logarithmic utility function used in Example 2.1 exhibits decreasing absolute risk aversion.[1] As de facto initial wealth declines in Figure 3.1, the increased risk aversion leads the DM to the more conservative, less risky action a_2 offering lower expected wealth, and this combination leads to the lower risk premium that Figure 3.2 shows. As she becomes more averse toward risk, she willingly gives up mean wealth to reduce the risk she bears.

7.2 Risk Preference and Information Value

This section investigates the role of the DM's attitude towards risk as a determinant of the demand value of information. The valuation of information by the risk neutral DM is a useful benchmark from which to compare how a risk averter would value the same source in the same decision problem. When valuing information, the risk neutral DM cares only about the impact on expected wealth that results from the use of the information. The risk averter cares also about changes in prospect variability, that is, changes in riskiness in the sense of Rothschild and Stiglitz (1970). Accordingly, the comparison of the value of imperfect information between risk averse and risk neutral DMs depends critically on the comparative impacts the use of the information has both on expected wealth and on prospect variability.

---

[1] For $u(W) = \log[W]$, $b(W) = W^{-1}$ and $b'(W) = -W^{-2} < 0$.

7.2.1 Comparison of the Risk Averter's Optimal Prospects with the Risk Neutral Benchmark

Useful inequalities for illustrating the comparative value of information arise by comparing optimal prospects with specific suboptimal ones. Comparing the prior optimal actions a_0^N and a_0^A, the optimality of a_0^A for the risk averter guarantees that

$$E_{w|a_0^A}\ u(W) \geq E_{w|a_0^N}\ u(W). \tag{7.41}$$

Similarly, with a_0^N being optimal under risk neutrality,

$$E_{w|a_0^N}\ [W] \geq E_{w|a_0^A}\ [W], \tag{7.42}$$

or, using (7.15),

$$\overline{W}_0^N \geq \overline{W}_0^A. \tag{7.43}$$

The relationships (7.33), (7.35), and (7.36) hold for any arbitrary prospect, including the optimal ones. For example, in the prior decision, under the concave utility function of a risk averter,

$$\overline{W}_0^A \geq R_0^A, \tag{7.44}$$

and under risk neutrality,

$$\overline{W}_0^N = R_0^N. \tag{7.45}$$

Combining (7.45) with (7.43) and (7.44) obtains the summarizing relationship between the uninformed reservation prices and means:

$$R_0^N = \overline{W}_0^N \geq \overline{W}_0^A \geq R_0^A. \tag{7.46}$$

Similar relationships hold for the costly informed decision. Since a_y^N maximizes expected wealth conditional on y, and the reduction ψ has no impact on the risk neutral decision,

$$\overline{W}_y^N(\psi) = \overline{W}_y^N - \psi \geq \overline{W}_y^A(\psi). \tag{7.47}$$

Taking the expectation with respect to p(y) shows $\overline{W}_I^N(\psi) = \overline{W}_I^N - \psi \geq \overline{W}_I^A(\psi)$. For the risk neutral DM, the preposterior expected wealth shifts down by ψ from what it would have been if there were no cost. In summary,

$$R_I^N(\psi) = \overline{W}_I^N(\psi) = \overline{W}_I^N - \psi \geq \overline{W}_I^A(\psi) \geq R_I^A(\psi). \tag{7.48}$$

7.2.2 Bounds on the Comparative Demand Value of Information

When comparing V_I^A to V_I^N, intuition might lead us to hypothesize that risk averters would seek information as a means of risk reduction, and hence tend to value it more than their risk neutral counterparts. This is not necessarily so; this subsection examines the conditions under which definitive comparisons are valid.

LaValle's General Bound

LaValle (1978) offers the most general bound on the value of information to a risk averter:

$$V_I^A \le V_I^N + R_0^N - R_0^A. \tag{7.49}$$

To show this, use the summarizing relationship (7.48), evaluated at $\psi = V_I^A$ so that (7.28) also holds,

$$\overline{W}_I^N(V_I^A) = \overline{W}_I^N - V_I^A \ge R_I^A(V_I^A) = R_0^A.$$

Hence,

$$\begin{aligned} V_I^A &\le \overline{W}_I^N - R_0^A \\ &\le V_I^N + R_0^N - R_0^A, \end{aligned} \tag{7.50}$$

where the final inequality follows from the definition of V_I^N given by (7.26) and from the equality (7.45).

The interesting thing about this bound is that the only input needed from the risk averse DM is the prior reservation price; no conditional decision rules need be determined. From (7.46), $R_0^N - R_0^A \ge 0$, so there is no general sign relationship between V_I^A and V_I^N without further conditions on the problem.

The reason is because the use of the information source increases the expected wealth and expected utility for all decision makers, but it does not necessarily leave unchanged the riskiness of the optimal informed prospect compared to the prior prospect. To the risk neutral DM any change in riskiness is inconsequential, but risk averters view altered riskiness as a significant factor that affects their overall valuation of the information.

An interesting problem-specific example in which $V_I^A \le V_I^N$ is when there is a risk free action in $\mathbf{a}$ that is the optimal prior choice for the risk neutral DM, as it is in Example 6.1 when $4/9 < p(x_1) < 5/9$. In this case all risk averters would also choose the risk free action, the reservation prices R_0^N and R_0^A would be the same, and from (7.49), risk averters would not value any information source by more than the risk neutral DM. Economically, even though the prior prospects $\tilde{W}_0^N$ and $\tilde{W}_0^A$ are identical and have zero riskiness, if the information structure is not useless the prospects $\tilde{W}_I^N$ and $\tilde{W}_I^A$ do have some variability. Irrespective of how the risk neutral DM values the source, no risk averse DM would value the information more because she views the increased riskiness as detrimental to her overall utility evaluation, even in the special case in which $\overline{W}_I^N = \overline{W}_I^A$.

*Bounds Based upon Rothschild–Stiglitz Variability

To build upon the preceding interpretation, equation (7.26) shows that $V_I^N = \overline{W}_I^N - \overline{W}_0^N$ for the risk neutral benchmark DM. The demand value for a risk averter is related to the difference in the risk averter's mean wealth in the following way.

(1) If $\tilde{W}_I^A$ is more R–S variable than $\tilde{W}_0^A$, then $V_I^A \le \overline{W}_I^A - \overline{W}_0^A$.

(2) If $\tilde{W}_I^A$ is less R–S variable than $\tilde{W}_0^A$, then $V_I^A \ge \overline{W}_I^A - \overline{W}_0^A$.

The gain in the mean is a source of information value, but in (1) the increased riskiness of the informed prospect is detrimental to the risk averter's overall valuation. In (2), the decreased riskiness is a source of value.

To show this, begin with the definition of the demand value of information V_I^A in the risk averse version of (7.25):

$$\int_W u(W - V_I^A)\, dF(W \mid a_I^A(V_I^A)) = \int_W u(W)\, dF(W \mid a_0^A).$$

The hypothesis in (1) asserts that, when adjusted to equal means,

$$\int_W u(W - \overline{W}_I^A + \overline{W}_0^A)\, dF(W \mid a_I^A) \le \int_W u(W)\, dF(W \mid a_0^A).$$

The left-hand side is further reduced if the DM uses the suboptimal decision rule $a_I^A(\psi)$,

$$\int_W u(W - \overline{W}_I^A + \overline{W}_0^A)\, dF(W \mid a_I^A(\psi)) \le \int_W u(W)\, dF(W \mid a_0^A),$$

including the specific rule $a_I^A(V_I^A)$:

$$\int_W u(W - \overline{W}_I^A + \overline{W}_0^A)\, dF(W \mid a_I^A(V_I^A)) \le \int_W u(W)\, dF(W \mid a_0^A).$$

Replacing the right-hand side using the definition (7.25) gives

$$\int_W u(W - \overline{W}_I^A + \overline{W}_0^A)\, dF(W \mid a_I^A(V_I^A)) \le \int_W u(W - V_I^A)\, dF(W \mid a_I^A(V_I^A)).$$

This inequality can hold only if $V_I^A \le \overline{W}_I^A - \overline{W}_0^A$.

The hypothesis in (2) is

$$\int_W u(W - \overline{W}_I^A + \overline{W}_0^A)\, dF(W \mid a_I^A) \ge \int_W u(W)\, dF(W \mid a_0^A).$$

Following the same approach as previously, substituting the definition (7.25) into the right-hand side, and forcing the DM to use the suboptimal decision rule a_I^A despite having paid for the information, yields

$$\int_W u(W - \overline{W}_I^A + \overline{W}_0^A)\, dF(W \mid a_I^A) \ge \int_W u(W - V_I^A)\, dF(W \mid a_I^A),$$

which is true when $V_I^A \ge \overline{W}_I^A - \overline{W}_0^A$.

A variation of (1), proven by Blair and Romano (1988), guarantees that the risk averter will not value information more than the risk neutral benchmark:

(3) If $\tilde{W}_I^A$ is more R–S variable than $\tilde{W}_0^N$, then $V_I^A \leq V_I^N + \overline{W}_I^A - \overline{W}_I^N$.

Here the hypothesis is

$$\int_W u(W - \overline{W}_I^A + \overline{W}_0^N)\, dF(W \mid a_I^A) \leq \int_W u(W)\, dF(W \mid a_0^N).$$

The demonstration follows exactly as before, after substituting the expected utility of the superior prospect $\tilde{W}_0^A$ in the right-hand side and using the fact $\overline{W}_0^N = \overline{W}_I^N - V_I^N$. When this sufficiency condition holds, it is assured that $V_I^A \leq V_I^N$, since $\overline{W}_I^A \leq \overline{W}_I^N$.

This result is most easily applied to the perfect information structure $\mathbf{I}\uparrow$. Under perfect information the state is precisely identified; there is no risk posterior to the receipt of any message. Every conditional prospect $\tilde{W}_y^u$ is degenerate with all its mass at the same wealth level for any u, hence $\tilde{W}_y^N$ is identical to $\tilde{W}_y^A$. All DMs choose the identical decision rules $a_{I\uparrow}^u$, which are unaffected by ψ. Thus the preposterior prospect $\tilde{W}_{I\uparrow}^u(\psi)$ is identical for all DMs. Suppose the two DMs have different initial prospects $\tilde{W}_0^A$ and $\tilde{W}_0^N$ and the identical perfectly informed prospect. Since $\overline{W}_{I\uparrow}^A = \overline{W}_{I\uparrow}^N$ yet $\overline{W}_0^A \leq \overline{W}_0^N$, the risk averter is guaranteed to get at least as great an increase in expected wealth as the risk neutral counterpart:

$$\overline{W}_{I\uparrow}^A - \overline{W}_0^A \geq \overline{W}_{I\uparrow}^N - \overline{W}_0^N = V_{I\uparrow}^N.$$

The content of (3) is that, to the risk averter, the comparative increase in mean wealth cannot be enough to compensate for the comparative increase in prospect variability.

Another illustration of this technique makes use of the conveniences of perfect information to compare the information valuation by two risk averters. Suppose two risk averters A_1 and A_2 have utility functions given by $u_1(\bullet)$ and $u_2(\bullet)$, respectively. Decision maker A_2 is more risk averse than A_1 in the sense of Ross (1981). The comparison is:

(4) If the perfect prospect $\tilde{W}_{I\uparrow}^u$ is less R–S variable than $\tilde{W}_0^{A_1}$, and if $\tilde{W}_0^{A_1}$ and $\tilde{W}_0^{A_2}$ are identical, then $V_{I\uparrow}^{A_2} \geq V_{I\uparrow}^{A_1}$.

When risk averter A_1 solves for the value of information and determines $V_{I\uparrow}^{A_1}$,

$$\int_W u_1(W - V_{I\uparrow}^{A_1})\, dF(W \mid a_{I\uparrow}^u) = \int_W u_1(W)\, dF(W \mid a_0^{A_1}),$$

she is stating her indifference between the two prospects $\tilde{W}_{I\uparrow}^{A_1}(V_{I\uparrow}^{A_1})$ and $\tilde{W}_0^{A_1}$. Since $\overline{W}_{I\uparrow}^{A_1}(V_{I\uparrow}^{A_1}) = \overline{W}_{I\uparrow}^u - V_{I\uparrow}^{A_1}$, and because the premise guarantees (2), $V_{I\uparrow}^{A_1} \geq \overline{W}_{I\uparrow}^u - \overline{W}_0^{A_1}$, it follows that $\overline{W}_{I\uparrow}^{A_1}(V_{I\uparrow}^{A_1}) \leq \overline{W}_0^{A_1}$. The DM A_1 is indifferent between a lower mean, less variable, costly informed prospect and a higher mean, more variable prior prospect. If DM A_2 is more risk averse and is offered exactly the same choice, she cannot prefer the more risky option:

$$\int_W u_2(W - V_{I\uparrow}^{A_1})\, dF(W \mid a_{I\uparrow}^{u}) \geq \int_W u_2(W)\, dF(W \mid a_0^{A_1}).$$

Now if $\tilde{W}_0^{A_1}$ and $\tilde{W}_0^{A_2}$ are identical,

$$\int_W u_2(W - V_{I\uparrow}^{A_1})\, dF(W \mid a_{I\uparrow}^{u}) \geq \int_W u_2(W)\, dF(W \mid a_0^{A_2}).$$

Replacing the right-hand side with DM A_2's expected-utility-equivalent informed decision,

$$\int_W u_2(W - V_{I\uparrow}^{A_1})\, dF(W \mid a_{I\uparrow}^{u}) \geq \int_W u_2(W - V_{I\uparrow}^{A_2})\, dF(W \mid a_{I\uparrow}^{u}),$$

which shows $V_{I\uparrow}^{A_2} \geq V_{I\uparrow}^{A_1}$. Hirshleifer and Riley (1992, page 202) present a graphical analysis of this situation.

*A Bound Requiring Only Risk Neutral Assessments

Although this kind of approach is of interest because it helps us to understand the relationship between risk preference and information value, a deficiency is that the results are both problem-specific and decision maker specific. The practical benefits are limited since to check for the satisfaction of the sufficiency conditions, the specific risk averse utility function must be known and in most cases the optimal decision rules determined. The universality of the decision rules and prospects under perfect information can lead to results not requiring the specification of u, but as the upcoming continuation of Example 3.1a shows, satisfaction of the sufficiency condition under perfect information does not imply satisfaction for all information structures.

The following approach, based on Lawrence (1992), concerns the relative values V_I^A and V_I^N for decision problems under imperfect information in which both the prior and the preposterior prospects can have different means and variabilities, but where $\tilde{W}_0^A$ and $\tilde{W}_I^A(\psi)$ need not be assessed. It offers a problem-specific sufficiency condition, requiring only risk neutral assessments and computations, under which no risk averse DM values imperfect information more than the risk neutral counterpart. In practice, satisfaction of the condition may be useful to the producer of the information, as it sets an upper bound on the demand price of any risk averse potential buyer facing the given decision problem. It also can be useful in the design of experiments that investigate empirical information behavior, as Section 9.3.3 discusses.

The results are derived by studying a subject familiar from Chapters 4 and 5, the preposterior mean, in this case of the risk neutral DM's terminal wealth. Defined as the mean of the risk neutral version of (7.21), the quantity $\overline{W}_y^N(\psi)$ is the expected wealth of the risk neutral DM who has paid ψ for an information structure and has received and responded optimally to the specific message y. Prior to the receipt of y, this quantity is a random variable, distributed according to the marginal distribution p(y). This prospect, the prior distribution of the posterior mean wealth of an optimizing risk neutral DM, is

$$\tilde{\overline{W}}_y^N(\psi) = \{ \overline{W}_y^N(\psi), p(y); \text{ for all } y \in \mathbf{Y} \}. \tag{7.51}$$

Since the risk neutral DM exhibits constant absolute risk aversion and simply maximizes expected wealth conditional on y, the magnitude of ψ affects only the mean of this prospect, not its variability.

The mean of $\tilde{\overline{W}}_y^N(\psi)$ is, using (7.20) and (7.47),

$$E_y \overline{W}_y^N(\psi) = \overline{W}_I^N(\psi) = \overline{W}_I^N - \psi.$$

With the notable exception of perfect information, this prospect is hypothetical in the sense that is not actually available to any DM, regardless of attitude towards risk. It does, however, give the risk neutral DM the same expected wealth (and hence expected utility) as the actual preposterior informed prospect $\tilde{W}_I^N(\psi)$. The advantage of focusing on the prospect $\tilde{\overline{W}}_y^N(\psi)$ is that it requires only risk neutral assessments yet plays the major role relating V_I^A to V_I^N.

Evaluated at $\psi = V_I^N$, $\overline{W}_I^N - V_I^N = \overline{W}_0^N$, so the two prospects $\tilde{\overline{W}}_y^N(V_I^N)$ and $\tilde{W}_0^N$ have the same mean, but perhaps not the same variability. The sufficiency condition is

(5) If $\tilde{\overline{W}}_y^N(V_I^N)$ is more R–S variable than $\tilde{W}_0^N$, then $V_I^A \leq V_I^N$.

The demonstration of (5) starts with (7.47), which shows $\overline{W}_y^N - \psi \geq \overline{W}_y^A(\psi)$. Any risk averter prefers more wealth to less, so

$$u(\overline{W}_y^N - \psi) \geq u(\overline{W}_y^A(\psi)).$$

Applying Jensen's inequality to the right-hand side,

$$u(\overline{W}_y^A(\psi)) = u(E_{w|a_y^A(\psi)}[W - \psi]) \geq E_{w|a_y^A(\psi)}\, u(W - \psi),$$

so

$$u(\overline{W}_y^N - \psi) \geq E_{w|a_y^A(\psi)}\, u(W - \psi)$$

for every y. Taking the expectation with respect to p(y),

$$E_y\, u(\overline{W}_y^N - \psi) \geq E_{w|a_I^A(\psi)}\, u(W - \psi),$$

shows that any risk averter would prefer the hypothetical prospect over the actual prospect chosen: by offering the risk averter the mean $\overline{W}_y^N(\psi)$ should y be received, enough risk has been "wrung out" to make the hypothetical prospect preferable.

Evaluated at $\psi = V_I^A$,

$$E_y\, u(\overline{W}_y^N - V_I^A) \geq E_{w|a_I^A(V_I^A)}\, u(W - V_I^A)$$

$$= E_{w|a_0^A}\ u(W)$$

$$\geq E_{w|a_0^N}\ u(W),$$

using the definition of V_I^A in (7.25) and the suboptimality of a_0^N for any risk averter, as in (7.41). Adding and subtracting V_I^N to the left-hand side and rearranging in light of (7.47) yields

$$E_y\ u(\overline{W}_y^N(V_I^N) + [V_I^N - V_I^A]) \geq E_{w|a_0^N}\ u(W). \tag{7.52}$$

The premise of (5) is

$$E_y\ u(\overline{W}_y^N(V_I^N)) \leq E_{w|a_0^N}\ u(W). \tag{7.53}$$

Both (7.52) and (7.53) can hold only if $V_I^A \leq V_I^N$.

The DM can determine whether the premise holds by the integral condition of the standard R–S variability test. As the following continuation of Example 3.1a shows, the satisfaction of the sufficiency condition depends upon the statistical informativeness of the information structure **I**.

♦ *Example 3.1a The Quadratic Perfect Competitor (Continued from Section 3.1.4)*

This example, a dichotomy with a continuous action space, can illustrate several of the results of this chapter. A perfectly competitive firm must choose a nonnegative production quantity $a \in \mathbf{a}$ prior to the realization of the random price $x \in \mathbf{X}$. Total revenue is xa, and suppose total cost is given by $FC + .5a^2$, where FC is the fixed cost. Hence, the payoff is the profit function $\pi(x, a) = xa - FC - .5a^2$. Given that initial wealth w is separable from the profit function, terminal wealth is

$$W = w + \pi(x, a) = w - FC + xa - .5a^2.$$

Assume there are two possible prices, so $\mathbf{X} = \{4, 8\}$ and that the initial knowledge is that $p(x_1) = .75$ and $p(x_2) = .25$. Finally, let w = \$9 and FC = \$3.

If the DM is risk neutral, desiring to choose the course of action that maximizes expected profit and hence expected terminal wealth, then the optimal production level for a given probability of ξ_1 of x_1 is $a_*^N(\xi_1)$, the solution to

$$t(\xi_1) = \max_a \{\xi_1[6 + 4a - .5a^2] + [1 - \xi_1][6 + 8a - .5a^2]\}.$$

Using the calculus, the optimal action is $a_*^N(\xi_1) = 4[2 - \xi_1]$, and the value of a decision is

$$t(\xi_1) = 8\xi_1^2 - 32\xi_1 + 38.$$

For $\xi_1 = p(x_1) = .75$, $a_0^N = 5$ and the value of the risk neutral prior decision is $t(\xi_1) = \overline{W}_0^N = \$18.50$. At $a_0^N = 5$, the prior prospect is

$$\tilde{W}_0^N = \{\$13.5, .75; \$33.5, .25\}. \tag{7.54}$$

Under perfect information, all decision makers choose the decision rules $a_{x_1}^u = 4$ and $a_{x_2}^u = 8$, giving the optimal informed prospect

$$\tilde{W}_{I\dagger}^u = \{\$14, .75; \$38, .25\},$$

a prospect with mean $\overline{W}_{I\dagger}^u = \$20$. Hence the risk neutral value of perfect information is $V_{I\dagger}^N = \$1.5$, and subtracting this amount from each terminal wealth in $\tilde{W}_{I\dagger}^u$ shows that the premise of (3) is met, ensuring that $V_{I\dagger}^A \leq \$1.5$ for all risk averters. Note that in this perfect information case, the comparison in (5) is identical to the comparison in (3).

The bound in (7.50) gives $V_{I\dagger}^A \leq 20 - R_0^A$, and requires no R–S comparability criterion to be met. For the risk averter with the utility function $u(W) = [W]^{\frac{1}{2}}$, the analysis in Section 3.1.4 shows $a_0^A = 4.7118$, $\overline{W}_0^A = \$18.46$, and $R_0^A = \$17.71$. Hence (7.50) gives the bound $V_{I\dagger}^A \leq \$2.29$. In addition, the premise of (2) is met, giving $V_{I\dagger}^A \leq \$1.54$. In fact, calculation shows $V_{I\dagger}^A = \$1.135$.

Now modeling imperfect information using (6.55), for the specified prior the posterior distributions are

$$\Pi(\theta) = \begin{bmatrix} p(x_1|y_1;\theta) & p(x_1|y_2;\theta) \\ p(x_2|y_1;\theta) & p(x_2|y_2;\theta) \end{bmatrix} = \begin{bmatrix} .25[3+\theta] & .75[1-\theta] \\ .25[1-\theta] & .25[1+3\theta] \end{bmatrix}.$$

The optimal decision rule for the risk neutral benchmark is

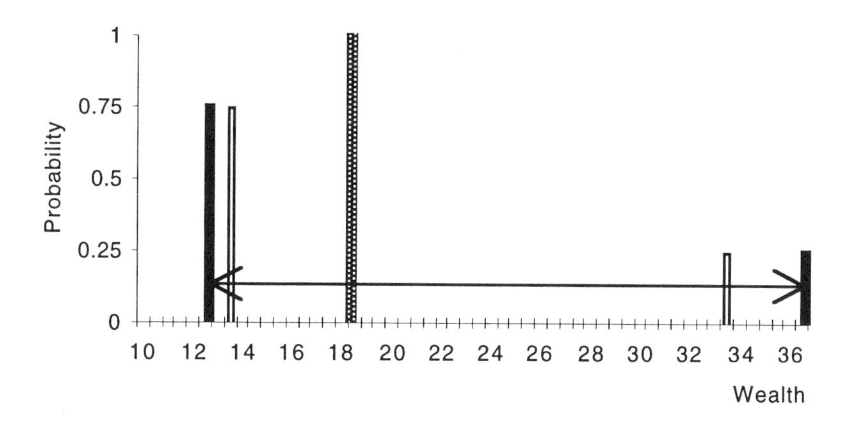

Figure 7.4. The adjusted preposterior prospect spreads with θ. When θ = 0, the prospect is degenerate with all its mass at the prior mean of \$18.50. The prior prospect is indicated by the lighter colored spikes; it is identical to the preposterior prospect when θ has risen to .8541. The prospect at perfect information, θ = 1, is indicated by the darker colored spikes.

$$a^N_{I(\theta)} = \{ a^N_{y_1}, a^N_{y_2} \} = \{5 - \theta, 5 + 3\theta\}.$$

Applying the data in the first row of $\Pi(\theta)$, the conditional posterior means are $\overline{W}^N_{y_1} = .5\theta^2 - 5\theta + 18.5$ and $\overline{W}^N_{y_2} = 4.5\theta^2 + 15\theta + 18.5$, making the preposterior mean $\overline{W}^N_{I(\theta)} = 1.5\theta^2 + 18.5$. The value of the information structure $\mathbf{I}(\theta)$ is $V^N_{I(\theta)} = 1.5\theta^2$. There is no region of useless information in this decision problem; every scintilla of informativeness changes the optimal action and all but the first of them contribute to the value of information.

Subtracting $V^N_{I(\theta)}$ from each conditional posterior mean yields the adjusted preposterior prospect

$$\tilde{\overline{W}}^N_y(V^N_{I(\theta)}) = \{-\theta^2 - 5\theta + 18.5, .75; 3\theta^2 + 15\theta + 18.5, .25\}; \quad (7.55)$$

an R–S comparison of (7.55) with the prior optimal prospect $\tilde{W}^N_0$ in (7.54) shows that the sufficiency condition is met only for highly informative structures. If $\theta = 0$, this prospect is degenerate with all its probability at the prior mean of \$18.5. As θ grows greater than zero, this prospect spreads out as shown in Figure 7.4. At $\theta = 1$, the comparison is identical to that in (3). At about $\theta = .8541$, the prospect becomes variable enough to satisfy the sufficiency condition in (5). The conclusion is that $V^A_{I(\theta)} \leq 1.5\theta^2$ for any risk averter whenever $\theta > .8541$. When $\theta < .8541$, the comparative valuation is decision maker specific. ♦

7.3 Nonlinear Models and Information Aversion

Although most discussions of the DM's preferences concentrate on her attitude towards bearing risk, the criterion she chooses to apply when making decisions also affects her valuation of information.[2] This section delves more deeply into the normative and descriptive validity of the expected utility criterion, the criterion under which the DM maximizes a preference function that is linear in the probabilities of the alternatives.

7.3.1 The Expected Utility Criterion

A prospect $\tilde{W}_k$ is a random variable, defined on terminal wealth, and induced by the choice of an action $a_k \in \mathbf{a}$. It is useful at times to generalize and drop the reference to any specific action and just consider a prospect as a random variable defined on terminal wealth without any explanation as to how it arises. A synonym for a prospect viewed in this sense is a *lottery*.

In general, an arbitrary finite prospect/lottery $\tilde{W}_k$ is defined as the listing

---

[2] Szaniawski (1967) considers the value of information for a DM choosing the minimax criterion.

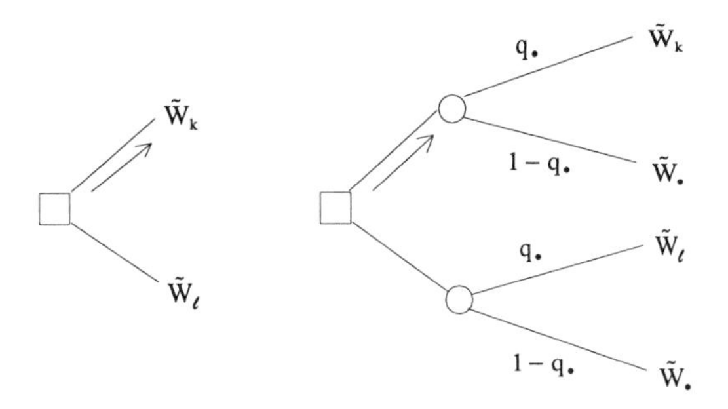

Figure 7.5. Suppose the DM chooses up when given the choice on the left. Then when facing the decision on the right, if she does not make the choice indicated by the arrow, she has violated the independence axiom.

$$\tilde{W}_k = \{w_{k1}, p_{k1}; \cdots ; w_{kh}, p_{kh}; \cdots ; w_{kH}, p_{kH}\}, \qquad (7.56)$$

where p_{kh} is the probability of obtaining wealth level w_{kh} in the kth prospect. It is convenient to order the w_{kh} in increasing magnitude, so that

$$w_{k1} < \cdots < w_{kh} < \cdots < w_{kH}.$$

One of the listed w_{kh} must ultimately occur, so coherence of the problem formulation requires

$$\Sigma_h \, p_{kh} = 1.$$

When choosing between available actions or their corresponding prospects, principles of choice such as dominance (among actions) and stochastic dominance (among prospects) are of limited usefulness. Choices are generally made from among the set of undominated actions, and prospects are seldom comparable by stochastic dominance. In order to decide which crop to plant in Example 2.1, or to choose between the prospects $\tilde{W}_1$ and $\tilde{W}_2$ in Example 2.2, the DM must reveal more details about the structure of her preferences.

A traditional approach is to present the DM with a set of common sense principles with which the DM agrees to abide. The decision theorist then shows the DM that acceptance of these principles, called axioms, logically requires the DM to make assessments and choices in a prescribed way. Kreps (1988) provides a good introduction to theory of choice via these techniques; Fishburn (1988) presents an advanced analysis. Some of the best known early systems of axioms include Von Neumann and Morgenstern (1947), Marschak (1950), Savage

(1954), and Anscombe and Aumann (1963). Each of these systems ultimately leads to the expected utility model—the criterion that the DM "should" choose the course of action that maximizes the mathematical expectation of utility.

The study and comparison of alternative axiom systems is beyond the scope here, but one very basic postulate is that the DM is able to express a preference ordering between two prospects $\tilde{W}_k$ and $\tilde{W}_\ell$, that is, is willing to state that one is strictly preferred to the other or there is indifference between the two. Symbolically, strict preference is denoted by $\triangleright$, and indifference by $\approx$. Then either $\tilde{W}_k \triangleright \tilde{W}_\ell$, or $\tilde{W}_\ell \triangleright \tilde{W}_k$, or $\tilde{W}_k \approx \tilde{W}_\ell$. Furthermore, it is assumed this preference can be represented by a preference function $\mathcal{U}(\bullet)$ such that

$$\tilde{W}_k \triangleright \tilde{W}_\ell \quad \text{if and only if } \mathcal{U}(\tilde{W}_k) \geq \mathcal{U}(\tilde{W}_\ell),$$

$$\tilde{W}_\ell \triangleright \tilde{W}_k \quad \text{if and only if } \mathcal{U}(\tilde{W}_\ell) \geq \mathcal{U}(\tilde{W}_k),$$

$$\tilde{W}_k \approx \tilde{W}_\ell \quad \text{if and only if } \mathcal{U}(\tilde{W}_k) = \mathcal{U}(\tilde{W}_\ell).$$

The important questions are the characteristics and the mathematical form of this preference function. Notice that this function is not the same thing as the Von Neumann–Morgenstern utility function for specific (and certain) levels of wealth, but it is reasonable to believe that $\mathcal{U}(\bullet)$ should in some way be related to $u(W)$.

The independence axiom is a second and more controversial postulate. On the left panel of Figure 7.5, suppose the DM is offered a simple choice between prospects $\tilde{W}_k$ and $\tilde{W}_\ell$, and states the preference $\tilde{W}_k \triangleright \tilde{W}_\ell$. How would (or should) the DM respond if now the choice problem were augmented with the opportunity of mixing $\tilde{W}_k$ and $\tilde{W}_\ell$ with a third prospect $\tilde{W}_\bullet$ according to the right panel in Figure 7.5? This opportunity shows a choice between compound prospects, that is, prospects comprised of subprospects. If nature chooses down at the first chance node, either option gives the DM the same prospect $\tilde{W}_\bullet$. But if nature chooses up, and this happens with probability $q_\bullet$, then the DM will wind up with either $\tilde{W}_k$ or $\tilde{W}_\ell$.

The DM might reason, "When nature chooses down, my preference doesn't matter; I get $\tilde{W}_\bullet$. When nature chooses up, I am in effect back to my original straight-up choice between $\tilde{W}_k$ and $\tilde{W}_\ell$, and it only makes sense to continue to prefer $\tilde{W}_k$." A DM who thinks this way is likely to accept the *independence axiom*:

> The DM prefers prospect $\tilde{W}_k$ over $\tilde{W}_\ell$ if and only if the DM also prefers the compound prospect $\{\tilde{W}_k, q_\bullet; \tilde{W}_\bullet, 1-q_\bullet\}$ over $\{\tilde{W}_\ell, q_\bullet; \tilde{W}_\bullet, 1-q_\bullet\}$ for any prospect $\tilde{W}_\bullet$ and all positive probabilities $q_\bullet$. An analogous statement holds for indifference.

Von Neumann and Morgenstern (1947) show that acceptance of the independence axiom, combined with the existence of a preference ordering, a technical continuity axiom, and the assumption that all probabilities are given exogenously, is sufficient to justify the expected utility hypothesis. If the probabilities are personal or subjective, Savage (1954) presents a more complex set of seven axioms that also lead to the criterion of expected utility. See Chapter 1 of Laffont (1989) for a discussion of these two axiom systems.

In symbols, under the *expected utility criterion* the preference function $\mathcal{U}(\bullet)$ takes a particularly simple functional form that is linear in the probabilities. Specifically, the preference index for a prospect $\tilde{W}_k$ is of the form

$$
\begin{aligned}
\mathcal{U}(\tilde{W}_k) &= \mathcal{U}(\{w_{k1}, p_{k1}; \cdots ; w_{kh}, p_{kh}; \cdots ; w_{kH}, p_{kH}\}) \\
&= u(w_{k1})p_{k1} + \cdots + u(w_{kh})p_{kh} + \cdots + u(w_{kH})p_{kH} \\
&= \Sigma_h\, u(w_{kh})p_{kh},
\end{aligned}
\qquad (7.57)
$$

where $u(\bullet)$ is the Von Neumann–Morgenstern utility function for wealth.

In words, the adherent to this criterion judges each available prospect by calculating the sum of the chance-weighted utility of each possible wealth level achievable in the prospect. This calculation produces a quantity termed the expected utility of the prospect. Assessing this for all available prospects, the DM is advised to choose the one that offers the highest preference index, that is, the prospect with the maximum expected utility.

This model is not the only reasonable mathematical form the preference function $\mathcal{U}(\bullet)$ can take. It is certainly the most well known, and definitely quite useful when applied to decision problems under uncertainty. Nevertheless, as the next subsection covers, alternative preference functions without the independence axiom can be quite interesting from the standpoint of the DM's evaluation of information.

7.3.2 *Troubles with the Expected Utility Model*

Not all is well with the expected utility model. Beginning with the famous Allais Paradox, and moving on to several other reasonable decision situations [Machina (1987)], there is considerable systematic empirical evidence that some DMs make choices that are logically inconsistent with the maximization of expected utility [MacCrimmon and Larsson (1979)]. From the prescriptive viewpoint, it is easy to pooh-pooh these results as simply mistaken reasoning, but from the descriptive viewpoint, such preferences may have unusual implications for the value of information and the demand for information in the marketplace.

♦ *Example 7.3a Allais' Problem*

Suppose the DM is given the choice between the following two prospects, where the monetary values are measured in millions of dollars,

$$\tilde{W}_1 = \{\$0, .00; \$1, 1.00; \$5, .00\};$$

$$\tilde{W}_2 = \{\$0, .01; \$1, .89; \$5, .10\}.$$

Prospect 1 is risk-free, in the sense that it is a degenerate prospect offering money with certainty. Prospect 2 is risky. The two prospects are not comparable via stochastic dominance so the choice depends upon the assessed utility function.

The Allais paradox involves choices from among four prospects. The DM first chooses between the two prospects $\tilde{W}_1$ and $\tilde{W}_2$, and then chooses between the following two additional prospects.

$$\tilde{W}_3 = \{\$0, .90; \$1, .00; \$5, .10\};$$

$$\tilde{W}_4 = \{\$0, 89; \$1, .11; \$5, .00\}.$$

Many subjects, including Savage (1954, pages 101–103) himself, choose $\tilde{W}_1$ over $\tilde{W}_2$ and $\tilde{W}_3$ over $\tilde{W}_4$. These preferences violate the independence axiom.

Assuming prospect $\tilde{W}_1$ is generated by action a_1, $\tilde{W}_2$ by a_2, and so on, Figure 7.6 puts the Allais prospects on two decision trees. The tree in the left panel is strategically equivalent to the choice between $\tilde{W}_1$ and $\tilde{W}_2$. Under either choice, at the first chance node the DM has a .89 chance of receiving \$1, and a .11 chance of immediately reaching another chance node. To be consistent with the independence axiom, if $a_1 \rhd a_2$, the DM must prefer the certainty of obtaining \$1 to the gamble that nets \$5 or \$0. The tree in the right panel, the choice between $\tilde{W}_3$ and $\tilde{W}_4$, is identical to the one on the left, except the lower branch at each first chance node yields \$0 instead of \$1. If nature chooses up, the DM faces the same outcome in either panel. Applying the independence axiom here, the preference $a_3 \rhd a_4$ implies now a preference for the gamble between \$5 and \$0 over the certainty of receiving \$1.

Under the independence axiom, writing $\tilde{W}_k = \{\$1, 10/11; \$1, 1/11\}$ and $\tilde{W}_\ell = \{\$0, 1/11; \$5, 10/11\}$, if $\tilde{W}_k \rhd \tilde{W}_\ell$, then $\{\tilde{W}_k, .11; \tilde{W}_\bullet, .89\} \rhd \{\tilde{W}_\ell\ .11; \tilde{W}_\bullet, .89\}$ for any $\tilde{W}_\bullet$. But in the observed choices at issue, if $\tilde{W}_\bullet = \{1, 1.00\}$, then $\tilde{W}_k \rhd \tilde{W}_\ell$, whereas if $\tilde{W}_\bullet = \{0, 1.00\}$, then $\tilde{W}_\ell \rhd \tilde{W}_k$. The Allais-type decision maker seems to be reasoning in the following way. "When the chances are good that I can receive a large sum, I prefer the certain prospect to the risky one. But when the chances are good that I get nothing anyway, I may as well go for it and take the risk." ♦

More generally, the prospect $\tilde{W}_\bullet$ in the definition of the independence axiom may not be irrelevant to the decision. The empirical evidence is that some people's preferences swing from more risky to less risky choices as the alternative $\tilde{W}_\bullet$ becomes better in the sense of first-order stochastic dominance. Allais (1979, page 441) describes the phenomenon as "the preference for security in the neighborhood of certainty."

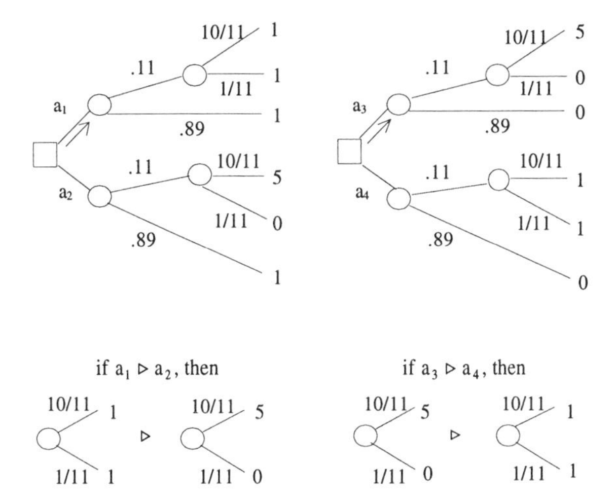

Figure 7.6. When the DM makes the choices indicated by the arrows, she is violating the independence axiom and reversing her choice between the two prospects shown at the bottom.

The observed violations have led recently to a number of alternative theories of choice that intend to better explain the empirical violations of the expected utility model, generally by dropping at least some aspects of the independence axiom. Machina (1987; 1989) lists several of the alternatives, collectively termed "nonexpected utility" models, "nonlinear expected utility," or "general preferences."

7.3.3 Aversion to Information

Preference structures that exclude or modify the independence axiom may exhibit the phenomenon of *aversion to information*, the preference for less information rather than more. Researchers have studied the conditions under which information aversion arises in several of the nonexpected utility models: Newman (1980) in the context of the "prospect theory" of Kahneman and Tversky (1979a); Keasey (1984) in the context of the "regret theory" of Loomes and Sugden (1982; 1987); and Schlee (1990) in the context of Quiggin's (1982) theory of "anticipated utility."

Wakker (1988), Machina (1989), Hilton (1990), Schlee (1991; 1997), and Safra and Sulganik (1995) study the topic in general. Machina (1989) presents a defense of the nonlinear models against the aversion to information arguments.

Schlee (1991) shows there is no aversion to perfect information when the model is framed as in Section 2.1. Hilton (1990) presents a clever example of a decision problem in which the choices boil down to the identical choices as in the Allais paradox. In Hilton's example, the risk neutral, expected-utility-maximizing DM assesses $V_I^N > 0$, yet a DM with Allais preferences assesses $\mathbf{U(D^* \mid I) < U(D^* \mid I\downarrow)}$.

Example 7.3b illustrates in a direct way how a violation of the independence axiom can lead to a preference for null information. It turns out in this demonstration, however, that every DM using the expected utility criterion assesses the information structure as useless, despite the fact that it offers statistical information.

♦ *Example 7.3b Industrial Policy*

The Commissioner for Industrial Investment in a distant nation is deciding which of two economic development projects the government should undertake: a_1: build an automobile industry and tool it to produce large and expensive luxury vehicles, or a_2: build the industry and tool it to produce small, fuel-efficient cars. The Commissioner identifies six alternative potential state descriptions of the world automobile market over the relevant planning horizon, descriptions that highlight the favorability of the economic situation and the availability of oil.

Table 7.3 presents the basic framing of the decision model, including a portion of the semantic description for each state, the payoff function giving the net benefits to the taxpayers from each of the two choices, and the prior probability of the states. In the assessment, large vehicles do better in a good economy, whereas small vehicles tend to do better the less available is oil (i.e., the higher is the relative price of oil). There is considerable prior belief that oil supplies will be tight over the planning horizon, situations that the Commissioner/DM thinks would lead to the substitution of new small cars for older, less fuel-efficient ones.

Table 7.3. Framing for Example 7.3b

State x_i	Description (economy, oil, •)	Payoff $\omega(w, x, a_1)$	Payoff $\omega(w, x, a_2)$	Prior Probability $p(x_i)$
x_1	(bad, abundant, •)	1	0	1/64
x_2	(bad, normal, •)	1	1	8/64
x_3	(bad, tight, •)	1	3	15/64
x_4	(good, abundant, •)	3	0	3/64
x_5	(good, normal, •)	3	1	8/64
x_6	(good, tight, •)	3	3	29/64

The two prior prospects are

$$\tilde{W}_1 = \{\$0, .00; \$1, \tfrac{3}{8}; \$3, \tfrac{5}{8}\} \text{ with } \overline{W}_1 = \$2.25;$$

$$\tilde{W}_2 = \{\$0, \tfrac{1}{16}; \$1, \tfrac{1}{4}; \$3, \tfrac{11}{16}\} \text{ with } \overline{W}_2 = \$2.31.$$

Suppose the DM's preference is $\tilde{W}_1 \triangleright \tilde{W}_2$, so $\tilde{W}_0^u = \tilde{W}_1$; the DM chooses a_1.

The information option is a study of the energy situation, with special reference to the market power of a worldwide oil cartel over the planning horizon. The source offers one of two potential messages.

> y_1: The cartel will either fall apart or be very powerful; the situation will not be normal, regardless of the world economy.
>
> y_2: The cartel will not fall apart, but may or may not have the discipline to keep oil supplies tight. Supplies will not be abundant, regardless of the world economy.

Each message is equally likely, $p(y_1) = p(y_2) = .50$. The DM assesses the following posterior distributions of the state, conditional on each message,

$$\Pi = \begin{bmatrix} p(x_1|y_1) & p(x_1|y_2) \\ p(x_2|y_1) & p(x_2|y_2) \\ p(x_3|y_1) & p(x_3|y_2) \\ p(x_4|y_1) & p(x_4|y_2) \\ p(x_5|y_1) & p(x_5|y_2) \\ p(x_6|y_1) & p(x_6|y_2) \end{bmatrix} = \begin{bmatrix} \frac{2}{64} & 0 \\ 0 & \frac{16}{64} \\ \frac{14}{64} & \frac{16}{64} \\ \frac{6}{64} & 0 \\ 0 & \frac{16}{64} \\ \frac{42}{64} & \frac{16}{64} \end{bmatrix}.$$

Conditional on message y_1, the lotteries for actions a_1 and a_2 are:

$$\text{if } y_1,\ \tilde{W}_1 = \{\$0, .00; \$1, .25; \$3, .75\} \equiv \tilde{W}_\ell, \text{ with } \overline{W}_\ell = \$2.50;$$

$$\text{if } y_1,\ \tilde{W}_2 = \{\$0, .125; \$1, .00; \$3, .875\} \equiv \tilde{W}_k, \text{ with } \overline{W}_k = \$2.625.$$

Conditional on message y_2, the lotteries for the two actions are identical:

$$\text{if } y_2,\ \tilde{W}_1 = \tilde{W}_2 = \{\$0, .00; \$1, .50; \$3, .50\} \equiv \tilde{W}_\bullet, \text{ with } \overline{W}_\bullet = \$2.00.$$

The reason for the peculiar naming is for convenience with the notation in the independence axiom.

Concerning the choice of action conditional on each message, the DM is indifferent between actions under message y_2; both result in the prospect $\tilde{W}_\bullet$. The two responses to y_1 are distinct.

Case 1. Suppose, after having received y_1, the DM chooses a_1; that is, $\tilde{W}_\ell \triangleright \tilde{W}_k$. Given that the prior choice in the uninformed decision is also a_1, the information source is useless. Without information, the optimal prospect is $\tilde{W}_0^u =$

{\$0, .00; \$1, 3/8; \$3, 5/8}, with information the optimal informed prospect [given $p(y_1) = p(y_2) = .50$] is the mixture $\tilde{W}_I^u = \{ \tilde{W}_\ell, .50; \tilde{W}_\bullet .50\}$ = {\$0, .00; \$1, 3/8; \$3, 5/8}. The information source has no impact upon the DM's choices in any consequential way; the source is useless despite the fact that it offers non-null statistical information.

Case 2. Suppose instead that the DM prefers $\tilde{W}_k$ and chooses a_2 having received y_1. Now the source has an impact upon action and is not useless. The informed prospect is $\tilde{W}_I^u = \{ \tilde{W}_k .50; \tilde{W}_\bullet, .50\}$ = {\$0, 1/16; \$1, 1/4; \$3, 11/16}. However, $\tilde{W}_I^u$ is identical to $\tilde{W}_2$ in the prior decision, a prospect the DM found inferior to $\tilde{W}_1$. The information source would have a detrimental effect on the DM; she rejects the use of this source even if it were free. These choices, a_1 in the prior decision, a_2 if y_1, and $a_1 \approx a_2$ if y_2, violate the independence axiom.

Preferences violate the independence axiom if $\tilde{W}_k \rhd \tilde{W}_\ell$ but $\{ \tilde{W}_\ell, q_\bullet; \tilde{W}_\bullet, 1-q_\bullet\} \rhd \{ \tilde{W}_k, q_\bullet; \tilde{W}_\bullet, 1-q_\bullet\}$. The DM in Case 2 prefers $\tilde{W}_k$ to $\tilde{W}_\ell$ when she has the knowledge that y_1 gives her, namely, that the energy situation will be extreme, not normal. On the other hand, without information the DM prefers the mixture distribution $\{ \tilde{W}_\ell, .50; \tilde{W}_\bullet, .50\}$ = {\$0, .00; \$1, 3/8; \$3, 5/8} = $\tilde{W}_0^u$. The Commissioner with these preferences will not seek information, simply choose a_1, and be done with it. Perhaps she should be concerned, however, that a subversive organization might threaten to perform the energy study and reveal the results! ♦

Casual observation does suggest that aversion to information does exist, and that such a DM's rationale for such behavior is not unreasonable. Some people refuse to be tested for the presence of a gene indicating a type of cancer, and might even pay not to receive the results if such a test were surreptitiously performed. The maxim "forewarned is forearmed" may be the motto that establishes that information has value, but one cannot summarily dismiss the opposite view—"ignorance is bliss" and "what I don't know won't hurt me."

This concludes the study of the valuation of information per se. Under the presumption that the value of alternative information structures has been or can be assessed, the next chapter turns to the choice of the optimal information structure from among the alternatives.

8 Information Demand and Procurement

Information, as a commodity that is tradeable as an economic good, is not a particular signal or message, but rather a set of potential signals or messages: an information structure. The decision on the optimal structure to possess, which Marschak (1971) terms the meta-decision, depends critically upon the available sources' statistical properties, pragmatic uses, and comparative costs. With the costs of information moving into the foreground, Chapter 8 studies the meta-decision by viewing information as a differentiated commodity available for purchase. The chapter concentrates on the normative theory of information demand and procurement, deferring to Chapter 9 the discussion of practical and descriptive issues such as how individuals actually choose sources and how the design of the organization's information system can influence those choices.

8.1 The Demand for Information

Section 1.5 presents the theory of the optimal choice of information structure in terms of a straightforward tradeoff between expected information value and cost. With that analysis as the starting point, this section develops a model of the demand for informativeness and expands on the Figure 1.4 characterization of optimal and suboptimal information possession. In addition, Section 8.1.2 uses the model to make a brief excursion into the social science of information, investigating some of the consequences of differential possession of informativeness among a group of information users.

8.1.1 The Value of the Costly Informed Decision

Suppose the marketplace provides decision makers with the option of choosing from among an indexed array of available information structures, each with specified statistical properties and cost. Whether a parameter θ can index informativeness in an operational sense depends upon the nature of the problem and the modeling techniques. In specific circumstances we have seen four examples of index parameters for statistical informativeness: the entropy measures, the correlation coefficient when the joint distribution of messages and states is bivariate normal, the sample size when sampling from a finite population, and the calibrated modeling system described in Section 6.2.4. More generally, the availability of an indexing of information structures by Blackwell's criterion (see Section 6.2) is sufficient, but it is not necessary. As McGuire (1972) notes and several of the case studies in Section 1.5.3 demonstrate, it may be possible to tailor a problem-specific indexing.

For modeling, assume the following technical specifications. The index is bounded, $0 \le \theta \le \bar{\theta}$, with $\theta = 0$ corresponding to null information and $\theta = \bar{\theta}$ to perfect information (i.e., precise identification of the state). Write $\mathbf{I}\downarrow \equiv \mathbf{I}(0)$. For the cost indexing $\mathbf{C}(\theta)$, $\theta = 0$ is a structure with no cost: $\mathbf{C}(0) = 0$, and higher values of θ imply greater cost: $\mathbf{C}'(\theta) > 0$.

The decision maker desires to maximize the expectation of utility given the available statistical information and wealth at the time of the choice. Without the use of any information source, the maximum expected utility is

$$\mathbf{U}(\mathbf{D}^* \mid \mathbf{I}(0), \mathbf{C}(0)) = \int_{\mathbf{X}} \mathrm{u}(\omega(\mathrm{w}, \mathrm{x}, \mathrm{a}_0^{\mathrm{u}}))\, \mathrm{dF}(\mathrm{x}). \tag{8.1}$$

Having purchased an information structure $\mathbf{I}(\theta)$ costing $\mathbf{C}(\theta)$, the preposterior maximum expected utility is

$$\mathbf{U}(\mathbf{D}^* \mid \mathbf{I}(\theta), \mathbf{C}(\theta)) = \int_{\mathbf{Y}} \int_{\mathbf{X}} \mathrm{u}(\omega(\mathrm{w} - \mathbf{C}(\theta), \mathrm{x}, \mathrm{a}_{\mathrm{y}}^{\mathrm{u}}(\theta, \mathbf{C}(\theta))))\, \mathrm{dF}(\mathrm{x}, \mathrm{y}; \theta), \tag{8.2}$$

where $\mathrm{a}_{\mathrm{y}}^{\mathrm{u}}(\theta, \mathbf{C}(\theta))$ denotes the optimal action, given message y from information structure $\mathbf{I}(\theta)$, when initial wealth has been reduced by $\mathbf{C}(\theta)$.

The meta-decision, the choice of the optimal information structure to possess, is the solution θ^* defined by

$$\max_{\theta} \mathbf{U}(\mathbf{D}^* \mid \mathbf{I}(\theta), \mathbf{C}(\theta)) = \mathbf{U}(\mathbf{D}^* \mid \mathbf{I}(\theta^*), \mathbf{C}(\theta^*)). \tag{8.3}$$

The quantity $\mathbf{U}(\mathbf{D}^* \mid \mathbf{I}(\theta^*), \mathbf{C}(\theta^*))$ is the preposterior expected utility from choosing $\mathbf{I}(\theta^*)$ at cost $\mathbf{C}(\theta^*)$, or the *value of the costly informed decision.* It does not measure the DM's gain from incorporating the information, as the expected utility $\mathbf{U}(\mathbf{D}^* \mid \mathbf{I}(0), \mathbf{C}(0))$ of the prior decision is available anyway.

Even when the function (8.2) is continuous and differentiable in θ, the use of the calculus does not fully characterize the optimal solution. The first step is to find the extreme points by setting

$$\mathbf{U}'(\mathbf{D}^* \mid \mathbf{I}(\theta), \mathbf{C}(\theta)) = 0. \tag{8.4}$$

Assuming fulfillment of second-order conditions, denote a global-maximum solution to (8.4) as θ_*. Additional factors influence the optimal choice. First, there is the possibility of corner solutions: if $\theta_* \le 0$, then $\theta^* = 0$. If $\theta_* \ge \bar{\theta}$, then $\theta^* = \bar{\theta}$. Second, the decision maker cannot be forced to purchase an information structure; the uninformed prior decision is always available. If

$$\mathbf{U}(\mathbf{D}^* \,|\, \mathbf{I}(\theta_*), \mathbf{C}(\theta_*)) \leq \mathbf{U}(\mathbf{D}^* \,|\, \mathbf{I}(0), \mathbf{C}(0)), \tag{8.5}$$

then the optimal decision is no information: $\theta^* = 0$. This conclusion is simply an expression of *Mooers' Law* in information science [Mooers (1960)]: information will not be incorporated whenever it is more "painful and troublesome" to have information than not to have it.

In summary, the value of the costly informed decision is

$$\mathbf{U}(\mathbf{D}^* \,|\, \mathbf{I}(\theta^*), \mathbf{C}(\theta^*)) = \tag{8.6}$$

$$\mathbf{U}(\mathbf{D}^* \,|\, \mathbf{I}(\bar{\theta}), \mathbf{C}(\bar{\theta})) \text{ if } \theta_* \geq \bar{\theta} \text{ and } \mathbf{U}(\mathbf{D}^* \,|\, \mathbf{I}(\theta_*), \mathbf{C}(\theta_*)) \geq \mathbf{U}(\mathbf{D}^* \,|\, \mathbf{I}(0), \mathbf{C}(0));$$

$$\mathbf{U}(\mathbf{D}^* \,|\, \mathbf{I}(\theta_*), \mathbf{C}(\theta_*)) \text{ if } \theta_* \leq \bar{\theta} \text{ and } \mathbf{U}(\mathbf{D}^* \,|\, \mathbf{I}(\theta_*), \mathbf{C}(\theta_*)) \geq \mathbf{U}(\mathbf{D}^* \,|\, \mathbf{I}(0), \mathbf{C}(0));$$

$$\mathbf{U}(\mathbf{D}^* \,|\, \mathbf{I}(0), \mathbf{C}(0) \quad \text{ if } \theta_* \leq 0 \text{ or if } \mathbf{U}(\mathbf{D}^* \,|\, \mathbf{I}(\theta_*), \mathbf{C}(\theta_*)) \leq \mathbf{U}(\mathbf{D}^* \,|\, \mathbf{I}(0), \mathbf{C}(0)).$$

As the focus now moves away from the individual and more towards the individual as a member of an organization, the analysis considers only the risk neutral cases. For that reason the superscript that identifies the DM's attitude towards risk is now unnecessary and is henceforth suppressed. In addition, the text returns to the notation that stresses the role of θ; write $V_{\mathbf{I}(\theta)} \equiv V(\theta)$.

In the risk neutral, separable version of (8.2),

$$\begin{aligned}\mathbf{U}(\mathbf{D}^* \,|\, \mathbf{I}(\theta), \mathbf{C}(\theta)) &= \int_{\mathbf{Y}} \int_{\mathbf{X}} \{w + \pi(x, a_y(\theta)) - \mathbf{C}(\theta)\}\, dF(x, y; \theta) \\ &= \mathbf{U}(\mathbf{D}^* \,|\, \mathbf{I}(\theta)) - \mathbf{C}(\theta) \\ &= V(\theta) - \mathbf{C}(\theta) + \mathbf{U}(\mathbf{D}^* \,|\, \mathbf{I}(0), \mathbf{C}(0)).\end{aligned} \tag{8.7}$$

Equation (1.11) defines the expected gain from incorporating costly information as, in this notation,

$$\mathbf{G}(\theta) = \mathbf{U}(\mathbf{D}^* \,|\, \mathbf{I}(\theta), \mathbf{C}(\theta)) - \mathbf{U}(\mathbf{D}^* \,|\, \mathbf{I}(0), \mathbf{C}(0)) = V(\theta) - \mathbf{C}(\theta). \tag{8.8}$$

In the risk neutral, separable case, the θ^* that maximizes $\mathbf{U}(\mathbf{D}^* \,|\, \mathbf{I}(\theta), \mathbf{C}(\theta))$ also maximizes $\mathbf{G}(\theta)$, since $\mathbf{U}(\mathbf{D}^* \,|\, \mathbf{I}(0), \mathbf{C}(0))$ is a constant with respect to θ. Should $\mathbf{G}(\theta_*) < 0$, then $\theta^* = 0$.

The demand curve for informativeness relates the per unit price of informativeness to the informativeness the optimizing DM desires to incorporate at that price. The modeling system of Section 6.2.4, in which the informativeness parameter θ enters the information structure linearly, is a simple approach for investigating such matters in the case of a finite state space. The following continuation of Example 5.4b illustrates. For additional analyses of information demand, see Kihlstrom (1974a; 1974b), Grossman, Kihlstrom, and Mirman (1977), Allen (1986), and Chavas (1993).

♦ *Example 5.4b A Betting Model (Continued from Section 5.4.1)*
Recall the problem in which a gambler with initial wealth w can bet a proportion of her wealth on the occurrence of either state x_1 or state x_2. For example, x_1 might be the event "team 1 beats the point spread," and event x_2 "team 2 beats the point spread." The space of actions is $\mathbf{a} = \{a: -1 \le a \le 1\}$, with $a > 0$ a bet on x_1, and $a < 0$ a bet on x_2. A correct bet returns twice the amount bet; an incorrect bet returns nothing. The terminal wealth from action a in state x_i is

$$\omega(w - \mathbf{C}(0), x_1, a) = w + aw = w[1 + a]$$

$$\omega(w - \mathbf{C}(0), x_2, a) = w - aw = w[1 - a].$$

Under risk neutrality, the expected profit from $a \in \mathbf{a}$ is

$$\begin{aligned} \mathbf{U}(\mathbf{D} \mid \mathbf{I}(0), \mathbf{C}(0), a) &= w[1 + a]p(x_1) + w[1 - a][1 - p(x_1)] \\ &= w[1 + a[2p(x_1) - 1]]. \end{aligned}$$

Hence, the prior optimal action is to bet everything: $a_0 = +1$ if $p(x_1) \ge .5$, $a_0 = -1$ if $p(x_1) \le .5$. Suppose the point spread adjusts so that without further information it is reasonable for everyone to believe that $p(x_1) = .5$. In this case the risk neutral gambler is indifferent between any action and

$$\mathbf{U}(\mathbf{D}^* \mid \mathbf{I}(0), \mathbf{C}(0)) = w. \tag{8.9}$$

Given the option of choosing from the sequence of costly information structures modeled by (6.55), suppose the expenditure must be made out of initial wealth, making $w - \mathbf{C}(\theta)$ the wealth available for wagering. Under the assumption that $p(x_1) = .5$, the informed posterior probabilities are

$$\Pi(\theta) = \begin{bmatrix} p(x_1|y_1;\theta) & p(x_1|y_2;\theta) \\ p(x_2|y_1;\theta) & p(x_2|y_2;\theta) \end{bmatrix} = \begin{bmatrix} \frac{1}{2}[1+\theta] & \frac{1}{2}[1-\theta] \\ \frac{1}{2}[1-\theta] & \frac{1}{2}[1+\theta] \end{bmatrix}. \tag{8.10}$$

Conditional on y_1, the costly expected utility of an action a is

$$\begin{aligned} \mathbf{U}(\mathbf{D} \mid \mathbf{I}(\theta), \mathbf{C}(\theta), y_1, a) &= \tfrac{1}{2}[w - \mathbf{C}(\theta)]\{[1 + a][1 + \theta] + [1 - a][1 - \theta]\} \\ &= [w - \mathbf{C}(\theta)][1 + a\theta], \end{aligned}$$

so the optimal decision rule is to bet all remaining wealth on state 1, $a_{y_1}(\theta) = +1$, for all θ. There is no region of useless information in this situation; the conditional expected utility is

$$\mathbf{U}(\mathbf{D}^* \mid \mathbf{I}(\theta), \mathbf{C}(\theta), y_1) = [w - \mathbf{C}(\theta)][1 + \theta].$$

A similar analysis also shows

$$\mathbf{U}(\mathbf{D}^* \mid \mathbf{I}(\theta), \mathbf{C}(\theta), y_2) = [w - \mathbf{C}(\theta)][1 + \theta],$$

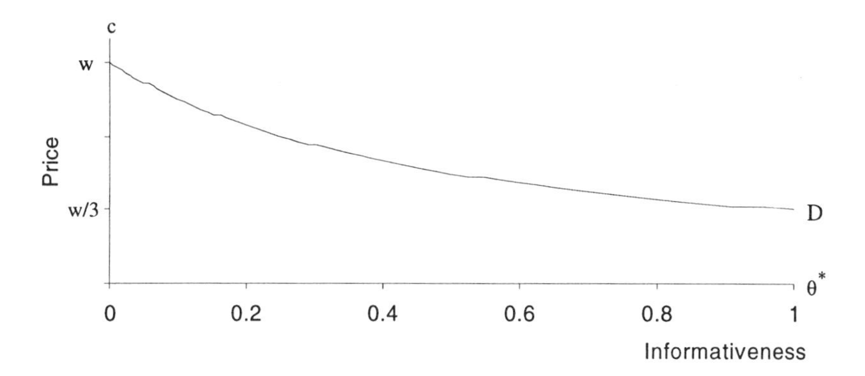

Figure 8.1. In Example 5.4b, the demand for informativeness shifts with initial wealth. There is no region of useless information.

so the preposterior expectation is

$$\mathbf{U}(\mathbf{D}^* \mid \mathbf{I}(\theta), \mathbf{C}(\theta)) = [w - \mathbf{C}(\theta)][1 + \theta]. \tag{8.11}$$

Evaluating the derivative of (8.11) with respect to θ (using the chain rule) characterizes the optimum as a marginal cost equals marginal revenue type result:

$$\mathbf{C}'(\theta) = [w - \mathbf{C}(\theta)]/[1 + \theta]. \tag{8.12}$$

For specificity, suppose the cost function is linear in θ: $\mathbf{C}(\theta) = c\theta$, where c is the per unit "price" of informativeness. The solution to (8.12) then becomes

$$\theta_* = [w - c]/2c,$$

but this must be further processed in line with (8.6) to determine the optimum. The optimal choice is perfect information whenever $\theta_* \geq 1$; $\theta^* = 1$ when $w \geq 3c$. The solution $\theta_* \leq 0$ when $w \leq c$; when wealth is this low compared to cost, $\theta^* = 0$ and no information is demanded. Figure 8.1 shows the demand curve for information as it depends upon w, c, and θ. The function has no discontinuities, is downward sloping, and increases (shifts to the right) with the initial wealth of the DM. Substituting the optimal demand $\theta^*(w, c)$ into (8.11) gives the value of the costly informed decision in the problem:

$$\begin{aligned} \mathbf{U}(\mathbf{D}^* \mid \mathbf{I}(\theta^*), \mathbf{C}(\theta^*)) &= 2[w - c] && \text{when } \theta^* = 1; \\ &= \tfrac{1}{4}\left[\frac{w^2}{c} + 2w + c\right] && \text{when } 0 \leq \theta^* \leq 1; \\ &= w && \text{when } \theta^* = 0. \; \blacklozenge \end{aligned} \tag{8.13}$$

8.1.2 Economic Consequences of Differential Information

The theory of endogenous informativeness can be applied to address economic issues outside the realm of normative decision theory. Consider the social consequences of any differential ability to afford the purchase of information. When comparing decision makers, the ones that choose to possess information structures with higher index θ are "more informed" in a quantifiable sense. To the extent that wealthier individuals in a community can afford and choose to obtain sources with greater informativeness, such individuals are able to make more profitable decisions, in a statistical sense. This subsection presents, in the context of the preceding wagering model, an informational explanation for the possibility of increasing inequality in the distribution of wealth based upon the ability to afford and possess (statistically) better information. This type of analysis brings up important social policy issues relevant to the Information Age, regarding, for example, the availability and affordability of educational information sources and structures.

♦ *Example 5.4b (Continued)*
Consider now a small community of wagerers, each facing the meta-decision (8.11) with different endowments of initial wealth. Since in (8.13) the individual demand for information is a normal good in the sense that it increases with initial wealth, the more wealthy members of the community are willing and able to take advantage of better information structures.

To run the model, assume a perfectly competitive and secret market, so that the only signals available to each individual are those coming from the information structure purchased. In other words, suppose no wagerer can view any other wagerer's bet, and that individual bets have no perceptible effects in the market. Figure 8.2 shows the results from wagering by a community of eight individuals with the given distribution of wealth. Each tick on the line represents a wagerer; above the tick is the initial wealth and below the tick is the optimal meta-decision of that individual. The posterior expected wealth after the wager, from (8.13), appears on the next line; this becomes initial wealth for the next round of wagering and leads to the associated meta-decision.

Figure 8.2 shows that the poorest individuals possess null information, and if they do bet, there is no expected gain. The wealthiest individuals possess perfect information and make a sure bet, with after-cost wealth doubling each time. The middle class purchases imperfect information and can expect to work its way up to the ability to afford perfect information. Although it is dangerous to draw any broad conclusions from such a rudimentary illustration, it is clear in this model that the distribution of wealth becomes increasingly unequal, the cause being informational. ♦

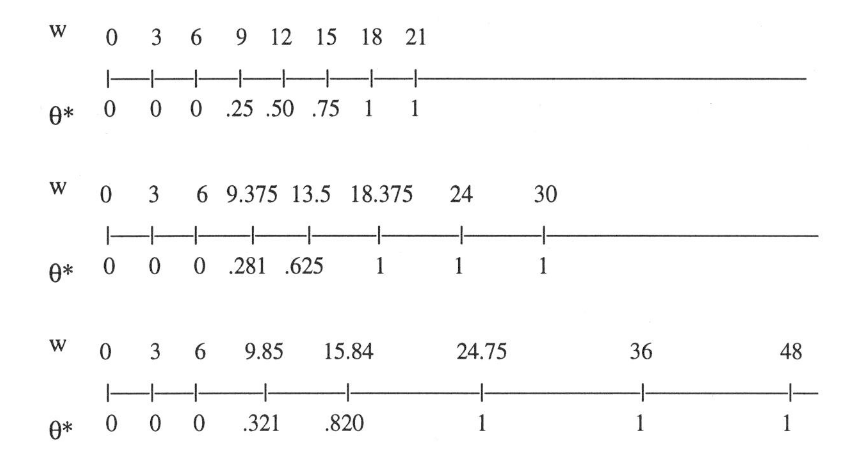

Figure 8.2. When the community's initial distribution of wealth is given by the top line, the differential ability to afford information leads to greater inequality.

The meta-decision is a problem antecedent to the analysis of the economic consequences of the resulting differential possession of information. When decision makers' informed decisions involve taking actions in the market, the consequences of those decisions can feed back upon the well-being of each DM. Uninformed individuals may be able to infer specific messages from simply monitoring these consequences in the market. Furthermore, as Section 5.5.2 points out, information possessed can be used strategically. These issues are well studied in the economics of information; for a modern treatment of many types of model, see Hirshleifer and Riley (1992).

For example, the analysis in Section 5.1.2 assesses the value of an economic forecaster to a specific farmer, but it may not be good methodology to assess the value of the forecaster to the perfectly competitive industry as a whole by simply adding up the forecaster's value to each user. The collective response to the information by the users can prevent the market price from being exogenous. See Lave (1963) for a discussion of the differences between the value of information to an individual user and the value of information to an industry; Babcock (1990) and Schlee (1996) are also relevant here. Hayami and Peterson (1972) and Bradford and Kelejian (1977) investigate the market impact of better statistical reporting about a competitive market. Indeed, Bradford and Kelejian (1981) use the modeling sequence (6.55) to assess the impact of greater informativeness on the distribution of income of the various participants in a competitive agricultural market.

8.1.3 Optimal and Suboptimal Information Possession

This subsection examines the DM's preposterior expected wealth from the costly incorporation of any of the various information structures she may choose, both optimal and suboptimal. As informativeness runs the gamut from null to perfect, it is possible to characterize null, useless, uneconomic, economic, optimal, and wasteful levels of information possession. In previous chapters we have seen several examples of useless information, nonnull information structures with no expected value. The following continuation of Example 5.4a illustrates that useless information complicates the analysis and causes a discontinuity in the demand curve.

♦ *Example 5.4a Fed Watching and Investing (Continued from Section 5.4.1)* Recall the one-period investment problem where the DM has a choice between a risk free Treasury Bill earning $[1 + k]$ per dollar invested and a bond whose return depends upon the unknown future policy of the Fed. The states are x_1: Fed tightens monetary policy, and x_2: Fed loosens monetary policy. If the Fed tightens, the return per dollar invested in the bond is $z_1[1+k]$; if the Fed loosens, it is $z_2[1+k]$, where z_1 and z_2 are parameters such that $z_1 \leq 1 \leq z_2$. Define also the quantity $\overline{z} = r_1 z_1 + r_2 z_2 > 1$, where $r_i \equiv p(x_i)$.

The analysis in Section 5.4 shows that the optimal uninformed action is to put all available wealth in the bond, $a_0 = 0$. The value of the prior decision is

$$\mathbf{U}(\mathbf{D}^* \,|\, \mathbf{I}(0), \mathbf{C}(0)) \;=\; w[1 + k]\,\overline{z}. \tag{8.14}$$

For a specific illustration, let $r_1 = .25$, $r_2 = .75$, $z_1 = .8$, $z_2 = 1.2$, $w = \$100$, and $k = .08$. Then $\overline{z} = 1.10$ and $\mathbf{U}(\mathbf{D}^* \,|\, \mathbf{I}(0), \mathbf{C}(0)) = \$118.80$.

Suppose now the decision maker has the choice from a sequence of calibrated information structures indexed by the parameter θ, with posterior probabilities

$$\Pi(\theta, r_1) \;=\; \begin{bmatrix} p(x_1|y_1;\theta,r_1) & p(x_1|y_2;\theta,r_1) \\ p(x_2|y_1;\theta,r_1) & p(x_2|y_2;\theta,r_1) \end{bmatrix}$$

$$= \begin{bmatrix} \theta+[1-\theta]r_1 & [1-\theta]r_1 \\ [1-\theta][1-r_1] & \theta+[1-\theta][1-r_1] \end{bmatrix}. \tag{8.15}$$

The informed situation models most simply if the information cost can be paid out of posterior dollars. Suppose the information sources provide credit: the informants lend the cost $\mathbf{C}(\theta)$ to their clients at the risk free rate k. That is, the full amount w can be invested and the decision maker pays $[1 + k]\mathbf{C}(\theta)$ at the end of the period. The net payoff is

$$\omega^{\#}(w, x_1, a, \mathbf{C}(\theta)) \;=\; w[1 + k][a + [1 - a]z_1] - [1 + k]\mathbf{C}(\theta);$$

$$\omega^{\#}(w, x_2, a, \mathbf{C}(\theta)) = w[1 + k][a + [1 - a]z_2] - [1 + k]\mathbf{C}(\theta).$$

Conditional on the receipt of message y_1,

$$\mathbf{U}(\mathbf{D} \mid \mathbf{I}(\theta), \mathbf{C}(\theta), y_1, a) = w[1 + k]\{a + [1 - a][z_1\theta + [1 - \theta]\bar{z}]\} - [1 + k]\mathbf{C}(\theta).$$

The optimal choice changes from the prior optimum $a_0 = 0$ to $a_{y_1}(\theta) = 1$ when $z_1\theta + [1 - \theta]\bar{z} \leq 1$; or when informativeness $\theta \geq [\bar{z} - 1]/[\bar{z} - z_1]$. Conditional on message y_2,

$$\mathbf{U}(\mathbf{D} \mid \mathbf{I}(\theta), \mathbf{C}(\theta), y_2, a) = w[1 + k]\{a + [1 - a][z_2\theta + [1 - \theta]\bar{z}]\} - [1 + k]\mathbf{C}(\theta),$$

so the optimal choice is $a_{y_2}(\theta) = 0$ for all θ, since $z_2\theta + [1 - \theta]\bar{z} > 1$.

Applying the optimal decision rule in each case and using the calibration property that the marginal on the messages is the same as the marginal on the states, the value of the costly informed decision is

$$\mathbf{U}(\mathbf{D}^* \mid \mathbf{I}(\theta), \mathbf{C}(\theta)) = \tag{8.16}$$

$$\begin{cases} w[1 + k]\bar{z} - [1 + k]\mathbf{C}(\theta) & \text{if } \theta \leq [\bar{z} - 1]/[\bar{z} - z_1] \\ w[1 + k]\{r_1 + r_2[z_2\theta + [1 - \theta]\bar{z}]\} - [1 + k]\mathbf{C}(\theta) & \text{if } \theta \geq [\bar{z} - 1]/[\bar{z} - z_1]. \end{cases}$$

This situation has a region of useless information. When the information structure is of relatively low statistical informativeness, the optimal response to any message does not change from the optimal choice in the prior uninformed decision. The source becomes potentially valuable only when there is sufficient statistical informativeness to be credible enough to lead the decision maker to take differential action depending upon the message received.

Evaluating $\mathbf{U}'(\mathbf{D}^* \mid \mathbf{I}(\theta), \mathbf{C}(\theta)) = 0$ amounts to setting marginal cost equal to marginal revenue:

$$\mathbf{C}'(\theta) = 0 \qquad \text{if } \theta \leq [\bar{z} - 1]/[\bar{z} - z_1];$$

$$\mathbf{C}'(\theta) = w[z_2 - \bar{z}][1 - r_1] \qquad \text{if } \theta \geq [\bar{z} - 1]/[\bar{z} - z_1].$$

In the useless case, the optimal solution can only be $\theta^* = 0$. In the more statistically informed case, the marginal revenue is clearly positive but the resulting solution θ_* must be further processed in line with (8.6).

In the numerical example the breakeven θ, at which the information stops being useless, is $\theta = [1.1 - 1]/[1.1 - .8] = 1/3$. Suppose the cost function is quadratic of the form $\mathbf{C}(\theta) = c\theta^2$, where c is the per unit price or cost of informativeness. Then (8.16) becomes

$$\mathbf{U}(\mathbf{D}^* \mid \mathbf{I}(\theta), \mathbf{C}(\theta)) = \begin{cases} 118.80 - 1.08c\theta^2 & \text{if } \theta \leq 1/3 \\ 116.10 + 8.1\theta - 1.08c\theta^2 & \text{if } \theta \geq 1/3. \end{cases} \tag{8.17}$$

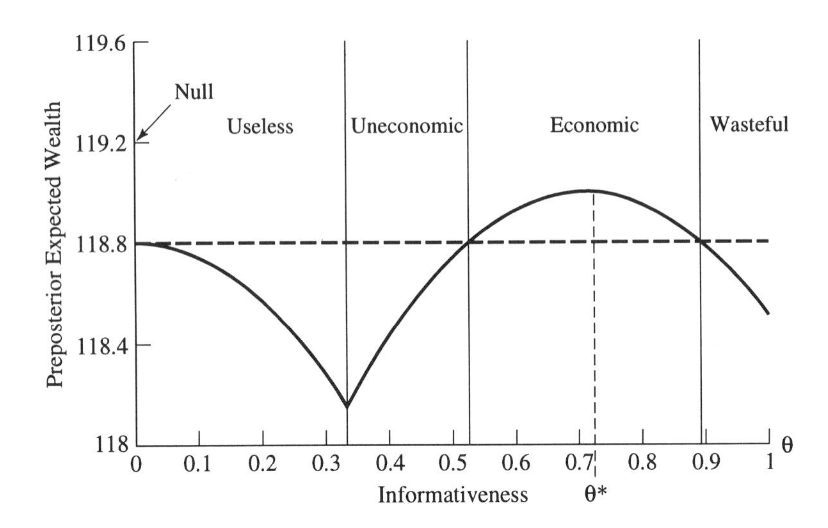

Figure 8.3. The DM's preposterior expected wealth is a function of the information structure she chooses to possess. Because of information cost, both too little and too much informativeness make the DM worse off than if she did not incorporate information at all.

Figure 8.3 graphs this function of θ for c = \$5.25. The base level of expected terminal wealth is \$118.80, the expectation achievable without the use of any information structure. The figure shows five regions, or degrees, of information possessed. Null statistical information, when $\theta = 0$, can never be of any pragmatic value. Useless information is statistically informative in Blackwell's sense, but in this situation cannot change actions and hence is of no pragmatic value; in specific problems, useless information need never be acquired, even when free. Uneconomic information can affect decisions and would be utilized if free, but it costs more than it is worth. Economic information has pragmatic value both gross and net, and in this region lies the optimal purchase of information. The meta-decision is $\theta^* = .7143$, yielding maximum expected wealth of \$118.99. Finally, wasteful information, although highly informative in the statistical sense, also costs more than it is worth.

The demand curve for information is generated by varying the cost parameter c. Figure 8.4 graphs the function (8.17) for alternate values of c. Taking the derivative of (8.17) with respect to θ yields the results $\theta_* = 0$ when $\theta \leq 1/3$ and $\theta_* = 3.75/c$ when $\theta \geq 1/3$. The graph for c = 6 illustrates the phenomenon (8.5): $\mathbf{U}(\mathbf{D}^* \,|\, \mathbf{I}(\theta), \mathbf{C}(\theta)) \leq \mathbf{U}(\mathbf{D}^* \,|\, \mathbf{I}(0), \mathbf{C}(0))$ for all θ and hence at the extreme point $\theta_* = .625$ the posterior expected wealth is less than that available with no information. In other words, at c = 6 every source $\mathbf{I}(\theta)$ is uneconomic so $\theta^* = 0$. The highest price a decision maker would pay to purchase an information structure is c = 5.625. The corresponding optimal structure $\theta^* = 2/3$ is the least statistically informative source that would be demanded in this problem. The quantity of information demanded increases as the price falls further, and any price lower than 3.75 leads the decision maker to purchase perfect information. Figure 8.5 depicts the demand curve for information in this problem under the sequence of calibrated information structures modeled by (8.15). The demand curve is well behaved except for the discontinuity. ♦

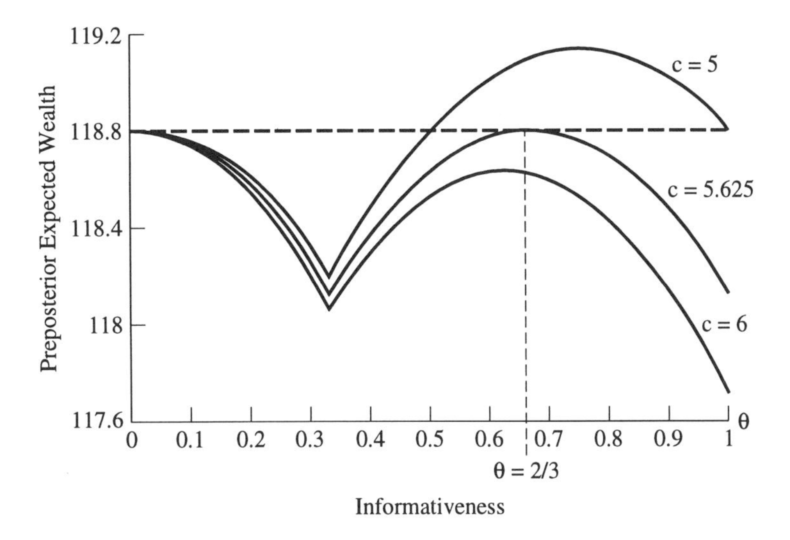

Figure 8.4. Studying the optimal meta-decision as it depends upon c, the per-unit cost of informativeness, the least informative information structure demanded is $\theta = 2/3$.

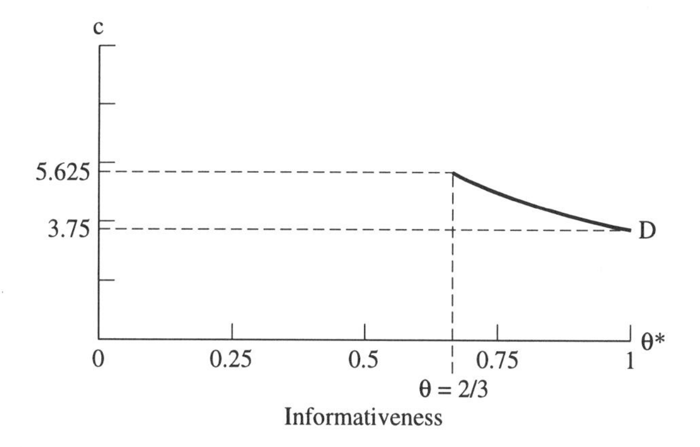

Figure 8.5. This demand curve exhibits a discontinuity.

Wilson (1975) provides further discussion of the economics of this situation. For related analysis in statistical decision problems in which the sample size is the index of informativeness and cost, see Raiffa and Schlaifer (1961, Section 5.5) and Pratt, Raiffa, and Schlaifer (1995, Chapter 14). Diagrams such as Figure 8.3 are also useful for illustrating the sensitivity of the preposterior net expected wealth [or, in light of (8.8), the expected information gain] to deviations from θ^*: how far the chosen θ can deviate from θ^* before there is significant detriment to the DM. Wendt (1969) discusses the importance of this "flatness" issue for the design of empirical studies on information choice.

The implicit assumption of this section is that the DM knows exactly what she would be getting from each member of the sequence of information structures available to her. This may not be so, especially when the alternatives being considered are interpersonal sources from outside the organization. Special techniques are necessary when the DM seeks to procure such sources, since the pecuniary interests of an information vendor may not coincide with the best interests of the DM and her organization. Section 8.2 explains.

8.2 Information Procurement

Suppose the decision maker seeks to procure the services of an outside information vendor, a firm or individual selling expertise that purports to improve decisions and resulting consequences. Marketplace examples of such informants include economic forecasters, financial advisors, consultants, lawyers, and spies. If the two parties come to contractual agreement, the informant performs an inquiry into the circumstances and communicates a report or message that the DM uses as the basis for a choice of action. When nature reveals the uncertain state of the world, the DM learns the consequences of this choice.

Viewing the DM as principal and the informant as agent, the problem is the design of a procurement contract that considers the two parties' differential revenues, costs, motivations, incentives, and knowledge of one another.[1] In his analysis of the business problem of evaluating and rewarding information sources, Savage (1971, page 798) points out that the appropriate incentive depends both upon the importance of the information to the DM and upon the effort the informant must undertake to produce the message for himself:

> The appropriate incentive for you to offer a respondent for his opinion depends not only on the importance for you of obtaining that opinion

[1] One interpretation of the expected value of information is that it is the maximum fixed fee the DM should be willing to pay for access to the source's messages. However, this calculation is not the same thing as negotiating the actual payment in a noncooperative environment, even if a fixed-fee contract were appropriate.

with a specified degree of accuracy but also on the difficulty for the respondent in obtaining it from himself. This makes the choice of a scoring rule designed to evoke the right degree of effort from the respondent on the various components of his task particularly subtle.

Following Savage's dictum that incentives for the informant should depend upon the importance of the information to the DM, the remainder of this chapter studies the optimal design of a procurement contract from the class of contracts that compensate the informant with a share of the contribution he makes to the DM's profitability. Nadiminti, Mukhopadhyay, and Kriebel (1996) mention this class of contract and argue that the information explosion may make it more common in the future. Since the economics of the situation has much in common with the recent literature on regulation in procurement [e.g., Baron and Myerson (1982); Laffont and Tirole (1986; 1993)], the solution to the DM's contracting problem combines the analytical approach of the new regulatory economics with the decision theory notion of the ex-post value of information.

8.2.1 The Informant as Agent of the DM

The informant's basic product is an information structure: a collection of potential messages the source might communicate combined with a specification of the statistical relationship between each potential message and each uncertain state of the world. If the informant would reveal the precise statistical model that generates the messages (e.g., the details of an econometric model), then p(x, y) can be assessed using methods in Chapter 4. Suppose the source is unwilling to provide the model and its statistical properties, perhaps because the model is proprietary (after all, the model is the source's technology) or because there is no precise statistical model. Oftentimes, the source is willing merely to provide assertions about the properties of p(x, y). The difficulty with assertions of informational prowess is that the source may find it advantageous not to reveal the complete truth about the information structure.

There are several circumstances in which it may be advantageous for the informant to make the communication of information variables different from his true beliefs. One clear situation is when the informant is a charlatan—after all, anyone can make forecasts or give advice. This vendor ballyhoos expertise in order to get the business, and then deceptively produces messages hoping to generate some fees before being detected. Another possibility, not uncommonly asserted in lawsuits between investors and financial advisors, is that the informant may be competent but has a conflict of interest; that is, the advice intends to induce actions with consequences favorable not to the DM-client, but to some other party or parties. On a more altruistic level, Lawrence (1991b, pages 438–439) documents an example of a forecaster who purposely biases his messages because he believes it to be in his clients' best interest. Winkler and Murphy

(1970) illustrate a fourth example, in which a probability forecaster is paid according to his Brier score [Brier (1950)], but "hedges" his messages depending upon his attitude towards risk. Finally, in the principal-agent context of this analysis, a discrepancy can arise in a poorly designed contract due to the DM's lack of knowledge about the informant's characteristics.

Osband (1989) is the first to formally incorporate another of the subtleties that Savage (1971) hints at: the informativeness is not exogenous but can be influenced by the informant's effort. The present approach assumes the informant can choose to produce one from a sequence of potential information structures, ordered by increasing informativeness to the DM. To produce a more informative structure, the informant must exert more effort and bear more cost in the inquiry.

The DM cannot observe this effort. For example, suppose the prior distribution of the random variable is symmetric and unimodal with mean $\overline{x}$. Upon hearing a forecast very near $\overline{x}$, how can the DM detect whether this message is the result of a careful considered analysis, an uninformed guess, or the result of a purposeful deception? After all, a highly capable informant should commonly forecast common events, but then again, maybe so should a charlatan.

In procuring the information service the DM faces both moral hazard and adverse selection: she directly observes neither the informant's effort nor the cost efficiency of that effort, meaning she does not know the information structure the informant produces and the monetary cost of producing it. At best she can observe only the informant's assertions of informativeness and efficiency. The possibility of a dishonest state of affairs serves as the motivation to search for contract designs that are crafted to protect the DM by coaxing the truth out of the self-interested informant. Since contract incentives that encourage the truth also affect the effort the informant undertakes, the informativeness of the source becomes endogenous to the DM.

In light of her lack of knowledge about the informant's efficiency, informativeness, and costs, the DM seeks to design a procurement contract that maximizes her expected gain by optimally trading off inducement to produce information value against the extraction of economic rent from the informant.[2] Since the contractual agreement can depend only upon what is observable by both parties or is communicated from one party to the other, the DM solves the problem by regulating the informant's compensation as a function of certain data she requires the informant to provide.

Much of the contract design problem involves ensuring honesty in the communication of two distinct types of data. As is typical in adverse-selection models, the agent must report his cost efficiency of effort, and the contract design is

[2] Economic rent is any payment to a resource in excess of the minimum amount necessary to bring forth that resource.

incentive compatible if it induces the informant to reveal the truth. In addition, the nature of this problem requires the communication of information variables: messages and their associated probability distributions. The contract is *strictly proper* [Savage (1971)] if it provides incentives to guarantee that the informant truthfully reveals the probability distributions he produces and believes to be true. Generalizing the original work on this subject by McCarthy (1956), the overall contract design is said to *keep the informant honest* if it is both incentive compatible and strictly proper.

Section 8.2.2 sets up the basic framework, defining the DM's problem, describing the informant's technology and costs, and presenting the notation and primary technical assumptions necessary for the subsequent analysis. Section 8.2.3 describes the general characterization of an agreement between the two parties that bases the compensation on the observable ex-post value to the DM of the messages the informant communicates. Section 8.3 develops the theory of the expected value of an information structure when there is a possible discrepancy between what the informant communicates and what he believes to be true, and then presents the design for the optimal value-based menu of contracts that keeps the informant honest. The informant then chooses from the menu according to his best interests. One of two brief examples shows that the self-selection feature in the contract [Melumad and Reichelstein (1989)] extracts enough rent to increase the DM's expected gain by nearly seven percent.

8.2.2 The Framework and Primary Assumptions

The DM faces a decision problem with an uncertain payoff $\pi(x, a)$ that depends upon the choice of action $a \in \mathbf{a}$ and the realization of a random variable $x \in \mathbf{X}$. Assume that both the action space $\mathbf{a}$ and state space $\mathbf{X}$ are compact subsets of finite-dimensional Euclidean space, and the payoff $\pi(x, a)$ is a bounded, real-valued function that is strictly concave and smooth, such that the partial derivative $\pi_a(x, a)$ exists and is everywhere continuous. The prior probability density function $p(x)$ is common knowledge. Without utilizing the informant, the solution for the DM is to choose the prior optimal action a_0 characterized by the first-order condition

$$\int_{\mathbf{X}} \pi_a(x, a_0)\, dF(x) = 0. \tag{8.18}$$

The assumptions guarantee the achievement of a maximum and a unique solution.

The DM also has the option of making use of an informant who offers to produce an information structure providing signals that presume to be pertinent to the actual realization of X. Assume the informant's technology allows him to choose to produce one from a sequence of information structures $\mathbf{I}(\theta)$ indexed by a continuous parameter θ belonging to an interval $[0, \bar{\theta}]$. An individual structure

$$\mathbf{I}(\theta) = \{\mathbf{Y}, p(x, y; \theta)\},$$

comprises 1) a space of potential signals $\mathbf{Y} = \{y\}$ that might result from the inquiry, assumed not to vary with θ, and 2) a joint probability density function of the signals and states $p(x, y; \theta)$, defined on $\mathbf{X} \times \mathbf{Y}$. For any $\mathbf{I}(\theta)$, assume the space $\mathbf{Y}$ is a compact subset of a finite-dimensional Euclidean space, and that the joint density $p(x, y; \theta)$ is absolutely continuous and twice differentiable in θ on the interval $[0, \bar{\theta}]$. The joint density is consistent with the common knowledge prior $p(x)$, and it embodies the marginal density $p(y; \theta)$ from which the signal is drawn, the conditional density of the state $p(x \mid y; \theta)$ for each signal y, and the likelihood of each signal given the state, $p(y \mid x; \theta)$.

The parameter θ fully specifies the information structure $\mathbf{I}(\theta)$, and it indexes an ordering of the sequence of structures according to the following definition of informativeness.

Definition 1. If $\theta' > \theta$, then the DM would not prefer to utilize $\mathbf{I}(\theta)$ over $\mathbf{I}(\theta')$ if both were available at no cost and with completely honest communication.

The information structure $\mathbf{I}(0)$ is the least informative and $\mathbf{I}(\bar{\theta})$ the most informative feasible structure.

The specific information structure $\mathbf{I}(\theta)$ that the profit-maximizing informant produces is a function of the effort he chooses to undertake, which is in turn a function of the compensation incentives the DM offers in a contract to which the two parties agree prior to the exertion of the effort. Effort is costly for the informant, and it is natural to postulate that it is more costly to produce and operate a more informative structure. Assume the informant can produce any structure $\mathbf{I}(\theta)$, $\theta \in [0, \bar{\theta}]$, according to the cost function

$$C(\theta) = ck(\theta), \tag{8.19}$$

where $k(\theta)$ is continuous, increasing, and strictly convex in θ: $k_\theta(\theta) > 0$ and $k_{\theta\theta}(\theta) > 0$ for every $\theta \in [0, \bar{\theta}]$. Here c is a continuous cost efficiency parameter, belonging to $[\underline{c}, \bar{c}]$, and known only to the informant. The informant with parameter $\underline{c} > 0$ is the most efficient type, able to produce any $\mathbf{I}(\theta)$ at the least cost.

The DM desires to procure and utilize the services of the type-c informant, yet she cannot directly observe c, θ, or the signal y that the informant draws in the inquiry using the structure $\mathbf{I}(\theta)$ he produces. The DM does observe a communicated message $\tilde{y}$, along with the informant's assertion that $\tilde{y}$ is a drawing from an information structure $\mathbf{I}(\tilde{\theta})$. The notation identifies a communicated variable by a superscript tilde (~). If the variable is without the tilde, then it is either true or believed by the communicator to be true. If it is advantageous to make the communications different from his true beliefs, the informant adopts a strategy of deception in which he translates the signal y from $\mathbf{I}(\theta)$ into a message $\tilde{y}$ consistent with $\mathbf{I}(\tilde{\theta})$.

The adaptation of the dual information structure (6.40) to this context allows the modeling of possible discrepancies between the actual and the communicated information variables. Considering the asserted $\mathbf{I}(\tilde{\theta})$ and the true $\mathbf{I}(\theta)$ as individual information structures, the interest lies in the properties of the trivariate density of the state, the communicated message, and the actual signal in the dual structure

$$\vartheta(\theta, \tilde{\theta}) = \{\mathbf{Y} \times \mathbf{Y}, p(x, y, \tilde{y}; \theta, \tilde{\theta})\}.$$

Given $\tilde{\theta}$ and θ, it is useful to write the trivariate density as

$$p(x, \tilde{y}, y; \tilde{\theta}, \theta) = p(x \mid \tilde{y}, y; \tilde{\theta}, \theta)\, p(\tilde{y} \mid y; \tilde{\theta}, \theta)\, p(y; \theta), \qquad (8.20)$$

where the right-hand side shows a factorization into the following conditional and marginal densities. 1) $p(x \mid \tilde{y}, y; \tilde{\theta}, \theta)$ is the posterior density of the state, given the communicated message and drawn signal, 2) $p(\tilde{y} \mid y; \tilde{\theta}, \theta)$ describes the informant's generation of the communication conditional on the signal he actually draws, and 3) $p(y; \theta)$ is the marginal density from which the informant draws the signal using the true information structure.

The informant chooses this trivariate density in response to the contract's incentives by choosing $\mathbf{I}(\theta)$ and $\mathbf{I}(\tilde{\theta})$ and by strategically devising the density $p(\tilde{y} \mid y; \tilde{\theta}, \theta)$. The next section describes an approach to contracting that provides incentives designed to keep the informant honest when he makes these choices.

8.2.3 The Contract Design Problem

In designing the contract the DM faces adverse selection (unknown c), moral hazard (unknown θ), and possible dishonesty in the communication of information variables. To solve the problem, the theory of incentives in procurement [Laffont and Tirole (1993)] suggests an approach in which the DM offers a menu of compensation contracts from which the informant is allowed to select. The menu not only offers a choice of compensation functions depending upon the announcement of the cost efficiency parameter $\tilde{c}$, it also includes a regulation function $\tilde{\theta}(\tilde{c})$ that insists the informant contract for the delivery of the specific information structure $\mathbf{I}(\tilde{\theta}(\tilde{c}))$ when he announces $\tilde{c}$.

There are four mutually observable items of data: an announcement $\tilde{c}$, a contractual agreement $\mathbf{I}(\tilde{\theta})$, a communication $\tilde{y}$, and the state realization x, so the compensation function in its most general form is $\mathbf{t}(\tilde{c}, \tilde{\theta}, \tilde{y}, x)$. This section proposes and studies a specific compensation function under which the two parties share the incremental payoff that results when the DM hires the informant and takes action in response to the communicated message $\tilde{y}$. This scheme requires the DM to reveal the details of her decision problem to the informant, making the payoff function $\pi(x, a)$ common knowledge. To develop this compensation function, the first task is to describe precisely how the DM responds after having received the message $\tilde{y}$.

In principle the DM should choose the action optimal under the posterior density $p(x \mid \tilde{y}, y; \tilde{\theta}, \theta)$, but she does not observe y and θ. She could provide a prior probability distribution for these variables, but using a prior for y and θ has the undesirable side effect of providing an additional source of uncertainty for the informant: he does not know precisely how the DM will respond to the message he sends because her decision rule is a function both of the message and the private a priori knowledge she utilizes. As the designer of the contract it is simpler for the DM to just announce that she will take any message she receives at face value as a drawing from a contractual structure $\mathbf{I}(\tilde{\theta})$. This announcement is a contract design characteristic; the DM is still allowing for the possibility $\tilde{y} \neq y$ and $\theta \neq \tilde{\theta}$. Under this contract specification, the DM chooses the action optimal under the conditional density $p(x \mid \tilde{y}; \tilde{\theta})$, the unique action that solves

$$\max_a \int_{\mathbf{X}} \pi(x, a)\, dF(x \mid \tilde{y}; \tilde{\theta}) = \int_{\mathbf{X}} \pi(x, a^*(\tilde{y}, \tilde{\theta}))\, dF(x \mid \tilde{y}; \tilde{\theta}), \quad (8.21)$$

where the new notation is $a_{\tilde{y}}^{N}(\tilde{\theta}) \equiv a^*(\tilde{y}, \tilde{\theta})$, an optimal decision rule that satisfies

$$\int_{\mathbf{X}} \pi_a(x, a^*(\tilde{y}, \tilde{\theta}))\, dF(x \mid \tilde{y}; \tilde{\theta}) = 0. \quad (8.22)$$

The strict concavity and differentiability of $\pi(x, a)$ in a, combined with the assumed existence and continuity of the partial derivative $p_\theta(x \mid \tilde{y}; \tilde{\theta})$ for every $\tilde{\theta} \in [0, \bar{\theta}]$ ensures that the function $a^*(\tilde{y}, \tilde{\theta})$ is unique, continuous, and differentiable in $\tilde{\theta}$ [see Kihlstrom (1974b), Section 2].

By asserting the way she will respond to any message $\tilde{y}$, the DM ensures that both parties know with certainty the function $a^*(\tilde{y}, \tilde{\theta})$ describing her response to $\tilde{y}$ under any contractual structure $\mathbf{I}(\tilde{\theta})$. This certain response provides an observable quantity that can serve as a common knowledge criterion for the compensation function. After the choice of action the state x occurs and the ex-post value of the message $\tilde{y}$,

$$\upsilon(x, \tilde{y}; \tilde{\theta}) = \pi(x, a^*(\tilde{y}, \tilde{\theta})) - \pi(x, a_0),$$

is the difference, in the realized state x, between the terminal payoff under action $a^*(\tilde{y}, \tilde{\theta})$ and the terminal payoff that would have resulted under the prior optimal action a_0. The ex-post value of the message $\tilde{y}$ can be positive or negative.

The message may result in an action more appropriate for the state that actually occurs, or it may in a sense steer the DM wrong and lead to a less favorable outcome than would otherwise have been achieved.

Because of the complex two-dimensional nature of this model, consider a menu of procurement contracts in which the informant's compensation function is linear in $\upsilon(x, \tilde{y}; \tilde{\theta}(\tilde{c}))$:

$$\mathbf{t}(\tilde{c}, \tilde{\theta}, \tilde{y}, x) = [\alpha(\tilde{c})][\upsilon(x, \tilde{y}; \tilde{\theta}(\tilde{c}))] + s(\tilde{c}), \tag{8.23}$$

where the share α, the fixed payment s, and the contractual informativeness $\tilde{\theta}$ are all regulated as a function of the announcement $\tilde{c}$. When $s < 0$ and $\alpha > 0$, the contract amounts to a fixed entrance fee paid to the DM, followed by the transfer of a fraction of the realized ex-post value. When $\alpha = 1$ the transfer is the entire ex-post value, meaning the DM essentially sells the decision to the informant for a fixed fee.

The timing of the events in the contracting process is important and it is convenient to summarize the preceding discussion into distinct stages.

Stage I. The initial offer. The DM reveals her decision problem and offers the informant a menu of contracts that specifies, as a function of $\tilde{c}$, the fixed payment $s(\tilde{c})$, the share $\alpha(\tilde{c})$ of the realized ex-post value, and the regulated informativeness $\tilde{\theta}(\tilde{c})$ that the informant must agree to deliver. At this time the DM also states that she will take the messages at face value, meaning she will choose her actions based solely on the assumption that any message she receives is a drawing from the contractual information structure $\mathbf{I}(\tilde{\theta}(\tilde{c}))$.

Stage II. Choice of a contract. The informant has the option to select one of the contracts and, if so, he agrees to deliver the information structure $\mathbf{I}(\tilde{\theta}(\tilde{c}))$ and to be compensated according to (8.23) with specified s and α. Although the agent cannot view the principal's action choice a, he knows the compensation structure ensures it is in the principal's interest to choose the action optimal under the message he sends. There is no further negotiation.

Stage III. Production of an information structure. The informant then exerts effort, bears the cost, and produces the information structure $\mathbf{I}(\theta)$, a structure possibly different from $\mathbf{I}(\tilde{\theta}(\tilde{c}))$. Note that when the actual informativeness is endogenous, the timing of events is different from the literature on strictly proper scoring rules. In Savage's (1971) elicitation problem the goal is to induce the informant to reveal what he already exogenously believes. Here the DM is trying to induce the informant to produce the information structure to which he previously agreed, and then to reveal the probability distributions he believes.

Stage IV. Drawing of the signal. After producing $\mathbf{I}(\theta)$, the informant draws the signal $y \in \mathbf{Y}$ in the inquiry.

Stage V. Communication of a message. The informant communicates a message $\tilde{y}$ to the DM, a message supposedly drawn using the contractual information structure $\mathbf{I}(\tilde{\theta}(\tilde{c}))$. If there is a discrepancy from Stage IV, then the informant is adopting a strategy of deception to translate y into $\tilde{y}$.
Stage VI. Action response by the DM. The DM then chooses the action $a^*(\tilde{y}, \tilde{\theta}(\tilde{c}))$, optimal posterior to the receipt of the message $\tilde{y}$ under the conditional density of the state she assumes to be true according to the contract.
Stage VII. State revelation and monetary transfer. Finally, nature reveals the uncertain state and the payments are made based upon the contract specifications and the realized ex-post value of the message, $\upsilon(x, \tilde{y}; \tilde{\theta}(\tilde{c}))$.

8.3 Optimal Incentive Contracts to Procure Information

The DM designs the compensation and regulation functions so as to maximize her expected gain from procurement while providing the informant with incentives to 1) announce his true efficiency parameter: $\tilde{c} = c$, 2) produce the same information structure that he contracts for: $\mathbf{I}(\theta) = \mathbf{I}(\tilde{\theta}(\tilde{c}))$, and 3) communicate the same signal that he draws: $\tilde{y} = y$. The revelation principle allows the DM to limit consideration to incentive compatible, strictly proper contracts that induce this honest behavior.

Approaching the design problem recursively, the natural break for the analysis is between Stages III and IV, a time posterior to announcing $\tilde{c}$, agreeing to $\mathbf{I}(\tilde{\theta}(\tilde{c}))$ and producing $\mathbf{I}(\theta)$, but prior to the drawing and optimal communication of any messages. After beginning with the theory of the value of information when there is a possible discrepancy between the contractual information structure and the structure the informant actually produces, this section presents the optimal design and illustrates it with two examples. The most technical of the proofs are relegated to the final subsection.

8.3.1 The Expected Value of Information

The regulated informant's realized profit from any policy of announcing, producing, and communicating is

$$\omega(c, \tilde{c}, \tilde{\theta}(\tilde{c}), \theta, \tilde{y}, x) = [\alpha(\tilde{c})][\upsilon(x, \tilde{y}; \tilde{\theta}(\tilde{c}))] - ck(\theta) + s(\tilde{c}). \quad (8.24)$$

At the beginning of Stage V, the type-c informant has announced that his efficiency is $\tilde{c}$, contracted to deliver $\mathbf{I}(\tilde{\theta}(\tilde{c}))$, accepted the compensation parameters $\alpha(\tilde{c})$ and $s(\tilde{c})$, produced $\mathbf{I}(\theta)$, drawn the signal y, and borne the cost. With c, $\tilde{c}$, $\tilde{\theta}(\tilde{c})$, and θ fixed, the informant's only remaining decision is to choose the optimal communication $\tilde{y}^*$.

In general, the relevant expectation is with respect to the conditional density $p(x \mid \tilde{y}, y;\ \tilde{\theta}(\tilde{c}), \theta)$, but from the informant's viewpoint, the choice of $\tilde{y}$ has no bearing on his true beliefs about the distribution of the random state variable X:

$$p(x \mid \tilde{y}, y;\ \tilde{\theta}(\tilde{c}), \theta) \ = \ p(x \mid y;\ \theta). \tag{8.25}$$

Note that (8.25) is the garbling condition G_3 in Section 6.2.3.

The informant's current decision problem is

$$\max_{\tilde{y}} \int_X \omega(c,\ \tilde{c},\ \tilde{\theta}(\tilde{c}), \theta,\ \tilde{y}, x)\, dF(x \mid y;\ \theta)$$

$$= \int_X \omega(c,\ \tilde{c},\ \tilde{\theta}(\tilde{c}), \theta,\ \tilde{y}^*, x)\, dF(x \mid y;\ \theta). \tag{8.26}$$

It is assumed this solution $\tilde{y}^*$ is unique, so that the optimal communication is the deterministic function $\tilde{y}^* = \tilde{y}^*(y,\ \tilde{\theta}(\tilde{c}),\ \theta)$. Hence, the informant chooses the conditional density $p(\tilde{y} \mid y;\ \tilde{\theta}(\tilde{c}), \theta)$ to be degenerate, with $p(\tilde{y} \mid y;\ \tilde{\theta}(\tilde{c}), \theta) = 1$ when $\tilde{y} = \tilde{y}^*$ and $= 0$ otherwise.

The contract design intends to ensure the strictly proper reporting of beliefs: at Stage V, the informant, having drawn signal y, must obtain the highest expected profit by communicating this signal and no other, for every $y \in \mathbf{Y}$. Condition [SP] is

$$[SP]: \int_X \omega(c,\ \tilde{c},\ \tilde{\theta}(\tilde{c}), \theta, y, x)\, dF(x \mid y;\ \theta)$$

$$\geq \int_X \omega(c,\ \tilde{c},\ \tilde{\theta}(\tilde{c}), \theta,\ \tilde{y}, x)\, dF(x \mid y;\ \theta) \text{ for every } \tilde{y} \neq y \text{ and each } y \in \mathbf{Y}.$$

Lemma 1 states that a sufficient condition for the satisfaction of condition [SP] is that the informant produce the same information structure for which he contracts.

Lemma 1. If $\mathbf{I}(\theta) = \mathbf{I}(\tilde{\theta}(\tilde{c}))$, then $\tilde{y}^* = \tilde{y}^*(y,\ \tilde{\theta}(\tilde{c}),\ \tilde{\theta}(\tilde{c})) = y$.

Proof. Under the premise expected profits are

$$\int_X \omega(c,\ \tilde{c},\ \tilde{\theta}(\tilde{c}),\ \tilde{\theta}(\tilde{c}),\ \tilde{y}, x)\, dF(x \mid y;\ \tilde{\theta}(\tilde{c}))$$

$$= \ [\alpha(\tilde{c})]\left\{\int_X \upsilon(x,\ \tilde{y};\ \tilde{\theta}(\tilde{c}))\, dF(x \mid y;\ \tilde{\theta}(\tilde{c}))\right\} - ck(\tilde{\theta}(\tilde{c})) + s(\tilde{c}). \tag{8.27}$$

The only variable component in (8.27) is the ex-post value $\upsilon(x,\ \tilde{y};\ \tilde{\theta}(\tilde{c})) = \pi(x, a^*(\tilde{y},\ \tilde{\theta}(\tilde{c}))) - \pi(x, a_0)$, so the informant maximizes his expected profits by maximizing his expectation of the DM's payoff:

$$\max_{\tilde{y}} \int_X \pi(x, a^*(\tilde{y},\ \tilde{\theta}(\tilde{c})))\, dF(x \mid y;\ \tilde{\theta}(\tilde{c})).$$

Having drawn y, this expectation is maximized by inducing the DM to take $a^*(y,\ \tilde{\theta}(\tilde{c}))$, the action optimal for y.

When the informant has produced the same information structure he contracted for, there can be no expected gain from communicating any message other than $\tilde{y} = y$. The importance of this lemma is that if the DM initially designs the contract to induce the informant in Stage III to produce $\mathbf{I}(\theta) = \mathbf{I}(\tilde{\theta}(\tilde{c}))$, then she can be assured the contract leads the informant to reveal his true signals.

Returning now to the general case with arbitrary $\mathbf{I}(\theta)$ and $\mathbf{I}(\tilde{\theta})$, the informant's expectation of the ex-post value of the optimal message $\tilde{y}^*$ is, given y,

$$\int_X \upsilon(x, \tilde{y}^*(y, \tilde{\theta}, \theta); \tilde{\theta})\, dF(x \mid y; \theta)$$

$$= \int_X \{\pi(x, a^*(\tilde{y}^*(y, \tilde{\theta}, \theta), \tilde{\theta})) - \pi(x, a_0)\}\, dF(x \mid y; \theta). \quad (8.28)$$

Prior to drawing the signal y, at the beginning of Stage IV, the expectation of (8.28) with respect to the marginal density that generates the signals, $p(y; \theta)$, is

$$\int_Y \int_X \upsilon(x, \tilde{y}^*(y, \tilde{\theta}, \theta); \tilde{\theta})\, dF(x, y; \theta)$$

$$= \int_Y \int_X \{\pi(x, a^*(\tilde{y}^*(y, \tilde{\theta}, \theta), \tilde{\theta}))\} dF(x, y; \theta) - \int_X \pi(x, a_0)\, dF(x)$$

$$= \breve{V}(\tilde{\theta}, \theta), \quad (8.29)$$

using the law of iterated expectation (2.40). The quantity $\breve{V}(\tilde{\theta}, \theta)$ is the expected value of producing the information structure $\mathbf{I}(\theta)$ after having contracted to deliver the structure $\mathbf{I}(\tilde{\theta})$ for decision making.

In the important strictly proper case in which the informant produces the contractual structure so that $\theta = \tilde{\theta}$, the expected value of information is, using Lemma 1,

$$\breve{V}(\tilde{\theta}, \tilde{\theta}) = \int_Y \int_X \{\pi(x, a^*(\tilde{y}^*(y, \tilde{\theta}, \tilde{\theta}), \tilde{\theta}))\} dF(x, y; \tilde{\theta}) - \int_X \pi(x, a_0)\, dF(x)$$

$$= \int_Y \int_X \{\pi(x, a^*(y, \tilde{\theta}))\} dF(x, y; \tilde{\theta}) - \int_X \pi(x, a_0)\, dF(x)$$

$$= V(\tilde{\theta}). \quad (8.30)$$

The quantity $V(\tilde{\theta})$ is the traditional definition of the expected value of imperfect information when there is no concern for dishonesty in communication.

The continuity and differentiability assumptions on the payoff and density functions guarantee that $V(\tilde{\theta})$ is twice differentiable in $\tilde{\theta}$. In fact, nondecreasingness of the derivative $V_{\tilde{\theta}}(\tilde{\theta})$ is the technical test the ordering of the information structures must satisfy to meet Definition 1: when $\tilde{\theta}' > \tilde{\theta}$, then $V(\tilde{\theta}') \geq V(\tilde{\theta})$, and this is met when $V_{\tilde{\theta}}(\tilde{\theta}) \geq 0$ for every $\tilde{\theta} \in [0, \bar{\theta}]$.

The subsequent analysis relies upon differentiability of $\breve{V}(\tilde{\theta}, \theta)$ in both $\tilde{\theta}$ and θ. This requires the following additional assumption. Either the optimal communication function $\tilde{y}^* = \tilde{y}^*(y, \tilde{\theta}, \theta)$ is continuous and differentiable in

$\tilde{\theta}$ and θ, or it is not a function of $\tilde{\theta}$ and θ [i.e., $\tilde{y}^* = \tilde{y}^{**}(y)$].[3] This assumption facilitates the proofs of the following two lemmas. The proofs appear in Section 8.3.5.

Lemma 2. Let the production be fixed at $\mathbf{I}(\theta)$. Maximum information value occurs by contracting for $\tilde{\theta} = \theta$. That is, $\breve{V}(\theta, \theta) \geq \breve{V}(\tilde{\theta}, \theta)$, or

$$\partial \breve{V}(\tilde{\theta}, \theta)/\partial \tilde{\theta}\Big|_{\tilde{\theta}=\theta} = \breve{V}_{\tilde{\theta}}(\theta, \theta) = 0.$$

Lemma 3. Let the contractual structure be fixed at $\mathbf{I}(\tilde{\theta})$. Then

$$\partial \breve{V}(\tilde{\theta}, \theta)/\partial \theta\Big|_{\theta=\tilde{\theta}} = \partial V(\tilde{\theta})/\partial \tilde{\theta},$$

or, equivalently, $\breve{V}_{\theta}(\tilde{\theta}, \tilde{\theta}) = V_{\tilde{\theta}}(\tilde{\theta})$.

The next subsection develops the specifications for the optimal initial menu of contracts the DM offers in Stage 1. The preceding two lemmas are useful in proving that the optimal contract design keeps the informant honest.

8.3.2 The Optimal Contract Design

The regulated informant's expected profit from any policy of announcing, producing, and optimally communicating is

$$\breve{\omega}(c, \tilde{c}, \tilde{\theta}(\tilde{c}), \theta) = \int_Y \int_X \omega(c, \tilde{c}, \tilde{\theta}(\tilde{c}), \theta, \tilde{y}^*(y, \tilde{\theta}(\tilde{c}), \theta), x)\, dF(x, y; \theta)$$

$$= [\alpha(\tilde{c})][\breve{V}(\tilde{\theta}(\tilde{c}), \theta)] - ck(\theta) + s(\tilde{c}). \quad (8.31)$$

Using the revelation principle, a contract design that induces the informant to behave honestly at every opportunity must satisfy the following three classes of constraints:

[IP]: $\breve{\omega}(c, c, \tilde{\theta}(c), \tilde{\theta}(c)) \geq 0.$

[IC]: $\breve{\omega}(c, c, \tilde{\theta}(c), \tilde{\theta}(c)) \geq \breve{\omega}(c, \tilde{c}, \tilde{\theta}(\tilde{c}), \theta)$ for every $\tilde{c} \neq c$ and $\theta \neq \tilde{\theta}(\tilde{c})$.

[SP]: $\int_X \omega(c, \tilde{c}, \tilde{\theta}(\tilde{c}), \theta, y, x)\, dF(x \mid y; \theta)$

$\geq \int_X \omega(c, \tilde{c}, \tilde{\theta}(\tilde{c}), \theta, \tilde{y}, x)\, dF(x \mid y; \theta)$ for every $\tilde{y} \neq y$ and each $y \in \mathbf{Y}$.

The [IP] constraint is the individual participation or rationality constraint that guarantees nonnegative economic profit to the honest informant. The incentive

[3] The first example in Section 8.3.4 illustrates the former possibility; the second example illustrates the latter.

compatibility constraint [IC] requires that the informant's profit be higher under honesty than under any other strategy involving misstatement of c and/or production of any information structure other than $\mathbf{I}(\tilde{\theta}(c))$.

At Stage III, the type-c informant has announced $\tilde{c}$ but still must determine the optimal production θ^* and thereby fix the optimal communication strategy $\tilde{y}^*(y, \tilde{\theta}(\tilde{c}), \theta)$. Assuming (8.31) is well behaved, the optimal production is the function $\theta^* = \theta^*(c, \tilde{c})$ characterized in the first-order condition

$$d\breve{\omega}(c, \tilde{c}, \tilde{\theta}(\tilde{c}), \theta)/d\theta = [\alpha(\tilde{c})][\breve{V}_\theta(\tilde{\theta}(\tilde{c}), \theta^*(c, \tilde{c}))] - ck_\theta(\theta^*(c, \tilde{c})) = 0.$$

Lemma 1 states that if this optimal production solution equals the contractual informativeness $\tilde{\theta}(\tilde{c})$, then the [SP] constraints are met. This justifies replacing [SP] with the single equality constraint

$$[SP']: \quad \theta^* = \theta^*(c, \tilde{c}) = \tilde{\theta}(\tilde{c}).$$

Substituting this into the [IC] constraint yields

$$[IC']: \quad \breve{\omega}(c, c, \tilde{\theta}(c), \tilde{\theta}(c)) \geq \breve{\omega}(c, \tilde{c}, \tilde{\theta}(\tilde{c}), \tilde{\theta}(\tilde{c})) \quad \text{for every } \tilde{c} \neq c.$$

The subsequent analysis develops the optimal contract to satisfy the [IP] and [IC′] constraints. This solution must then be checked to ensure the three original constraints [IP], [IC], and [SP] are all met.

When $\theta^* = \tilde{\theta}(\tilde{c})$, (8.30) applies and the informant's profit function is

$$\hat{\omega}(c, \tilde{c}) = [\alpha(\tilde{c})][V(\tilde{\theta}(\tilde{c}))] - ck(\tilde{\theta}(\tilde{c})) + s(\tilde{c}). \tag{8.32}$$

Considering only incentive compatible contracts that induce the truthful announcement of c, when $\tilde{c} = c$,

$$\varpi(c) = [\alpha(c)][V(\tilde{\theta}(c))] - ck(\tilde{\theta}(c)) + s(c). \tag{8.33}$$

To ensure that c is reported honestly,

$$\varpi(c) = \max_{\tilde{c}} \hat{\omega}(c, \tilde{c}). \tag{8.34}$$

for all c in $[\underline{c}, \bar{c}]$. The [IP] constraint becomes

$$[IP']: \quad \varpi(c) \geq 0.$$

Lemma 4 is a standard result in the theory of incentive contracts.

Lemma 4. The necessary and sufficient conditions for the functions $\varpi(c)$ and $\tilde{\theta}(c)$ to be incentive compatible are

$$[IC'\text{-FOC}]: \varpi(c) = \int_c^{\bar{c}} k(\tilde{\theta}(t))\, dt,$$

and

[IC′-SOC]: $\tilde{\theta}_c(c) \leq 0.$

The value in [IC′-FOC] is the rent the DM gives up to the informant with efficiency c in order to achieve the truthful revelation of c. The condition [IC′-SOC] states that the more inefficient the informant claims to be [higher $\tilde{c}$], the lower the informativeness for which he will be allowed to contract. The proof of this lemma appears in the Section 8.3.5.

The DM's gain from using an honest type-c informant is, for the as yet unchosen functions $\tilde{\theta}(c)$, $\alpha(c)$, and $s(c)$,

$$\mathbf{G}(c) = [1 - \alpha(c)][V(\tilde{\theta}(c))] - s(c) = V(\tilde{\theta}(c)) - [\alpha(c)][V(\tilde{\theta}(c))] - s(c).$$

Prior to receiving any report from the informant, let the DM have prior beliefs about c embodied in a continuous and strictly positive density function $f(c) > 0$ for all c in $[\underline{c}, \bar{c}]$. This prior is assumed to be statistically independent of the trivariate density (8.20) and its factorizations. Under f(c), the DM's problem is

$$\max_{\alpha(\cdot), s(\cdot), \tilde{\theta}(\cdot)} E_c \mathbf{G}(c) = \int_{\underline{c}}^{\bar{c}} \{V(\tilde{\theta}(c)) - [\alpha(c)][V(\tilde{\theta}(c))] - s(c)\} f(c)\, dc,$$

subject to

[IP′]: $\varpi(c) \geq 0;$

[IC′-FOC]: $\varpi(c) = \int_c^{\bar{c}} k(\tilde{\theta}(t))\, dt;$

[IC′-SOC]: $\tilde{\theta}_c(c) \leq 0.$

In addition, it must be shown that at the optimal design the constraint [SP′], $\theta^* = \tilde{\theta}(\tilde{c})$, holds in the informant's decision making.

With the informant's profit as given in (8.33), the DM's gain is

$$\mathbf{G}(c) = V(\tilde{\theta}(c)) - ck(\tilde{\theta}(c)) - \varpi(c). \quad (8.35)$$

Out of the total value expected to be produced, the DM's gain is the residual after covering the cost of the informant's inquiry and giving up the rent necessary to ensure the truthful revelation of c. Substituting the [IC′-FOC] constraint into (8.35), the expected information gain is

$$E_c \mathbf{G}(c) = \int_{\underline{c}}^{\bar{c}} \{V(\tilde{\theta}(c)) - ck(\tilde{\theta}(c)) - \int_c^{\bar{c}} k(\tilde{\theta}(t))\, dt\} f(c)\, dc. \quad (8.36)$$

Ignoring the [IC′-SOC] constraint for now, writing F(c) for the cumulative distribution function, defining $h(c) \equiv F(c)/f(c)$ as the hazard rate of the distribution of the efficiency parameter, and integrating (8.36) by parts, the DM's problem becomes

$$\max_{\tilde{\theta}(\cdot)} E_c \mathbf{G}(c) = \int_{\underline{c}}^{\bar{c}} \{V(\tilde{\theta}(c)) - [c + h(c)]\, k(\tilde{\theta}(c))\}\, f(c)\, dc. \quad (8.37)$$

The solution to this problem for each c yields the optimal regulation function $\tilde{\theta}^*(c)$, providing that it satisfies the remaining incentive compatibility requirement $\tilde{\theta}_c^*(c) \le 0$.

The first-order condition, identifying $\tilde{\theta}^* = \tilde{\theta}^*(c)$, is that marginal revenue equal marginal cost:

$$V_{\tilde{\theta}}(\tilde{\theta}^*(c)) - [c + h(c)]\; k_{\tilde{\theta}}(\tilde{\theta}^*(c)) = 0. \quad (8.38)$$

The second-order condition is that marginal cost must increase faster than marginal revenue:

$$V_{\tilde{\theta}\tilde{\theta}}(\tilde{\theta}^*(c)) < [c + h(c)]\; k_{\tilde{\theta}\tilde{\theta}}(\tilde{\theta}^*(c)). \quad (8.39)$$

This condition is important in this model because, depending upon the specifics of the problem and the technical nature of the ordering on the information structures via θ, the function $V(\tilde{\theta})$ may very well be convex in $\tilde{\theta}$.

Differentiating (8.38) to see if $\tilde{\theta}^*(c)$ satisfies the [IC′-SOC] constraint,

$$\tilde{\theta}_c^*(c) = \frac{[1+h_c(c)]k_{\tilde{\theta}}(\tilde{\theta}^*(c))}{V_{\tilde{\theta}\tilde{\theta}}(\tilde{\theta}^*(c)) - [c+h(c)]k_{\tilde{\theta}\tilde{\theta}}(\tilde{\theta}^*(c))}.$$

The denominator is negative at the optimum by the second-order condition (8.39). The numerator is nonnegative as long as $h_c(c) \ge -1$, making $\tilde{\theta}_c^*(c) \le 0$.

In addition, the optimal function $\tilde{\theta}^*(c)$ characterized in (8.38) may have corner solutions:

a) shut down: $\tilde{\theta}^*(c) = 0$ for $c > \bar{c}'$, where $\bar{c}'$ solves $\tilde{\theta}^*(\bar{c}') = 0$;

b) maximum informativeness: $\tilde{\theta}^*(c) = \bar{\theta}$ for $c < \underline{c}'$, where $\underline{c}'$ solves $\tilde{\theta}^*(\underline{c}') = \bar{\theta}$.

Both of these conditions make use of the monotonicity of $\tilde{\theta}^*(c)$.

8.3.3 Implementation

The following contract implements the optimal regulation function $\tilde{\theta}^*(\bullet)$ and keeps the informant honest.

$$\alpha^*(\tilde{c}) = \tilde{c}[\tilde{c} + h(\tilde{c})]^{-1}; \quad (8.40)$$

$$s^*(\tilde{c}) = -[\alpha^*(\tilde{c})][V(\tilde{\theta}^*(\tilde{c}))] + \tilde{c}k(\tilde{\theta}^*(\tilde{c})) + \int_{\tilde{c}}^{\bar{c}} k(\tilde{\theta}^*(t))\, dt. \quad (8.41)$$

Note that the share depends only on the announced efficiency $\tilde{c}$ and the hazard rate of the DM's prior probability distribution on c. If c is known with certainty,

$h(\tilde{c}) = 0$ and $\alpha^*(\tilde{c}) = 1$; the DM sells the decision to the informant. The fixed fee is set to ensure the honest informant's expected profits (8.33) are as required by [IC′-FOC].

**Proof.* Facing the menu in Stage II, but not having made any announcements or decisions, the informant's expected profits are

$$\breve{\omega}(c, \tilde{c}, \tilde{\theta}^*(\tilde{c}), \theta) = [\alpha^*(\tilde{c})][\breve{V}(\tilde{\theta}^*(\tilde{c}), \theta)] - ck(\theta)$$
$$- [\alpha^*(\tilde{c})][V(\tilde{\theta}^*(\tilde{c}))] + \tilde{c}k(\tilde{\theta}^*(\tilde{c})) + \int_{\tilde{c}}^{\bar{c}} k(\tilde{\theta}^*(t))\, dt,$$

with the decision variables $\tilde{c}$ and θ. The first-order conditions are

$$\breve{\omega}_\theta(c, \tilde{c}, \tilde{\theta}^*(\tilde{c}), \theta) = [\alpha^*(\tilde{c})][\breve{V}_\theta(\tilde{\theta}^*(\tilde{c}), \theta)] - ck_\theta(\theta)$$
$$= \breve{V}_\theta(\tilde{\theta}^*(\tilde{c}), \theta) - [c/\tilde{c}][\tilde{c} + h(\tilde{c})]\, k_\theta(\theta) = 0, \qquad (8.42)$$

using (8.40), and

$$\breve{\omega}_{\tilde{c}}(c, \tilde{c}, \tilde{\theta}^*(\tilde{c}), \theta) = [\alpha^*(\tilde{c})][\breve{V}_{\tilde{c}}(\tilde{\theta}^*(\tilde{c}), \theta)] + [\alpha^*_{\tilde{c}}(\tilde{c})][\breve{V}(\tilde{\theta}^*(\tilde{c}), \theta)]$$
$$- [\alpha^*(\tilde{c})][V_{\tilde{c}}(\tilde{\theta}^*(\tilde{c}))] - [\alpha^*_{\tilde{c}}(\tilde{c})][V(\tilde{\theta}^*(\tilde{c}))]$$
$$+ \tilde{c}k_{\tilde{c}}(\tilde{\theta}^*(\tilde{c})) + k(\tilde{\theta}^*(\tilde{c})) - k(\tilde{\theta}^*(\tilde{c})) = 0. \qquad (8.43)$$

Evaluating using the chain rule, substituting from (8.40), and rearranging yields

$$\breve{\omega}_{\tilde{c}}(c, \tilde{c}, \tilde{\theta}^*(\tilde{c}), \theta) = [\alpha^*(\tilde{c})][\breve{V}_{\tilde{\theta}}(\tilde{\theta}^*(\tilde{c}), \theta)][\tilde{\theta}^*_{\tilde{c}}(\tilde{c})]$$
$$+ [\alpha^*_{\tilde{c}}(\tilde{c})][\breve{V}(\tilde{\theta}^*(\tilde{c}), \theta) - V(\tilde{\theta}^*(\tilde{c}))]$$
$$- [\alpha^*(\tilde{c})][\tilde{\theta}^*_{\tilde{c}}(\tilde{c})]\{ V_{\tilde{\theta}}(\tilde{\theta}^*(\tilde{c})) - [\tilde{c} + h(\tilde{c})]\, k_{\tilde{\theta}}(\tilde{\theta}^*(\tilde{c}))\} = 0.$$

The first two terms vanish when production is fixed at $\theta = \tilde{\theta}^*(\tilde{c})$. The first term is zero because $V_{\tilde{\theta}}(\tilde{\theta}^*(\tilde{c}), \tilde{\theta}^*(\tilde{c})) = 0$ by Lemma 2. The second term is identically zero because $\breve{V}(\tilde{\theta}^*(\tilde{c}), \tilde{\theta}^*(\tilde{c})) = V(\tilde{\theta}^*(\tilde{c}))$, as in (8.30). The third term is zero because it is a multiple of the vanishing first-order condition (8.38) that defines $\tilde{\theta}^*(\bullet)$ for any c, including $\tilde{c}$. This establishes that the contract satisfies the condition [SP′]; hence it is strictly proper and the constraint [SP] is met.

Substituting $\tilde{\theta}^*(\tilde{c})$ for θ in the remaining first-order condition (8.42), the quantity

$$\breve{V}_\theta(\tilde{\theta}^*(\tilde{c}), \tilde{\theta}^*(\tilde{c})) - [c/\tilde{c}][\tilde{c} + h(\tilde{c})]\, k_\theta(\tilde{\theta}^*(\tilde{c}))$$

vanishes when $\tilde{c} = c$, since, using Lemma 3 and the fact that $k_\theta(\bullet) = k_{\tilde{\theta}}(\bullet)$, it again becomes the DM's first-order condition (8.38) that fixes the optimal function $\tilde{\theta}^*(\bullet)$.

Finally, Lemma 1 ensures that the informant will communicate the signal he draws. Hence, at Stage II the profit-maximizing informant facing these opportunities will announce $\tilde{c} = c$, will produce the same informativeness as contracted: $\theta^* = \tilde{\theta}^*(c)$, and will transmit $\tilde{y} = y$.

8.3.4 Examples

This section briefly presents some examples. The first studies the optimal procurement of an economic forecaster when the forecast message and the state realization are distributed bivariate normal and the DM's payoff is quadratic in the action, and the second considers the acquisition of an informant in a binary decision problem with two states and two messages.

♦ *Example 8.3a Procuring a Forecaster*

Suppose the random variable X is on the real line and any signal y is a point forecast of X such that the joint density of the state and the forecast is distributed bivariate standard normal. A Blackwell-indexing in this case is $\theta = \rho^2$, the square of the correlation coefficient between the two. If the informant produces $\mathbf{I}(\theta)$ then the joint density of the state and any forecast signal y is given as

$$p(x, y; \theta) \sim \mathbf{BN}(\bar{x} = 0,\ \sigma_x^2 = 1;\ \bar{y} = 0,\ \sigma_y^2 = 1; \theta = \rho^2),$$

and the posterior density of the state conditional on y is

$$p(x \mid y; \theta) \sim \mathbf{N}(\bar{x}_{y;\theta} = y\theta^{\frac{1}{2}}, \sigma^2_{x|y;\theta} = 1 - \theta; \theta = \rho^2).$$

The DM faces a decision problem with payoff

$$\pi(x, a) = ax - \tfrac{1}{2}a^2,$$

a payoff function that is continuous in both x and a. The optimal prior decision is $a_0 = 0$, yielding expected payoff $E_x\ \pi(x, a_0) = 0$.

To design the contract to hire this forecaster, the DM must obtain $\tilde{\theta}^*(\tilde{c})$, the optimal regulation function that determines the information structure she insists the informant contract for as a function of the revealed efficiency $\tilde{c}$. To do so using (8.38), the DM first ascertains the information value function $\breve{V}(\tilde{\theta}, \theta)$ and its honest variant $V(\tilde{\theta})$.

Taking any communication (point forecast) $\tilde{y}$ at face value, the DM's conditional expected payoff $a\bar{x}_{\tilde{y};\tilde{\theta}} - \frac{1}{2}a^2$ is maximized at

$$a^*(\tilde{y}, \tilde{\theta}) = \bar{x}_{\tilde{y};\tilde{\theta}} = \tilde{y}\tilde{\theta}^{\frac{1}{2}}.$$

Hence, the ex-post value of the message is

$$\upsilon(x, \tilde{y}; \tilde{\theta}) = \pi(x, a^*(\tilde{y}, \tilde{\theta})) - \pi(x, a_0) = x\tilde{y}\tilde{\theta}^{\frac{1}{2}} - \tfrac{1}{2}\tilde{y}^2\tilde{\theta}.$$

Since he knows both y and θ, the informant's expectation of the DM's payoff is

$$\int_X \pi(x, a^*(\tilde{y}, \tilde{\theta}))\, dF(x \mid y; \theta) = y\tilde{y}\theta^{\frac{1}{2}}\tilde{\theta}^{\frac{1}{2}} - \tfrac{1}{2}\tilde{y}^2\tilde{\theta}. \qquad (8.44)$$

The message $\tilde{y}^*$ that maximizes (8.44) is

$$\tilde{y}^*(y, \tilde{\theta}, \theta) = y\theta^{\frac{1}{2}}\tilde{\theta}^{-\frac{1}{2}},$$

meaning that the DM takes the optimal action

$$a^*(\tilde{y}^*(y, \tilde{\theta}, \theta), \tilde{\theta}) = y\theta^{\frac{1}{2}}.$$

Thus, under this strategy of deception, the informant is always able to trick the DM into taking the action optimal under the informant's true belief. This yields the information value function

$$\breve{V}(\tilde{\theta}, \theta) = \int_Y \int_X \upsilon(x, \tilde{y}^*(y, \tilde{\theta}, \theta); \tilde{\theta})\, dF(x, y; \theta) = \tfrac{1}{2}\theta; \qquad (8.45)$$

it is proportional to the true squared correlation coefficient between the state and the forecast signal.

To model the cost of producing $\mathbf{I}(\theta)$, consider the following information production function:

$$\theta = 1 - \exp\{-\phi\varepsilon\},$$

where ε is the informant's effort and ϕ is an index of technological efficiency such that $\partial\theta/\partial\phi = [\varepsilon]\exp\{-\phi\varepsilon\} > 0$. An informant with larger ϕ can provide greater θ for the same effort ε. The inverse function is

$$\varepsilon = -\frac{1}{\phi}\log[1 - \theta].$$

Suppose the cost equation is $\mathcal{C} = \gamma\varepsilon$, where γ is the accounting cost per unit of effort. The cost function is then

$$\mathbf{C}(\theta) = -c\log[1 - \theta] = ck(\theta),$$

where $c \equiv \gamma/\phi$. The higher is c the less efficient is the informant via some combination of the economic cost of performing a given effort and the technological ability to transform effort into informativeness.[4] Under this cost function, with c > 0 it is infinitely costly to produce perfect information, that is, $\bar{\theta} = 1$.

---

[4] The contract design intends to prevent the following types of statements from the informant, unless they are true. "This will be a very difficult project for us to undertake (translation: ε will be high), and it will require us to put our best people on it (translation: γ will be high). Therefore, our fee must be high." In fact, the informant

The DM must provide the density f(c) and assess the corresponding hazard rate function h(c). The optimal share is $\alpha^*(c) = c[c + h(c)]^{-1}$. Since the honest variant of (8.45), $V(\tilde{\theta}) = \frac{1}{2}\tilde{\theta}$ is continuous in $\tilde{\theta}$, the first-order condition (8.38) applies and determines the optimal regulation function as the solution to

$$V_{\tilde{\theta}}(\tilde{\theta}) - [c + h(c)]\ k_{\tilde{\theta}}(\tilde{\theta}) \ = \ \tfrac{1}{2} - [c + h(c)][1 - \theta]^{-1} \ = \ 0,$$

which is $\tilde{\theta}^*(c) = 1 - 2[c + h(c)]$ as long as $[c + h(c)] < \frac{1}{2}$. The second-order condition (8.39) holds, and differentiating $\tilde{\theta}^*(c)$ with respect to c gives $\tilde{\theta}_c(c) = -2[1 + h_c(c)]$, so the solution satisfies the incentive compatibility constraint [IC′-SOC] as long as $h_c(c) \geq -1$.

Consider the case in which the prior distribution of c is uniform with density function $f(c) = [\bar{c} - \underline{c}]^{-1}$. Then in this case the hazard rate is $h(c) = c - \underline{c}$ and the optimal regulation function is $\tilde{\theta}^*(c) = 1 - 4c + 2\underline{c}$ for $c \leq \frac{1}{4} + \frac{1}{2}\underline{c}$ and $\tilde{\theta}^*(c) = 0$ for larger values of c. The optimal share is $\alpha^*(c) = c[2c - \underline{c}]^{-1}$. Constraining $\bar{c} \leq \frac{1}{4} + \frac{1}{2}\underline{c}$ to avoid the complication of the corner solution, the fixed payment is, after performing the integration required in (8.41),

$$s^*(c) \ = \ -c[1 - 4c + 2\underline{c}][4c - 2\underline{c}]^{-1} - c - \tfrac{1}{2}\underline{c}\log[4c - 2\underline{c}] + \varphi(\underline{c}, \bar{c}),$$

where $\varphi(\underline{c}, \bar{c}) = \bar{c} - [\bar{c} - \frac{1}{2}\underline{c}]\log[4\bar{c} - 2\underline{c}]$.

Replacing the c in $\tilde{\theta}^*(c)$, $\alpha^*(c)$, and $s^*(c)$ with $\tilde{c}$ and offering the three functions to the informant as a contract offer, the type-c informant's profit function is

$$\breve{\omega}(c, \tilde{c}, \tilde{\theta}^*(\tilde{c}), \theta) \ = \ \tilde{c}[2\tilde{c} - \underline{c}]^{-1}[\tfrac{1}{2}\theta] + c\log[1 - \theta]$$
$$- \ \tilde{c}[1 - 4\tilde{c} + 2\underline{c}][4\tilde{c} - 2\underline{c}]^{-1} - \tilde{c} - \tfrac{1}{2}\underline{c}\log[4\tilde{c} - 2\underline{c}] + \varphi(\underline{c}, \bar{c}).$$

Differentiation shows the informant desires to produce $\theta^* = 1 - 4\tilde{c} + 2\underline{c}$ and announce $\tilde{c} = c$.

If $\bar{c} = .26$ and $\underline{c} = .02$, then the DM's expected gain from the procurement is, in the format of (8.37),

$$E_c\,\mathbf{G}(c) \ = \ \int_{.02}^{.26} \{.52 - 2c + [2c - .02]\log[4c - .04]\}\frac{1}{.24}\,dc \ = \ .11134.$$

Table 8.1. The Optimal Distribution of Information Value when c = .05

Gross Information Value	.4200
DM's Information Gain	.1917
Payment to Informant	.2283
Cost of Inquiry	.0916
Profit to Informant	.1367

could be merely repackaging a previous study; selling the same thing many times is an old trick that earns healthy rent in the consulting business.

The informant with $c = .05$ accepts a contract with $\alpha^* = .625$, $s^* = -.03417$, and $\tilde{\theta}^* = .84 = \theta^*$. Table 8.1 presents the expected distribution of the total information value under this agreement. ♦

♦ *Example 8.3b Procurement in a Binary Problem*
Consider a binary decision problem with two states $\mathbf{X} = \{x_1, x_2\}$ and two signals $\mathbf{Y} = \{y_1, y_2\}$. The joint density of the states and signals is

$$\rho(\theta) = \begin{bmatrix} p(x_1, y_1; \theta) & p(x_1, y_2; \theta) \\ p(x_2, y_1; \theta) & p(x_2, y_2; \theta) \end{bmatrix} = \begin{bmatrix} \frac{1}{4}[1+\theta] & \frac{1}{4}[1-\theta] \\ \frac{1}{4}[1-\theta] & \frac{1}{4}[1+\theta] \end{bmatrix},$$

where $\theta \in [0, 1]$ is a Blackwell-indexing, $p(x_1) = p(x_2) = \frac{1}{2}$, and $p(y_1; \theta) = p(y_2; \theta) = \frac{1}{2}$.

Suppose the DM's payoff is $\pi(x_1, a) = \frac{1}{2} + 2a - a^2$ and $\pi(x_2, a) = \frac{3}{2} - a^2$, so under the equiprobable prior distribution, $a_0 = \frac{1}{2}$ and $E_x\, \pi(x, a_0) = \frac{5}{4}$. If the contract calls for the information structure $\mathbf{I}(\tilde{\theta})$, then $a^*(\tilde{y}_1, \tilde{\theta}) = \frac{1}{2}[1 + \tilde{\theta}]$, $a^*(\tilde{y}_2, \tilde{\theta}) = \frac{1}{2}[1 - \tilde{\theta}]$, and the ex-post value of each state–message combination is:

$$\upsilon(x_1, \tilde{y}_1; \tilde{\theta}) = \upsilon(x_2, \tilde{y}_2; \tilde{\theta}) = \tfrac{1}{4}[2\tilde{\theta} - \tilde{\theta}^2];$$

$$\upsilon(x_1, \tilde{y}_2; \tilde{\theta}) = \upsilon(x_2, \tilde{y}_1; \tilde{\theta}) = \tfrac{1}{4}[-2\tilde{\theta} - \tilde{\theta}^2].$$

It is straightforward to show that the optimal communication strategy for the informant who has produced $\mathbf{I}(\theta)$ and drawn y is independent of θ and $\tilde{\theta}$: $\tilde{y}^*(y_1, \tilde{\theta}, \theta) = y_1$ and $\tilde{y}^*(y_2, \tilde{\theta}, \theta) = y_2$. The expected value of information is

$$\breve{V}(\tilde{\theta}, \theta) = \tfrac{1}{4}[2\tilde{\theta}\theta - \tilde{\theta}^2].$$

To develop a specific contract, suppose $\mathbf{C}(\theta) = ck(\theta) = c\theta^3$, $c \in [\frac{1}{6}, \frac{1}{2}]$, and $f(c) = [\frac{1}{2} - \frac{1}{6}]^{-1} = 3$. Then the following contract is optimal. $\alpha^*(c) = 6c[12c - 1]^{-1}$, $s^*(c) = -\frac{1}{2}c[12c - 1]^{-3} + \frac{1}{24}[12c - 1]^{-2} - \frac{1}{600}$, and $\tilde{\theta}^*(c) = [12c - 1]^{-1}$. Under this contract, the DM's expected gain is

$$E_c\, \mathbf{G}(c) = \int_{\frac{1}{6}}^{\frac{1}{2}} \{\tfrac{1}{4}[12c - 1]^{-2} - [2c - \tfrac{1}{6}][12c - 1]^{-3}\} 3\, dc = \tfrac{1}{60}. \quad (8.46)$$

To compare this result with a contract that does not have the self-selection feature, suppose the DM does not care about rent extraction and simply announces that the two compensation parameters are $\hat{\alpha}$ and $\hat{s}$, allowing the informant to respond with the $\tilde{\theta}$ he will deliver. With the compensation parameters exogenous to the informant, Lemma 2 implies that the informant's profits are maximized by announcing the same $\tilde{\theta}$ he intends to produce; there is no incentive for any discrepancy between $\tilde{\theta}$ and θ. Informant c $[\geq \frac{1}{6}]$ has profits under this offer of $\frac{1}{4}\hat{\alpha}\theta^2 - c\theta^3 + \hat{s}$, and desires to produce $\theta^* = \frac{1}{6}\hat{\alpha}c^{-1}$. Informant c's optimal profits are $\frac{1}{432}\hat{\alpha}^3 c^{-2} + \hat{s}$, and to tax this away from the least efficient type $[c = \frac{1}{2}]$, the DM chooses $\hat{s}^* = -\frac{1}{108}\hat{\alpha}^3$. The DM chooses $\hat{\alpha}^*$ to maximize her expected gain, which is

$$E_c\,\mathbf{G}(c) = \int_{\frac{1}{6}}^{\frac{1}{2}} \{\tfrac{1}{144}[1 - \hat{\alpha}][\hat{\alpha}c^{-1}]^2 + [\tfrac{1}{108}\hat{\alpha}^3]\}3\,dc.$$

The solution is $\hat{\alpha}^* = \frac{3}{4}$, giving $\hat{s}^* = -\frac{1}{256}$, and evaluating the DM's expected gain at this optimum yields

$$E_c\,\mathbf{G}(\hat{\alpha}^*, \hat{s}^*) = \tfrac{1}{64}. \tag{8.47}$$

Comparing (8.46) with (8.47), the gain from the self-selection feature is $6\frac{2}{3}\%$.♦

*8.3.5 *Proofs of Lemmas 2, 3, and 4*

This subsection presents the proofs for the main results stated in this section.

Proof of Lemma 2, $\breve{V}_{\tilde{\theta}}(\theta, \theta) = 0$. The first derivative of $\breve{V}(\tilde{\theta}, \theta)$ in (8.29) with respect to $\tilde{\theta}$ is

$$\breve{V}_{\tilde{\theta}}(\tilde{\theta}, \theta) = \int_Y \int_X \{\pi_{\tilde{\theta}}(x, a^*(\tilde{y}^*(y, \tilde{\theta}, \theta), \tilde{\theta}))\}dF(x, y; \tilde{\theta})$$

$$= \int_Y \int_X \{[\pi_a(x, a^*(\tilde{y}^*(y, \tilde{\theta}, \theta), \tilde{\theta}))][\alpha^*_{\tilde{\theta}}(\tilde{y}^*(y, \tilde{\theta}, \theta), \tilde{\theta})]\}dF(x, y; \tilde{\theta}).$$

Evaluated at $\tilde{\theta} = \theta$, Lemma 1 ensures that $\tilde{y}^*(y, \theta, \theta) = y$, so

$$\breve{V}_{\tilde{\theta}}(\theta, \theta) = \int_Y \int_X \{[\pi_a(x, a^*(y, \theta))][\alpha^*_{\tilde{\theta}}(y, \theta)]\}dF(x, y; \theta) = 0$$

since, as in (8.22),

$$\int_X \pi_a(x, a^*(y, \theta))\, dF(x \mid y; \theta) = 0$$

by the definition of $a^*(y, \theta)$.

Proof of Lemma 3, $\breve{V}_\theta(\tilde{\theta}, \tilde{\theta}) = V_{\tilde{\theta}}(\tilde{\theta})$. The first derivative of $V(\tilde{\theta})$ in (8.30) is

$$V_{\tilde{\theta}}(\tilde{\theta}) = \int_Y \int_X \pi_{\tilde{\theta}}(x, a^*(y, \tilde{\theta}))\, dF(x, y; \tilde{\theta}) + \pi(x, a^*(y, \tilde{\theta}))\, dF_{\tilde{\theta}}(x, y; \tilde{\theta})$$

$$= \int_Y \int_X [\pi_a(x, a^*(y, \tilde{\theta}))][\alpha^*_{\tilde{\theta}}(y, \tilde{\theta})]\, dF(x, y; \tilde{\theta})$$

$$+ \pi(x, a^*(y, \tilde{\theta}))\, dF_{\tilde{\theta}}(x, y; \tilde{\theta}). \tag{8.48}$$

Next, the first partial derivative of $\breve{V}(\tilde{\theta}, \theta)$ in (8.29) with respect to θ is

$$\breve{V}_\theta(\tilde{\theta}, \theta) = \int_Y \int_X \pi_\theta(x, a^*(\tilde{y}^*(y, \tilde{\theta}, \theta), \tilde{\theta}))\, dF(x, y; \theta)$$

$$+ \pi(x, a^*(\tilde{y}^*(y, \tilde{\theta}, \theta), \tilde{\theta}))\, dF_\theta(x, y; \theta)$$

$$= \int_Y \int_X [\pi_a(x, a^*(\tilde{y}^*(y, \tilde{\theta}, \theta), \tilde{\theta}))][\alpha_\theta^*(\tilde{y}^*(y, \tilde{\theta}, \theta), \tilde{\theta})]\, dF(x, y; \theta)$$

$$+ \pi(x, a^*(\tilde{y}^*(y, \tilde{\theta}, \theta), \tilde{\theta}))\, dF_\theta(x, y; \theta).$$

Evaluating this at $\theta = \tilde{\theta}$ and using Lemma 1,

$$\breve{V}_\theta(\tilde{\theta}, \tilde{\theta}) = \int_Y \int_X [\pi_a(x, a^*(y, \tilde{\theta}))][\alpha_\theta^*(y, \tilde{\theta})]\, dF(x, y; \tilde{\theta})$$

$$+ \pi(x, a^*(y, \tilde{\theta}))\, dF_\theta(x, y; \tilde{\theta}).$$

This is identical to (8.48) since $\alpha_\theta^*(\bullet) = \alpha_{\tilde{\theta}}^*(\bullet)$ and $F_\theta(\bullet) = F_{\tilde{\theta}}(\bullet)$.

Proof of Lemma 4, necessity. The proof of this result follows closely the approach of Baron and Myerson (1982, Section 3). Equation (8.33) gives the informant's expected profit when his true efficiency is c, but if it is actually $\tilde{c} > c$, then

$$\varpi(\tilde{c}) = [\alpha(\tilde{c})][V(\tilde{\theta}(\tilde{c}))] - \tilde{c}k(\tilde{\theta}(\tilde{c})) + s(\tilde{c}). \tag{8.49}$$

Using (8.32), (8.33), and (8.49), to ensure incentive compatibility (8.34),

$$\varpi(c) \geq \hat{\omega}(c, \tilde{c}) = \varpi(\tilde{c}) + [\tilde{c} - c]k(\tilde{\theta}(\tilde{c})). \tag{8.50}$$

Also, interchanging the roles of c and $\tilde{c}$,

$$[\tilde{c} - c]k(\tilde{\theta}(c)) \geq \varpi(c) - \varpi(\tilde{c}) \geq [\tilde{c} - c]k(\tilde{\theta}(\tilde{c})). \tag{8.51}$$

Dividing both sides of (8.51) by $\tilde{c} - c \geq 0$ and taking the limit as $\tilde{c} \to c$,

$$\lim_{\tilde{c} \to c} \frac{\varpi(c) - \varpi(\tilde{c})}{\tilde{c} - c} = -\varpi'(c) = k(\tilde{\theta}(c)). \tag{8.52}$$

Integrating (8.52) between c and $\bar{c}$ and setting $\varpi(\bar{c}) = 0$ yields [IC′-FOC]. Equation (8.51) states that when $\tilde{c} > c$,

$$k(\tilde{\theta}(c)) \geq k(\tilde{\theta}(\tilde{c})), \tag{8.53}$$

and since $k_\theta(\theta) > 0$, this implies that the regulation function $\tilde{\theta}(c)$ must be continuous and nonincreasing in c, which is [IC′-SOC].

Proof of Lemma 4, sufficiency. Evaluating [IC′-FOC] at $\tilde{c}$ and substituting into (8.50),

$$\hat{\omega}(c, \tilde{c}) = \int_{\tilde{c}}^{\bar{c}} k(\tilde{\theta}(t))\, dt + [\tilde{c} - c]k(\tilde{\theta}(\tilde{c}))$$

$$= \int_c^{\bar{c}} k(\tilde{\theta}(t))\, dt - \int_c^{\tilde{c}} k(\tilde{\theta}(t))\, dt + [\tilde{c} - c]k(\tilde{\theta}(\tilde{c}))$$

$$= \varpi(c) - \int_{c}^{\tilde{c}} k(\tilde{\theta}(t))\, dt + [\tilde{c} - c]k(\tilde{\theta}(\tilde{c}))$$

$$= \varpi(c) - \int_{c}^{\tilde{c}} [k(\tilde{\theta}(t)) - k(\tilde{\theta}(\tilde{c}))]\, dt,$$

since $k(\tilde{\theta}(\tilde{c}))$ is a constant function. The integral is positive because of (8.53), ensuring $\varpi(c) \geq \hat{\omega}(c, \tilde{c})$.

The DM's ability to access an interpersonal external information source such as the informant is merely one component of the broad information system the DM's organization can provide. With decision makers and other users choosing sources and applying information more or less consistently with the normative prescriptions of this and previous chapters, the next chapter turns to the issues of system design and its impact upon information demand, procurement, and incorporation.

9 Economics of Valuable Information Systems

Having completed the presentation of the normative theory of information valuation and choice, this final chapter investigates the feasibility of applying it to the user-oriented design and evaluation of an organization's information system. This broader viewpoint requires aggregation from the level of the individual DM to the collective whole, and raises a host of new issues regarding the sociology, politics, and psychology of information use within the environment of an organization. Fundamentally, this requires us to question the extent to which normatively optimal behavior is actually observed, and whether managerial initiatives to affect both system design and the broader organizational culture can cause behavior changes in directions that are consistent with economic theory. The first three sections of this chapter concern essentially empirical issues involving the information use environment, the activities of the system, and people's ability to assess value and respond to system incentives and other situation-specific conditions. In general, experimental results indicate that behavior is qualitatively consistent with decision theory, but with room for improvement. The fourth section presents an aggregative model to explain how the information system that maximizes the organization's expected information gain is determined by the interaction of the nature of the decision problems the users face, the behavior of the users, the incentives the design of the system gives to those users, and the investments the organization makes.

9.1 Information Use Environments

The introduction in Section 1.6.2 describes the information use environment as the fundamental building block for information system design. In Taylor's (1986; 1991) conceptualization, an understanding of the information use environment requires an identification and classification of the potential users and the types of decision problems they face, along with an analysis of the social, cultural, and political milieu within the organization. Since the value and gain from information are highly dependent upon the characteristics of the decision maker and her specific decision problem, user surveys are a natural and fruitful technique for developing this understanding. The first purpose of a user study is to determine the nexus between the users' information needs and the decision problems they face. Then, by examining the characteristics of the sources the users choose to access, the organization learns the kinds of activities and enhancements the system can provide to facilitate information gain. This section reviews empirical evidence from information use studies of decision making in the business and scientific/technical domains.

9.1.1 Business Environments

User studies of business environments tend to focus on the needs and behavior of executive managers. Chapter 5 presents numerous examples of the decision problems managers face and the resulting information needs; common decisions regard personnel, purchasing, production, inventory, pricing, and marketing efforts. Managers also need to plan, and have a need to scan a wide variety of events external to the organization both for decision making and monitoring purposes. The most common conclusion in user studies is that managers find interpersonal sources, particularly face-to-face meetings, to be among the most valuable. In a well-respected study, Grinyer and Norburn (1975) find that companies exhibiting more person-to-person communication tend to make more use of relevant information and ultimately exhibit better financial performance. Indeed, to the extent they can promote interpersonal communication, it is not unconventional to consider both the organization's hierarchical structure and the architectural arrangement of the physical space to be legitimate concerns for information system design.

McLeod and Jones (1986) analyze detailed logs of the information choice behavior of five senior executives over a two-week period. The logs report the accessing of a grand total of 1,454 sources, for an average of 29 per business day. Documents comprise 61% of the total, with letters and memos as the leading media, and 39% are interpersonal sources, primarily via telephone calls. For each source accessed, the subjects assess a value index from 0 to 10. It is unclear whether this is a preposterior, conditional, or ex-post assessment, but the discussion indicates it is a conditional one, assessed after obtaining the message and in anticipation of taking action in response. The most valued source is the scheduled meeting, followed in order by the unscheduled meeting, touring, and social meetings, all interpersonal sources. The memo from a subordinate is the most valuable written source. The executives report they receive many messages with little or no value.

Daft, Lengel, and Trevino (1989) investigate why managers prefer interpersonal sources for decision making. They argue that many decision problems in an organization are so unstructured, ambiguous, and poorly understood that significant effort is necessary for simply framing the issues. Pooling opinions and developing consensus ("shared meaning") is how problems get solved, and interpersonal give-and-take, rather than data gathering, is the way these ambiguous situations get resolved. Using a sample of 95 managers, they find evidence that supports the hypothesis that the more ambiguous the situation, the more that oral media are preferred to written.

The well-run meeting has many characteristics that contribute to information gain. Whether the purpose of the meeting is to make a decision or just to share information, people are generally well prepared and ready to explain the meaning and significance of events, judge each other's credibility and general informativeness, and receive situation reports and guidance. The advantages over email are the additional informativeness that comes from the verbal and nonverbal signals that only face-to-face communication can provide, along with the possibility of the increased frankness, organizational culture permitting, that can come from a lack of documentation.

Another important set of interpersonal sources is the *invisible college*, an informal network of friends, colleagues, and experts [Cronin (1982)]. Although it is difficult to isolate its contributions, the invisible college nevertheless comprises an oft-used set of information sources in many domains, as Baldwin and Rice (1997) discuss in their analysis of the information-seeking behavior of securities analysts.

McKinnon and Bruns (1992) perform detailed field-study interviews with 73 managers from 12 manufacturing corporations, emphasizing the routine needs for information and the sources chosen. Production and operations mangers, as "hands-on" decision makers, tend to focus on data producing sources that provide frequent physical counts: new orders, inventory levels, output and defective counts, and other data developed on the shop floor. Because of the need for timeliness, these data are often passed on to the manager verbally, before formal reports are even available. Managers in sales and marketing rely on interpersonal sources, especially ones external to the firm: the customer, of course, is a major information source, as are sources that can provide social information about customers, can generate names of potential customers, and can assist in the monitoring of competitors. Sales sees itself as the liaison between the customer and the rest of the company, and so needs an internal information system that can coordinate between customer information requests and the production, logistics, and billing functions, that is, that helps prevent the "run-around" that can lose a customer. McKinnon and Bruns find that DMs in operations, production, and sales have little immediate need for financial reports. Income and variance reports are valuable for assessing the effectiveness of decision rules and overall management performance, but they are not needed on a daily basis. Less frequent reporting of financial results allows day-to-day blips to be smoothed out, making it easier to spot trends.

There is quite a bit of research, much of it going under the name "environmental scanning," on the need for information about random variables external to the organization: matters in the political, economic, and sociocultural realms. One particularly important question is the extent to which the uncertainty, complexity, and ambiguity of the external environment are factors in information search and choice. There are two common empirical approaches: surveys that correlate individuals' perceptions of environmental uncertainty with observations on their information search, and laboratory studies that observe behavior changes under controlled circumstances. Culnan (1983) and Daft, Sormunen, and Parks (1988) are examples of the former methodology; Schroeder and Benbasat (1975) is an example of the latter.[1]

Sampling 362 professionals at the headquarters of two corporations, Culnan (1983) correlates the frequency of choice among nine information sources of all types with perceptions on the accessibility of each source and an index of each subject's perception of how complex her job environment is. Frequency of source choice is significantly positively correlated with source accessibility, as economic theory would suggest. Frequency of source use is also positively correlated with environmental complexity, but the importance of this effect seems secondary.

Daft, Sormunen, and Parks (1988) present a model of the external information use environment of a strategically oriented chief executive officer, and apply it to compare information use and financial performance in a sample of 50 single-business manufacturing firms. In personal interviews, either the CEO or another high officer describes the information use environment and reveals the frequency of choice of various information sources. The authors build an index of strategic uncertainty for each executive's environment, and find that it is significantly positively correlated with frequency of information use. Moreover, higher performing firms (as measured by return on assets) have higher correlations than lower performing ones, and show greater breadth and focus in their information use. Another supported hypothesis is that greater strategic uncertainty leads CEOs to make comparatively more frequent use of interpersonal sources over documents.

The computer simulation experiment of Schroeder and Benbasat (1975) illustrates why the relationship between environmental uncertainty and information

---

[1] As Section 6.3.4 shows, there is no general theoretical relationship between the uncertainty or volatility of the environment and the value of information. There are identifiable circumstances, however, in which greater uncertainty, in the sense of Rothschild–Stiglitz variability (see Section 6.3.2), is associated with greater information value.

demand may not be monotonic. The experiment presents 51 business students with a multiperiod inventory management problem in which each subject decides when and how much of a product to order. Each also has the option to purchase any number from among 76 different accounting reports containing data in various levels of detail. The criterion is to minimize total cost over a simulated 150-day period. The random state variable is the daily demand for the product, which for each subject can have low, medium, or high standard deviation. The average number of purchased reports is about 21 for the low variability environment, 24 for the medium, but only 17 for those facing the most variability. The explanation is similar to the discussion in Sections 1.4.5 and 6.3.4 When the environment is volatile, the DM may simply take a more conservative prior action: in the inventory problem, dealing with the uncertainty by holding larger stocks instead of purchasing information. It is interesting to note that the reports the high uncertainty group most commonly choose to access are the ones with high-detail, current information.

9.1.2 Scientific and Technical Environments

In an ideal user study for the purpose of a decision-theoretic evaluation of information, the basic unit of analysis would be a complete, well-defined decision problem. The survey would be a diary of the entire experience of incorporating information and solving the problem, from the decision to seek through the choice of action and ultimately to the final realization of the outcome. In practice, most surveys are much less ambitious. With that said, Allen's (1977) long-term examination of information use in a matched-case sample of complex R&D projects is a remarkable example of a user study.

Allen finds 17 instances in which the United States government awarded contracts to multiple competing organizations to solve the same R&D problem, and convinces 33 of the awardees to participate in a detailed case history of each team's problem solution. Government technical monitors then judge the relative quality of the alternative solutions, allowing Allen to separate the higher performing teams from the lower performing ones. The study then compares the information use behavior associated with more and less successful decision making results.

The projects are mostly associated with the space program of the 1960s, and the solution to each problem is generally some type of engineering design. The design reported to the government is the action chosen; this interacts with the random state variables to determine the performance of the design, which is the aspect the government technical experts judge. Presumably the basis for the design the team submits is a decision rule derived from the incorporation of all the messages processed over the course of the project.

The *solution development record* is the primary survey instrument for measuring the effect of any specific message on the solution of the problem. Given a specified action space, that is, a set of potential problem solutions, each week the subjects estimate the subjective probability that each available action will ultimately be chosen as the solution. If a new action is identified as a possibility, it is added to the action space. When one action achieves a probability of one and the research stops, the problem is solved. Each week, the subjects also identify the information sources chosen and accessed. Although a comparison of the sources processed and the changes in the probabilities of alternative actions does not measure the value of information in a strict sense, it does measure in a meaningful way the pragmatic impact of each message received in a complex, dynamic, and real situation.

A major conclusion of the study is the overwhelming importance of interpersonal sources, both internal and external to the team. Indeed, Allen (1977, page 121) states that a successful team cannot sustain itself without consistently importing new information from outside sources. When it does not, performance suffers, as Katz and Allen (1982) document in an analysis of the "not invented here" syndrome. Studying the communication patterns within the organization, Allen (1977) finds a small group of key people whom others often choose as information sources, the *technological gatekeepers*. These boundary spanning individuals are distinguished by the combination of extensive contacts outside the organization, vociferous reading, and great depth of understanding of the subject matter.

Turning now to some of the specific results, for the 17 projects there are 494 messages that are credited with producing new ideas, that is, new potential solutions to the problem. Of these, over 40% come from interpersonal sources other than government officials; the broadcast literature and internal company reports account for less than 20% of the total. The government, having an incentive to share ideas between the competitors, provides a little less than 30% of the idea-generating messages.

The higher performing teams tend to make less use of the literature and more use of internal communication than their lower performing counterparts. Concerning the time pattern of source choice, the use of the literature is most common in the first third of the project duration. Compared to the better performers, the lower rated teams tend to make relatively greater use of the literature and external interpersonal sources in the very early stages of the project, and relatively greater use of internal technical staff later in the project. Since Allen shows that accessibility is the most important determinant of the first choice of source, a poorer performer's initial choice of impersonal and external sources may reflect a psychological cost from not wanting to appear uninformed or naive in front of colleagues.

Along these lines, Dewhirst (1971) investigates what he calls the "information-sharing norms" of the organization as a cultural aspect of the information use environment. The use of interpersonal sources, shown time and again to be a most efficient means for DMs to obtain messages, may be impeded by the perception of a psychological cost to seeking information from colleagues. To the extent this perceived cost is part of the culture of the organization, it forces the access of more costly and perhaps less informative sources. The study asks 298 engineers and scientists about the source of their most recently obtained valuable information, and about their perception whether information-sharing norms within the organization are strong, moderate, or weak. The evidence indicates that weaker perceived sharing norms tend to push users from interpersonal sources to written ones.

Compared to businesspeople and engineers, scientists make greater use of archival sources, especially the formal literature. In an analysis of the use environment of a corporate research center, Mote (1962) finds that the information requirements of scientists, and hence their use of an information center, depends upon the extent to which the scientists are solving problems that require multidisciplinary approaches. The explanation is that when the subject matter is less well defined the literature is less well organized and the scientists are more likely to seek assistance from the information system.

Not all information use environments encompass decision making. In Machlup's (1962) classification, higher education offers an environment that instills intellectual knowledge; this is best viewed as primarily a monitoring activity. With no specific decision problems to anchor the information use environment, the techniques of decision theory are not well suited for understanding information subsystems that serve a primarily monitoring clientele, such as a university library. Such situations are better handled by other approaches [see Saracevic and Kantor (1997)].

9.1.3 User Assessment of Information Value

This subsection reviews some user studies that request dollar estimates of the value of information in a systemwide context. Care must be taken when interpreting reported value, as the experimental design can affect the meaning of the measured results. For example, if the survey questions are not clear, the respondent may report cost savings rather than information value. In addition, the point in time that the survey is administered has a bearing on the results. If the survey is given prior to cognition, the reported value could be an estimate of the preposterior expected value of the source. If it is given after cognition, the report could be a conditional measure of the expected value of the message, prior to the realization of the state. If sufficient time has elapsed for the state to be realized, the report could be an ex-post measure such as (1.1).

Griffiths and King (1993) consolidate the results from a series of surveys of the users of special libraries: document-providing subsystems of large organizations that primarily serve scientific and technical personnel. In the surveys, one complete use of the information system is the substantive reading of one document: in the language of this book, the user cognition of one message. For the last-read document, either a journal article, a book, or an unpublished report, the survey asks each respondent about the consequences of the reading and the costs of user processing in terms of time and money. The questions are asked posterior to user cognition, and hence posterior to the most recent use of the system. At the time of the survey, the user has already made an affirmative decision to seek information, identified and chosen an information source, and obtained, accepted, and processed the message. The survey asks for the user's estimate of the value of the document's information, which Griffiths and King call the *consequential value*. Consequential value is clearly not a preposterior measure.

Griffiths and King present their results in a highly aggregated form. They create a prototype user, one who reads 198 documents per year, working in a prototype organization. The prototypes are amalgams of results from somewhere between 8 and 21 organizations. The prototype user spends 253 hours per year reading, for an average of 1.28 hours per reading. For 1,892 observations, Griffiths and King (1993, page 80) find 74% of journal article readings reporting zero consequential value, another 12.5% reporting a minimal amount, but about 2% reporting value in excess of $10,000. The frequency distribution of the reported consequential value decays similarly to that of an exponential distribution. Kantor (1995) finds precisely the same pattern in his user surveys.

The Griffiths and King (1993, Chapter 5) results are summarized as follows.

- Journals: 59% of journal readings are for decision making, and 31% are for monitoring; the average reading time is 0.83 hours; 26% of the readings report consequential value; $310 is the average value per reading.
- Books: 61% of book readings are for decision making, and 27% are for monitoring; the average reading time is 1.91 hours; 42% of the readings report consequential value; $650 is the average value per reading.
- Internal Reports: 78% of report readings are for decision making, and 5% are for monitoring; the average reading time is 1.61 hours; 50% of the readings report consequential value; $1,090 is the average value per reading.

The average consequential value for journal articles is lowest because 59% of the uses are for decision, but only 26% of the readings report consequential value. About the same proportion of book readings is for decision, but since a higher proportion of book readings report positive value, the average dollar value is much higher. Reports are substantially read for decision making, and half of them were valuable, making the average dollar value very high.

Gallagher (1974) surveys the systemwide value of an information source that creates a computer-generated periodic cost accounting report. This is one broadcast source, used by many different DMs to solve many different problems. In the organization he investigates, there are 103 managers who receive this report, and he asks them the maximum amount they would pay each year for this report if it were discontinued internally and purchased from an outside vendor. The histogram of the 52 respondents willing to assess this preposterior value shows the same pattern that Griffiths and King find—a large number of assessments ascribing minimal value, a very few extremely high assessments, and a pattern in between that decays nearly exponentially. The mean reported value of this source is $2,819, and the median is $550. The highest values are assessed by managers in upper middle-level line positions.

Section 9.4 presents a model that is consistent with this pattern of user-reported value assessment. Before turning to the theory, two additional practical matters require consideration. The next section turns to a more detailed examination of the system activities that can promote greater information value and gain for the organization. Section 9.3 reviews the extent to which users are able to respond to the system's incentives and assess information value accurately and without bias.

9.2 System Design and Information Gain

At the theoretical level, the organization needs information about all random variables whose realizations combine with actions to determine outcomes, but only when the expected information gain is positive. At the practical level of system design, the organization must make decisions about specific classes of users and types of uses that the resources of the system desire to serve. One interesting mechanism for these decisions is Rockart's (1979) advice that each DM identify her *critical success factors*, the key decision problems she faces that, if solved well, will ensure the achievement of the organization's goals. Upon prioritization of these problems, the system should then work to provide cost-effective access to the sources, internal and external, that are relevant to these vital areas. An inventory of available data sources, technology, and human expertise is helpful; Burk and Horton (1988) is a practical guide for this inventory. Design must also provide incentives for users to work efficiently within the system.

Optimal design involves 1) a thorough understanding of the information use environment; 2) fixed-cost investments in an internal infrastructure of data resources, technological capability, human expertise, and physical capital; 3) decisions on the willingness to finance access to external data sources, including consulting services; and 4) decisions on system data processing activities to imbue the infrastructure with the capability to transform data into messages in the way that maximizes the expected information gain. This section describes these system activities. As Mason and Sassone (1978) point out, studying these activities one by one is useful for assessing the impact of marginal changes in the system, such as the addition or subtraction of individual sources and services. For example, Ragowsky, Ahituv, and Neumann (1996) use a survey technique to relate the benefits of an individual system application to the organization-specific characteristics of the information use environment.

9.2.1 The Gain-Producing Activities of an Information System

In the view of both the organization and the users, the broad information system is an instrument with three uses: decision making, monitoring, and intermediate data processing. Decision making and monitoring are terminal uses of the system; intermediate data processing facilitates a terminal use.

One decision making use of the system is the optimal incorporation of information into one decision problem. Depending upon the problem, a decision making use can be quite involved, with many intermediate steps including several rounds of identification, choice, message access, and cognition before the final choice of action and resolution of the problem. A decision-making use does not necessarily lead to information value, but the nature and character of the steps in Figure 1.1, as designed in the system and executed by the user, are the critical factors creating the potential for value and net gain. A monitoring use of the system is similar, but it excludes any decision making application and is likely to be less involved.

As an intermediate data processing instrument, the system itself serves as a data producing information source by crafting original messages for communication to decision making and monitoring users. This type of processing gives the organization the ability to adapt to the specific decision problems and monitoring needs of the terminal users, hopefully leading to cost savings and/or better decisions. Intermediate data processing may be executed by an agent of one of the subsystems (e.g., a librarian, information analyst, tax accountant, or staff economist) whose job is to facilitate information processing by decision makers and monitors within the organization. Most systems also provide intermediate data processing in the form of sophisticated computer software applications such as decision support models and search engines.

Research in information science sees the organization's information system as a "value-adding" mechanism. The phrase "value of information" [Griffiths (1982); Repo (1989); Dessimoz (1995)] is generally used in a broad sense to mean the net or after-cost value of the information system, a concept this book calls the organization's information gain. To illustrate the distinction, a ceteris paribus reduction in the cost of information is valuable to the organization, but it does not directly give value to the information. It does give direct cost savings, which are a source of information gain. Hence, when researchers in information science talk of adding value to information sources, systems, and markets [Mowshowitz (1992); Taylor (1986); Kuhlen (1995)], it is important to distinguish between the system processing activities that increase the gain by reducing the costs of processing from those intended to increase informativeness, the source's or system's potential to create information value in a decision making use. Activities that increase informativeness are costly; this is another justification for the postulate that the expected cost of information increases with informativeness. Recall also from Figure 1.5 that cost reductions are value-adding activities in an indirect sense, since activities that reduce the minimum cost of achieving a given level of informativeness increase the optimal informativeness to incorporate. This chapter uses the word "gain-producing" to encompass both value enhancement and cost reduction within the information system.

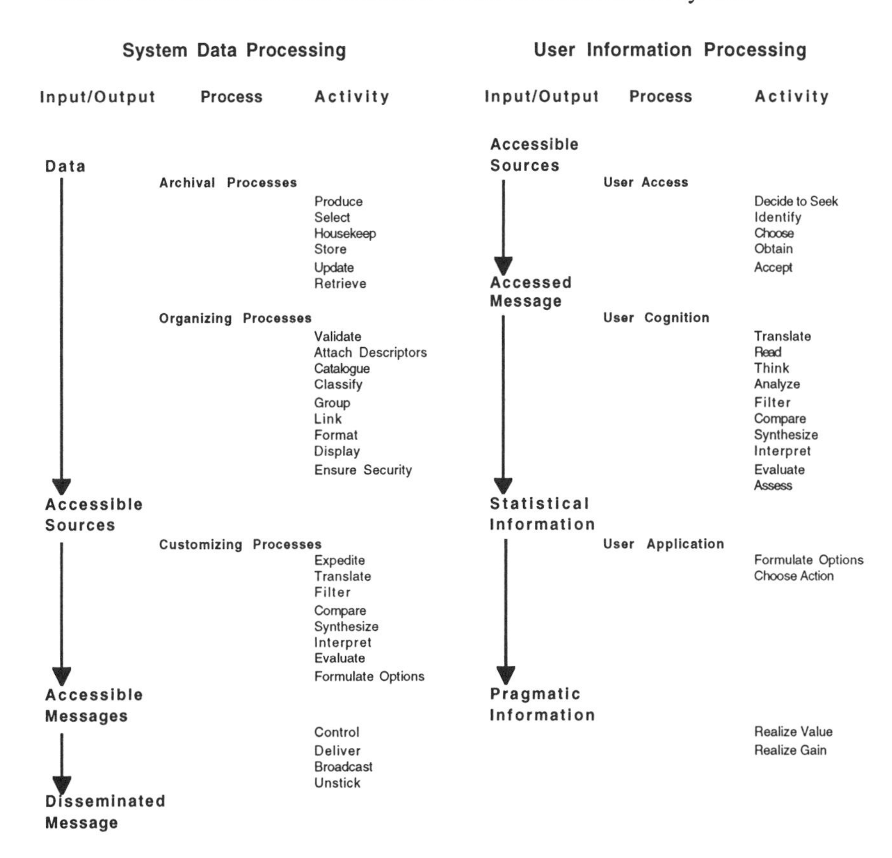

Figure 9.1. Gain-producing information processing in the organization.

Figure 9.1, an expansion of Taylor's (1986, page 6) value-added spectrum, details the gain-producing processes and activities within the organization that system design can potentially influence. A detailed discussion of this figure follows.

9.2.2 System Data Processing

System data processing implements the system's responsibilities in the optimal design. From the organization's view, the purpose of system data processing is to enhance the probability that any incorporation of information by the users is completed at the minimum cost of achieving a specified level of informativeness. System processing can be subdivided into *archiving* activities, *organizing* activities, and *customizing* activities. Archiving and organizing activities are antecedent to any user interface with the system, and the end product is a cogent collection of data sources awaiting access by a user. Customizing activities are the system's active, problem-specific contribution to user information processing. It often involves intermediate data processing uses of the system (i.e., the system as a data producing or broadcast source), and the end product is a message which is either accessible or disseminated.

Archiving and Organizing Processes

Archiving activities involve 1) the selection of sources to acquire and store internally, based upon decisions about the nature and scope of the decision problems to which the system aspires to offer convenience and informativeness; 2) housekeeping, such as scrubbing incoming data to ensure they are clean and weeding out internal sources that are no longer cost-effective; 3) decisions on updating existing sources for timeliness and currency, such as adding recent data to a time series or obtaining a new edition of a book; and 4) decisions on storage and retrieval technologies, including which data may be accessed in real-time and which with delay.

The new electronic environment is changing the nature of archiving, both for the organization and for the individual. Although the proprietary record, including the documentation and analysis of the organization's transactions, generally remains to be managed in-house, there is no longer as much need to accumulate collections from the common record. The philosophy of archiving is moving, as Saracevic and Kantor (1997) put it, from "just-in-case" to "just-in-time." As an example of the benefits, quantitative models and empirical research in library operations research find that physical proximity is an important determinant of library use [Hayes and Borko (1983)]. To the extent that new technologies make the distance from the system less relevant in the future, the cost of access declines and use increases, providing the expectation of greater information gain for the organization. These innovations are not completely beneficial; the possible substitution of Internet access to journals for personal subscriptions raises membership concerns in the professional organizations that sponsor the journals [Varian (1997)].

There are a large number of firms selling information products that either add to the common record or amount to slightly different ways to access different pieces of the common record. The common record being so voluminous and growing, most firms' piece is not very large. For example, according to Williams (1997) the online database segment of the market in 1996 had 2,938 producers producing 10,033 databases, for an average per firm of 3.41. This contrasts with 1985, when 1,210 producers supplied 3,010 databases, averaging 2.49 each. The market structure of the data industry can best be described as monopolistic competition.

Organizing activities enhance the potential for reliable and efficient access. One important organizing activity is the augmentation of the common and proprietary records using keywords, subject headings, abstracts, indicators of validity, and other pertinent descriptors. These data about data are called *metadata*, and they can increase information gain both by cost saving and value enhancement. Using the results in Section 6.2, this type of augmentation increases informativeness in the sense of Blackwell. It also allows for greater efficiency in sorting and retrieval, and is especially effective when it is standardized. As an example, the Federal Geographic Data Committee has adopted standards for geospatial data; a discussion is currently available at the Website www.fgdc.gov.

Validation is a valuable component of metadata, providing an accurate description of a record's sources, methods of gathering and/or compilation, possible biases, and so on. Validation is currently important for database products, but in the future world of data overload, it may also be useful in preliminary filtering as a vouching device, for example, by identifying a particular author as a Nobel Prize winner or a journal as being refereed. The user's perception of the credibility of a source is an important dimension of informativeness.

Cataloguing and classifying are traditional organizing activities. Griffiths and King's (1993) research suggests that considerable information gain arises when decision makers avoid actions that "reinvent the wheel." In a survey of 647 research scientists, Martyn (1964) reports 43 instances in which the scientists unintentionally duplicated previous research due to belated discovery of the relevant document. This makes a strong case that organizations should catalogue and centralize internal reports. A related organizing activity is to group and link together similar information sources, for example, by creating Internet pages to collect sources relevant to specific classes of decision problems.

There is considerable empirical evidence that the proper format and display of a source's message can enhance information gain. Blocher, Moffie, and Zmud

(1985) offer evidence that the format of a report can affect decision making in ways that depend upon the specific decision problem. The experiment presents auditors with a series of decision problems, each with known prior probabilities and payoff function, but having details that make the problem either simple or complex. There is an information source that offers relevant and accurate financial reports, either in a tabular format or a color-graphic format. Upon ex-post assessment of the quality of each decision, the experimenters find better performance from the color-graphic chart for the simple task, but that the table induces better performance when the task is complex. For additional examples, see the review in Dickson, Senn, and Chervany (1977) of a series of laboratory experiments on the effects of information presentation on decision making.

Finally, ensuring the security of the archived collection, especially the proprietary record, is an organizing activity whose nature is changing as more and more of the data are archived electronically. Example 5.5 hints at the value of industrial espionage; Schweizer (1996) sounds the alarm.

Customizing Processes: The System as Source

Customizing takes place in a domain of user access, cognition, and application activities that can be undertaken either by the system or by the individual user; note the intersection of customizing activities with user processing activities in Figure 9.1. System design must specify the kinds of processing the system can more efficiently provide, and how much is to be left to the users. The system's treatment of translation services provides a simple example of alternative design specifications. The system could automatically translate all foreign language documents as a part of organizing, or it could offer to translate upon request of a user, which would be a customizing activity, or it could leave it to the users to obtain translation services externally.

Filtering is an important and common custom processing activity. Filtering aids the user's choice of source by screening alternative sources and identifying those expected to be the most informative to the use at hand. An example is a computer-aided bibliographic database search, an activity that can be performed either by the human resources of the system or directly by the user. Another is a recommender system [Resnick and Varian (1997)], which can be helpful for both filtering and vouching. The rise of the Internet and the application of powerful search engines are dramatically reducing the cost of source identification.

Information science studies filtering partly as a problem of optimal *retrieval.* Precision and recall are two basic measures of the success of a filtering activity. *Precision* is the proportion of identified sources that are relevant to a specific user's specific information need, and *recall* is the proportion of relevant sources that the search identifies. In an experiment that pits two-person teams against a prespecified opponent in a war game that includes tactics and negotiation,

Streufert (1973) finds that increasing the precision of a fixed number of messages leads to more instances of integrated and strategic (complex) decision making.

When information system design moves away from the physical archiving of documents and toward electronic access from external vendors, the organization trades fixed costs for variable. This makes it more important to filter for informativeness prior to the decision to obtain the message. The pragmatic informativeness of a specific source, and the rank ordering by informativeness of all potential sources, is not only use-specific, it is user-specific because it depends upon each individual's initial knowledge and ability to understand the message. A document containing the latest treatise on quantum physics may be highly informative to a professional physicist, but be uninformative to (over the head of) a freshman student in Physics 101, irrelevant to a layman, and mere coloring paper for a child. This dimension of informativeness is called *situational* or *cognitive relevance* in the literature on information retrieval; see Saracevic and Kantor (1997). The organization desires to avoid the purchase of documents that get rejected on sight because of improper situational relevance, perhaps because the level of analysis is too simple to contain information or too difficult for the DM to cognitively process.

As Eisenberg and Barry (1988) point out, it is not enough for filtering to merely exclude the irrelevant sources and include all relevant ones. The cost of achieving a given level of informativeness in an information structure that combines the messages from multiple sources depends upon the order that each source in the composite group is accessed and cognitively processed; because of the efficiencies of prerequisite knowledge and the waste of redundancy, some sequences can achieve a given level of understanding using less processing time. Allen (1977) and McLeod and Jones (1986) discuss how the information use environment can affect this sequencing. Assuming that upon completion of the task the user can rank-order all processed sources by their perceived informativeness, Tague-Sutcliffe (1995) proposes a logarithmic measure of the informativeness of a composite of information sources.

The system's services may go further and select a group of sources, analyze them, and present a synthesis or annotated bibliography to the user. Getting even closer to the problem, interpersonal sources and artificial intelligence technology may assist the user's cognition and application, presenting analysis and interpretation of meaning, and perhaps evaluating decision options. Dhar and Stein (1997) explore the design of data producing sources that help with decision making. Decision Support Systems (DSS) are models, housed on computers, that assist the DM in accessing, summarizing, interpreting, and ultimately applying information for decision making. A sophisticated DSS attempts to model human reasoning, and may include some combination of accounting, economic, and an optimization submodels. "Reject this applicant" might be the output of a credit scoring DSS that intends to determine to whom the DM should make loans. The *intelligence density* of an application is the framework Dhar and Stein use to catalogue the various characteristics that contribute to overall information gain. Aspects of intelligence density include closeness of the recommended decision to optimal, the ability to explain and justify the decision, timeliness, and cost characteristics such as generalizability, the quality and cost of the inputs required, and user friendliness.

In a laboratory test of the potential gain from using a DSS, van Bruggen, Smidts, and Wierenga (1998) measure profit performance in a marketing simulation game as it depends upon the availability of an application that can perform "what if" analyses. The subjects with access to the DSS outperform those who do not. The beneficial effect is especially strong for those subjects who score lower in analytical ability on a separate test. See also Sharda, Barr, and McDonnell (1988).

Customizing Processes: The System as Control Mechanism

The nature and control of message dissemination (i.e., the custom processing of accessible messages into disseminated messages) comprises the final component of system data processing. Dissemination may take place upon the initiative and/or effort of either the system or the users, and messages may be available to only one user, to a selected group, or broadly available to all. For example, rather than having a large number of users each independently bearing the cost to access the system for similar purposes, the organization may find it economical for the system to serve as a broadcast source by disseminating messages from selected sources and inviting users to accept them. Such services include putting up displays for browsing, offering current awareness, journal routing and other source identification (scanning) services, sponsoring educational conferences, and automatically disseminating internal messages such as accounting and sales reports. Although many of these services offer natural ways to use the system as a monitoring instrument, messages found by monitoring can certainly turn out relevant in decision making; this phenomenon is sometimes called serendipity.

The term "information overload" describes the observation that the number of data sources available is in excess of the ability of decision makers to choose wisely from among them and process their messages into information. Messages can appear without user request or need, such as advertising, which is a collateral message emanating from some broadcast sources. Some data producing sources would disseminate their messages universally. There is also undoubtedly a certain amount of time wasted monitoring data that could not possibly be relevant to any of the organization's decisions, such as "surfing the Internet." Lost and wasted time is clearly part of the cost of the system.

Glazer, Steckel, and Winer (1992) identify a potentially deleterious effect from the frequent and routine dissemination of messages from multiple sources. In a complex environment with many distinct action variables that must be managed, the outcome function may be more sensitive to changes in some actions than others; after all, some decisions are more important than others. To the extent that making a report easier to access can deflect attention from more important decisions to less, organizational performance suffers. Glazer et al. test this hypothesis in the context of a marketing simulation game that requires subjects to make production, pricing, advertising, and product positioning decisions. The game offers a number of different market research studies, but rather than allowing the subjects to choose from among all of them, the experimental treatments simulate alternative dissemination policies by either requiring or precluding the purchase of specific reports. The result is that the experimenter is able to entrap the subjects into misdirecting their attention toward less consequential decisions. The subjects employ good decision rules based upon the messages they obtain, but by not concentrating on the most important issues, overall performance suffers.

Control, in a broader sense than the maintenance of security, is therefore important. Cyert and March (1963, pages 107–110) place information handling rules such as routing and filtering among the organization's key standard operating procedures. Critical questions involve inclusion and exclusion of messages from particular sources to particular users: Who should know what? Who has seen what? Who keeps the flow of irrelevant messages down? How is the flow from proprietary sources controlled? These system design matters are particularly relevant in the context of modern management approaches to the "Information Based Organization;" see Vincent (1990), Fletcher and Diamond (1995), and Choo (1998). As an example, Mukhopadhyay, Kekre, and Kalathur (1995) assess the gain from the installation of Electronic Data Interchange technology between Chrysler Corporation and its suppliers at about $60 per vehicle, due to improved coordination of materials flows.

As a component of the information use environment that management can potentially influence, Dewhirst's (1971) results suggest that improved sharing norms is a mechanism by which system design can affect information gain. The installation of a technology that broadens the potential for access and usage might promote this, but in and of itself does not cause greater willingness to share information internally. When people's jobs and roles are defined by the information they have access to, they may view its possession as a source of power and be unwilling to share it.

Davenport, Eccles, and Prusak (1992) identify these models of information politics: 1) technocratic utopianism, which concentrates on technological infrastructure and in its straw-man form views technology as the end rather than the means, showing little interest in pragmatic issues; 2) anarchy, where each individual fends for herself and little is shareable; 3) feudalism, where each department or division head has complete control over her information sources and determines what becomes available between divisions; 4) monarchy, which dictates rules from the top but can devolve into feudalism or anarchy upon the demise of the monarch, unless there are "constitutional" safeguards; and 5) federalism, a negotiated sharing of information based upon recognition of its value to the organization as a whole. The emphasis under federalism is stewardship rather than ownership of information. Ranking the models, the authors advocate federalism based upon commonality of vocabulary and accessibility of information, despite the fact it is difficult to achieve and sustain. A benevolent monarchy is second best, being the most efficient in information management. Feudalism has the least to recommend it.

Simpson and Prusak (1995) argue that information overload is to some extent a symptom of a suboptimal division of responsibility between system processing and user processing. The (partial) solution to information overload is not simply to have the system do more of the processing; receiving raw data without analysis or filtering for relevance is just as uninformative as a report with all kinds of insights and advice written by people who, crudely put, don't know what they're talking about. The optimal division of responsibility is situation-specific and can best be ascertained by communication and coordination between the users and the system's agents, acting together as a team.

The economic theory of teams studies the control of message dissemination among groups of individuals working together to achieve a common goal. Radner (1961; 1962) and Marschak and Radner (1972) consider the allocation and application of information within teams: what messages should get to which individuals, and when. The team theory models have changed over the decades. In the early applied analyses, such as Beckmann (1958) and McGuire (1961), the costs of communication are a primary focus. The decision problem Beckmann investigates, reservation policy for airline flights, is not that different from the problem airlines face today, but the optimal solution and the expected payoff to the airline have changed considerably. Modern analyses [Radner (1993)] assume zero communication costs and focus on the relationships between information processing and hierarchical structures for communication within the organization. For example, Aoki (1986) considers the differences between horizontal and vertical dissemination of messages within the organization; see also Geanakoplos and Milgrom (1991) and Prat (1996). Bassan and Scarsini (1995) present a theoretical model for message dissemination within the political environment of the benevolent monarch.

Many studies of information use in business environments call for system design to provide enough flexibility so that each user can self-customize: define and obtain the precise information she needs [e.g., McKinnon and Bruns (1992), page 208]. To a great extent, the new technology of archiving and organizing, particularly the maturing of database and network technology, is making this feasible. See, for example, Chapter 4 of Dhar and Stein (1997). It is a question for good management whether such investments in technology can increase the organization's information gain.

Turning to a somewhat different issue, von Hippel (1994) investigates the causes and effects of messages that are expensive to access, *sticky information*. Obtaining the message from a chosen source can be costly because some interpersonal sources may decline to be accessed for political or other reasons, or because of the sheer magnitude of the data, boundaries between organizations caused by trade secrecy, or the way the information source is encoded. The latter is particularly important when obtaining information about technology; the message may be embedded in software, require software to decode, or be embodied in some physical object that is expensive both to obtain and to decode. In Teece's (1977) study of 26 international technology transfer projects, transfer costs averaged 19% of total project costs, even with both sides willing to work together as a team. Von Hippel (1994) describes how this costliness affects the management of problem solving tasks.

Once the message has been obtained,[2] the matter is out of the system's domain and into the hands of the user. Upon sight, the user can dispose of the message, file it away for possible future reference, or accept it for cognitive processing. Only after spending the time and effort on cognition can the user ascertain if the message contains any information. If not, the system has not operated efficiently.

9.2.3 Design and Performance

This chapter has mentioned several studies that relate the information use environment and the system design to the organization's performance. Care is warranted when interpreting such results. Good ex-ante system design only creates the potential for information gain and successful performance. There is no guarantee because performance is necessarily an ex-post measurement, meaningful after the realizations of the random variables. In any specific decision making use

[2] An ironic observation about research in information science is that a nontrivial subset of the literature is difficult to obtain, in some cases prohibitively expensive. Not only is some of the work proprietary, done under contract for specific organizations, but there is an unfortunate amount of "gray literature," publications never made available through easily accessible channels. In addition, interesting work is untranslated and hence unavailable in English, as Mayère (1997) and the references in Wersig's (1997) review of the theory of information science attest.

(trial), random variation interacts with design and decision to determine gain and performance. Even over a number of trials, a given design yields different performance outcomes depending upon the specific combination of state realizations. The saying of the baseball manager Branch Rickey comes to mind: "Luck is the residue of design." If information gain is expected to occur, then it should be accurately measurable in aggregate performance only after a large number of trials.

From a macro perspective, an important question is the relationship between the investment in the technological infrastructure and the organization's ultimate profitability and productivity. One line of research uses production function approaches that include expenditures on information systems as one of the factors of production [Hayes and Erickson (1982); Braunstein (1985); Brynjolfsson and Hitt (1996)]. Research that finds no relationship between productivity and investment in information technology sometimes calls the result the *productivity paradox*. The counterarguments are that productivity is a poorly measured variable and that it takes time for new innovations to work their way through the economy and show up in the statistics; Brynjolfsson and Hitt (1996) argue that the paradox, to the extent that it ever did exist, disappeared in the early 1990s. Another explanation of the productivity paradox is that some researchers are equating investments in computers with investments in the information system; certainly computer hardware and software are only one component of the organization's system for information. An alternative approach [Koenig (1990; 1992)] is to relate the performance of the organization to the attitude towards information in the organization, as measured by survey.

From a micro perspective, laboratory studies that control the random variations are useful for isolating particular effects and testing for consistency with decision theory. Porat and Haas (1969) perform a laboratory simulation that places subjects in a competitive business environment as the managers of a single-product firm. In each stage of the experiment, the subject decides on production, price, and advertising, and sets a profit goal. There are four treatments, each differing essentially by the Blackwell-informativeness of the information source the experiment provides gratis to the subjects. The results show significant improvement in realized profits between the treatments having the most difference in informativeness. Mock (1969) gives subjects a complex economic problem, draws a specific sequence of realizations for the random variables, and compares observed profitability as it depends upon whether the data are available in real-time or with delay. Subjects with more timely data average higher profits—for this specific sequence of state realizations.

Matters of system design and choice of source require decisions based upon ex-ante assessments. In addition to the issue of whether the application of information improves performance, at least in a statistical sense, it is important to question whether people are capable of adequately assessing information value and whether they respond to incentives and other situation-specific characteristics in ways that are consistent with the theory. This is the subject matter of the next section.

9.3 Experiments in Ex-Ante Information Behavior

9.3.1 Normative and Descriptive Economics

Applied economics comprises three things: advice on how a person ought to behave in order to be a rational, calculating *homo economicus*, observations on how people actually do behave, and observations and predictions of the social and market consequences of the way people actually behave. As far as the descriptive validity of the present normative approach is concerned, there is no question but that people make errors in judgment and in decision making, and that the same errors are common enough to be easily identified and classified; see Hogarth and Makridakis (1981) for a thorough review of this from a business standpoint. Sometimes when researchers observe people not behaving precisely the way a particular economic theory says they should, they reject the real-world applicability of the theory and advocate other paradigms. This conclusion throws the baby out with the bath water; the more progressive approach is to investigate whether people behave sufficiently close to the prescriptions of normative economics that the theory can provide insights about economic phenomena. This section takes a look at the empirical evidence about the consistency of individual behavior with the principles of decision theory.[3]

Reasonable people can debate whether decision theory has reached its potential as a normative guide to decision making, but the fact is that information is sought and obtained, and decisions are made on the basis of current understanding. The most successful models, as Arrow (1985) points out, are grounded on the assumption that individuals optimize in the face of constraints. The constraints may well reflect the true costs of obtaining information and making hard decisions and dealing with multiple uncertainties. Common sense, heuristics, and intuition can certainly be rational ways to make decisions. Marschak (1964) argues that the problem of understanding peoples' limited capacity for finding optimal decisions is in fact the problem of understanding the costs of decision making in a world in which good decision making skills are a scarce resource.

[3] Section 7.3 has already considered the basic consistency of observed behavior with the hypothesis of expected utility and the impacts of nonexpected utility on the value of information. Marschak (1964) provides some additional experimental tests for the basic postulates of decision theory.

Part of good management is to remedy the failure of others in the organization to make the optimal decisions; another part is to exploit the suboptimal decision making of one's competitors. Hence, Marschak reasons, it is useful to study the behavior of both successful DMs and below-average ones. As Section 4.1 discusses, there is reason to be optimistic that people can learn to perform better. Indeed, Hogarth and Makridakis' threefold recommendation for dealing with peoples' failures is greater organizational use of decision-theoretic concepts, particularly sensitivity analysis; the assessment of information value; and the multiattribute utility approach of Keeney and Raiffa (1976).

Wason (1960) presents evidence of a serious violation of the principles of decision theory: the phenomenon of accepting messages that confirm existing beliefs or support prespecified actions, while ignoring disconfirming evidence. This behavior essentially convolutes the decision rule. Rather than intending to take action on the basis of a message not known in advance, the action is chosen and a message is then found to justify it. If the information source cannot change the prior action, it is useless and offers only cost and negative gain to the organization. Emshoff and Mitroff (1978) describe several case studies of information selection intended to do little more than support preconceived opinions. Rosenthal (1963) performs an experiment that can be interpreted as indicating how the views of the boss become reflected in the results of a staff's analysis. Cosier (1978) tests some remedies for this cultural problem in the information use environment, and finds benefit from a cultural acceptance of "devil's advocacy." Nevertheless, as long as bosses prefer sycophantic subordinates, this suboptimal technique can flourish.

Feldman and March (1981) suggest that organizational culture can give individuals the incentive to gather information for purposes other than decision making and monitoring. Gathering information can serve as a symbol of competence, an instrument for strategic manipulation, and a mechanism for covering one's posterior, both statistical and anatomical, in the event of an unfavorable outcome. In addition, the activity of gathering information can serve as a substitute for actually having to make a decision; politicians who do not want to commit to a particular position are quick to advocate "thorough study and review" of the issue by an "independent, blue-ribbon" commission. The consequence of such incentives is an organizational overuse of the information system above the decision-theoretic norm.

Stripping away these issues of organizational behavior, the key questions revolve around people's ex-ante or preposterior capability to adequately assess information value and to respond to incentives and other problem-specific characteristics in ways that are consistent with the theory. Ward Edwards is the pioneer in comparing "real with ideal" in Bayesian statistical decision making; see Edwards (1965) and Peterson and Beach (1967). Another approach uses the Brunswik (1952) lens model, a staple in psychology that is quite adaptable to the Bayesian analysis of information behavior; see Slovic and Lichtenstein (1971).

In empirical studies the common treatment effects include varying the payoff function, prior state distribution, informativeness, and cost per unit of informativeness. The subjects may face simple decision problems involving cards, urns, or spinners, or more complex problems with substantive content. The advantage of the former design is that the experimenter can calculate the risk-neutral optimal behavior and compare it qualitatively and quantitatively with the experimental results. The latter design places the subject in a more realistic situation, but it confounds the experiment with extraneous factors that make interpretation less straightforward. One type of experiment makes the informativeness endogenous to the DM, either by allowing the subject to choose a fixed sample size or to decide when to stop looking based on the messages already received and processed (called sequential sampling or optional stopping). This is useful for studying search behavior and the responsiveness to incentives. Another type offers DMs exogenous information structures and asks them for their demand price; this tests the ability to assess value. The next subsections take these two types in turn.

Most studies find qualitative correspondence with the normative model, but a divergence from the risk neutral optimum. In the typical terminology, "overbuying" means the willingness to purchase an information structure that is more informative than the risk neutral benchmark: in terms of Figure 8.3, informativeness to the right of θ^*. "Underbuying" is the opposite. Similarly, "overvaluing" ("undervaluing") means expressing a bid price for an information structure greater (less) than the normative amount V_I^N.

The subject's attitude toward risk is a confounding factor that is difficult to control for in this type of experiment. We know from Chapters 3 and 7 that risk preference affects the choice of action and that a risk averter's demand price can be greater than or less than that of her risk neutral counterpart, and any divergence between V_I^A and the benchmark V_I^N does not necessarily reflect genuine over- or undervaluing of information. Most studies, however, fall back to the position that the amounts of money the subjects themselves are risking is so little that an insistence on risk neutrality is warranted.

9.3.2 Experiments in Information Acquisition

Stigler's (1961) classic theory proposes that individuals search for information up to the point at which the marginal value of another query equals its marginal cost. Naturally, higher marginal cost should result in less search. In a laboratory test of Stigler's problem of shopping for the lowest price, Urbany (1986) varies search cost, the dispersion of market prices, and the informativeness of the information source telling about the price dispersion. The subject's objective is essentially to minimize the cost of purchase plus the actual and opportunity costs of search. The results are consistent with the theory. The number of searches (stores shopped) decreases as cost per search increases, and those subjects with up-front access to the more informative source have less need for further search. Schotter and Braunstein's (1981) experimental study of job search also obtains results consistent with the basic economic theory.

Irwin and Smith (1957) perform a straightforward and uncluttered test of the effects of information cost, problem stakes, and environmental uncertainty on the informativeness that subjects choose to incorporate. In the experiment, each subject chooses to see numbered cards, one by one, until she is willing to decide whether the mean of the entire pack is greater than or less than zero. The more cards seen, the more informative the evidence, but each card costs either a half cent or a cent, depending upon the treatment. Additional treatments vary the payment for a correct decision, the mean of the numbers in the deck, and the standard deviation of those numbers. At the cost of one cent each, the subjects on average choose 16.6 cards, and at one half cent each they choose 4 more cards on average. The subjects choose more cards the higher the stakes and the greater the environmental uncertainty.

For given information costs, many decision problems exhibit the normative characteristic that optimal informativeness increases with some measure of the magnitude of the payoffs involved (i.e., the stakes of the problem). O'Connor, Peterson, and Palmer (1972) test for an empirical effect between stakes and information purchase, as do Irwin and Smith (1957), but with a twist: in a binomial sampling problem, the authors rig the stakes and costs so that the expected information gain is zero for any sample size. Hence, a risk neutral subject should be indifferent about how many observations she chooses. Rather than actual purchases being randomly distributed, the results show a clear bias for purchasing larger sample sizes, the larger the stakes. The authors' explanation for this result is a lack of risk neutrality on the part of the subjects.

Wald (1947) shows that the optimal sequential sampling procedure results in greater information gain than taking the optimal fixed sample size. To test the descriptive validity of this theorem, Fried and Peterson (1969) offer subjects a binomial sampling experiment that alternates between choosing a fixed sample size and allowing them to observe a random drawing, one by one, until stopping and deciding which of two populations is being sampled. The subjects show the ability to take partial advantage of the superiority of optional stopping, but do not take full advantage because they apparently use a suboptimal stopping criterion. Snapper and Peterson (1971) expand on the sequential aspects of this approach. Both studies find evidence supporting the hypothesis that subjects have a bias for overbuying observations from less informative sources.

In a card-drawing decision problem in which the sample size is the index of informativeness, Green, Halbert, and Minas (1964) calculate the normatively optimal fixed-size sample to draw for various combinations of payoff, prior, and likelihood. For each treatment, the subject requests to buy a batch of n cards before making the decision. The cost per card is not varied, and for several of the treatments it is optimal to demand no cards. The results show the subjects behaving qualitatively like Bayesians, while exhibiting both overbuying and underbuying, depending on the treatment. The most interesting result is a tendency to purchase wasteful information, a willingness to purchase cards when the normative optimum is to take no cards. This is a decision with negative expected information gain.

Lanzetta and Kanareff (1962) perform a different kind of experiment in which subjects are asked to solve a series of 25 complex problems. The example problem gives a brief description about a mental patient and then asks the subject to choose from among six actions. The subject can buy from zero to five additional and relevant messages, one at a time, but must make a decision within three minutes. The subject wins money only if her decision is correct. In fact, unbeknownst to the subject, the actual decision does not matter; she is declared correct solely as a function of how many messages she buys. If she buys none, she has no chance of being correct, one message gives her a 20% chance, two messages a 40% chance, and so on through to five messages, which gives her the certainty of winning the payoff every time. Buying all five messages maximizes expected net payoff, but even after 25 trials, the subjects do not learn this. With the messages free, the subjects on average buy fewer than four messages, and when each message costs a nickel, they average about two purchases.

Lanzetta and Kanareff's results have been used as evidence that people tend to underestimate informativeness, learn slowly about optimal purchasing, and underbuy information. Note, however, that money is not the only cost of information here. The problems are timed, meaning the time taken to cognitively process another message takes away from the time available to choose the optimal action. Hence, even when the monetary cost is zero, the messages are not free. When proper consideration is given to the cost of cognitive processing, perhaps underbuying is not occurring.

The most realistic class of information acquisition studies gives the subject the choice of several alternative information sources and allows her to access and cognitively process them, one by one, until coming to a terminal decision. Examples include Kanarick, Huntington, and Petersen (1969), Lim and O'Connor (1996), and the work of Connolly (1988) and his associates. The experimental design can either offer a mixture of source informativeness, or offer all sources with the same informativeness, but varying it by trial. Kanarick et al. use decks of cards, so that precise composite-message likelihoods can be calculated; the costs of the sources are varied systematically. Lim and O'Connor give subjects the task of forecasting the sales of a soft drink at the beach; possible sources, each with differing informativeness, include data on the daily high temperature, the number of visitors to the beach, and a time series forecasting model. Connolly has subjects bet on the point spreads in football games, affording them the opportunity to consult with experts of varying cost and informativeness.

Comparing the chosen composite information structure with the prespecified optimum for each trial, the experiments observe both underbuying and overbuying, with suboptimal choice among the alternatives. The quantitative performance is poor enough to lead Connolly (1988) to conclude that human skills are lacking when it comes to striking the balance between information costs and information value. One ad hoc explanation, at least for underbuying, is that the observation of cost-avoiding source selection may be due to the fact that information cost is a certainty, whereas information value is prospective.

An issue of economic importance is the effect of constraints on such things as the number of sources available and the budget for information processing. Several studies show a tendency to respond to changes in constraints that are in fact not binding and hence should be irrelevant to the decision. In an optional stopping problem, Pitz (1968) constrains the sample size to either 5, 10, or 20, and finds that as the constraint is tightened, the subjects choose smaller samples, even under circumstances in which the optimum is less than the constraint. Levine, Samet, and Brahlek (1975) is a most interesting experiment that controls both the access to information and the budget for it. In a sequential sampling task to determine which of four urns is the correct state, it costs the subject one resource unit to request access to a source. The experimenter then comes back with some metadata that tells the subject whether the source is of high, medium, or low informativeness. The subject then decides whether to pass on this source or obtain its message; obtaining the message costs two additional resource units. The subjects can consult up to either 16 or 24 sources, and have enough resources available to be able to purchase a specified percentage of the cost of looking at all of them. On average, the subjects request 8.79 sources before taking action when 16 are available, and 11.85 when up to 24 may be accessed. The subjects also request and look at more sources the more resources they have. The subjects pass most frequently on the low informativeness sources, and they are more particular in what they look at when availability is 16, but the budget does not affect this aspect significantly. Overall, there is a tendency to overbuy, yet on average the subjects only expend about 57% of available resources.

The grand conclusion from the literature of expert resolution (Section 4.2.3), information retrieval (Section 9.2.2), and psychology is that it is a difficult task to efficiently create a composite information structure via the access and cognitive processing of messages from multiple sources. This would seems to be an arena where education and technology can work together to improve human performance.

9.3.3 Experiments in Value Assessment

For experiments in which the subjects assess the demand-price value of an exogenous information structure, there must be a mechanism to elicit the true maximum amount the subject is willing to pay. One mechanism is to offer the same problem to the subject with many trials differing by the cost of the information. The cost at which the decision changes from purchasing to not purchasing the source is the estimate of the subject's demand price. A difficulty can develop if the subject rejects the source at one price but then accepts it at a higher one; some type of overt or covert intervention by the experimenter is necessary to ensure this inconsistency does not arise. A second method is to require the subject to bid directly for the source against a random drawing. If the subject's bid is higher than the random draw, the subject buys the source and pays the drawn price. If the bid is less than the draw, the subject does not get access to the source and must make the prior decision. It can be shown that the optimal bid is the subject's true demand price, although as Marschak (1964) points out, it is best to demonstrate clearly to each subject why this is in fact optimal.[4]

Wendt (1969) asks 17 student subjects to bid for information in a straightforward binary (two-state, two-message, and two-action) decision problem. The payoff functions are symmetric with $\pi(x_1, a_1) = \pi(x_2, a_2) = +100$ and $\pi(x_1, a_2) = \pi(x_2, a_1) = -100$. The likelihood matrix is symmetric with $p(y_1 | x_1) = p(y_2 | x_2)$ and varying between .55 and 1.00 in increments of .05. The alternative treatments for the prior are $p(x_1) = .5, .7$, or .9. For the latter two priors, this sets up a subset of the informativeness treatments in which the sources are useless, that is, in which optimal action cannot change regardless of the message. Comparing the bids with the risk neutral optima, 16 of the 17 subjects respond qualitatively to the treatments in the direction the normative theory recommends. Quantitatively, the subjects are willing to pay more than the risk neutral prescription, especially for the structures with lower informativeness. The subjects show a definite penchant for purchasing useless information.

The book by Green, Robinson, and Fitzroy (1967) contains the results from a series of studies in which subjects directly face small, finite-model decision problems. The experiments systematically vary all the relevant problem attributes: payoffs, prior probabilities, informativeness, the action space, and the cost of information. The subjects, both students and executives, are asked to pretend they are marketing managers making decisions on problems with stakes in the tens of thousands of dollars. The experiments test both information buying and

[4] If the demand price < draw < bid, the subject must unnecessarily pay more than the source is worth. If the demand price > draw > bid, the subject unnecessarily misses out on buying a source expected to provide gain. Setting demand price = bid ensures neither of these undesirable results can occur.

valuation; the subject's demand value for information is inferred from changes in the decision to seek as information cost is varied. The general conclusions are that subjects respond to treatments in the qualitatively proper way, but there is a strong tendency to overvalue information sources.

There is a problem with this type of study: the presumption that the DMs are all risk neutral, so that any deviation from the risk neutral optimum is not consistent with Bayesian decision theory. As we have seen in Chapter 7, risk averse individuals are willing at times to trade away a prospect with higher expected wealth for one with lower variability. Even if the risk averter chooses actions identical to the risk neutral counterpart, normative value assessments can be quite different. Consider the data from Example 2.1 in Table 3.1, in which for the same imperfect information structure **I**, $V_I^N = \$1.60$ and $V_I^A = \$3.97$. If we give a subject this problem and she assesses a value of \$3, this reflects overvaluation if she is risk neutral, but undervaluation if she happens to exhibit the assumed logarithmic utility function.

In one of the information buying experiments, Green et al. (1967) offer 45 subjects a binary decision problem with the following payoff matrix,

$$\begin{bmatrix} \pi(x_1,a_1) & \pi(x_2,a_1) \\ \pi(x_1,a_2) & \pi(x_2,a_2) \end{bmatrix} = \begin{bmatrix} 100{,}000 & 20{,}000 \\ 80{,}000 & 32{,}000 \end{bmatrix}.$$

The prior is $p(x_1) = p(x_2) = .5$, and the subjects may choose to purchase, at varying cost, one of four information sources whose posterior probabilities are given by the upcoming equation (9.8) with $\theta = 0$ (null information), .4, .8, or 1.0 (perfect information). In 60% of the trials, the subjects choose the risk neutral optimal informativeness, with the more common error being to overbuy. Even though action a_1 is the risk neutral prior optimal choice a_0^N, in about one-third of the trials, the subjects choose action a_2, a choice with lower expected payoff, but also less variability. This choice does not necessarily mean the subject has made a mistake; there are risk averse utility functions for which this choice is optimal. Subjects who maximize the expected utility of wealth are certainly exhibiting Bayesian behavior, and such decisions, as we have seen, can have a dramatic effect on the normative value of information.

The results in Lawrence (1992), discussed in Section 7.2.2, suggest a simple modification to the payoff matrix that can control for this type of bias. Consider the following matrix,

$$\begin{bmatrix} \pi(x_1,a_1) & \pi(x_2,a_1) \\ \pi(x_1,a_2) & \pi(x_2,a_2) \end{bmatrix} = \begin{bmatrix} 80{,}000 & 0 \\ 60{,}000 & 40{,}000 \end{bmatrix}.$$

With all other characteristics of the problem the same, the risk neutral optimal prior decision is the less variable choice a_2; risk averters also prefer a_2. Lawrence's (1992) sufficiency theorem shows that $V_I^A \leq V_I^N$ for all **I** with $\theta \geq .6$. Hence, when subjects are asked to assess the value of any of these more informative sources, an observation greater than V_I^N reflects bona fide overvaluation of the information source, rather than a confounding due to risk preference.

In another approach to dealing with such biases in reported value assessment, Hilton, Swieringa, and Hoskin (1981) divorce the problem of information valuation from the problem of action selection. The authors accomplish this by forcing the subjects to use a DSS that chooses actions using the risk neutral criterion. The problem involves drawing alternative fixed-size samples from an urn of uncertain composition. For each of six sample sizes (informativeness levels), the experiment elicits the demand price by varying the cost of the sample and finding the price at which the subject changes her decision to purchase. Comparing the aggregate average demand price for each informativeness level with the risk neutral benchmark, the authors do not reject the hypothesis that the two values are equal. In other words, separating information valuation from action selection tends to lessen the extent of overvaluation. There is still considerable individual variation; a cluster analysis of the 97 subjects classifies 45 of them as accurate risk neutral assessors, 22 of them as assessors who undervalue, and 30 who overvalue.

Ronen and Falk (1973) present some qualitative evidence of consistency between the elicited information value and the theory. The experiments ask subjects for a preposterior bid for information in a sequence of accounting-related decision problems. In one of the experiments, 64 students bid on perfect information in 9 problems constructed so that the expected information value increases monotonically with the entropy of the prior distribution (see Section 2.3.3). Calculating Kendall's τ for the correlation of the rankings (1 through 9) of entropy with the rankings of bid prices, it is remarkable that 56 of the subjects show significant positive rank correlation, as the theory predicts. Only 2 show significant negative correlation.

Continuing with the idea of separating information valuation from action selection, Hilton and Swieringa (1981) offer subjects a series of treatments in which the risk neutral demand price increases with the Rothschild–Stiglitz variability of the state distribution (see Sections 6.3.2 and 7.1). Although the assessed demand prices are increasing with variability and hence qualitatively consistent with the theory, there is a definite tendency for overvaluation.

Whether the experimental design involves cards, spinners, and urns, or is cluttered up with substantive detail, the general conclusion of this section is that DMs are qualitatively adept at behaving like Bayesians. This arms us with confidence that users respond to incentives in the system in ways that are qualitatively consistent with the decision theory paradigm.

9.4 A Decision-Theoretic Model for System Design

The organization's goal is to design a system that maximizes the expectation of the total information gain. There are a couple of methods for applying decision-theoretic notions to information system evaluation and design at the organizationwide level. One approach [Ahituv (1980)] is to use decision theory to identify a set of attributes that affect the organization's information value or gain, and combine them using the multiattribute utility theory of Keeney and Raiffa (1976) to provide an overall evaluation. Hammitt and Cave (1991) implement this approach in the context of the allocation of a research budget. Pasa and Shugan (1996) investigate the value of a marketing research subsystem as a function of such things as environmental uncertainty, the stakes, and industry factors. Measurement is a key difficulty here, requiring judicious choice of the appropriate proxies.

This section develops a more direct aggregation from the individual to the whole based upon the decision theory approach to information and organization developed most fully by Marschak (1974) and Marschak and Radner (1972). This framework has been applied to accounting information subsystems by, among others, Mock (1973; 1976), Butterworth (1972), Demski (1972), Feltham (1972), and Itami (1977), but the integration of decision theory into the design and evaluation of more general information systems has been slower. From the more general perspective, this section sketches a normative model to explain user behavior as it depends on the information use environment and the incentives and services the system provides. Upon aggregation, the model characterizes the optimal system design in terms of organizational tradeoffs between expected information value and cost. The ultimate goal of this approach is a decision-theoretic integration of information system design, user behavior, and organizational performance.

9.4.1 The Framework

Expanding upon the discussion surrounding Figure 1.2, the unit of production is one terminal use of the information system, either as a decision making or as a monitoring instrument. In the notation, each terminal use of the system is indexed by the subscript τ, and has associated with it a user variable cost $\mathcal{UC}_\tau$, and a system variable cost $\mathcal{SC}_\tau$. Just as steel, glass, plastic, and rubber are intermediate goods that feed into the production of an automobile, an intermediate data processing use feeds into a terminal use. All such variable costs should be allocated to the terminal use to which it contributes. The total fixed cost of system, $\mathcal{FC}$, are all costs independent of terminal use. These include system fixed cost such as the funding for archiving and organizing, and the fixed cost to the users of the time spent learning to interface with the system, time that could be spent on other activities for the organization.

Let $\upsilon_\tau(x, y)$, as in (1.1), denote the ex-post consequential value of the information generated in terminal use τ of the system. This quantity is zero for all monitoring and some decision making uses. Given good accounting estimates of user and system variable costs, the organization's gain that results from terminal use τ is

$$\mathcal{G}_\tau = \upsilon_\tau(x, y) - \mathcal{UC}_\tau - \mathcal{SC}_\tau. \tag{9.1}$$

The organization's realized total information gain is $\mathcal{OG} = -\mathcal{FC} + \Sigma_\tau \mathcal{G}_\tau$, as in (1.3). This accounts for the total gain, and as an accounting model it is useful as far as it goes.

The assumption of optimizing behavior is the mechanism that breathes economic life into an accounting model. Here, the basic assumption is that users solve their information processing problem optimally, using criteria consistent with the goals of the organization. The user, being closest to the need for information, is modeled as the manager of a team comprising herself and the agents of the information system. The model assumes each user, given the overall system as it presents itself, manages the resources of the team with the objective of maximizing the expected information gain to the organization from each use. This assumption opens the door to the study of the consequences of this behavior for the design and management of information systems.

There is an economic rationale for the assumption that the user solves the decision problem in the most cost-effective manner, from the viewpoint of the organization. Economic theory holds that, in equilibrium, employees are paid the value of their marginal product; in other words, salary is equal to the incremental contribution that the employee makes to the organization's profitability. Hence, it is in the user's pecuniary interest to maximize the organization's information gain.

There is an important complication: although the user is fully cognizant of her own costs, she may have significantly less knowledge of system costs. The optimizing organization, of course, is cognizant of all costs, and designs the incentives of the system with this asymmetry of knowledge in mind. It is a matter of indifference to the organization whether one dollar's worth of time is spent out of the budget of the superior, the subordinate, or the system, if the same informativeness results. The organization needs to provide incentives that ensure the user applies the combination of resources that minimizes the total organizational costs of achieving the optimal level of informativeness.

Simpson and Prusak (1995) describe one company that requires users to estimate the information value whenever they desire to apply the system's services, and the system follows up later to obtain another estimate of the value, presumably this time an ex-post measure. Another option, user charges, serve to remind the user that system-budgeted resources are not free and should not be used capriciously. This is the purpose of funny money in an organization: to give signals to employees about the true costs and provide incentives to allocate the organization's resources optimally. Bowonder and Miyake (1992) present a case study of integrated information management in a large industrial corporation.

9.4.2 A Theory of Information Production and Cost

The key component of the economic model is the user's production function for information; the informativeness of the information processing in terminal use τ is a function of 1) the effort the employees and agents of the organization undertake, and 2) the technical relationship between the input of effort and the output of informativeness, an index of the productivity of the system that is summarized as the "effectiveness" of the system. In its most general form, the information production function is

$$\theta_\tau = f_\tau(\varepsilon_\tau, \phi), \tag{9.2}$$

where θ_τ is the index of informativeness in terminal use τ, generated as a function of the effort applied by the organization ε_τ and the effectiveness parameter ϕ. The total effort the organization puts in is under the management of the user, and the effectiveness is determined by the organization's decisions on design and investments in the system.

The total effort of the organization ε_τ is the total time the employees and agents expend on the terminal use τ: the time spent identifying and choosing sources plus the time spent obtaining, understanding, and applying the resulting messages. The basic hypothesis is that the more effort the organization puts in, the greater the informativeness extracted. For a given ϕ, it takes more effort to find more informative sources and to evaluate the meaning of more informative messages. The effectiveness parameter ϕ has a positive effect on the productivity of effort: the higher ϕ is, the more informativeness can be generated by a given amount of effort. Equivalently, the higher ϕ is, the less effort is necessary to generate the same informativeness.

The formal model assumes θ_τ is a one-dimensional summary of informativeness, and it is reasonable to postulate diminishing returns to information processing effort. Suppose an information structure has a maximum potential informativeness $\bar{\theta}_\tau$, achievable by devoting infinite effort to its processing. In other words, assume the information production function is such that informativeness is concave, nondecreasing, and bounded in ε_τ, with $\theta_\tau \rightarrow \bar{\theta}_\tau$ as $\varepsilon_\tau \rightarrow \infty$ for any ϕ. Since the optimal effort is unlikely to be infinite, in this model the informativeness of an information structure is endogenous because effort is a choice variable for the user.

In most real cases informativeness is multidimensional,[5] highly user- and problem-dependent, subjective, and ex-ante difficult to measure. This characterization is not always true; there are several examples in Chapters 5 and 6 in which informativeness is summarized by a one-dimensional measure, such as sample size (Example 5.2), uncertainty removed (Example 5.4b), correlation coefficient (Sections 5.1.2 and 5.2.4), and the theoretical model (6.55). In other cases informativeness can be measured by proxy or ex-post from user surveys, such as Tague-Sutcliffe's (1995) measure of retrieval informativeness. Nevertheless, especially when considering the incorporation of information from multiple sources, it may be necessary to accept that ex-ante composite informativeness is not observable or too costly to observe.

In other words, the informativeness of an information structure is something that is assessed and determined internally by the user. The informativeness index is a technical way of modeling the answer to a question that users really do ask themselves or others: "What might I get out of this source if I choose to access its message and invest a certain amount of time and effort to understand it?" There is no presumption that any DM-user of an information system formally performs any analysis. Fortunately, informativeness is a choice variable and can be "optimized out" in a formal theory, leaving only the observable consequences of the choices made.

Effort is costly to the organization. Let γ be the per unit accounting cost per unit of the organization's effort. Then the organization's total variable cost is

$$\mathcal{C}_\tau = \gamma\varepsilon_\tau. \tag{9.3}$$

The translation of effort into the equivalent amount of the organization's money (the estimation of γ) is an important empirical problem with many nuances.

To develop a specific cost function, consider the information production function first applied in Section 8.3.4:

$$\theta_\tau = 1 - \exp\{-\phi\varepsilon_\tau\}, \tag{9.4}$$

where the index of effectiveness ϕ is such that $\partial\theta_\tau/\partial\phi = [\varepsilon_\tau]\exp\{-\phi\varepsilon_\tau\} > 0$. A system with larger ϕ can provide greater θ_τ for the same effort ε_τ. The upper graph in Figure 9.2 depicts this production function for two values of ϕ, $\phi' < \phi''$. The inverse function is

$$\varepsilon_\tau = -\frac{1}{\phi}\log[1 - \theta_\tau]. \tag{9.5}$$

---

[5] Zmud's (1978) factor analysis of 35 subjects judging the informativeness of various reports identifies eight dimensions.

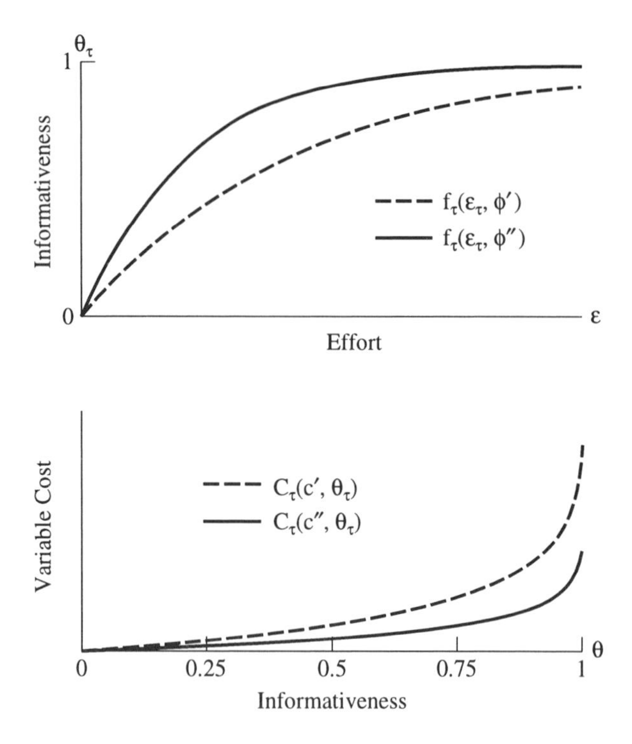

Figure 9.2. An increase in the effectiveness parameter from ϕ' to ϕ'' increases the production of informativeness for a given effort, and lowers the organization's variable cost of achieving a given level of informativeness.

Applying the cost equation (9.3), the cost function is

$$C_\tau(c, \theta_\tau) = -c \log[1 - \theta_\tau] = ck(\theta_\tau), \tag{9.6}$$

where $c \equiv \gamma/\phi$ is the cost parameter. The higher c is the less efficient is the system via some combination of the economic cost of performing a given effort and the technological ability to transform effort into informativeness. Under this cost function, with $c > 0$ it is infinitely costly to produce perfect information, that is, to achieve $\overline{\theta}_\tau = 1$. The lower graph in Figure 9.2 shows this cost function for two values of c, $c' > c''$. Examples of system activities that lower the cost function (i.e., reduce the minimum cost of achieving a given level of informativeness) include improved management, more efficient technology, and interpersonal sources with greater knowledge.

Hence the theory establishes that the user has an important control over the cost of information: she can alter the effort she and the organization undertake in performing the analysis, thereby affecting the informativeness she extracts from the system. The postulate is that it is more costly for a user to make a more informative use of the system.

9.4.3 Information Gain in a Canonical Decision Problem

To model the value side of the net gain, this section creates a prototype organization in which the employees and agents face a set of decision problems with identical structure but different stakes. Assume that over the course of a specified time period, the employees and agents of the organization face N decision problems, each of which has the same canonical structure but involves different stakes. Indexing each individual problem with the subscript τ, the canonical problem has two actions $\mathbf{a} = \{a_1, a_2\}$, two states $\mathbf{X} = \{x_1, x_2\}$, and the payoff function $\pi_\tau(x, a)$ depicted in Table 9.1.

Table 9.1. The Canonical Decision Problem

	x_1 = Situation Favorable	x_2 = Situation Unfavorable
a_1 = develop	w_τ	$-w_\tau$
a_2 = do not develop	0	0

To give the canonical problem an interpretation, a_1 can mean "develop a new product," and a_2 mean "do not develop." Depending on the realization of the state, the choice a_1 either gains or loses the organization $\$w_\tau$; this amount completely characterizes the stakes of the canonical problem τ. The organization, not knowing the stakes of the problem before it arises, properly views w_τ as the realization of a random variable with probability density function $p(w_\tau)$. In this model the individual DM knows the stakes; contrast this with the approach of Yovits, Foulk, and Rose (1981), in which the payoffs are random variables in the DM's mind and can be learned via experimentation.

Adopting Laplace's principle of insufficient reason, assume the prior distribution of the state for each problem is $p(x_1) = p(x_2) = \frac{1}{2}$. Then $E_x\, \pi_\tau(x, a_1) = E_x\, \pi_\tau(x, a_2) = 0$. Although the DM is strictly speaking indifferent between the actions, suppose the organization opts for conservatism and insists on the choice a_2. Then the optimal prior action is to do nothing, $a_0 = a_2$, and

$$\max_a E_x\, \pi_\tau(x, a) = E_x\, \pi_\tau(x, a_0) = 0, \tag{9.7}$$

for every canonical decision problem τ.

The DM also has the option to use the organization's information system. The informativeness the DM derives from the system depends on her effort and on the effectiveness of the system. Whatever information source the DM ultimately chooses, assume that the semantic content of the message accepted can be summarized into one of two messages: y_1 = "the situation is favorable for state x_1," and y_2 = "the situation is favorable for state x_2."

The statistical informativeness of the system toward decision problem τ is summarized by the parameter θ_τ in the posterior distribution of the states given by the matrix (9.8):

$$\Pi(\theta_\tau) = \begin{bmatrix} p(x_1|y_1;\theta_\tau) & p(x_1|y_2;\theta_\tau) \\ p(x_2|y_1;\theta_\tau) & p(x_2|y_2;\theta_\tau) \end{bmatrix} = \begin{bmatrix} \frac{1}{2}[1+\theta_\tau] & \frac{1}{2}[1-\theta_\tau] \\ \frac{1}{2}[1-\theta_\tau] & \frac{1}{2}[1+\theta_\tau] \end{bmatrix}. \quad (9.8)$$

Here, $0 \le \theta_\tau \le 1$. When $\theta_\tau = 1$, the system offers perfect information: depending on the message, either $p(x_1 | y_1;\ \theta_\tau) = 1$ or $p(x_2 | y_2;\ \theta_\tau) = 1$, so the state is precisely identified. At the other extreme, $\theta_\tau = 0$ is null information: $p(x_1 | y_1;\ \theta_\tau) = p(x_2 | y_2;\ \theta_\tau) = \frac{1}{2}$, which is the same knowledge already embodied in the prior distribution.

Conditional on receiving the message y_1, the expected outcome from responding with action a_1 is

$$\begin{aligned} E_{x|y_1} \pi_\tau(x, a_1) &= \pi_\tau(x_1, a_1)\, p(x_1 | y_1;\ \theta_\tau) + \pi_\tau(x_2, a_1)\, p(x_2 | y_1;\ \theta_\tau) \\ &= \tfrac{1}{2} w_\tau[1 + \theta_\tau] - \tfrac{1}{2} w_\tau[1 - \theta_\tau] \\ &= w_\tau \theta_\tau \ \ge\ 0. \end{aligned} \quad (9.9)$$

Hence, the optimal response $a_{y_1} = a_1$ and the conditional value of information defined by (3.29) is, writing $V_{y;\,\theta} \equiv V(y;\ \theta)$,

$$V_\tau(y_1;\ \theta_\tau) = E_{x|y_1}\{\pi_\tau(x,\ a_{y_1}) - \pi_\tau(x,\ a_0)\} = w_\tau \theta_\tau. \quad (9.10)$$

Conditional on the message y_2, the expected outcome from responding with action a_1 is

$$E_{x|y_2} \pi_\tau(x, a_1) = \tfrac{1}{2} w_\tau[1 - \theta_\tau] - \tfrac{1}{2} w_\tau[1 + \theta_\tau] = -\ w_\tau \theta_\tau \ \le\ 0, \quad (9.11)$$

so $a_{y_2} = a_2$ and

$$V_\tau(y_2;\ \theta_\tau) = E_{x|y_2}\{\pi_\tau(x,\ a_{y_2}) - \pi_\tau(x,\ a_0)\} = 0. \quad (9.12)$$

Given that the marginal distribution of the messages is $p(y_1;\ \theta_\tau) = p(y_2;\ \theta_\tau) = \frac{1}{2}$, the expected value of information is

$$E_y\ V_\tau(y;\ \theta_\tau) = \tfrac{1}{2} w_\tau \theta_\tau + \tfrac{1}{2}[0] = \tfrac{1}{2} w_\tau \theta_\tau \equiv \tilde{V}_\tau(w_\tau,\ \theta_\tau). \quad (9.13)$$

In the canonical decision problem, the expected value of information increases directly with the stakes w_τ and the statistical informativeness θ_τ that the user chooses to extract from the system.

With the cost function (9.6), the user determines θ_τ^* as in (1.12):

$$\max_\theta \mathbf{G}_\tau(w_\tau,\ c,\ \theta_\tau) = \tilde{V}_\tau(w_\tau,\ \theta_\tau) - \mathbf{C}_\tau(c,\ \theta_\tau) = \tfrac{1}{2} w_\tau \theta_\tau + c \log[1 - \theta_\tau]. \quad (9.14)$$

The optimal informativeness depends on the stakes and on the cost parameter $c \equiv \gamma/\phi$, which comprises the system effectiveness and the cost of effort: $\theta^*_\tau = f_\tau(w_\tau, c)$. In this illustration, evaluating the derivative

$$dG_\tau(w_\tau, c, \theta_\tau) / d\theta_\tau = \tfrac{1}{2}w_\tau - c[1 - \theta_\tau]^{-1},$$

yields the optimum as

$$\theta^*_\tau = f_\tau(w_\tau, c) = \begin{cases} 1 - [2c/w_\tau] & \text{if } w_\tau \geq 2c \\ 0 & \text{if } w_\tau \leq 2c. \end{cases} \tag{9.15}$$

For sufficiently large stakes, the optimal informativeness increases as the cost parameter c decreases. If c is too large relative to the stakes of the problem, the optimal solution $\theta^*_\tau = 0$ means the user does not seek information and immediately solves the uninformed problem. Equation (9.15) describes the demand curve for informativeness as it depends upon c, the price of informativeness. Figure 9.3 depicts this demand curve; an increase in the stakes leads to an increase in demand, shifting the curve to the right. Using (9.5), optimal effort is

$$\varepsilon^*_\tau = -\frac{1}{\phi}\log[2c/w_\tau] \tag{9.16}$$

if $w_\tau > 2c$, and 0 otherwise.

Depending upon whether the user enters the system, the expected information gain from decision problem τ is $G_\tau(w_\tau, c, \theta^*_\tau) = \frac{1}{2}w_\tau\theta^*_\tau + c\log[1 - \theta^*_\tau]$. Substituting in the optimal choice function gives $G_\tau(w_\tau, c, f_\tau(w_\tau, c)) \equiv \tilde{G}^*_\tau(w_\tau, c)$:

$$\tilde{G}^*_\tau(w_\tau, c) = \begin{cases} \tfrac{1}{2}w_\tau - c + c\log[2c/w_\tau] & \text{if } w_\tau \geq 2c \\ 0 & \text{if } w_\tau \leq 2c. \end{cases} \tag{9.17}$$

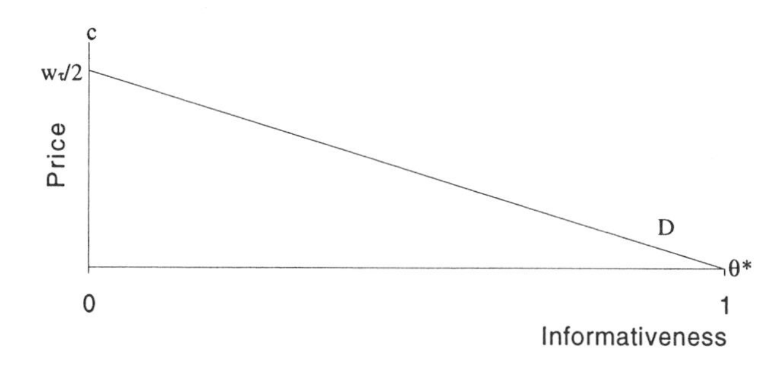

Figure 9.3. The demand curve for informativeness shifts with the stakes in the canonical problem. Because of the assumed prior distribution, there is no region of useless information.

The quantity $\tilde{G}_\tau^*(w_\tau, c)$ is the expected information gain to the organization from a decision problem with stakes w_τ when the cost parameter of the system design is c. Note that for every $w_\tau > 2c$, $\partial \tilde{G}_\tau^*(w_\tau, c)/\partial w_\tau = \frac{1}{2} - c/w_\tau > 0$ and $\partial \tilde{G}_\tau^*(w_\tau, c)/\partial c = \log[2c/w_\tau] < 0$. The expected gain increases as the stakes increase and decreases as the cost parameter increases.

Both optimal informativeness and the expected gain increase with the system effectiveness parameter ϕ, but evaluating the derivative of (9.16) with respect to ϕ, optimal effort may go up or down as a result of improved system effectiveness. On the one hand, higher ϕ means less effort is needed to achieve a given level of informativeness, but on the other hand, desiring to incorporate more informativeness requires more effort; the net impact of ϕ on ε_τ^* is ambiguous.

This conclusion is consistent with empirical work by Todd and Benbasat (1992). These researchers investigate the impact on users from improving system effectiveness through the provision of a DSS. In a search problem to find an apartment, the subjects using the decision aid significantly reduce their effort, while not changing the "amount" of information they observe. Even if the optimal informativeness to incorporate is inelastic and does not increase significantly with ϕ, the more efficient production of informativeness increases the organization's information gain, as it frees up time for additional endeavors relevant to the organization's benefit.

9.4.4 Reported Results from a Survey

Suppose now the prototype organization administers a user survey similar to the type discussed in Section 9.1.3. Although in an actual survey informativeness is not observable, such a survey can observe 1) the source the user chooses to process, 2) the effort and other costs borne in the processing, and 3) the user's estimate of the value of the source's information. An analysis of hypothetical results allows a better understanding of what actual survey data would be measuring in the context of an economic model with optimizing behavior.

The organization views the stakes w_τ in any problem τ as a random variable. Suppose there are N = 15,360 decision problems that arise during one time period. To simplify the exposition, assume the stakes are distributed uniformly across six possible values: $w_\tau = 0, 2, 4, 6, 8, 10$. An exponential distribution, characterized by a large number of problems with low stakes, and a small number with large stakes, is an alternative that might fit actual data better.

Consider three possible values for c: $c_1 = \frac{1}{2}$, $c_2 = 1$, and $c_3 = 2$. Since $c \equiv \gamma/\phi$, lower c means more effectiveness in the system (i.e., higher ϕ for a specified γ). Out of the 15,360 decision problems, a certain number of decision makers choose not to seek information, and therefore do not make a decision making use of the system and are not observed by the survey. The switchpoint is $w_\tau = 2c$, so the nonusers number 2,560 if $c = \frac{1}{2}$, 5,120 if $c = 1$, and 7,680 if $c = 2$.

The hypothesis: the more effective is the system, given the accounting parameter γ, the greater the utilization of the system. It is important to remember, however, that maximizing the total information gain is the goal of the organization, not maximizing system use.

Table 9.2 uses the solution (9.15) to show the optimal θ_τ^* for different combinations of w_τ and c. Note that the extracted informativeness increases with w_τ and decreases with c (increases with ϕ for a specified γ).

Table 9.2. Optimal Informativeness as a Function of Stakes and System Effectiveness

		w_τ					
		0	2	4	6	8	10
	$\frac{1}{2}$	0.0	.5	.75	0.83	0.87	0.9
c	1	0.0	0.0	.50	0.66	0.75	0.8
	2	0.0	0.0	0.0	0.33	0.50	0.6

The posterior distribution of the states under the optimal informativeness θ_τ^* is derived by inserting (9.15) into (9.8); for those circumstances with $\theta_\tau^* > 0$,

$$\Pi(\theta_\tau^*) = \begin{bmatrix} p(x_1|y_1;\theta_\tau^*) & p(x_1|y_2;\theta_\tau^*) \\ p(x_2|y_1;\theta_\tau^*) & p(x_2|y_2;\theta_\tau^*) \end{bmatrix} = \begin{bmatrix} 1-[c/w_\tau] & c/w_\tau \\ c/w_\tau & 1-[c/w_\tau] \end{bmatrix}. \quad (9.18)$$

For $\theta_\tau^* > 0$, the joint probabilities of all state-message combinations are given by, since $p(y_1;\theta_\tau) = p(y_2;\theta_\tau) = \frac{1}{2}$,

$$\rho(\theta_\tau^*) = \begin{bmatrix} p(x_1,y_1;\theta_\tau^*) & p(x_1,y_2;\theta_\tau^*) \\ p(x_2,y_1;\theta_\tau^*) & p(x_2,y_2;\theta_\tau^*) \end{bmatrix} = \begin{bmatrix} \frac{1}{2}-[c/2w_\tau] & \frac{1}{2}c/w_\tau \\ \frac{1}{2}c/w_\tau & \frac{1}{2}-[c/2w_\tau] \end{bmatrix}. \quad (9.19)$$

Turning now to the reported consequential value, in the canonical problem there are a large number of observations reporting 0 value, even though all the observations are on decision making uses. All users who process the message y_2 report zero value because there is no impact on action. Since $p(y_2;\theta_\tau) = \frac{1}{2}$, this is half of all responses. This result is peculiar to this model and such observations do not reflect a false start due to insufficient information. Those users who process message y_1 do report consequential value. The question is, what exactly are they reporting?

Suppose the users are reporting the ex-post consequential value $\upsilon_\tau(x, y;\theta_\tau^*)$. The possible reports would be

$$\begin{bmatrix} \upsilon_\tau(x_1,y_1;\theta_\tau^*) & \upsilon_\tau(x_1,y_2;\theta_\tau^*) \\ \upsilon_\tau(x_2,y_1;\theta_\tau^*) & \upsilon_\tau(x_2,y_2;\theta_\tau^*) \end{bmatrix} = \begin{bmatrix} w_\tau & 0 \\ -w_\tau & 0 \end{bmatrix}. \quad (9.20)$$

Note the possibility of negative consequential value: "I would have been better off without it!" The joint probability $p(x_i, y_j;\theta_\tau^*)$, from (9.19), gives the chance any observed user ($w_\tau > 2c$) would report the ex-post value $\upsilon_\tau(x_i, y_j;\theta_\tau^*)$. Figure 9.4 presents the histogram of reported consequential value for the case c = 1. As an example of the calculation to obtain this hypothetical histogram, there are 2,560 decision problems with $w_\tau = 4$, and all would be observed in the survey. Half would receive message y_2 and report 0 as the ex-post value, $\frac{1}{2} - \frac{1}{8} = 37.5\%$ of them would report $w_\tau = 4$, and the remaining 12.5% would report $-w_\tau = -4$.

The histogram in Figure 9. 4 does not resemble the distribution that Griffiths and King (1993, page 80) report. Even if the distribution of stakes were exponential, with the negative values this does not seem to be what the actual surveys are measuring. Since the Griffiths–King survey takes place immediately after cognition and application, it could be that the realization of the state has not yet occurred and the respondents are actually reporting the conditional value of the message $V_\tau(y;\ \theta_\tau^*) = E_{x|y}\ \upsilon_\tau(x,\ y;\ \theta_\tau^*)$. In other words, reported consequential value is the expected ex-post value of the message they have applied, before the ultimate consequences are known.

Under this timing for the survey, evaluating (9.10) and (9.12) using (9.15) yields the possible reports

$$[V_\tau(y_1;\ \theta_\tau^*),\ V_\tau(y_2;\ \theta_\tau^*)] \ = \ [w_\tau - 2c,\ 0]. \tag{9.21}$$

Here, the processing of y_2 still leads to a reported value of zero, but it is interesting that the processing of y_1 leads to a reported value somewhat less than the stakes. The DM-user is hedging her report due to continued uncertainty about the outcome of the decision.

Figure 9.5 provides the histograms of reported consequential value for each of the three alternative values of c. Table 9.3 contains some summary data on each of these distributions.

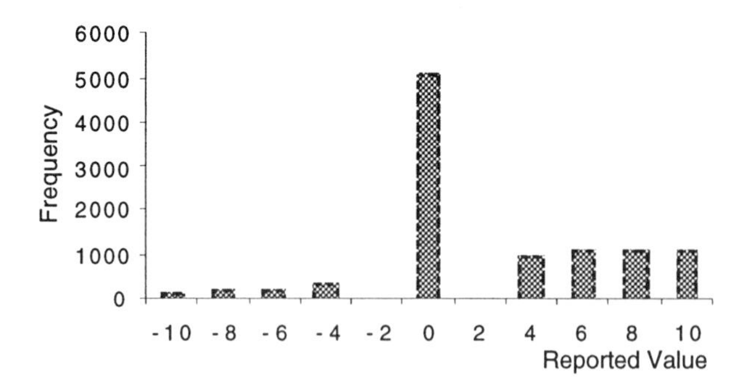

Figure 9.4. If the survey is administered after the final resolution of the decision problem, the respondents are reporting the ex-post value, and the results should include a small number of negative observations.

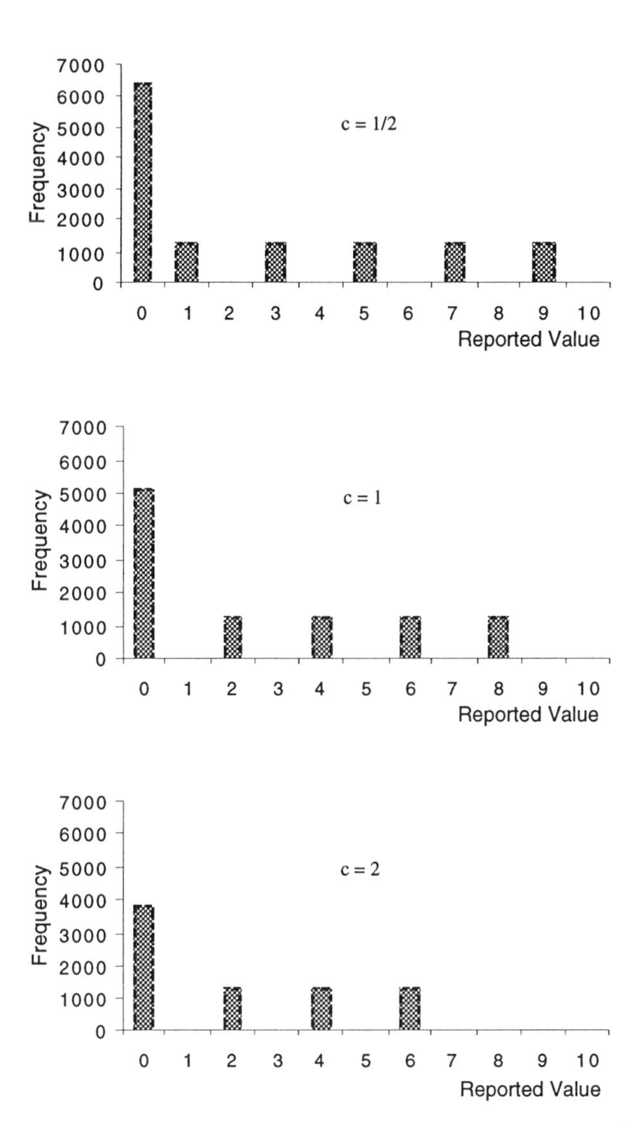

Figure 9.5. If the respondents are reporting the conditional value of information, all the observations are nonnegative. The graphs depict how the effectiveness parameter (inversely related to c, for a given γ) affects the results.

The total reported consequential value can serve as an index of the informativeness of the system. This is not to say, however, that the system $c = \frac{1}{2}$ is optimal for the organization because it says nothing about the costs of achieving that level of effectiveness. The goal is to maximize total information gain, not information value and not the system's technological effectiveness. If $c = \frac{1}{2}$ costs $500,000 while $c = 1$ costs $10,000, clearly the latter system provides the organization with more information gain. Greater effectiveness may lead to both more system value and system cost. This is the final economic question: find the optimal c^* that maximizes the organization's expected information gain.

Table 9.3. Summary Results on the Hypothetical Survey for Different Values of c

		Total Decision Problems	Total Nonusers	Total Users at Zero	Total Value	Mean Value/ Problem
	$\frac{1}{2}$	15,360	2,560	6,400	$32,000	$2.083
c	1	15,360	5,120	5,120	$25,600	$1.667
	2	15,360	7,680	3,840	$15,360	$1.000

9.4.5 *Characterization of the Organization's Optimal System*

This subsection studies the prototype organization's problem of designing the optimal information system. The organization views the stakes w_τ as a random variable, defined on a space **W** of monetary amounts, with the density function $p(w_\tau)$. The expected incremental gain to the organization from an arbitrary problem τ is

$$\overline{\mathcal{G}}_\tau(c) = \int_{\mathbf{W}} \tilde{G}_\iota^*(w_\tau, c)\, p(w_\tau)\, dw_\tau. \tag{9.22}$$

In the illustration, there is no incremental gain when $w_\tau \leq 2c$, so the expected incremental gain is

$$\overline{\mathcal{G}}_\tau(c) = \int_{2c}^{\infty} \{\tfrac{1}{2} w_\tau - c + c \log[2c/w_\tau]\}\, p(w_\tau)\, dw_\tau. \tag{9.23}$$

Suppose w_τ is distributed uniformly between 0 and W. The expected incremental gain evaluates to

$$\begin{aligned} \overline{\mathcal{G}}_\tau(c) &= \int_{2c}^{W} \{\tfrac{1}{2} w_\tau - c + c \log[2c/w_\tau]\} W^{-1}\, dw_\tau \\ &= \tfrac{1}{4} W - c^2/W + c \log[2c/W]. \end{aligned} \tag{9.24}$$

Note that $d\overline{\mathcal{G}}_\tau(c)/dc < 0$.

Let $\mathcal{FC}(c)$ be the fixed cost of achieving c, a function that decreases with c (and hence increases with the effectiveness parameter ϕ). Summing over all N decision making uses and subtracting the fixed cost of providing the system gives the organization's expected information gain,

$$\overline{\mathcal{OG}}(c) = -\mathcal{FC}(c) + \Sigma_\tau \overline{\mathcal{G}}_\tau(c) = -\mathcal{FC}(c) + N\overline{\mathcal{G}}_\tau(c). \tag{9.25}$$

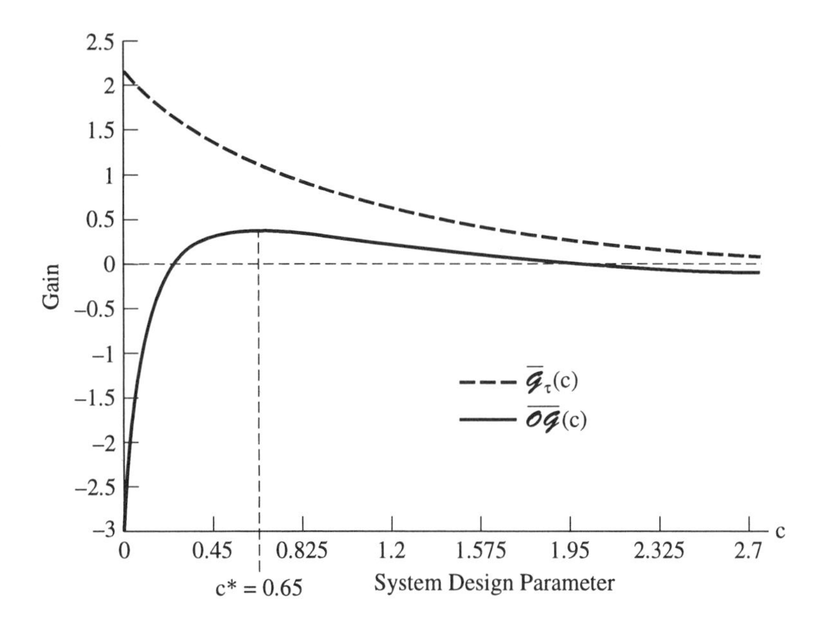

Figure 9.6. The greater the system effectiveness parameter ϕ, the larger the expected incremental gain in any canonical decision problem. Since the organization bears a higher fixed cost to provide greater system effectiveness, the optimal system design trades off the counterbalancing forces.

Equation (9.25) is the model's version of the accounting relationship (1.3). The optimal system design is the value of the choice parameter c that

$$\max_c \overline{\mathcal{OG}}(c) = -\mathcal{FC}(c) + N\overline{\mathcal{G}}_\tau(c). \tag{9.26}$$

The quantity $\overline{\mathcal{OG}}(c^*)$ is the organization's expected information gain from the optimally designed information system.

Suppose $\mathcal{FC}(c) = .5N/c$. Then, using (9.24) and (9.26), the optimal system c^* maximizes

$$\max_c \overline{\mathcal{OG}}(c) = -.5N/c + \tfrac{1}{4}NW - Nc^2/W + Nc\log[2c/W]. \tag{9.27}$$

This equation is difficult to solve analytically. Setting W = 10 and N = 1, spreadsheet calculations show $c^* = 0.65$, with the expected incremental gain per use at \$1.1316, and the expected information gain at \$0.3623. Figure 9.6 graphs the functions (9.24) and (9.27) as a function of c.

9.5 Postlude

At one level, the system design problem is deceptively simple: 1) allow managers efficient access to the statistical information they need to scan the environments that offer potential gain; 2) design the system so that it is flexible enough so that it can serve information needs, user by user; 3) give the DMs pragmatic information, not statistical information (i.e., get messages into the hands of people who can act upon them); 4) set up communication networks so that pragmatic information developed in one use, but also pragmatic in other uses, can be accessed efficiently; and 5) if a particular decision problem is cut-and-dried, provide a DSS to make the decision, thereby freeing up managerial time.

Aside from the obvious deficiency that these assertions say nothing about the cost of doing these things, Ackoff (1967), in his classic article entitled "Management Misinformation Systems," argues that the preceding design principles are based upon assumptions that may not be justified. Going through each principle one by one, it becomes apparent that there is a prerequisite that must be satisfied to give these assertions validity, prerequisites that in most cases involve the ideas of decision theory.

Ackoff states that the first design principle is based upon the assumption that most managers operate in an environment in which there is a lack of relevant information. The true problem, as he sees it, is not the lack of relevant information; it is the oversupply of irrelevant information. Perhaps this information overload is exacerbated by the tendency to overbuy and overvalue information that Section 9.3 documents. The prerequisite solution is for system design to concentrate more on precision in filtering and retrieval, while recognizing that relevance is often individual-specific.

Designing the system to serve the information needs of each user assumes that managers need the information they want. Ackoff argues that managers cannot know their information needs until they understand the decision problems they face. The prerequisite solution is some kind of structured thinking, if not formal model building, about the decisions each manager faces. Without sound framing of the decision problems, managers' information wants will include much that is irrelevant, contributing to information overload.

Providing only pragmatic information to decision makers presumes that the managers not only know what they need, but also how to incorporate the information so as to improve decisions and information gains. To do this, the prerequisite is that managers know how to value and use information, especially in complex situations.

Ackoff questions whether improved communication within the organization can actually improve organizational performance. Despite the rather strong evidence that interpersonal communication is beneficial, he argues that an alternative solution is an organizational structure that places all decisions requiring the same information under a common authority, making the sharing less necessary.

The idea that the organization should provide a DSS to make straightforward decisions is premised on the notion that the manager does not need to understand how the system works, just how to use it. The problem here, as Ackoff sees it, is that black box solutions are no better than the programmer's understanding of the problem. To judge the quality of the DSS, the manager must understand the logic of the decision problem; again, proper framing is the prerequisite solution.

This book ends with the same thought it began with in the Preface: in the future Information Age, people, either technically or heuristically, are going to have to frame decisions and assess information value, cost, and gain within complex contexts. These assessments depend upon economic, statistical, technological, and human factors, making broad synthesis a necessity. As we have seen, many disciplines in addition to decision theory have important roles to play in this synthesis. In the ideal, the well-designed, integrated information management function does not have to be an overhead cost; it can be a profit center.

References

Ackoff, R. L., 1967, Management Misinformation Systems. *Management Science*, 14, 147–156.

Adams, R. M., K. J. Bryant, B. A. McCarl, D. M. Legler, J. O'Brien, A. Solow, and R. Weiher, 1995, Value of Improved Long-Range Weather Information. *Contemporary Economic Policy*, 13, 10–19.

Ahituv, N., 1980, A Systematic Approach Toward Assessing the Value of an Information System. *MIS Quarterly*, 4, 61–75.

Ahituv, N., and Y. Wand, 1984, Comparative Estimation of Information Under Two Business Objectives. *Decision Sciences,* 15, 31–51.

Ahituv, N., and B. Ronen, 1988, Orthogonal Information Structures—A Model to Evaluate the Information Provided by a Second Opinion. *Decision Sciences*, 19, 255–268.

Akerlof, G., 1970, The Market for Lemons: Qualitative Uncertainty and the Market Mechanism. *Quarterly Journal of Economics*, 84, 488–500.

Allais, M., 1979, The So-Called Allais Paradox and Rational Decisions Under Uncertainty. *Expected Utility Hypotheses and the Allais Paradox* (M. Allais and O. Hagen, eds.), D. Reidel, Dordrecht, Holland, 437–681.

Allen, B., 1986, The Demand for (Differentiated) Information. *Review of Economic Studies*, 53, 311–323.

Allen, T. J., 1977, *Managing the Flow of Technology: Technology Transfer and the Dissemination of Technological Information Within the R&D Organization.* MIT Press, Cambridge, MA.

Anscombe, F. J., and R. J. Aumann, 1963, A Definition of Subjective Probability. *Annals of Mathematical Statistics*, 34, 199–205.

Antonovitz, F., and T. Roe, 1986, A Theoretical and Empirical Approach to the Value of Information in Risky Markets. *Review of Economics and Statistics*, 68, 105–114.

Aoki, M., 1986, Horizontal vs. Vertical Information Structure of the Firm. *American Economic Review*, 76, 971–983.

Arrow, K. J., 1965, *Aspects of the Theory of Risk Bearing.* Yrjö Jahnssonin Säätio, Helsinki.

Arrow, K. J., 1972, The Value of and Demand for Information. *Decision and Organization* (C. B. McGuire and R. Radner, eds.), North Holland, Amsterdam, 131–139.

Arrow, K. J., 1985, Informational Structure of the Firm. *American Economic Review Proceedings*, 75, 303–307.

Arrow, K. J., and R. C. Lind, 1970, Uncertainty and the Evaluation of Public Investment Decisions. *American Economic Review*, 60, 364–378.

Arrow, K. J., T. E. Harris, and J. Marschak, 1951, Optimal Inventory Policy. *Econometrica*, 19, 250–272.

Åström, K. J., 1970, *Introduction to Stochastic Control Theory.* Academic Press, New York and London.

Avriel, M., and A. C. Williams, 1970, The Value of Information and Stochastic Programming. *Operations Research*, 18, 947–954.

Babcock, B. A., 1990, The Value of Weather Information in Market Equilibrium. *American Journal of Agricultural Economics*, 72, 63–72.

Baldwin, N. S., and R. E. Rice, 1997, Information-Seeking Behavior of Securities Analysts: Individual and Institutional Influences, Information Sources and Channels, and Outcomes. *Journal of the American Society for Information Science*, 48, 674–693.

Baquet, A. E., A. N. Halter, and F. S. Conklin, 1976, The Value of Frost Forecasting: a Bayesian Approach. *American Journal of Agricultural Economics*, 58, 511–520.

Baron, D. P., 1971, Information in Two-Stage Programming Under Uncertainty. *Naval Research Logistics Quarterly*, 18, 169–176.

Baron, D. P., and R. Myerson, 1982, Regulating a Monopolist with Unknown Costs. *Econometrica*, 50, 911–930.

Barza, M., and S. G. Pauker, 1980, The Decision to Biopsy, Treat, or Wait in Suspected Herpes Encephalitis. *Annals of Internal Medicine*, 92, 641–649.

Bassan, B., and M. Scarsini, 1995, On the Value of Information in Multi-Agent Decision Theory. *Journal of Mathematical Economics*, 24, 557–576.

Bawden, D., 1997, The Nature of Prediction and the Information Future: Arthur C. Clarke's Odyssey Vision. *Aslib Proceedings*, 49, 57–60.

Beckmann, M. J., 1958, Decision and Team Problems in Airline Reservations. *Econometrica*, 26, 134–145.

Bellman, R. E., 1961, *Adaptive Control Processes: A Guided Tour.* Princeton University Press, Princeton, NJ.

Bellman, R. E., and R. Kalaba, 1957, Dynamic Programming and Statistical Communication Theory. *Proceedings of the National Academy of Sciences*, 43, 749–751.

Bereanu, B., 1966, On Stochastic Linear Programming. The Laplace Transform of the Distribution of the Optimum and Applications. *Journal of Mathematical Analysis and Applications*, 15, 280–294.

Berger, J. O., 1985, *Statistical Decision Theory and Bayesian Analysis, 2nd Edition.* Springer-Verlag, New York.

Bernknopf, R. L., D. S. Brookshire, M. McKee, and D. R. Soller, 1997, Estimating the Social Value of Geologic Map Information: A Regulatory Application. *Journal of Environmental Economics and Management*, 32, 204–218.

Best, D. P., 1996, Business Process and Information Management. *The Fourth Resource* (D. P. Best, ed.), Aslib/Gower, London.

Birge, J. R., 1995, Models and Model Value in Stochastic Programming. *Annals of Operations Research*, 59, 1–18.

Birge, J. R., and F. Louveaux, 1997, *Introduction to Stochastic Programming.* Springer-Verlag, New York.

Blackwell, D., 1951, Comparison of Experiments. *Proceedings of the Second Berkeley Symposium on Mathematical Statistics and Probability* (J. Neyman, ed.), 93–102.

Blackwell, D., 1953, Equivalent Comparisons of Experiments. *Annals of Mathematical Statistics*, 24, 265–273.

Blackwell, D., and M. A. Girshick, 1954, *Theory of Games and Statistical Decisions*. John Wiley, New York.

Blair, R. D., and R. E. Romano, 1988, The Influence of Attitudes Toward Risk on the Value of Forecasting. *Quarterly Journal of Economics*, 103, 387–396.

Blattberg, R. C., and S. J. Hoch, 1990, Database Models and Managerial Intuition: 50% Model + 50% Manager. *Management Science*, 36, 887–899.

Blocher, E. J., R. P. Moffie, and R. W. Zmud, 1985, How Best to Communicate Numerical Data. *Internal Auditor*, 42, 38–42.

Bohnenblust, H. F., L. S. Shapley, and S. Sherman, 1949, *Reconnaissance in Game Theory*. RM-208, RAND, Santa Monica, CA.

Bookstein, A., and S. T. Klein, 1990, Compression, Information Theory, and Grammars: A Unified Approach. *ACM Transactions on Information Systems*, 8, 27–49.

Borch, K. H., 1968, *The Economics of Uncertainty*. Princeton University Press, Princeton.

Boulding, K. E., 1966, The Economics of Knowledge and the Knowledge of Economics. *American Economic Review Papers and Proceedings*, 56, 1–13.

Bowonder, B., and T. Miyake, 1992, Creating and Sustaining Competitiveness: Information Management Strategies of Nippon Steel Corporation. *International Journal of Information Management*, 12, 39–56.

Bradford, D. F., and H. H. Kelejian, 1977, The Value of Information for Crop Forecasting in a Market System: Some Theoretical Issues. *Review of Economic Studies*, 44, 519–531.

Bradford, D. F., and H. H. Kelejian, 1981, The Value of Information in a Storage Model with Open- and Closed-Loop Controls. *Journal of Economic Dynamics and Control*, 3, 307–317.

Braunstein, Y. M., 1982, The Functioning of Information Markets. *Information Reports and Bibliographies*, 11, 3–20.

Braunstein, Y. M., 1985, Information as a Factor of Production: Substitutability and Productivity. *The Information Society*, 3, 261–273.

Brier, G. W., 1950, Verification of Forecasts Expressed in Terms of Probability. *Monthly Weather Review*, 78, 1–3.

Brown, R. V., A. S. Kahr, and C. Peterson, 1974, *Decision Analysis for the Manager*. Holt, Rinehart and Winston, New York.

Brunswik, E., 1952, *The Conceptual Framework of Psychology*. University of Chicago Press, Chicago, IL.

Brynjolfsson, E., and L. Hitt, 1996, Paradox Lost? Firm-Level Evidence on the Returns to Information Systems Spending. *Management Science*, 42, 541–558.

Burk, C. F., and F. W. Horton, 1988, *InfoMap: A Complete Guide to Discovering Corporate Information Resources*. Prentice-Hall, Englewood Cliffs, NJ.

Bush, V., 1945, As We May Think. *Atlantic Monthly*, 176, 101–108.

Butterworth, J. E., 1972, The Accounting System as Information Function. *Journal of Accounting Research*, 10, 1–27.

Casson, M., 1997, *Information and Organization*. Clarendon Press, Oxford.

Chan, Y.-S., 1981, A Note on Risk and the Value of Information. *Journal of Economic Theory*, 25, 461–465.

Chavas, J.-P., 1993, On the Demand for Information. *Economic Modelling*, 10, 398–407.

Chavas, J.-P., P. M. Kristjanson, and P. Matlon, 1991, On the Role of Information in Decision Making. The Case of Sorghum Yield in Burkina Faso. *Journal of Development Economics*, 35, 261–280.

Cherry, C., 1966, *On Human Communication: A Review, a Survey, and a Criticism, 2nd Edition.* MIT Press, Cambridge, MA.

Choo, C. W., 1998, *The Knowing Organization: How Organizations Use Information to Construct Meaning, Create Knowledge, and Make Decisions.* Oxford University Press, New York.

Chow, G., 1975, *Analysis and Control of Dynamic Economic Systems.* John Wiley, New York.

Clayton, D. G., 1978, A Model for Association in Bivariate Life Tables and Its Application in Epidemiological Studies of Familial Tendency in Chronic Disease Incidence. *Biometrika*, 65, 141–151.

Clemen, R. T., 1991, *Making Hard Decisions.* PWS-Kent, Boston.

Clemen, R. T., and R. L. Winkler, 1985, Limits for the Precision and Value of Information from Dependent Sources. *Operations Research*, 33, 427–442.

Clemen, R. T., A. H. Murphy, and R. L. Winkler, 1995, Screening Probability Forecasts: Contrasts Between Choosing and Combining. *International Journal of Forecasting*, 11, 133–146.

Cook, R. D., and M. E. Johnson, 1981, A Family of Distributions for Modeling Non-Elliptically Symmetric Multivariate Data. *Journal of the Royal Statistical Society B*, 43, 210–218.

Connolly, T., 1988, Studies of Information-Purchase Processes. *Human Judgment: The SJT View* (B. Brehmer and C. R. B. Joyce, eds.), North-Holland, Amsterdam, 401–425.

Cosier, R. A., 1978, The Effects of Three Potential Aids for Making Strategic Decisions on Prediction Accuracy. *Organizational Behavior and Human Performance*, 22, 295–306.

Cox, D. R., 1958, Two Further Applications of a Model for Binary Regression. *Biometrika*, 45, 563–565.

Cox, D. R., 1970, *The Analysis of Binary Data.* Methuen and Company, London.

Crémer, J., 1982, A Simple Proof of Blackwell's "Comparison of Experiments" Theorem. *Journal of Economic Theory*, 27, 439–443.

Cronin, B., 1982, Invisible Colleges and Information Transfer: A Review and Commentary with Particular Reference to the Social Sciences. *Journal of Documentation*, 38, 212–236.

Cronin, B., and E. Davenport, 1991, *Elements of Information Management.* Scarecrow Press, Metuchen, NJ.

Culnan, M. J., 1983, Environmental Scanning: The Effects of Task Complexity and Source Accessibility on Information Gathering Behavior. *Decision Sciences*, 14, 194–206.

Cyert, R. M., and J. G. March, 1963, *A Behavioral Theory of the Firm.* Prentice-Hall, Englewood Cliffs, NJ.

Daft, R. L., R. H. Lengel, and L. K. Trevino, 1989, Message Equivocality, Media Selection, and Manager Performance: Implications for Information Systems. *MIS Quarterly*, 13, 355–366.

Daft, R. L., J. Sormunen, and D. Parks, 1988, Chief Executive Scanning, Environmental Characteristics, and Company Performance: An Empirical Study. *Strategic Management Journal*, 9, 123–139.

D'Agostino, R. B., and M. A. Stephens, 1986, *Goodness of Fit Tests*. Marcel Dekker, New York.

Dakins, M. E., J. E. Toll, M. J. Small, and K. P. Brand, 1996, Risk-Based Environmental Remediation: Bayesian Monte Carlo Analysis and the Expected Value of Sample Information. *Risk Analysis*, 16, 67–79.

Davenport, T. H., R. G. Eccles, and L. Prusak, 1992, Information Politics. *Sloan Management Review*, 34, 53–65.

Davis, D. R., and W. M. Dvoranchik, 1971, Evaluation of the Worth of Additional Data. *Water Resources Bulletin*, 7, 700–707.

Dawid, A. P., 1982, The Well-Calibrated Bayesian. *Journal of the American Statistical Association*, 77, 605–613.

DeGroot, M. H., 1962, Uncertainty, Information, and the Sequential Design of Experiments. *Annals of Mathematical Statistics*, 33, 404–419.

DeGroot, M. H., 1970, *Optimal Statistical Decisions*. McGraw-Hill, New York.

DeGroot, M. H., and S. E. Fienberg, 1982, Assessing Probability Assessors: Calibration and Refinement. *Statistical Decision Theory and Related Topics III, Volume I* (J. O. Berger and S. S. Gupta, eds.), Academic Press, New York, 291–314.

DeGroot, M. H., and S. E. Fienberg, 1986, Comparing Probability Forecasters: Basic Binary Concepts and Multivariate Extensions. *Bayesian Inference and Decision Techniques* (P. Goel and A. Zellner, eds.), Elsevier, Holland, 247–264.

Demski, J. S., 1972, *Information Analysis*. Addison-Wesley, Reading MA.

Dessimoz, J.-D., 1995, Quantitative Assessment and Economical Evaluation of Information and Knowledge. Paper presented at the International Colloquium on the Economics of Information, ENSSIB, Lyon, France.

Dewhirst, H. D., 1971, Influence of Perceived Information-Sharing Norms on Communication Channel Utilization. *Academy of Management Journal*, 14, 305–315.

Dhar, V., and R. Stein, 1997, *Seven Methods for Transforming Corporate Data into Business Intelligence*. Prentice Hall, Upper Saddle River, NJ.

Diamond, P. A., and J. E. Stiglitz, 1974, Increases in Risk and in Risk Aversion. *Journal of Economic Theory*, 8, 337–360.

Dickson, G. W., J. A. Senn, and N. L. Chervany, 1977, Research in Management Information Systems: The Minnesota Experiments. *Management Science*, 23, 913–923.

Drèze, J. H., and F. Modigliani, 1972, Consumption Decisions Under Uncertainty. *Journal of Economic Theory*, 5, 308–335.

Dulá, J. H., 1992, An Upper Bound on the Expectation of Simplicial Functions of Multivariate Random Variables. *Mathematical Programming*, 55, 69–80.

Dvoretzky, A., A. Wald, and J. Wolfowitz, 1951, Elimination of Randomization in Certain Statistical Decision Procedures and Zero-Sum Two-Person Games. *Annals of Mathematical Statistics*, 22, 1–21.

Economist, 1996, The Hitchhiker's Guide to Cybernomics. September 28, 3–46.

Edirisinghe, N. C. P., and W. T. Ziemba, 1994, Bounds for Two-Stage Stochastic Programs with Fixed Recourse. *Mathematics of Operations Research*, 19, 292–313.

Edwards, W., 1965, Optimal Strategies for Seeking Information: Models for Statistics, Choice Reaction Times, and Human Information Processing. *Journal of Mathematical Psychology*, 2, 312–329.

Eisenberg, M., and C. Barry, 1988, Order Effects: A Study of the Possible Influence of Presentation Order on User Judgments of Document Relevance. *Journal of the American Society for Information Science*, 39, 293–300.

Elderton, W. P., and N. L. Johnson, 1969, *Systems of Frequency Curves*. Cambridge Press, London.

Ellger, C., 1991, The Importance of the Quaternary (Information) Sector for Spatial Development: the Case of Baden-Württemberg. *De-Industrialisation and New Industrialisation in Britain and Germany* (T. Wild and P. Jones, eds.), Anglo-German Foundation for the Study of Industrial Society, London, 283–302.

Emshoff, J. R., and I. I. Mitroff, 1978, Improving the Effectiveness of Corporate Planning. *Business Horizons*, 21, 49–60.

Epstein, L. G., 1980, Decision Making and the Temporal Resolution of Uncertainty. *International Economic Review*, 21, 269–283.

Evans, J. S., N. C. Hawkins, and J. D. Graham, 1988, The Value of Monitoring for Radon in the Home: A Decision Analysis. *JAPCA*, 38, 1380–1385.

Feldman, M. S., and J. G. March, 1981, Information in Organizations as Signal and Symbol. *Administrative Science Quarterly*, 26, 171–186.

Feltham, G. A., 1972, *Information Evaluation*. Studies in Accounting Research #5, American Accounting Association.

Ferguson, T. S., 1967, *Mathematical Statistics: A Decision Theoretic Approach*. Academic Press, New York.

Finkel, A. M., and J. S. Evans, 1987, Evaluating the Benefits of Uncertainty Reduction in Environmental Health Risk Management. *JAPCA*, 37, 1164–1171.

Fishburn, P., 1988, *Nonlinear Preference and Utility Theory*. Johns Hopkins University Press, Baltimore, MD.

Fletcher, P. D., and L. Diamond, 1995, The Information Based Organization. Paper presented at the International Colloquium on the Economics of Information, ENSSIB, Lyon, France.

Fox, K. A., J. K. Sengupta, and E. Thorbecke, 1973, *Theory of Quantitative Economic Policy with Applications to Economic Growth, Stabilization, and Planning, 2nd Edition*. North-Holland, Amsterdam.

Frank, M. J., 1979, On the Simultaneous Associativity of F(x, y) and x + y − F(x, y). *Aequationes Mathematicae*, 19, 194–226.

Frees, E. W., and E. A. Valdez, 1997, Understanding Relationships Using Copulas. *North American Actuarial Journal*, 2, 1–25.

Freixas, X, and J.-J. Laffont, 1984, On the Irreversibility Effect. *Bayesian Models in Economic Theory* (M. Boyer and R. E. Kihlstrom, eds.), North-Holland, Amsterdam, 105–114.

Fried, L. S., and C. R. Peterson, 1969, Information Seeking: Optional Versus Fixed Stopping. *Journal of Experimental Psychology*, 80, 525–529.

Friedman, B. M., 1979, The Information Value of Observing Monetary Policy Deliberations. *Journal of Economic Dynamics and Control*, 1, 383–393.

Friedman, M., and L. J. Savage, 1948, The Utility Analysis of Choices Involving Risk. *Journal of Political Economy*, 56, 279–304.

Fuller, W. A., 1996, *Introduction to Statistical Time Series, 2nd Edition*. Wiley, New York.

Futrell, G., 1968–1986, Hog Situation. *Iowa Outlook Letter*, Iowa State University, Ames, IA.

Gaba, A., and R. L. Winkler, 1995, The Impact of Testing Errors on Value of Information: A Quality Control Example. *Journal of Risk and Uncertainty*, 10, 5–13.

Gallagher, C. A., 1974, Perceptions of the Value of a Management Information System. *Academy of Management Journal*, 17, 46–55.

Gates, B., 1995, *The Road Ahead.* Viking, New York.

Geanakoplos, J., and P. Milgrom, 1991, A Theory of Hierarchies Based on Limited Managerial Attention. *Journal of the Japanese and International Economies*, 5, 205–225.

Genest, C., and L.-P. Rivest, 1993, Statistical Inference Procedures for Bivariate Archimedean Copulas. *Journal of the American Statistical Association*, 88, 1034–1043.

Genest, C., and J. V. Zidek, 1986, Combining Probability Distributions: A Critique and an Annotated Bibliography. *Statistical Science*, 1, 114–135.

Getz, M., 1988, More Benefits of Automation. *College and Research Libraries*, 49, 534–544.

Gilboa, I., and E. Lehrer, 1991, The Value of Information—An Axiomatic Approach. *Journal of Mathematical Economics*, 20, 443–459.

Gioia, D. A., 1992, Pinto Fires and Personal Ethics: A Script Analysis of Missed Opportunities. *Journal of Business Ethics*, 11, 379–389.

Glazer, R., J. H. Steckel, and R. S. Winer, 1992, Locally Rational Decision Making: The Distracting Effect of Information on Managerial Performance. *Management Science*, 38, 212–226.

Gnanadesikan, R., 1996, *Methods for Statistical Data Analysis of Multivariate Observations, 2nd Edition.* Wiley, New York.

Gould, J. P., 1974, Risk, Stochastic Preference, and the Value of Information. *Journal of Economic Theory*, 8, 64–84.

Green, P. E., M. H. Halbert, and J. S. Minas, 1964, An Experiment in Information Buying. *Journal of Advertising Research*, 4, 17–23.

Green, P. E., P. J. Robinson, and P. T. Fitzroy, 1967, *Experiments on the Value of Information in Simulated Marketing Environments*. Allyn and Bacon, Boston, MA.

Grettenberg, T. L., 1964, The Ordering of Finite Experiments. *Transactions of the Third Prague Conference on Information Theory, Statistical Decision Functions, Random Processes*, Czechoslovak Academy of Sciences, Prague, 193–206.

Griffiths, J.-M., 1982, The Value of Information and Related Systems, Products, and Services. *Annual Review of Information Science and Technology, Volume 17* (M. E. Williams, ed.), Knowledge Industry Publications, White Plains, NY, 269–284.

Griffiths, J.-M., and D. W. King, 1993, *Special Libraries: Increasing the Information Edge*. Special Libraries Association, Washington, DC.

Grinyer, P. H., and D. Norburn, 1975, Planning for Existing Markets: Perceptions of Executives and Financial Performance. *Journal of the Royal Statistical Society A*, 138, 70–97.

Grossman, S. J., R. E. Kihlstrom, and L. J. Mirman, 1977, A Bayesian Approach to the Production of Information and Learning by Doing. *Review of Economic Studies*, 44, 533–547.

Gumbel, E. J., 1960, Bivariate Exponential Distributions. *Journal of the American Statistical Association*, 55, 698–707.

Hammitt, J. K., and J. A. K. Cave, 1991, *Research Planning for Food Safety*. R-3946-ASPE/NCTR, RAND, Santa Monica, CA.

Hanoch, G., and H. Levy, 1969, The Efficiency Analysis of Choices Involving Risk. *Review of Economic Studies*, 36, 335–346.

Hanrahan, M. S., 1972, Optimum Swine Production and Marketing Strategies with Limited Farrowing and Feeding Space. Unpublished Master's thesis, Iowa State University, Ames, IA.

Hausch, D. B., and W. T. Ziemba, 1983, Bounds on the Value of Information in Uncertain Decision Problems II. *Stochastics*, 10, 181–217.

Hayami, Y. and W. Peterson, 1972, Social Returns to Public Information Services: Statistical Reporting of U.S. Farm Commodities. *American Economic Review*, 62, 119–130.

Hayenga, M., et al., 1985, *The U.S. Pork Sector: Changing Structure and Organization*. Iowa State Press, Ames, IA.

Hayes, R. M., 1995, The Fine Structure of Community Information Economies. Paper presented at the International Colloquium on the Economics of Information, ENSSIB, Lyon, France.

Hayes, R. M., 1997, Economics of Information. *International Encyclopedia of Information and Library Science* (J. Feather and P. Sturges, eds.), Routledge, London.

Hayes, R. M., and H. Borko, 1983, Mathematical Models of Information System Use. *Information Processing and Management*, 19, 173–186.

Hayes, R. M., and T. Erickson, 1982, Added Value as a Function of Purchases of Information Services. *The Information Society*, 1, 307–338.

Hendrickson, A. D., and R. J. Buehler, 1971, Proper Scores for Probability Forecasters. *Annals of Mathematical Statistics*, 42, 1916–1921.

Henry, C., 1974, Investment Decisions Under Uncertainty: The "Irreversibility Effect." *American Economic Review*, 64, 1006–1012.

Hess, J., 1982, Risk and the Gain from Information. *Journal of Economic Theory*, 27, 231–238.

Hildreth, C., 1963, Bayesian Statisticians and Remote Clients. *Econometrica*, 31, 422–438.

Hilton, R. W., 1979, The Determinants of Cost Information Value: An Illustrative Analysis. *Journal of Accounting Research*, 17, 411–435.

Hilton, R. W., 1980, Integrating Normative and Descriptive Theories of Information Processing. *Journal of Accounting Research*, 18, 477–505.

Hilton, R. W., 1981, The Determinants of Information Value: Synthesizing Some General Results. *Management Science*, 27, 57–64.

Hilton, R. W., 1990, Failure of Blackwell's Theorem Under Machina's Generalization of Expected-Utility Analysis Without the Independence Axiom. *Journal of Economic Behavior and Organization*, 13, 233–244.

Hilton, R. W., and R. J. Swieringa, 1981, Perception of Initial Uncertainty as a Determinant of Information Value. *Journal of Accounting Research*, 19, 109–119.

Hilton, R. W., R. J. Swieringa, and R. E. Hoskin, 1981, Perception of Accuracy as a Determinant of Information Value. *Journal of Accounting Research*, 19, 86–108.

Hirshleifer, J., 1973, Where Are We in the Theory of Information? *American Economic Review*, 63, 31–39.

Hirshleifer, J., and J. G. Riley, 1992, *The Analytics of Uncertainty and Information*. Cambridge Press, Cambridge, UK.

Ho, T. S. Y., and R. Michaely, 1988, Information Quality and Market Efficiency. *Journal of Financial and Quantitative Analysis*, 23, 53–70.

Hogarth, R. M., 1975, Cognitive Processes and the Assessment of Subjective Probability Distributions. *Journal of the American Statistical Association*, 70, 271–289.

Hogarth, R. M., and S. Makridakis, 1981, Forecasting and Planning: An Evaluation. *Management Science*, 27, 115–138.

Hogg, R. V., and A. T. Craig, 1978, *Introduction to Mathematical Statistics, 4th Edition*. Macmillan, New York.

Horowitz, I., and P. Thompson, 1995, The Sophisticated Decision Maker: All Work and No Pay? *Omega, The International Journal of Management Science*, 23, 1–11.

Howard, R. A., 1966, Information Value Theory. *IEEE Transactions on System Science and Cybernetics*, ssc-2, 22–26.

Howard, R. A., 1971, Proximal Decision Analysis. *Management Science*, 17, 507–541.

Howard, R. A., J. E. Matheson, and D. W. North, 1972, The Decision to Seed Hurricanes. *Science*, 176, 1191–1202.

Huber, G. P., 1974, Methods for Quantifying Subjective Probabilities and Multi-Attribute Utilities. *Decision Sciences*, 5, 430–458.

Hurwicz, L., 1960, Optimality and Informational Efficiency in Resource Allocation Processes. *Mathematical Methods in the Social Sciences, 1959* (K. J. Arrow, S. Karlin, and P. Suppes, eds.), Stanford Press, Stanford CA, 27–46.

Hurwicz, L., 1972, On Informationally Decentralized Systems. *Decision and Organization* (C. B. McGuire and R. Radner, eds.), North-Holland, Amsterdam.

Ijiri, Y., and H. Itami, 1973, Quadratic Cost-Volume Relationship and Timing of Demand Information. *Accounting Review*, 48, 724–737.

Iman, R. L., and W. J. Conover, 1980, Small Sample Sensitivity Analysis Techniques for Computer Models, with an Application to Risk Assessment. *Communications in Statistics*, A9, 1749–1842.

Iman, R. L., and W. J. Conover, 1982, A Distribution-Free Approach to Inducing Rank Correlation Among Input Variables. *Communications in Statistics*, B11, 311–334.

Iman, R. L., and J. C. Helton, 1988, An Investigation of Uncertainty and Sensitivity Analysis Techniques for Computer Models. *Risk Analysis*, 8, 71–90.

Irwin, F. W., and W. A. S. Smith, 1957, Value, Cost, and Information as Determiners of Decision. *Journal of Experimental Psychology*, 54, 229–232.

Itami, H., 1977, *Adaptive Behavior: Management Control and Information Analysis*. Studies in Accounting Research #15, American Accounting Association.

James, B. R., and R. A. Freeze, 1993, The Worth of Data in Predicting Aquitard Continuity in Hydrogeological Design. *Water Resources Research*, 29, 2049–2065.

Johnson, N. L., and S. Kotz, 1970, *Continuous Univariate Distributions*. John Wiley, New York.

Johnson, N. L., S. Kotz, and N. Balakrishnan, 1994, *Continuous Univariate Distributions, 2nd Edition*. John Wiley, New York.

Jones, R. A., and J. M. Ostroy, 1984, Flexibility and Uncertainty. *Review of Economic Studies*, 51, 13–32.

Jouini, M. N., and R. T. Clemen, 1996, Copula Models for Aggregating Expert Opinions. *Operations Research*, 44, 444–457.

Kahneman, D., and A. Tversky, 1979a, Prospect Theory: An Analysis of Decision Under Risk. *Econometrica*, 47, 263–91.

Kahneman, D., and A. Tversky, 1979b, Intuitive Predictions: Biases and Corrective Procedures. *Forecasting. TIMS Studies in the Management Sciences Volume 12* (S. Makridakis, and S. C. Wheelwright, eds.), North-Holland, Amsterdam, 313–328.

Kall, P., and S. W. Wallace, 1994, *Stochastic Programming*. John Wiley, Chichester.

Kalman, R. E., 1960, A New Approach to Linear Filtering and Prediction Problems. *Journal of Basic Engineering*, 82, 34–45.

Kalman, R. E., and R. S. Bucy, 1961, New Results in Linear Filtering and Prediction Theory. *Journal of Basic Engineering*, 83, 95–107.

Kanarick, A. F., J. M. Huntington, and R. C. Petersen, 1969, Multi-Source Information Acquisition with Optional Stopping. *Human Factors*, 11, 379–386.

Kantor, P. B., 1979, A Review of Library Operations Research. *Library Research*, 1, 295–345.

Kantor, P. B., 1995, Of Time and the Library: New Approaches to Assessing the Impact of the Library on Individuals and Institutions. Paper presented at the International Colloquium on the Economics of Information, ENSSIB, Lyon, France.

Karlin, S., 1960, Dynamic Inventory Policy with Varying Stochastic Demands. *Management Science*, 6, 231–258.

Katz, R. W., B. G. Brown, and A. H. Murphy, 1987, Decision-Analytic Assessment of the Economic Value of Weather Forecasts: The Fallowing/Planting Problem. *Journal of Forecasting*, 6, 77–89.

Katz, R., and T. J. Allen, 1982, Investigating the Not Invented Here (NIH) Syndrome: A Look at the Performance, Tenure, and Communication Patterns of 50 R&D Project Groups. *R&D Management*, 12, 7–19.

Keasey, K., 1984, Regret Theory and Information: A Note. *Economic Journal*, 94, 645–48.

Keeney, R. L., 1992, *Value-Focused Thinking: A Path to Creative Decisionmaking*. Harvard University Press, Cambridge, MA.

Keeney, R. L., and H. Raiffa, 1976, *Decisions with Multiple Objectives: Preferences and Value Tradeoffs*. John Wiley, New York.

Kelly, J. L., 1956, A New Interpretation of the Information Rate. *Bell System Technical Journal*, 35, 917–926.

Kelly, M., 1991, The Value of the Option to "Wait and See." *Economics Letters*, 36, 147–151.

Kiefer, N. M., 1989, A Value Function Arising in the Economics of Information. *Journal of Economic Dynamics and Control*, 13, 201–223.

Kihlstrom, R. E., 1974a, A Bayesian Model of Demand for Information about Product Quality. *International Economic Review*, 15, 99–118.

Kihlstrom, R. E., 1974b, A General Theory of Demand for Information about Product Quality. *Journal of Economic Theory*, 8, 413–439.

King, W. R., and B. J. Epstein, 1983, Assessing Information System Value: An Experimental Study. *Decision Sciences*, 14, 34–45.

Kingma, B. R., 1996, *The Economics of Access versus Ownership: The Costs and Benefits of Access to Scholarly Articles via Interlibrary Loan and Journal Subscriptions*. Haworth Press, New York.

Klugman, S. A., and R. A. Parsa, 1999, Fitting Bivariate Loss Distributions with Copulas. *Insurance: Mathematics and Economics*, forthcoming.

Koenig, M. E. D., 1990, Information Services and Downstream Productivity. *Annual Review of Information Science and Technology, Volume 25* (M. E. Williams, ed.), Knowledge Industry Publications, White Plains, NY, 55–86.

Koenig, M. E. D., 1992, The Importance of Information Services for Productivity "Under-Recognized" and "Under-Invested." *Special Libraries*, Fall, 199–210.

Kraft, D. H., and B. R. Boyce, 1991, *Operations Research for Libraries and Information Agencies*. Academic Press, San Diego.

Kreps, D. M., 1988, *Notes on the Theory of Choice*. Westview Press, Boulder CO.

Krzysztofowicz, R., 1992, Bayesian Correlation Score: A Utilitarian Measure of Forecast Skill. *Monthly Weather Review*, 120, 208–219.

Kuhlen, R., 1995, Value-Added Effects of Information Markets. Paper presented at the International Colloquium on the Economics of Information, ENSSIB, Lyon, France.

Kwon, Y. K., J. C. Fellingham, and D. P. Newman, 1979, Stochastic Dominance and Information Value. *Journal of Economic Theory*, 20, 213–230.

Laffont, J.-J., 1976, Risk, Stochastic Preference, and the Value of Information: A Comment. *Journal of Economic Theory*, 12, 483–487.

Laffont, J.-J., 1989, *The Economics of Uncertainty and Information*. MIT Press, Cambridge, MA.

Laffont, J.-J. and J. Tirole, 1986, Using Cost Observation to Regulate Firms. *Journal of Political Economy*, 94, 614–641.

Laffont, J.-J. and J. Tirole, 1993, *A Theory of Incentives in Procurement and Regulation*. MIT Press, Cambridge, MA.

Lanzetta, J. T., and V. T. Kanareff, 1962, Information Cost, Amount of Payoff, and Level of Aspiration as Determinants of Information Seeking in Decision Making. *Behavioral Science*, 7, 459–473.

LaValle, I. H., 1967, A Bayesian Approach to an Individual Player's Choice of Bid in Competitive Sealed Auctions. *Management Science*, 13, 584–597.

LaValle, I. H., 1968, On Cash Equivalents and Information Evaluation Under Uncertainty. *Journal of the American Statistical Association*, 63, 252–290.

LaValle, I. H., 1978, *Fundamentals of Decision Analysis*. Holt, Rinehart and Winston, New York.

LaValle, I. H., 1980, On Value and Strategic Role of Information in Semi-Normalized Decisions. *Operations Research*, 28, 129–138.

Lave, L. B., 1963, The Value of Better Weather Information to the Raisin Industry. *Econometrica*, 31, 151–164.

Lave, L. B., and G. S. Omenn, 1986, Cost-Effectiveness of Short-Term Tests for Carcinogenicity. *Nature*, 324, 29–34.

Lave, L. B., and G. S. Omenn, 1988, Screening Toxic Chemicals: How Accurate Must Tests Be? *Journal of the American College of Toxicology*, 7, 565–574.

Lawrence, D. B., 1976, The Value of Information in Decision Making: A Bibliography. *Setting Statistical Priorities. Report of the Panel on Methodology for Statistical Priorities* (I. R. Savage et al., eds.), National Academy of Sciences, Washington, DC, 145–172.

Lawrence, D. B., 1987, The Assessment of the Expected Value of Information in the Binary Decision Model. *Managerial and Decision Economics*, 8, 301–306.

Lawrence, D. B., 1991a, Managerial Evaluation of Exogenous Forecast Sources. *Managerial and Decision Economics*, 12, 249–259.

Lawrence, D. B., 1991b, Models for the Assessment of the Value of Forecast Information. *Journal of Forecasting*, 10, 425–443.

Lawrence, D. B., 1992, Attitude Towards Risk, Prospect Variability, and the Value of Imperfect Information. *Southern Economic Journal*, 59, 194–209.

Lawrence, D. B., 1997, Evaluation et Acquisition d'une Source d'Information. *La Société Informationelle: Enjeux Sociaux et Approches Economiques* (A. Mayère, ed.), L'Harmattan, Paris, 197–213.

Lawrence, D. B., and T. G. Watkins, 1986, Rural Banking Markets and Holding Company Entry. *Journal of Economics and Business*, 38, 123–130.

Leitch, G., and J. E. Tanner, 1991, Economic Forecast Evaluation: Profits Versus the Conventional Error Measures. *American Economic Review*, 81, 580–590.

Levine, J. M., M. G. Samet, and R. E. Brahlek, 1975, Information Seeking with Limitations on Available Information and Resources. *Human Factors*, 17, 502–513.

Lichtenstein, S., B. Fischhoff, and L. D. Phillips, 1982, Calibration of Probabilities: The State of the Art to 1980. *Judgment Under Uncertainty: Heuristics and Biases* (D. Kahneman et al., eds.), Cambridge University Press, Cambridge, 306–334.

Lim, J. S., and M. O'Connor, 1996, Judgmental Forecasting with Interactive Forecasting Support Systems. *Decision Support Systems*, 16, 339–357.

Lindley, D. V., 1972, *Bayesian Statistics, A Review*. Society for Industrial and Applied Mathematics, Philadelphia.

Lindley, D. V., 1985, *Making Decisions, 2nd Edition*. John Wiley, London.

Lindley, D. V., A. Tversky, and R. V. Brown, 1979, On the Reconciliation of Probability Assessments. *Journal of the Royal Statistical Society Series A*, 142, 146–180.

Loomes, G., and R. Sugden, 1982, Regret Theory: An Alternative Theory of Rational Choice Under Uncertainty. *Economic Journal*, 92, 805–824.

Loomes, G., and R. Sugden, 1987, Some Implications of a More General Form of Regret Theory. *Journal of Economic Theory*, 41, 270–287.

Losee, R. M., 1990, *The Science of Information*. Academic Press, San Diego.

MacCrimmon, K. R., and S. Larsson, 1979, Utility Theory: Axioms Versus "Paradoxes." *Expected Utility Hypotheses and the Allais Paradox* (M. Allais and O. Hagen, eds.), D. Reidel, Dordrecht, Holland, 333–409.

Machina, M. J., 1982, "Expected Utility" Analysis Without the Independence Axiom. *Econometrica*, 50, 277–323.

Machina, M. J., 1987, Choice Under Uncertainty: Problems Solved and Unsolved. *Journal of Economic Perspectives*, 1, 121–154.

Machina, M. J., 1989, Dynamic Consistency and Non-Expected Utility Models of Choice Under Uncertainty. *Journal of Economic Literature*, 27, 1622–1668.

Machlup, F., 1962, *The Production and Distribution of Knowledge in the United States*. Princeton University Press, Princeton, NJ.

Madansky, A., 1959, Bounds on the Expectation of a Convex Function of a Multivariate Random Variable. *Annals of Mathematical Statistics*, 30, 743–746.

Madansky, A., 1960, Inequalities for Stochastic Linear Programming Problems. *Management Science*, 6, 197–204.

Markowitz, H., and N. Usmen, 1996, The Likelihood of Various Stock Market Return Distributions. Part 1: Principles of Inference; Part 2: Empirical Results. *Journal of Risk and Uncertainty*, 13, 207–247.

Marschak, J., 1950, Rational Behavior, Uncertain Prospects, and Expected Utility. *Econometrica*, 18, 111–141. (Errata. *Econometrica*, 18, 312).
Marschak, J., 1954, Towards an Economic Theory of Organization and Information. *Decision Processes* (R. M. Thrall et al., eds.), John Wiley, New York, 187–220.
Marschak, J., 1959, Remarks on the Economics of Information. *Contributions to Scientific Research in Management.* Western Data Processing Center, University of California, Los Angeles, 79–100.
Marschak, J., 1963, On Adaptive Programming. *Management Science*, 9, 517–526.
Marschak, J., 1964, Actual Versus Consistent Decision Behavior. *Behavioral Science*, 9, 103–110.
Marschak, J., 1971, Economics of Information Systems. *Journal of the American Statistical Association*, 66, 192–219.
Marschak, J., 1972, Optimal Systems for Information and Decision. *Techniques of Optimization* (A. V. Balakrishnan, ed.), Academic Press, New York, 355–370.
Marschak, J., 1974, *Economic Information, Decision, and Prediction, Volume 2*. D. Reidel, Holland.
Marschak, J., and K. Miyasawa, 1968, Economic Comparability of Information Systems. *International Economic Review*, 9, 137–174.
Marschak, J., and R. Radner, 1972, *Economic Theory of Teams*. Yale Press, New Haven, CT.
Martyn, J., 1964, Unintentional Duplication of Research. *New Scientist*, 21, 338.
Mason, R. M., and P. G. Sassone, 1978, A Lower Bound Cost Benefit Model for Information Services. *Information Processing and Management*, 14, 71–83.
Mayère, A., 1997, *La Société Informationelle: Enjeux Sociaux et Approches Economiques*. L'Harmattan, Paris.
McCall, J. J., 1965, The Economics of Information and Optimal Stopping Rules. *Journal of Business of the University of Chicago*, 38, 300–317.
McCarthy, J., 1956, Measures of the Value of Information. *Proceedings of the National Academy of Sciences*, 42, 654–655.
McGuire, C. B., 1961, Some Team Models of a Sales Organization. *Management Science*, 7, 101–130.
McGuire, C. B., 1972, Comparison of Information Structures. *Decision and Organization* (C. B. McGuire and R. Radner, eds.), North Holland, Amsterdam, 101–130.
McKay, M. D., W. J. Conover, and R. J. Beckman, 1979, A Comparison of Three Methods for Selecting Values of Input Variables in the Analysis of Output from a Computer Code. *Technometrics*, 21, 239–245.
McKinnon, S. M., and W. J. Bruns, 1992, *The Information Mosaic*. Harvard Business School Press, Boston, MA.
McLeod, R., and J. W. Jones, 1986, Making Executive Information Systems More Effective. *Business Horizons*, 29, 29–37.
Meinhold, R. J., and N. D. Singpurwalla, 1983, Understanding the Kalman Filter. *The American Statistician*, 37, 123–127.
Melumad, N. D., and S. Reichelstein, 1989, Value of Communication in Agencies. *Journal of Economic Theory*, 47, 334–368.
Menou, M. J., 1993, *Measuring the Impact of Information on Development*. International Development Research Centre, Ottawa.
Milgrom, P., 1981, Good News and Bad News: Representation Theorems and Applications. *Bell Journal of Economics*, 12, 380–391.

Milgrom, P., and R. J. Weber, 1982, The Value of Information in a Sealed-Bid Auction. *Journal of Mathematical Economics*, 10, 105–114.

Mills, J. P., 1926, Table of the Ratio: Area to Bounding Ordinate, for any Portion of the Normal Curve. *Biometrika*, 18, 395–400.

Miyasawa, K., 1968, Information Structures in Stochastic Programming Problems. *Management Science*, 14, 275–291.

Mock, T. J., 1969, Comparative Values of Information Structures. *Empirical Research in Accounting: Selected Studies, 1969*, supplement to *Journal of Accounting Research*, 7, 124–159.

Mock, T. J., 1973, The Value of Budget Information. *Accounting Review*, 48, 520–534.

Mock, T. J., 1976, *Measurement and Accounting Information Criteria*. Studies in Accounting Research, #13, American Accounting Association.

Mokyr, J., 1997, Are We Living in the Middle of an Industrial Revolution? *Federal Reserve Bank of Kansas City Economic Review*, 82, 31–43.

Mooers, C. N., 1960, Mooers' Law or, Why Some Retrieval Systems Are Used and Others Are Not. *American Documentation*, 11, ii.

Morris, J. R., 1974, The Logarithmic Investor's Decision to Acquire Costly Information. *Management Science*, 21, 383–391.

Morris, P. A., 1974, Decision Analysis Expert Use. *Management Science,* 20, 1233–1241.

Morris, P. A., 1983, An Axiomatic Approach to Expert Resolution. *Management Science*, 29, 24–32.

Mote, L. J. B., 1962, Reasons for the Variations in the Information Needs of Scientists. *Journal of Documentation*, 18, 169–175.

Mount, K., and S. Reiter, 1974, The Informational Size of Message Spaces. *Journal of Economic Theory*, 8, 161–192.

Mowshowitz, A., 1992, On the Market Value of Information Commodities. I. The Nature of Information and Information Commodities; II. Supply Price; III. Demand Price. *Journal of the American Society for Information Science*, 43, 225–248.

Mukhopadhyay, T., S. Kekre, and S. Kalathur, 1995, Business Value of Information Technology: A Study of Electronic Data Interchange. *MIS Quarterly*, 19, 137–156.

Murota, T., 1988, Demand and Supply Values of Information. *Information Economics and Policy*, 3, 25–34.

Murphy, A. H., 1973, A New Vector Partition of the Probability Score. *Journal of Applied Meteorology*, 12, 595-600.

Murphy, A. H., and H. Daan, 1985, Forecast Evaluation. *Probability, Statistics, and Decision Making in the Atmospheric Sciences* (A. H. Murphy and R. W. Katz, eds.), Westview Press, London, 379–437.

Murphy, A. H., and J. C. Thompson, 1977, On the Nature of the Nonexistence of Ordinal Relationships Between Measures of the Accuracy and Value of Probability Forecasts: An Example. *Journal of Applied Meteorology*, 16, 1015–1021.

Murphy, A. H., and R. L. Winkler, 1977, The Use of Credible Intervals in Temperature Forecasting: Some Experimental Results. *Decision Making and Change in Human Affairs* (H. Jungermann and G. De Zeeuw, eds.), D. Reidel, Holland, 45–56.

Murphy, A. H., and R. L. Winkler, 1987, A General Framework for Forecast Verification. *Monthly Weather Review*, 115, 1330–1338.

Murphy, A. H., and R. L. Winkler, 1992, Diagnostic Verification of Probability Forecasts. *International Journal of Forecasting*, 7, 435–455.

Nadiminti, R., T. Mukhopadhyay, and C. H. Kriebel, 1996, Risk Aversion and the Value of Information. *Decision Support Systems*, 16, 241–254.

Nelson, R., 1961, Uncertainty, Prediction and Competitive Equilibrium. *Quarterly Journal of Economics*, 75, 41–62.

Nelson, R., and S. Winter, 1964, The Weather Forecasting System. *Quarterly Journal of Economics*, 78, 420–441.

Newman, D. P., 1980, Prospect Theory: Implications for Information Evaluation. *Accounting Organizations and Society*, 5, 217–230.

Newman, J. W., 1971, *Management Applications of Decision Theory*. Harper and Row, New York.

Nordhaus, W. D., 1994a, *Managing the Global Commons: The Economics of Climate Change*. MIT Press, Cambridge, MA.

Nordhaus, W. D., 1994b, Expert Opinion on Climatic Change. *American Scientist*, 82, 45–51.

Nordhaus, W. D., and D. Popp, 1997, What is the Value of Scientific Knowledge? An Application to Global Warming Using the PRICE Model. *Energy Journal*, 18, 1–45.

O'Connor, M. F., C. R. Peterson, and T. J. Palmer, 1972, Stakes and Probabilities in Information Purchase. *Organizational Behavior and Human Performance*, 7, 43–52.

Ohlson, J. A., 1975, The Complete Ordering of Information Alternatives for a Class of Portfolio-Selection Models. *Journal of Accounting Research*, 13, 267–282.

Ohlson, J. A., 1979, Residual (API) Analysis and the Private Value of Information. *Journal of Accounting Research*, 17, 506–527.

Osband, K., 1989, Optimal Forecasting Incentives. *Journal of Political Economy*, 97, 1091–1112.

Pasa, M., and S. M. Shugan, 1996, The Value of Marketing Expertise. *Management Science*, 42, 370–388.

Pauker, S. P., and S. G. Pauker, 1987, The Amniocentesis Decision: Ten Years of Decision Analytic Experience. *Birth Defects*, 23, 151–169.

Pearl, J., 1978, An Economic Basis for Certain Methods of Evaluating Probabilistic Forecasts. *International Journal of Man-Machine Studies*, 10, 175–183.

Pearson, K., 1968, *Tables of the Incomplete Beta Function, 2nd Edition*. Cambridge Press, London.

Peck, S. C., and T. J. Teisberg, 1996, Uncertainty and the Value of Information with Stochastic Losses from Global Warming. *Risk Analysis*, 16, 227–235.

Peizer, D. B., and J. W. Pratt, 1968, A Normal Approximation for Binomial, F, Beta, and Other Common, Related Tail Probabilities, I. *Journal of the American Statistical Association*, 63, 1416–1456.

Peterson, C. R., and L. R. Beach, 1967, Man as an Intuitive Statistician. *Psychological Bulletin*, 68, 29–46.

Pethig, R., 1994, Optimal Pollution Control, Irreversibilities, and the Value of Future Information. *Annals of Operations Research*, 54, 217–235.

Pfanzagl, J., 1959, A General Theory of Measurement Applications to Utility. *Naval Research Logistics Quarterly*, 6, 283–294.

Pindyck, R. S., and D. L. Rubinfeld, 1991, *Econometric Models and Economic Forecasts, 3rd Edition*. McGraw-Hill, New York.

Pitz, G. F., 1968, Information Seeking When Available Information is Limited. *Journal of Experimental Psychology*, 76, 25-34.

Plackett, R. L., 1965, A Class of Bivariate Distributions. *Journal of the American Statistical Association*, 60, 516–522.

Porat, A. M., and J. A. Haas, 1969, Information Effects on Decision-Making. *Behavioral Science*, 14, 98–104.

Porat, M. U., 1977, *The Information Economy*. U. S. Government Printing Office, Washington, DC.

Powell, P., 1992, Information Technology Evaluation: Is It Different? *Journal of the Operational Research Society*, 43, 29–42.

Prat, A., 1996, Shared Knowledge vs. Diversified Knowledge in Teams. *Journal of the Japanese and International Economies*, 10, 181–195.

Pratt, J. W., 1964, Risk Aversion in the Small and in the Large. *Econometrica*, 32, 122–136.

Pratt, J. W., H. Raiffa, and R. O. Schlaifer, 1995, *Introduction to Statistical Decision Theory*. MIT Press, Cambridge.

Quiggin, J., 1982, A Theory of Anticipated Utility. *Journal of Economic Behavior and Organization*, 3, 323–343.

Radner, R., 1961, The Evaluation of Information in Organizations. *Proceedings of the Fourth Berkeley Symposium on Mathematical Statistics and Probability, Volume 1*, University of California Press, Berkeley, CA, 491–530.

Radner, R., 1962, Team Decision Problems. *Annals of Mathematical Statistics*, 33, 857–881.

Radner, R., 1993, The Organization of Decentralized Information Processing. *Econometrica*, 61, 1109–1146.

Radner, R., and J. E. Stiglitz, 1984, A Nonconcavity in the Value of Information. *Bayesian Models in Economic Theory* (M. Boyer and R. E. Kihlstrom, eds.), Elsevier Science Publishers, New York, 33–52.

Ragowsky, A., N. Ahituv, and S. Neumann, 1996, Identifying the Value and Importance of an Information System Application. *Information and Management*, 31, 89–102.

Raiffa, H., 1968, *Decision Analysis: Introductory Lectures on Choices Under Uncertainty*. Addison-Wesley, Reading MA.

Raiffa, H., and R. O. Schlaifer, 1961, *Applied Statistical Decision Theory*. Division of Research, The Harvard School of Business Administration, Boston.

Real, L. A., 1993, Animal Choice Behavior and the Evolution of Cognitive Architecture. *Science*, 253, 980–986.

Reichard, E. G., and J. S. Evans, 1989, Assessing the Value of Hydrogeologic Information for Risk-Based Remedial Action Decisions. *Water Resources Research*, 25, 1451–1460.

Repo, A. J., 1989, The Value of Information: Approaches in Economics, Accounting, and Management Science. *Journal of the American Society for Information Science*, 40, 68–85.

Resnick, P., and H. R. Varian, 1997, Recommender Systems. *Communications of the ACM*, 40, 56–58.

Rockart, J. F., 1979, Chief Executives Define Their Own Data Needs. *Harvard Business Review*, 47, 81–93.

Ronen, J., and G. Falk, 1973, Accounting Aggregation and the Entropy Measure: An Experimental Approach. *Accounting Review*, 48, 696–717.

Rosenthal, R., 1963, On the Social Psychology of the Psychological Experiment: The Experimenter's Hypothesis as Unintended Determinant of Experimental Results. *American Scientist*, 51, 268–283.

Ross, S. A., 1981, Some Stronger Measures of Risk Aversion in the Small and the Large with Applications. *Econometrica*, 49, 621–638.

Rothschild, M., and J. E. Stiglitz, 1970, Increasing Risk: I. A Definition. *Journal of Economic Theory*, 2, 225–243. (Addendum to Increasing Risk. *Journal of Economic Theory*, 5, 306).

Safra, Z., and E. Sulganik, 1995, On the Nonexistence of Blackwell's Theorem-Type Results with General Preference Relations. *Journal of Risk and Uncertainty*, 10, 187–201.

Samuelson, P. A., 1969, Lifetime Portfolio Selection by Dynamic Stochastic Programming. *Review of Economics and Statistics*, 51, 239–246.

Samuelson, P. A., 1970, The Fundamental Approximation Theorem of Portfolio Analysis in Terms of Means, Variances, and Higher Moments. *Review of Economic Studies*, 37, 537–542.

Saracevic, T., and P. B. Kantor, 1997, Studying the Value of Library and Information Services. Part I. Establishing a Theoretical Framework; Part II. Methodology and Taxonomy. *Journal of the American Society for Information Science*, 48, 527–563.

Savage, L. J., 1954, *The Foundations of Statistics*. John Wiley, New York.

Savage, L. J., 1971, Elicitation of Personal Probabilities and Expectations. *Journal of the American Statistical Association*, 66, 783–801.

Schelling, T. C., 1996, Global Decisions for the Very Long Term: Intergenerational and International Discounting. *Wise Choices: Decisions, Games, and Negotiations* (R. J. Zeckhauser, R. L. Keeney, and J. K. Sebenius, eds.), Harvard Business School Press, Boston, MA, 152–166.

Schlaifer, R. O., 1969, *Analysis of Decisions Under Uncertainty*. McGraw-Hill, New York.

Schlee, E. E., 1990, The Value of Information in Anticipated Utility Theory. *Journal of Risk and Uncertainty*, 3, 83–92.

Schlee, E. E., 1991, The Value of Perfect Information in Nonlinear Utility Theory. *Theory and Decision*, 30, 127–131.

Schlee, E. E., 1996, The Value of Information about Product Quality. *Rand Journal of Economics*, 27, 803–815.

Schlee, E. E., 1997, The Sure Thing Principle and the Value of Information. *Theory and Decision*, 42, 21–36.

Schotter, A., and Y. M. Braunstein, 1981, Economic Search: An Experimental Study. *Economic Inquiry*, 19, 1–25.

Schroeder, R. G., and I. Benbasat, 1975, An Experimental Evaluation of the Relationship of Uncertainty in the Environment to Information Used by Decision Makers. *Decision Sciences*, 6, 556–567.

Schweizer, P., 1996, The Growth of Economic Espionage: America is Target Number One. *Foreign Affairs*, 75, 9–14.

Shannon, C. E., 1948, A Mathematical Theory of Communication. *Bell System Technical Journal*, 27, 379–423.

Sharda, R., S. H. Barr, and J. C. McDonnell, 1988, Decision Support System Effectiveness: A Review and an Empirical Test. *Management Science*, 34, 139–159.

Simon, H. A., 1956, Dynamic Programming Under Uncertainty with a Quadratic Criterion Function. *Econometrica*, 24, 74–81.

Simpson, C. W., and L. Prusak, 1995, Troubles with Information Overload—Moving from Quantity to Quality in Information Provision. *International Journal of Information Management,* 15, 413–425.

Singh, N., 1991, Posterior-Preserving Information Improvements and Principal-Agent Relationships. *Journal of Economic Theory*, 55, 192–202.

Slovic, P., and S. Lichtenstein, 1971, Comparison of Bayesian and Regression Approaches to the Study of Information Processing in Judgment. *Organizational Behavior and Human Performance*, 6, 649–744.

Slovic, P., B. Fischhoff, and S. Lichtenstein, 1977, Behavioral Decision Theory. *Annual Review of Psychology*, 28, 1–39.

Smith, J. Q., 1988, *Decision Analysis. A Bayesian Approach.* Chapman and Hall, London.

Snapper, K. J., and C. R. Peterson, 1971, Information Seeking and Data Diagnosticity. *Journal of Experimental Psychology*, 87, 429–433.

Snyder, H., and E. Davenport, 1997, *Costing and Pricing in the Digital Age: A Practical Guide for Information Services.* Neal-Schuman, New York.

Song, J.-S., and P. H. Zipkin, 1996, Inventory Control with Information About Supply Conditions. *Management Science*, 42, 1409–1419.

Spetzler, C. S., and C.-A. S. Staël von Holstein, 1975, Probability Encoding in Decision Analysis. *Management Science*, 22, 340–358.

Staël von Holstein, C.-A. S., 1970, *Assessment and Evaluation of Subjective Probability Distributions.* Economic Research Institute, Stockholm.

Stigler, G. J., 1961, The Economics of Information. *Journal of Political Economy*, 69, 213–225.

Streufert, S. C., 1973, Effects of Information Relevance on Decision Making in Complex Environments. *Memory & Cognition*, 1, 224–228.

Swinton, S. M., and R. P. King, 1994, The Value of Pest Information in a Dynamic Setting: The Case of Weed Control. *American Journal of Agricultural Economics*, 76, 36–46.

Sulganik, E., and I. Zilcha, 1997, The Value of Information: The Case of Signal-Dependent Opportunity Sets. *Journal of Economic Dynamics and Control*, 21, 1615–1625.

Szaniawski, K., 1967, The Value of Perfect Information. *Synthese*, 17, 408–424.

Tague-Sutcliffe, J., 1995, *Measuring Information.* Academic Press, San Diego, CA.

Taylor, A. C., J. S. Evans, and T. E. McKone, 1993, The Value of Animal Test Information in Environmental Control Decisions. *Risk Analysis*, 13, 403–412.

Taylor, R. S., 1986, *Value-Added Processes in Information Systems.* Ablex Publishing, Norwood, NJ.

Taylor, R. S., 1991, Information Use Environments. *Progress in Communication Science* (B. Dervin and M. J. Voigt, eds.), Ablex Publishing, Norwood, NJ, 217–254.

Teece, D. J., 1977, Technology Transfer by Multinational Firms: The Resource Cost of Transferring Technological Know-How. *Economic Journal*, 87, 242–261.

Theil, H., 1957, A Note on Certainty Equivalence in Dynamic Planning. *Econometrica*, 25, 346–349.

Theil, H., 1965, *Economic Forecasts and Policy, 2nd Revised Edition*. North Holland, Amsterdam.

Theil, H., 1967, *Economics and Information Theory*. North-Holland, Amsterdam.

Thompson, K. M., and J. S. Evans, 1997, The Value of Improved National Exposure Information for Perchloroethylene (Perc): A Case Study for Dry Cleaners. *Risk Analysis*, 17, 253–271.

Todd, P., and Benbasat, I., 1992, The Use of Information in Decision Making: An Experimental Investigation of the Impact of Computer-Based Decision Aids. *MIS Quarterly*, 16, 373–393.

Torgersen, E., 1991, *Comparison of Statistical Experiments*. Cambridge University Press, New York.

Tversky, A., and D. Kahneman, 1974, Judgment Under Uncertainty: Heuristics and Biases. *Science*, 185, 1124–1131.

United States Department of Agriculture, 1968–1987, *Agricultural Prices*. U.S. Government Printing Office, Washington, DC.

Urbany, J. E., 1986, An Experimental Examination of the Economics of Information. *Journal of Consumer Research*, 13, 257–271.

van Bruggen, G. H., A. Smidts, and B. Wierenga, 1998, Improving Decision Making by Means of a Marketing Decision Support System. *Management Science*, 44, 645–658.

Vardeman, S., and G. Meeden, 1983, Calibration, Sufficiency, and Domination Considerations for Bayesian Probability Assessors. *Journal of the American Statistical Association*, 78, 808–816.

Varian, H. R., 1997, The AEA's Electronic Publishing Plans: A Progress Report. *Journal of Economic Perspectives*, 11, 95–104.

Vincent, D. R., 1990, *The Information-Based Corporation: Stakeholder Economics and the Technology Investment*. Dow Jones-Irwin, Homewood, IL.

von Hippel, E., 1994, "Sticky Information" and the Locus of Problem Solving: Implications for Innovation. *Management Science*, 40, 429–439.

von Neumann, J., and O. Morgenstern, 1947, *Theory of Games and Economic Behavior, 2nd Edition*. Princeton University Press, Princeton.

Wagner, J. M., and O. Berman, 1995, Models for Planning Capacity Expansion of Convenience Stores Under Uncertain Demand and the Value of Information. *Annals of Operations Research*, 59, 19–44.

Wagner, J. M., U. Shamir, and H. R. Nemati, 1992, Groundwater Quality Management Under Uncertainty: Stochastic Programming Approaches and the Value of Information. *Water Resources Research*, 28, 1233–1246.

Wakker, P., 1988, Nonexpected Utility as Aversion of Information. *Journal of Behavioral Decision Making*, 1, 169–175.

Wald, A., 1947, *Sequential Analysis*. Wiley, New York.

Wallsten, T. S., and D. V. Budescu, 1983, Encoding Subjective Probabilities: A Psychological and Psychometric Review. *Management Science*, 29, 151–173.

Ward, S. C., and C. B. Chapman, 1988, Developing Competitive Bids: A Framework for Information Processing. *Journal of the Operational Research Society*, 39, 123–134.

Wason, P. C., 1960, On the Failure to Eliminate Hypotheses in a Conceptual Task. *Quarterly Journal of Experimental Psychology*, 12, 129–140.

Weinstein, M. C., 1983, Cost-Effective Priorities for Cancer Prevention. *Science*, 221, 17–23.

Weinstein, M. C., 1996, Decision Analysis in Health and Medicine: Two Decades of Progress and Challenges. *Wise Choices: Decisions, Games, and Negotiations* (R. J. Zeckhauser, R. L. Keeney, and J. K. Sebenius, eds.), Harvard Business School Press, Boston, MA, 169–184.

Wendt, D., 1969, Value of Information for Decisions. *Journal of Mathematical Psychology*, 6, 430–443.

Wersig, G., 1997, Information Theory. *International Encyclopedia of Information and Library Science* (J. Feather and P. Sturges, eds.), Routledge, London.

Whiteman, C. H., 1996, Bayesian Prediction Under Asymmetric Linear Loss: Forecasting State Tax Revenues in Iowa. *Modelling and Prediction Honoring Seymour Geisser* (J. C. Lee, W. O. Johnson, and A. Zellner, eds.), Springer-Verlag, New York, 149–166.

Willemain, T. R., 1995, Model Formulation: What Experts Think About and When. *Operations Research*, 43, 916–932.

Williams, M. E., 1997, The State of Databases Today: 1997. *Gale Directory of Databases* (K. L. Nolan, ed.), Gale, Detroit, xvii–xxix.

Wilson, R., 1975, Informational Economies of Scale. *Bell Journal of Economics*, 6, 184–195.

Wilson, T. D., 1994, Information Needs and Uses: Fifty Years of Progress? *Fifty Years of Information Progress* (B. C. Vickery, ed.), Aslib, London.

Wilson, T. D., 1997, Information Management. *International Encyclopedia of Information and Library Science* (J. Feather and P. Sturges, eds.), Routledge, London.

Winkler, R. L., 1967, The Assessment of Prior Distributions in Bayesian Analysis, *Journal of the American Statistical Association*, 62, 776–800.

Winkler, R. L., 1969, Scoring Rules and the Evaluation of Probability Assessors. *Journal of the American Statistical Association*, 64, 1073–1078.

Winkler, R. L., 1972, A Decision-Theoretic Approach to Interval Estimation. *Journal of the American Statistical Association*, 67, 187–191.

Winkler, R. L., 1986, Expert Resolution. *Management Science*, 32, 298–303.

Winkler, R. L., and A. H. Murphy, 1970, Nonlinear Utility and the Probability Score. *Journal of Applied Meteorology*, 9, 143–148.

Yovits, M. C., C. R. Foulk, and L. L. Rose, 1981, Information Flow and Analysis: Theory, Simulation, and Experiments. I. Basic Theoretical and Conceptual Development; II. Simulation, Examples, and Results. *Journal of the American Society for Information Science*, 30, 187–210.

Zacharias, T. P., M. Y. Huh, and D. M. Brandon, 1990, Information in a Dynamic Management Model: An Application to Plant-Tissue Analysis and Fertilisation Scheduling. *European Review of Agricultural Economics*, 17, 85–97.

Ziemba, W. T., and J. E. Butterworth, 1975, Bounds on the Value of Information in Uncertain Decision Problems. *Stochastics*, 1, 361–378.

Zmud, R. W., 1978, An Empirical Investigation of the Dimensionality of the Concept of Information. *Decision Sciences*, 9, 187–195.

Acknowledgments

The quotation on page 37 is reprinted from R. S. Taylor, *Value Added Processes in Information Systems*, pages 4–5. Permission granted by Ablex Publishing Company, Greenwich, CT.

The quotation on page 105 is reprinted with permission from D. V. Lindley, *Bayesian Statistics, A Review*, page 9. Copyright 1972 by the Society for Industrial and Applied Mathematics. All rights reserved.

The quotation beginning on page 276 is reprinted from L. J. Savage, Elicitation of Personal Probabilities and Expectations, *Journal of the American Statistical Association*, 66, page 798. Permission granted by the American Statistical Association.

Symbol Glossary

a	an action
a_x	the optimal action, conditional on the certainty of state x
$a^*(\tilde{y}, \tilde{\theta})$	alternate notation for the optimal conditional decision rule, given informativeness $\tilde{\theta}$ and risk neutrality
a_0^u	the optimal prior action given u
a_y^u	the optimal action, conditional on message y, given u
$a_y^u(\psi)$	the optimal action, conditional on message y, given u and initial wealth reduction ψ
$a_{\mathbf{I}}^u$	the optimal deterministic decision rule, given **I** and u
$\mathbf{a}$	the space of actions
A	multipurpose; a number or a counter
A	superscript indicating a risk averse decision maker
α	multipurpose; either a parameter or a number, generally between zero and one
$\alpha(\tilde{c})$	the informant's compensation share, as a function of the announced $\tilde{c}$
b	multipurpose; a number or a parameter, substantively the coefficient of absolute risk aversion
bi	the binomial distribution
B	multipurpose; a number or a counter
B_0^u	the buying price of the prior optimal decision given u
B_y^u	the buying price of the conditional optimal decision given u
B	a Blackwell quasi-garbling matrix
BN	the bivariate normal distribution
β	multipurpose; a parameter or a number, also the indicator of the beta distribution or beta function
$\boldsymbol{\beta}$	a quantity measuring skewness or kurtosis
c	multipurpose; a number or a parameter, substantively the cost parameter for information
$\underline{c}$	minimum possible value of the cost parameter c
$\overline{c}$	maximum possible value of the cost parameter c
$\tilde{c}$	announced cost parameter c
C	multipurpose; a number, a point on the real line

CVXH	the convex hull of a set
$\mathbf{C}(\bullet)$	a cost function for information
$\mathcal{C}$	the observed variable cost of information processing
d	the differential operator
$\mathbf{d}(y)$	a conditional decision rule
$\mathbf{d}_I^u$	the optimal decision rule, given **I** and u
$\mathbf{d}$	a matrix of conditional decision rules
D	multipurpose; a number, a point on the real line
DM	the decision maker
D	a decision problem
$\mathcal{D}$	the discount or impatience coefficient
δ	the simplex on the action space **a**
Δ	the difference operator
Δ	the length of delay (Chapter 5)
e	multipurpose; a number or a parameter
exp	the exponential function
E	the expectations operator
ε	the effort undertaken in information processing(Chapters 1, 8, and 9)
ε	a random variable (Chapters 5 and 7)
$\mathfrak{I}$	a fixed quantity
$f(\bullet)$	general indicator for a function, substantively a probability density function with specified characteristics
$F(\bullet)$	a left-tail cumulative distribution function (cdf)
FC	a fixed cost
$\mathcal{FC}$	the fixed cost of an information system
ϕ	multipurpose; a parameter or a member of an arbitrary set, substantively the efficiency or effectiveness parameter in an information production function
Φ	an arbitrary set
$g(\bullet)$	general indicator for a function
g_y^u	the conditional incremental expected wealth from message y, given u
g_I^u	the preposterior incremental wealth of **I**, given u
$G(\bullet)$	general indicator for a function
G_0^u	the prior incremental gain in the reservation price given u
G_y^u	the conditional incremental gain from the message y, given u
G_I^u	the cash-equivalent gain from **I**, given u
$\mathbf{G}(\bullet)$	the expected gain from information in a decision problem
$\mathcal{G}_\tau$	the realized incremental gain from information in terminal use τ

$\bar{\mathcal{G}}_{\tau}(\bullet)$	the expected incremental gain to the organization in terminal use τ
γ	a parameter
Γ	a garbling matrix
$\Gamma(\bullet)$	a right-tail cumulative distribution function (cdf)
h	a counter
$h(\bullet)$	the hazard rate function of a probability distribution
hb	the hyperbinomial distribution
H	the number of elements in a finite set
$H(\mathbf{I}\downarrow)$	the entropy of the prior distribution p(x)
$H(\mathbf{I})$	the expected entropy or equivocation of **I**
η	a random variable
i	a counter identifying a specific state
ι	the risk or insurance premium
I_x	the left-tail cdf of the standard beta distribution, tabled by Pearson
I	an information structure
$\mathbf{I}\downarrow$	the null information structure
$\mathbf{I}\uparrow$	the perfect information structure
ϑ	a dual information structure
j	a counter; multipurpose but usually identifying a specific message
J	a counter identifying a specific message
$J(\mathbf{I})$	the information transmitted or uncertainty removed by **I**
$\varphi(\bullet)$	general indicator for a function
k	a counter; multipurpose but usually indicating a specific action or prospect resulting from a specific action
k	an interest rate in an investment problem (Chapters 5 and 8)
$k(\bullet)$	the technical factor in an information cost function
K	the number of actions in a finite action space
κ	multipurpose; a counter or a parameter
$\log[\bullet]$	the natural logarithm of the argument
ℓ	a counter
L	superscript indicating a risk loving decision maker
L	the length of a line segment
$\mathbf{L}(\bullet)$	a loss function
$\mathcal{L}$	a Lagrangian function
λ	a Lagrangian multiplier
$\boldsymbol{\lambda}$	a finite matrix of likelihoods
Λ	a number, a point on the real line
m	the number of states in a finite state space

M	length of memory
MC	marginal cost
MV	marginal value
μ_k	a quantity measuring an empirical moment
n	the number of messages in a finite message space
n′	a parameter of the beta distribution
N	the number of actual or potential observations
N	superscript indicating a risk neutral decision maker
N	the normal distribution
ℵ	the utility possibility set
ν	a parameter
$\mathcal{OG}$	the organization's realized information gain
$\overline{\mathcal{OG}}(\bullet)$	the organization's expected information gain
p_{kh}	the probability of wealth level h in prospect k
p(a)	a probability distribution for the DM's action
p(x)	the prior probability distribution of the state
$p(\bar{x}_y)$	the prior distribution of the posterior mean; the preposterior mean
p(x | y)	the posterior probability distribution of the state, conditional on the message
p(x, y)	the joint probability distribution of the state and the message
p(y)	the marginal probability distribution of the message
p(y | x)	the likelihood of the message, conditional on the state
$p(w_\tau)$	the probability distribution of the stakes in the canonical decisions
$p(W \mid a_k)$	the probability distribution for obtaining terminal wealth W having chosen a_k
$\pi(\bullet)$	the payoff function
Π	a finite matrix of posterior probabilities
Π_j	the jth column of the matrix Π
$\Pi_{ij}(\theta, r_1)$	the posterior probability of state i given message j, as a function of informativeness and prior
Π_h	the posterior probability of a tolerance range, given observation $\tilde{y}_h$
q	a probability that mixes a prospect
q	a finite vector of message probabilities
Q	diagonalization matrix of the vector **q**
θ	index of the informativeness of an information structure
$\bar{\theta}$	the maximum potential value of the informativeness index
$\tilde{\theta}$	the informativeness that the informant asserts

$\tilde{\theta}(\tilde{c})$	the regulated informativeness given the informant's announced cost efficiency
Θ	the set of potential information structures
r_i	alternate notation for the prior probability of state x_i
r'	a parameter of the beta distribution
$\mathbf{r}$	a finite vector of prior probabilities
R_s	remainder in an s-term Taylor series expansion
R_0^{u}	the reservation price of the prior decision, given u
$\tilde{R}_0^A$	the reservation price of a suboptimal prior decision by a risk averter
$R_k^{\mathrm{u}}(\psi)$	the prior reservation price of action a_k, given u and wealth reduction ψ
R_y^{u}	the conditional reservation price from the message y, given u
$R_{\mathbf{I}}^{\mathrm{u}}$	the reservation price of the informed decision, given $\mathbf{I}$ and u
$\mathbf{R}$	diagonalization matrix of the vector $\mathbf{r}$
$\Re_h$	the prior probability of a tolerance range given observation $\tilde{y}_h$
ρ	the correlation coefficient
$\boldsymbol{\rho}$	a finite matrix of joint probabilities
s	multipurpose; a number, a parameter, an index, often a dummy variable
$s(\tilde{c})$	the fixed fee of the informant's compensation, given the announced $\tilde{c}$
$\mathbf{S}$	a Markov matrix reducing the informativeness of the matrix Π
$\mathcal{SC}_\tau$	accounting measure of system variable cost in terminal use τ
σ_x^2	the unconditional variance of the random variable X
σ_y^2	the unconditional variance of the random variable Y
$\sigma_{x\mid y}^2$	the conditional variance of the random variable X, given y
$\sigma_{y\mid x}^2$	the conditional variance of the random variable Y, given x
$\sigma_{\bar{x}_y}^2$	the variance of the preposterior mean
σ_ε^2	the variance of a sequence of independent, identically distributed random variables $\varepsilon(s)$
σ_η^2	the variance of a sequence of independent, identically distributed measurement errors $\eta(s)$
$\sigma_{s\mid t}^2$	the variance of the stochastic process x(s), given the available y_t
Σ	summation operator
t	multipurpose indicator or counter; the current time stage, a point on the real line, or a dummy variable
$t(\xi)$	the value of the optimized decision under the distribution ξ
$\mathbf{t}(\bullet)$	the informant's general compensation function
T	superscript indicating the transpose of a matrix
T	the planning horizon

$T(\bullet)$	the integral condition for second-degree stochastic dominance
τ	subscript identifying a terminal use of the information system
$\mathcal{T}$	the set of available utility consequences
u	superscript indicating no specification of attitude towards risk
$u(\bullet)$	the utility function
$\mu_{x_i}(p(a))$	the expected utility of p(a), conditional on x_i
$\mu_{x_i}(\mathbf{d}(y))$	the expected utility of $\mathbf{d}(y)$, conditional on x_i
$\mu(p(a))$	the expected utility characteristic of p(a)
$\mu_{x_i}(\mathbf{d}, \mathbf{I})$	the conditional expected utility of **d**, under **I**, given x_i
$\mu(\mathbf{d}, \mathbf{I})$	the conditional expected utility characteristic of **d** under **I**
$\breve{\mu}(a_k(\xi))$	the expected utility of outcome from a_k under ξ
$\breve{\mathbf{u}}(a_k)$	the utility consequence of action a_k
$\mathbf{u}$	matrix of utilities
$U(\mathbf{D} \mid \bullet)$	the expected utility or value of a decision **D**
$U(\mathbf{D}^* \mid \bullet)$	the expected utility or value of a decision **D**, after an optimization
$\mathcal{U}(\bullet)$	preference function toward prospects
$\mathcal{UC}_\tau$	accounting measure of user variable cost in terminal use τ
$V(\bullet)$	an information value function, generally under risk neutrality
$\breve{V}(\tilde{\theta}, \theta)$	the expected value of the information structure $\mathbf{I}(\theta)$ when the alternate structure $\mathbf{I}(\tilde{\theta})$ is used for decision making
V_y^u	the conditional value of the message y, given u
$V_{\mathbf{I}}^u$	the demand price value of the information structure **I**, given u
$\hat{V}_{\mathbf{I}}^u$	the utility increment value of the information structure **I**, given u
$\breve{V}_{\mathbf{I}}^u$	hypothetical demand value for a suboptimal informed decision
$\tilde{V}_{\mathbf{I}}^u$	the supply price value of the information structure **I**, given u
$\mathcal{V}_{\mathbf{I}}^u$	an alternate demand price for **I**, given u, when information cost is paid from posterior wealth
$\upsilon(x, \bullet)$	the ex-post value of the message, in terms of payoff
$\hat{\upsilon}^u(x, \bullet)$	the ex-post value of the message, in terms of outcome
$\hat{\upsilon}(x, \bullet)$	the ex-post value of the message, in terms of utility increment
w	initial wealth
w_τ	stakes of the payoff in the canonical problem τ
w_{kh}	wealth level h in prospect/lottery k
W	terminal wealth
$\overline{W}_0^u$	the expected terminal wealth of the optimal prior decision, given u
$\overline{W}_k(\psi)$	the expected terminal wealth from action a_k, given wealth reduction ψ
$\overline{W}_y^u$	the conditional expected wealth from the message y, given u

$\overline{W}_I^u$	the preposterior expected wealth from the informed decision, given **I** and u
$\tilde{W}_k(\psi)$	a prospect induced by the action a_k, adjusted by wealth reduction ψ
$\tilde{W}_0^u$	the optimal prior prospect given u
$\tilde{W}_y^u$	the conditional optimal prospect from the message y, given u
$\tilde{W}_I^u$	the preposterior optimal informed prospect, given **I** and u
$\overline{\tilde{W}}_y^N(\psi)$	the costly prior distribution of the risk neutral posterior mean
W	the space of potential wealths
ω	a parameter; multipurpose
$\omega(\bullet)$	the outcome function
$\omega^{\#}(\bullet)$	an outcome function with separable information cost
$\breve{\omega}(\bullet)$	the regulated informant's expected profit from any policy of announcing, producing, and optimally communicating
$\hat{\omega}(\bullet)$	the regulated informant's expected profit when he produces as contracted
$\overline{\omega}(c)$	the regulated informant's expected profit under truthful communication
Ω	a class of decision problems with specified characteristics
x	a state of nature
x_b	a breakeven value where the optimal action changes
$x(s)$	a stochastic state realization at time stage s
$x'_w(a_k)$	a partitioning of **X** such that the action a_k yields wealth outcome W
$\bar{x}$	the unconditional mean of the random variable X
$\bar{x}_y$	the mean of the random variable X, conditional on the message y
$\bar{x}_t(s)$	the mean of the stochastic process x(s), given the available y_t
$\bar{x}^{(\ell)}(t)$	the left-hand unconditional partial expectation of X
$\bar{x}_y^{(\ell)}(t)$	the left-hand conditional partial expectation of X, given y
$\bar{x}^{(r)}(t)$	the right-hand unconditional partial expectation of X
$\bar{x}_y^{(r)}(t)$	the right-hand conditional partial expectation of X, given y
$\tilde{x}_h$	an empirically observed state realization
X	a random state variable
$\times$	alternate random state variable; generally one component of a multi-category state description
X	the state space
ξ_i	a probability for the state x_i
ξ	a probability distribution on the finite state space $\mathbf{X}^m$
Ξ	the simplex on the finite state space **X**
y	a message
$y_j(x_i)$	a probabilistic message stating the probability of state x_i

$\bar{y}$	the mean of the random variable Y
$\bar{y}_x$	the mean of the random variable Y, conditional on x
$\tilde{y}$	a message communicated by the informant
$\tilde{y}^*(\bullet)$	the informant's optimal communication
$\tilde{y}_h$	an empirically observed message or forecast statement
$\tilde{y}(t)$	the innovation at time stage t
Y	a random variable, the message an information structure will provide
Y	the message space
ψ	a nonstochastic reduction in wealth
z	a realization of a random variable Z
z_b	a breakeven value where the optimal action changes
$\bar{z}$	the mean of the random variable Z
Z	a random variable; generally an alternate state variable
ζ	a parameter

Author Index

—D—

—E—

—F—

—G—

—H—

—I—

—J—

—K—

—L—

—M—

—N—

—O—

—P—

—Q—

—R—

—S—

—T—

—U—

—V—

Subject Index

—D—

—J—

—K—

—L—

—M—

—N—

—O—

—P—

—R—

—S—

—T—

—U—

—V—

—W—